HUMAN RESOURCE MANAGEMENT
THE CANADIAN DYNAMIC

SHIMON L. DOLAN

University of Montreal

RANDALL S. SCHULER

Stern School of Business

Nelson Canada

I(T)P™
International Thomson Publishing
The trademark ITP is used under license

Published in 1994 by
Nelson Canada
A Division of Thomson Canada Limited
1120 Birchmount Road
Scarborough, Ontario M1K 5G4

Canadian Cataloguing in Publication Data

Dolan, Shimon
    Human resource management: the Canadian dynamic

Includes bibliographical references and index.
ISBN 0–17–603541–9

1. Personnel management – Canada.   I. Schuler,
Randall S.   II. Title

HF5549.2.C3D65   1993   658.3'00971   C93–093785–6

Acquisitions Editor   John Horne
Editorial Manager   Nicole Gnutzman
Developmental Editor   Yuval Kashdan
Art Director   Bruce Bond
Cover Design   Hania Fil
Text Design   Hania Fil
Cover and chapter opening photographs   Alex Murchison

Printed and bound in Canada
1 2 3 4 5   BG   97 96 95 94

Acknowledgments

Statistical information was provided through the cooperation of Statistics Canada. Readers may obtain further information or copies of related publications by writing to: Publication Sales, Statistics Canada, Ottawa, Ontario K1A 0T6, by calling 1-613-951-7277, or national toll-free 1-800-267-6677. Readers may also facsimile their order by dialing 1-613-951-1584.

Dedicated to my children, Keren and Tommy,
whom I love dearly (S.L.D.)

BRIEF CONTENTS

C O N T E N T S

Chapter Eight

Indirect Compensation 235

Chapter Nine

Performance Appraisal: Methods Procedures 261

Chapter Ten

Performance Appraisal: Applications and Improvements 299

CHAPTER FIFTEEN
EMPLOYEE RIGHTS   463

CHAPTER SIXTEEN
LABOUR RELATIONS   485

CHAPTER SEVENTEEN
INTERNATIONAL AND MULTINATIONAL HRM   525

CHAPTER EIGHTEEN

HR EFFECTIVENESS: RESEARCH AND PRACTICE   565

PREFACE

We approached the writing of *Human Resource Management: The Canadian Dynamic* with four objectives in mind: to *simplify*, *expand*, *update*, and *render the material stimulating*. We believe that the end result is one of the most current, comprehensive, and thought-provoking HRM texts in the field. As much as possible, this edition intends to prepare HR professionals for the 1990s.

Use of Simplified Language and Terminology. We focused our efforts on avoiding redundancies in the writing, using language that would be easily understood by students and practitioners alike, and avoiding abstract examples and jargon. The result, we believe, is a clear and more readable text.

Focus on the Expanded Role of HRM. Our efforts toward expansion also included major editing and restructuring of the chapters and themes. Four new chapters highlight the expanding scope and role of HRM: Strategic Aspects of HRM, Career Management and Planning, International and Multinational HRM, and HR Effectiveness. We also changed the structure and content of the existing chapters considerably. Staffing is now covered in two chapters; similarly, compensation is covered in two chapters: Direct Compensation (Chapter 7) and Indirect Compensation (Chapter 8). Unions and the collective bargaining process are covered in one integrated chapter: Labour Relations. Up-to-date material on quality of work life and productivity is featured in Contemporary Forms of Managing Human Resources (Chapter 13). All the chapters in the book highlight the growing importance of human resource management topics and their relation to the needs of business.

Use of Up-to-Date Examples and Terminology. We replaced or updated illustrative examples that amplify the theoretical content of the various chapters, and we integrated more current research and information pertaining to both legal and normative aspects of managing people at work in Canada. We attempted to provide the latest information about legal developments and statutory regulations about federal and provincial norms; however, changes may have occurred since the book was written.

The change in the title of the book reflects our use of up-to-date terminology. While during the 1980s the term "personnel" was frequently used to denote the department or section responsible for managing people, the 1990s have witnessed an evolution. The term personnel is not used very often; the same function has taken the label human resource management. Consequently, we decided to use only human resource management in the title of the book. It suggested throughout that this evolution denotes significant changes in philosophy and practice in HRM in Canadian firms.

Inclusion of Stimulating Material. Our experience is that a comprehensive text in any field can be technically sound but still be a boring exercise for the reader. In *Human Resource Management: The Canadian Dynamic* significant emphasis is placed on selecting and presenting material that will foster interest, curiosity, and even excitement on behalf of the reader. In our efforts to render the material stimulating, we focused on a number of factors. First, a significant emphasis was placed on real organizational applications. The latter take various forms: (a) each chapter begins with a Keynote Address by a senior executive in a Canadian firm or organization; (b) relevant articles taken from journals and professional publications appear as HRM in the News Vignettes, and profiles of Canadian companies are featured in HRM Dynamics; (c) each chapter has a section on computer applications; and (d) cases derived from the authors' consulting experience, or taken from current literature, are featured at the end of each chapter.

We also included our own "two cents" (i.e., ideas and opinions about controversial issues). We took the liberty (and the risk) of adding a personal touch—our opinion on numerous issues. Although we fully recognize that this could be a "double-edged sword," we decided to adapt this strategy, which has been used successfully in our classes. We hope that this fresh view will stimulate and provoke further thinking about current human resource concerns.

We maintained an inherent logic between the chapters and within each chapter. The first section describes the challenges and opportunities in managing people at work, with special emphasis on The Growing Importance of HRM (Chapter 1) and on the Strategic Aspects of HRM (Chapter 2). The second section presents the foundation for many HR activities—Job Analysis (Chapter 3), and Human Resource Planning (Chapter 4). This is followed by a discussion of the staffing function in Recruitment of Human Resources (Chapter 5), and in Selection and Orientation (Chapter 6). Next comes the issue of compensation, which has been divided into: Direct Compensation (Chapter 7) and Indirect Compensation (Chapter 8). This is followed by two chapters that describe the core of appraising employees. In Chapter 9, the methods and procedures of appraising employees are presented, and in Chapter 10, various applications and improvements are described. In the next section we deal with enhancing human potential. We present the basics of Training and Development (Chapter 11) in organizations, as well as Career Management and Planning (Chapter 12). The theme of improving the organization has also been divided into two: Contemporary Forms of Managing Human Resources (Chapter 13) and Health and Safety at Work (Chapter 14). Maintaining effective work relationships has been divided into two: Employee Rights (Chapter 15), and Labour Relations (Chapter 16). Finally, the last section presents a global view of managing human resources: International and Multinational HRM (Chapter 17) and HR Effectiveness: Research and Practice (Chapter 18).

To facilitate the understanding of the complexities involved in managing human resources in Canada several essential features are stressed consistently throughout the eighteen chapters.

HRM in the News Vignettes. This feature is placed strategically in the chapters. It aims to illustrate contemporary concerns in the management of human resources. It portrays recent examples taken from sources such as *The Montreal Gazette, The Globe and Mail, Canadian Business*; and monthly information service report bulletins such as *Human Resource Management in Canada.*

Chapter Pedagogy. A strong pedagogy supports the content of the book. Each chapter contains a Summary and Review and Analysis Questions. Key concepts are shown in bold type and defined in the Glossary. These features help to focus, review, and elaborate on the essential ideas of each chapter. Two additional aids include a set of up-to-date important references in the form of notes at the end of each chapter, and a convenient index for a quick retrieval of subjects at the end of the book.

Cases. A concise case at the end of each chapter applies the material previously discussed. The cases depict various business settings from public to private sector, from pulp and paper companies to high-tech industries, and from relatively small companies to rather large firms.

Whether you are a full-time student or part-time student enrolled in an HRM course, we hope that you will find *Human Resource Management: The Canadian Dynamic* stimulating and thought-provoking as well as informative and practical.

ACKNOWLEDGMENTS

In writing this book, we have benefited from the counsel, advice and assistance of many colleagues. But first, we wish to thank our former students whose collective experience with the first edition provided the impetus for this edition. Second, we wish to thank the CEOs and senior HR executives who granted us the Keynote Addresses and permitted us to share their views in this text. They include in alphabetical order:

Mr. Richard Barton, President and CEO, **Xerox Canada**
Mr. Kenneth S. Benson, Vice-President Personnel and Administration, **Canadian Pacific**
Mr. Peter Broadhurst, Vice-President Employee Relations, **Litton Systems Canada Ltd.**
Mrs. Shirley Carr, Former President, **Canadian Labour Congress**
Mr. John Cleghorn, President and COO, **Royal Bank of Canada**

Mr. Ross Coyles, Director Job Measurement, **Hay Group**
Mr. Pierre Girard, Corporate Vice-President Human Resources, **St-Hubert Group**
Mr. Yves Gosselin, Vice-President Staffing and Organizational Development, **Northern Telecom**
Mr. Peter A.W. Green, President, **Alcatel Canada Wire Inc.**
Dr. E.R. Israel, General Manager, Skill Dynamics Canada, An IBM Canada Company
Mr. Ron Kirschner, President and CEO, **Ivanhoe Inc.**
Mr. Yoshida Kogyo, President and CEO, **YKK Canada**
Mr. Charles A. Labarge, Vice-President Personnel Resources, **Bell Canada**
Mr. Don Morrison, President, **Avco Financial**
Dr. Louise Piché, Vice-President Human Resources, **Canadian National**
Mr. Arthur Sawchuk, President and CEO, **Dupont Canada**
Mr. Bob Swenor, Senior Vice-President, **Dofasco**
Mr. James Whitelaw, Senior Vice-President Human Resources, **Air Canada.**

We also wish to extend our thanks to the following individuals, whose encouragement and ideas have been directly or indirectly incorporated into this text: Professor Abe Korman (Baruch College, CUNY) for comments and suggestions for Chapter 12; Mr. Robert Saggers (Saggers Management Consultants) for ideas regarding HRM concerns among practitioners; Ms. Gaetin Haince (Montreal Trust) for comments and suggestions for Chapter 5; Mr. Denis Morin (Laval University) for comments for Chapters 9 and 10; Professor Luis Gomez-Mejia, Arizona State University, for comments and suggestions for Chapters 7 and 8; Professor Jean Guy Bergeron, The University of Montreal reviewed Chapter 16. His comments were most appreciated, although only a few were incorporated due to a divergence of opinions pertaining to the role and functions of unions in the labour relations system in Canada. A special thank you is due to Andrew Templer (University of Windsor); Andrew was very instrumental in commenting on an early version of the book; he was also most generous in supplying materials that were used in preparing Chapter 18. Other useful comments were made by the following reviewers selected by Nelson Canada:

Merle Ace	University of British Columbia
Monica Belcourt	York University
Doug Bicknell	University of Saskatchewan
R.G. Bradford	University of Alberta
Ronald L. Crawford	Concordia University
Gene Deszca	Wilfrid Laurier University
Stephen J. Havlovic	Simon Fraser University
David D. Dimick	York University
Harish C. Jain	McMaster University
Ian G. McGinty	University of Guelph

About 200 undergraduate students at McGill University, and forty executive MBA students at Concordia University served as our "guinea pigs" for trying out and experimenting with this text. Their feedback and general willingness to assist in the process are acknowledged.
Finally we wish to thank Nelson Canada's staff for their professional assistance. In particular, we wish to thank Yuval Kashdan for his editorial help pertaining to early versions of the manuscript, and Marg Bukta for her help in editing the final version of the book. The book would not have been published without the continual encouragement and support of Peter Jackson, and the dedication and meticulous care of Nicole Gnutzman.

Shimon L. Dolan	Randall S. Schuler
Montreal	New York

January 1993

CHAPTER ONE

THE GROWING IMPORTANCE OF HUMAN RESOURCE MANAGEMENT

KEYNOTE ADDRESS

Don Morrison
President, Avco Financial Services Canada Limited

Employees: The Deciding Factor

Canadian business is involved in an intensive campaign to increase productivity and to gain in the battle for international competitiveness. Consequently, focus is intensifying on conventional strategies such as streamlined operations, research and development, information technologies, and product development.

However, the largest operating expense of any large organization, its people, all too often does not receive the attention and development it deserves. We as senior management in Canadian companies often take a confined view of the human resources function. That is, a traditional emphasis on the basics such as compensation, benefits, recruitment, training, and the like are covered but we don't explore employee satisfaction, involvement, and values to the extent we should.

Avco Canada provides financial products and services to Canadians coast-to-coast through approximately 250 offices. Our employee base reflects varying levels of age, experience, nationality, cultures, and values. As such, we view our collective employee capability as the ultimate deciding factor in whether customers will continue to do business with us.

Simply put, it makes sound business sense, based on this diversity of today's employee, to foster innovation and creativity toward a common goal. Rather than simply developing a nice credo that states our employees are our greatest asset, and then going on to "more important" subjects, such as profitability, return on equity and other financial measurements, we have invested considerable resources and energy toward developing employee involvement and satisfaction.

The pillar of our human resource focus is the employee involvement process, which is the cultural environment that we have built at our company. Put in place following intensive customer research in the early 1980s, our quality effort requires and rewards extensive employee participation. In fact, every single Avco employee, from newly hired clerical staff to the president, participates on a quality team that meets a minimum of once per month. Approximately one-third of our employees have been provided organizational, leadership, and problem-solving training to help them effectively facilitate these teams. Avco Canada quality teams have researched, developed and implemented more than 1,350 ideas that have literally knocked down some thirty years of process and work systems paving the way to a better way of doing business. The cumulative savings or additional revenue generated from these team efforts for our company, since 1985, is more than nine million dollars.

To support our culture, core values that clearly articulate the company we want to be have been developed and our formal reward and recognition systems have been developed in alignment with these values. All employees negotiate and set goals with clear action plans and are measured to specified standards. Human resource and quality goals comprise a significant portion of these goals. Thus, an employee's performance in relation to these goals helps determine salary increases.

Our human resource group plays a proactive role in the day-to-day management of our organization, working hand-in-hand with operations, marketing, legal, treasury, and other functions to deliver service across the country. For example, our international human resource function is spearheading a senior operations management development program that focuses on five key performance dimensions, or roles. These dimensions work against traditional business paradigms of control and micro management, and include modules relating to roles of communicator, coach, manager, diagnostician, and trainer. In addition, the human resource group helps to develop team-building exercises and work processes we call "Teamsharing" in order to increase employee productivity, participation, and job satisfaction. We fully expect this investment in participatory schemes to pay off in increased loyalty and business.

Management strategies in today's business climate must be customer-focused and driven by employees as the agents of change. The immediate challenge, and opportunity, for Canadian business is to effectively tap into the inherent creativity and innovation of our employees. Although all levels of management and all levels of employees must share this vision, the human resource group should be the facilitators and guardians of this strategy. Thus, the role of the human resource group in the future will most likely become more and more important.

•　•　•

The Keynote Address by Mr. Morrison highlights the essential ideas that will be discussed in this book. It points out the increased importance of human resources in organizations today and the critical need to develop "a strategy" for remaining competitive in today's global economy, and it indicates that a wise strategy would be to satisfy internal customers (i.e., employees) as well as external customers in order to increase the firm's bottom line. Although Avco Financial has placed emphasis on quality and customer satisfaction through a "teamsharing" human resource (HR) strategy, it did not neglect the more traditional HR functions, such as recruitment, performance appraisal, compensation and incentive plans, as well as training. While other Canadian companies have chosen different strategies, one thing is clear: there is an increasingly important role for human resource management (HRM) in selecting, supporting, and implementing programs and strategies that will make the organization effective.

HR managers and departments are able to be more critical of today's organizations for a number of reasons: (1) organizations are more concerned than ever about managing human resources effectively because they understand the potential difference to profitability, growth, and even their own survival; (2) Human resources is seen as the department with the expertise to implement programs and policies that will facilitate effective management; and (3) HRM is a growing profession and organizations are beginning to realize that not just anybody can be assigned to the HR department; it takes skill and know-how in HRM to demonstrate effectiveness.

Although some organizations still use the term *personnel* for the department that deals with recruitment, selection, compensation, and training, the phrase *human resource management* is rapidly supplanting it. This change recognizes the vital role that human resources play in an organization, the challenges inherent in managing them effectively, and the growing body of knowledge and professionalism surrounding HRM. In return for this recognition, HR departments in organizations must successfully face the contemporary challenges.

Effective HRM enables organizations to enhance the quality of work life for their employees because it is based upon respect and concern for individual rights and preferences. Nonetheless, effective HRM still requires a thorough understanding of the numerous functions and activities that will be presented in this book.

•　•　•

HR THEMES, FUNCTIONS, AND ACTIVITIES

This book deals with the fundamental task of defining and analyzing jobs in organizations. In addition it is organized around eight themes that cover the general functions and activities of an HR department:

- Planning HR needs
- Staffing the organization's HR needs
- Compensating and motivating employees
- Appraising employee behaviour
- Enhancing human potential
- Improving the organization
- Maintaining effective work relationships
- Globalizing HRM

Although the HR departments of many organizations may not be currently performing all these functions, the trend is clearly moving in that direction. Consequently, it is useful to provide a broad description of the functions here.

Planning HR Needs

The planning function involves two major activities: (1) *strategic planning,* involving long-term planning and synchronizing the HR needs with the corporate strategic needs (i.e., growth, product or service diversity, downsizing, profit margins, market share, financial obligations, etc.); and (2) *short- and medium-range planning.* These two activities are essential for effectively performing many other HR activities. For example, they help indicate (a) how many and what types of employees the organization needs now and in future; (b) how the employees will be obtained (e.g., from outside recruiting or by internal transfers and promotions); and (c) the training needs that the organization will have. These activities can be viewed as the major factors influencing the staffing and development functions of the entire organization.

Although these activities are very important, most organizations have only recently incorporated them into routine HR operations. A recent survey conducted by the Conference Board of Canada indicates that, in the future, HR planning and its linkage to strategic business plans will be the single most important aspect of HR activity.[1]

Staffing the Organization's HR Needs

Once the organization's HR needs and links to the general business strategy have been determined, positions need to be filled. Staffing involves *recruiting* job applicants (candidates), *selecting* the most appropriate applicants for the available jobs, and *orienting and placing* the new job candidates.

These staffing activities apply to external candidates (those not currently employed by the organization) as well as to internal candidates (those currently employed). For the external recruitment, the organization must cast a wide net to ensure a full and fair search for job candidates. Recruiting is an extremely important HR function because the greater the number of applicants, the more selective an organization can be in its hiring. After the candidates have been identified, they must be selected. Common selection procedures include obtaining completed application forms or résumés; interviewing candidates; checking education, background, experience, and references; conducting various forms of tests; and holding various types of simulation. All procedures must comply with various federal and provincial human rights legislation, and, in principle, the final decision must be job related. In other words, selection procedures must result in a match between a candidate's ability and the abilities required by the job.

Compensating and Motivating Employees

Once employees are on the job, it becomes necessary to determine how well they are doing and to reward them accordingly. If they are not doing well, one must determine why. This may indicate that the reward structure needs to be changed, or that employee training is necessary, or that some type of motivation should be provided.

There are several aspects to compensation. Employees are generally rewarded on the basis of the value of the job, their personal contributions, and their performance. Although rewards based on performance can increase an employee's motivation to perform, other forms of compensation are given simply for being a member of the organization. The latter is commonly referred to as indirect compensation and is given to make the organization more attractive to new hires as well as to retain existing employees. The value and structure of both direct and indirect compensation needs to be rational and the process involves a careful analysis by the HR department.

Which form of compensation is most fair? Which form is most effective for the organization? How can jobs be evaluated fairly to determine their value? These concerns and others have an impact on the compensating activity, which includes: (1) administering direct compensation as well as designing performance-based pay systems, and (2) administering indirect compensation benefits to employees in the organization.

Although performance appraisal may not be desired by certain supervisors and many employees, it is critically important for measuring and monitoring an employee's contribution. Based on such evaluations, decisions are made regarding promotions, transfers, and training as well as de-hiring. Not all employees give continued good performance. Some may be chronically absent, some may be alcoholics or have chemical dependencies, and some may repeatedly be late to work. However, with the rise of employee rights, greater social responsibility, and the high cost of replacing employees, organizations may find it preferable to assist employees in correcting their undesired behaviour rather than to terminate them.

Appraising Employee Behaviour

Two areas in which HRM interest has grown in recent years are *training and development* and *career management and planning*. Determining, designing, and implementing employee training and development programs to increase employee ability, performance, and growth is of increased concern. Additionally, due to the staggering costs of turnover, many organizations develop policies and career paths aimed to assist employees in developing careers within the organization. The challenge is immense: the 1990s are characterized by limited growth and, thus, traditional career plans are very limited.

Training and development activities are used by many firms as one of the most important strategies to remain competitive. With the rapidly changing technologies, and with the need to have a workforce that is continually able to perform new tasks, the HR department is facing important challenges.

Enhancing Human Potential

There has been rapid growth in the past few years of activities that involve enhancing *quality of work life* and implementing *productivity* improvement programs as well as ameliorating *health and safety* at work. Through various innovations in the structure and forms of managing people, organizations are exploring ways and means to increase productivity and quality of work life for their employees. These two concepts are intimately linked because increased productivity is to be expected from a more content workforce. Experiments involving flattening organizational structure and increasing employee participation and responsibility are on the rise.

Similarly, organizations attempt to improve the work environment by making it less hazardous. While in the past the primary health and safety focus was on the physical work environment, there is a growing concern about the psychological work environment, since it is becoming apparent that if either environment is poor, productivity will suffer. In ameliorating the two types of work environments, both increased quality of work life and

Improving the Organization

productivity gains are likely to be achieved. In Canada, organizations must comply with federal and provincial laws covering occupational health and safety; these laws have a special influence in establishing and maintaining effective work relationships.

Maintaining Effective Work Relationships

When the organization has hired the employees it needs, it must take good care of them. In addition to compensation and a healthy and safe environment, it must provide conditions that will make it attractive for them to stay. As part of this function, organizations must establish and maintain effective working relationships with employees. This is achieved through a number of activities: (1) recognizing and respecting employee rights; (2) understanding why employees unionize and the functions and structure of the union; (3) bargaining and settling grievances with employees and the organizations representing them.

Increasingly, employees are gaining more rights. Consequently, employment decisions such as discharges, layoffs, and demotions must be made with care and evidence. It is important that the managers of the organization be aware of their employees' rights. The HR manager is in an excellent position to inform line managers of these rights.

Globalizing HRM

As the world becomes more interdependent, it is paramount that we understand and learn from HR activities in other countries. On the one hand, HR managers need to focus particularly on those countries that have achieved astonishing economic results, such as Japan and Germany; on the other hand, since many Canadian companies are or will become multinational (i.e., have branches, divisions, and plants in other countries), we need to develop and implement HRM policies that have international applications. Additionally, as attempts to become competitive are increasing, research and assessment of HRM is a universal concern for all organizations.

RELATIONSHIPS INFLUENCING HR FUNCTIONS AND ACTIVITIES

Rather than viewing HRM as a set of eight separate functions and activities, it is more appropriate to view the systemic relationships among them. That is, one activity's performance often depends on another's. (Because of this interdependence, a section in each chapter of the book briefly describes the most extensive and important relationships of each activity. Only the most critical relationships are described.) Moreover, all HR functions and activities are operating within the constraints of the internal and external environment. That is, all eight functions should be viewed as a unit, necessarily interrelated, and subject to a multitude of forces and events that help shape an organization's HR policies.

Internal Influences

Several features within organizations influence HR activities, including top management, organizational strategy, culture, technology, structure, and size. For example, top management's values help shape corporate culture, and strategy helps determine organizational structure. The key idea, however, is to understand how and why each of these factors within the internal environment influences HR practices.

TOP-MANAGEMENT SUPPORT. Top management determines how important HRM will be in an organization. If top management minimizes the importance of people to the organization's overall success, so will line managers. In turn, those in the HR department will perform only the most routine activities. A likely consequence will be to hold the HR functions as "reactive" to management needs rather than "proactive." Over the years, the general shift from *personnel* to *HRM* denotes a shift in top management's view of the importance and functions of this department. A recent survey of Quebec's largest corporations found a major shift in the perception of chief executive officers (CEOs) regarding the role and importance of their HR departments. Results show some very important trends:

91 percent of all respondents believe that the relative influence of HRM has significantly increased over the past five years and will most likely continue to rise; in large organizations, the senior HR officer has been normally found to be part of the corporate strategic team; these officers report benefiting from the strong support of their CEOs and the other managers.[2]

STRATEGY.   Organizations are increasingly linking HRM to corporate strategy. The corporate strategy determines which general characteristics organizations require in their employees. A strategy, for instance, will inform employees about such organizational concerns as: short-term vs. long-term focus; quality vs. quantity; high risk vs. low risk; flexibility vs. rigidity; independent vs. dependent behaviour; or conformity vs. autonomy and discretion, to name a few.[3] These characteristics, although partially constrained by the organizational technology and structure, affect the specific skills, knowledge, and abilities that employees need to perform their jobs. Because HR activities are capable of fostering the required employee characteristics, once a strategy is selected, these activities are influenced. The nature of this influence is so critical that it will be elaborated later in this chapter in the trends and crises section.

CULTURE.   Corporate culture represents the organization's value system. Strongly influenced by top management, it identifies people's values and the assumptions made about their willingness to work, their ethics, and the way they should be treated.[4] Culture often comes to be reflected in the company's HR practices. For example, companies such as DOFASCO developed a culture of caring for and respecting their employees. The company motto reflects this view: "Our product is steel, our strength is people." Other Canadian companies have adopted cultures ranging from an attempt to guarantee secured employment to policies of providing child care, employee assistance programs, and much more. More about these contemporary cultures appears in Chapter 13. What is clear, however, is that corporate culture has a significant impact on HR functions and activities, since activities normally articulate corporate culture. The actual selection of HR practices forms a menu of available choices and is dictated by the prevailing corporate culture.

TECHNOLOGY AND STRUCTURE.   Technology generally refers to the equipment and knowledge used to produce goods and services. It is well known that the prevailing technology to manufacture automobiles is the assembly line, while the educational technology offered to college and university students emphasizes lectures. Assembly-line technology has a distinct impact on the way jobs are designed and the type of employees that will be hired or trained to manufacture cars. Because education is highly dependent on the quality of lecturers, emphasis on selection, monitoring, and training of professors will be entirely different. With the economic crunch and quality and productivity crises, traditional technology and the host of HR activities associated with them are currently being challenged. In fact, the entire concept of the so-called "technological imperative" is being questioned. Although it was once believed that the assembly line was the most efficient way to produce cars, this belief has been rapidly changing. Assembly-line technology is giving way to newer forms of technology, such as craft or batch technology.[5]

Additionally, organizational structure is becoming flatter. With modern technology and computers, close supervision becomes unnecessary; human inspectors are being replaced by electronic inspectors, and work is being performed at flexible hours and often away from the physical plant. The trend has been for companies to restructure themselves to be most effective in terms of quality and cost. This has often been carried out through reduction in the number of levels of employees and by decentralizing the decision-making process (i.e., flatter structures).

SIZE. Organizational size is also an important factor in HR activities. With some exceptions, the larger the organization, the more developed its internal labour market and the less reliant it is on the external labour market. With more reliance on the internal labour market, the organization has more discretion in determining several HR policies. For example, decisions on how to pay its employees, how to evaluate them, how to classify jobs, and how to determine career paths are less dependent on the external labour market.

External Influences

Major components of the external environment influencing HR functions and activities include the *economy*, *national and international competitors*, *demographics* of the labour force, *social values*, and *laws and regulations*. Because the demographics, legal requirements, and social values issues are critical factors contributing to the growing importance of HRM, they are described in this chapter as well as in Chapter 4.

THE ECONOMY. The national, provincial, and local economies can have a significant impact on HR activities. A strong economy tends to decrease the unemployment, increase wages, make recruitment more important, increase the desirability of training, and prepare employers to negotiate with more militant employees and their unions. By contrast, a weak economy tends to increase unemployment, diminish wage demands, make recruitment less important, and reduce the need for training and development of current employees. HRM has a major role to play in both types of economies, although the priorities and nature of their respective activities and functions will change.

INTERNATIONAL COMPETITION. HRM is being affected not only by the immediate external environment, but also by the international economy and the free trade agreements with the U.S.A. and Mexico, which have increased the level of competition and forced Canadian corporations to become more competitive, flexible, and bottom-line oriented.

OBJECTIVES OF HRM

The eight separate HR functions and their related activities are important because they contribute to the realization of several organizational objectives. These have been classified for presentation purposes into three categories: *explicit*, *implicit* and *long-term* or *bottom-line*. These three categories, which by no means are to be regarded as mutually exclusive, are illustrated in Exhibit 1.1. The exhibit also depicts the logic and sequence for the chapters in the book.

Explicit Objectives

There are four major explicit objectives of effective HRM:

- To attract potentially qualified job applicants;
- To retain the desirable employees;
- To motivate the employees;
- To help employees grow, develop, and realize their potential in the organization.

To attract potentially qualified job applicants, it is not sufficient to have an elaborate recruiting program. Attractive compensation and training programs may also be required. And so it is with any of the other HR functions and activities: performing one effectively requires consideration of the others. Because of the importance and prevalence of this systemic relationship of the HR functions and activities, a section in each chapter is devoted to describing the relationships *most relevant* to the topic of that chapter.

HR functions and activities are important largely because they serve to attract, retain, and motivate employees, but it is widely acknowledged that by doing an effective job in realizing these explicit objectives, they positively affect the bottom line. Conversely, a

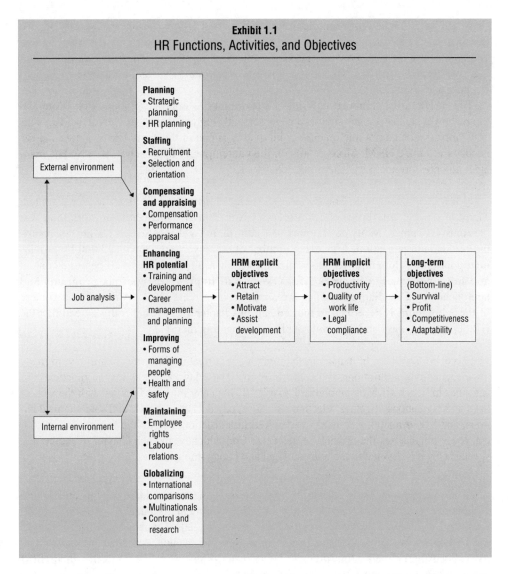

Exhibit 1.1
HR Functions, Activities, and Objectives

External environment

Job analysis

Internal environment

Planning
• Strategic planning
• HR planning

Staffing
• Recruitment
• Selection and orientation

Compensating and appraising
• Compensation
• Performance appraisal

Enhancing HR potential
• Training and development
• Career management and planning

Improving
• Forms of managing people
• Health and safety

Maintaining
• Employee rights
• Labour relations

Globalizing
• International comparisons
• Multinationals
• Control and research

HRM explicit objectives
• Attract
• Retain
• Motivate
• Assist development

HRM implicit objectives
• Productivity
• Quality of work life
• Legal compliance

Long-term objectives
(Bottom-line)
• Survival
• Profit
• Competitiveness
• Adaptability

poor selection of an employee or a poorly designed program to maintain employee motivation renders the employee unsatisfied and performance suffers.

There are three implicit HR objectives: improvement of productivity, improvement of quality of work life, and ensuring legal compliance. Although several HR functions and activities may serve the four explicit objectives discussed above, each may also serve these three implicit objectives, and once again it results in bottom-line long-term benefits to the organization.

Implicit Objectives

PRODUCTIVITY. Productivity is an important goal for any organization. HRM can do many things to improve productivity through people. In fact, recognizing this, the most productive organizations in North America differ from the less productive ones in their treatment of HR departments. The two major areas in which HR managers can make a significant contribution toward productivity improvements, according to the Conference Board of Canada survey, are work organization and design. The report suggests that traditionally structured work, where employee tasks and responsibilities are described in detail, blocks creativity, restricts the ability to contribute and add value, and affects productivity.[6]

At Du Pont Canada, for example, traditional work design is giving way to a broadened concept. While an operator's job in one plant consisted of monitoring valves and gauges and controlling the flow process, the job has changed to include scheduling work (including time off and overtime), scheduling delivery of raw materials, and occasionally evaluating peer performance.

Today, HRM has a unique and timely opportunity to improve productivity. More and more, however, that means increasing output with higher quality than ever before. This new emphasis on combining quantity with quality is one of the many forces increasing the need for effective HRM. More details on the contemporary approaches used by HR managers to boost productivity is found in Chapter 13.

QUALITY OF WORK LIFE.   The dissatisfying nature of many jobs is no longer disputed. Many of today's employees prefer a greater level of involvement in their work than was previously assumed. Many desire more self-control and a chance to make a greater contribution to the organization. A growing number of employers are convinced that by providing opportunities for employees to realize these new aspirations, they will be more content and thus their quality of work life (QWL) will improve. Numerous programs and approaches by Canadian companies are aimed at improving QWL. Although the content of these programs is described in more detail in Chapter 13, it is generally agreed that the HR department plays an important role in implementing them.

LEGAL COMPLIANCE.   In managing their employees, organizations must comply with many laws, regulations, arbitrations, and court decisions. These laws affect almost all functions and activities in which HRM is involved. Today's HR manager must be familiar with the web of laws and regulations affecting selection decisions, pay decisions, health and safety considerations, and labour relations, to name a few. Recent legislation, both at the federal and provincial level, emphasizes the rights of employees. Consequently, in each chapter of the book a special section is devoted to the relevant legal and policy implications.

Long-Term Objectives

Long-term objectives, or the bottom line, refers to the organization's profitability and competitiveness, or, in the case of nonprofit and government organizations, to survival and the ability to do more with the same or fewer resources. HRM makes a significant impact on the bottom line through its contribution to the four explicit and three implicit objectives. Focusing on the bottom line and being result oriented are the ways in which HRM can gain recognition and respect in organizations.

THE GROWING IMPORTANCE OF HRM

The 1990s are sure to usher in a whirlwind of change for HR departments everywhere. This decade is witnessing trends that will reverberate through companies worldwide, and Canadian firms will not be able to escape them. Today's highly competitive, volatile economic environment, a rapidly shrinking labour pool, greater workforce diversity including the increasing presence of women, the balancing of work life and family life, the customers' insistence on quality products and services at reduced costs, and the repercussions of drugs, alcohol, and diseases such as AIDS in the workplace are just some of the issues that will render the input of HR departments more critical to organizations' success. HR departments are expected to be more resourceful and their ingenuity will be tested. In fact, in order for organizations not only to survive but to succeed in the coming decade, HR departments will have to aggressively meet these challenges head-on. Already, there seems to be a wider recognition that some functions and activities emphasized in the past will no longer be important in the future; rather, other functions and activities will assume more importance.

Consequently, the growing importance of HRM is largely due to several trends and crises in society in general and in the world of work in particular. Added to this is the recognition that HRM can significantly influence the goals of organizations. In order to depict the major events that influenced the growth in importance of HRM, six major trends and crises have been identified: (1) increased competition and, therefore, the need to be competitive; (2) the costs and benefits associated with HR utilization; (3) the productivity crisis; (4) the increasing pace and complexity of social, cultural, legal, demographic, and educational changes; (5) the symptoms of dysfunction in the workplace; and (6) trends for the 1990s.

"The most important characteristic of today's business environment—and therefore the yardstick against which managerial techniques must be measured—is the new competition."[7] The world is becoming a single market and consequently, as accurately described in the following HRM in the News Vignette, competition is becoming fierce.

Increased Competition

Future Canadian competitiveness will be less dependent on traditional competitive tools as their efficacy is slowly being eroded. Instead, competitive strength will be increasingly contingent on new tools of which HRM is one. "The winning organization of the future will be the one that can best attract, retain, and motivate employees with drive, talent, and skills."[8]

HRM IN THE NEWS VIGNETTE

Creating a Competitive Canada

The central fact of economic activity in the world today is that the institutional changes which have taken place in the past decade or so—the collapse of the Soviet Union (and its economy), the unification of Germany, the approaching economic integration of Europe, free trade agreements in North America—combined with the great technological changes in transportation and communication, have created one single place in which to do business—in the world.... With the exception of agricultural products and a few other goods and services, there are no longer any highly protected markets.

The obvious and already apparent consequence of this change is the development of true global competition for most products and services. And those firms which can produce products at the lowest possible price will survive; those that cannot will not.

Only a decade or so ago, corporate executives could avoid responding to international change by producing, with the help of various protective measures or subsidies, only for their domestic market. However, with the decline of the barriers to movement of capital, goods, information and services, it is no longer a feasible strategy, unless the firm is a low-cost producer in world terms, to limit one's operations to one home market. The reality is that unless a company is managed globally for the purpose of producing at the lowest possible cost, some other company will come and take away the domestic market. Firms have no choice but to manage in the context of international markets. There is no place to hide.

Forward-thinking executives have recognized the change and are managing accordingly. Successful companies are planning globally and managing locally. They are removing layers of head-office management and getting away from hierarchical reporting systems. They are, in the vernacular, becoming "lean." They are using materials and technology regardless of their nationality, and are producing at the lowest possible cost.... There is, in fact, a great managerial revolution taking place. And no company can avoid the impact of the revolution.

Source: Excerpts from a feature article of the same title by J. Gillies, in a special issue, "Corporate Strategy 1992," Inside Guide Magazine 5, 6 (December 1991): 7. Reprinted with permission.

HR Costs

Today, with payroll costs running anywhere between 50 and 80 percent of total expenses, corporations realize it pays to be concerned with human resources. An important consequence of this awareness is the need for HR departments to be more cost conscious and to demonstrate their contribution to the organization by implementing cost saving programs without deterring from the traditional HR objectives. HR departments are expected to develop human resources in such a way that significant reductions in accidents, absenteeism, and error rates will occur, along with significant increases in morale and in the quality of product or service. Here are a few examples of typical costs and possible benefits pertaining to HR indicators:

- A recent survey of absenteeism in the Canadian pulp and paper industry found the average absence rate to be around 5.5 percent (which is also the standard rate prevailing in the Canadian industry).[9] Thus, it is estimated that a 5 percent absence rate costs a 1,000-employee firm $1.5 million a year. For paper mills reporting up to 15.8 percent absence rate the costs are three times higher.

- Recent studies of Canadian nurses in the hospital industry, especially those working in "high stress units" such as emergency wards and intensive care, found an alarming rate of turnover. Within a one-year period, about 20 percent of nurses quit their job in the unit and many more have expressed their intention to quit in the future.[10] With an estimated cost of about $5,000 per single nurse replacement, it is costing each hospital (having about 500 nurses on staff in these units), about $2.5 million every five years (assuming 100 percent turnover within this period).

- Accidents are also very costly to organizations. Although many more details about this topic are provided in Chapter 14, one example is provided here. The survey cited above for the Canadian pulp and paper industry, also found the average time lost due to work-related injuries or illness to be around 8.5 percent, ranging from companies experiencing 57 percent to those having only 0.10 percent. Due to different regulations and policies pertaining to workers' compensation, calculation of a firm's actual cost varies across provinces. Nonetheless, it is basically accepted that the direct and indirect costs are staggering.

- One researcher asserts that in a ten-year period the cost to Canadian industry of not using scientific methods in employee selection exceeds $55.6 billion. According to this researcher, the entire loss can be recuperated by a total investment of $1.3 billion in developing valid and reliable selection tools and approaches.[11]

Productivity Crisis

Although Canada ranked third among the world's seven leading industrial nations in productivity gains during the late 1970s, the data gathered during the 1980s and projections made by many economists for the 1990s suggest that a real productivity crisis will confront Canadian workers in this decade. Canada had a productivity gain of 4.2 percent in 1978 compared with Japan's 8.3 percent or France's 4.9 percent. All the other industrial nations reported smaller increments for that year: West Germany, 3.7 percent; Italy, 2.9 percent; the U.S.A., 2.5 percent; and Great Britain, 1.6 percent. The decline in Canadian productivity began, according to a study conducted by the consulting firm Caron Belanger Woods Gordon, in that year. Rather than comparing Canadian productivity to that of other nations, they analyzed the productivity trends and showed a systematic decline in productivity gains.[12] In the past few years Canadian productivity growth was limited to less than 3 percent annually, while the economies of the U.S.A., Japan, Germany, and even that of Spain pulled ahead significantly. In fact, if the trend continues, Spain will replace Canada in the ranks of the seven leading industrial nations of the world.

Undoubtedly, many factors are contributing to this productivity crisis—changes in technology, capital investment, capacity utilization and work flow, and government policies. Nonetheless, HRM is central to productivity, since more effective utilization of human resources may be the best hope for stopping the slide in productivity.

Several ongoing changes in the cultural and education levels and the social order in Canada have also made HRM more important. For example, between the early 1970s and mid 1980s the participation rate of women in the labour force increased from 38 percent to 53 percent.[13] In the 1990s the participation rate of women in the workforce is expected to increase due to the popularity of part-time work. During the 1990s the number of workers in the 18 to 24 age group will decline, while the number in the 35 to 44 age group will rise. Already in Canada, the proportion of younger workers between the ages of 15 and 24 years dropped from roughly one in four in the mid 1970s to one in five in the 1980s. This results from the coming-of-age of the "baby-bust" generation and is producing the worst labour shortage in twenty years. Although this problem is not creating an overall shortage of workers, it is affecting how those workers are able to fit available jobs. Because this baby-bust generation does not comprise enough youthful workers to fill the bottom level of the typical corporate pyramid, companies are being challenged to devise ingenious methods of wooing the increasingly choosy entry-level worker.

The current workforce is generally becoming more knowledgeable and better informed. Whereas in the early 1970s only one of every ten workers had a college degree, in the 1980s one of every five workers who entered the labour force had one, and the ratio is expected to be even higher in the 1990s. These high-quality human resources are potentially more productive. This potential, however, presents a real challenge to organizations. As society becomes better informed, it also tends to become more critical, less accepting of authority, and more cynical. Young workers appear to be particularly cynical about decisions made by supervisors and, correspondingly, more resistant to authority. Older workers, however, still tend to reflect earlier values of society and are, therefore, more inclined to be organization people, to accept authority, and to seek primarily the satisfaction of lower-level needs at work. Thus, effective HRM requires not only knowing how to manage and channel the skills of the young workers but also knowing how to manage a workforce with a mixed set of values. Other workforce characteristics are described in Chapter 4.

Pace and Complexity of Change

Rapid social change has been accompanied by changes in the relationship between the worker and the job. Some of the terms used to describe what is happening in the workplace include *stress*, *worker alienation*, *boredom*, and *job dissatisfaction*. These symptoms are often associated with decreasing motivation, increasing counterproductive behaviour, and more worker demands. Where they do exist, however, it appears that they can be eliminated through HR programs designed to involve employees more fully in decisions on the job.

A series of articles in the *Financial Post* reported the conclusions of a survey of top Canadian businesses that echoed the conclusions of Peters and Waterman's *In Search of Excellence*. They basically found that the best-run corporations in Canada are those that emphasize "people management": processes and structures through which managers deal with each other, their subordinates, their customers, and others in their environment.[14] Such findings have advanced the cause of improved HRM in organizations. HR officers have reported being pushed into the limelight of executive committee meetings and challenged to answer such questions as "What can we do to change the 'culture' of the firm?" and "How can we get our employees more involved?"

Symptoms in the Workplace

The work ethic among Canadian workers remains strong, with most workers ready to put in long hours to improve their economic positions. There are many anecdotes drawn from Canadian companies that show that in spite of the utilization of old technologies and a history of labour relations plagued with conflicts, mistrust can be changed. A case in point is the GM Ste Thérèse plant in Quebec. Until the mid 1980s the symptoms of the workplace were alarming, which led to a significant productivity decline. As GM was just about to close down the plant, an agreement was reached among management, labour, and the government to change the climate and methods of work. After implementing numerous HR programs and altering the plant culture, the plant became one of GM's most productive. Even during the hard economic times in 1991 and 1992, and despite GM's decision to significantly reduce its workforce worldwide, the Ste Thérèse plant expanded production to a new line previously manufactured by a California plant.

Another workplace symptom is the desire for a more explicit statement of employee rights. Among the rights employees desire are the right to work, to know what one's job and its requirements are, to participate in decisions, to be appraised fairly using objective performance criteria, to be accountable, and to be able to take risks and make mistakes.

Brief Evolution of HRM in Canada

An authoritative history of HRM in Canada has yet to be written. Nonetheless, many of the developments in this area reflect a combination of British and U.S. influences. Three major forces have helped to shape the evolution of the role of HR departments in Canadian business: (1) the slow change in general management philosophy, moving since the beginning of the century from the management of "things" to the management of "people"; (2) the political pressures that were eventually translated into laws; and (3) the changes in the values of the larger society of which Canadian business is a part.

Although HRM can be very important to an organization, organizations have not always viewed the HR department that way. This was due, in part, to the limited role it often played: "To many businessmen, including many chief executives, the people who worked in 'personnel' appeared to be a bunch of drones whose apparent missions in life were to create paperwork, recruit secretaries who couldn't type, and send around memos whose impertinence was exceeded only by their irrelevance."[15]

As a result of this perception, personnel directors seemed to be accomplishing nothing of any true importance. Today, for reasons already described, HR departments in many organizations are much more vital. Organizations are recognizing the prevalent crises and trends and the impact that HRM can have on the bottom-line organizational goals. Consequently, the HR department is now becoming a key corporate division and the executives who are being put in charge of these departments are as interested in profits as any other executives.

Trends for the Year 2000

Due to all the events suggested above, the functions and activities of HRM are likely to change in the future. While no one can predict with precision what will be the nature and scope of these changes, several emerging trends appear in recent surveys of senior HR executives. The common denominator for these surveys is that HRM will occupy a significantly more important role in Canadian organizations.[16]

INCREASE IN STRATEGIC INVOLVEMENT. Traditionally, HR departments had a relatively limited involvement in the total organization's affairs and goals. Now it seems that this is changing. All surveys indicate increased input from HR executives in developing corporate strategies, in addition to serving on operational planning and finance committees. Most senior HR officers in organizations bear the title of vice president, and report directly to the CEO. Thus, they are expected in the future to have closer links with the decision makers; to set up HR policies, practices, and programs that will help the firm better meet its strategic goals; and, in general, to affirm their presence through greater involvement in other aspects of the business. These changes, according to several researchers, are driven by three fundamental beliefs: (1) employee performance depends to a large extent on HR activities; (2) the quality of strategic decisions taken by top management is tied to the quality of HR data used in the decision-making process; and (3) successful implementation of strategic goals and objectives is contingent upon how well HR activities such as selection, performance appraisal, training and development, and compensation are carried out.[17] In addition, all surveys indicate that HR departments, via the respective HR senior executive, are expected to be much more proactive than reactive. This means that they will have to develop tools to maximize organizational and individual flexibility as well as make an important contribution to the resolution of conflicts inside and outside the organization. More information about the evolution and anticipated activities and functions pertaining to strategic HRM is provided in Chapter 2.

INCREASE IN STRATEGIC PARTNERSHIP WITH LINE MANAGEMENT. Many respondents indicate that in order to maintain their importance in the organization as well as increasing the likelihood of implementing successful HR programs, a new partnership with line managers will be created. Traditionally, HR roles vis-à-vis line managers had been those of a control agency, a service agency, and an advisor agency. In more and more organizations, the HR control function is delegated to line managers. Especially in large organizations, HR executives assume the role of internal consultant by offering their know-how to help line managers resolve operational problems. Two examples illustrate this shift. The first case is that of General Electric Canada, where the HR department has been transformed into an "organizational effectiveness centre" that provides, through its permanent staff, in-house counselling to various divisions in need of their expertise. In the second case, that of Northern Telecom Canada, the shift from bureaucratic approach to consultative approach was influenced by bottom-line needs. For instance, in the past HR managers developed merit pay guidelines, pay-off matrices, and a host of delivery systems for line managers to adopt. Presently, however, the trend is to move from organization-wide compensation approaches toward holding the line manager accountable for his or her compensation costs. Consequently, the line manager needs more latitude and flexibility to meet his or her labour market demands.

NEW PRIORITIES FOR FUNCTIONS AND ACTIVITIES. In addition to increases in strategic orientation, all surveys indicate an increase in importance of "work effectiveness issues." These are activities and programs designed to lead to higher levels of work quality and quantity, such as productivity improvement programs, and improved HR research designed to control and test effectiveness. However, slight differences exist between the surveys conducted in Ontario and those conducted in Quebec with regard to the emerging trends (next five years). Exhibit 1.2 shows the top five areas of priority.

As far as the common denominators, it appears that training and development are going to increase in importance in the 1990s. This trend is further explained in Chapter 11. It also appears that sensitivity to employee needs will be an important priority for the 1990s, either in the form of communications, attitude surveys, or personal counselling. On the other hand, while it is suggested that equity issues will preoccupy Ontario HR executives, their colleagues in Quebec will place more importance on minimizing labour costs and developing programs for increasing union–management cooperation.

Exhibit 1.2
Trends in Importance for HR Functions and Activities for the 1990s

RANK ORDER	PRENTICE–HALL SURVEY (ONTARIO)	DOLAN ET AL. SURVEY (QUEBEC)
1	Pay equity	Communications programs
2	Equal employment opportunity	Reducing labour costs
3	Personal problems counselling	Union–management cooperation (conflict resolution)
4	Employee attitude surveys	Training and development
5	Training and development	Staffing

Note: It is worth mentioning that the differences observed in Exhibit 1.2 might be due to the different methodologies used.

ORGANIZING THE HR DEPARTMENT

HRM in the Organization

Based on the discussion thus far, it is evident that for the HR department to be effective, it must not only be thoroughly involved in the organization but also be well organized. While there are no fixed rules regarding the organization of HR departments, there are some commonly established criteria that may guide their structuring.

It should be clear that effective HRM is proactive and open; it can simultaneously be engaged in implementing the many functions and activities listed in the earlier discussion. Thus the organization of HRM should be carried out bearing in mind its ability to respond to the following:

- The need to enable HR managers to assume different roles, as discussed in the next section;
- The need to facilitate HR staff work by facilitating access to where the action is;
- The need to enable a fair and consistent application of HR policies, regardless of how small or large or diversified the organization is;
- The need for the department's views to be an integral part of HR policy;
- The need for the HR department to have sufficient power and authority to help ensure that HR policies will be implemented affirmatively, legally, and without discrimination;
- The need for the HR department not just to react to personnel crises but to be active and innovative in dealing with HRM.

These six issues affect the *organization* of HR departments. An HR department can be organized so that it effectively addresses only one or two of these issues. The way top management views HR activities and what it is willing to let the HR department do will determine this organization. The importance that an organization assigns to HRM is often reflected by its position in the hierarchy. This in turn helps determine the number of roles HRM plays and the levels at which they are played.

HRM IN THE HIERARCHY. For the effective fulfillment of the various roles an HR department must assume, top HR managers should also be at the top of the organizational hierarchy. In fact, according to recent surveys, in more and more Canadian corporations the top HR manager is placed in second position in the hierarchy, usually at the VP level and equivalent to other VPs such as production, marketing, and finance.

Being at the top allows the HR manager to play a part in HR policy formulation and to have the power necessary for its fair and consistent implementation. When HRM has this much importance, it is likely to be performing operational, managerial, and strategic HR activities.

In addition to these considerations, it is imperative that an HR department be adequately staffed with professionals who are capable of assuming various roles.

HR managers can play several roles in an organization. The more roles they play, the more likely it is that they will be effective in improving the organization's productivity, enhancing QWL in the organization, and complying with all the necessary laws and regulations related to HR utilization. Although traditionally HR roles are primarily viewed as *staff* or advisory in capacity, it has been suggested that with the increase in importance of this department and with more involvement in corporate strategic decision processes, other roles have been added over the years. One interesting classification is to identify five major roles: policy formulator, provider and delegator, auditor, innovator, and adapter.

HR Roles

POLICY FORMULATOR ROLE. One role the HR department can play is that of providing information for top-management use, more specifically at the strategic level. The information may contain employee concerns and information about the impact of the external environment as well as ideas about helping the company gain a competitive edge.

HR staff can also advise in the process of policy formulation. The chief executive may still make policy statements, but these could be regarded as drafts of policy. Formal adoption of a final policy can take place after other executives, such as the HR manager and line managers, have had a chance to comment. St. Hubert B-B-Q as well as Noranda Mines, for example, have an executive committee composed of the senior vice-presidents. Any policy that has implications on employees is tested there first. The senior HR officer is a member of this committee, which not only helps ensure extensive informational input into HR policies but also increases the likelihood of a decision being accepted.

PROVIDER AND DELEGATOR ROLE. In reality, HR programs succeed because line managers (at managerial and operational levels) make them succeed. The "bread-and-butter" job of the HR department, therefore, is to enable line managers to make things happen. In the more traditional HR activities, such as selecting, interviewing, training, evaluating, compensating, rewarding, counselling, promoting, and firing, the department is basically providing a service to line managers. Since the line managers are ultimately responsible for their employees, many of them need these services. The HR department can also assist line managers by providing information about, and interpreting, equity legislation, jurisprudence, and court decisions, as well as health and safety standards.

The responsibilities of the HR department are to provide the services needed by the line managers on a day-to-day basis, to keep them informed of regulations and legislation regarding HRM, and to provide an adequate supply of job candidates for line managers to select from. To fulfil these responsibilities, however, the department must be accessible or the HR manager will lose touch with the line managers' needs. Consider this typical statement made by a line manager: "If only the personnel people would visit us sometime, they might better understand what it is we do."[18] Consequently, the HR staff should be as close as possible to where the people and problems are.

AUDITOR ROLE. Although HR managers may delegate much of the implementation of HR activities to line managers, the department is still responsible for seeing that activities are implemented fairly and consistently. This is especially true today because of fair employment legislation. Various provincial and federal regulations are making increasingly sophisticated demands on organizations. Responses to these regulations can best be made by a central group supplied with accurate information, the needed expertise, and the support of top management.

Expertise is also needed for implementing many HR activities, such as distributing employee benefits. Because having personnel experts is costly, organizations hire as few as possible and centralize them. Their expertise then filters to other areas of the organization.

In organizations that have several locations and several divisions or units, tension often exists between the need for decentralization and the need for having the expertise necessary to comply with complex regulations and to advise the best methods to carry out HR activities.

Furthermore, as costs of HRM are increasing, HR departments are also beginning to assume the responsibility for measuring the costs and benefits of various HR policies in the organization. There are many methods devised to carry out this assessment, but the one that is becoming more popular is the "Personnel Audit." More information about the assessment activities is provided in Chapter 18.

Part of the auditor role also involves control and research. This involves keeping and analyzing records on a wide variety of important HR matters, varying from those required by the government, such as employment equity and workers' compensation, to those that indicate employees' level of performance, motivation, absenteeism, and the like. The task of conducting this research and assessment is becoming easier with the introduction of computer technologies, and especially with the implementation of Human Resource Information Systems (HRIS).

INNOVATOR ROLE.   An important and ever-expanding role for the HR department is that of providing up-to-date application of current techniques and developing and exploring innovative approaches to personnel problems and concerns. The innovative role must be in tune with the times and the set of issues confronting a particular company. In periods of rising inflation and escalating wage and salary demands, the emphasis may be on compensation issues and negotiations with militant unions. On the other hand, in times of curbing operations, retrenchment, and downsizing, more creative work arrangements and lay-off plans may be needed.

Today, the HR issues demanding innovative approaches and solutions revolve around how to improve productivity, with much greater emphasis on customer satisfaction and QWL for the employees, while complying with a myriad of laws and regulations. Also, HRM needs to innovate in assisting the organization to deal with high uncertainty, high need for energy conservation, and intense international competition.

ADAPTER ROLE.   The need for organizations to constantly adapt new technologies, structuring processes, cultures, and procedures is increasing in view of enhanced competition. Their HR departments are expected to become a change agent, having the necessary skills to facilitate organizational change and to maintain organizational flexibility and adaptability.

Because these departments are experiencing the same pressures as the rest in the organizations they work for, they are streamlining and automating their operations and focusing services on critical tasks. In fact, in the "flat" organization, HR departments are normally a small, high performing, no-hassle staff function.

Centralization vs. Decentralization

The organizing concept of centralization vs. decentralization relates to the trade-off made between getting HRM to where the action is and applying policies fairly and systematically. It also relates to the balance between the benefits of having HR generalists and HR specialists. Under *centralization,* the essential decision making and policy formulation are done at one location (headquarters); under *decentralization,* the essential decision making and policy formulation are done at several locations (in the divisions or departments of the organization).

With the recent increases in regulatory requirements for use of human resources and the increased expertise necessary to deal with complex personnel functions, organizations are moving away from HR generalists toward HR specialists. At the same time, organizations, especially larger ones, are moving HR staff into the organization's divisions. As a result, the trend is to centralize some routine aspects of HRM and to decentralize all other activities.

Thus, in a large, multi-divisional organization (e.g., banks, insurance companies, retail chains), there is generally a corporate HR department staffed primarily with specialists and several divisional HR departments staffed largely with generalists. The corporate department, then, is involved in developing and coordinating HR policies as well as in strategic planning. In many cases the corporate HR department also oversees the regular functions for employees of the headquarters. As the division grows, it begins to hire its own specialists and to administer most of its HR needs. This often results in duplication of services and conflicts. However, sometimes duplication can be advantageous. For example, the design of training and development programs may be centralized, while the implementation may be decentralized.

All in all there are five major factors that influence a company's decision to centralize or decentralize. These are depicted in Exhibit 1.3. The grid presents some of the options and rationales for determining the optimal internal structure of the HR department. The key to this grid is that the structure must support the chosen business strategy.

One of the most widely accepted principles of HRM is that it ought to be the responsibility of all managers. This is reinforced in light of the increased openness and a conviction that it will be impossible to leave it to a group of HR specialists. With the increased number of professional employees, it is even suggested that each employee in the organization, not only those who occupy a supervisory role, will be responsible for HRM.

MANAGERS AND SUPERVISORS. HRM is the task of individuals who have specialized in, and are primarily responsible for, human resources. It is also the task of individuals not specialized in, but often responsible for, the day-to-day implementation of personnel functions and activities (line supervisors and line managers). This is not meant to imply that the HR manager never implements personnel functions and activities or that the HR manager does not get involved in their development and administration. Indeed, line and HR managers are interdependent in the effective management of human resources. As suggested previously, HRM cannot be effective without the support and direction of top management. Top-management influence is best shown by the roles that it allows the HR manager and the department to play.

THE EMPLOYEES. Employees are increasingly taking an active role in HRM. For example, they may be asked to appraise their own performance or the performance of their colleagues. Employees may also help determine their own performance standards and goals. It is no longer uncommon for employees to write their own job descriptions. Perhaps most significantly, employees are taking a more active role in managing their own careers, assessing their own needs and values, and designing their own jobs. Nonetheless, HR departments must help guide this process to ensure that individual plans are congruent with organizational objectives.

Many small organizations do not have individuals performing the HR function on a full-time basis. As the organizations grow, the HR department begins to emerge. There are no strict rules about when to create such a function or department. It depends on the size and complexity of the organization as well as the importance attached to the function by the CEO and other top executives. Very often, at the beginning, the founder or CEO looks after HR activities. As he or she is obliged to spend more time on other aspects of the operation, the tasks are delegated to an employee who later on becomes the HR manager. Other reasons for the creation of the department may include the volume of work in the HR area; operational HR problems such as setting up pension plans and insurances; or the emergence of indicators showing a serious HR problem such as high absenteeism, high turnover, etc.

Who Is Responsible for HRM?

HRM Size, Payroll, and Budgets

Exhibit 1.3
Human Resource Department Structural Design Considerations

FACTOR	FULLY CENTRALIZED	SOME DECENTRALIZED FUNCTIONS	MAXIMUM DECENTRALIZATION
(A) Type and structure of the total business	• single product • functional structure • single location (or multi-location but very standardized)	• functional but "units" starting to form • multiple locations	• multi products (or unique approach to a single business) • profit centres • high divisional autonomy • global
(B) Business realities	• economy of scale • low margins • productivity focus • sometimes a mature industry	• same as fully centralized, but new HR concerns need a structural response	• success of business dependent on a fast, flexible, local response
(C) Level of HR flexibility deemed essential	• almost none	• some	• considerable
(D) Required HR role	• service oriented • high implementation effort • HR seen as guardians of most "people concerns" • Low HR staffing ratios	• still service oriented but shift to a goal orientation—central services are very cost effective • line managers take on more HR management responsibilities	• designers/consultants to line managers • tight centralized HR planning and compensation control for top 10% of managers • proactive on new corporate-wide programs • high HR staffing ratios
(E) Strategy for organizational change	• continued centralization of key decision making • more top-down than bottom-up	• careful selection and re-structuring of various HR systems to address critical needs	• local organization culture seen as a strategic issue to be exploited • line managers fully accountable for good HR management

Source: R. Dods, Principal, William M. Mercer Ltd. Reprinted in Conference Board of Canada, *Report 41–89*, 1989, 14. Reprinted with permission from Robert A. Dods.

Although there are no yardsticks, often *HR ratios* are used to indicate the standards within a certain industry. Two types of HR ratios are used. A *regular ratio* indicates the number of employees in the HR department divided by the total number of employees in the firm; normally the ratio is expressed in relation to groups of 100 employees. A *refined HR ratio* refers to the number of professionals or expert employees (excluding clerical and secretarial employees) divided by the total number of employees in the organization. General surveys concerning these ratios show considerable range. For instance, the

Canadian 1988 Prentice–Hall survey showed that there was one HR specialist for every 571 employees on the average, while the Conference Board of Canada survey reports a median of 8.7 HR personnel per 1,000 employees, or almost one for every 120 employees.[19] Nonetheless, both surveys found that the larger, more "white-collar" and less unionized the workforce, the larger the specialized HR function tends to be. A recent survey in Quebec found that on average, 1.4 percent of the employees work in the HR department of an organization, and 0.7 percent are HR professionals (i.e., refined ratio).[20]

The size of the HR department is closely tied to its payroll costs. Measuring payroll costs in terms of salaries/wages and benefits, the 1988 Conference Board of Canada survey, which was based on data compiled from forty-six firms, indicates that the HR function cost an average of 1.6 percent of the total company payroll. However, the HR payroll costs per employee decreased as the size of the workforce increased. It basically points out that there is an advantage of scale to the organization, where initial relative payroll is more expensive, but this diminishes as the organization becomes larger. Conversely, smaller firms have proportionally more HR professionals because of reduced economies of scale and also because they perform administrative services that are not always part of the responsibilities of the HR function. Finally, a significant predictor of HR ratios is related to the type of industry. For instance, the Conference Board survey found the median ratio in nonmanufacturing firms to be significantly higher than in the manufacturing firms, 9 HR personnel per 1,000 employees compared with 7.6 HR personnel respectively.

The money allocated by organizations to their HR department continues to increase each year. For example, a survey conducted in the early 1980s points out that the per-employee personnel cost across industries was about $385. That figure rose to about $582 in 1988. Nonmanufacturing businesses tend to spend less than manufacturing firms, where the median HR payroll costs per employee are $580 and $639 respectively.[21] Due to the increase in importance and roles of HR departments, it is safe to assume that an increase in their budgets will continue although the payroll portion of it will be reduced.

STAFFING THE HR DEPARTMENT

Qualities of the HR Manager and Staff

How effectively an organization's human resources are managed depends in large part upon the quality of the people in the HR department. Given the changes in the work environment and the emerging roles of the HR professionals, the ideal characteristics of such a manager should include the features outlined below.[22]

BETTER KNOWLEDGE OF BUSINESS MANAGEMENT. If HR managers wish to be part of the executive team and contribute in a real way, they must acquire a better understanding of the firm's business objectives and the means that must be employed to attain them. They must have solid training in strategic planning, understand financial statements, be familiar with sales, marketing and production techniques, and know how to use modern technical tools such as data processing and management information systems. CEOs have often deplored HR managers' overall lack of general business training. This often affects their credibility, even within their own fields.

GREATER UNDERSTANDING OF ECONOMIC PHENOMENA. The globalization of markets, the internationalization of corporations, and the ever-growing insistence on quality, require HR professionals to be more familiar with economic issues, since they will be requested to advise their firms on productivity matters. The economic factors that bear direct impact on HR manager resourcefulness include issues such as: competitiveness in the context of labour costs; international transfers; compensation programs; and the balance between internal equity and the need to remain competitive within various markets where the firm may operate through its various profit centres.

GREATER ANALYTICAL ABILITIES. Due to the emerging roles that businesses wish to assign to the HR managers, they are being asked more often to manage *processes* rather than *activities*, they will be more often consulted for advice when the decision-making processes are blocked because of unresolved conflicts or unwillingness to change manifested by certain groups within the company. Consequently, HR managers will have to develop good analytical skills in diagnosis and problem solving.

COMPETENT LEADERSHIP. Unlike what happened in the past, one's position in the hierarchy alone will not be sufficient to assume future HR responsibilities. The HR manager's personal credibility, based on recognizable abilities, such as the power to convince and to influence, and skills in being accepted by different groups (especially top management) will become the determining factor in HRM success. Knowing how to influence decision-makers without always having the authority, and being able to sell and defend their positions is difficult and challenging, but HR managers will not be able to escape this role.

GREATER PROPENSITY FOR ACTION. To be part of the decision-making team, HR managers must be prepared to take a proactive approach. Instead of waiting for others to come to them with problems, they must have the foresight to be able to approach people while things are happening. HR managers can no longer afford to remain secluded in their own territory; rather, they must act in their colleagues' territory without, however, being a threat to them. In other words, HR managers cannot be effective by retreating to a policy that proved successful in the past, namely "don't rock the boat"; they will be forced to play on centre stage, where decisions and business risks are involved, and where they may categorically fail if wrong advice is given.

GREATER SKILL AS A "DEVELOPER." Because survival is becoming more and more contingent on adaptation, the HR manager needs to be intimately involved in the tumultuous structural changes of the organization. The HR professional must help develop plans and strategies, aiming to equip the company with the necessary workforce, both in quantity and quality; to assist in the motivation and retention of employees whose organization is downsizing or rapidly expanding; and to help manage succession by planning the key employees in the firm.

HEIGHTENED POLITICAL AWARENESS. HR managers need to develop political skills, not in the sense of playing games in the organizational arena, but to integrate all resources and rally them around basic objectives and values of the firm. Changing organizational cultures requires great political skill.

GREATER CUSTOMER ORIENTATION. Although this quality may contradict others mentioned above, it should be emphasized that the HR managers need at all times to be able to balance the requisition for services from the external environment, from top management, and from the employees. As organizations are attempting to become "good corporate citizens," HR professionals must be attentive to the needs of the surrounding community. In addition to this scanning capacity, however, they must be conversant with matters concerning equity and justice within the firm. HR managers will be the ones who will detect QWL problems and suggest remedies. Consequently, even though HR managers are expected to become more business oriented, they will still be expected to remain the guardians of employees' rights and to retain the spirit of service which they have shown all along.

Thus far, the general qualities of senior HR executives were described. What qualities do the rest of the HR staff need and where do these people come in? In order to answer these questions it may be necessary to differentiate between an HR *generalist* and an HR *specialist*.

Differentiating between HR Generalists and HR Specialists

HR GENERALISTS. Line positions are one important source for HR staff. A brief tour by a line supervisor in a personnel position, usually as a personnel generalist, can convey to the HR department the knowledge, language, needs, and requirements of the line. As a result, the HR department can more effectively fill its service role. Another source of HR talent is current nonmanagerial employees. In many organizations HR positions are staffed with former hourly employees. Like line managers, these people bring with them information about the needs and attitudes of employees.

HR generalists should possess many of the same qualities as HR specialists, but the level of expertise in a personnel specialty generally need not be at the same depth. The generalist, however, needs to have a moderate level of expertise in many HR activities and must be able to obtain more specialized knowledge when it is needed.

HR SPECIALISTS. Staff specialists should have skills related to the specialty, an awareness of the relationship of that specialty to other HR activities, and a knowledge of the organization and where the HR department fits in. Specialists who are new to an organization should also develop an appreciation for its political realities. Further, specialist staff should remember that they are not in business to promote the latest fads—and companies are not in business to perpetuate HR departments. Universities are an important source of HR specialists. Since specialists may work at almost any HR activity, qualified applicants can come from specialized programs in law, industrial/organizational psychology, labour and industrial relations, counselling, organizational development, and medical and health sciences.

As a field of employment, HRM is becoming very attractive. It offers numerous different types of jobs, many of which are comparable to those associated with other entry-level business career choices such as accounting and marketing. Starting salaries for specialists are also competitive to the extent that many graduate business and management schools offer programs (M.B.A.) with specialization in human resources. This is a relatively recent trend, which reflects the competitive career options for graduates of such programs. In addition, there is a high level of professionalism beginning to emerge in association with the field of HRM.

HRM AS A CAREER

As suggested above HR job holders are paid competitively. However, there is a wide disparity in pay levels due to the size of the organization, the exact title and job responsibility, the type of industry, and the province in which the firm is located. Moreover, the numbers may change in relation to the economic cycle. Having said this, some data relating to the profile and pay of the most senior HR managers are provided for illustrative purposes.

Profile of Senior HR Managers

A survey conducted in Quebec in 1989 found that basic salary (i.e., bonuses and benefits excluded) varies between $135,000 (highest) and $35,000 (lowest) for senior managers, with the mean at about $67,294. On the other hand, the same survey revealed that only 25 percent of all senior executives made more than $70,000 a year. And further, it has been shown that amongst the lower-level HR directors, 30 percent were females who earned on the average 33 percent less than male directors (means of $40,000 vs. $60,000 respectively).[23] Salaries and bonuses are generally higher for individuals in larger organizations with more experience and more education. In addition, salaries are often higher in large metropolitan areas.

The same survey also found that the senior HR executive has about 12.4 years' experience in HRM and approximately 5.3 years of other administrative experience. The average age of a typical senior HR executive is 44 years in large organizations (over 2,000 employees) and 39 years for the smaller organizations. Among the 138 executives studied, over 50 percent had completed undergraduate university studies and 21 percent possessed graduate degrees (M.B.A., Law, M.A., or M.Sc.). The profile suggests that the field is staffed with many more professionals that ever before.

Professionalism in HRM

Whether or not HRM could be classified as a profession is debatable. Although many practitioners, academics, and HR associations would like it to happen, HRM has not yet achieved the status of other professions such as law, medicine, or even psychology. These other professions require a minimum education and licensing in order to practise. This is done with a view to protecting the public/client and ensures a minimum of professional conduct. On the other hand, other criteria commonly used by other types of professions have been also adapted by HR managers and their respective professional associations. One of the characteristics of a professional is a clear adherence to a code of ethics. As an extension of this, some HR researchers have identified the following criteria for true HR professionals:

1. The HR manager must regard the obligation to implement public objectives and to protect the public interest as more important than blind loyalty to an employer's preferences.
2. In daily practice, the professional must thoroughly understand the problems assigned and must undertake whatever study and research is required to assure continuing competence and the best of professional attention.
3. The practitioner must maintain a high standard of personal honesty and integrity in every phase of daily practice.
4. The professional must give thoughtful consideration to the personal interest, welfare, and dignity of all employees who are affected by his or her prescriptions, recommendations, and actions.
5. Professionals must make very sure that the organizations that represent them maintain a high regard and respect for the public interest and that they never overlook the importance of the personal interests and dignity of employees.[24]

According to available information, except for Ontario, none of Canada's other HRM associations have adopted a "professional code of ethics," although such a code is most desirable. In the U.S.A., on the other hand, the Society for Human Resource Management (formerly, American Society for Personnel Administration, ASPA) has recently adopted one that could provide an example for Canadian counterparts. (See Exhibit 1.4.)

Who are professional HR managers in Canada? Many signs of increased professionalism are evident. They include a rise in the average education, rise in their importance in the organization, and the relatively high participation in professional associations and activities. On the other hand, the absence of formal licensing and a clear code of ethics indicates that there still is room for improvement before Canadian HR managers become "real professionals." In a recent survey of senior executives, members of the Human Resource Professional Association of Quebec, respondents were asked to rate their opinions on a number of professional criteria (e.g., the role of HR practice, training, institutional control, and ethics). Based on a scale from (1) Totally Disagree to (4) Totally Agree, 86 percent of the respondents believed that HR practitioners should possess academic degrees or diplomas pertinent to the discipline, and that this should constitute a prerequisite to practice. When asked whether HRM should be regulated and overseen by a professional

Exhibit 1.4
Society for Human Resource Management — Code of Ethics

SOCIETY FOR

HUMAN

RESOURCE

MANAGEMENT

Code of Ethics

As a member of the Society for Human Resource Management, I pledge myself to:

* Maintain the highest standards of professional and personal conduct.

* Strive for personal growth in the field of human resource management.

* Support the Society's goals and objectives for developing the human resource management profession.

* Encourage my employer to make the fair and equitable treatment of all employees a primary concern.

* Strive to make my employer profitable both in monetary terms and through the support and encouragement of effective employment practices.

* Instill in the employees and the public a sense of confidence about the conduct and intentions of my employer.

* Maintain loyalty to my employer and pursue its objectives in ways that are consistent with the public interest.

* Uphold all laws and regulations relating to my employer's activities.

* Refrain from using my official positions, either regular or volunteer, to secure special privilege, gain or benefit for myself.

* Maintain the confidentiality of privileged information.

* Improve public understanding of the role of human resource management.

This Code of Ethics for members of the Society for Human Resource Management has been adopted to promote and maintain the highest standards of personal conduct and professional standards among its members. Adherence to this code is required for membership in the Society and serves to assure public confidence in the integrity and service of human resource management professionals.

Source: Society for Human Resource Management, "Code of Ethics." Reprinted with permission from SHRM, 606 N. Washington St., Alexandria, VA 22314, U.S.A.

corporation, responses were divided: 43 percent were basically against this idea while 57 percent favoured such regulation. Furthermore, when asked whether most competent non-human-resource managers could satisfactorily perform in HRM without extensive training, 73 percent said no. Similarly, 78 percent of the respondents supported the assertion that HRM should be bound by a professional code of ethics. Because of the fast obsolescence in knowledge, 91 percent of the respondents strongly supported the suggestion to require HR managers to take at least one academic course or seminar every year to update their knowledge and skills. However, when confronted with the dilemma regarding the extent to which HRM should be encouraged to conform to corporate policies and practices, even when they conflict with their own professional code of ethics, 82 percent of the respondents believed that corporate policies should dominate in such cases.[25]

Professional Certification or Accreditation

In 1976 the American Society for Personnel Administration (ASPA) helped establish an independent institute called the AAI (ASPA Accreditation Institute). The Institute adopted the name Personnel Accreditation Institute (PAI) in 1979 and was renamed Human Resource Certification Institute in 1990.

The Institute presently grants two levels of designation: (1) basic, which is PHR (Professional in Human Resources), and (2) senior, which is SPHR (Senior Professional in Human Resources). As of late 1990, 8,000 individuals had been certified, while a far greater number, who had expressed interest, had failed to meet the established criteria. Presently, the Institute administers two national exams on two dates each year in fifty-seven U.S. cities. Students who have majored in the HR field may sit for the exam within one year of their graduation date, but do not earn their certification until other criteria are met as well. In order to maintain certification, it is necessary to demonstrate currency in the field every three years.

With the exception of the Province of Ontario, Canada has been lagging behind in the move toward certification of HR professionals. In Ontario, there is a professional designation, CHRP (Certified Human Resource Practitioner), and a code of ethics must be signed and adhered to in order to qualify. As of the fall of 1993, mandatory comprehensive provincial examinations for all HR graduates will form part of the standard requirements for HRM education at an Ontario college or university.

Other provinces, such as Quebec, have "softer" legislation with regard to allied professions such as industrial relations and psychology. The title of Industrial Relations Consultant is reserved for individuals who have successfully completed an Industrial Relations college degree program, or have practised for at least five years. Similarly, no individual can call himself or herself a psychologist if he or she is not a member of the association/corporation of psychologists. In order to become a member in these associations (which include the allied Industrial/Organizational Psychologists), all provincial regulations (with the exception of Quebec) require the individual to hold a Ph.D. degree (Masters degree for Quebec). It is hoped that tighter professional control will further boost the image of the HR profession and will attract even more competent individuals to this field.

PLAN OF THIS BOOK

Purposes

This book is intended to serve readers by fulfilling several specific purposes:
* To increase your expertise in the functions and activities of HRM;
* To assist you in being an effective HR manager;
* To present the complexities, challenges, and trade-offs involved in being an effective HR manager;
* To instill a concern for professionalism in HRM;

- To provide a "menu" and "frame of reference" for line managers who are concerned with HR issues.

The three major themes in this book include: (1) the ideal way to manage human resources, which encompasses theories, models, and research evidence; (2) the practical way to manage human resources, which encompasses applications and realities in Canadian business; and (3) the legal perspectives. Each of these is integral in illustrating the importance of HRM and in demonstrating how it can help organizations effectively utilize their human resources.

Themes

MODELS, THEORY, AND RESEARCH. A major aim of this book is to provide the most current and useful information related to HRM. Thus, frequent use is made of current research and theory related to the effective use and management of human resources. You will receive extensive information that will enable you to set up an "ideal" method of HRM in your organization. A description of all the current HR functions and activities will be provided, together with an explanation of why they may or may not work. With this knowledge you can decide how to make HR functions and activities work better. Assisting you in this is the section on assessment at the end of most chapters. It contains suggestions on what data to gather in order to make assessments and, in turn, improvements on each activity. As is the case for other professions, HRM requires a great deal of information. Computer technology enables HR professionals to improve the decision-making process. For this reason, a small section on computer applications has been added to each chapter in the text. Much of the information in this section has been provided for illustrative purposes. It is not intended to be exhaustive.

APPLICATIONS AND PRACTICAL CONSIDERATIONS. Examples from Canadian organizations and HR managers are used to provide illustrations of the challenges and practical realities of the HR activities being examined. Each chapter begins with a Keynote Address by a CEO, President, or Senior VP of a large Canadian organization. Many short, real-life scenarios and quotations, called HRM in the News Vignette, illustrate that the material discussed in this book is not theoretical but represents real business concerns. Cases are included at the end of the chapters to provide you with the opportunity to deal with the challenges and practical realities first-hand.

LEGAL PERSPECTIVE. Because of the increased impact of various legislation, wherever possible, the legal and policy implications in relation to HR functions and activities are specified. You should be aware, however, that laws and regulations cited in the text are valid up to 1992 and may have changed by the time you read this book. You should also be aware that although all HR activities are subject to legal influence, some are more influenced than others and thus the relevant chapters contain much more legal material. For instance, Chapter 15 is entirely devoted to legal issues pertaining to employee rights; Chapter 14 (health and safety) and Chapter 16 (labour relations) also have extensive sections of legal content. Conversely, in other chapters only the most relevant information is provided.

Knowledge of effective HR functions and activities is vital for anyone working in organizations, but particularly for managers and especially HR staff. This is true whether the organization you work in is private or public, large or small, slow-growing or fast-growing.

Many of the readers of this book will be students who are introduced to HR for the first time. The material has been carefully selected to provide you with a taste of the field along

For Whom Is This Book Written?

with concrete information enabling you to pursue a career in human resources. Selected references are provided to enable you to examine many of the topics discussed in much more detail. These references are contained in the endnotes of each chapter along with points of clarification or explanation. Consider the endnotes as an additional source of useful information. All in all, this book will help you develop the first set of HRM values, which will be instrumental in pursuing a professional career in the field. Finally, the book may serve you later on in your career as a "refresher."

Postscript

Each chapter contains a Postscript section, which appears after the Summary section. The Postscript does not necessarily add to the conventional wisdom of a theme or activity presented; rather it enables the authors to "add their two cents" in the form of opinion, future prediction, their position on a controversial issue, and the like. You may not, nor necessarily should you, agree with the ideas presented. However, you may find some comments to be thought-provoking. You will also notice that the content of each of the postscripts does not fall into any logical order. It was simply a matter of "picking and choosing" whatever was believed to be relevant to the chapter content. We hope that you will understand it in this context.

SUMMARY

This chapter examines the growing importance of the functions and activities of HRM, defines it, and lists its purposes. Because of the increasing complexity of HRM, nearly all organizations have established an HR department. Not all of these departments, however, perform all the HR functions and activities discussed in this chapter. A department's functions and activities, and the way it performs them, depend greatly on the roles it plays in the organization and the stature of its leader, the senior HR executive. The various roles that an HR department plays in the organization are discussed. Organizations that are most concerned with effective HRM allow their HR departments to play all the roles. When this occurs, it is likely that the HR departments have demonstrated their value to their organizations by showing how they contribute to the productivity, QWL, and legal compliance—all purposes associated with the organization's bottom-line criteria.

REVIEW AND ANALYSIS QUESTIONS

1. The text describes how internal and external influences affect HR functions and activities. Do you agree with these explanations? What other factor(s) would you add?
2. HR objectives were divided into three levels: explicit, implicit, and long-term. Can you think of a different way to describe the various HR objectives?
3. Select at least two factors that contribute to the growing importance of HRM in today's organizations and elaborate on their importance.
4. Discuss the major considerations in structuring the HR department in a centralized vs. decentralized fashion.
5. Elaborate on at least three roles of the HR manager.
6. What are the emerging qualities needed from senior HR executives? Why?
7. What is the essence of the debate concerning HRM professionalism? What is your opinion?

A BROADER VIEW SEIZES MORE OPPORTUNITIES:
THE ROAD TO BECOMING THE NEXT CEO

Bob French, corporate vice-president in charge of human resources, is now finally able to take a pause from the continuous stream of fire-fighting activity he has been engaged in since he came to Bancroft ten years ago! Like many of his colleagues in other firms, Bob's knowledge of HRM came as much from doing it as anything else.

His constant fire fighting tended to keep him pretty narrowly focused. Because of his workload, he rarely read personnel and human resources journals or attended professional conferences. However, recently, things have been easing up. He has been able to recruit and train almost all the division managers in charge of human resources. Now they can do most of the fire fighting—at least that's what Bob is planning on. And he has been doing more reading than ever before. Of course, Bob has not been totally out of touch with the rest of the world or the growing importance of HR planning. When he started filling the slots for division HR managers, he made sure that it was a learning experience for him. Bob always required job candidates to prepare a one-hour talk on the state of research and practice in different areas of HRM, such as selection, appraisal, compensation, and training. He would even invite M.B.A. candidates who had no course work in personnel and ask them to relate their field of interest to HRM.

Bob is planning to become the CEO of Bancroft or some other firm of similar or larger size within the next five to seven years. He thinks he can achieve this if he remains in human resources and does an outstanding job. He will have to be outstanding by all standards, both internal and external to the firm. From his interviews during the past three years, Bob knows that it is imperative to move HRM in a strategic direction while at the same time doing the best possible job with the "nuts and bolts" activities.

During a moment of reflection, Bob begins to scratch some notes on his large white desk pad. In the middle is Bancroft. To its left are its suppliers and to its right are its customers. In his head are all the HR practices he is so familiar with. He has a hunch that there must be a way to use the firm's expertise in performance appraisal and training to help Bancroft be more effective. Bancroft has been learning tremendously from its five-year drive to improve quality, but during the past year quality gains have slowed. Bancroft must continue to improve its quality, but large internal quality gains are becoming more and more difficult to achieve as Bancroft climbs the learning curve. Bob wonders: How can he help Bancroft experience the excitement of seeing large gains in quality improvement again? Bob circles the list of suppliers and begins to formulate a plan that will improve his chances of becoming CEO. He now seeks your advice on exactly what to do and how to go about doing it.

Case Questions

1. What can Bob do with his suppliers to help gain a competitive advantage using HR activities?
2. Is Bob realistic in thinking HRM can really help his firm be better by working with their suppliers?
3. Can Bob become a CEO by being effective in HR?

NOTES

1. P.P. Benimadhu, "Human Resource Management: Charting a New Course," *Report 41–89* (Ottawa: Conference Board of Canada, May 1989), 15, chart 5.
2. See S.L. Dolan, "Critical Issues in the Management of Human Resources in the 90s," *Human Resources* (Israel), 4, 44 (1991): 8–13; S.L. Dolan, V.P. Hogue, and J. Harbottle, "Lévolution des tendances en gestion des ressources humaines au Québec," in *25 Years of Industrial Relations In Quebec*, ed. R. Blouin (Montreal: Yvon Blais Inc., 1990), 777–89.
3. For an interesting discussion about general employee characteristics to complement an organization strategy see: R.S. Schuler, "Personnel and Human Resource Management Choices and Organizational Strategy," in *Readings in Personnel and Human Resource Management*, 3rd ed., ed. R.S. Schuler, S.A. Youngblood, and V. Huber (St. Paul, Minn.: West Publishing Co., 1988), particularly the table on p. 27.

4. Organizational culture and work ethics have become so critical an issue for researchers and practitioners around the globe that 1986 saw the establishment of the International Society for the Study of Work and Organizational Values (ISSWOV). The Society organizes international conferences and publishes a newsletter with the aim of exchanging views and ideas among international scholars regarding work ethics and organizational culture.

5. A. Taylor III, "Back to the Future at Saturn," *Fortune* 113, 3 (August 1988), 63–72.

6. Benimadhu, "Human Resource Management," 18.

7. D.Q. Mills, *The New Competitors* (New York: Wiley, 1985), 18.

8. Conference Board of Canada, *Report 41–89*, vi 2.

9. See S.L. Dolan and C. Leonard, *Survey on Absenteeism in the Canadian Pulp and Paper Industry*, Report prepared for the Canadian Pulp and Paper Industry Association, September 1991, 6; For the Canadian figures see R. Beaupré, "L'absence au travail, maladie et affaires personnelles," Les Publications du Québec, Québec, 1990.

10. M.R. van Ameringen, et al., "Lack of Professional Latitude and Role Problems as Correlates of Propensity to Quit among Nursing Staff in Quebec Hospitals," in *Proceedings of the Second International Conference on Work Values* (Prague: The International Society for the Study of Work and Organizational Values, 1990), 63–71.

11. T. Janz, "Forecasting the Costs and Benefits of Traditional versus Scientific Employment Selection Methods in Canada to the Year 1990," in *Canadian Readings in Personnel and Human Resource Management*, ed. S.L. Dolan and R.S. Schuler (St. Paul, Minn.: West Publishing Co., 1987), 103–11.

12. "Productivité: l'impartatif en affaires pour les années 80," *Le Monde des Affaires*, 18 (1984): 13.

13. Statistics Canada, "Women in Canada: A Statistical Report," *Catalogue 89–503E*, March 1985.

14. T.J. Peters and R.H. Waterman, Jr., "In Search of Excellence: Lessons from America's Best-run Companies," in *The Financial Post* (June 6, 13, 20, and 27, 1981). The study was conducted by the MacKinsey Canada Office, the management consulting firm for which Peters and Waterman (at the time) worked.

15. H.E. Meyer, "Personnel Directors Are Becoming the New Corporate Heroes," *Fortune* 113, 2 (February 1976), 84–89.

16. This section is based on information found in the following four major surveys and reports: (1) "1988 Prentice–Hall Survey," reported in *Human Resource Management in Canada*, January 1990: 15,046–49; seventy-seven organizations participated to this survey; (2) "At the dawn of the 21st century: An overview of changes awaiting the profession," *Report of the membership relations committee of the Association of Human Resource Professionals of the Province of Quebec*, published 16 May 1989; (3) P.P. Benimadhu, "Human Resource Management: Charting a New Course," *Report 41–89*, The Conference Board of Canada, May 1989. This report was based on a meeting of a handful of senior HR executives who participated in a special conference on the subject; (4) "Strategic Human Resource Management: Old and New Concerns," a survey conducted in 1989 by S.L. Dolan and J. Harbottle, from the University of Montreal, in conjunction with the Association of Human Resource Professionals of the Province of Quebec; 135 senior HR executives responded to this survey.

17. M.A. Devanna, C.J. Fombrum, and N.M. Tichy, *Strategic Human Resource Management* (New York: Wiley, 1984), 51.

18. F.K. Foulkes, "Organizing and Staffing the Personnel Function," *Harvard Business Review*, May–June 1977, 142–54.

19. *Human Resource Management in Canada*, January 1990, 15,053–54.

20. From Dolan and Harbottle, "Strategic Human Resource Management: Old and New Concerns" (Results were presented at the annual conference of the Association of Human Resources Professionals of the Province of Quebec, Montreal, April 1990).

21. Conference Board of Canada, *Report 41–89*, 24.

22. Based on Membership Relations Committee Report, "At the Dawn of the 21st Century: Human Resource Management—An overview of changes awaiting the profession" (Paper delivered at a meeting of Association of Human Resource Professionals of the Province of Quebec, Montreal, 16 May 1989).

23. Dolan and Harbottle, "Strategic Human Resource Management."

24. D. Yoder and H. Heneman Jr., "PAIR Jobs, Qualifications and Careers," in *PAIR, ASPA Handbook of Personnel and Industrial Relations*, ed. D. Yoder and H. Heneman Jr. (Washington, D.C.: BNA, 1979), vol. 8, 19–58.

25. S.L. Dolan and K. Cannings, "Professional and Organizational Values in Human Resource Management" (Unpublished manuscript, 1993).

CHAPTER TWO

STRATEGIC ASPECTS OF HRM

KEYNOTE ADDRESS
Yves Gosselin*
Vice-President Staffing and OD, Northern Telecom

Northern Telecom Vision 2000

"Leadership is a theme common to everything we do, including our approach to recruiting and hiring the brightest minds on campus." (Paul G. Stern, Chairman and CEO, Northern Telecom)

To support its vision of being the world's leading telecommunications equipment supplier (Vision 2000), Northern Telecom has launched a series of initiatives that now constitute the core elements of its strategic human resources policy. Vision 2000 is underpinned by a set of core values, the guiding philosophy of the company.

CORE VALUES

Excellence	• We have only one standard—excellence.
Teamwork	• We share one vision—we are one team.
Customers	• We create superior value for our customers.
Commitment	• We do what we say we do.
Innovation	• We embrace change and reward innovation.
People	• Our people are our strength.

Our strategic human resources policy aligns a number of human resource functions, such as recruitment and selection, training and development, career planning and management succession, to the core values specified above. We have also established mechanisms enabling fine tuning to reflect our corporate strategic objectives.

Our human resource strategy starts with the unequivocal statement that Vision 2000 will be achieved through recruiting the brightest minds on campus. Our aim in recruiting and developing talented people is to tap the most potent economic stimulus of all—idea power. Our leading-edge innovation for attracting the top graduates is to offer them a three-year employment contract, which demonstrates our commitment to ensuring a successful beginning to their careers.

We have thoroughly studied success at Northern Telecom as well as success factors and "best-practice" experience from other companies to generate our own leadership profile. This profile defines the excellent leader in the context of Northern Telecom. Essentially, it outlines the company's expectations in terms of experiences and competencies and in terms of behaviour—actions and attitudes evident on the job. The profile continuously evolves as the company and the business environment change.

To supplement the skills, competencies, and experiences gained from the various assignments and to mobilize all managers and individual contributors behind Vision 2000, Northern Telecom has introduced a comprehensive curriculum of leadership development. Specific programs have been designed to help individuals succeed in the important transitions in their careers. Programs range from Entry Leadership Forum designed for new grads, through Leadership Forum for first-line managers, to Global Leadership Forum for senior executives. People management is a key element of the leadership curriculum.

To ensure that individual performance and development are managed in harmony with the company's needs and goals, Northern Telecom has a program in place called Managing for Achievement (MFA). The MFA program encourages employees to engage in regular reviews of development and performance with their colleagues and managers. It is the key vehicle to record and track individual performance toward objectives as well as personal growth through individual development.

Talent management, called Key Resource Development (KRD), is an integral part of MFA. Through an annual review of all developmental plans of employees, the process identifies the top 5 percent—the most promising employees—including those of exceptionally high potential, minorities and females, or persons designated

* Yves Gosselin was VP for Northern Telecom until 1993.

for global assignments. Special attention is given to these persons in terms of assignments as well as increased contact with senior management. The information collected in these reviews forms the basis of Northern Telecom's human resource planning. Regrouped in talent pools according to their functions and levels, these employees represent the strength for the future. Successors to the key positions are identified from these pools of talented people.

Finally, to keep these programs effective and truly useful, they are being continuously examined by human resource practitioners and by line managers with the goal of keeping them closely linked to the needs of the business.

.   .   .

The Keynote Address by Yves Gosselin of Northern Telecom illustrates very clearly the major preoccupations of companies that wish to succeed in the years to come. It is also evident from the presentation that strategic HRM has many different components. These include policies, culture, values, and practices. While Northern Telecom has labelled their strategic HRM effort "Vision 2000," other companies will use different names. Although diverse in content, the common denominator for all strategic HRM is the multiple linkages and integration of its various components to a coherent strategic need of the organization.

.   .   .

STRATEGIC HRM

Concept and Definitions

There is no generally accepted definition of strategic HRM. Some view it as an extension of HR planning; others see it as a way management gains competitive advantage and comes to grips with ill-defined and tough-to-solve HR problems.[1] Despite the variation in perspectives, today the element that most clearly distinguishes *strategic* HR management from previous forms of HR management is the attempt to link it directly to business strategy. Based on these viewpoints, *strategic human resource management* can be defined as "All those activities affecting the behaviour of individuals in their efforts to formulate and implement the strategic needs of the business."[2]

However, in order to implement strategic HRM certain conditions need to be met. Based on many interviews with senior Canadian executives of important corporations, one author identifies seven principles that should be considered in order to facilitate effective strategic HRM:

1. There should be an overall corporate purpose, and the HR dimensions of that purpose should be evident.
2. There should exist a process for developing a strategy within the organization and there should be an explicit consideration of HR dimensions.
3. Effective linkages should exist on a continuing basis to ensure the integration of HR considerations with the organization's decision-making process.
4. The office of the CEO should provide the climate for integrating HR considerations to the needs of the business.
5. The organization at all levels should establish responsibility and accountability for HRM.
6. Initiatives in HRM should be relevant to the needs of business.
7. It should include the responsibility to identify and interact in the social, political, technological, and economic environments in which the organization is and will be doing business.[3]

Before embarking on details of the various components and mechanisms for implementing strategic HRM, a brief review of its evolution and importance is presented.

Evolution and Importance

In order to understand the concept of strategic HRM, it is essential first and foremost to comprehend the notion of strategy in general. In fact, it is important to note that the concept of strategy is not in itself an entirely modern one. Writing in 300 B.C., the Chinese philosopher Sun Tzu, author of the *Ping-fa* described the art of strategy as based upon winning victories by analysis, calculation, and manoeuvring before confrontations, and requiring the improvement of the skills needed to act strategically. Theoretical developments were made in the area of military strategy by such authors as the well-known German military theorist Klausewitz in the 19th century.[4]

Whereas strategizing has been an integral part of political and military theory for centuries, it is only recently (i.e., over the past thirty years) that researchers and practitioners have been studying its business applications. The work in business theory is significant in that it stands in contrast to certain of the basic assumptions of rationality advanced in early neoclassical management, whereby the underlying assumption was that there exists a single actor, the entrepreneur–owner–operator, who can affect the sole goal of profit maximization. Today, we know that competition obviates the possibility of influencing the market, with the exceptional cases being imperfect competition and monopoly. Contrasting with such economic determinism, the concept of strategy introduces a greater degree of voluntarism.

In the broad arena of economics, finance, and administration, we witnessed over the years the development of models geared to understanding how strategy is linked to and influences a great number of factors, such as organizational structure and behaviour, product and organizational life-cycles, and, of course, profits and survivability.

In the field of HRM, however, developments are more recent and tentative. Two principal streams seem to be emerging: one has its focal point on planning and modelling; the other places the emphasis on issues such as strategic choices and discretion.

Consequently, various definitions of strategy are in circulation. The term is often used "idiosyncratically": among game theorists, for example, strategies are concrete actions or rules for choosing actions in a conflict situation, while for others strategy implies "long-term" or "high-level" planning, and yet others refer to it as broad gauge issues of mission.[5] One of the definitions that bridges strategy with HR suggests that it can be best understood as "the means by which the firm fully utilizes its structure, processes, competencies, and resources to take advantage of environmental opportunities and minimize the impact of externally imposed threats to accomplish its objectives." This results in the need to implement two HR *fits:* (1) with the business, and (2) with the diverse HR structures, processes, and competencies within and among themselves.[6]

Historically, planning models and theories preceded other types of thinking. Nonetheless, HR planning theories have contributed significantly to the development of conceptual models of the strategic business–human resource linkage. As will be mentioned in the next chapter, some HR experts consider forecasting as the core element. Planning theory was preoccupied initially with the task of HR planning for large corporations. It was later complemented by career planning. Recent years, however, have been characterized by attempts to integrate the planning process into the web of managing and harmonizing the diverse functional activities that comprise HRM.

The many-faceted elements that comprise the contemporary models of strategic HRM include:

- Identifying the major theme or thrust of HR practices in different strategies;
- Describing how organizations can gain competitive advantage through selected HR practices;
- Describing different HR issues within different strategy phases and in different stages of a product life cycle;
- Tailoring HR practices to specific strategies based on employee characteristics necessary to meet strategic demands.

ELEMENTS IN STRATEGIC HRM

Environmental Scanning and Analysis

Most organizations recognize that analysis of the company's macro-environment is required in corporate planning. However, only a few organizations have actually scanned this same environment for its HR implications. While the specific environmental interests vary depending on the industry and the business strategy, dimensions in the environment that should be tapped include the social, educational, demographic, political/legal, and economic trends and events.

In the social arena, for example, organizations should be alert to societal values. During periods of high unemployment, some companies boost their image by demonstrating good corporate citizenship; for example, once a week the *Montreal Gazette* provides free advertisement space for unemployed people seeking employment opportunities.

In the educational arena, potential difficulties may arise due to shortages of some skilled workers. Consequently, some organizations get involved with technical schools, colleges, and universities to set up specific joint programs for training people in acquiring these skills (see Chapter 11).

With respect to political and legal trends, emerging concerns pertaining to the impact of the free trade agreements with the U.S.A. and Mexico loom on the horizon. Finally, analysis of economic conditions and the effect of global competition provide useful information for corporate planning and the role of the HR department in the strategy adopted.

A matrix of a scanning strategy pertaining to these dimensions can be developed. As shown in Exhibit 2.1, scanning can be undertaken by adhering to one of three approaches: irregular, regular, or continuous. Simultaneously, scanning strategy may consider the following parameters: media, scope, motivation, nature, time frame for data, time frame for decision impact, and, finally, the organizational responsibility.

Exhibit 2.1
An Environmental Scanning Framework

	SCANNING APPROACH		
	Irregular	Regular	Continuous
Media for Scanning	Ad hoc studies	Periodically updated studies	Structural data-collection and processing systems
Scope of Scanning	Specific events	Selected events	Broad range of environmental systems
Motivation for Activity	Crisis initiated	Decision and issue oriented	Planning process oriented
Temporal Nature of Activity	Reactive	Proactive	Proactive
Time Frame for Data	Retrospective	Contemporary	Prospective
Time Frame for Decision Impact	Current/near-term	Near-term	Near-term/long-term
Organizational Responsibility	Various staff functions	Various staff functions	Environmental scanning unit

Source: Adapted from and based on Lorenz P. Schrenk, "Environmental Scanning," in *Human Resource Management: Evolving Roles and Responsibilities*, ed. L. Dyer (Washington: BNA/SHRM, 1989), 1–88.

Linking HR to Business Planning

Sixty-seven percent of respondents of a recent survey by the Conference Board of Canada indicated that linking HR planning to the strategic business plan will be a significant HR issue in the next few years.[7] The integration of HR planning into the corporate plan is imperative for business success. Respondents of the same survey indicated that many well-conceived business plans went awry because the HR implications of a strategic thrust were not considered.

If there is an increasing emphasis upon more strategic HRM, it is because of the belief that it can contribute to greater organizational effectiveness and enhance bottom-line contributions. The literature on the impact of HR activities on organizational effectiveness shows the presence of a number of dimensions associated with strategic management in the more effective organizations: the use of a long-term perspective, controlling for outcomes through the use of objective criteria, and monitoring performance by taking account of the multiple constituencies served by the HR department.

Linkage between HR planning and strategy is vital because it fosters HR strategies that parallel and support the firm's business plans. Employee characteristics and HR policies vary depending on the strategy chosen by the firm.[8] For instance, employee characteristics and HR policies will be different if a firm adopts an entrepreneurial strategy instead of a rationalization/maximize-the-profit strategy. In the case of the entrepreneurial strategy, the organization needs to adopt HR policies that lead employees to be innovative and risk taking. For example, one of the HR functions, the performance appraisal process, should be designed rather loosely with incomplete integration, emphasizing results criteria, be future-oriented, encourage high employee participation, and recognize the accomplishment of groups rather than single individuals. In contrast, the rationalization/maximize-the-profit strategy used by organizations at a mature stage, needs employees to focus on high output, low risk, and highly repetitive behaviour in the short term. Consequently, the performance appraisal process best suited to enable the organization to achieve its business objectives will focus on results criteria, require low employee involvement, and centre on the evaluation of the individual.

Similarly, all facets of the HR function—recruitment, selection, compensation, training, and development—will have to be adapted for the two different strategies if HRM is to become responsive to the business needs of an individual organization's strategy.

While there are well over a dozen frameworks for studying and understanding strategy types, Exhibit 2.2 describes five critical characteristics of typical corporate strategies. They are critical because they suggest the employee characteristics necessary to meet strategic demands. Exhibit 2.3 identifies some key general employee characteristics.

Exhibit 2.2
Characteristics of Typical Corporate Strategies

Entrepreneurial: In this strategy, projects with high financial risk are undertaken, minimal policies and procedures are in place, there are insufficient resources to satisfy all customer demands, and there are multiple priorities to satisfy all customer demands. The focus here is on the short run and getting the operation off the ground.

Dynamic Growth Strategy: Here risk taking on projects is more modest. There is a constant dilemma between doing current work and building support for the future. Policies and procedures are starting to be written, since there is a need for more control and structure for an ever-expanding operation.

Extract Profit/Rationalization Strategy: The focus here is on maintaining existing profit levels. Modest cost-cutting efforts and employee terminations may occur. Controlling systems and structure are well developed, along with an extensive set of policies and procedures.

Liquidation/Divestiture Strategy: The focus of this strategy involves selling off assets, cutting further losses, and reducing the workforce as much as possible. Little or no thought is given to trying to save the operation, as declining profits are likely to continue.

Turnaround Strategy: The focus of this strategy is to save the operation. Although cost-cutting efforts and employee reductions are made, they are short-term programs for long-run survival. Worker morale may be somewhat depressed.

Exhibit 2.3
General Employee Characteristics to Complement Corporate Strategy

Repetitive, Predictable Behaviour .... Creative, Innovative Behaviour

Short-Term Focus .... Long-Term Focus

Cooperative, Interdependent Behaviour .... Independent, Autonomous Behaviour

Low Concern for High Quantity .... High Concern for High Quantity

Low Concern for Quality .... High Concern for Quality

Low-Risk Orientation .... High-Risk Orientation

Concern for Process .... Concern for Results

Preference to Avoid Responsibility .... Preference to Assume Responsibility

Inflexible to Change .... Flexible to Change

Low Task Orientation .... High Task Orientation

Low Organizational Identification .... High Organizational Identification

Focus on Efficiency .... Focus on Effectiveness

Source: R.S. Schuler "Personnel and Human Resource Management—Choices and Organization Strategy," in *Canadian Readings in Personnel and Human Resource Management*, ed. S.L. Dolan and R.S. Schuler (St. Paul, Minn.: West Publishing Co., 1987), 8. Reprinted with permission.

Employee characteristics are matched on the basis of business characteristics, and then HR practices can be matched with strategy. Further discussion of this matching process is found in the section Strategic Policies and Practices in HR Activities. To this list, specific characteristics in terms of employees' skills, knowledge, and abilities can be added to consider the match with specific job requirements. The latter is discussed in detail in Chapter 6, and is therefore omitted here.

MODELS AND APPROACHES TO STRATEGIC HRM

Schuler's 5–P Model [9]

As mentioned earlier, a variety of models and theories of strategic HRM exist. In this section only two models, which emphasize different strategic aspects of HRM, are presented: (1) the Schuler 5–P Model, and (2) the Dolan and Harbottle Model.

The 5–P Model of strategic HRM joins many HR activities to the strategic needs of the business. Categorizing HR activities as strategic or not depends upon whether they are systematically linked to the strategic needs of the business, not whether they are done in the long term rather than short term, or whether they focus on senior managers rather than nonmanagerial employees.

The 5–P Model attempts to link several HR activities that tend to be treated separately by practitioners and academics alike. Additionally, the model highlights the impact of HR activities when they are linked to the strategic needs of the business. According to the model, there are *five* HR activities that affect the behaviour of individuals at different levels in the organization: (1) HR Philosophy, (2) HR Policies, (3) HR Programs, (4) HR Practices, and (5) HR Process.

HR Philosophy is a statement of how the organization views its human resources, what role they play in the overall success of the business, and how they are to be treated and managed. Some organizations refer to these as *culture*. A firm's HR philosophy can be found in its *statement of business values*. For example, see the Core Values statement for Northern Telecom, in the Keynote Address section.

HR Policies are statements that provide guidelines for action on people-related business issues, and for the development of HR programs and practices based upon the strategic needs of the business. People-related business issues may include the need to hire skilled workers, to improve worker productivity, or to reduce health and safety costs. HR policies might provide guidelines suggesting means for solving these issues in a creative, innovative way.

HR Programs are coordinated HR efforts specifically intended to initiate, disseminate, and sustain strategic organizational change efforts necessitated by strategic business needs. For example, Chrysler's strategic effort to change its image by emphasizing quality and backing it up with an unprecedented warranty evolved at the top-management level and was then filtered down throughout the entire organization. What the programs have in common is the fact that they are generated by the strategic intentions and directions the firm is taking, and that they involve HR issues. They also share the reality of having *strategic goals* that are used to target and measure the effectiveness of the HR program. Current HR programs deriving from strategic business needs address the following questions:

- What is the nature of the corporate culture? Is it supportive of the business?
- Will the organization be able to cope with future challenges in its present form?
- What kind of people and how many will be required?
- Are performance levels high enough to meet demands for increased profitability, innovation, higher productivity, better quality, and improved customer service?
- What is the level of commitment to the company?
- Are there any potential constraints, such as skill shortages or labour relations problems?

Once the fundamental issues and questions are identified, HR programs can be formulated. These programs are typically associated with the term *HR strategy*, hence they represent the plans and programs meant to address strategic HR issues facing the organization.

HR Practices address all employees in the organization, but somewhat differently, depending upon their roles. There are three categories of roles in organizations: leadership, managerial, and operational. Leadership roles include establishing direction, aligning people, motivating and inspiring individuals, and causing dramatic and useful change; managerial roles are the traditional roles of planning, directing, delegating, organizing, and coordinating; operational roles are those necessary to deliver the service or produce the products.

Once the role behaviours are identified, HR practices can then be developed to cue and reinforce employee performance in these roles. Because different roles require different cues, organizations have different practices for different employees.

HR Process addresses the issue of *how* all these other HR activities are identified, formulated, and implemented. For example, some companies choose a process of complete involvement and participation, while others prefer to use a consultative process, and yet others still employ an authoritative process (i.e., all decisions are made by a few at the top). HR process thus seems to vary along a continuum from extensive participation by all employees to no participation by any employees. Two continua could be used to differentiate between the formulation and implementation, but it appears that there is a need for consistency across these two dimensions of process. This need for consistency also appears to be evident across all strategic HR activities.

The HR department is placed in an ideal situation to assume responsibility for the 5–Ps of strategic HRM. In general it can:

- Assist in the formulation of the firm's strategic directions and needs;
- Identify the HR philosophies or culture consistent with the business needs;
- Develop and implement HR policies, programs, and practices consistent with the HR culture;
- Ensure that the HR process is consistent with the other HR activities.

Dolan and Harbottle Approach[10]

The approach developed by Dolan and Harbottle is a normative one. Instead of focusing on the nature of linkages between strategic HR and strategic business, the aim is to explain the emergence of strategic HRM. It is assumed that different organizational conditions and varying levels of strategic/operational styles of business, and of HRM, create a discretionary margin for HR strategic input to corporate business decisions. Traditionally, it is expected that HRM and corporate strategy will be synchronized. In reality, however, some HR departments have more impact on (and strategic input into) corporate strategy than others. The question, though, is: What explains these differences?

In order to explain the emergence of strategic HRM and its true alliance with strategic business objectives, a political model pertaining to the concept of *dominant coalition* is proposed. In order to understand the conditions and circumstances that favour the HR department becoming part of the dominant coalition, one critical dimension associated with strategic HRM and two sub-dimensions should be understood: the critical dimension is *strategic influence*, and the sub-dimensions are *strategic relations* and *control and power over information processing*. Exhibit 2.4 portrays these linkages.

Strategic influence is the first and most important dimension, as it implies being given the opportunity to develop and enhance HR objectives and goals consistent with the business strategy and goals. Corporate commitment, and in particular the support of the CEO, is a contributing factor explaining the influence of senior HR executives.

Strategic influence can be conceptualized as consisting of two dimensions: the one is technical and the other managerial. Technical is defined in terms of the expertise in the

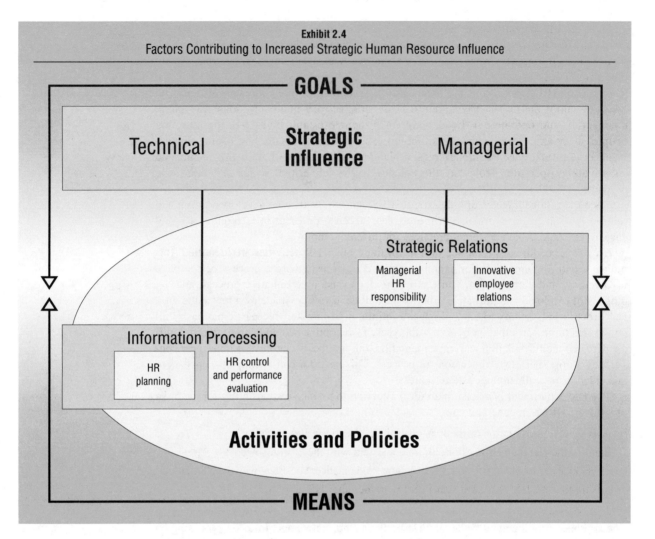

Exhibit 2.4
Factors Contributing to Increased Strategic Human Resource Influence

GOALS

Technical   **Strategic Influence**   Managerial

Strategic Relations

| Managerial HR responsibility | Innovative employee relations |

Information Processing

| HR planning | HR control and performance evaluation |

Activities and Policies

MEANS

form of planning or other strategic and control activities that can increase the probability of success for the organization. The managerial dimension is associated with the activities of resource allocation and coordination.

The strategic influence of HR managers in organizations is manifested through strategic relations and information processing. These are hypothesized as contributing to the adoption of a strategic style of HRM through strategic influence (with its technical and managerial dimensions).

Strategic relations means the level of innovation; proactive HR practices that facilitate relationships with key constituencies, namely the CEO. It is proposed that innovative and proactive HR departments would be in a position to have more strategic influence than HR departments for whom such an approach in unimportant. Activities with upper management, such as executive training and development, will also fall into the category of high visibility and, consequently, more influence.

In the conduct of these activities, considerable information, and therefore power, can be obtained and be used to exercise HRM strategic influence. An HR department that is sensitive to the needs of its most important constituents will most likely increase its influence. From this perspective, strategic choices will be made regarding relationships with each of the constituencies served by the HR department.

Additionally, HR departments that are more advanced in implementing planning and control systems and techniques (i.e., information processing) are more influential. However, harmonizing the diverse HR activities can be accomplished where the senior HR managers possess the aptitudes and analytical skills. HR information processing systems enable HRM to use forecasts and to develop rapidly varying scenarios and simulations, thus providing the organization with detailed analysis of the implications of different business strategies. Furthermore, return on investment and cost–benefit models (see Chapter 18) can be used to generate optimal business HR scenarios. These quantitative methods are essential to answering the bottom-line questions of other executives. This results in increased prestige, and consequently leads to increased strategic influence. In sum, the model suggests the following as an explanation of the degree and scope of involvement of HR managers in strategic corporate affairs:

- A higher degree of accountability for HR staff in the practice and responsibilities of non-HR functions will increase their strategic influence,
- Greater organizational priorities accorded to those activities that cater to senior (non-HR) managers are likely to be accompanied by increased strategic influence for the HR department,
- Innovative and proactive HR policies are likely to attract the attention of senior constituents and will eventually lead to increased influence of the HR department,
- Strategic influence will be increased where HR activities and policies are developed with a long-term planning horizon,
- The greater and the more sophisticated the arsenal used by the HR department for control and information processing, the greater their strategic influence.

HRM IN THE NEWS VIGNETTE

"Put me in Coach" — Human Resource Managers in the 1990s

"Put me in a coach, I'm ready to play." These words evoke images of the athlete who practises hard and diligently, but for some reason never gets into the game. Ignored by the coach, except when the game has been either won or lost, the player wonders about his role on the team. "Is all the hard work and preparation worth it? Why doesn't the coach put me into the game when it really matters?" The situation eats at him until his self-confidence begins to weaken. "How well will I play if I ever get into the game in an important situation?" The position of many people working in the human resources function is analogous to our enthusiastic but apprehensive athlete.

Historically many senior managers have seen and treated "personnel" as a dumping ground. "He can't make it in the line, but he's good with people. Put him in personnel." Given this attitude, it is not surprising that many human resources professionals never get into the corporate game when it matters—when strategies are being developed and critical decisions are being made.

This exclusion of human resource managers from the real game is strange, given the fact that almost every corporate annual report contains the statement that "people are our most important asset." And what annual general meeting could pass without the CEOs stating emphatically that everything that has been achieved was the result of the marvellous efforts of the organization's people. And yet, the senior human resources professional, the person whose job description outlines responsibility for the people side of the organization, is left on the bench when important planning and decision making take place.

The Game Will Change in the 1990s

Will this situation continue in the 1990s? In some organizations, it will. But in many more, the coaches—veteran and new—are recognizing that the game has changed. It is ironic that during an era being dubbed the age of technology or the information explosion, senior managers everywhere are starting to understand that people really are the critical asset. If people are not performing to their full potential, the company will not perform to its full potential.

Not only the game has changed—so has the team. Our athlete, referred to above as "he," could just as easily be "she." Several key players on the team may also be women. The male image traditionally associated with sports does not fit with most of today's companies. The macho management style is disappearing and is being replaced by a finesse orientation based on an understanding of what makes people tick.

This awakening of senior management is reflected in current business literature, which is focusing strongly on leadership as the key to improving corporate performance. Leadership is all about people—getting them excited about the organization and its goals, excited about corporate, team, and personal performance.

The game has changed and the athlete on the bench is now a critical player. If leadership is all about vision, values, culture, goals and motivation, the role of the human resources executive is to put all the human resources management elements in place to support the vision and the values, create the culture, and achieve the goals. Without those elements, the mission statement will become empty words and the leadership challenge will not be met.

The senior human resources manager will be counted on to use a total systems approach to address the people component of the organization's strategy The diagram depicts in the outer ring the organization's vision as driving the mission, values, culture, and objectives and goals. All of these, together, form the framework within which the human resources professional develops the many components of the total human resource management system.

The challenge does not lie within any one of the elements of the system. Many human resources professionals are skilled in addressing each element on a single-issue basis. The development of a compensation program which will ensure internal equity and market competitiveness is not particularly difficult. Similarly, developing performance appraisal plans or training and development programs is old hat for many.

What makes the game challenging and new is the need to start with the vision, values, and culture and develop each of the elements in a fashion which will drive the organization towards achieving them. As well, the elements should be mutually supportive and must not pull in opposite directions.

The Human Resource Management Elements

Let us examine each of the elements briefly:

- Expectations and objectives should relate clearly to the organization's mission and goals. An organization dedicated to sales must be dominated by sales-related, as opposed to administrative, goals.

- Job and team design needs to be consistent with the culture and the values. It is inconsistent for an organization that says it values individuality and creativity to design assembly line-type jobs whereby the employee understands only a part of the total process and has little opportunity for creative input. An organization which says that it values teamwork should design jobs so that teamwork is not only possible but required.

- Development and training should reflect the values and priorities of the organization. This implies not only strong focus in training activities, but also the need to make training programs fit with the personality of the organization. For example, a company that wants to be objective or results oriented should ensure that its development and training programs promote the setting and achieving of individual and group objectives.

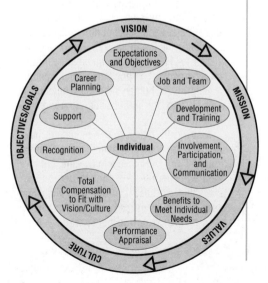

- Involvement, participation, and communication all should reflect the organization in a consistent and persistent fashion. If the enterprise places a high value on employee involvement and participation, the human resources professionals should ensure that organization of work and consultative mechanisms are appropriate and are in place. Consistency with development and training is critical; an organization that values participation should ensure that its training program content reflects these values.

- Benefits to meet individual needs reflect the growing diversity of the work force and the need for human resources professionals to ensure that, to the extent possible, the fringe benefits programs meet the individual needs of employees. This is particularly important for a company which places high value on the individual and his or her unique contribution.

- Performance appraisal approaches and systems come in a number of forms, many of which are not particularly useful. This is often an area of internal inconsistency. Some corporations talk about their results orientation and then appraise employee performance on the basis of personality traits or nonquantitative factors. The message is all wrong. Constructed and used properly, the performance appraisal system can be a great support to the vision and values, but to do so, it has to reflect the organization's priorities.

- Total compensation should fit with the vision, values, and culture. Total compensation programs can include base salary, variable performance related to components such as bonuses or commissions, and share ownership programs. Properly constructed programs can do an enormous amount to send strong messages and influence behaviour towards organizational priorities. A firm which says that it values performance and then awards standard salary increases or bonuses regardless of performance is sending a powerfully inconsistent message. A company that says that it wants its employees to act like owners, but does not give them any way to actually be an owner, is in a similar situation.

- Recognition of the performance of individuals or teams is critical to the system. Recognition programs do not have to cost a lot, but they can be strong motivators. It is critical to ensure that the results and behaviours recognized are consistent with the values and the vision. Organizations that value the contribution of all employees should ensure that the efforts of employees at all levels, not just managers or professional staff, receive recognition. A firm which values excellence in service recognizes those who excel in this area, not just the top sales people.

- Support for employees should be important to all organizations. Support programs can include employee assistance programs, fitness, day care, and so on. It is especially critical for a company whose values state a high concern for its people that support programs in place.

- Career planning needs to reflect the organization's people values. A company which talks about employee loyalty and its commitment to its staff, but then leaves people to fend for themselves when it comes to career planning and development, is giving a contradictory, demotivating message.

The Challenge to the Human Resources Function

The human resources function faces the tremendous challenge of having all the programs, policies, and approaches that touch individual employees in synchronization with the company vision and with each other. Meeting the challenge requires, first of all, insight into the organization's future directions and what they mean in terms of the total human resources management system. In many instances, it has to be the senior human resources manager who adds the people (values, culture), dimension to the business aspects of the vision and mission statements.

Next, a careful review of each element of the framework is required. Each has to be assessed in light of the vision, mission, culture, and objectives. Does what we have now fit? Will it move us closer to where we want to be? What changes are required? What are the priorities? How quickly can we implement the changes?

Finally, determination and leadership possibly represent the biggest change of all for the human resources function. Human resources professionals should become the champions of change, not passive order takers. It is the history of order taking that has kept them on the bench for so long. Willingness to jump into the fray and play an active, leading role will get them back into the game.

Human Resources Professionals Are Ready To Go

Is our athlete ready? In many cases, the answer is a resounding "Yes." Generally speaking, human resources professionals are well educated and trained. Many have the interpersonal skills required for that task. Are they prepared to take the risks inherent in throwing themselves into the action? Again, for many, the answer is "Yes." For others, long accustomed to the passive, order-taking approach, the challenge will be too great. In these cases, companies serious about their future will make changes in their human resources staff. Organizations which really understand the importance of people to their success will not tolerate a lack of leadership from this function.

The future is exciting for the human resources function. It promises a new game, and a chance to be a key player. There are, of course, other aspects to the coming years that will be of importance—increasing government regulation of the workplace comes to mind immediately. It is the role of supporting the business strategies, however, that will create an entirely new dimension and challenge for human resources professionals in many, many organizations.

To complete our analogy, the game will get increasingly tough and competitive. The team will need new skills to succeed on a long-term basis. Our athlete can add that critical dimension if he or she can rise to the occasion. In the coming years, coaches will be telling our athlete to get in the game. They will be counting on our athlete to score. They will be counting on our athlete to be a team leader. That is the future for human resources management.

Source: Featured article by C. Pratt, Senior Vice-President Human Resources, Noranda Inc. Appeared in: *Business Quarterly* 58, 4 (Spring 1989): 58–60. Reprinted with permission.

STRATEGIC POLICIES AND PRACTICES IN HR ACTIVITIES

Strategy implementation involves choosing specific HR practices that will reinforce the behaviour needed to implement the organization's strategy. Exhibit 2.5 organizes these choices into six categories. The exhibit defines opposite ends of each practice continuum. Clearly, an intermediate choice is also possible for most of the practices.

Effectively linking strategy and HRM requires more than selection from a series of practice choices. The challenge is to develop configurations of HR practice choices that together contribute to the implementation of the organization's strategy.

Strategic HR Planning

Planning choices include a wide range of alternatives, as will be described in Chapter 4. Organizations that view the planning and forecasting process as largely informal and short term are likely to have a different strategic outlook from those with a more formal, long-term approach. Surprisingly, although many organizations recognize the importance of long-term planning, few do it properly.

It is also important to note that, in addition to the level of formality and time horizon, strategic HR planning should include both an external and internal focus. The external focus relates to HR relationships with the corporate planning group and other functional departments. For example, the HR representatives should participate in the market analysis, be aware of the internal financial position, and be involved in the environmental analyses that are essential to strategy formulation.

The internal aspects of strategic HR planning relate to the HR relationship with other managers and areas within the HRM group. Planning at this level is more narrow and it is directed toward issues of strategy implementation.[11]

Exhibit 2.5
Choices in HR Practices that Can Be Matched with Competitive Strategies

1. Planning Choices

Informal ⟷ Formal
Short Term ⟷ Long Term
Explicit Job Analysis ⟷ Implicit Job Analysis
Job Simplification ⟷ Job Enrichment
Low Employee Involvement ⟷ High Employee Involvement

2. Staffing Choices

Internal Sources ⟷ External Sources
Narrow Paths ⟷ Broad Paths
Single Ladder ⟷ Multiple Ladders
Explicit Criteria ⟷ Implicit Criteria
Limited Socialization ⟷ Extensive Socialization
Closed Procedures ⟷ Open Procedures

3. Appraising Choices

Behavioral Criteria ⟷ Results Criteria
Purposes: Development, Remedial, Maintenance
Low Employee Participation ⟷ High Employee Participation
Short-Term Criteria ⟷ Long-Term Criteria
Individual Criteria ⟷ Group Criteria

4. Compensating Choices

Low Base Salaries ⟷ High Base Salaries
Internal Equity ⟷ External Equity
Few Perks ⟷ Many Perks
Standard, Fixed Package ⟷ Flexible Package
Low Participation ⟷ High Participation
No Incentives ⟷ Many Incentives
Short-Term Incentives ⟷ Long-Term Incentives
No Employment Security ⟷ High Employment Security
Hierarchical ⟷ High Participation

5. Training and Development

Short Term ⟷ Long Term
Narrow Application ⟷ Broad Application
Productivity Emphasis ⟷ Quality of Work Life Emphasis
Spontaneous, Unplanned ⟷ Planned, Systematic
Individual Orientation ⟷ Group Orientation
Low Participation ⟷ High Participation

6. Labour Relations Choices

Union Avoidance ⟷ Cooperation with Union
Confrontation ⟷ Collaboration
Low Respect for Employee Rights ⟷ High Respect for Employee Rights
Formal Relationship ⟷ Informal Relationship
Secretive ⟷ Open

Source: Adapted from R.S. Schuler and S.E. Jackson, "Linking Competitive Strategies with Human Resource Management Practices,"*Academy of Management Executive* 1, 3 (1987): 207–19.

Strategic Staffing

Many staffing decisions have implications for strategy implementation. For example, whether the company hires from the outside or relies primarily on internal sources will determine the opportunities for current employees, and in this way will influence career management and promotion, which in turn will influence rewards, training and development, and the overall QWL for the firm's employees.

A related issue, which characterizes the 1990s, pertains to mergers and acquisitions as well as de-hiring or layoffs during periods of downsizing. Because of market opportunities (in the case of mergers and acquisitions) or a sudden need to downsize because of market conditions, many organizations find themselves making staffing decisions that are rarely tied to careful strategic analysis. In some organizations, decisions are made "overnight" due to the pressing need to staff new positions. It is only recently that corporations are beginning to realize that market conditions will most likely remain hectic and unpredictable, and consequently a long-term strategy is required. While previously succession planning for senior managers was given much attention due to its strategic importance, increasingly practitioners and academics are paying attention to emerging strategic staffing issues, such as the succession of boards of directors and the acquisition of employees.

Strategic Elements in Performance Appraisal

Performance appraisal has gained increasing importance as an HR practice due to the increased demand for innovation, competition for specific talents, and the impact of technology on the nature of jobs. Consequently, there are mounting reasons for integrating this activity into a strategic perspective. Performance appraisal is a key element in the success of implementing or retaining corporate strategy, since it embodies the actions and results exhibited by employees in order to make the strategy work. For example, if a company wishes to adopt a Total Quality Management (TQM) approach, performance appraisal would likely incorporate "quality and customer satisfaction" goals for employees and call for behaviours that focus on developing a broader sensitivity to customer needs.

In spite of its potential importance in the strategic management process, performance appraisal is not receiving the proper attention. Much of this lack of attention is due to the fact that managers and employees alike are frustrated with the existing performance appraisal system. Although the obstacles to performance appraisal are described in detail in Chapters 9 and 10, it should be mentioned here that many managers do not like to use the system, and employees do not find the system in place to be valid and reliable. Consequently, it is of the utmost importance to tune-up and adjust the performance appraisal system to assess the behaviours needed to achieve a strategic objective.

Strategic Compensation Systems[12]

The choices made in respect of reward are particularly important in implementing a strategy. Perhaps more than any area of HRM, the reward structure communicates the overall philosophy and strategy of the organization. Furthermore, reward choices overlap many other areas of HRM. For example, compensation strategy normally overlaps the performance appraisal system.

In order to devise a strategic compensation plan, there are three questions, and multiple facets in each, to be addressed. These include:

1. What will be the basis of pay (job vs. skills; performance vs. seniority; short- vs. long-term orientation; risk aversion vs. risk taking; corporate vs. division performance; internal vs. external equity; hierarchical vs. egalitarian; and qualitative vs. quantitative measures of performance)?

2. What are some design considerations (pay level vs. market; fixed pay vs. incentives, frequency of raises, or bonuses; intrinsic vs. extrinsic rewards)?

3. What will be the administrative framework (centralization vs. decentralization of pay

policies; open vs. secret; participation vs. nonparticipation; and bureaucratic vs. flexible policies)?

Each of the above questions should be answered in detail and the results should be compared to the conditions in a particular organization or unit. If the conditions are favourable and they support the organization's corporate strategy, then implementation should follow. For example, in order for a performance-contingent pay policy to be effective, six important conditions must be met:

- Pay and performance must be loosely coupled; otherwise they may inadvertently produce the opposite results of what was intended. The tighter the coupling, the more likely it will result in problems pertaining to local rationality; measurement difficulties will be compounded, inflexibility will be institutionalized, and inequity issues will mushroom.
- Avoid mechanistic systems—attempts to use performance-contingent pay in a purely mechanistic manner are almost certainly doomed to failure.
- It is necessary to nurture the belief that performance makes a difference.
- Provide multiple layers of rewards—no single pay for performance "will do the trick" because they all have negative side effects.
- Do not ignore nonfinancial incentives.
- Performance-contingent pay systems must be customized to each firm's unique situation.[13]

Once the critical dimensions of a compensation system have been determined, specific types of rewards that support these dimensions should be delineated.

An organization's philosophy and strategy are inextricably linked with its approach to improve the current or future performance of its employees. Organizations that are not committed to improving the performance of their own workforce will instead seek to hire skilled employees from outside. It is a matter of trade-off, since training and developing employees is both costly and time consuming.

However, if the company decides to do its training, it must ensure that the programs are linked to the overall strategic objectives. Further, it should be recognized that objectives for training are different from those of development (more information will be provided in Chapter 11).

All in all, companies that invested handsomely in training and development are convinced that it affects the bottom line even if results are not always obvious in the short term. One benefit that may arise when linking a strategic business plan to HR training and development is reduced costs. Another benefit is that employees are more aware of what their future in the company will be like, and it results in more commitment to the firm.

In our day and age, it is evident that in order to succeed in business, an organization must have well-trained personnel that can react to any situation.

Strategic HR Training and Development

Strategic HRM with regard to labour relations has a number of facets. First, if the company is about to expand, merge, or acquire a new firm, strategies pertaining to the role of unions and costs of labour are critical determinants. For example, in order to reduce labour cost or to benefit from a nonunion strategy, a company may choose an area that is known for its anti-union sentiments. However, once employees are represented by a union, the firm may choose to adhere to confrontational or cooperative relationships.

Incorporating labour relations issues into the strategic management process has both benefits and drawbacks. In formulating strategy, unions could provide necessary input from employees. In addition implementation of other HR policies may be smoother under good labour–management relationships. For example, a joint union–management

Strategic Labour Relations

committee produces good results when devising and enforcing policies to reduce accidents and to solve other health and safety problems.

One of the key themes emerging in strategic HRM in the 1990s stresses the need for innovation. In order to enhance competitiveness through facilitation of innovation, it is necessary to restructure labour–management relations in four key areas.[14]

- *Worker input or "say":* The absence of worker "say" is likely to lead to dysfunctions such as low morale, work disruption, and high turnover.
- *Flexibility:* Flexibility in production is especially important in the Canadian unionized sector, where old feuds between labour and management have led to comprehensive collective agreements that can run into hundreds of pages. Consequently, the extensive rules governing the workplace often rob it of its ability to quickly change production schedules in response to a dynamic market.
- *Sharing:* If there were some assurances that the "pie" was being divided equitably, workers' need for sharing in the fruits of labour would be met.
- *Security:* There are numerous problems in making participative, flexible, and equitable HRM systems work in the absence of some measure of employment security. This does not necessarily imply a lifetime employment guarantee, but it means the implementation of a variety of policies that will enhance security. This might include assurance for reducing subcontracting, investing more in training, and increasing opportunities for transfers to other jobs before layoffs occur. A strategy that will be needed is one that respects some priorities and enhances procedural justice.

TRENDS IN STRATEGIC HRM

Assessing HRM Strategies

Assessing HRM strategies means two things: (1) assessing the congruencies of the HR policies with the corporate strategy and objectives, and (2) determining the extent to which the end results of these congruencies contribute to the bottom line. Because the latter is discussed in detail in Chapter 18 (i.e., control and evaluation of HRM), this section is reserved to discuss strategic options for assessing congruency of fit.

A critical question to ask is: to what extent are HR practices and policies coordinated with the process of strategic management? In order to facilitate the assessment, a number of scholars have investigated the corporate and business strategies of a range of organizations across different industries. The most popular strategic typology, which can be helpful for analyzing the congruency with HRM strategy, includes the *grand strategy, adaptive strategy,* and *competitive strategy.*

GRAND STRATEGY. This represents a major plan of action for achieving the sales and earnings goals of the firm as a whole. The three grand strategy options often discussed are: *stability*, *growth*, and *turnaround*.

Stability strategies imply keeping the status quo—continuing to serve customers in the same manner in the same market domain and seeking only a modest improvement of performance. Firms that adhere to such strategies see the environment as offering limited opportunities. *Growth* strategies may imply a number of possibilities: exploiting new markets or products and providing opportunities for people to grow internally within the firm. When a business is in decline due to a recession or other reasons, *turnaround* strategies may include cost reduction, asset reduction, and overall downsizing. Each of these subdimensions calls for different HR policies and practices.

ADAPTIVE STRATEGY. Whereas grand strategies apply to entire organizations, adaptive business strategies are applicable to units within the organization. All in all, an adaptive business strategy aims at establishing congruence between the organization and its external environment. The three broad approaches to it include: the *prospector*, the *defender*, and the *analyzer*.[15]

Organizations that follow a *prospector* strategy are continually testing product and market opportunities. They create change to which competitors must react; they normally operate in a dynamic and growing environment; they need to have a flexible internal structure and systems in order to facilitate innovation. In contrast, the *defender* firm is concerned with stability; instead of making major changes in its technology and structure, the defender organization concentrates on improving the efficiency of existing methods. The *analyzer* strategy is to maintain a stable business core while innovating on the perimeter. It represents the middle ground between the other two strategies.

COMPETITIVE STRATEGY. This typology is based on Porter's well-known typology distinguishing three competitive business strategies: *differentiation, cost leadership,* and *focus*.[16]

A *differentiation* strategy involves an attempt to set a firm's products or services apart from those of its competitors. Advertising, product features, or technology may achieve a product or service perceived as unique. A firm pursuing *cost leadership* seeks efficiencies in production and uses tight controls to gain a competitive edge. It enables the company to price at or below the competition while maintaining quality and greater than average profit margins. The *focus* strategy emphasizes a specific market, product line, or customer group. Within this market, the focused organization may compete on the basis of either differentiation or cost leadership.

Computer Applications

Global competition is putting increasing pressures on Canadian managers to make faster and better business decisions. In the HR arena, managers must control labour costs; motivate employees to high quality, customer-oriented performance; and continuously search out new and better ways of doing both. Consequently, the potential for the use of HR information technology to contribute to the competitive advantage of the firm is enormous. Nonetheless, survey after survey shows that the majority of the firms have invested in HR computer applications to manage more traditional functions: employee records, payroll, and compensation and benefits administration.[17] In contrast to these traditional computer applications, Exhibit 2.6 illustrates how HR can divide its work and address related decisions for advancing the competitive strategies of the firm. The three strategies suggested below, resemble those mentioned above. They include:

- *Cost leadership strategy:* A strategy aimed at becoming a low-cost producer in its industry; sources of cost advantage include economies of scale, proprietary technology, or favoured access to important supply sources (people, raw materials, etc.).
- *Quality/customer satisfaction strategy:* A strategy aimed at improving existing work methods, products or services, and customer relations as a means of commanding premium prices; it is also concerned with cost reductions, but only in areas that do not directly affect customers' perceptions of quality or value.
- *Innovation strategy:* A strategy that emphasizes the creation of new operations and management methods, technology, or products and services.

Exhibit 2.6 illustrates various matchings of HR objectives with types of computer applications. Three categories of applications are suggested:

- *Transaction processing/reporting/tracking applications:* These best support routine, high volume HR decisions with well-defined information needs and outcomes. They may include calculation of overtime pay, document reviews, employee transfers, etc.
- *Expert systems applications:* These improve decisions for which the "right" outcomes are determined through expert knowledge and experience. They are also based on rules, but the rules are complex, derived from careful analyses of expert decisions. For example, determining the quality of recruits based on historical records, examining whether the training procedures for two groups of employees yield the same results, etc.

Exhibit 2.6
Matching Computer Applications with HR Strategic Competitive Objectives

HR Competitive Objectives	Transaction Processing/ Reporting/Tracking Systems	Expert Systems	Decision Support Systems
Cost Leadership: People Working Harder	• Reduces paper handling • Standardizes entry and reporting • Increases processing accuracy • Increases report turnaround • Early warning of goal deviations	• Decreases need for HR experts • Helps spread database and training costs over entire workforce	• Increases chance of innovation for HR cost controls
Quality/Customer Satisfaction: People Working Smarter	• Increases time for HR quality initiatives • Enables custom reports and data entry • Increases awareness of HR information and can lead to its improvement	• Enables line employees to make HR decisions informed by HR expertise • Increases customizing of HR programs • Increases line satisfaction with/ understanding of HR	• Increases chance of innovations for HR quality/customer satisfaction
Innovation: People Working with Vision	• Increases time for HR innovation • Awareness of goal deviations sparks discoveries	• Increases time for HR innovation • Line understanding of HR sparks collaboration and discovery	• Powerful support for discovery • Shortens discovery process • Fast testing, reporting, and documentation of new finds

Source: R. Broderick and J.W. Boudreau, "Human Resource Management, Information Technology, and the Competitive Edge," *Academy of Management Executive* 6, 2 (1992): 12. Reprinted with permission.

• *Decision support system applications:* These improve decisions for which the rules are changing or not well defined, and the "right" outcomes are unknown. For example: What is the right level of sales force hiring and training to maintain optimal sales?

In sum, among the types of automated systems that HR managers can use in pursuing strategic issues are: (1) dedicated application software, (2) dedicated database, (3) general purpose inquiry software, (4) interface software, and (5) packages combining several of these forms.[18] Like any other systems, each has its advantages and disadvantages.

Dedicated application software was developed to support a particular need, for example, payroll processing. Most dedicated systems are relatively inflexible and are difficult to adapt and maintain. Consequently, they are of limited value for any long-term strategic purposes. Likewise, dedicated databases are likely to be poorly maintained and become obsolete when the developer or sponsor moves on.

General purpose inquiry software is a more recent development, but with the potential for providing cost-effective and relatively easy-to-use support for strategic HRM. These may include report writers and query software capable of retrieving and extracting data from files and databases. The big advantage of this software is flexibility pertaining to strategic questions. Additionally, problem-oriented software, such as spreadsheets, statistical packages, and modelling tools are also suited to respond to strategic information needs.

Finally, sophisticated interface software is now being developed to help link and translate output between types of problem-oriented software. Recently developed packages include a variety of applications that combine inquiry; problem solving, which interfaces with decision support systems; and an executive information system.[19]

S U M M A R Y

This chapter described the dynamic and complex environment in which the HR function operates and the importance of confronting it through a strategic approach. In order to develop an effective response to dealing with both internal users (i.e., corporate decision makers) and external pressures, companies need to develop HR policies and practices that will be congruent with the overall business strategic needs. All in all, it has been suggested that HR strategy that fits with the firm's strategy will most likely create a competitive edge.

In order to increase the congruency, elements in strategic HR management were described and three different models were presented so as to illustrate the relevant parameters to consider in developing a strategy via the use of the contingency approach. Additionally, a few examples were drawn from selected strategic HR activities, namely planning, staffing, performance appraisal, compensation, and labour relations.

Obviously, the entire field of strategic HRM is in its infancy. But, considering the volume of articles, papers, and research results published in this domain, it is evident that even if theory and models are imperfect, the need is there to find ways of linking HR policies and practices to business strategic and long-term plans.

P O S T S C R I P T

If you read any recent article about management, or more specifically on HRM, chances are that the word *strategy* will be repeated at least a dozen times. The impression that one has is that HR managers and academics have discovered a new concept. And, like any new concept it has mushroomed and become so popular that in many circles it is the "in" thing to talk about. How can a responsible HR manager (or a university professor in an academic setting) deny that he or she is using a strategic approach in their organization (research)? It is like admitting that one is incompetent; it is like denying "mother nature."

Unfortunately, strategic HRM has become a panacea to solve not only all organizational problems but also to boost the image of the users. Until strategy was "discovered," it was very difficult for HR practitioners to demonstrate their usefulness to the organization. Historically, "personnel" used to be the dumping ground for ineffective line managers (see HRM in the News Vignette). And even when this view had changed, HR managers were still confronted with the difficulty of justifying their existence. More specifically, most HR activities did not lead to tangible outcomes. (Even today, many managers believe that HRM is an art, not a science consisting of a definite body of knowledge.) Consequently, HR managers were frustrated. But, fortunately, there was a saviour on the horizon—strategic thinking. Now HR managers can become part of the ball game traditionally left to other managers in finance, marketing, production, etc.

But, by examining the evolution of strategic theories, models, and thinking one can realize that this is not a modern-day concept. Even within the broader field of management, contingency approaches, fit theories, long-term perspective, and the like (all components of strategic thinking) have been known to be around for over fifty years.

Nobody is trying to suggest that strategic HRM is not important. On the contrary, the essence of this chapter is to demonstrate its usefulness. However, a strong word of caution should be attached to the context in which it is discussed and presented. Much more remains to be done. Strategic thinking is the first step in refocusing HR managers' attention from the execution of traditional roles to activities that are long term in nature. There is no doubt that shifts in thinking are taking place. But the limitations of the tools and techniques available to the HR manager in applying this approach do not justify viewing it as a panacea.

REVIEW AND ANALYSIS QUESTIONS

1. Why is strategic HRM becoming important today?

2. In what way(s) could human resources be linked to business planning?

3. Can you apply some of the principles listed in Schuler's 5–P model to an organization that you are familiar with?

4. How can the HR department gain strategic influence in the organization? Use Dolan and Harbottle as reference.

5. "Strategy implementation involves choosing specific HR practices." Explain and illustrate this by an example.

6. One typology of general business strategy involves "grand," "adaptive," and "competitive." Explain the differences between these concepts.

7. You have been recently appointed to become the senior HR officer for Lotus Corporation (makers of Lotus 1-2-3). Your principal task is to devise an HRM strategy. From your general knowledge about this company (or other well-known software development companies) list the principal steps to be undertaken and questions to be asked in order to carry this assignment.

CASE STUDY

YES, WE HAVE NO FRESH PASTRIES

While the margin on fresh pastries is more than double those on pre-packaged donuts and cakes, the pastry business is, well, just that: another business. It is different from the business of running a grocery store. At least, if "grocery store" is defined as the traditional high-volume, low-margin, limited-selection, space-driven, discount-driven, 40,000-square-foot grocery store. But what if it is defined as a high-margin, high-volume, expanded-selection, customer-driven, service-oriented, 40,000-square-foot grocery store? If we change the definition, can we sell fresh pastries?

"Of course," said the top team at Miracle Food Mart, a Toronto-based retail grocery operation with stores in Ontario and Quebec. Five years ago the top team decided that competing with the new 100,000-square-foot stores was not a viable merchandising strategy. Their volume and the size of their parking lots were so much greater.

Competing with them would not be possible because it would mean moving from all the current, space-bound locations and uprooting relationships with all its current customers, suppliers, and communities. Obviously, even the world's greatest patisserie wouldn't be able to do enough volume to justify 40,000 square feet.

The top team got back to the basic questions: What business are we in? Who are our competitors? and, Given that we aren't moving the stores, what do our customers want?

Answers to the above questions essentially resulted in the company deciding to embrace the newer definition of what a grocery store is, i.e., a customer-driven, service-oriented store with an expanded selection of items. From an individual store perspective this would mean the elimination of many of the current items to make room for more brand items and higher margin items. The latter meant having a deli section (with the smells of barbecued chicken); an expanded fresh fruit section (more tropical fruits); a variety of small, ethnic food booths (for eating in or taking home); and, yes, a pastry shop.

All this sounded great to Bill Bennett, vice-president in charge of Miracle Food Mart's 23,000 employees. Asked by the others on the top team if he could "deliver the people on this one," he answered: "No problem." To himself, Bill was asking questions like: Where do I start? What does this new store strategy really mean for my people? What does it mean for human resources?

Case Questions

1. Which employees does Bill need to change for the new strategy to be successful?
2. What changes does Bill need to make? Does he only need to change some HR practices, like compensation?
3. How should Bill make the necessary changes?

NOTES

1. See, for example, P.H. Mirvis, "Formulating and Implementing a HR Strategy," *Human Resource Management* 24, 4 (1985): 385–412; and D. Ulrich, "Organizational Capability as a Competitive Advantage: Human Resource Professionals as Strategic Partners," *Human Resource Planning* 10, 4 (1987): 169–84.
2. R.S. Schuler, "Strategic Human Resource Management: Linking the People with the Strategic Needs of the Business," *Organizational Dynamics* 21, 1 (Summer 1992): 18–32.
3. J.R. Nininger, *Managing Human Resources* (Ottawa: Conference Board of Canada, 1982).
4. A. Losovski, *La Grève est un combat* (Montreal: Librairie Progressive, 1976).
5. See R.P. Rumlet, "Evaluation of Strategy: Theory and Models," in *Strategic Management*, ed. D.E. Scendel and C.W. Hofer (Boston: Little Brown, 1979), 196–215.
6. L. Baird and I. Meshoulam, "The HRS Matrix: Managing the Human Resource Function Strategically," *Human Resource Planning* 7, 1(1984): 1–21.
7. P.P. Benimadhu, "Human Resource Management: Charting a New Course," *Report 41–89* (Ottawa: Conference Board of Canada, May 1989).
8. The ensuing discussion is based on R.S. Schuler, "Personnel and Human Resource Management—Choices and Organization Strategy," in *Canadian Readings in Personnel and Human Resource Management*, ed. S.L. Dolan and R.S. Schuler.(St. Paul, Minn.: West Publishing Co., 1987), 3–26.
9. The discussion is based on Schuler, "Strategic Human Resource Management."
10. Based on S.L. Dolan and J.G. Harbottle, "Strategic Changes in Human Resources" (Paper presented at the annual meeting of the Association of Human Resource Professionals of the Province of Quebec, Montreal, 17 April 1989); and J.G. Harbottle, "Strategic Human Resource Management: Influence, Relations, Policies and Practices—an exploratory empirical study of Quebec firms," (Unpublished Paper, April 1990).
11. J.E. Butler, G.R. Ferris, and N.K. Napier, *Strategy and Human Resource Management* (Cincinnati: South-Western Publishers, 1991), especially Chapter 5.
12. The ensuing discussion is based on material from a workshop on "Strategic Aspects of Compensation," prepared and given by L. Gomez-Mejia and D. Balkin to senior executives of Hydro-Quebec, Montreal, 18 November 1991. Material is used with permission of the contributors.
13. For more information on these and other related strategic compensation issues, see L. Gomez-Mejia, and D. Balkin, *Compensation, Organizational Strategy, and Firm Performance* (Cincinnati: South-Western Publishing, 1992).
14. For an elaborate discussion of this subject, see A. Verma, "The Prospects for Innovation in Canadian Industrial Relations in the 1990s," *Discussion Paper #QPIR 1991–5*, Kingston, Industrial Relations Centre, Queens University.
15. R.E. Miles and C.C. Snow, *Organizational Strategy, Structure and Process* (New York: McGraw–Hill, 1978); and R.E. Miles and C.C. Snow, "Designing Strategic Human Resource Systems," *Organizational Dynamics* 13 (1984): 36–52.
16. M.E. Porter, *Competitive Strategy: Techniques for Analyzing Industries and Competitors* (New York: Free Press, 1980).
17. R. Broderick and J.W. Boudreau, "Human Resource Automation for Competitive Advantage: Case Studies of Ten Leaders,"

Working Paper # 90–04, Center for Advanced Human Resource Studies, School of Industrial and Labour Relations, Cornell University.

18. R.R. Louis, "Using Computers to Support Strategic Management of Human Resources," in *Using Computers in Human Resources*, ed. S.E. Forrer and Z. Leibowitz (San Francisco: Jossey–Bass Publishers, 1991), 54–111.

19. For an excellent reference and specification of HRM systems, including information on vendors, see V.R. Ceriello and C. Freeman, *Human Resource Management Systems: Strategies, Tactics, and Techniques* (Lexington: Lexington Books, 1991).

CHAPTER THREE

JOB ANALYSIS

KEYNOTE ADDRESS
Ross Coyles
Director, Job Measurement, Hay Management Consultants

The Importance of Job Analysis

Whether organizations operate in a heavily legislation-laden jurisdiction or in an open, free-market economy, effective job analysis will continue to be a critical component of organization and human resources effectiveness. Effective job analysis will not only provide a process to identify, collect, examine and record job information, but it must also provide fundamental and sound job understanding. Through job analysis, organizations can then readily satisfy many of the basic information demands placed on them by such programs as pay and employment equity; but they can also assess and describe structures and opportunities in a more salient and appropriate manner—in ways that will allow their people to contribute more.

Organizations will continue to downsize, rightsize, and bytesize; effective job analysis will continue to provide significant insights into a basic building block of an organization—the job. Rather than simply documenting (and perhaps reinforcing) the status quo, effective job analysis must contribute significantly to improving selection, training, development, and motivation of people in environments where change will continue to be constant. Static or outdated terms and definitions, if used in job analysis, are obviously contrary to the needs of tomorrow's organizations. A fully developed frame of reference, incorporating a job's accountabilities, the work required of the incumbent, and the organizational context will allow both the organization and its employees to achieve. The opportunities provided by a well-constructed job analysis process should far outweigh the constraints.

Job analysis must not inhibit employee behaviour; rather, it must discern a job's key components and provide people with enough relevant information from which they can get the job done. For jobs do not exist as entities on their own; at any given time they are a (sometimes) subtle amalgam of an organization's requirements and the characteristics of the job holders. At Hay we have always considered job analysis to be a cornerstone of organizational and human resource effectiveness. We continue to refine basic approaches to job content analysis for use in job evaluation, performance management, "job ladder" progression, etc., and are presently developing more integrated approaches to job analysis, incorporating characteristics of successful, individual performance with the job's content. These integrated approaches not only provide a comprehensive and cost-effective way of defining the job, but they describe how and where employees can add value to their job and their organizational unit. The integrated approach's utility far exceeds basic content analysis in many job levels and in most organizations.

Will organizations continue to change? Will they continue to refine and improve those processes that lead to organization and human resources effectiveness? To readily respond to these actions they must continue to develop processes that will assess and analyze jobs in a more effective and efficient manner and in a way that is consistent with their organization's philosophy and sensitive to its culture and values. Effective job analysis has assisted organization improvement in the past; there is no reason to believe this will change as we move ahead.

· · ·

The Keynote Address by Ross Coyles confirms many HR experts' fundamental belief in the importance of job analysis despite the crises and challenges organizations are confronted with today. Job analysis has dominated many HR activities and will continue to do so, although its content and the methods to be used in carrying out this activity will most likely be different in the future.

· · ·

Almost all the functions and activities of HRM and the behaviour and attitudes of employees have their roots at the interface of employees and their jobs. Jobs are the link between individuals and organizational structure and outputs. When employees act in capacities that make good use of their abilities and skills, the organization is able to gain by transactions with the environment. Thus, from an HR perspective, job analysis is the basic process on which most other HR activities depend. Its aim is to provide managers with detailed information about how the organization performs its functions and thus goes about achieving its goals and objectives.

Job analysis is the process of describing and recording the purpose of a job; its major duties and activities; the conditions under which it is performed; and the necessary skills, knowledge, and attitudes (SKAs). Job analysis often results in two principal tasks, a **job description** and a **job specification,** as shown in Exhibit 3.1.

JOB ANALYSIS

In addition to assisting in a variety of HR decisions, such as selection, promotion, performance appraisal, and other functions and activities, as shown in Exhibit 3.1, job analysis is necessary to validate the methods and techniques used in making these decisions. Job analysis is also important because it provides the basis for establishing or reassessing the following broader organizational concerns:

Purposes and Importance of Job Analysis

- *Organizational structure*: It helps in deciding how the overall tasks of the organization should be divided into business units, divisions, departments, work units, etc.
- *Job structure*: It helps in deciding how tasks should be clustered into positions and job families.
- *Degree of authority*: It helps in understanding the way decision-making authority is allocated.
- *Span of control*: It helps in understanding the reporting relationships in an organization, and how many and what kinds of people report to each superior.
- *Employment equity goal*: It helps to design a process for ensuring that protected groups are represented in various jobs and job families.
- *Performance standards*: As performance standards are set in relation to the job, individual and group performance can be assessed.
- *Employee redundancy*: Job analysis helps to identify employee redundancies during mergers, acquisitions, and downsizing.
- *Guidance*: It guides supervisors and incumbents in writing references and preparing résumés for employees leaving and seeking new employment.

Job analysis has extensive relationships with other HR activities, as well as with the goals and characteristics of the organization. Some of the more important aspects are outlined below.

Job Analysis Relationships and Influences

ORGANIZATIONAL GOALS. The design of jobs not only reflects the design and technology of the organization, but also its goals. Jobs are in fact very explicit statements by organizations of what they have determined to be the most appropriate means for accomplishing their goals. Furthermore, the stated goals and the subsequent standards of excellence that an organization establishes give clear cues to employees about what is important and where their efforts are required. Since goals help determine the products and environments of organizations, they also help determine the criteria against which workers will be evaluated.

TECHNOLOGY. The type of technology being used by, and available for, an organization is also critical because it determines what types of job designs are possible and what types of

Exhibit 3.1
Relationships and Aspects of Job Analysis

```
                    ┌──────────────────┐   ┌──────────────┐
                    │ Organizational   │   │ Legal        │
                    │ structure        │   │ environment  │
                    │ and technology   │   │              │
                    └──────────────────┘   └──────────────┘

              ┌──────────────────┐
              │ Job              │
              │ descriptions     │
              │ • Purposes       │
              │ • Duties         │
              │ • Standards      │
              └──────────────────┘

┌──────────────┐              ┌────────────────────────────┐   ┌────────────────────┐
│              │              │ Other HR activities        │   │ Bottom line        │
│ Job analysis │              │ • HR planning              │   │ • Survival         │
│              │              │ • Recruitment and selection│   │ • Profitability    │
│              │              │ • Performance appraisal    │   │ • Competitiveness  │
│              │              │ • Compensation             │   │ • Adaptability     │
└──────────────┘              │ • Training                 │   └────────────────────┘
                              │ • Career planning          │
              ┌──────────────────┐  └────────────────────┘
              │ Job              │
              │ specifications   │
              │ • Skills         │
              │ • Knowledge      │
              │ • Abilities      │
              └──────────────────┘

              ┌──────────────────┐   ┌──────────────────┐
              │ Job design       │   │ Job context      │
              │ considerations   │   │ considerations   │
              └──────────────────┘   └──────────────────┘
```

jobs are appropriate for various organizational designs. For example, Canadian automobile manufacturers, with huge investments in plants and machinery to make cars on assembly lines, find it almost impossible to convert their car-making technology so that groups of workers make the cars. The result is that most assembly jobs remain fairly segmented and repetitive. Furthermore, assembly-line technology determines the structure or design of the organization and, in turn, the most appropriate types of job designs.

HUMAN RESOURCE PLANNING. Job analysis helps to decide how successors should be planned for in various succession plans. Also, it helps determine the types of employees needed when companies are planning to diversify their products or services, as well as to change or alter technologies. Part of the planning is also the compliance with legal considerations, as illustrated in the next section.

RECRUITMENT AND SELECTION. On the basis of job analysis and in conjunction with HR planning, the organization can determine whom to recruit. Without job analysis, the organization would be unable to specify what types of job applicants are needed, and when and where they are needed. This, in turn, can have negative consequences for organizational productivity and the validity of its selection procedures and decisions. Only with job analysis information can an organization specifically demonstrate that its selection procedures are job related.

APPRAISING PERFORMANCE AND TRAINING. To effectively evaluate employee performance, the appraisal method used must reflect the important duties of the job. Only by examining the skills required for a job (as defined in the job specifications) can the organization train and promote employees in conjunction with its HR needs.

COMPENSATION. Job analysis plays a critical role in compensation activities. It is on the basis of the job analysis that a job's worth is determined. Job analysis also determines whether the pay level is fair in relation to that of other jobs. That is, job analysis helps ensure that employees in jobs of equal worth receive the same pay. It can also be used to provide insights into "comparable worth" considerations.

CAREER MANAGEMENT AND PLANNING. Job analysis guides employees in preparing themselves to realize their career aspirations. The advertised job descriptions and job specifications can help them decide on the type of training and development they should choose in order to pursue their career.

Today, the legal need for selection tests and performance appraisals that accurately predict job performance has made job analysis much more important. The various federal and provincial human rights legislations admonish the personnel specialist to do a thorough job analysis before selecting a personnel test or developing a measure of job performance. Specific requirements will be discussed in more detail in Chapter 6, but one main requirement is that selection devices should be "content valid." This means that test items should,

Legal Considerations in Job Analysis

HRM IN THE NEWS VIGNETTE
Grandiose Titles are Passé, but Still Fit the Empty-Suit Crowd

We live in a world where a "sanitation engineer picks up garbage, an "assistant vice-president, reproduction technology" might be a mailroom clerk in charge of photocopying and "personal financial savant," the latest euphemism for stockbroker. We know that corporate nomenclature is a study in highfalutin semantics. Yet we continue to believe that job titles matter.

…ICI Canada, a multinational paint and chemical manufacturer that is currently decentralizing management, is a good example of how a flatter corporate structure streamlines titles. Keith Willard, who runs personnel at ICI, observes that the head of the paint division is called president, while the head of automotive paint is general manager. "Titles don't mean a heck of a lot around here," he says. Even so, he deals with people who would prefer a better title to a pay raise.

…Certainly, requesting a lofty title has been known to confer worth within an organization. One Bay Streeter insisted on the title of "Chief" economist, even though he was the only economist. The move prevented anyone coming in over his head and allowed him to build an empire.

…Some employees seek an important-sounding title in the hope that when they change jobs their new employer will be impressed. But most quickly learn that job titles aren't transferable; they vary too much between companies. The notable exceptions are old-guard financial services companies. … "Within a bank," says Willard, "someone's title reveals which dining room he eats in, how many weeks of vacation he has, how many square feet his office is, and how many windows he has."

…Imperilled and imprecise as inflated titles are, they continue to matter because they feed inflated egos. But these, too, will be cut down to size eventually.

Source: Excerpts from a feature article by A. Kingston, *Financial Times of Canada*, 25 February 1991, 15. Reprinted wth permission.

as much as possible, represent the actual on-the-job behaviour being measured. A case in point is the miner who was refused employment because he needed eyeglasses and therefore did not pass the physical examinations that were called for during the selection process. Medical evidence in this case proved that poor vision corrected by glasses would not hinder performance of a timberman in this type of job. Consequently, the Canadian Human Rights Commission awarded the miner $8,162.05 for lost wages plus the offer of another job.[1]

KEY CONSIDERATIONS IN JOB ANALYSIS

Job Design and Job Analysis

Because job design is concerned with job characteristics, duties, and purposes, it is intimately related to job analysis, in that it may have a profound influence on employee productivity and QWL. Unfortunately, this influence can be negative, for example, when it results in employee boredom, absenteeism, and sabotage. On the other hand, this influence can be positive if it leads to feelings of greater achievement, responsibility, challenge, and meaningfulness. How would you define a job so an employee would feel positive about it and motivated by it? An understanding of job design qualities can make this task easier to perform. Chapter 13 provides examples of how job design qualities have been used to produce beneficial effects, such as increased employee satisfaction and job involvement, and lowered absenteeism and turnover.

JOB DESIGN QUALITIES. There are three job design qualities: *characteristics, duties*, and *purposes*.

Characteristics. There are several critical job design characteristics. These include:

- *Skill variety*: The degree to which a job requires a variety of different activities in carrying out the work, involving the use of a number of different skills and talents of the person;
- *Job significance*: The degree to which a job has substantial importance on the lives of other people, whether those people are in the immediate organization or in the world at large;
- *Job identity*: The degree to which a job requires completion of a "whole" and identifiable piece of work, that is, doing a job from beginning to end with a visible outcome;
- *Autonomy*: The degree to which a job provides substantial freedom, independence, and discretion to the individual in scheduling the work and in determining the procedures to be used in carrying it out;
- *Job feedback:* The degree to which carrying out the work activities required by the job provides the individual with direct and clear information about the effectiveness of his or her performance;.
- *Cognitive job elements*: The specific parts (elements) of a job, such as communicating, decision making, analyzing, or information processing;
- *Physical job elements*: The elements or specific parts of a job, such as lifting, lighting, colouring, sound, speed, and positioning.

 The importance of these characteristics is their association with the job outcomes; for example, by themselves the physical job elements help determine who can perform a job. Therefore, jobs can be more or less accessible to all job applicants based on the physical job elements. In combination, several of these characteristics may influence employee motivation, performance, absenteeism, and turnover.

Duties. The specific activities and behaviours that constitute the job are called duties. Note, however, that different employees may engage in different behaviour in carrying out a duty. As described later in this chapter, these duties are generally derived from the job analysis.

Purposes. The critical aspect of a job is the reason for its creation and existence. Why does the job exist? How and why does it relate to the final product or goal of the organization? The design of a job whose purpose is to contribute only a small part of the total product of an organization will be quite different from that of a job whose purpose is to contribute a large part to the total product. The former may be designed into small, simple segments with minimal job identity and skill variety. The latter may be designed into larger, more complex segments with greater job identity and skill variety. In essence, the intention of each job vis-à-vis the final product of the organization influences its design.

In Chapter 1, a concern for the decline in the productivity and QWL of Canadian companies was expressed. In trying to explain this phenomenon, many people point to the design of the jobs in organizations and their relationship with changing workforce values. They claim that most jobs are too simple and repetitive. Furthermore, many workers could do a lot more than they are now doing and could be using more skills. Organizations, however, should resist the temptation to overcompensate for this by designing jobs with more complexity, before considering the appropriateness of the job analysis. Failure to analyze the characteristics of the individuals and the characteristics of an organization's values may result in the selection of an inappropriate job design. Consequently, two characteristics should be analyzed: individuals and organizational technological systems.

INDIVIDUAL CHARACTERISTICS. Knowledge of an individual's characteristics is critical to determining the appropriate and feasible job design. If jobs are to be enriched successfully, employees must have the knowledge relevant to performing the new tasks. It may be useful to match individuals with jobs on the basis of their SKAs. One way to learn more about individual characteristics would be to administer a questionnaire such as the one shown in Exhibit 3.2 (Job Activity Preference Questionnaire (JAPQ)), which measures individual preferences on 150 job elements, four of which are shown in this exhibit. Other ways may include the personality measures and interest tests described in Chapter 6.

ORGANIZATIONAL TECHNOLOGICAL SYSTEMS. The *technological system* of an organization refers to the machines, methods, and materials that are used to produce the organization's product. The type of technology (in the system) can strongly influence the content of job analysis. The assembly line is often used as an example of a technology that requires extremely repetitive and very simple jobs. Jobs that skilled workers and some managers perform are generally the opposite of assembly-line jobs. Both skilled workers and managers can often control the pace of their work and can use a variety of skills. Organizations can make the same product using very different types of technology, and thus the content of the job will be different.

Although job analysis is an old HR tool, renewed interest has been spurred in part by organizational efforts to become more competitive and profitable and, in part, by the need to comply with numerous federal and provincial legal requirements. As a consequence, organizations want to know about all aspects of job analysis because it yields crucial information in every facet of HR operation; it reveals needs that HR initiatives are intended to rectify or anticipate.

WHAT SHOULD BE ANALYZED? Because job analysis is a process of describing and recording many aspects of jobs, it is obvious that the work should include an investigation

Collecting Job Analysis Information

Exhibit 3.2
Job Elements of a Job Activity Preference Questionnaire

How important would you like each of the following job elements (job activities) to be in your work? Use the rating scale in giving your responses. Your total response score suggests how much you would prefer a job with these elements.

Rating Scale
0 No importance
1 Very minor
2 Low
3 Average
4 High
5 Extreme importance

I. Perceptual Interpretation

_____   1. Using colour perception (telling the difference between things by colour)

_____   2. Recognizing sound patterns (Morse code, heartbeats, etc.)

_____   3. Recognizing sounds by loudness, pitch, or tone quality (tuning pianos, repairing sound systems, etc.)

_____   4. Estimating speed of moving parts (rpm of a motor, speed of lathes, etc.)

_____   5. Estimating speed of moving objects (vehicles, materials on conveyor belt, etc.)

_____   6. Estimating speed of processes (chemical reactions, assembly operations, timing of food preparation, etc.)

☐   Total (your score on Dimension I)

II. Information Processing

_____   7. Combining information (combining information, as to prepare a weather report, to fly a plane, etc.)

_____   8. Analyzing information (interpreting financial reports, determining why an engine will not run, diagnosing an illness, etc.)

_____   9. Gathering, grouping, or classifying information (preparing reports, filing correspondence, etc.)

_____   10. Coding or decoding (receiving Morse code, translating languages, shorthand, etc.)

☐   Total (your score on Dimension II)

III. Handling and Manipulating Activities

_____   11. Arranging or positioning (placing objects, materials, etc., in a specific position or arrangement)

_____   12. Physically handling objects, materials, etc.

_____   13. Feeding/off-bearing (feeding materials into a machine or removing materials from a machine or piece of equipment)

_____   14. Hand–arm manipulation (activities involving hand and arm movements, as in repairing automobiles, packaging products, etc.)

☐   Total (your score on Dimension III)

IV. Communication of Decisions and Judgements

_____   15. Advising (using legal, financial, scientific, clinical, spiritual, or other professional principles to counsel individuals)

_____   16. Negotiating (dealing with others to reach an agreement or solution, e.g., labour bargaining, diplomatic relations, etc.)

_____   17. Persuading (as in selling, political campaigning, etc.)

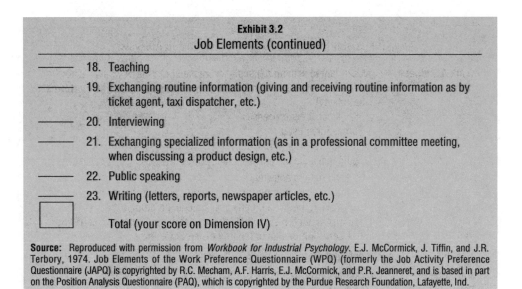

Exhibit 3.2
Job Elements (continued)

——— 18. Teaching

——— 19. Exchanging routine information (giving and receiving routine information as by ticket agent, taxi dispatcher, etc.)

——— 20. Interviewing

——— 21. Exchanging specialized information (as in a professional committee meeting, when discussing a product design, etc.)

——— 22. Public speaking

——— 23. Writing (letters, reports, newspaper articles, etc.)

☐ Total (your score on Dimension IV)

Source: Reproduced with permission from *Workbook for Industrial Psychology*. E.J. McCormick, J. Tiffin, and J.R. Terbory, 1974. Job Elements of the Work Preference Questionnaire (WPQ) (formerly the Job Activity Preference Questionnaire (JAPQ) is copyrighted by R.C. Mecham, A.F. Harris, E.J. McCormick, and P.R. Jeanneret, and is based in part on the Position Analysis Questionnaire (PAQ), which is copyrighted by the Purdue Research Foundation, Lafayette, Ind.

of what employees do in their job. Typically, information is collected by someone in the HR department in cooperation with a supervisor. It is becoming more common (and less expensive) for the incumbent, or the person in the job, to also provide job information. However, before beginning to collect the information, it is important to understand that a number of different perspectives can be applied, each oriented toward a slightly different goal. These can be used separately or in combination to yield the information desired. They include:

- *Actual activities*: What incumbents really do in their job;
- *Perceptions*: What incumbents believe they do in their job;
- *Standards*: What incumbents should do in their job;
- *Plans*: What incumbents tend to do in future jobs;
- *Motivation*: What incumbents want to do in their job;
- *Ability*: What incumbents are able to do in their job;
- *Potential*: What incumbents are capable of doing but they are not doing presently;
- *Future*: What incumbents are expected to do in their job in the future.

While conducting the job analysis there is a trade-off among validity, reliability, and costs associated with each perspective. All in all, the greater the need for accurate and relevant information (i.e., the core of validity and reliability), the greater the time and costs of obtaining the information. Each perspective is appropriate for a particular use.

Traditionally, the information obtained in job analysis is based on job incumbent perceptions that are validated by their superiors. The typical content of the information collected is shown in Exhibit 3.3

The traditional process of conducting job analysis consists of a number of steps. First, the analysts familiarize themselves with the position(s) to be investigated; then, they have to decide about the nature of the results they wish to obtain; the third step involves selecting the most appropriate approach to use for valid and reliable results; then, they have to select the tool(s) to be used in gathering the information; this is followed by the actual conduct of the analysis and the information gathering; the next step is compiling and verifying the validity of the information collected; and, finally, a decision is made about monitoring and when next to gather the information.

Data Collection Methods and Processes

Exhibit 3.3
Types of Information Obtained through Job Analysis

Work Activities	Job-oriented activities (usually expressed in terms of what is accomplished; sometimes indicating how, why, and when a worker performs the activity)
	    work activities/processes
	    procedures used
	    activity records (films, etc.)
	    personal accountability/responsibility
	Worker-oriented activities
	    human behaviours performed in work (sensing, decision
	        making, performing physical actions, communicating, etc.)
	    elemental motions (such as those used in methods analysis)
	    personal job demands (energy expenditure, etc.)

Machine, Tools, Equipment, and Word Aids Used

Job-Related Tangibles and Intangibles	Materials processed Products made Knowledge dealt with or applied (such as law or chemistry) Services rendered (such as laundering or repairing)
Work Performance	Work measurement (time taken) Work standards Error analysis Other aspects
Job Context	Physical working conditions Work schedule Organizational context Social context Incentives (financial and nonfinancial)
Personal Requirements	Job-related knowledge/skills (education, training, work experience, etc.) Personal attributes (aptitudes, physical characteristics, personality, interests, etc.)

Source: Adapted from E.J. McCormick, "Job and Task Analysis," in *Handbook of Industrial and Organizational Psychology*, ed. M.D. Dunnette (New York: Wiley, 1983), 652–53.

There may be as many methods for gathering information as there are job aspects to describe. Some of the more commonly used methods are: (1) observations and recording via mechanical devices, such as stop watches, counters, and films; (2) interviews with job incumbent(s); (3) conferences with job analysts or experts; (4) diaries kept by job incumbents; (5) structured and unstructured questionnaires filled out by incumbents or by observers, such as the supervisor or job analyst. There are three aspects to consider in choosing the appropriate method: validity, reliability, and cost. Both reliability and validity can be increased by using multiple methods. Here are some general descriptions of the principal methods.

OBSERVATIONS. Historically this was the first method. Frederick Taylor advocated it early in the century and it provided the foundation for his "scientific management" approach. Other industrial engineers, using photographs taken in quick succession, were able to dissect the physical movements of labourers and reassemble them in more efficient and productive ways. The advantage of a third party observer is the objectivity and credibility not available in information supplied by job incumbents. The disadvantages include the fact that the mere observation can influence the behaviour of the job incumbent, it is meaningless for jobs requiring mental effort, and it is not effective for jobs with a long job cycle. To illustrate the inappropriateness of observations, here is the case of the McGill University students' project. In this case, students were asked to select a method and use it for describing the job of junior programmers at IBM. The students, who had wrongly chosen the observation method, reported back to the class that IBM programmers spent most of their time "drinking coffee and smoking cigarettes.[2] Evidently this was not the case. Finally, it is important to note that if observation is being used, it should include a number of job incumbents. This will ensure that the observation did not pick up the unique behaviour of a single individual, but rather the analysis will assemble the typical behaviour for all job incumbents. In order to do that, a job analyst records the type or frequency of behaviour on an observation sheet, which is normally prepared in advance.

INTERVIEW WITH JOB INCUMBENT. This consists of asking a job incumbent a series of questions about the job. The major advantage of the interview is its potential for probing and give-and-take between the analyst, the job incumbent, and the supervisor. One disadvantage of the interview is that the quality of information provided depends to a large extent on the rapport established between the interviewer and the job incumbent. Other disadvantages may include the fact that an interview is time consuming and is perceptual and thus subjective in nature.

CONFERENCE WITH JOB ANALYSTS/EXPERTS. This is similar to the interview method, except that a number of people are involved. This results in better validity and reliability, since groups tend to do better than individuals on open-ended problem solving. Consequently, this method is used for new jobs and also for charting down future job descriptions. The disadvantage has to do with its relatively high cost and also the fact that basically perceptions are tapped.

DIARIES. The job incumbent is asked to record his or her activities at regular intervals in a diary or log. There is a page or two for each day. Diaries are effective for jobs covering a relatively long cycle. The major disadvantages include the concentration on activities rather than results. Also, because it is so personal, some important details may be missing.

QUESTIONNAIRES. This is a very common way to collect data. However, in general there are two types of questionnaires: structured, and open or unstructured. In a structured questionnaire respondents check a scale, fill in blanks, or circle a multiple choice response. In an unstructured questionnaire, respondents write essays on specific questions. The advantages of questionnaires are that they are relatively inexpensive and that they can be easily analyzed with computers. As with other methods, the disadvantage is the perception and subjectivity of the responses. Some of the instruments used will be described later in the chapter.

On a more practical note, it should be mentioned that reviewing past job descriptions in the organization can be a good start for familiarizing the analyst with the job and for deciding which method might be more appropriate. Similarly, contacting colleagues in other organizations and requesting copies of their job description as well as looking for background information in specialized books, such as the *Canadian Classification and Dictionary of Occupations* or the *Dictionary of Occupational Titles*, is recommended.

Finally, a few words about the choice of analyst should be mentioned, since it is very important. Although job analysis can be conducted by the HR department, attention should be paid to the training and experience of those who were assigned to overview the process. Research generally suggests that professional job analysts conduct a more reliable and valid analysis. Reliance on less experienced analysts may produce biased results. For example, female analysts may focus on fatigue, visual strain, and interpersonal relations, while male analysts may emphasize working conditions and physical effort. Research also indicates that supervisors and incumbents rate the worth of incumbent jobs more positively than do outside consultants.

Job Descriptions and Job Specifications

The outcomes generated through job analysis are the job descriptions and job specifications. Typically, a single job description lists several aspects of a job along with the necessary SKAs (i.e., the worker specifications of them). Job descriptions should be detailed enough so that the reader can understand (1) what is to be done (the domains, behaviour, duties, and results); (2) what products are to be generated (the purposes of the job); (3) what work standards are applied (e.g., quality and quantity); (4) under what conditions the job will be performed; and (5) the task characteristics of the job. Consequently, the final job analysis documents should probably include the parameters listed below.

1. *Job title r*efers to a group of positions that are identical in their significant duties. In contrast, a *position description* refers to a collection of duties performed by a single person. Titles can be deceptive; jobs in different departments or in different organizations may have the same title but different duties. Thus, in determining whether jobs are similar for purposes of pay or selection procedures, an analyst should focus on the degree of overlap in duties rather than on the similarity in titles.

2. *Department* and/or division where the job is located.

3. *Date* the job was analyzed will show when the description was, and should be, updated.

4. *Name* of the incumbent (optional) and name of the job analyst are useful for record keeping purposes. However, for job evaluation purposes, incumbent names should be omitted; otherwise they may inappropriately bias evaluators.

5. *Job summary* or job objective is an abstract of the job; it can be used for job posting, recruitment advertisements, and salary surveys.

6. *Supervision received and given* identifies reporting relationships. If supervision is given, the duties associated with it should be detailed under the major job duties.

7. *Major duties and responsibilities* identifies the duties and underlying tasks that make up a product or service. Duties are a collection of tasks that recur and are not trivial. For maximum information, duties should be prioritized in terms of the time spent and the importance; a duty may take little time but be critical to job success.

8. *Job specifications* delineate the experience, education, training, licensing, and SKAs needed to perform a job. *Knowledge* relates to the body of information in a particular subject area that, if applied, makes adequate performance of the job possible (e.g., knowledge of FORTRAN; knowledge of labour laws). The terms *skill* and *ability*, often used interchangeably, relate to observable capabilities to perform a learned behaviour (e.g., operating a crane). The requirements should be limited to the *minimum* qualifications a new employee can be expected to bring to the job.

9. *Job context* deals with the environment that surrounds a job. For instance, work may be conducted outdoors (e.g., construction), in remote areas (e.g., an oil rig), in low temperature (e.g., freezers) or in a closed place (e.g., air traffic control tower). It may involve extensive standing (e.g., bank tellers), or exposure to fumes (e.g., fibreglass fabricator), noise (e.g., drill press operator), diseases (e.g., laboratory technician), or stress (e.g., emergency room nurse). Information on these job components provides an understanding of the setting in which work is conducted.[3]

Regardless of what is included in the job description, it is important that it be worded effectively. For job descriptions many job analysts suggest:

- A terse, direct style should be used.
- The present tense should be used throughout.

- Each sentence should begin with an active verb.
- Each sentence must reflect an objective, either specifically stated or implied in such manner as to be obvious to the reader. A single verb may sometimes reflect both the objective and worker action.
- All words should impart necessary information; others should be omitted. Every precaution should be taken to use words that have only one possible connotation and that specifically describe the manner in which the work is accomplished.
- The description of tasks should reflect the assigned work performed and worker traits ratings.

An example of a typical job analysis document is provided in Exhibit 3.4. The example was taken from Henry Birks & Sons Limited, which is one of Canada's largest jewellery retail chains. Note that this job description also provides information regarding performance standards that are integrated into the scope of responsibilities. In addition, job purposes are implied from the percentages assigned to the key functions in the introductory section. Notice also that in the culture of this organization, the result of the job analysis is entitled Job Outline, although in fact it is a job description.

There are many procedures that can be used to determine what job information to collect, how to collect it, from whom to collect it, and how to organize and present it in job descriptions and job specifications. Some of the options for conducting the job analysis have been discussed before. However, because many more organizations today prefer to use structured procedures, they are discussed in more detail in this section. **Structured job analysis** refers to fixed forms and processes or systems that are used to gather the job analysis data. One way to describe structured techniques is by dividing them into two types: those focusing on aspects of the job (*job-focused*) and those focusing on aspects of the individual (*person-focused*). Some of the typical techniques in both categories are described here.

FUNCTIONAL JOB ANALYSIS (FJA). The United States Training and Employment Service (USTES) in the U.S. Department of Labour developed **functional job analysis** to describe the nature of jobs in terms of people, data, and things and to develop job summaries, job descriptions, and employee specifications. FJA was designed to improve job placement and counselling for workers registering for employment at local state employment offices. Today, many aspects of FJA are used by a number of private and public organizations.

FJA is both a conceptual system for defining the dimensions of worker activity and a method of measuring levels of worker activity. The fundamental premises of FJA are:

- A fundamental distinction must be made between what gets done and what workers do to get things done. For example, bus drivers do not carry passengers;.they drive vehicles and collect fares.
- Jobs are concerned with data, people, and things.
- In relation to things, workers draw on physical resources; in relation to data, on mental resources; and in relation to people, on interpersonal resources.
- All jobs require the worker to relate to data, people, and things to some degree.
- Although employees' behaviour or the tasks they perform can apparently be described in an infinite number of ways, there are only a few definitive functions involved. Thus, in interacting with machines, workers feed, tend, operate, and set up; in the case of vehicles or related machines, they drive or control them. Although these functions vary in difficulty and content, each draws on a relatively narrow and specific range of worker characteristics and qualifications for effective performance.

STRUCTURED JOB ANALYSIS METHODS

Job-Focused Techniques

Exhibit 3.4
Job Outline

JOB TITLE: Sales Associate	**CODE**

Store #/ Dept.: 280 / Montreal - Downtown
Title of Immediate Superior: Sales Supervisor
Present Incumbent(s): Mary Brown
                   Joe Smith
Completed by: Louise Bouchard
Area Manager's Authorization: Jim Tremblay / Jan. 20th, 1992

JOB OBJECTIVE:

Under the supervision of the Sales Supervisor, the Sales Associate is responsible for prompt and courteous service to customers in order to maximize sales and customer service, so as to promote the Company's image of quality and professionalism.

KEY JOB FUNCTIONS:

80%	Maximizes sales and customer service
5%	Maintains merchandise display
5%	Records all transactions on register
5%	Completes necessary paper work
5%	Performs necessary housekeeping duties
100%	

SCOPE OF RESPONSIBILITIES:

A) Dimensions: Average sales volume $60,000/yr. (1991)
                      Average no. of transactions 500/yr.

B) Relationships: • Deals directly with customers

                      • Promotes team work with co-workers

(Job Titles and   • May provide guidance to more junior
# of Employees)   Sales Associates

NATURE/WORKING ENVIRONMENT:

A) [   ] Office [X] Store [   ] Other (Specify) _____

B) Effort: • Must stand throughout work period
            • Environment is fast paced with many interruptions

QUALIFICATIONS: (Minimum Qualifications Required to Access Job)

A) General Work Experience or Equivalent Formal Education:
                       • High school or equivalent

B) Related Work Experience: • 5 years of selling experience (Retail or Service indust.)

C) Other: • Fluently bilingual (French and English)

                       • Excellent communications skills

Exhibit 3.4
Job Outline (continued)

JOB TITLE:	CODE
Sales Associate	

DUTIES PERFORMED: (Begin each point with an Action Verb)

1. Practises professional salesmanship within the guidelines of store policy and department procedures to achieve maximum sales and provide the highest level of customer satisfaction.

2. Promotes customer satisfaction, in a friendly way, as the most important consideration in every transaction. Ensures that special orders are handled efficiently.

3. Maintains a neat, organized, and well-stocked merchandise area. Ensures that merchandise is properly ticketed and attractively displayed. Communicates stock replenishment needs to supervisor.

4. Develops and maintains product knowledge of merchandise available from assigned department as well as what other departments carry. Is aware of and implements store policies and department procedures.

5. Responsible for adherence to all loss prevention policies, credit policies, and procedures, i.e., credit terms, discounts, return and exchange procedures, opening of new accounts, account authorizations, and cheque approvals.

6. Responsible for accuracy of salesbill completion. Daily register balancing and other report processing required.

7. May assist in training other less experienced sales associates in product knowledge and sales techniques.

8. Performs other duties as assigned by supervisor or manager.

FOR HUMAN RESOURCES USE ONLY

Job Title:

Job Code:

Store #/ Dept.:

Reviewed by:

Authorized Use

GROUP

_____   _____
Date   Signature

- The functions appropriate to dealing with data, people, or things are hierarchical and ordinal, proceeding from the complex to the simple. Thus, to indicate that a particular function, say compiling data, reflects the requirements of a job is to say that it also includes the requirements of lower functions, such as comparing, and that it excludes the requirements of higher functions, such as analyzing.[4]

The worker functions associated with data, people, and things are listed in Exhibit 3.5. The USTES has used these worker functions as a basis for describing over 30,000 job titles in the *Dictionary of Occupational Titles* (*DOT*). Employment and Immigration Canada created the *Canadian Classification and Dictionary of Occupations* (*CCDO*). The latter uses an alphanumeric code to arrange jobs into occupational groups. This classification is based on, among other things, the kind of work performed, the materials or equipment used or produced, the standards to be met, the education or training required, the working conditions, and the relationship of the job-holder to co-workers.[5] Presently, the Department of Employment and Immigration is preparing a new format to allow for pay equity considerations.

An HR manager who has to prepare job descriptions and job specifications can start with the *Canadian Classification and Dictionary of Occupations* to determine the general job analysis information, and use the *Handbook for Analyzing Jobs* for more specific resource planning.

Exhibit 3.5
Functions Associated with Data, People, and Things

DATA	PEOPLE	THINGS
0 synthesizing	0 mentoring	0 setting up
1 coordinating	1 negotiating	1 precision working
2 analyzing	2 instructing	2 operating/controlling
3 compiling	3 supervising	3 driving/operating
4 computing	4 diverting	4 manipulating
5 copying	5 persuading	5 tending
6 comparing	6 speaking/signalling	6 feeding/offbearing
	7 serving	7 handling
	8 taking instructions/helping	

Source: Adapted from U.S. Department of Labor, Employment Service, Training and Development Administration, *Handbook for Analyzing Jobs* (Washington, D.C.: Government Printing Office, 1972), 73.

MANAGEMENT POSITION DESCRIPTION QUESTIONNAIRE. Although the FJA approach is complete, it requires considerable training to use well and is quite narrative in nature. The narrative portions tend to be less reliable than more quantitative techniques, such as the **Management Position Description Questionnaire (MPDQ)**. This method of job analysis relies upon the checklist method to analyze jobs. It contains 197 items related to the concerns and responsibilities of managers, their demands and restrictions, and miscellaneous characteristics. These items have been condensed into thirteen job factors including:

- Product, market, and financial planning
- Coordination of other organizational units and personnel
- Internal business control
- Products and services responsibility
- Public and customer relations

- Advanced consulting
- Autonomy of action
- Approval of financial commitments
- Staff service
- Supervision
- Complexity and stress
- Advanced financial responsibility
- Broad personnel responsibility

The MPDQ is designed for managerial positions, but responses to the items vary by managerial level within any organization and among different organizations. The MPDQ is appropriate for evaluating managerial jobs, determining the training needs of employees moving into these jobs, creating job families and placing new managerial jobs into the right job family, compensating these jobs, and developing selection procedures and performance appraisal forms.

THE HAY PLAN. Another method of analyzing managerial jobs is the **Hay Plan**, which is used by a large number of organizations. Although less structured than the MPDQ and PAQ, it is systematically tied into a job evaluation and compensation system. Thus, use of the Hay Plan allows an organization to maintain consistency not only in how it describes managerial jobs, but also in how it rewards them. The purposes of the Hay Plan are management development, placement, and recruitment; job evaluation; measurement of the execution of a job against specific standards of accountability; and organization analysis.

The Hay Plan begins with an interview between the job analyst and the job incumbent. The information that is gathered relates to four aspects of the incumbent's job: the objectives, the dimensions, the nature and scope of the position, and the accountability objectives. Information about the objectives allows the reader of the job description to know why the job exists in the organization and for what reason it is paid. Information about dimensions conveys to the reader how much of the "show" the incumbent runs and the magnitude of the end results affected by his or her actions.

The core of the Hay job description is the information about the nature and scope of the position, which covers five crucial aspects:

- How the position fits into the organization, including reference to significant organizational and outside relationships.
- The general composition of supporting staff. This includes a thumbnail sketch of each major function of any staff under the incumbent's position—size, type, and the reason for its existence.
- The general nature of the technical, managerial, and human relationship know-how required.
- The nature of the problem solving required: what are the key problems that must be solved by this job, and how variable are they?
- The nature and source of control or of the freedom to solve problems and act, whether supervisory, procedural, vocational, or professional.

Information related to the accountability objectives tells what end results the job exists to achieve and the incumbent is held accountable for. There are four areas of accountability: organization (including staffing, developing, and maintaining the organization); strategic planning; tactical planning, execution, and directing the attainment of objectives; and review and control.

Because the Hay Plan is based on information gathered in an interview (as opposed to the checklist method in the MPDQ), the success of the Plan depends upon the skills of the interviewer. Interviewers can be trained to collect information useful for job descriptions, job evaluation, and compensation. The Hay Plan results in one organization can be compared with those in other organizations to ensure external pay comparability. The Hay Plan is discussed further in Chapter 7, Direct Compensation.

JOB INFORMATION MATRIX SYSTEM (JIMS). The JIMS is designed to collect information on such issues as: (1) what does the employee *do* on the job? (2) what equipment or tools does the employee *use*? (3) what does the employee *have* to know? (4) what are the employee's *responsibilities*? and (5) under *what conditions* does the employee have to perform? The JIMS can be completed by the job incumbent and/or by supervisors. The advantage of the JIMS is its standardization and thus the possibility to computerize responses. However, a work analyst is still needed to monitor analysis. This technique can be used with great success with some occupations, but is very limited to white-collar jobs.

OCCUPATIONAL ANALYSIS INVENTORY (OAI). This technique integrates job-oriented elements with person-oriented elements. It also covers work goals. The OAI uses over 600 elements organized in five clusters: (1) information received, (2) mental activities, (3) work behaviour, (4) work goals, and (5) work context. These are rated by supervisors or workers on three scales: significance, occurrence, and applicability. The first two scales are six-pointed; the third is dichotomous. Although the results of the OAI are very specific, its drawback is the voluminous number of elements. On the other hand, it could be used very effectively for assessing training needs.

METHODS ANALYSIS. **Methods analysis** focuses on analyzing a *job element*, the smallest identifiable component of a job. The need for methods analysis often results from (1) changes in tools and equipment, (2) changes in product design, (3) changes in materials, (4) modifications of equipment and procedures to accommodate handicapped workers, and (5) health and safety concerns.

While HR managers have downplayed the importance of methods analysis in recent years, it is still widely used in manufacturing settings. In fact, the increased use of new technologies, collectively referred to as *programmable automation*, has increased the need for methods analysis. These new processes include computer-aided design (CAD), computer-aided manufacturing (CAM), computer-aided engineering (CAE), and computer-integrated manufacturing (CIM). Unfortunately, many manufacturers have acquired new technology much in the way a family buys a new car: drive out the old, drive in the new, enjoy the more comfortable, faster, smoother, more economical ride, and life continues. Such an approach can mean disaster for a manufacturing firm; if the company fails to understand and prepare for the markedly different ways of production with the new technologies, they will become as much an inconvenience as a benefit, but a lot more expensive. Thus, it is increasingly important to study and document work processes, and it is in this context that methods analysis comes in handy.

While conventional job analysis procedures and structured procedures generally focus on describing the job and its general duties, the conditions under which the duties are performed, and the levels of authority, accountability and know-how required, methods analysis describes how to do the job as efficiently and effectively as possible. Although methods analysis could be used for many jobs, it is more frequently applied to nonmanagerial jobs. In these jobs, individual activity units can often be identified more readily.

Methods analysis, which had its origins in industrial engineering, may take different forms. In addition to charting the flow processes and the worker–machine interaction, methods analysis concentrates on work measurement (or time study) and work sampling.

In essence, **work measurement** determines standard times for all units of work activity in a given task or job. Combining these times gives a standard time for the entire job. These standard times can be used as a basis for wage-incentive plans (incentives generally are given for work performance that takes less than the standard time), cost determination, cost estimates for new products, and balancing production lines and work crews. Establishing standard times is challenging, since the time it takes to do a job can be influenced as much by the individual doing the job as by the nature of the job itself. Consequently, determining standard times often requires measurement of the "actual effort" the individual is exerting and the "real effort" required. This process often involves some guess work. Common methods of collecting time data and determining standard times include the stopwatch time studies, standard data, predetermined time systems, and work sampling for determining standard time.

Work sampling is the process of taking instantaneous samples of the work activities of individuals or groups of individuals. Work sampling can be done in several ways: the job analyst can observe the incumbent at predetermined times; a camera can be set to take photographs at predetermined times; or at a given signal, all incumbents can record their activity at that moment. The activities from these observations are timed and classified into predetermined categories. The result is a description of the activities by classification of a job and the percentage of time for each activity. A recent study that examined the difference between *successful* managers and *effective* managers used this approach. It has been found that successful managers, those who moved up the hierarchy, spent more time on networking activities than the effective managers. The latter, defined as those who have achieved a high level of quality and quantity of work performance, spent more time on routine communication with their subordinates as well as on human resource aspects of management.[6]

Person-Focused Techniques

In addition to the job-focused techniques that describe jobs in terms of task or activity statements that culminate in a definition of the person-oriented content of the jobs, there are the person-focused or behaviour-focused techniques that are behavioural statements resulting in the definition of the person-oriented content of jobs. Some of the more known techniques are described in this section.

POSITION ANALYSIS QUESTIONNAIRE (PAQ). The **PAQ** is a structured questionnaire containing 187 job elements. Seven additional items relating to amount of pay are included for research purposes only. The PAQ is organized into six divisions:

- *Information input*: Where and how does the worker get the information used in performing the job? Examples are the use of written materials and near-visual differentiation.
- *Mental processes*: What reasoning, decision-making, planning, and information-processing activities are involved in performing the job? Examples are the level of reasoning in problem solving and coding/decoding.
- *Work output*: What physical activities does the worker perform, and what tools or devices are used? Examples are the use of keyboard devices and assembling/disassembling.
- *Relationships with other people*: What relationships with other people are required in performing the job? Examples are instructing and contacts with the public or customers.
- *Job context*: In what physical or social contexts is the work performed? Examples are high temperatures and interpersonal conflict situations.
- *Other job characteristics*: What other activities, conditions, or characteristics are relevant to the job?[7]

Each element is also rated on one of six rating scales. The scales are: (1) extent of use, (2) importance of the job, (3) amount of time, (4) possibility of occurrence, (5) applicability, and (6) other. Using these six divisions and six rating scales, the nature of jobs is essentially determined in terms of communication/decision making/social responsibilities; performance of skilled activities; physical activity and related environmental conditions; operation of vehicles and equipment; and processing of information. Using these five dimensions, jobs can be compared and clustered. The job clusters can then be used for staffing decisions and the development of job descriptions and specifications.

While task inventories limit comparisons of jobs within occupations, the PAQ's reliance on person-oriented traits allows it to be applied to a variety of jobs and organizations without modification. Responses to the items are analyzed by computer to produce a job profile that indicates how a particular job compares with other jobs with regard to the six elements detailed above. The PAQ database also contains information about the relationships among PAQ responses, job aptitudes, and labour market pay rates. Thus, this tool has a potential for selection and job evaluation as well as being a job analysis technique.

POSITION DESCRIPTION QUESTIONNAIRE (PDQ). Closely modelled after the PAQ, the technique was developed by Control Data Corporation and lends itself easily to quantification of results and thus to computer analysis. Unfortunately, it has been specifically tailored to Control Data's needs and proves costly to adapt to other organizations.

JOB ELEMENT INVENTORY (JEI). Another technique which is closely modelled after the PAQ but has wider applications. It was designed as an aid in selecting employees for the U.S. Civil Service. An *element* is an item of knowledge, a skill, an ability, or a personal characteristic linked somehow to job success. It contains a 153-item JEI and is very simple to use. It has been designed for completion by incumbents. A simple three-point scale indicates whether each element (1) is not present in the job, (2) is present but not important, or (3) is present and is important. The chief advantages of this technique are its simplicity and the cost savings associated with having incumbents, rather than trained analysts, complete the instrument. Additionally, since the response scale is numerical, results can be stored in a database and analyzed by computers.[8]

PHYSICAL ABILITIES ANALYSIS (PAA). A subject subset of abilities and job demands used to analyze jobs is physical proficiency. The **PAA** uses nine abilities to analyze the physical requirements of tasks. The nine abilities and examples of each include:

- *Dynamic strength*: This is defined as the ability to exert muscular force repeatedly or continuously over time.
- *Trunk strength*: This is a derivative of the dynamic strength factor and is characterized by resistance of trunk muscles to fatigue over repeated use.
- *Static strength*: This is the force that an individual exerts in lifting, pushing, pulling, or carrying external objects.
- *Explosive strength*: This is characterized by the ability to expend a maximum of energy in one or a series of maximum thrusts.
- *Extent flexibility*: This involves the ability to extend the trunk, arms, and/or legs through a range of motions in either the frontal, sagittal, or transverse planes.
- *Dynamic flexibility*: This contrasts with extent flexibility in that it involves the capacity to make rapid, repeated flexing movements, in which the resilience of the muscles in recovering from distension is critical.
- *Gross body equilibrium*: This is the ability to maintain balance in either an unstable position or when opposing forces are pulling.

- *Stamina*: This is synonymous with cardiovascular endurance and enables the performance of prolonged bouts of aerobic work without experiencing fatigue or exhaustion.[9]

In analyzing jobs with the PAA, seven-point scales are used to determine the extent to which each job requires each of the seven abilities (from maximum performance to minimum performance). With the presence of many voluntary affirmative action programs, the need for organizations to know the precise physical requirements for jobs is increasing. Thus, the information from the PAA can be very instrumental, along with job design, in accommodating workers to jobs.

THE CRITICAL INCIDENT TECHNIQUE (CIT). This technique is more frequently used for developing behavioural criteria. The CIT requires those knowledgeable about a job to describe to a job analyst the critical job incidents (i.e., those incidents that they have observed over the past six to twelve months that represent effective and ineffective performance). The job analyst may prompt those describing the incidents by asking them to write down five key things an incumbent must be good at, or to identify the most effective job incumbent and describe that person's behaviour.[10]

Those describing the incidents are also asked to describe what led up to the incident, what were the consequences of the behaviour, and whether the behaviour was under the control of the incumbent. After a number of critical incidents have been described and recorded, they are rated by their frequency of occurrence, importance, and the extent of ability required to perform them. This information, often concerning a few hundred incidents for each job, is then clustered into job dimensions. These dimensions, which may often utilize only a subset of all the critical incidents obtained, can then be used to describe the job. They can also be used to develop performance appraisal forms, particularly Behaviourally Anchored Rating Scales (described in Chapter 9).

The major disadvantages of this job analysis method are the time required to gather descriptions of the incidents and the difficulty of identifying average performance; these methods often elicit the extremes of performance (e.g., ineffective or effective or very bad or very good) and omit examples of what is average performance. This disadvantage, however, can be overcome by obtaining examples of multiple level performance. An attempt to do so has been done through the **Extended CIT.**

Instead of beginning by having incumbents or others knowledgeable about the jobs list examples of effective and ineffective behaviour, the Extended CIT begins by having incumbents identify *job domains*.[11] These domains are essentially umbrellas under which many specific tasks can be included. For example, a job domain for a manager may be *training*. Specific tasks that can be placed under this domain include: informally and formally teaching employees to learn new job skills, engaging in self-study on and off the job, and orienting new employees to the job and the organization.

The specific tasks that come under a given domain may vary from organization to organization. Consequently, after the job domains have been identified (often ten to twenty per job) and defined, the job analyst lists the tasks to be performed in each domain. The analyst lists these tasks after asking the incumbents to write examples or scenarios that reflect three different levels of performance for each domain. In describing these scenarios, the incumbents list what the main event is, the behaviour of the people in the scenario, and the consequences of that behaviour. Using scenarios collected from the incumbents, the analyst writes task statements. Each statement is essentially an example of one behaviour (or several in a domain that is described in the scenarios), indicating if they actually perform the tasks, how frequently, the difficulty in doing so, and the importance of the task.

With the information obtained thus far, job descriptions can be written. The Extended CIT can, however, be used to develop performance appraisal forms, to appraise performance, and to spot training needs. This is done by having the incumbents (again, a different group to ensure validity) estimate the level of performance each task statement represents and place it in one of the domains identified initially by a previous group of incumbents. If the incumbents are then asked to describe the abilities (physical and mental) necessary to perform the tasks in each domain, selection procedures can be developed. In this step the incumbents are presented with a list of abilities together with short definitions, and asked to indicate the amount needed to satisfactorily perform the tasks in each domain. Once these abilities are identified, they can also be used to write the job specifications or a job description.

Although the Extended CIT takes more time to develop than the CIT method, it does gather a great deal more information from the incumbents, such as the needed abilities, performance levels, and the domains of the jobs. The Extended CIT also goes through several additional development steps. Both, however, are based on the identification of job behaviour and, as such, both are useful in performance appraisal and training.

ASSESSING JOB ANALYSIS METHODS

Confronted with the eleven alternative job analysis methods (six job-focused and five person-focused), the question is: which is the best method to use? The appropriateness of a specific job analysis method depends upon two major sets of considerations: the usefulness for other HR activities and the extent to which the method addresses some practical concerns.[12] Nonetheless, it should be mentioned that the assessment of job analysis methods provided here is meant to be suggestive, not exhaustive and definitive.

Instrumentality of Job Analysis Methods

Earlier in the section on the relationships and influences between job analysis and other HR activities, it was indicated that the purposes of job analysis are to serve in:

- Human resource planning
- Recruitment and selection
- Performance appraisal
- Training and development
- Compensation
- Career management and planning

An assessment of how well these activities are served by each job analysis method is summarized in Exhibit 3.6.

Practical Concerns

Several practical concerns are also useful in assessing each job analysis method. These concerns are:

- *Versatility/suitability:* the method's appropriateness for analyzing a variety of jobs;
- *Standardization:* the extent to which the method yields norms that allow comparisons with different sources of job analysis data collection and at different times;
- *User acceptability:* the user's acceptance of the method including its forms;
- *User understandability/involvement:* the extent to which those who are using the method, or are affected by its results, know what the method is about and are involved in the collection of the job analysis information;
- *Training required:* the degree of training needed by those involved in using the method;
- *Readiness to use:* the extent to which the method is ready to be used for a job;
- *Time for completion:* the time required for the method to be implemented and the results of the method obtained;

- *Reliability and validity:* the consistency of the results obtained with the method and the accuracy of those results in describing the duties, their importance, and the skills and abilities required to do the duties;
- *Costs:* the amount of overall benefit or value to be gained by the organization in using the method in relationship to the costs incurred in its use.

Using these several practical concerns, the assessment of each job analysis method is presented in Exhibit 3.7.[13] Rating is done using a five-point scale, ranging from (1) served to a very limited extent, to (5) served to a great extent.

Exhibit 3.6
Assessment of Instrumentality of Job Analysis Methods

	HR PLANNING	RECRUITMENT AND SELECTION	PERFORMANCE APPRAISAL	TRAINING AND DEVELOPMENT	COMPENSATION	CAREER PLANNING
Job-Focused Techniques						
FJA	4	4	3	4	3	5
MPDQ	4	4	3	3	3	4
HAY	3	4	4	3	5	3
JIMS	3	4	4	4	3	4
OAI	4	4	3	5	3	4
METHODS ANALYSIS	3	3	4	2	3	3
Person-Focused Techniques						
PAQ	4	4	3	3	3	4
PDQ	4	4	3	3	3	4
JEI	4	4	4	4	4	4
PAA	2	4	2	2	2	2
CIT	4	4	4	4	3	2

Note: The techniques are rated from (1) the least instrumental, to (5) the most instrumental.

Exhibit 3.7
Assessment of Job Analysis Methods Against Several Practical Concerns

CONCERN	FJA	MPDQ	HAY	JIMS	OAI	PAQ	PDQ	JEI	PAA	CIT
Versatility/Suitability	5	4	4	4	4	4	3	4	3	5
Standardization	5	5	5	5	5	5	5	5	4	3
User Acceptability	4	4	4	4	4	4	4	5	3	4
Understandability	4	4	5	4	4	4	4	5	3	5
Training Required	3	3	3	3	3	3	4	4	3	4
Readiness to Use	5	5	5	4	4	5	4	4	3	3
Time for Completion	4	4	4	4	3	3	3	4	3	3
Reliability and Validity	4	4	4	4	4	3	3	3	3	3
Costs	4	4	4	4	3	3	2	3	3	3

Note: Methods analysis was omitted from this assessment.

Exhibit 3.8
CN Job Document

JOB NUMBER

MISSION AND VISION: "To meet customers' transportation and distribution needs by being the best at moving their goods on time, safely, and damage free. As we accomplish our mission, CN will be a long-term business success by being close to our customers, first in service, first in quality, environmentally responsible, cost effective and financially sound, and a challenging and fulfilling place to work."

THESE OBJECTIVES SHOULD BE REFLECTED IN YOUR JOB DOCUMENT WHERE APPROPRIATE.

EFFECTIVE DATE:
TITLE:
TERRITORY:
ORGANIZATION:
FUNCTION:
ACTIVITY:
LOCATION:

FIRST LEVEL SUPERIOR   JOB NUMBER :
TITLE : MANAGER SENIOR, MARKET

SECOND LEVEL SUPERIOR   JOB NUMBER :
TITLE :

PURPOSE OF POSITION :

KNOWLEDGE AND SKILLS :

QUANTITATIVE DATA

SUPERVISION :

BUDGET - DIRECT RESPONSIBILITY :

OTHER :

JOB RESPONSIBILITIES
MAJOR RESPONSIBILITY 1 :   PERCENT OF TIME :

MAJOR RESPONSIBILITY 2 :   PERCENT OF TIME :

MAJOR RESPONSIBILITY 3 :   PERCENT OF TIME :

MAJOR RESPONSIBILITY 4 :   PERCENT OF TIME :

GUIDANCE AND AUTHORITY
MAJOR DECISION 1 :

DECISION ENVIRONMENT :

WORKING RELATIONSHIPS

MOST FREQUENT CONTACT 1 :

NATURE OR PURPOSE:

OTHER INFORMATION
WORKING CONDITIONS :

While there are software systems specifically designed to aid in preparing job descriptions and job specifications, all in all companies are using relevant information as part of their Human Resource Information System (HRIS). Because an HRIS contains many sub-systems and thus is used extensively in an overall HR planning, it will be discussed in more detail in Chapter 4. In order to illustrate the use of one sub-system with application to job analysis, the "Job Document System," which is part of the Canadian National HRIS, is described here.

Computer Applications

The job document is designed to describe a position, stating its purpose, its responsibilities, and the main tasks related to the discharging of these responsibilities. The job document, thus, provides the basis for many other HR activities such as job evaluation, HR planning, recruitment, selection and placement, and training and development.

Employees can fill out blank document forms for input by HR managers. Exhibit 3.8 is a blank version of the job document. Similar documents are used in other organizations.

S U M M A R Y

The person–job interface is of vital importance to organizations today. This interface helps determine employee performance, satisfaction, and job involvement. Job analysis provides the foundation for many HR activities. Through the analysis, both the job description and the job specification are generated. Although the task of conducting the job analysis is highly technical and not always exciting, because of its importance it should not be neglected by HR departments. The tendency is to conduct analyses from time to time, but those are not sufficiently updated to reflect changes in the content of the job and the responsibilities of the job holder. The challenge, therefore, is finding the best or most appropriate way to analyze jobs. Because there are so many different methods and techniques, it becomes important to first identify and assess the appropriateness of the method to be used in the organization. For clarity, the techniques were divided in this chapter into two categories: job-focused and person-focused. Additionally, it is important to understand that some methods might be more instrumental for compensation and yet others might best serve the training and development activity. After the numerous methods were described, they were assessed using an instrumentality matrix that reflects their usefulness vis-à-vis several HR activities and functions. A final selection can then be made taking into consideration several practical concerns.

P O S T S C R I P T

Managers and employees alike have great difficulty with job descriptions. Although they understand the need for it, they often note that by the time a job description has been completed, today's organizational dynamics, brought about by fierce competition in the marketplace, have already caused changes in the job. Consequently, job analysis is given low priority by HR managers. This is reinforced by the mere fact that the conduct (or supervision) of the job analysis process is very technical and boring. HR managers prefer to be engaged in more creative HR activities. Often when management consultants confront HR managers with the problem of negligence in the conduct and update of job analysis, the typical reply is: "I'm too busy doing my job and so are many of our employees, so we don't have time to write job descriptions."

Traditionally, job descriptions are often characterized by rigid, standardized language that reflects the way most jobs are designed. Job analysis provides a framework for conformity to job holders with similar occupations or family of occupations. In fact, many jobs appear in organizational charts illustrated in boxes, which is a metaphor for rigidity and boundaries. This goes against a contemporary trend, especially with a highly educated workforce, whereby each employee prides himself or herself in being unique (rather than one of many) and engaging in explicit and implicit behaviours that are never described in a traditional job analysis.

The dilemma is: how to continue to write job descriptions and specifications without limiting the behaviour of the employees. This will be one of the challenges in the upcoming years. Some of the guidelines for developing a flexible job description might take into consideration the following ideas:

- Create "user-friendly" job descriptions where the employees involved will always be part of the process of finalizing it (through negotiation or other means); allow for periodic changes as suggested and discussed by the employees; and listen carefully to the rationale employees advance for indicating why their job is "different" from someone else's bearing a similar or identical job title. They might have good reasons.

- Instead of the traditional way of writing job descriptions by listing duties, see if you can specify "outputs." Since the ultimate goal is to produce (or serve), the outputs should be specified. It is acknowledged that this prescription is easier said than done, but some companies have already adopted this idea and are in the process of implementing it.[14]

- Add to the traditional job description some information that will guide the job holders in getting results effectively. Describe the norms and the culture of the work group. For example, a senior manager in BCE (Bell Canada Enterprises) recently complained that if he had known that he was expected to work late nights and weekends on a regular basis, he would never have taken the job in the first place.[15] Attempts should be made to describe the relationships that are important for getting the job done.

REVIEW AND ANALYSIS QUESTIONS

1. Why is job analysis so important as an HR activity?
2. What are some legal issues (federal or provincial) related to job analysis?
3. Choose any two methods of job-focused job analysis techniques and describe their advantages and disadvantages.
4. Choose any two methods of person-focused job analysis techniques and describe their advantages and disadvantages.
5. Discuss and review the important considerations in selecting job analysis methods.
6. In a nutshell, how might job analysis activities be assessed in terms of their importance to organizations?

CASE STUDY

THE PROJECT DIRECTOR

Dr. Betsy Morales has just been appointed Project Director of a research project on the effects of career counselling practices on university women. The previous director was fired after only six months on the job. The project is expected to be finished in two years, and funding sources expect quarterly progress reports. The project is six months behind schedule, half the funds for the first year have been spent, and the staff, which was selected by the previous director, is experiencing severe conflicts and low morale. Dr. Morales' challenge is to devise a plan to successfully complete the first year's objectives with the existing staff, remaining funds, and limited time available.

Canadian College was founded in 1912 as a private, independent, undergraduate, nonprofit institution. The main campus of Canadian College grew steadily since its founding to a size of over 10,000 full-time students, and 3,600 part-time students. It continues to be a respected undergraduate institution with future plans to offer graduate degrees in some areas.

As with many other colleges, Canadian College has begun to suffer the consequences of a reduced student-age population and cuts in financial aid to undergraduate students. In order to expand the potential student market, the board of trustees decided to initiate graduate programs. However, the College lacks the required research component at the graduate level. Once several research projects are underway, the president plans to develop an Institute for Social Research. He feels the College could gain more visibility.

Dr. Smith, Vice-President for External Resources, was mandated to accomplish this task. He needed to get many research proposals going, and he reviewed many of the Requests for Proposals (RFP) that had been offered by different federal and provincial agencies and foundations. Several proposals were of particular interest. He had expected the faculty to become interested in proposal writing, but he did not get the desired response. Although the faculty was informed of the new interest in research, it was not given any reason to become involved in the process with Dr. Smith. Many faculty members, particularly those without tenure, wanted to become the project director for any winning proposal that they wrote. Some also wanted to know whether they would be relieved of teaching duties for a period of time while directing a project and/or whether they would have a raise. Since the College had not established any clear guidelines on these issues, Dr. Smith was ambiguous in his replies.

Finally, Dr. Smith decided to hire a consultant to initiate the research thrust. The first research project awarded was a study on the effects of career counselling practices on university women. It was a two-year project, with funds for the second year contingent upon successful completion of the first year's objectives. Dr. Smith was very happy with this award, since it would fit nicely into the plans for the Institute for Social Research. To direct this project, he thought a woman was appropriate. He decided to hire Elizabeth Boone, an experienced professional with an M.A. in Education, who had been working as a counsellor in another College Upward Bound program.

After six months as director of the research projects, Elizabeth Boone was fired. She was very bitter about her experience at Canadian College. This was what she had to say:

This project has left me angry and frustrated. I don't think I have ever been in such a situation. I am not an expert on women's issues, but it is something that interests me and that I wanted to learn more about. I have an M.A. in Education, and three years' experience as an Upward Bound counsellor. With good staff, I wouldn't have had any problem with this project. But I didn't have any luck at all with the staff. I admit that this was in part because I didn't have any experience in hiring, but also I was under strong pressure to hire certain persons.

Aside from my friend Zayra, who was very helpful, I was stuck with an arrogant doctorate student recommended by Dr. Smith. She carried around her books on research methods and statistics almost as a banner of how much she knew. And then there was Victoria, whom I hired because of all her counselling experience. It turned out that she was always showing off about her experience, almost as if my younger age was a problem. Her husband was chronically ill and she was absent a lot. I would not be surprised if she quits. Even the secretary was a problem. I mean, she was efficient. But, I think the position of secretary is very personal and confidential, and I would have liked to choose my own. Yet, the College has this policy of giving priority to current clerical personnel when new positions open, and I had no input in deciding who would be my secretary.

With such a weak staff, I found myself doing all the work alone, and trying to get advice from people outside the College. I'm sure that while I sought advice, they were probably gossiping behind my back. I should add that I have a very difficult family life, with four children from my first marriage and three from my husband's first marriage living at home. Yet I gave this project so much energy. I was very excited by the subject of this project, and also the prospect of more money and status. I did all the work that was done for this project alone. Yet, instead of firing the staff, I got fired.

Following this event, the president called upon Dr. Betsy Morales to be the project director. In a private meeting with Dr. Morales, he acknowledged that morale among the team was very low, they were behind schedule in terms of progress, and remaining funds were limited. In order to help Dr. Morales carry out her new duties effectively, he prepared a short project staff background information sheet, as described in Exhibit 3.9.

Exhibit 3.9
Research Project Staff

Dr. Betsy Morales, Director: Ph.D., Education, Simon Fraser University, 1975. Seven years as executive director of the provincial Commission on the Status of Women and ten years as member of the faculty of the School of Education at Canada College.

Zayra Lin, Researcher: M.A., Education, University of Toronto, 1982. Ten years' experience as curriculum developer for a public school district, with particular expertise in the development of audio-visual educational materials.

Exhibit 3.9
Research Project Staff (continued)

Grace Peters, Researcher: M.A., Clinical Psychology, Memorial University of Newfoundland, 1985. Presently finishing doctorate dissertation in clinical psychology, York University. Seven years' experience as a clinical psychologist in a higher education environment, with particular expertise in research methodology.

Victoria Humphreys, Counselling Specialist: M.A., Educational Counselling, McGill University, 1972. Twenty years' experience as school counsellor at elementary and secondary levels.

Gloria Mosca, Secretary: Secretarial Sciences, Canada College, 1983. Nine years of increasingly complex clerical duties at a junior college.

Case Questions

1. What mistakes were committed by Elizabeth Boone, the first project director?
2. Demonstrate the systematic relations among job analysis, reward systems, performance appraisal, and staff development as portrayed in this case.
3. If you were Betsy Morales (the new project leader), how would you proceed to overcome the problems?

NOTES

1. Case reported in *Human Resource Management in Canada*, Report Bulletin No. 24, 1985, 3.
2. Reported by a team of students at McGill University who conducted a job analysis as part of the requirements for the course in Human Resource Management for Professor Dolan, Winter 1989.
3. R.J. Plachy, "Writing Job Descriptions that Get Results," *Personnel*, October 1987, 56–63.
4. For more information, see S.A. Fine, "Functional Job Analysis: An Approach to a Technology for Manpower Planning," *Personnel Journal*, November 1974, 813–18; Department of Labour, *Dictionary of Occupational Titles*, vol. 2 3rd ed. (Washington, D.C.: Government Printing Office, 1965); Department of Labor, Manpower Administration, *Handbook for Analyzing Jobs* (Washington, D.C.: Government Printing Office, 1972); Department of Labor, *Task Analysis Inventories: A Method of Collecting Job Information* (Washington, D.C.: Government Printing Office, 1973); and J. Markowitz, "Four Methods of Job Analysis," *Training and Development Journal*, September 1981, 112–21.
5. Canada Employment and Immigration, *Canadian Classification and Dictionary of Occupations*, vol. 5 (Ottawa: Queen's Printer, 1971), 1–2; the CCDO was revised in 1985 (Employment Equity Legislation Introduced, News Release, 1985).
6. F. Luthans, R.M. Hodgetts, and S.A. Rosenkrantz, *Real Managers* (Cambridge: Ballinger Publishing, 1988).
7. E.J. McCormick and J. Tiffin, *Industrial Psychology*, 6th ed. (Englewood Cliffs, N.J.: Prentice–Hall, 1974), 53. Reprinted with the permission of Prentice–Hall, Inc. The Position Analysis Questionnaire (PAQ) is copyrighted by the Purdue Research Foundation. The PAQ and related materials are available through the University Book Store, 360 West State Street, West Lafayette, Ind., 47906. Further information is available through PAQ Data Processing Division at that address. For a description of the validation of a short form of the PAQ, see S.M. Colarelli, S.A. Stumpf, and S.J. Wall, "Cross-Validation of a Short Form of the Position Description Questionnaire," *Educational and Psychological Measurement* 42 (1982): 1279–83. The PAQ has been adopted for professional and managerial jobs. For a description of this, see J.C. Mitchell and E.J. McCormick, "Development of the PMPQ: A Structural Job Analysis Questionnaire for the Study of Professional and Managerial Positions" (Purdue Research Foundation, Purdue University, *PMPQ Report #1*, 1979).
8. R.J. Harvey et al., "Dimensionality of the Job Element Inventory, A Simplified Worker-Oriented Job Analysis Questionnaire," *Journal of Applied Psychology* 73 (1988): 639–46.
9. C.P. Sparks, "Job Analysis," in *Personnel Management*, ed. K.M. Rowland and G.R. Ferris (Boston: Allyn and Bacon, Inc., 1982), 92. These physical proficiencies are taken from the extensive work of E.A. Fleishmann, *Structure and Measurement of Physical Fitness* (Englewood Cliffs, N.J.: Prentice–Hall, 1964); "Toward a Taxonomy of Human Performance," *American Psychologist* 30 (1975): 1 017–32; and "Evaluating Physical Abilities Required by Jobs," *Personnel Administrator* 42 (1979): 82–92.

10. J.C. Flanagan, "The Critical Incident Technique," *Psychology Bulletin* 51 (1954): 327–58.

11. Extended CIT was developed by and is described in S. Zedeck, S.J. Jackson, and A. Adelman, *A Selection Procedures Reference Manual* (Berkeley: University of California, 1980).

12. Much of the following discussion of assessing job analysis methods is based on the extremely thorough work reported by R.A. Ash and E.L. Levine, in "Evaluation of Seven Job Analyses" (Unpublished manuscript, University of South Florida, 17 July 1981). See also E.L. Levine, R.A. Ash, and N. Bennett, "Exploratory Comparative Study of Four Job Analysis Methods," *Journal of Applied Psychology* 65 (1980): 524–35; and R.A. Ash and E.L. Levine, "A Framework for Evaluating Job Analysis Methods," *Personnel*, November–December 1980, 53–59.

13. Note that the assessments of the job analysis methods presented in Exhibits 3.7 and 3.8 represent extrapolation from several sources including job analysts (the Ash and Levine study cited), and academic researchers, discussion with several management consultants and an evaluation of the written documents describing each method. As some methods might have been refined since this book was written, the reader is encouraged to use his or her own judgement to complete the missing details.

14. See P. McLagen, "Flexible Job Models: A Productivity Strategy for the Information Age," in J.P. Campbell et al., *Productivity in organizations: New Perspectives from Industrial and Organizational Psychology* (San Francisco: Jossey–Bass, 1988).

15. Information was provided during a stress management crisis intervention program conducted by one of the authors of this text at BCE during 1990.

CHAPTER FOUR

HUMAN RESOURCE PLANNING

KEYNOTE ADDRESS
Charles A. Labarge
Vice-President Personnel Resources, Bell Canada

Human Resource Planning at Bell Canada

Bell Canada, the largest Canadian telecommunications operating company, markets a full range of state-of-the-art products and services to more than seven million business and residence customers in Ontario, Québec, and parts of the Northwest Territories.

At Bell Canada, our mission and values form the foundation for building our plans, while the strategic course and supporting commitments establish the overall approach for charting our future. Successful human resources planning depends on an understanding of the corporate planning strategies.

The corporate planning framework is comprised of three components: strategic planning, tactical planning, and resource management. Strategic planning addresses the longer-term directions, goals, and objectives, and the principal policies and plans for achieving corporate goals. It addresses the external and internal factors and critical issues facing our organization in the future. The strategic plan defines the business the company will pursue, the organizational capabilities, and the economic and noneconomic contribution it intends to make to its shareholders, employees, customers, and communities.

Tactical planning contains more specific plans. While the focus of strategic planning is on what business we should be in and the direction in which we should be going, the tactical plan is a transition plan focusing on how the organization is going to get there within a one-year time-frame. Our business units' annual business plans identify the prioritized programs to be implemented, and the financial and performance objectives necessary to achieve the results expected in the strategic plan for that year.

The third component, resource management, identifies the annual budgetary guidelines for resources needed to meet the financial and performance objectives. Planning is the key process to set directions and plans for our employees to meet corporate objectives. It is through people that we will achieve our goals and through people that we will live our mission "to be a world leader in helping people communicate and manage information."

AN INTEGRATED PLANNING PROCESS.

Human resources planning is an integral part of Bell Canada strategies evolution. The need for people with increasingly specialized skills, higher managerial potential, a commitment to achieve continuous improvement in a rapidly changing environment, and professional qualifications in disciplines that did not exist before is and will continue to be an overriding business concern of the organization.

In each of the company's strategic thrusts, our people will make the difference in successfully accomplishing these thrusts. We will stay ahead of the competition if we have employees who possess the right set of skills; if we provide those employees with the opportunity to enhance those skills; and if we provide for flexible evaluation and rewards systems that will motivate employees and optimize their contribution to our strategic directions.

Recognizing that human resources are critical to the success of our company and to the attainment of our mission, it follows that we must be alert to the evolving external trends and issues that can influence the attitudes and values of individuals and that, in turn, may dictate a need for changes in our various policies and revolutionize our traditional way of doing things.

Our future success is dependent on our ability to anticipate, identify, adapt, and manage change. Human resources can provide a unique and sustained competitive advantage. Therefore, effective human resources planning is mandatory to ensure overall organization success. The interrelation between the corporate and human resources strategy setting is schematized in Exhibit 4.1.

Similar to the corporate planning framework, the integrated human resources planning process is comprised of strategic planning, tactical planning, and results management.

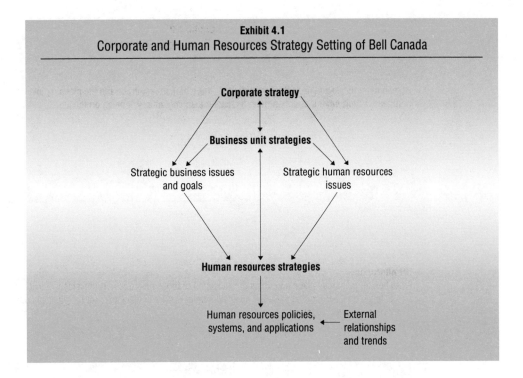

Exhibit 4.1
Corporate and Human Resources Strategy Setting of Bell Canada

HUMAN RESOURCES STRATEGIC PLANNING.

The human resources strategic plan identifies strategies and human resources needs covering a three- to five-year planning horizon. Long-term objectives and key integrated programs are developed in sync with the corporate strategies and business unit plans. Development of this plan requires input from company executives, personnel management, and key business units.

The strategic planning process begins with an assessment of the organization's mission, directions, goals, and objectives. Environmental scenarios are developed dealing with the state of the economy, anticipated regulatory or legal impacts, competitive factors, technological change, and social change with effects on organizational goals and objectives.

With our continuous commitment to employees, employee survey results are key inputs to our planning analysis. The company's employee demographics are also analyzed, including the human resources requirements of present jobs. A forecast is prepared covering the number and type of employees needed to meet future job requirements and organizational goals and objectives. Employee requirements are determined with the identification of shortages, surpluses, and training demands. Policies, programs, and processes are devel-

oped or enhanced to address the client demands (see Exhibit 4.2).

HUMAN RESOURCES TACTICAL PLANNING.

The human resources tactical plan, also called the personnel business plan, contains the major thrusts, key objectives, and deliverables in support of the human resource strategic plan. In other words, it reflects the annual plans and commitments to achieve or progress toward the strategic goals.

The main drivers for this plan are the corporate and human resources strategies, the current status and key issues obtained from an operational analysis of the company entities, which includes the business units' business plans.

Thrusts and priorities are communicated and discussed with the personnel business units, which identify the work programs for the year. The work programs are prioritized in light of the corporate and personnel priorities. In addition to line support work, such as the identification of placement needs, employee development, staff shortages, surpluses, etc., the work programs identify the human resources processes that will be developed or enhanced. A load-to-capacity analysis is then performed, priorities are firmed up, budget allocations

Exhibit 4.2
Major Human Resources Processes

HR Planning
Human resources planning is the forecasting of future human resources and the planning initiatives required for recruitment, selection, training, career planning, and well-being on the job.

HR Allocation
From human resources planning comes the allocation of those resources. At this stage, activities and efforts focus on ensuring that the most qualified employees are in place to meet the business objectives. Supporting processes deal with:

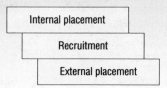

HR Development
This segment refers to activities and programs aimed at increasing individual performance by developing employees needed to meet the business objectives. Training, development, and education supporting processes include:

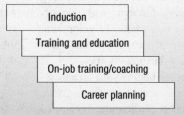

HR Utilization
Ensuring that we retain and motivate competent employees within the organization is critical to the company's success. Some of the supporting processes in HR utilization are:

HR process effectiveness and efficiency drive a multitude of business decisions. Each process exists to make a contribution to one or more organizational goals.

are addressed, and commitments for deliverables are obtained prior to publishing the plan.

RESULTS MANAGEMENT.

The results management component provides the executives with an ongoing mechanism for monitoring the implementation and results of the strategic and tactical plans. This process is concerned with plan execution, including the activities of reporting, commu- nicating, and modifying the plans in order to meet the desired results. Quarterly results are obtained from the business units and analyzed, and a status report is produced providing feedback to all personnel groups, highlighting the accomplishments compared to commitments made and areas needing attention.

EFFECTIVE MANAGEMENT OF CHANGE.

The 1990s promise to be a decade in which there will be a major transformation in the composition of our workforce. The aging population, entry into the workplace of diverse groups of people, technological advances, and an increasingly competitive environment are emphasizing the continuing need for strategic human resource planning and swift implementation of new programs.

Human resource planning has a critical role to play in anticipating and managing people issues in order to effectively manage changes and ensure the realization of the company's vision. The integrated planning process described is an ongoing live mechanism that needs commitment from all levels of management in order to ensure that sound and realistic directions, plans, and programs are produced in line with corporate strategies.

* * *

The discussion of Bell Canada's HRP shows the multiple linkages it has to other planning processes in the company, including corporate strategy, business unity strategies, and, of course, human resources strategy. As Bell prepares for significant changes in the future, becoming more flexible and adaptive, the human resource planning function will become more critical.

HRP is also tied to annual tactical planning in which both line managers and HR managers share responsibility. Exhibit 4.2 shows the flow from HR planning to other important HR functions, such as HR allocation of resources, HR development, and HR utilization. As will be shown in this chapter, HRP is the base upon which effective human resource management is constructed.

* * *

HUMAN RESOURCE PLANNING

In general terms, human resource planning (HRP) is one of the first steps of any effective HRM program. More specifically, HRP involves forecasting the HR needs for the organization and planning the steps necessary to meet these needs.

WHAT IS HRP? It is a process of developing and implementing plans and programs used to ensure that the right number and type of individuals are available at the right time and place to fulfil organizational needs. As such, HRP is directly tied to strategic business planning. Because of the trend toward more strategic involvement by HRM (discussed in Chapter 2), HRP is one of the fastest growing and most important areas in HRM. HRP helps ensure that organizations fulfil their business plans for the future in terms of financial objectives, output goals, product mix, technologies, and resource requirements. Once their business plans are determined, often with the assistance of the HR department, the HR planner assists in developing workable organizational structures and in determining the number and types of employees that will be required to meet financial and output goals. After workable structures and the requirements for individuals are identified, the HR planner develops programs to implement the structure and to obtain the individuals.

Purposes and Importance of HRP

IMPORTANCE OF HRP IN THEORY. HRP is important to an organization because it serves many purposes. A major purpose is to identify future organizational demands and supplies of human resources, and to develop programs to eliminate any discrepancies, taking into consideration the best interests of the individual and the organization. HRP can also reduce the expenses associated with excessive turnover and absenteeism, low productivity, and an unproductive training program.

IMPORTANCE OF HRP IN PRACTICE. How important is HRP amongst practitioners? The answer is a paradox: HRP is more important than ever, but not important enough. In a survey conducted by Hay of 927 HR professionals, some 51 percent said that top management considers HRP to be "very important" or "fairly important," while only 16 percent thought that HRP was either "unimportant" or "neglected" in their organizations. However, when asked about the nature of their HRP programs, only 20 percent said that they were "formal"; another 45 percent indicated that they were developed, but "informal"; a large 34 percent admitted that they were "rudimentary."[1]

WHAT IS BEHIND THIS APPARENTLY CONFLICTING MESSAGE? Is HRP one of those weather-like corporate activities that everyone talks about but nobody can act on? Perhaps so—until recently. But now, demographic and business exigencies will push HRP to the forefront. Organizations that find the way to plan for their HR needs will begin to enjoy a competitive advantage. The elaborate presentation of HRP in Bell Canada (see Keynote Address) highlights its growing importance and actual use; it is critical to the success of organizational strategy and planning.

Today, we are well aware of the shift in the demographics of the workforce. While the baby boom produced a glut of professional and managerial talent, the generation now entering behind them is dramatically smaller. Thus, at the middle and upper ends of the management and professional hierarchy, we have severe competition for responsibility and career growth.

By contrast, the entry-level population that will occupy many of the rapidly increasing knowledge jobs is beginning to shrink dramatically. While the past five years have seen a concentration on streamlining and downsizing organizations, the next decade will see these activities occupying the same stage with efforts to attract, develop, and retain key professional and managerial employees.

Certainly productivity has always been a critical issue. Now, and in the future, doing more for less while being more competitive may be the most pressing issue we face. New technologies are constantly being substituted for direct labour. Work redesign will maximize the utilization of scarce skills. Individuals will face greater accountability for achieving organizational goals. This will require the HRP professionals to examine the efficiency of staffing levels, the mix of positions, and the development of talent and job design, so that workers' talents are better matched to their tasks. They will work with those who have been displaced and those whose jobs have become redundant. As new technologies, such as state-of-the-art information systems, robots, and office automation are introduced, these planning professionals will be called upon to answer questions such as: How can the workforce assimilate these new technologies? What impact will these new technologies have on job design and on the organizational structure? Which skills will we need and which not?

HRP professionals are also concerned with the problem of the aging workforce, permanent unemployment, and the economic impact of shifting from a manufacturing to a service economy. As HRP becomes more measured and pragmatic in its approach, professionals will have to be more knowledgeable.

PURPOSES OF HRP. The purposes of HRP are to

- Reduce HRM costs by helping management anticipate shortages or surpluses of human resources and correct these imbalances before they become unmanageable and expensive;
- Provide a better basis for planning employee development that makes optimum use of workers' attitudes;
- Improve the overall business planning process;
- Provide more opportunities for women and minority groups in future growth plans, and identify the specific skills available;
- Promote greater awareness of the importance of sound HRM throughout all levels of the organization;
- Provide a tool for evaluating the effect of alternative HR actions and policies.[2]

All of these purposes are now more easily attained than ever before, thanks to computer technology. This allows vast numbers of job-related records to be maintained on each employee, in essence creating an HR information system (this will be described in detail later). These records, which include information on employee job preferences, work experiences, and performance evaluations, provide a job history of each employee in an organization and a complete set of information on the jobs and positions in it. This in turn can be used to facilitate the purposes of HRP in the interests of the individual as well as the organization.

All of these purposes in part explain the recent and growing importance of HRP. A large number of environmental and organizational changes also explain its importance. These changes are making it necessary for HRM to be more future-oriented, comprehensive, and integrative.

This perspective has a number of fundamental attributes: (1) it considers HR costs to be an investment rather than an uncontrollable expense; (2) it is proactive rather than reactive, or passive, in its approach to developing HR policies and resolving HR problems; (3) it is characterized by a change in HRM role perspective: the previous emphasis on the completion of HRM transactions is being replaced by a future-oriented approach in which the HR department acts as a controller of the organization's human resources; (4) it recognizes that there must be an explicit link between HRP and other organizational functions, such as strategic planning, economic and market forecasting, and investment and facilities planning; (5) it recognizes that such HR activities as recruitment, selection, labour relations, compensation and benefits, training, organizational planning, and career management must be visualized as dynamic interconnecting activities rather than a series of separate, nonintegrated functions; and (6) it focuses on approaches that further both organizational and individual goals.

One environmental change that is making HRP more important is recent legislation in combination with voluntary province-wide pressure in support of affirmative action and other employment matters. Equal Employment Opportunity and the Occupational Safety and Health Acts were established in many provinces in response to pressures and influences from the International Labour Office (ILO) and U.S. case law.

Another important environmental change involves predictions about shortages in blue-collar occupations and entry-level white-collar occupations by the year 2000, such as in tool and die making, bricklaying, and other skilled crafts. Along with shortages of certain types of individuals, there is a growing abundance of other job seekers — those in the 35- to 44-year-old age group. As discussed later in this chapter, the number of people entering this age group is increasing faster than the number of jobs available for them. Consequently, many of these people can probably anticipate relatively static income and rivalry with older workers for some period of time.

The new retirement options available to workers are also causing a shift in concern for staffing positions, but not in the direction expected. Workers now have options ranging from early retirement in their mid-50s to retirement in their 70s. However, more workers are staying on the job longer than anticipated. This fact, coupled with the protection given to employees under various human rights laws, has caused organizations to devote more time to managing these senior employees.

The increasing potential for managerial obsolescence is another critical change. Rapid changes in knowledge are making it difficult for professionals, engineers, and managers to remain current at their jobs. Consequently, they must be provided with the opportunity for continued training. However, organizations are not sure how to do this, nor do they always recognize the potential for obsolescence. Nevertheless, the unsolved problem of professional obsolescence posed by the production of knowledge is a threat to the growth potential of organizations and society as a whole.

The general expansion and diversification of organizations due to global competition also makes HRP more important. Trends toward multinational operations are attended by difficulties in transferring workers and in operations and staffing in foreign cultures.

Another compelling reason for HRP is the investment an organization makes in its human resources. Human assets, as opposed to some other assets, can increase in value. An employee who develops skills and abilities becomes a more valuable resource. Because an organization makes investments in its personnel either through direct training or job assignments, it is important that employees be used effectively throughout their careers. The dollar value of a trained, flexible, motivated, and productive workforce is difficult to determine, although attempts are being made to do so. At Upjohn Pharmaceutical Company, a series of indexes has been developed to reflect the relationships between employee costs (treated as an investment) and organizational performance.[3] The indexes include:

- Pretax Earnings/Total Employees
- After Tax Earnings/Total Employees
- Sales/Total Employees
- Pretax Earnings/Employee Costs
- Employee Costs/Value Added
- Capital Costs/Value Added
- Pretax Earnings/Value Added
- Value Added/Sales

In addition, an increasing number of organization leaders are acknowledging that the quality of the workforce can be responsible for significant differences in short- and long-run performances. Many corporate executives are concluding that insufficient or unqualified human resources are at least as serious a production bottleneck as a scarcity of capital, and that HR investments are as important a factor in company planning as the acquisition of plants, equipment, or materials.

The final reason for the increased emphasis on HR planning and programming is the growing resistance of employees to change and relocation. There is also a growing emphasis on self-evaluation and on valuing loyalty and dedication to the organization. All these changes make it more difficult for the organization to assume it can move its employees around arbitrarily, thus increasing the necessity of planning ahead.

HRP is important because it influences almost all of the other HR activities. Although all these relationships are important, only the most critical are discussed, as shown in Exhibit 4.3.

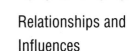

Relationships and Influences

JOB ANALYSIS. In order to be engaged in HRP, both job descriptions and job specifications are required; without them, planning is impossible.

RECRUITMENT AND SELECTION. HRP helps determine the staffing needs of an organization. In conjunction with job analysis, it indicates how many and what types of people need to be recruited. Recruitment influences the pool of available job applicants, which in turn influences the needs for selection and placement. Thus, HRP can be viewed as a major input into an organization's staffing function. This relationship is highlighted again in Chapters 5 and 6, on recruitment and selection.

TRAINING AND DEVELOPMENT. HRP helps the organization forecast shortages in the labour force and also areas where obsolescence may occur. This helps the organization train its employees and ensure that they possess the latest relevant skills.

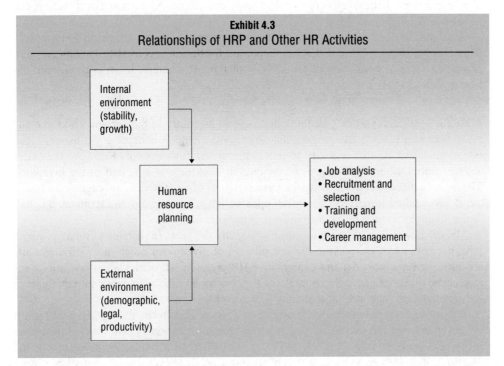

Exhibit 4.3
Relationships of HRP and Other HR Activities

- Internal environment (stability, growth)
- Human resource planning
- External environment (demographic, legal, productivity)
- • Job analysis
  • Recruitment and selection
  • Training and development
  • Career management

CAREER MANAGEMENT. HRP helps career management programs aid an organization in retaining valued employees and keeping them from becoming obsolete. Furthermore, along with career planning by employees, HRP helps reduce employee turnover and absenteeism. The organization can plan on a larger supply of qualified human resources and, therefore, has a smaller need for additional people. Further discussion on this will be provided in Chapter 12.

FOUR PHASES OF HRP

HRP is based on the determination of an organization's HR needs—the identification of both the HR supply and demand. Although these estimations are critical, until recently most organizations have avoided making them or engaging in any of the four phases of HRP, which are as follows:

1. Gathering, analyzing, and forecasting data in order to develop an HR supply forecast (and create a HR information system), and demand forecast (and add to the HR information system);
2. Establishing HR objectives and policies and gaining approval and support for them from top management;
3. Designing and implementing plans and action programs in such areas as recruitment, training, and promotion that will enable the organization to achieve its HR objectives;
4. Controlling and evaluating HRM plans and programs to facilitate progress toward HR objectives.

Exhibit 4.4 shows the relationships among these phases as well as corporate goals and environmental components.

Phase 1: Gathering, Analyzing, and Forecasting Supply and Demand Data

The first phase of HRP involves developing data that can be used to determine corporate objectives, policies, and plans, as well as HR objectives and policies. As shown in Exhibit 4.4, the HR inventory and forecast are influenced in turn by these same factors. The interaction of these aspects of HRP helps determine the current HR situation and future needs.

As shown in Exhibit 4.5 (which further elaborates the phases shown in Exhibit 4.4), there are five steps in Phase 1. Each is important for the success of HR planning and programming. Step 1, consisting of an analysis of the HR situation in an organization, has four aspects.

ANALYSIS. HR analysis may begin with taking an inventory of the current workforce and the current jobs in the organization. Analysis of both elements is necessary if the organization is to determine its capability to meet current and future needs. Knowing the skills, abilities, interests, and preferences of the current workforce is only half of the inventory. The other half consists in knowing the characteristics of current jobs and organization, and the skills required to perform them. An updated job analysis program facilitates this half of the inventory as well as the matching of employees and jobs.

Manual inventories have been used successfully for years in matching employees with jobs, but computers are making the compilation of inventories much more efficient, and are allowing for a more dynamic, integrative HR program. Through computers, employees in separate divisions and different areas of the country are finding it easier to participate in the organization's network for matching jobs and employees.

A common computer-oriented information system used in the management of human resources is often referred to as a human resource information system (HRIS) or human resource management system (HRMS). An HRIS/HRMS provides an inventory of the positions and skills existing in a given organization. However, these systems are more

Exhibit 4.4
The Human Resource Planning and Programming Process

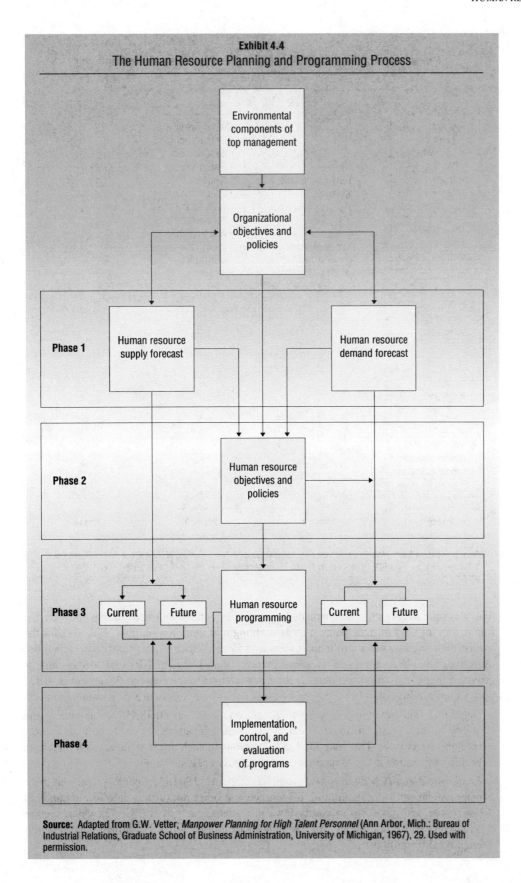

Source: Adapted from G.W. Vetter; *Manpower Planning for High Talent Personnel* (Ann Arbor, Mich.: Bureau of Industrial Relations, Graduate School of Business Administration, University of Michigan, 1967), 29. Used with permission.

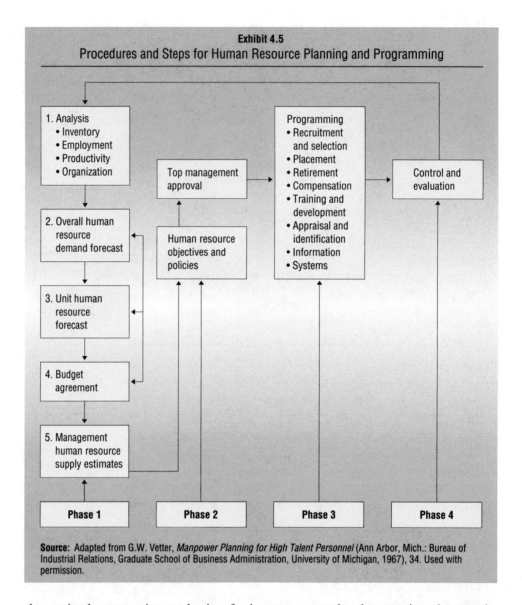

Exhibit 4.5
Procedures and Steps for Human Resource Planning and Programming

Source: Adapted from G.W. Vetter, *Manpower Planning for High Talent Personnel* (Ann Arbor, Mich.: Bureau of Industrial Relations, Graduate School of Business Administration, University of Michigan, 1967), 34. Used with permission.

than a simple aggregation mechanism for inventory control and accounting; they are the foundation for a set of management tools enabling managers to establish objectives for the use of their organization's human resources and to measure the extent to which those objectives have been achieved. Detailed presentation of several HRIS/HRMS systems is provided in the section on computer technology later on in the chapter. A number of HRM policy applications could be advanced by proper set-up of HRIS/HRMS in organizations:[4]

- *Organizational demography, planning, and analysis*: An HRIS/HRMS enhances the ability to track basic attributes such as age, sex, educational level, length of service, race, etc., over time. This may facilitate decisions in such areas as succession planning, benefits/utilization analysis, and wage/productivity analysis.

- *Employment equity planning and monitoring*: An HRIS/HRMS could greatly enhance employment equity programming for women and other minorities; therefore it can help the company to conform to equity laws in Canada, such as Bill C–62, which require employers that come under Canada Labour Code and federal contractors to develop employment equity plans.

- *Scenario-building and forecasting*: HRIS/HRMS outputs can be used as a basis for forecasting the effects of alternative scenarios. This could aid in identifying future skills shortages or surpluses, career pathing, comparing past and projected recruitment, promotion, turnover patterns for high and low performing employees, etc.
- *Productivity analysis and program evaluation*: An HRIS/HRMS could be used to monitor the effects of training programs and other productivity improvement programs on various performance measures.

An HR analysis also examines the probable future composition of society's workforce. Often this aspect is based on wage, occupational, and industrial groups. Historical data on workforce composition, along with current demographic and economic data, are used to make HR projections. These are not specific to any single organization, but they can often provide an organization with useful information for its HR plans, particularly for long-term needs.

The third aspect of HR analysis involves the determination of labour productivity and its probable productivity in the future. Projected employee turnover and absenteeism, for example, influence the productivity of an organization's workforce at any time, and thus, its future HR needs. These projections might also suggest a need to analyze the reasons for turnover and absenteeism, and then form the basis for strategies to deal with them. It should be noted, however, that under certain circumstances, increased turnover is desirable. For example, if an organization suddenly finds itself with too many employees, increased turnover, especially among poor performers, might be welcomed.

The final aspect of the first step in HRP is the examination and projection of organizational structure. This helps determine the probable size of the top, middle, and lower levels of the organization, for both managers and nonmanagers. In addition, it provides information about changes in the organization's HR needs and about specific activities or functional areas that can be expected to experience particularly severe growth or contraction.

The type of organization is a major factor determining both structure and degree of change. As organizations become more technologically complex and face more complex and dynamic environments, more complex structures will evolve—with more departments and a greater variety of occupations. Thus, the type of organization and its environment play an important role, not only in determining the organization's structure, but in providing information useful for forecasting its HR needs.

HR DEMAND FORECAST. An organization's demand for human resources can be determined by a variety of forecasting methods, both simple and complex. Forecasting results in approximations—not absolutes or certainties. The quality of the forecast depends on the accuracy of information and the predictability of events. The shorter the time horizon, the more predictable the events and the more accurate the information. For example, organizations are generally able to estimate how many undergraduates they may need for the coming year, but are less successful at forecasting their needs for the next five years.

A recent study in Canada indicates that only 27 percent of surveyed companies engaged in formal HRP. Among them, the planning span varied considerably from small firms (mode 1 year) to medium and large firms (mode 5 years). This suggests that small firms are more concerned about short-term planning, while larger firms are more concerned with the long term.[5]

Two classes of forecasting techniques are frequently used to project the organization's demand for human resources. These are judgmental forecast and conventional statistical projections. **Judgemental forecasting** is done by experts who assist in preparing the forecasts. The most common method of estimating HR demand is **managerial estimates**. Estimates are made by top managers (top-down). Alternatively, the review process begins at lower levels (bottom-up) and is passed up for refinement. In financial institutions, such as banks and trusts, a bottom-up approach is used, where each branch passes its estimates to the head office. The success of these estimates depends on the quality of the information provided to the judgmental experts. Useful information can include data on current and projected productivity levels, market demand, and sales forecasts, as well as current staffing levels and mobility information.

A successful judgmental process is carried on through the **Delphi technique**. At a Delphi meeting, a large number of experts take turns presenting a forecast statement and assumptions. An intermediary passes each expert's forecast and assumptions to the others, who then make revisions in their own forecasts. This process continues until a viable composite forecast emerges. The composite may represent specific projections or a range of projections, depending on the positions of the experts.

The Delphi technique is based on "decision theory"; it combines the advantages of an individual decision-making process with the advantages of a group decision process, and at the same time eliminates some of the problems associated with each. For instance, group process is preferred over individual process under the following circumstances: (a) when a consensus is reached, and (b) when no particular individual dominates the group. The Delphi technique uses group input without domination and aims at reaching a consensus. Consequently, it has been shown to produce better one-year forecasts than many other quantitative techniques.[6] Delphi techniques, however, do have some limitations. There may be difficulties, for example, in integrating the opinions of the experts. This technique appears to be particularly useful for generating insights into highly unstructured or undeveloped subject areas, such as HRP.

A related method is the **nominal grouping technique**. Several people sit around a conference table and independently list their ideas on a sheet of paper. After ten to twenty minutes, they take turns expressing their ideas to the group. As these ideas are presented, they are recorded on larger sheets of paper so that everyone can see all the ideas and refer to them in later parts of the session.

Although the two techniques are similar in process, the Delphi technique is more frequently used to generate predictions, and the nominal grouping technique is used more for identifying current organizational problems and potential solutions to them. Both of these judgmental forecasting techniques are less complex and rely less on data than those based on the statistical methods discussed next.

The most common **statistical projection** procedures are simple linear regression and multiple linear regression analyses. In **simple linear regression** analysis, a projection of future demand is based on a past relationship between the organization's employment level and a variable related to employment, such as sales. If a relationship can be established between the level of sales and the level of employment, predictions of future sales can be used to make predictions of future employment. Although there may be a relationship between sales and employment, the relationship is often influenced by an organizational learning phenomenon. For example, the level of sales may double, but the level of employment necessary to meet this increase may be less than double. And if sales double again, the incremental amount of employment necessary to meet this new doubling may be even less than that necessary to meet the first doubling of sales. An organizational learning curve can usually be determined by logarithmic calculations. Once the learning curve has been determined, more accurate projections of future employment levels can be established.

Multiple linear regression analysis is an extension of simple linear regression analysis. Instead of relating employment to one other variable related to it, several variables are used. For example, instead of using only sales to predict employment demand, productivity and equipment-use data may also be used. Because it incorporates several variables related to employment, multiple regression analysis may produce more accurate demand forecasts than linear regression analysis. It appears, however, that only relatively large organizations use multiple regression analysis.

In addition to these two regression techniques, several other statistical techniques are used to forecast staffing needs. Such techniques include:

- *Productivity ratios*—where historical data are used to examine the past level of a productivity index.[7]
- *Human resource ratios*—where past HR data are examined to determine historical relationships among the employees in various jobs or job categories. Regression analysis is then used to project total or key group HR requirements for various job categories.[8]
- *Time series analysis*—where past staffing levels are used to project future HR requirements. Past staffing levels are examined in view of isolating seasonal and cyclical variations, long-term trends, and random movement. Long-term trends are then extrapolated using a moving average technique, exponential smoothing procedure, or a regression technique.[9]
- *Stochastic analysis*—where the likelihood of landing a series of contracts is combined with the HR requirements of each contract to estimate expected staffing requirements. The potential application area relates to government contractors and the construction industry.[10]

RECONCILING THE BUDGET. The third aspect in the first phase of HR planning and programming puts the whole activity into economic perspective. The personnel forecast must be expressed in dollars terms, and this figure must be compatible with the organization's profit objectives and budget limitations. Of course, the budget reconciliation process may also point up the importance of adjusting the budget to accommodate the HR plan. This reconciliation stage also provides an opportunity to align the objectives and policies of the HR department and the organization.

FORECASTING HR SUPPLIES. Although forecasted supply can be derived from both internal and external sources of information, the internal source is generally most crucial and most available. As with forecasting demand, there are basically two techniques to help forecast internal labour supply: judgmental and statistical. Once made, the supply forecast can then be compared with the HR demand forecast to help determine, among other things, action programming for identifying HR talent and balancing supply and demand forecasts. However, most current forecasting of labour supply and demand is short range and is used for the purposes of budgeting and controlling costs. Forecasts for a five-year period, when done, are used in planning corporate strategy, and facilities, and identifying managerial replacements.

Two judgmental techniques used by organizations to make supply forecasts are replacement planning and succession planning. **Replacement planning** uses charts that show the names of the current occupants of positions in the organization and the names of likely replacements. Replacement charts make potential vacancies readily apparent, based on the present performance levels of employees currently in jobs. Openings are most likely to occur in those jobs in which the incumbents are not outstanding performers. Incumbents are listed directly under the job title. Those individuals likely to fill the potential vacancies are listed directly under the incumbent. Such a listing can provide the organization with a good estimate of what jobs are likely to become vacant and who will be ready to fill them.

Succession planning is similar to replacement planning except that succession planning tends to be longer term, more developmental, and more flexible. Although succession planning is widely practised, many employers using it tend to emphasize the characteristics of the managers and downplay the characteristics of the positions to which these managers may eventually be promoted.

Statistical techniques are less common in forecasting supply. In the past, these techniques were not widely used because of inadequate databases, lack of software programs, shortages of trained professionals to use them, and the restrictive conditions under which the models are applicable. They are now, however, gaining popularity.

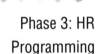

Phase 2: Establishing HR Objectives and Policies

As was shown in Exhibit 4.4, Phase 2 in the HRP process is setting HR objectives and policies. These objectives and policies are directly related to corporate objectives and policies. The impact of the organization's objectives, policies, and plans on HRP would seem difficult to deny, but according to one survey, only about 25 percent of the organizations achieve a substantial link between general institutional planning and their HRP. An additional 45 percent reported only some link, while 20 percent had no link at all.[11]

Though it may seem that in the past HRP activity was too often divorced from the mainstream operations of the organization, the HR department is more and more involved in determining an organization's goals, plans, and objectives, and thus linkages exist between corporate and HR policies.

Phase 3: HR Programming

The third phase is an important extension of HRP. After the assessment of an organization's needs, action programming must be developed to serve those needs. These action programs may be designed to increase the supply of the right employees in the organization (if the forecasts in Phase 1 showed that demand exceeded supply) or to decrease the number of current employees (if the forecasts showed that supply exceeded demand). Two such programs are illustrated here.

ATTRACTION: NEW ORGANIZATIONAL STRUCTURES. The HR planner assists in developing a workable organizational structure. Workable structures serve the objectives of planning and programming, which are to attract, retain, and motivate employees. It appears, however, that present organizational structures may not be as workable as they once were. Changes in our society, particularly in workforce values, have seriously undermined the traditional relationship between organizations and their members. This has led to a crisis that may only be resolved by the development of new organizational forms. Chapter 13 discusses these emerging structures in more detail.

In general, present organizational structures or forms can be characterized by supervisory control; minimal employee participation in workplace decisions; top-down communications; an emphasis on extrinsic rewards to attract, retain, and motivate employees (rewards such as pay, promotion, and status symbols); narrowly designed jobs with narrow job descriptions; and a primary concern for productivity and fitting people to jobs. This primary concern translates into selecting people on the basis of their technical SKAs to meet the demands of the job.

Sensing that these present organizational structure characteristics are no longer appropriate for attracting, retaining and motivating individuals, some organizations, such as Honeywell and Control Data, are engaging in alternative structures. These structures can be characterized by greater employee self-control; more employee participation in workplace decisions; bottom-up as well as top-down communications; recognition of employee rights; an emphasis on intrinsic rewards (such as senses of responsibility, meaningfulness, and achievement) and extrinsic rewards; more broadly designed jobs that allow more worker discretion; and primary concerns for QWL, productivity, and fitting jobs to people. These primary concerns translate into selecting individuals on the basis of their technical skills and knowledge and also on the basis of job and organizational characteristics to match the personality, interests, and preferences of the individuals.

REDUCTION: DEALING WITH JOB LOSS. Due to economic and technological conditions in the past few years, layoffs have become an increasing phenomenon. Organizations therefore must become sensitive in dealing with the effects of these conditions on employees and either try to minimize them or eliminate the necessity for layoffs. This can be achieved through redundancy planning. **Redundancy planning** is essentially HRP associated with the process of laying off employees who are no longer needed—they are redundant. Involved in this planning may be outplacement counselling, buy-outs, job skill retraining, and job transfer opportunities.

Unions, of course, can also play a central role in redundancy planning. In one of Kruger's Pulp & Paper divisions in Montreal, union and management got together and established a redundancy plan that included such programs as attrition and early retirement. Other unions view redundancy planning as part of their participation in QWL projects. They view it as a necessary trade-off for increasing their voice in traditional management areas.

Thus HR programming and planning may help an organization reduce the bottlenecks, discussed later, as well as avoid or reduce the number of redundant workers by making sure that counselling programs are provided and that potentially redundant employees are made aware of the counselling. It is important that both layoffs and counselling efforts not be used as methods of "getting rid of" older workers. And it is especially important that employees do not perceive them as such.

Control and evaluation of HR plans and programs are essential to the effective management of human resources; Exhibit 4.4 shows program control and evaluation as the last phase of HRP. Efforts in this area are clearly aimed at quantifying the value of human resources and recognizing them as an asset to the organization.

Phase 4: HRP Control and Evaluation

An HRIS/HRMS facilitates program control and evaluation by allowing for more rapid and frequent collection of data to back up the forecast. This data collection is important, not only as a means of control, but also as a method for evaluating plans and programs and making adjustments.

The collection of data should occur at the end of each year and at fixed intervals during the year, and evaluation of it should occur at the same time in order to hasten revisions of existing forecasts and programs. The revisions will likely influence short-term, intermediate, and long-term forecasts.

Evaluation of HR plans and programs is an important process not only for determining the effectiveness of HRP, but also for demonstrating the significance of both HRP and the HR department in the organization as a whole.

Possible criteria or standards for evaluating HRP include:

- Actual staffing levels vs. established staffing requirements;
- Productivity levels vs. established goals;
- Actual HRM flow rates vs. desired rates;
- Programs implemented vs. action plans;
- Program results vs. expected outcomes (e.g., improved applicant flows, reduced quit rates, improved replacement ratios);
- Labour and program costs vs. budgets;
- Ratios of program results (benefits) to program costs.

HRP Roadblocks

One of the key roadblocks to developing HRP has been the lack of top-management support. This has also prevented the HR department from playing all of its roles as discussed in Chapter 1. HRM can help overcome this roadblock with data and bottom-line (dollars and cents) facts that demonstrate the effectiveness of HRP and HRM.

Another roadblock is the difficulty in integrating all the HR activities so necessary to make HRP work. A challenge for HR managers is to create an HRM system in which all the functions and activities discussed in Chapter 1 are integrated and coordinated with the business plan.

A third roadblock is the lack of involvement of line managers. Failure to involve line management in the design, development, and implementation of an HRP system is a common oversight for first-time planners. HR managers are often tempted to develop or adopt highly quantitative approaches to planning. These often have little pragmatic value to line managers dealing with problems such as reducing excessive turnover, identifying and training replacements for key positions, and forecasting staffing needs. HRP, to be effective, must serve the line managers' needs.

IMPORTANT CHANGES INFLUENCING HRP IN THE 90s

The job of HRP encompasses the whole range of societal, demographic, economic, and government regulatory factors that influence changes in an organization's workforce. Just as HRM is concerned with the "whole persons," HRP must be increasingly aware of the total external environment that will shape the workforce and its concerns, as well as the particular environment that is influencing the current workforce.

HRM IN THE NEWS VIGNETTE

New Approaches to Managing a Fluctuating Workforce During The Recession

Bell has adopted a set of measures to increase its room to manoeuvre in managing its fluctuating workforce requirements. These measures are intended to help the company weather the recession without having to resort to layoffs or early retirement plans.

The new, fully voluntary programs adds special options to leaves of absence for personal or educational reasons, in addition to the existing possibilities for reducing hours and for job sharing. [Employees are able] to take advantage of other alternatives, such as improved pension conditions for those who wish to work part time prior to pension, and special benefit in the case of voluntary termination.

In the face of the ongoing recession, Bell has adopted new measures to manage its workforce surplus—which numbers some 2,500 employees throughout the company— in relation to the budget, and increase its short-term flexibility.

New Measures Adopted:

* Leaves of absence for personal reason up to one year—Health plan and SPP premiums paid by company; permission to work elsewhere; full service credit; guarantee of re-employment; continuation of concession telephone-service.

* Leave of absence for educational purposes up to four years—tuition reimbursement; education allowances; insurance, health plan and SPP premiums paid by company; full service credit; guarantee of summer employment and of re-employment; continuation of concession telephone-service.

* Improved pension conditions for employees who wish to work part time prior to pension.

* Special conditions for voluntary termination.

Existing Measures:

* Reduction in overtime

* Reduction in use of outside human resources

* Hiring freeze

* Voluntary freeze

* Temporary reduction in work hours (e.g., reclassification to part-time for a certain period)

* Job sharing

Source: Excerpt from *Bell News* 38, 6 (23 March 1992): 4. Reprinted with permission.

There are several significant changes taking place in the Canadian population and, hence, in the nature of the labour force. In addition, substantial changes are occurring in the nature of jobs and the dominance of certain industries.

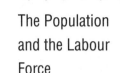

The Population and the Labour Force

SLOWER LABOUR FORCE INCREASE. The counter clerk handing you your Burger King sandwich next time may not be the usual teenager. Rather, it may be some teenager's grandparent! The major reason is the shrinking supply of young workers. After more than two decades of growth, the nation's population between 16 and 24 years of age has peaked. This age group will continue to decline as a percentage of the total labour force and of the population. In the meantime, the numbers in the 25 to 54 age group (especially the 35 to 44 segment) will continue to rise. The 35 to 44 age group is expected to increase 32 percent between 1985 and 1995, from 3,565,000 to 4,705,000. These projections are made by Canada Employment and Immigration, which publishes both short- and long-term labour force projections. One document, the Ford Occupational Imbalance Listing (FOIL), is a quarterly publication that estimates both labour market demand (by occupation) and supply characteristics. A longer-term projection is provided by the Canada Occupational Forecasting Program (COFP). Statistics Canada also publishes reports on a monthly, quarterly, and annual basis.

The number of people in the labour force continued to grow at the end of the 1980s, but at a slower pace than in the years before. In the first half of 1990 the workforce increased 1.3 percent, compared to a 1.7 percent increase in 1989 and 2 percent in 1988 and 1987. During the 1970s, average yearly increases amounted to 3.2 percent, as the large baby-boom generation entered the job market.[12] The strongest growth came—like previous years—from women 25 years and over (especially ages 25 to 44), with a participation rate of 57.9 percent in 1989, compared to 54.6 percent in 1985.

The proportion of men 25 years and over in the labour force drifted down. In 1989, 77 percent of men were in the workforce. The declining participation rate for men was caused almost exclusively by men aged 55 and over. Their participation rate dropped to less than 40 percent in the first half of 1990. One reason for the decline is the better pension options, but it also reflects fewer opportunities for the unemployed in this age category.

DECREASING PARTICIPATION OF YOUNG WORKERS. The number of young people (15 to 24 years of age) in the workforce declined again in the second half of the 1980s. Their level fell to 2.6 million in June 1990, compared with an average 2.7 million in 1989 and a peak level of over 3 million in 1981. This decline can be understood as one result of the aging labour force, as the baby-boom generation approaches middle age and fertility rates have dropped.[13]

Data for 1990 show, for the first time since 1982, that the labour force participation rate of young people also might have entered an era of decline. After the 1981–82 recession, the participation rate of young women and men was strong and had climbed up again to 69 percent in 1987. The mainly continuous increase in participation, which was due especially to the involvement of students, had until 1990 moderated the effect on the labour force of the declining population in this age group (youth population decreased from 4.6 million in 1981 to 3.7 million in June 1990). Together with the strong participation of women, this decline will influence the exodus of male workers, which in turn will be reflected in the future composition of the labour force.

CHANGES IN FEMALE EMPLOYMENT. The increase in the rate of women's employment has been related considerably to the growing numbers of them working part time, despite the fact that the proportion of people working part time has declined slightly since the mid 1980s.

Women with a high level of education were the most likely ones to be employed. In 1988, 76 percent of women with a university degree, 69 percent with a post-secondary certificate or diploma, and 62 percent with some post-secondary training were employed.[14]

Employment gains have been observed especially among women aged 25 to 54. The percentage employed in this age category rose in 1989 to 68.9 percent, from 61.9 percent in 1985. Statistics also showed a significant rise in employment among married women and women with children. In 1988, 57 percent of married women with pre-school children and 70 percent with children aged 6 to 15 had jobs.

Despite shifts in the types of jobs women held, in 1989 72 percent of women were employed in so-called traditional low-paying jobs, such as clerical positions, sales, service, health care, etc. On the other hand, the number of female managers and administrators doubled between 1982 and 1989, with 11 percent of women working in these fields in 1989.

PERMANENT PART-TIME WORK.   Part-time employment and especially permanent part-time is growing in Canada. The trend in part-time employment is related to both structural and cyclical factors. Many changes have taken place in the structure and composition of the labour force. In addition to the increased participation of women, there is a sharp shift from the goods producing industries to the service industries as well as strong growth in white-collar employment, areas where there are more part-time employment opportunities due to the nature of the market.

In 1986, part-time workers in Canada worked an average 14.5 hours per week compared to 37.9 hours for full-timers. Many studies have shown that part-time workers do not receive the same wage and benefits coverage as full-time workers.

From an HRP perspective, however, part-time employment offers flexibility in staffing and scheduling of work. Very often, part-time employees are used to staff continuous operations, weekend and evening work, and seasonal activities. Part-time work may actually increase productivity in some jobs, particularly where the jobs are routine and monotonous.

DISADVANTAGED GROUPS AND MINORITIES.   In recent years, the role of disabled people in the Canadian workforce has changed. New technologies have helped more disabled people to participate and perform in a variety of jobs. Additionally, special training programs are available to accommodate these individuals. However, despite a slight increase in participation, a much smaller proportion of disabled people have jobs. Only 40 percent of the 1.8 million disabled people in Canada aged 15 to 64 were employed in 1986, compared with 70 percent of nondisabled people. Nonetheless, the participation rate of this group will most likely increase in the future with the parallel growth of the various equity opportunities.[15]

According to the 1986 census, black Canadians and native people continued to experience higher unemployment rates due to their greater presence in low-paid unskilled jobs, which are especially vulnerable during low economic cycles.

LABOUR FORCE POPULATION PROJECTIONS.   Exhibit 4.6 shows projections of the labour force by age and gender. The projection assumes a medium growth scenario with a constant fertility rate of 1.67 births per woman and immigration of 200,000 per year. It is projected that the number of young workers will continue to decline at least until 1995. This could lead to a shortage of young skilled workers as well as a shortage of young people who are willing to do low-wage jobs, like washing dishes or serving at McDonald's.

The number of women in the workforce will increase at a higher rate than the number of men, which might intensify competition in regard to who gets hired, promoted, etc.

The aging of the labour force will accelerate, leading to a surplus of people in the 35 to 44 age category at least until the year 2000. Career opportunities will be restricted; there will be too many qualified workers and too few jobs available, especially if the economy grows slowly and organizations continue to downsize and become flatter in structure.[16]

Exhibit 4.6
Labour Force Projections by Age and Gender

Age, Both Sexes	PROJECTED NUMBERS		
	1995	2000	2011
15 and over	22,373,300	23,752,200	26,434,800
15 to 24	3,807,700	3,874,900	3,982,700
25 to 54	12,596,500	13,185,400	13,375,000
25 to 34	4,528,200	4,206,500	4,246,300
35 to 44	4,562,600	4,854,100	4,300,900
45 to 54	3,505,700	4,124,800	4,827,800
55 and over	5,969,100	6,691,900	9,077,600
55 to 64	2,454,900	2,778,400	4,152,600
65 and over	3,514,200	3,913,500	4,925,000
Total no. of women 15 and over	14,232,200	14,940,900	16,239,400
Total no. of men 15 and over	13,735,400	14,343,300	15,450,500

Source: *Population Projections for Canada, Provinces and Territories, 1989–2000*, Statistics Canada, Catalogue no. 91–520. Reproduced with the permission of the Minister of Industry, Science and Technology, 1993.

More dramatic is the phenomenon of the "greying" of the workforce. By 2011, one-quarter of the Canadian workforce will be in the 55 to 64 age category.

CHANGES IN REQUIRED TRAINING AND IN OCCUPATIONAL STRUCTURE. According to a recent study prepared by the Hudson Institute, the Canadian occupational structure will change dramatically by the year 2000. As can be seen in Exhibit 4.7, the fastest growing occupations include: natural, computer, and math scientists (51.5 percent); technicians (40 percent); sales and marketing (30.9 percent); managerial, librarians, writers, artists, entertainers, athletes, and lawyers, all at about 25 percent.

Connected to these changes is the reality of shortages of skilled workers. Most studies predict that between 1991 and 2000, two-thirds of Canadian jobs created will require more than twelve years of education, and 50 percent will require more than seventeen years of education. Fortunately, many Canadians are beginning to understand the necessity to upgrade their skill level. In a recent survey released by Statistics Canada, 29 percent of the 9,338 respondents wanted more educational qualifications to prepare for a first job, 33 percent to improve their career, 10 percent to change their career, and 10 percent to improve their income.[17] The difference between *current* and *future* years of education required for the Canadian workforce is depicted in Exhibit 4.8.

Most major companies devote substantial resources to economic forecasting, in addition to subscribing to the macroeconomic analyses of banks, insurance companies, private economists, and government agencies. Since economic conditions are certain to affect the future workforce and conditions of employment, these conditions should be considered in HRP.

GENERAL ECONOMIC CONDITIONS. One trend that will certainly affect HRP is the relative stagnation in the growth rate of productivity. Currently, the rate of inflation is at a

Trends and
Changes in the
Economy

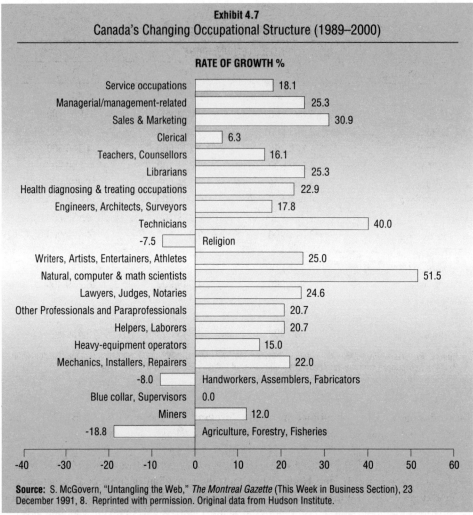

Exhibit 4.7
Canada's Changing Occupational Structure (1989–2000)

RATE OF GROWTH %

Occupation	Rate
Service occupations	18.1
Managerial/management-related	25.3
Sales & Marketing	30.9
Clerical	6.3
Teachers, Counsellors	16.1
Librarians	25.3
Health diagnosing & treating occupations	22.9
Engineers, Architects, Surveyors	17.8
Technicians	40.0
Religion	-7.5
Writers, Artists, Entertainers, Athletes	25.0
Natural, computer & math scientists	51.5
Lawyers, Judges, Notaries	24.6
Other Professionals and Paraprofessionals	20.7
Helpers, Laborers	20.7
Heavy-equipment operators	15.0
Mechanics, Installers, Repairers	22.0
Handworkers, Assemblers, Fabricators	-8.0
Blue collar, Supervisors	0.0
Miners	12.0
Agriculture, Forestry, Fisheries	-18.8

Source: S. McGovern, "Untangling the Web," *The Montreal Gazette* (This Week in Business Section), 23 December 1991, 8. Reprinted with permission. Original data from Hudson Institute.

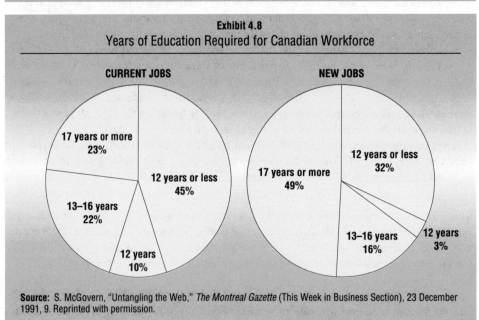

Exhibit 4.8
Years of Education Required for Canadian Workforce

CURRENT JOBS

- 17 years or more 23%
- 12 years or less 45%
- 13–16 years 22%
- 12 years 10%

NEW JOBS

- 12 years or less 32%
- 17 years or more 49%
- 13–16 years 16%
- 12 years 3%

Source: S. McGovern, "Untangling the Web," *The Montreal Gazette* (This Week in Business Section), 23 December 1991, 9. Reprinted with permission.

moderate level and is not a major consideration in HRP. Yet, if inflation were to increase, say to 7 percent, the cost of most goods sold would double in about ten years. Similarly, wages and salaries (to keep up with inflation) would double. Higher inflation would also influence the cost of employer-paid fringe benefits, and further enhance the need for productivity gains and better workforce utilization. Consequently, faced with stagnation in productivity rates, a possible renewal of high inflation, and continued intense international competition, organizations are now becoming concerned with increasing productivity. This concern in turn is causing a significant economic shift toward increased automation, the use of robots, and advanced technologies.

TECHNOLOGIES, AUTOMATION, AND ROBOTS. The technologies in which Canada is advancing most rapidly and which have the most potential for enhancing productivity and workforce utilization are: microelectronics, artificial intelligence, materials research, material surfaces, biotechnology, geology, and oil and energy exploration. A significant application of microelectronics will result in increased automation (and computerization) and the use of robots. Although using these products increases productivity dramatically, it also has a dramatic effect on the size of workforce required and the pride and self-esteem of employees.

In 1990 Canada's industrial robot population was approximately 1,500, of which between 950 and 1,000 were in Ontario and about 300 in Quebec. It is feared that, although advances in robotics can help people by eliminating dull and dangerous jobs, their use may also take away the pride, self-respect, and earnings of those displaced. Robots may also eliminate jobs. Thus, the HRP needs of the organization must be altered when robots are considered. Where use of robots is necessary, redundancy planning may be especially useful.

Changing Social Values

Closely linked with changes in the population, the labour force, and the economy are changes in social values, interests, and preferences. These changes are particularly important for HRP in values relating to *work, mobility*, and *retirement*.

VALUES TOWARD WORK. Productivity stagnation is often related to the decline or disappearance of the value that the workforce places on hard work. According to some, however:

> *The work ethic has not disappeared. People today are willing to work hard at "good" jobs, providing they have the freedom to influence the nature of their jobs and to pursue their own lifestyles.*[18]

People still value work, but the type of work that interests them has changed. They want jobs with challenge and they want jobs in which they are provided with the freedom to make some decisions. As suggested by survey results at General Electric and AT&T, however, people do not necessarily seek or desire rapid promotion, especially when it involves transferring to another geographic location. They do tend to seek influence and control—characteristics of the job and work situation integral to QWL.[19] What QWL represents, then, is personal control, self respect, and power to influence what is going on.

VALUES TOWARD MOBILITY. The values employees attach to work significantly affect their feelings about moving from job to job, especially when it entails moving from one region of the country to another. Like the recently changing employee values toward work, the new values against mobility are having significant impact on HRM, particularly in recruiting, training, promoting, and motivating managers and professionals. Large companies like Bell Canada, CN, and Air Canada are having a more difficult time getting their employees to move. This growing reluctance, however, may have some benefits for companies—in the past five years, the average cost to a company of moving a homeowning employee has tripled.

VALUES TOWARD RETIREMENT. Many fear the golden years might become just brass. The North American predilection for early retirement appears to be waning, slowing a trend of the 1970s that would have put the average retirement age below 55 by the year 2000. Many workers are bypassing provisions for early retirement (age 55 or 60) and even staying past the traditional retirement age of 65. This is largely in response to inflation rates, concerns over the stability of the social insurance system, and federal and provincial legislation protecting the older employee.

One significant consequence of this change in value toward retirement is the bottleneck it creates in the promotional paths for younger employees, particularly women and those belonging to minorities. Note that later retirement adds to the problems for HR managers caused by the changing demographics of the larger 35- to 44-year-old workforce group discussed earlier. HR managers will need to play the role of innovator very astutely to accommodate the older workforce and yet still retain and motivate the younger one.

TRENDS IN HRP

Assessing HRP

Without effective HRP, an organization may find itself with a plant or office but without the people to run it. Organizations can no longer assume that the right number of appropriately qualified people will be ready when and where the organization wants them. So, on a broad level, HRP activity can be assessed on the basis of whether or not the organization has the people it needs: are the right people at the right place, time, and price (salary)?

At more specific levels, HRP activities can be assessed by how effectively they (along with recruitment) attract new employees, deal with job loss, and adapt to the changing characteristics of the environment. Since an important part of HRP is forecasting, HRP can be assessed by how well its forecasts (whether of specific HRM needs or of specific environmental trends) compare with reality. Accuracy here can be very crucial, since it is unlikely that HRP can do well on a broad level if it fails to do well in forecasting. Another important criterion against which HRP can be assessed is the selection and appropriateness of the tools it uses to engage in its activities and the success in linking them to corporate goals. One of the critical tools developed over the past few years, the human resource information system, is discussed in the next section.

Computer Applications

Computer technology can be divided into different categories, two of which are presented here: (a) human resource information systems, the most important development tool for HR planners; and (b) other computer applications specific to HRP.

WHAT IS HRIS? The **human resource information system** (**HRIS**) has been designed to analyze information related to human resources in order to engage in better planning, thereby making better decisions. An HRIS can provide timely data relating to HR issues. The ultimate goal of HRIS is to help the HR department attain its short- and long-term objectives.

The functioning of an HR department with the assistance of an HRIS is a fairly new concept that has not been fully explored. Many organizations that already have an HRIS in place do not take full advantage of it. Some are not using it as a tool for forecasting. Rather, it is simply used as a database containing personnel information about employees. However, as more and more organizations analyze the potential uses of their HRIS, they realize that information contained in this type of system should not only be accessed by the HR department but by line managers as well.

Traditionally, an HRIS has been used by corporate HR professionals who were able to perform more efficiently with the assistance of systems tracking information on job applicants, training levels, payroll, and benefit options. However, more progressive companies let their line managers access the system. Ontario Hydro, for example, moved its HRIS out of the head office environment into the workplace of line managers. Ontario Hydro's decision was based on a fundamental belief that decisions in the employment cycle start and end with the line managers. Line managers need to have the "book on their people" and they need this information to be handy. Managers need to know what human resources are available, what skills their people possess, when they are available, and what new skills they plan to gain. Thus, giving line managers access has simplified the decision-making process.

Exhibit 4.9 shows the multiple possible uses of an HRIS. However, according to numerous studies, these systems are not properly used. Some of the major problems in their application include:

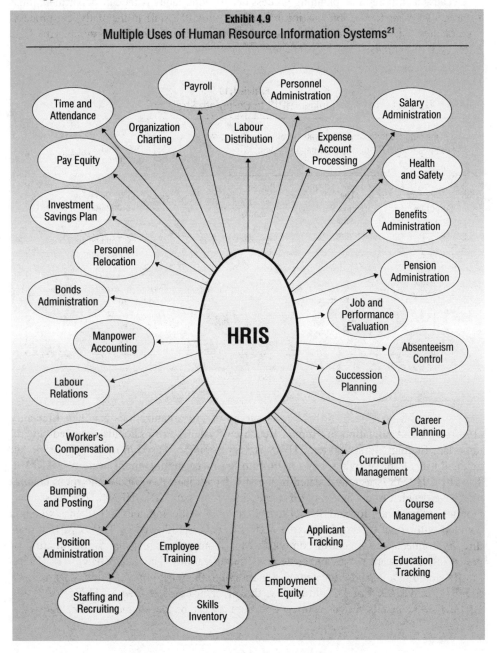

Exhibit 4.9
Multiple Uses of Human Resource Information Systems[21]

- Having little impact on serving a line manager's need for people data;
- Consisting of a series of separate HR applications with little or no integration;
- Focusing on back-office issues;
- Requiring too many records and forms;
- Costing too much to maintain and modify.[20]

LINKING HRIS TO CORPORATE STRATEGY. In Chapter 2 emphasis was placed on the vital link between the organization's strategic goals and the processes that ensure a workforce is capable of achieving them. With this realization, the HRIS can assist corporations in attaining this vital link by helping them to quickly and efficiently analyze and plan their HR needs to fulfil their strategy.

Because a corporation's planning process occurs continuously, the HR department must have ready access to key information in order to assist the staff in the analytical process. One of the best ways for the department to provide this information is via an HRIS, as depicted in Exhibit 4.10.

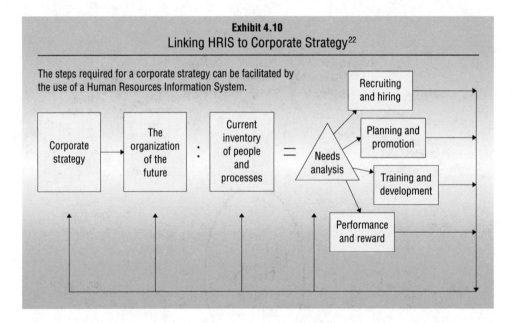

Exhibit 4.10
Linking HRIS to Corporate Strategy[22]

The steps required for a corporate strategy can be facilitated by the use of a Human Resources Information System.

Corporate strategy → The organization of the future · Current inventory of people and processes = Needs analysis → Recruiting and hiring / Planning and promotion / Training and development / Performance and reward

HRIS IN CANADIAN ORGANIZATIONS. A survey of 513 organizations conducted recently (1990) by the Association of Human Resource Systems Professionals revealed several important findings. First, the term HRIS is very commonly used in many industries, but gradually this term is giving way to "**human resource management system**" (**HRMS**). The HRIS/HRMS is usually located in the HR department. Also, more and more companies have decided to exclude payroll processing from their HRIS/HRMS. The most commonly used hardware for an HRIS/HRMS is the personal computer (40 percent), which is coupled with some type of local area network. This is followed by keyboard terminals directly connected to a central computer. Most companies are using a combination of prepackaged software with some customized modifications. The data of HRIS/HRMS are mostly stored in a database located on a mainframe; the most popular databases are: *IMS*, *FOCUS*, and *DB2*. For PC databases, the most popular is *dBase*. The core of the HRIS/HRMS contains various applications, but they can be placed under four categories:

1. HR administration and workforce planning;
2. Compensation and affirmative action—employment equity;
3. Benefits and staffing;
4. Health and safety, payroll, and labour relations.

The survey also indicates that the majority of companies have more than half of these applications integrated in one HRIS/HRMS, rather than operating them as separate systems.

OTHER HRP COMPUTER APPLICATIONS. Although many opportunities exist for computer use in HRP, two applications stand alone. These can be part of HRIS/HRMS, but they can also constitute a separate activity: forecasting and succession planning.

In order to do forecasting, HR planners use spreadsheets and statistical packages. There are a few forecasting packages on the market, but they are not widely used because they require extensive customization and implementation.

Programs dealing with succession planning, on the other hand, can be easily tailored to meet individual needs. Therefore, it is more common for HR departments to buy them than to devote in-house data-processing resources to design and develop them. Among the available systems are *Executive Track II* (ExcuTRACK), which features "succession domino scenarios" that show the implications of various succession moves, and *Management Succession Planning* (MSP), which offers several approaches to succession designation.

A variety of articles have been written about the considerations for choosing HRP software. The criteria are varied and complex. Nonetheless, here are some major points to consider:

- What functions do you want your planning system to perform?
- How do you hope to use such a system?
- Who will be using it?
- Does the package meet your requirements or do you need a customized system?
- Will the system run on a microcomputer? This is a much less costly option than running it on a main frame.
- If you buy, what is the vendor's reputation for support, reliability, etc.?[23]

S U M M A R Y

HRP is needed because society is changing; changes in the global market, in the labour force, in general economic conditions, and in values and in legislation are forcing organizations to prepare themselves in advance of these changes.

Because of these changes, HR departments must develop strategic and operational plans for all activities associated with HR utilization. These plans describe the broad range, long-term goals of HRM, and should be tied into the strategic plans of the rest of the organization.

HR departments must pay careful attention to accomplishing each of the four phases of HRP. The first phase is to determine what resources the organization has at present, and what it will be like in the future, in order to develop a forecast of HR needs. In the second phase, the objectives and policies of the HR department must be compatible with the overall objectives of the organization. Action programs must be developed and implemented in the third phase. To help ensure their effectiveness, the fourth phase stipulates an evaluation of the implementation and administration of each program. On the basis of the results of the evaluation, the programs can then be modified as necessary. Roadblocks exist that increase the challenge of HRP, namely, the lack of top-management support. This support, however, can be gained by showing top management that the potential benefits of HRP include reduced HRM costs, better employee development, improved overall organizational planning, more opportunities for a better-balanced and more integrated workforce, greater awareness of the importance of HRM in the total organization, and tools to evaluate the effectiveness of alternative HR actions and policies.

Although HRP is a complex task, the job of planners is becoming easier with the introduction of computer technology. Many organizations are using an integrated HRIS/HRMS, which can significantly increase the efficiency of the decision processes involved in planning.

P O S T S C R I P T

A relatively unique feature of the Canadian labour force is the large number of immigrants brought in over the past thirty years. These have been important since some of them fulfilled the traditional role of taking the most menial and lowest paying jobs in society. However, other groups of immigrants filled a large proportion of the skilled and semi-skilled positions. Recently, however, the European supply of trade professionals is drastically dropping and they are being replaced by less skilled visible minorities (Orientals, Blacks, East Indians). This results in two problems in the labour force: (a) a chronic shortage of skilled labour, even during periods of high unemployment, and (b) an increase in ethnic prejudice, which creates a host of new problems for many employers.

In order to deal with these two recent trends, Canadian employers need to develop long-term HRP strategies. In so far as the first problem is concerned, companies can no longer count on skilled immigrants to fill badly needed positions. Rather, they will have to spend more energy (and money) on retraining their present workforce. The second problem should also be seen as a long-term problem. While in many other countries the immigrant population assimilates fairly quickly through a process commonly known as the "melting pot," in Canada, due to a policy of encouraging cultural diversity (the common metaphor is "mosaic"), many ethnic groups retain their culture, ethics, and work values for substantially longer periods. This means that they have different approaches to work. There might be various implications to this diversity. A variety of stereotypes and prejudices that affect relations between ethnic groups within the workplace need to be considered as part of the strategic HRP policy.

R E V I E W   A N D   A N A L Y S I S   Q U E S T I O N S

1. What is the essential goal of HRP?
2. If HRP is so complex, why do companies still engage in it?
3. Discuss typical roadblocks to HRP and how each might be removed.
4. Provide a step-by-step overview of the four phases of HRP.
5. Identify and describe the most commonly used method of judgmental forecasting. What are its advantages and disadvantages?
6. Why are quantitative/statistical methods of forecasting limited?
7. What are the major demographic and occupational changes affecting the supply of and demand for labour in the future?
8. What are the two most salient outcomes of evaluating HR plans and programs?
9. What is an HRIS/HRMS? How is it related to HRP?
10. What are the implications of managing a diversified workforce?

CASE STUDY

DUMP-IT INC. EXPANDS

Horace Dumpitt, Jr., chairman of the board of Dump-it Inc., has decided to increase the scope of the firm's operations by developing a new division devoted to the collection and disposal of hazardous industrial wastes. Dump-it Inc. was founded in 1929 by Horace Dumpitt, Sr. Initially, the company's main operations involved the collection and burial of household wastes. Through hard work and astute business decisions, Dump-it Inc. has grown into a large full-service organization dealing with all aspects of household and light commercial waste collection and disposal. Disposal and recycling of chemical and medical waste, therefore, would represent a logical avenue for corporate expansion. The public in general, and organizations in particular, are willing these days to pay more money for proper treatment and disposal of such waste. Dumpitt Jr. has entrusted the crucial task of developing a plan for the expansion to his daughter Emanuelle, a recent M.B.A. graduate.

Conscious of the recent awareness of the ecology movement (i.e., "Green Party") and the federal government's (as well as many provincial governments') hazardous waste treatment and disposal legislation, Emanuelle recognizes that the field presents an opportunity to capitalize and increase business markedly. As a result of all these regulations and the AIDS epidemic scare, the disposal price of a ton of regular hazardous waste has increased from approximately $500 per ton in 1985 to $900 per ton in 1992, and the disposal of medical waste (such as needles and other hospital refuse) was even more lucrative.

The Dump-it Corporate Planning Division has concluded that the company could derive 35 to 40 percent profit, after taxes, if a new chemical waste treatment and disposal division could be developed and placed in operation in the near future. Market entry is not anticipated to present a problem, since the company has been in the disposal business in excess of sixty years and is fully cognizant of the political, economic, and practical ramifications of market entry. Further, the company's considerable size and prestige are sufficient to prevent competitors from blocking entry.

Emanuelle has concluded, therefore, that her major problem is to determine the staff requisite for rapid and efficient implementation of the new division. Due to a depressed market in construction and high vacancy rates for office space, Emanuelle has been able to lease a large amount of office space adjacent to the main Dump-it parking lot at very attractive terms. Consequently, she has been able to eliminate any potential relocation expense with respect to employees selected for transfer to the new division. Nevertheless, Emanuelle realizes that the transfer of existing employees may create gaps in the existing Dump-it organization structure and that a whole cadre of new employees will have to be hired. She has concluded that Dump-it must, therefore, make provisions to assemble the staff to carry out this new effort.

Case Questions

1. Is Emanuelle right? Will a whole cadre of new employees have to be hired?
2. When should Emanuelle have developed HR plans to meet potential expansion needs?
3. What steps should Emanuelle take to ensure that Dump-it will be able to staff the new division?
4. Who should be involved with Emanuelle in developing the HR plans for Dump-it?

NOTES

1. Hay Group Inc., "The Planning Paradox: Human Resources Planning—Trends and Issues," *Management Memo* No. 340, 1986.
2. E.W. Vetter, *Manpower Planning for High Talent Personnel* (Ann Arbor, Mich.: Bureau of Industrial Relations, Graduate School of Business, The University of Michigan, 1967); and D.B. Gehrman, "Objective-Based Human Resource Planning," *Personnel Administrator*, December 1982, 71–75.
3. H.L. Dahl and K.S. Morgan, "Return on Investment in Human Resources," (Unpublished manuscript, Upjohn Company, 1982) cited by G. Milkovich, L. Dyer, and T. Mahoney in *Human Resource Management in the 1980s*, ed. S.J. Carrol and R.S. Schuler (Washington, D.C., BNA, 1983).

4. The implications were extracted from: E.B. Harvey, and J.H. Blakely, "Maximizing Use of Human Resource Information Systems (HRIS)," in *Canadian Readings in Personnel and Human Resource Management*, ed. S.L. Dolan and R.S. Schuler (St. Paul, Minn.: West Publishing Co., 1987), 444–60.

5. S.L. Dolan, V.P. Hogue, and J. Harbottle, "L'évolution des tendances en gestion des ressources humaines au Québec," in *25 Years of Industrial Relations in Quebec*, ed. R. Blouin, (Montreal: Yvon Blais Inc., 1990), 777–89; S.L. Dolan, "A Survey of the Perceived Effectiveness of Human Resources Management among Vice Presidents of Human Resource Management in Quebec" (Paper presented at the Annual Meeting of the Administrative Science Association of Canada (ASAC), Montreal, June 1989).

6. M.J. Gannon, *Organizational Behavior* (Boston: Little Brown, 1979), 97.

7. For more information, see S. Makridaki and S.C. Wheelwright, eds., *Forecasting* (New York: North–Holland Publishing Co., 1979).

8. See, for example, J.R. Hinrichs and R.F. Morrison, "Human Resource Planning in Support of Research and Development," *Human Resources Planning* 3 (1980): 201–10.

9. E.H. Burack and N.J. Mathys, *Human Resource Planning: A Pragmatic Approach to Manpower Staffing and Development* (Lake Forest, Ill.: Brace–Park, 1979).

10. N.K. Kwak, W.A. Garrett, Jr., and S. Barone, "A Stochastic Model of Demand Forecasting for Technical Manpower Training," *Management Science* 23 (1977): 1 089–98.

11. E.H. Burack and T.G. Gutteridge, "Institutional Manpower Planning: Rhetoric Versus Reality," *California Management Review* 20, 3 (1978): 18.

12. J.A.B. Parliament, "Labour Force Trends: Two Decades in Review," *Canadian Social Trends*, Autumn 1990, 17–19.

13. H. Pold, "The Labour Market: Mid-Year Report," *Perspectives*, Autumn 1990, 2–8.

14. J.A.B. Parliament, "Women Employed Outside the Home," *Canadian Social Trends*, Summer 1989, 2–6.

15. G.L. Cohen, "Disabled Workers," *Perspectives*, Winter 1989, 31–37.

16. D. Stoffman, "Completely Predictable People," *Report on Business Magazine*, 1990, 78–84.

17. Cited in "Sources," *Perspectives*, Autumn 1990, 67–68.

18. See "Expectations That Can No Longer Be Met," *Business Week*, 30 June 1980, 84.

19. J.J. Mansell and T. Runkin, "Changing Organizations: The Quality of Working Life Process," *Ontario Quality of Life Centre, Occasional Papers Series No. 4*, September 1983.

20. Information has been assembled from a brochure of the Human Resource Information Management section of Towers Perrin Company, supplied by Brian Beatty, 19 December 1991.

21. R. Teti and C. Carreiro, "Human Resources Information Systems" (Unpublished paper submitted to Professor Dolan as part of the requirement in Human Resource Management, McGill University, Fall 1991).

22. Teti and Carreiro, "Human Resources Information Systems," 8.

23. A. Piebalgs, "The Use of Computers in Human Resource Planning," in *Human Resources Management in Canada*, 1987, 20,542.

CHAPTER FIVE

RECRUITMENT OF HUMAN RESOURCES

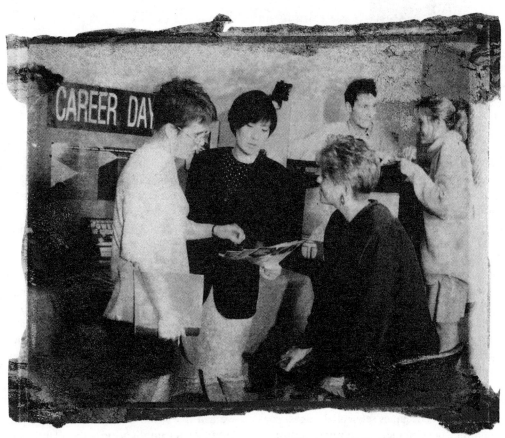

KEYNOTE ADDRESS
Louise Piché
Vice-President Human Resources, Canadian National

Reflections on Employment Equity

Canadian National (CN) launched its employment equity program in 1984. A full ten years prior to this, CN initiated a program intended to employ and promote more women. That program had some modest successes but, in the light of subsequent events, was found inadequate.

The subsequent events involve the charge, upheld by a tribunal of the Canadian Human Rights Commission, of systemic discrimination against women in blue-collar jobs brought against CN by Action Travail des Femmes. The tribunal's decision generated a lot of critical press and, frankly, made us feel pretty uncomfortable. It eventually led to the Supreme Court's landmark decision recognizing special programs or affirmative action.

Corporate discomfort is a powerful force. CN's executive was challenged by the circumstances. So much so that it became determined to see the women's program, affirmative action, employment equity—whatever you choose to call it — visibly successful at CN.

Simply put, the strategy was to get measurable results and get them fast. This priority was clear enough, but it stood conventional practice on its head. The latter takes plenty of time and occupies sequential stages: conception, planning, development, experiment, adjustment, implementation, monitoring, and reporting. This process is time-tested and perfectly valid. We did not use it.

We adopted two complementary strategic paths: one to implement, monitor, and report; the other to carry communications and information to facilitate—or, if necessary, force—development and adjustment in scope, focus, and fine-tuning. Each path would carry two-way traffic. On the implementation path, goals and techniques would go top-down; initiatives and reporting, bottom-up. Communications tools and techniques would be top-down; program needs and information, bottom-up. We needed and got corporate support for and commitment to the employment equity program on both strategic lines: immediate implementation and communi-

nications. The creation of a high profile position in 1984 to steer the employment equity thrust reinforced the message of the CEO that "a top priority will be to get immediate, measurable results."

We pursued our communication line with in-house publications, public meetings, and the development of audio-visual materials and advertising norms. We asked each department in CN to set realistic goals and time-tables to produce the "measurable results" required. We held a series of workshops focusing on neutral processes and content with designated employment equity coordinators from all parts of the organization.

Every year since, about 25 percent of all our recruits in nontraditional occupations have been women. Also, the number of women at all levels of management has been increasing steadily. Representation of visible minorities, disabled people, and Natives has also risen constantly. Attitudes amongst CN employees are increasingly positive and proactive. However, to the extent that our experience has been successful, specific characteristics should be noted: (1) the depth of commitment to it—before we embarked on employment equity, we had five years of legal debate in attempting to contemplate its implications; the result led to thorough analysis and maturity; (2) the approach—employment equity became a condition of doing business, precisely the same approach as to any other serious corporate goal. This represented a fundamental shift away from the voluntary approach that characterized efforts a decade ago; (3) a recognition that full implementation of employment equity results in better HR systems. The experience indicates that making women more secure results in a more serene and productive work environment for everyone. These effects are expanding as the program is broadened to include other groups.

Employment equity legislation requires compliance. It is almost always possible to distinguish between the spirit and the letter of the law. The spirit, which is reflected through the Charter of Rights and Freedoms or the Labour Code, reflects social consensus on the repugnancy of discriminatory employment practices. Merely obeying the letter of the law is, in the case of employment equity, an option that defies social consensus. However, it is important to say that persuasion should prevail over coercion, popularization over impo-

sition. The implementation of an employment equity program should be an interest, a principle, and a pragmatism. Perhaps the best way to respect a principle is to ensure that, once it is accepted as such, it is reasonable and sensible for everyone to put it into practice.

. . .

The Keynote Address by Louise Piché describes the challenges and successes in implementing an employment equity program. As will be discussed in this chapter, employment equity is high on the agenda for HR managers, especially in the context of recruitment, for legal reasons as well as due to normative pressures. While other Canadian companies are currently complying with the law and implementing employment equity programs, information about the CN experience is of

critical importance due to its historical context: CN was the first company in Canada required by the courts to implement such a program. Thus, the evolution in its corporate attitudes, as well as its employees' perceptions, is fascinating. According to the information cited above, it seems that a change from exhibiting passive compliance to proactive promotion of employment equity has taken place in CN over the past few years. The process should be of interest to all HR professionals.

. . .

INTRODUCTION TO RECRUITMENT

Recruitment is important because the success of an organization's hiring program depends on it. Recruiting a large pool of potentially qualified applicants helps an organization select those who will perform well. Recruitment is also important to the organization's fulfilment of its equal employment opportunity commitments. This chapter discusses the purposes of recruitment, the relationship of the recruitment activity to other personnel activities and functions, internal and external sources of job applicants, and legal issues related to recruitment, and it provides an assessment of the recruitment activity.

Recruitment is generally defined as a set of activities and processes used to obtain sufficient numbers of highly qualified people so that the organization can select the most appropriate people to fill its job needs. In addition, recruitment should be concerned with meeting the needs of job candidates. In other words, recruitment not only attracts individuals to the organization but also increases the chance of retaining them once they are hired. Of course, the recruitment activity must be done in compliance with an extensive set of rules and legal regulations.

Purposes and Importance of Recruitment

The general purpose of recruitment is to provide a pool of potentially qualified job candidates to select from. More specifically, the purposes of recruitment are to:

- Determine the present and future recruitment needs of the organization in conjunction with the HRP and job analysis activity;
- Increase the pool of qualified job applicants at minimum cost to the organization;
- Increase the success rate of the selection process by reducing the number of obviously underqualified or overqualified job applicants;
- Reduce the probability that job applicants, once recruited and selected, will leave the organization after only a short time;
- Meet the organization's responsibility for employment equity and other legal and social obligations regarding the composition of its workforce;
- Increase organizational and individual effectiveness in the short and long term;
- Evaluate the effectiveness of various techniques and locations of recruiting for all types of job applicants.[1]

Conducting all these activities effectively enables the organization to avoid costly legal battles and settlements and to select only those applicants who are indeed qualified. Because recruiting is as much concerned with getting job applicants to stay once selected as it is with getting an initial pool of potentially qualified job applicants, it should also lead to a higher QWL.

Recruitment Relationships and Influences

STRATEGIC AND HR PLANNING. Recruiting programs are developed around three components: strategic business planning, job/role planning, and HR planning. Strategic business planning determines the organization's goals, future products and services, growth rate, location, legal environment, and structure. Job/role planning, which follows strategic business planning, specifies what needs to be done at all levels in order to meet the strategic business plans. HRP determines what types of jobs the organization needs to fill, and thus, the SKAS needed by job applicants.

As part of HRP, programs are established in close coordination with recruiting to indicate where and how the individuals with the needed SKAS will be found. Results of past recruiting efforts can be used to determine where particular types of individuals may be located again. Caution must be used here, however, because use of past sources may result in the organization's inability to fulfil its legal responsibilities, such as affirmative action for minorities, women, and the handicapped.

It should be apparent that the recruitment process, to be done effectively, requires a great deal of information. This information must also be centralized so that all the HR activities related to recruitment can be coordinated. An HRIS can be useful for recruitment, since it can rapidly simulate organizational changes and conditions and thereby determine future HR needs.

JOB ANALYSIS. Although HRP identifies the organization's job needs, it is job analysis that is essential for identifying the necessary SKAS and the appropriate individual preferences, interests, and personality (PIP) traits for each job type in each organizational setting. It is very difficult, if not impossible, to do effective recruiting unless the job qualifications are defined, preferably upon initiation of the employment requisition. No internal or external recruiting should begin until there is a clear and concise statement of the education, skills, and experience requirements and the salary range for the job. In larger organizations, this information is readily available in job descriptions and salary structures. Yet numerous hours and dollars are spent in recruiting, particularly recruiting advertising, where the applicant is required to play a "guessing game" about the job qualifications required.

TRAINING AND DEVELOPMENT. If recruiting activities produce a large pool of qualified job applicants, the need for employee training may be minimal. But if recruiting activities produce a large, but unqualified, pool of job applicants, the organization will be faced with heavy training costs. Some organizations have no choice but to recruit people who are not yet ready to perform on the job. This usually results from a shortage of skills within the labour market. Recruiting decisions often include a trade-off: should the organization expand its labour market and import skilled workers from other markets (regions or countries) or should the organization settle for less qualified candidates and assume a massive investment in training? This dilemma is somewhat typical of the aeronautic industry in Canada during rapid growth periods.[2]

CAREER MANAGEMENT AND PLANNING. If the organization has a clear policy on recruitment from within, it can also assist individuals in planning their career. In contrast, if recruitment is done unsystematically, employees have difficulty devising their career plans.

THE EXTERNAL ENVIRONMENT. Often, the type of employee an organization needs depends upon the external environment. In times of national economic recession, some executives may worry about whether they can find a job, but chief financial officers and others who can cut costs still get calls from recruiters. Once hired, these cost cutters can help the HR department revise its medical and life insurance plans in order to achieve benefit cost control.

RECRUITMENT, SELECTION, AND EMPLOYMENT EQUITY

For most companies in Canada, legal considerations, obligations, and requirements play a critical role in the recruitment activities as well as in other staffing decisions. Because much of the legislation facing HRM is directed at employment decisions, which involve both recruitment and selection (i.e., hiring and firing), this section will discuss both. The legal requirements are becoming so numerous and complex that employment equity legislation is becoming a first consideration in making employment decisions. The burden of complying with this web of laws and regulations is the responsibility of the HR manager.

This section summarizes the most important features of employment equity in Canada. The description is applicable to all staffing decisions, thus it is pertinent to this chapter as well as the next. Furthermore, because there is pending legislation in several provinces, the emphasis in this section will be primarily on federal laws and regulations.

Exhibit 5.1
Components of the Recruitment Activity

Strategic and HR planning

Job analysis

Legal considerations

Recruitment
• How many
• Where
• What type

Internal
• Sources:
  Promote
  Transfer
• Methods:
  Posting
  Employee referrals

External
• Sources:
  Walk-ins
  Agencies
  Schools
  Trade ass'ns/unions
• Methods:
  Radio and TV
  Newspaper
  Trade journal
  Acquisitions/mergers

Recruitment activities
• Realistic interview
• Expanding career and job opportunities
• Alternative work arrangements

Pool of potentially qualified applicants

External environment

Concepts and Definitions

Before moving into the discussion of employment equity, we should explain some terms or concepts that will be used throughout the chapter. "Employment equity" is concerned with **discrimination**. Discrimination can be of two types—*intentional*, which we are all aware of, and *unintentional or systemic discrimination*.

Employment equity itself can be defined as:

> *A comprehensive process adopted to ensure equitable representation of designated groups throughout the workplace and to remedy and prevent the effects of intentional and systemic discrimination.*[3]

Or, more simply put by Employment and Immigration Canada:

> *Employment equity means ensuring that all job applicants and employees have a fair chance in the workplace. It is achieved when no person is denied employment opportunities or benefits for reasons unrelated to ability.*

The basic premise of employment equity is that if discriminatory barriers are eliminated, the workplace should reasonably reflect the labour pool. This should not be confused with "pay equity," which is intended to rectify the historical undervaluation of women's work (see Chapter 7).

It is the HR professional's job to ensure that employment equity is implemented and plans and procedures are undertaken to achieve it. Employment equity is a growing responsibility and it has an effect on many areas within the HR department.

INDIRECT OR SYSTEMIC DISCRIMINATION. Systemic discrimination can occur when a seemingly neutral policy has an adverse effect on one of the groups protected under human rights legislation. Methods of assessing qualifications for employment have evolved over time to suit the needs of a particular type of worker in a particular type of labour market.

Nonetheless, the Canadian Human Rights Act (as well as numerous boards of inquiry in several provinces) has borrowed the legal definition of discrimination from U.S. case law. Systemic discrimination refers to any employment system or practice that, while equitable in intent and application, has a differential and negative impact on women or minorities. In the U.S.A. the concept of systemic discrimination was articulated by the Supreme Court in *Griggs vs. Duke Power Co. (1971)*. In this case the court indicated that intent does not matter; the consequences of an employer's actions determine whether it may have discriminated under Title VII of the Civil Rights Act. Systemic discrimination is pervasive in Canadian employment systems. Often it can only be detected by a statistical examination of the results of an employment practice that measures the ratio of successful women and minority applicants to successful major group members.

THE LEGAL STATUS OF THE SYSTEMIC DISCRIMINATION CONCEPT. The approach adopted in the Griggs case, which was a watershed for U.S. jurisprudence, also became the prevailing view in Canada, where the process, though similar, has been somewhat slower. Proving intent has been an important concept in Anglo–Canadian law. In *Dritnell vs. Michael Brent Personnel Place (1968)* and *MacBean vs. Village of Plaster Rock (1975)*, boards of inquiry in two provinces found that intention or motive must be evident to prove discrimination. A 1975 case seemed to severely limit the chances for a systemic interpretation when in *Ryan vs. Chief of Police, Town of North Sydney*, the board of inquiry rejected the idea that a height and weight requirement constituted employment discrimination against women because of its very heavy adverse impact on female applicants. This was followed by what must be considered Canada's "Griggs" case, *Singh vs. Security and Investigation Services Ltd. (1976)*. In this case, Singh would not wear the traditional hat of the company's uniform for religious reasons. Again, this case involved a crucial change in approach—discrimination was defined by the board in terms of its effect on the protected group rather than the intent or motivation of the alleged violation.

Although the board took a clear position, it also recognized that business necessity was an acceptable defence. It stated:

> *First, one decides whether the employee's request is important and valid, i.e., not trivial or arbitrary. Second, one determines the extent of the inconvenience that would be caused to the employer if the request were granted. Finally, the inconvenience to the employer and the importance of the request from the standpoint of the employee must be balanced.*

Subsequently, the Singh case was supported by a number of similar decisions. In *Colfer vs. Ottawa Board of Commissioners of Police (1979)*, an Ontario board found height (5' 9") and weight (160 lbs.) requirements to be discriminatory, and in *Foster vs. B.C. Forest Products Ltd.*, (*1985*) a British Columbia board found that a height/weight requirement had an adverse impact and was not a good indicator of strength or the ability to do a job.

Despite these decisions, a number of issues could have severely limited the impact of a systemic approach. First, the "business necessity" defence can present a substantial obstacle. Difficulties arise if the complainant is forced not only to prove a negative proposition but also to assume the responsibility, including costs, for presenting evidence on technical matters. Courts have generally held, however, that once the basic elements of the case have been proven—prima facie evidence of discrimination—the onus shifts to the respondent to establish business necessity. Such reasoning was found in Foster and Colfer as well as in *Bone vs. CFL (1979)* and *Robertson vs. Metropolitan Investigation Security (Canada Ltd.) (1979)*.

A second problem can arise in reference to the acceptability of vague and subjective definitions of "business necessity." The Colfer decision, however, made it clear that evidence in support of business necessity must demonstrate an acceptable level of rigor. In an important decision in 1982, the Supreme Court of Canada ruled unanimously against a mandatory retirement age of 60 for firefighters in the Borough of Etobicoke. The defence of a bona fide occupational requirement was rejected as insufficient because it was impressionistic and relied on general assertions. Evidence to support the Borough's claim must, the court ruled, cover the detailed nature of the duties to be performed, the conditions existing in the workplace, and the effect of these conditions particularly on those near retirement age.

Settlements and decisions relating to religious accommodation and weight and height requirements, for example, have helped define what constitutes systemic discrimination in federal and provincial jurisdiction. Some landmark cases explain the evolution and present state in this regard. For instance, a setback of the federal view occurred in 1983, when a Federal Court of Appeal ruled (2–1) that Sections 7 and 10 of the Canadian Human Rights Act are not sufficiently comprehensive to include indirect or systemic discrimination (*CNR vs. K.S. Bhinder*). The court concluded that some missing words, found in the U.S. 1964 Civil Rights Act, were necessary if the existing Canadian Act was to be interpreted to include systemic. However, a recent decision of the Supreme Court of Canada in the case of *Central Alberta Dairy Pool vs. Alberta (Human Rights Commission) (1990)* reversed the previous rulings and set the current jurisprudence with regard to the definition of direct discrimination. Following six years of legal battle, the court concluded that the employer cannot discriminate against an employee whose religion requires him to observe the sabbath on a particular day, and that the employer is required to seek accommodation for such individuals. Until this decision, employers were not bound by the various human rights charters to make such accommodations.

ANALYSIS OF SYSTEMIC DISCRIMINATION. Systemic discrimination is not necessarily the result of conscious attempts to exclude certain groups. For this reason it does not involve an examination of motivation and intent, but an analysis of results and empirical validity. Employers intent on identifying and removing systemic discrimination must therefore ascertain where target group workers are under-represented, given their availability according to requisite skills. If certain restrictive or exclusionary practices are indicated by an analysis of the composition of the workforce, they can be analyzed more intensively.

The goal of this analysis is to determine whether or not employment practices having an adverse impact are necessary for the safe and efficient operation of the enterprise. This determination requires two steps. First, it is imperative to ask whether there is an alternative system or practice able to meet the employer's objective with little or no differential race or sex impact. If a suitable alternative does exist, the exclusionary practice cannot be justified as "necessary." Second, if no alternative exists, it is necessary to analyze the validity of the practice. This means assessing, by objective methods, whether or not a practice has accomplished its predictive or evaluative function.

The systemic approach, with its emphasis on impact and business necessity rather than on intent, provides an objective measure for determining whether or not discrimination exists. It downplays the question of individual blame and concentrates on rationalizing employment systems based on valid business need; solutions are oriented toward achievement of realistic goals rather than attitudinal change.

Despite the emphasis on systemic discrimination, intentional discrimination, whether individual or broadly based, must not be ignored. Both forms of discrimination adversely affect certain groups, therefore both must be understood so that HR managers can develop effective remedies capable of eliminating or reducing discrimination.

BONA FIDE OCCUPATIONAL QUALIFICATIONS AND SENIORITY SYSTEMS. All jurisdictions have a bona fide occupational qualification exemption in respect to sex discrimination in employment. The burden of proof, however, rests with the employer in all provincial jurisdictions except for New Brunswick.

Manitoba's Human Rights Commission has, for example, set out some fundamental principles regarding Bona Fide Occupational Requirements (BFORS). To ensure equality of opportunity, application forms and interviews should be designed so as to select persons solely on the basis of: (1) genuine qualifications relevant only to job performance, and (2) individual merits rather than group stereotypes.

In *Maureen Stanley et al. vs. RCMP (1987)*, the Canadian Human Rights Commission (CHRC) ruled that a requirement for prison guards to be of the same sex as the inmates in police cells constitutes a BFOR. However, in many other cases the ruling went the other way. For example, in 1987 the Federal Court of Appeal upheld a CHRC decision that found that bus company's policy of refusing to employ new drivers over the age of 35 was not a BFOR and was therefore illegal discrimination on the basis of age.

Seniority systems in unionized companies, if specified in the collective agreement, may discriminate against women if, for example, males acquire more seniority than females. In such cases males will obtain more rights, such as preferred jobs and preferred schedules, and a lower possibility of layoff through the application of the last-in-first-out rule.

In Canada there are provincial and federal laws that often overlap and provide unique regulations for the HR professional. Along with these laws are the provincial and CHRC rulings, which often stipulate removal of barriers and positive action steps as part of case settlements. Determining exactly what an organization's equal employment obligations are is made more complex by this extensive web of federal, provincial, and local legislation, guidelines, and the decisions of quasi-judicial bodies (such as a panel of arbitrators). Some of the most important developments affecting employment (with a special emphasis on staffing considerations) are outlined below.

Background and Evolution of Employment Equity

Government commitment to equal rights in employment has grown steadily since the Second World War. For many decades following Confederation, Canadian jurisprudence provided little assistance in establishing the legal right to equitable treatment. There can be little doubt that the remarkable achievements of the Universal Declaration of Human Rights, proclaimed by the United Nations General Assembly on 10 December 1948, was a key catalyst. This was followed by the International Labour Organization's (ILO) adoption of the equal remuneration for male and female workers for work of equal value. What followed in Canada was a decade of fair practices legislation in the area of employment, beginning with Ontario's Fair Employment Practices Act (1951) and including two federal acts, the Canada Fair Employment Practices Act (1953) and the Female Employees Equal Pay Act (1956).

In 1958 the ILO provided another important foundation for government action when it adopted the Discrimination (Employment and Occupation) Convention (No.111). This Convention required each ratifying country to promote equality of opportunity and treatment in employment, with the aim of eliminating discrimination. Canada ratified the Convention in 1964.

This corresponded with the emergence of new legislative initiatives in many provincial jurisdictions. Spurred in part by the work of the ILO and in part by the conservative interpretation applied by the courts, new human rights legislation was passed in all provinces. Perhaps most importantly, the administration of the new Acts was eventually placed in the hands of provincial human rights commissions, where a more proactive and developmental approach could be expected.

A commitment to equal rights is increasing at the federal level. The 1970 Royal Commission on the Status of Women, numerous studies on the economic position of native people, the Special House of Commons Committee on the Disabled and the Handicapped, the Special Committee on Participation of Visible Minorities in Canadian Society, the ratification of the International Covenants on Human Rights, the Federal Action Plan for Women, the Canadian Human Rights Act, and the Charter of Rights and Freedoms have all arisen from a deep-rooted concern with making the ideal of equality a social and economic reality.

The **Canadian Human Rights Act** became effective in 1978. The Act established the CHRC to enforce anti-discrimination laws and to promote observance of human rights and equality. The government has also instituted an affirmative action program in the private sector to test the effectiveness of voluntary programs in removing employment discrimination and correcting the effects of past discrimination. Besides prohibiting intentional discrimination on a wide variety of grounds (including six physical handicaps), the Act explicitly accepts the systemic definition of discrimination that formed the basis of American affirmative action and anti-discrimination programs. Under this definition, the CHRC examines the impact of an employment decision or transaction, rather than the employer's intent, to determine whether it is discriminatory. The Canadian Human Rights Act also explicitly permits the implementation of special programs that will prevent or reduce disadvantages to certain designated groups or remedy the effects of past discrimination against those groups. The Act also gives the CHRC the power to order the implementation of affirmative action programs where discrimination has been found.

Canada further confirmed its commitment to the principle of affirmative action in passing the Constitution Act of 1982. As of 17 April 1985, under Section 15(2) of the Charter of Rights and Freedoms, the legality of special programs of affirmative action cannot be questioned. The courts are now entitled, pursuant to Section 24, to order ameliorative measures for disadvantaged groups.

In 1983 the Abella Commission on Equality in Employment was appointed. This stemmed from the American experience, as well as from mounting public pressure for government action in defining more specifically the appropriate remedies in cases of discrimination. Judge Abella was to inquire into the most efficient, effective, and equitable means of promoting employment opportunities for, and eliminating systemic discrimination against, four designated groups: *women, disabled people, native people,* and *visible minorities.* The inclusion of visible minorities was significant in that prior to that date visible or racial minorities had not been designated as a target group for employment programs on a national basis. In its final report the Commission recommended that organizations set mandatory equity programs.

In August 1984, a federal human rights tribunal issued its first decision with regard to *mandatory* affirmative action programs. The tribunal ordered CN to hire women for one in four nontraditional or blue-collar jobs in its St. Lawrence region until they held 13 percent of such jobs. CN was also required to implement a series of other measures, varying from abandoning certain mechanical aptitude tests to modifying the way it publicizes available jobs. The decision arose from a complaint laid in 1979 by a Montreal lobby group (Action Travail de Femmes). The goal of 13 percent would roughly correspond to the proportion of women in blue-collar jobs in industry generally.

In response to the Abella Commission, a number of changes have been introduced in the Act; one pertains to the issue of responsibility. Where an employee is in a position of authority (i.e., part of the "directing mind" of the organization), the employer will be held responsible for the actions of that employee through the "organic" theory of corporate responsibility, unless *all* the following conditions are met: (a) the employer did not consent to the discrimination, (b) the employer exercised "all due diligence" to prevent the discrimination, and (c) the employer acted subsequently to mitigate or avoid the effects of the discrimination. One of the goals in amending the Act was to provide a leadership role and to establish a complementary relationship to the CHRC.

In another direct response to the Abella Commission, the federal government established in 1987 the Employment Equity Act, the mandatory Federal Contractors Program, and Treasury Board Employment Equity Guidelines for federal departments and Crown corporations. There was a sense that only strong leadership and strong measures could correct the existing inequalities in the Canadian workplace.

The purpose of this Act was to achieve equality in the workplace. No person should be denied employment or benefits for reasons unrelated to ability. To fulfil that goal the Act's aims were to reverse the conditions that undermine the employment prospects of the four groups mentioned above.

The Act, through the legislated employment equity program, requires that federally regulated employers and Crown corporations with 100 or more employees must identify and eliminate barriers, implement employment equity plans and programs, achieve a representative workforce, and report annually on their results. These reports are tabled in the House of Commons and are also distributed to major public libraries across Canada. This reporting and public scrutiny is an important ingredient of the Act. It encourages employers to carry out their requirements and demonstrate their actions for all to see, and at the same time makes this same information available to any employee groups or other interested parties. Employers who fail to report may be fined up to $50,000.

Since the Act was passed there is still much evidence to suggest that employment equity has yet to be achieved for the four designated groups.[4] Based on the reports submitted to the federal government by the organizations subject to the Act, it is clear that most organizations have not succeeded in achieving a representative workforce. Although some organizations have succeeded in achieving employment equity, it was implemented for members of visible minorities and women rather than for the other groups.

An organization's ability to achieve a representative workforce should be influenced by the characteristics of the organization's HR department, because HRM is usually assigned responsibility for the employment equity programs and because these programs are often closely related to other HR activities such as recruitment.

Implementation of an employment equity program produces an HR system that is fairer and more efficient. It also broadens the pool of candidates for jobs and strengthens internal recruitment. In order for HR policies to be supportive of the equity programs, the following is suggested:

- Regular HRM audits should be conducted in order to ensure that other HR policies and procedures are bias-free and adhere to the Act.
- Appeal systems should be installed to provide employees with a mechanism to report employment equity violations.
- Employee development policies and procedures should be set to increase the number of designated group members eligible for promotion.
- An HRIS should be used to facilitate the identification and tracking of designated group members and to make it easier to monitor the progress toward employment equity goals.
- "Women friendly" HR policies, such as child-care centres and flextime, should be offered in order to attract, retain, and develop women who bear the responsibility of child care.[5]

This program is administered by the Employment and Immigration Commission. The goals are the same as the Employment Equity Act; however, they operate differently. Any contractor with 100 or more employees, bidding on government contracts worth $200,000

The Employment Equity Act: Facts and Challenges to HRM

Equity and the Federal Contractors Program

or more, is required to identify and remove artificial barriers to the selection, hiring, promotion, and training of the designated groups as a condition of their bid. As reported in the 1989 *Employment Equity Annual Report:*

> *1,270 organizations representing close to one million employees, have affirmed their commitment to employment equity. A total of 744 employers have received contracts making them subject to review.*

Failure to make a satisfactory commitment to employment equity could result in a bid being made invalid.

Similar programs exist in the City of Toronto and in the Province of Quebec. In Quebec, this program applies to groups receiving subsidies from the government as well. The president of the Quebec Human Rights Commission, Lewis Caron, in a speech on 22 March 1991, indicated that 154 forms have been completed to date. Of these, seventy-three have been awarded contracts.

It could be argued that, to a certain extent, contract compliance is voluntary, but once a firm is committed, the same implementation issues apply as under the legislative program—data collection; planning and analysis; goals and timetables; and reports (formal reporting is not part of the programs but they are subject to audits).

Suggestions have been made that the federal government should also extend this commitment to the broader public sector by requiring employment equity implementation in all agencies receiving public monies. A regulated program would thereby reach a larger employer universe without the need for further legislation.

Canadian and Provincial Human Rights Acts

The Canadian Human Rights Act states that every individual should have an equal opportunity with other individuals to have the life that he or she desires, which is consistent with his or her duties and obligations as a member of society without being hindered in or prevented from doing so by discriminating practices based on race, national or ethnic origin, colour, religion, age, marital status, or conviction for an offence for which a pardon has been granted, or by discriminatory employment practices based on physical handicap. The federal Act also prohibits discrimination with respect to recruitment, selection, promotion, transfer, training, and termination.

Each of the ten provinces and the two territories have enacted their own human rights acts, most of which are similar to the federal law. Exhibit 5.2 shows the prohibited grounds of discrimination in employment in Canada.

The complementary relationship of the Employment Equity Act and the CHRC stems from the fact that copies of the annual reports are filed with the latter. As a result they can monitor these target groups and also have the authority to initiate an investigation where reasonable grounds of systemic discrimination exist. Individuals may also file complaints with the CHRC against an employer.

Based on the reports filed for the 1987 calendar year the CHRC received :

> *11 complaints on the employment practices of employers. It also requested that 19 employers cooperate in a joint review of their equity situation. Seventeen complied, and the commission has initiated a complaint investigation against the others.*[6]

Implications for companies are costly, since HR managers must now develop new information systems to track and report all this information. At the very least, they will be required to make changes to their existing systems. This has in fact led to the development of new specialists in HRM who must be aware of all the steps to implementing an employment equity policy.

Exhibit 5.2
Prohibited Grounds of Discrimination in Employment

	Federal	British Columbia	Alberta	Saskatchewan	Manitoba	Ontario	Quebec	New Brunswick	Prince Edward Island	Nova Scotia	Newfoundland	Northwest Territories	Yukon
Race	●	●	●	●	●	●	●	●	●	●	●	●	●
National or ethnic origin[1]	●				●	●	●	●	●	●	●		●
Ancestry			●	●	●	●	●					●	●
Nationality or citizenship				●	●	●					●		
Place of origin			●	●	●	●		●			●		
Colour	●	●	●	●	●	●	●	●	●	●	●	●	●
Religion	●	●		●	●		●	●	●	●	●		●
Creed[2]			●	●		●				●	●	●	●
Age	●	●	●	●	●	●	●	●	●	●	●	●	
		45-65	18+	18-65		18-65		18+		40-65	19-65		
Sex	●	●	●	●	●	●	●	●	●	●	●	●	●
Pregnancy or childbirth	●		●	●		●							
Marital status[3]	●	●	●	●	●	●	●	●	●	●	●	●	●
Family status[3]	●				●	●	●				●		
Pardoned offence	●						●				●		
Record of criminal conviction		●				●	●						
Physical handicap or disability	●	●	●	●	●	●	●	●	●	●	●	●	
Mental handicap or disability	●				●	●	●	●	●	●	●	●	
Dependence on alcohol or drug	●												
Place of residence												●	
Political belief		●			●		●		●		●		
Assignment, attachment or seizure of pay[4]											●		
Source of income													
Social condition[4]							●						
Language							●						
Social origin[4]											●		
Sexual orientation[5]						●	●						
Harassment[5]	●					●	●				●		

1. New Brunswick includes only "national origin."
2. Creed usually means religious beliefs.
3. Quebec uses the term "civil status."
4. In Quebec's charter, "social condition" includes assignment, attachment or seizure of pay and social origin.
5. The federal, Ontario and Quebec statutes ban harassment on all proscribed grounds. Ontario, Nova Scotia and Newfoundland also ban sexual solicitation.

Source: Reproduced with the permission of the Canadian Human Rights Commission.

EXHIBIT 5.3

Employment Equity Data Sheet Used by the Federal Business Development Bank

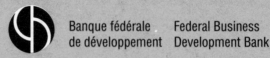

Banque fédérale   Federal Business
de développement   Development Bank

Canadä

ÉQUITÉ EN MATIÈRE D'EMPLOI

EMPLOYMENT EQUITY

Équité en matière d'emploi

En tant que société de la Couronne, la Banque est fière de participer à la promotion de l'équité en matière d'emploi par la mise en place d'un programme interne visant à éliminer les obstacles à une représentation équitable de la population canadienne au sein de l'organisation.

La mise sur pied d'un tel programme nécessite, entre autres, l'analyse des candidatures aux postes comblés par recrutement externe ainsi que l'analyse de la main d'oeuvre active de la Banque. Cette analyse n'est possible qu'à la condition que chaque postulant(e) et employé(e) veuille bien nous transmettre CONFIDENTIELLEMENT ET VOLONTAIREMENT les renseignements demandés dans le questionnaire ci-joint et le retourner dans l'enveloppe adressée au Chef, Personnel.

La Loi canadienne sur les droits de la personne autorise l'employeur à recueillir les données nécessaires à certains programmes destinés à éliminer les désavantages que subissent, sur le plan de l'emploi, des groupes particuliers et plus spécifiquement, les femmes, les autochtones, les membres des minorités visibles et les personnes atteintes de déficiences.

La Banque est soumise à la Loi sur la protection des renseignements personnels et le droit de chque personne à cette protection sera maintenu.

Nous vous remercions de votre contribution et si des informations supplémentaires s'avéraient nécessaires, n'hésitez pas à communiquer avec Cécile Cournoyer, Chef, Politiques et programmes de dotation au (514) 496-2589.

Employment Equity

As a Crown Corporation, the Bank is proud to actively participate in the promotion of employment equity by implementing an internal program aimed at eliminating obstacles to an equitable representation of the Canadian population in the workplace.

Implementation of such a program requires, among other things, an analysis of applications received for jobs offered through external recruiting and the analysis of the Bank's workforce. This analysis is only possible if applicants and employees complete the enclosed questionnaire and return it in the envelope addressed to the Manager, Personnel. Completion of the questionnaire is VOLUNTARY and will be kept STRICTLY CONFIDENTIAL.

The Canadian Human Rights Act permits employers to collect the data they require to plan and support special programs which are designed to eliminate disadvantages in employment for certain groups and more specifically, women, aboriginal peoples, members of visible minorities and persons with disabilities.

The Bank is subject to the Privacy Act and individual rights concerning access to personal information will be maintained.

We thank you for your cooperation and if you need any further information please contact Cécile Cournoyer, Manager, Staffing Policies and Programs at (514) 496-2589.

S. Desjardins

Vice-President, Human Resources and Administration
Vice-présidente, Ressources humaines et administration

FOR FBDB EMPLOYEE USE ONLY/
À L'USAGE DE L'EMPLOYÉ(E) DE BFD SEULEMENT

PERSONAL IDENTIFICATION NO.

Nº D'IDENTIFICATION PERSONNELLE

FOR FBDB EMPLOYEE USE ONLY/
À L'USAGE DE L'EMPLOYÉ(E) DE BFD SEULEMENT

NOM/NAME _____

EMPLOI POSTULÉ/POSITION APPLIED FOR

LIEU/LOCATION _____

Nous vous conseillons de lire tout le questionnaire avant de commencer à cocher les cases qui s'appliquent à votre cas.

It is recommended that you read the entire questionnaire before checking the boxes which apply to you.

AUTO-IDENTIFICATION

Veuillez cocher les cases appropriées

SELF-IDENTIFICATION

Please check the appropriate boxes

SEXE **SEX**

1.
Indiques si vous êtes de sexe:

| Féminin | F | Female |
| Masculin | M | Male |

1.
Please indicate whether you are:

AUTOCHTONES

L'expression «autochtone» désigne les Indiens inscrits et non-inscrits, les Inuits et les Métis qui résident au Canada.

ABORIGINAL PEOPLES

Aboriginal peoples are persons in Canada who identify themselves to be Status Indian, Non-Status Indian, Inuit or Métis

2.
Vous considérez-vous comme faisant parti des autochtones?

| Oui | Y | Yes |
| Non | N | No |

2.
Do you consider yourself to be an aboriginal person?

If no, go directly to question 4

Si non, passez à la question 4

3.
Si oui, indiquez à quel groupe vous appartenez,
(*Ne cochez qu'une seule case.*)

Passez ensuite à la question 6

Inuit	A	Inuit
Métis	B	Métis
Indien inscrit	C	Status Indian
Indien non-inscrit	D	Non-Status Indian

3.
If yes, please specify to which group you belong.
(*Check only one category.*)

Then go to question 6

PERSONNES APPARTENANT À DES MINORITÉS VISIBLES

PERSONS FROM VISIBLE MINORITY GROUPS

Les personnes appartenant à des minorités visibles sont celles dont la race ou la couleur est différente de celle de la majorité de la population du Canada.

Members of visible minority groups are persons of race or colour other than that of the majority of the population in Canada.

4.

Appartenez-vous à une minorité visible?

Oui [Y] Yes
Non [N] No

4.

Are you a member of a visible minority group?

Si non, passez à la question 6

If no, go directly to question 6

5.

Si oui, indiquez à quel groupe vous appartenez. (*Ne cochez qu'une seule case.*)

Noir(e) d'Afrique	[A]	Black from Africa
des Antilles	[B]	from Antilles
d'Amérique	[C]	from America
Noir(e) — autre	[D]	Black — other
Chinois(e)	[E]	Chinese
Japonais(e)	[F]	Japanese
Coréen(ne)	[G]	Korean
Philippin(e)	[H]	Filipino
Indo – Pakistanais(e) (Asie du Sud)	[I]	Indo-Pakistani (South Asia)
Asiatique de l'Ouest ou Arabe (Moyen-Orient)	[J]	West Asian or Arab (Middle East)
Asiatique du Sud-Est (Birmanie, Cambodge, Laos, Thaïlande, Vietnam, etc.)	[K]	South East Asian (Burma Kampuchesa, Laos Thailand, Vietnam, etc.)
Autre minorité visible Veuillez préciser	[L]	Other visible minority Please Specify

5.

If yes, please indicate which visible minority group. (*Check only one category.*)

PERSONNES ATTEINTES DE DÉFICIENCES

PERSONS WITH DISABILITIES

Les personnes atteintes de déficiences sont celles qui, à des fins d'emploi, se considèrent comme étant grandement handicapées en raison d'une ou de plusieurs déficiences physiques ou mentales. de difficultés d'apprentissage, de troubles psychiatriques ou sensoriels qui persistent, ou qui croient qu'un employeur éventuel serait susceptible de les considérer comme telles.

Persons with disabilities include those persons who, for purposes of employment, consider themselves, or believe that a potential employer would likely consider them, disadvantaged by reason of any persistent physical, mental, psychiatric, learning or sensory impairment.

6.
Vous estimez-vous désavantagé(e) dans votre carrière à cause d'une déficience persistante d'ordre physique, mental, psychiatrique, sensoriel ou causant des difficultés d'apprentissage?

Oui [Y] Yes
Non [N] No

6.
Do you consider yourself to be disadvantaged in your career by reason of any persistent physical, mental psychiatric, learning or sensory impairment?

7.
Si oui, dans quelle catégorie se classe votre déficience? (*Cochez toutes les cases requises.*)

7.
If yes, please indicate which applies to you. (*Check all applicable boxes.*)

Coordination ou dextérité déficiente	X	Coordination or dexterity impairment
Troubles moteurs (usage constant d'un fauteuil roulant, amputation, etc.)	X	Mobility impairment (confinement to a wheelchair, amputation, etc.)
Défaut d'élocution	X	Speech impairment
Mutisme	X	Muteness
Troubles visuels (sauf ce qui peut être corrigé par des verres ou des lentilles cornéennes	X	Visual impairment (except if it can be corrected by glasses or contact lenses
Cécité	X	Blindness
Troubles auditifs (surdité partielle)	X	Hearing impairment (partial hearing)
Surdité	X	Deafness
Handicap physique non visible (épilepsie, hémophilie, etc.)	X	Non-visible physical impairment (Epilepsy, Hemophilia, etc.)
Maladie ou handicap mental	X	Mental handicap/illness
Difficultés d'apprentissage	X	Learning disability
Autres types de déficiences	X	Other impairment
Veuillez préciser		Other specify

MERCI DE VOTRE COLLABORATION

THANK YOU FOR YOUR COOPERATION

Source: Reproduced with the permission of the Federal Business Development Bank.

Implementing Employment Equity

An Employer shall, in consultation with such persons as have been designated by the employees to act as their representatives or, where a bargaining agent represents the employees, in consultation with the bargaining agent, implement employment equity...[7]

As can be seen, it is the responsibility of the employer to adopt a program that will achieve equality in the workplace. Five stages are necessary to achieve this.

PHASE 1: PREPARATION. The process begins with senior management. There must be a commitment to these values at the top of the organization and these must in turn be communicated to middle managers. Responsibility and accountability should be assigned to a senior member of management, usually within human resources, to see that the goals are in fact carried out.

There must be some form of communication strategy in place. The ultimate goal is to ensure a positive environment in which to implement the program and to promote voluntary self-identification of the target groups. To be effective, a communication program will identify the purposes of the self-identification process, address their concerns, and encourage their full participation. This can be accomplished through memos from senior management, meetings and seminars, and production of videos.

The whole process, therefore, revolves around the participation of top management and the voluntary disclosure by employees of information about their status. In order to do reporting there must be a collection process for this information.

PHASE 2: ANALYSIS. This stage identifies the problem areas the employer may have. It basically compares all the internal data gathered on the designated groups to external data. One of the greatest challenges in implementing a policy comes from the difficulty employers face in obtaining this voluntary information from employees. This in turn creates the frustration of filing reports based on incomplete information. Programs developed on bad data will only lead to further problems at some later stage.

Employment equity practitioners recommend that relevant data be collected at the time of application and hiring, upon promotion or transfer, and at training courses for permanent, part-time, and casual workers. An employment equity questionnaire, completed anonymously, is often used for this purpose. A sample Federal Business Development Bank questionnaire is shown in Exhibit 5.3.

Once the data are gathered, an analysis can be made to determine where underrepresentation occurs and appropriate plans can be made to rectify the situation. A review of employment systems to identify barriers to these groups must be made. Information on hiring, promotions, and availability of training in these groups must be analyzed.

PHASE 3: PLANNING. The analysis must then produce a plan to remedy the areas identified by affirmative action. The goal, of course, is to increase representation of the groups in the firm. This plan should be closely linked to other organizational plans, particularly the HR staffing plan. The equity plan should contain numerical goals for hiring, training, and promotion along with time frames to accomplish these goals. It should also identify those responsible for implementation and have some format for evaluation of the progress or completion of the objectives. To date, employers have reported some real difficulties in meeting their plan. These may relate to the highly specialized staff required and the lack of designated candidates within this group. Economic or organizational changes, such as recession or downsizing and mergers, also present stumbling blocks to organizations.

PHASE 4: IMPLEMENTATION. The means used to meet these goals are as varied as the companies themselves. Quotas on hiring visible minorities or native people have been used. At least 50 percent of university recruits being females and more participation of females in special management programs are other examples of how these plans can be implemented. The HRM in the News Vignette shows how some Ontario colleges as well as the University of Ottawa are trying to implement the program, although they are aware that it may cause *reverse discrimination*.

PHASE 5: MONITORING. As with any plan, the goals must be monitored. This can be as simple as a count of the various numerical goals set. The accountability factor mentioned previously is an important ingredient in this process. In short, these corporate goals should be dealt with in the same way other goal commitments are handled.

In addition to the internal monitoring for federally legislated companies, there is the annual external filing of public reports that will monitor the ongoing achievement of corporate plans.

It will take time to effect this social change, for there is a time lag in developing plans and having them monitored. There is also a time lag resulting from challenges to the system and the consequent legal delays. The Ontario Ministry of Citizenship stated in its July

---

HRM IN THE NEWS VIGNETTE
Losing His Job to Women, Professor Bewails Reverse Discrimination

At Toronto's Ryerson Polytechnical Institute, woman's gain is Phillip Ferreira's loss. His contract job as a professor of philosophy is being replaced later this year by a permanent position, and men are being told not to apply. The post-secondary school is trying to change its gender balance. Just one of the seven philosophy professors on permanent staff is a woman.

Mr. Ferreira...finds that neither his head nor his heart accepts the reasons why he must look elsewhere for work. "I can, on philosophical grounds, always justify equitable hiring practices and I can certainly support and defend any practices that do away with discrimination," he said in an interview. "But what I personally cannot defend is any sort of blatant reverse discrimination."

Ron Bontekoe, who also teaches philosophy on contract at Ryerson, said he has taken a permanent position at the University of Hawaii for next year because employment equity at Canadian schools restricts his job chances.

Ryerson, like the Ontario College of Art, has developed a strong employment equity program to redress an imbalance of men and woman among the full-time teaching staff.

At the Ontario College of Art, all vacancies created by retirement over the next decade are to be filled by women. At Ryerson, the figure is about 80 per cent over the same period and several of Ryerson's vacancies

are "targeted"—held for women, unless no qualified women can be found within two years.

The two schools have the country's toughest employment equity programs among post-secondary institutions. At the University of Ottawa, which the Association of Universities and Colleges in Canada considers an equity leader, 40 per cent of new full-time positions annually are to be filled by women.

The University of Ottawa considers that a reasonable goal, since women make up 32 per cent of doctoral graduates in Canada, said Hélène Carrière, coordinator of the school's equity program.

Larry Gray, Ryerson's vice-president of faculty and staff affairs, said he agrees with Mr. Ferreira that he is being discriminated against. "I sympathize with his pain, but I don't know what else I can say to him, other than there's never been a theological guarantee of fairness." As for legislated guarantees of fairness—human rights codes, for example—Mr. Gray said that "there are now legislated discriminations, which are acceptable." Ryerson received permission from the Ontario Human Rights Commission for its employment equity program.

Source: Excerpts from a feature article of the same title by Sean Fine, *The Globe and Mail*, 21 January, 1990, Reprinted with permission.

1989 Discussion Paper on Employment Equity that "it will not produce change overnight, since improvements depend on the rate of growth and turnover in jobs." It is also recognized that many of the issues faced by disadvantaged groups do not have their source in the workplace and cannot be rectified by changes to the employment system alone.

OTHER CONSIDERATIONS. Occasionally, recruiting efforts are found to be discriminatory, even when unintended. For example, gender labelling of jobs and stereotyping can result in the exclusion of women and minorities. This was illustrated by a study of the Canadian Broadcasting Corporation. Among other findings, the study reported that (1) most jobs in the CBC were segregated, and (2) when a woman did summon enough courage to apply for one of these "men only" jobs, she was actively discouraged by the male interviewers.[8]

SOURCES AND METHODS FOR OBTAINING JOB APPLICANTS

Internal Sources

Internal sources include present employees, friends of employees, former employees, and former applicants. Promotions, demotions, and transfers can also provide applicants for departments within the organization.

PROMOTIONS. The case for promotion from within rests on several sound arguments. One is that internal employees are better qualified. "Even jobs that do not seem unique require familiarity with the people, procedures, policies, and special characteristics of the organization in which they are performed."[9] Another is that employees are likely to feel more secure and to associate their long-term interests with the organization that provides them the first choice of job opportunities. Availability of promotions within an organization can also motivate employees to perform, and internal promotion can be much less expensive to the organization in terms of both time and money.

By comparison, luring applicants from outside the organization can be an expensive process. The costs to the company of relocating the new recruit and his or her family may range from $10,000 to $50,000. Further, the new recruit is often brought in at a higher salary than those currently in similar positions in the organization. The result, especially if the new recruit fails to contribute as expected, is dissatisfaction among the current employees. In addition, the incentive value of promotions diminishes.[10]

Disadvantages of a **promotion-within policy** may include an inability to find the best qualified person. Also, in-fighting, inbreeding, and lack of varied perspectives and interests may result. If an organization has a policy of promotion from within, it must identify, select, and pressure candidates to accept the promotions. When done during times of rapid organizational growth, almost any employee may be promoted, regardless of qualifications, because the organization faces a managerial shortage. Rapid growth may temporarily obscure managerial deficiencies, but when the growth rate abates the company will be faced with a surplus of managers whose poor performance cannot be covered.

Based upon these advantages and disadvantages, most organizations use a combination of internal promotion and external recruiting. Many tend to obtain particular types of employees from particular sources, for example, to hire highly trained professionals and high-level managers from the outside rather than to promote from within.

TRANSFERS. Another way to recruit internally is by transferring current employees without promotion. Transfers are often important in providing employees with the more broad-based view of the organization often necessary for future promotions. Thus, providing transfers can be a way of getting job applicants from outside the organization as well as inside. Recent trends suggest that transfers or promotions that involve relocation may not be as attractive as they once were, except for companies that engage in some sort of relocation counselling. Approximately 60 percent of the 500 largest Canadian companies now use this type of service to relocate their employees.[11]

One of the major issues in promoting or transferring candidates from within is whether seniority or performance/merit should be used as the criterion. Unions seem to prefer promotion and transfer based on seniority: organizations prefer promotion or transfer based on ability. Occasionally the criterion for promotions is personal judgment, particularly for middle- and upper-level managerial positions. It is difficult to defend this criterion under legal guidelines. Therefore many organizations use test results from managerial assessment centres as one alternative to personal judgments and impressions. Since assessment centres are used more frequently as a selection device than as a recruiting device, they are discussed more extensively in Chapter 6.

JOB ROTATION. Whereas transfers are usually permanent, job rotations are usually temporary. Job rotation has been used effectively to expose management trainees to various aspects of organizational life. It has also been used to relieve job burnout for employees in high-stress occupations. For example, some hospitals in Quebec are currently devising policies to swap nurses who work in emergency rooms or intensive care units (high-stress environments) with those working in other wards. Job rotation is also considered part of career management and planning, and thus is discussed in Chapter 12.

Internal Methods

There are many methods for internally advertising job vacancies. Candidates can be identified by word of mouth, from company personnel records, promotion lists, and from the skills inventory list generated by an organization's HRIS. Since the "notice on the bulletin board" (job posting) and employees referrals are the most frequently used methods, they are discussed first.

JOB POSTING. In essence, a **job posting** extends an open invitation to all employees, through prominent display of notice, to apply for a job vacancy. A job posting:

1. Provides opportunities for employee growth and development;
2. Provides equal opportunity for advancement to all employees;
3. Creates a greater openness in the organization by making opportunities known to all employees;
4. Increases staff awareness regarding salary grades, job descriptions, general promotion and transfer procedures, and what comprises effective to outstanding job performance;
5. Communicates organization goals and objectives while allowing each individual the opportunity to self-select the best possible "fit" for himself or herself in the organizational job structure.[12]

Although job postings are usually found on bulletin boards, they can also be found in company newsletters, circulated in employee lounges, and announced at staff meetings. Generally, all openings except for management positions are posted. Sometimes specific salary information is posted, but job grade and pay range are more typical. Job posting is beneficial for organizations because it improves morale, provides employees with the opportunity for job variety, facilitates a better matching of employee skills and needs, and fills positions at a low cost.

There are, however, several disadvantages to job posting that counteract these benefits. They include:

- The process of filling vacancies is lengthened.
- The morale of unsuccessful candidates may suffer if feedback is not timely or carefully handled.
- Choices can be more difficult for the selecting manager if two or three almost equally qualified candidates are encountered.

- Information about the posted jobs, such as salary or position grade, may trigger objections from employees who perceive inequities with their position evaluations or salaries.
- Supervisory–subordinate relationships may be jeopardized by subordinates who frequently attempt to bid out of their work units.

EMPLOYEE REFERRAL PROGRAMS (ERPs).   These are essentially word-of-mouth advertisements that generally involve rewarding employees for referring skilled job applicants to an organization. This method has proved to be a low cost-per-hire way of recruiting applicants, even though in many cases the applicants come from outside the organization. The underlying assumption is that the current employee knows the company and its culture and has a good understanding about what the job really involves. Thus, as the recruitment process entails a "sale" process, current employees are in the best position to do this.[13]

For successful referrals, employees may receive a financial bonus (in some companies, it may exceed $500), especially if they refer someone with a skill that is in high demand. Toronto-based Sun Life Assurance of Canada set up "Sun Power," a program to help recruit employees with special skills. A bonus of up to $1,000 is offered to employees who help find a suitable candidate.[14] An ERP starts with a clear goal and rules. The program must pinpoint people with particular skills and qualifications. For instance, White Spot Ltd., a restaurant and catering chain in Vancouver, offers $500 to employees who recruit at the managerial level, but no bonus for recruiting hourly staff.[15] Furthermore, to ensure fairness and clarity, the ERP must include guidelines specifying when and how the employee will receive the award. Sun Life, for example, gives half the bonus when the candidate joins the company and the other half six months later after the new hire completes the probationary period.

One major concern with an ERP is potential discrimination: individuals may be likely to refer those who are of the same race or sex. While this may not necessarily preclude fulfilling affirmative action program obligations, there are potential legal problems. In addition, cliques and nepotism may develop, having negative effects on work.

SKILLS INVENTORY.   Another method of internal recruiting is to use the skill-related information contained in personnel files, but much time and effort is required to get it. A formal skills inventory aggregates this information through the use of an HRIS or HRMS. Any data then can be quantified, coded, and included in a skills inventory.

Common information includes name, employee number, job classification, prior jobs, prior experience, specific skills and knowledge, education, licences, publications, and salary levels. The results of formal assessments, such as those obtained in assessment centres, during work samples tests, and with job interest inventories, can also be included. Because the collection and maintenance of a skills inventory is time consuming, it is used more frequently by organizations that set up this database for other HR purposes.

External Sources

Recruiting internally does not always produce enough qualified job applicants. This is especially true for organizations that are growing rapidly or that have a large demand for high-talent professional, skilled, and managerial employees. Therefore, organizations need to recruit from external sources. Recruiting from the outside has a number of advantages, including bringing in people with new ideas. It is often cheaper and easier to hire an already trained professional or skilled employee, particularly when the organization has an immediate demand for scarce labour skills and talents. External sources can also supply temporary employees, who provide the organization with much more flexibility than permanent ones.

Information about the supply of certain types of labour is published monthly by Employment and Immigration Canada, provincial departments of labour, industry associations, newsletters, and local Canada Employment Centres. There are over 800 Employment Centres spread all over Canada. More than 23,000 employees willing to assist employers in meeting their recruitment needs work in these centres. Information regarding labour force characteristics on a national, provincial, or even city-by-city (in some cases) basis is contained in the monthly *Labour Force Survey*, published by Statistics Canada. A related service of Statistics Canada is the Help Wanted Index (HWI). It is published four times a year and helps track the help wanted advertisements placed in eighteen major newspapers across Canada. The survey attempts to indicate the number of jobs available.

Although reliable information for the 1990s is not available, past surveys by the Economic Council of Canada suggest that in the late 1970s and early 1980s the single most frequent method of job search for all unemployed persons in Canada, regardless of occupation, education, and sex, was the informal method of contacting employers directly.[16] The same survey shows, in descending order of importance, the use of Canada Employment Centres, ads in the newspapers, and checking with friends and relatives. Exhibit 5.4 shows the relative costs and time requirements pertaining to some of these methods.

Exhibit 5.4
Cost and Time Variations of External Recruiting Sources

SOURCE	APPROXIMATE COST (RELATIVE TO OTHER SOURCES)	AVERAGE LENGTH OF TIME TO FILL A POSITION
Walk-ins	Low	Daily
Canada (and Quebec) Employment Centres	Low	Varies (contingent on market conditions). In a normal market it takes about 2–4 months.
Private Employment Agencies	Medium	Varies (contingent on market conditions). In a normal market, it takes between a week to 1 month.
Executive Search Firms	High	Varies (contingent on market conditions). In normal times it takes about 6 months to fill a senior executive position, 3 months for middle management, and 1–2 months for a staff position.
Professional/Trade Associations	Medium	6–12 months
Technical and Educational Institutions	Medium	6–12 months

Note: Estimates of costs and time have been computed based on information supplied by several executive search companies in the Montreal region.

WALK-INS. In the walk-in method, individuals become applicants by walking into an organization's employment office. This method, like employee referrals, is relatively informal and inexpensive and is almost as effective as employee referrals for retaining applicants once hired. Unlike referrals, however, nonreferred applicants may know less about the specific jobs available and usually come without the implicit recommendation of a current employee. This may be a disadvantage since current employees may be reluctant to recommend unsatisfactory applicants.

Although walk-ins may be a relatively inexpensive source of applicants, this method is not used extensively when it comes to managerial, professional, and sales applicants. It tends to be a passive source of applicants and thus may not provide the specific types of applicants needed to fulfil affirmative action and equal employment considerations. These drawbacks may be reduced by attracting walk-ins with open house events. These events can attract all types of applicants from the nearby community, but sufficient numbers of some applicants can only be attained by also using other sources.

EMPLOYMENT AGENCIES.   Employment agencies are the second most popular source of employment for Canadians. The public employment agencies in Canada are the Canada Employment Centres (CECS). As indicated earlier, the CECS exist in every province and their work is coordinated by the Employment and Immigration Department, which has recently developed a nationwide computerized "job bank" to which all provincial employment offices are connected. When an employer has a job opening, the personnel department notifies the CEC of the job and its requirements. Typically, this information is immediately posted at the CEC's job information centre. Prospective employees discuss the job opening with a CEC counsellor who interviews the candidate and finds out if his or her qualifications meet the requirements. If the counsellor's assessment is positive, a referral is made to the firm. The effectiveness of the CEC's placement activity has been studied and the results are mixed. Although the CEC is the second most important source for recruiting, the agency exposes to the labour market only one in three job seekers, and actually places only one in five. Furthermore, almost half of the vacancies filled are in clerical, sales, and service occupations; very few placements are made in primary, managerial, and professional occupations.[17]

Private employment agencies tend to serve two groups of job applicants: (1) professional and managerial workers, and (2) skilled workers. The agencies dealing with the skilled group often provide applicants that employers would have difficulty finding otherwise. Many employers looking for skilled workers do not have the resources to do their own recruiting or have only temporary or seasonal demands for skilled labour. Private agencies therefore play a major role in recruiting professional and managerial applicants.

Executive search firms have been growing steadily in Canada. With most of the growth taking place in the past fifteen years, the estimated annual market for their services is about $40 million.[18] Some search firms claim that they are not employment agencies because they do not find jobs for people; instead, what they do is find people for jobs. The fees charged by these agencies range up to 33 percent of the first year's total salary and bonus package for the job to be filled. The search firm gets this money whether or not they find someone who is eventually selected for the job. Even if the firm is successful in finding someone who is hired, the cost may be much greater than the fees charged. This is because in the pre-screening process, the search firm may have rejected a candidate who would have done well or may have placed a candidate who will not do well. These two errors, discussed in Chapter 6 as false negative and false positive respectively, represent additional costs to the organization. To minimize costs, the organization should closely monitor the search firm's activities.

It is estimated that there are at least thirty Canadian firms (some are branches of multinational management consulting firms) offering executive search services. Note that the agencies may identify (pre-screen) job applicants who are already working with other organizations. Consequently, in addition to its expense, this method of dealing with a potential candidate is apt to be very secretive.

Executive search firms normally establish contacts with many client organizations. Their motto is that the best candidate for a job is somebody who is not necessarily looking for one. For that reason, many refer to executive search officers as "head-hunters." The underlying assumption for the search is that senior executives could always be lured to other organizations if the job content and the compensation attached to it are right. In 1988 the Sobeco Group published the results of their survey of 300 senior executives (presidents and vice-presidents), which shows that 70 percent of them will consider changing jobs within the next five years.[19]

The only serious drawback to using an executive search firm is cost. Unfortunately, many Canadian firms seem to be very loyal to the search firm they initially selected and only in a few cases is a real cost–benefit analysis carried out to determine the quality of the services. However, with changes in management philosophies and pressure to become competitive, this cavalier approach will most likely disappear.

TEMPORARY HELP AGENCIES. Whereas private recruiting agencies provide applicants for full-time positions, temporary help agencies provide applicants for part-time positions. Their use is growing as skilled and semiskilled individuals find it preferable to work less than a forty-hour week, or at least on their own schedule. Temporary employees (temps) also have a chance to work in a variety of organizations; consequently, they have the opportunity to satisfy preferences for workplace variety. Though temps may receive higher direct compensation than the organization's permanent staff, they generally forego indirect compensation (i.e., benefits, which are discussed in Chapter 8).

Organizations are using temporary help agencies more than ever because workers with certain skills can only be obtained through them. This is especially true for small companies that are not very visible or cannot spend the time to recruit on their own. According to Ted Turner, vice-president of the Canadian Association of Temporary Services, the growth rate of the temp industry was twenty times that of the regular workforce.[20] This is reinforced by U.S. data that show a similar trend. In a survey conducted by the Administrative Management Society, (AMS), 91 percent of the firms surveyed use temporary services. The principal reason given was to alleviate overloads, to assist with special projects, and to replace employees who are absent or on vacation. The AMS survey also found that:

- Temps are used every week by 36 percent of the respondents;
- The usual length of service for a temp is one to four weeks;
- Most temps are hired for clerical duties and secretarial help.[21]

TRADE ASSOCIATIONS AND LABOUR ORGANIZATIONS. In some industries, such as the construction industry, skilled workers are recruited through the local labour organization. Since those contractors often hire seasonal workers, a union hiring hall is a convenient channel for attracting many candidates.

Trade and professional associations are also important sources for recruiting. They often have newsletters, which can be used to post employment opportunities. The annual meetings can also provide employers and potential job applicants with an opportunity to meet. Some communities and schools have picked up on this idea and now bring together large numbers of employers and job seekers at "job fairs." Of course, these fairs provide limited interview time and thus serve only as an initial step in the recruitment process, but they are an efficient recruiting source for both employers and individuals.

TECHNICAL AND EDUCATIONAL INSTITUTIONS. High schools, vocational and technical schools, and colleges and universities are important sources of recruits for most organizations, although their importance varies depending on the type of applicant sought. For example, if an organization is recruiting for managerial, technical, or professional applicants, colleges and universities are the most important source. When an organization is seeking plant/service and clerical employees, high schools or vocational schools would be more effective sources.

Recruiting at colleges and universities is often an expensive process, even if it eventually produces job offers and acceptances. U.S. studies have shown that approximately 30 percent of the applicants hired from college leave the organization within the first five years. This rate of turnover is even higher for graduate management students (M.B.A.s).[22]

Some people attribute this high turnover rate to the lack of job challenge. Organizations claim, however, that people just out of college have unrealistic expectations. Partly because of the expense, organizations are questioning the necessity of hiring college graduates for some jobs. Many universities, on the other hand, suggest that on-campus recruitment is the most popular method for students looking for their first job, and they provide placement and counselling centres that facilitate the job search for their graduates.

External Methods

RADIO AND TELEVISION. Some organizations looking for applicants of all types engage in extensive advertising on radio and television, in the local paper, and in national newspapers such as *The Financial Post* or *The Globe and Mail*. Companies are reluctant to use these media because they fear: (a) it is too expensive, (b) it will make the company look desperate, or (c) it will damage the firm's conservative image. Yet, organizations that are "desperate" to reach certain types of job applicants, such as skilled workers, use these media. In reality, however, there is nothing desperate about using radio or television. Rather it is the *content* and *delivery* that may imply some level of desperation. Recognizing this, organizations are increasing their recruitment expenditures for carefully designed radio and television advertisements with very favourable results.

NEWSPAPERS AND TRADE JOURNALS. Newspapers have traditionally been the most common method of external recruiting. They reach a large number of potential applicants at a relatively low cost per hire. Newspaper ads are used to recruit all types of positions, from the most unskilled to the most highly skilled and top managerial positions. Ads range from the simple and matter-of-fact to highly creative eye-catching. The average advertising cost for high-level jobs is in excess of $4,000 per professional person recruited.[23]

Trade journals enable organizations to aim at a much more specific group of potential applicants. Ads in trade journals are often more creative and professional and the paper stock quality is better than newsprint. Unfortunately, long lead times are required and thus the ads can become outdated.

Preparing ads to be placed in newspapers and trade journals requires considerable skill. Many organizations hire advertising firms to do this rather than spend the time and money to do it themselves. Selecting an advertising agency must be done with as much care as is used in selecting a private recruiting agency. A typical advertisement is shown in Exhibit 5.5.

COMPUTERIZED SERVICES. An external method of growing popularity is the computerized recruiting service. It provides a place to both list job openings and locate job applicants. Some recruiting firms collect systematic information from multiple sources and make their data bank available to customers. Customers can hook into the data bank via a computer terminal and can find qualified people in a few minutes (it might take seven or eight hours to do the same search by going through paper résumés). Other companies supply their customers with a CD that is updated a number of times each year.

ACQUISITIONS AND MERGERS. A significant result of the merger or acquisition process is a large pool of employees, some of whom may no longer be necessary in the new organization in their old capacity. Consequently, the new organization has a large number of potential job applicants (although they are current employees) who are already qualified. A merger or acquisition may create new jobs and may also require the retention of old jobs. For these new jobs, the pool of employees rendered redundant becomes the pool of potentially qualified applicants. For the old jobs (those unchanged), the pool of employees is formed by the most qualified people currently employed in those positions.

In contrast to other external methods, acquisitions and mergers enable an organization to obtain a large pool of highly qualified individuals quickly, thus potentially facilitating its strategic plans. An organization may be able to pursue a strategic business plan, such as

Exhibit 5.5
A Typical Newspaper Advertisement

BOEING

BOEING CANADA TECHNOLOGY LTD., WINNIPEG DIVISION, has made the commitment to be a "World Class" manufacturer and to strengthen its leadership position in the Aerospace Industry. We are now seeking an individual to accept the challenges of working in this environment in the following area:

Senior Systems Analyst
CATIA Specialist

This position offers a challenging opportunity for a highly motivated individual to provide systems management/technical support in the installation, development and maintenance in a (mainframe) CAD/CAM/CIM environment. This individual should have strong communication skills to provide support and consultation for end user products and services.

The successful candidate will possess a degree or diploma in Computer Science or Engineering plus at least 4 years related experience in systems support of manufacturing/aerospace applications. Sound knowledge of CATIA modules with emphasis on manufacturing integration plus experience with MVS/ESA, TSO/ISPF, DFDSS, RACF and data communications facilities are required.

Boeing is an equal opportunity employer offering a competitive salary and benefits. Interested candidates may forward a detailed résumé to the Human Resources Department at:

Boeing Winnipeg
99 Murray Park Road
Winnipeg, Manitoba
R3J 3M6

Quality
Planemaker
to the World

having a sudden abundance of talent enter a new product line, that would be impossible using other recruiting methods. However, mergers and acquisitions require the displacement of excess employees and the integration of a large number of employees into a new organization rather quickly. Consequently, recruiting via acquisitions and mergers needs to be closely tied in with HR planning and selection.

Which of the many methods described above is the best for recruiting each occupational group? Based upon a survey of HR executives conducted by the Bureau of National Affairs, the best methods, or those most effective, varied across occupations. For example,

Assessment of Methods

private employment agencies were most effective for applicants in sales, professional, technical, and management positions, whereas walk-ins were most effective for office/clerical and plant/service applicants.

While the results of the survey are informative, they only represent the executives' perceptions regarding what is effective. If a cost–benefit analysis were done on each method, the results could be quite different. Such an analysis would require that the costs involved in using a method of recruiting be measured and then compared to the benefits derived. The costs of travel, hotel, and salary incurred by a recruiter visiting a college campus, for example, would be easy to determine. The benefits from the college recruiting, however, can be very difficult to measure (especially in dollar amounts). Is the length of time an applicant stays on the job once hired a benefit from recruiting? If it is, how is the value of this benefit determined? Can it be translated into dollars and cents? Presently, it appears difficult to determine the monetary benefits of recruiting methods. It might be more feasible, for example, to record the length of time that hired applicants acquired by each recruiting method stay on the job, and then compare the results. These results can then be compared with the costs of each method.

Another way the utility of each method can be determined is by comparing the number of potentially qualified applicants hired by each method for each occupational group. The methods resulting in the hiring of the most qualified applicants in each group may be determined the most effective, even if not the least expensive.

INCREASING THE POOL OF POTENTIALLY QUALIFIED APPLICANTS

Although organizations may use both external and internal sources of recruitment, they may not always obtain a sufficient or desired number of the applicants they want, or retain those employees of most value to the organization. This is especially true in highly competitive markets and for highly skilled individuals.[42] The organization can, however, enhance recruitment through the enticements it offers, such as relocation assistance, career development programs, or child-care services. It is an added benefit that many things companies are doing to increase applicant pools also increase the probability that, once hired, the applicant-employee will stay.

Before looking at what the organization can do to attract potentially qualified applicants (PQAs), it is useful to look first at the applicants. That is, if organizations want to attract candidates, it is necessary to know *what* attracts them and *how* they are attracted. In essence, to know how candidates are attracted, one must know where they get their information regarding job availability. To gain a competitive edge, organizations must also understand and meet the needs of job seekers. To increase the likelihood of successful recruitment, a number of strategies can be used.

Conveying Job and Organizational Information

The traditional approach to recruiting involves matching the job applicant's SKAs, with the demands of the job. The more recent approach to recruiting adds to this concern with matching the job applicant's PIPs with the job and the organizational culture. Effective HRM strives to not only match individuals with jobs, but to ensure long retention.

Achieving both is possible by (1) devoting attention to the job interview, (2) having a job matching program, (3) carefully timing recruitment procedures, (4) developing policies regarding job offer acceptances, and (5) expanding career and job options.

JOB INTERVIEW.   A vital aspect of the recruitment process is the interview. A good interview provides the applicant with a realistic preview of the job. A good interview can be an enticement for an applicant to join an organization, just a bad interview can turn away many applicants.

The quality of the interview can partially determine whether or not an applicant will accept a job, if offered. Other things being equal, the chances of a person's accepting a job offer increase when interviewers show interest and concern for the applicant. In addition, it has been found that college students feel most positive toward the recruitment interview when they can take at least half of the interview time to ask questions of the interviewer and when they are not embarrassed or put on the spot by the interviewer.

The content of the recruitment interview is also important. Organizations often assume that it is in their best interest to tell a job applicant only the positive aspects of the organization. But it has been reported in studies by the life insurance industry that providing realistic (positive and negative) information actually increases the number of eventual recruits. In addition, those who receive realistic job information are less likely to quit once they accept the job.[24]

In some cases, when candidates receive inaccurate information about the company, they have sued for misrepresentation. The HRM in the News Vignette shows one such case. Although the company lost initially, it won the case in an appeal, but, in any event, was forced to spend a considerable amount for legal defence and other expenses. The firm's reputation was damaged, regardless of winning the case in court.

Assuming the job applicants pass an initial screening, they should be given the opportunity to have an interview with a potential supervisor and even co-workers. The interview with the potential supervisor is crucial, for this is the person who often makes the final decision.

JOB MATCHING. Job matching is a systematic effort to identify people's SKAs and PIPs of people and to match them to the job openings. Increasing pressure on organizations to maintain effective recruitment, selection, and placement of new and current employees may make an automated job-matching system worthwhile. For example, Citibank's job-matching system for nonprofessional employees evolved from an automated system designed to monitor job requisition and internal placement processes. The system is currently used to identify suitable positions for staff members who wish to transfer or who are seeking another job due to technological displacement or reorganization, and to ensure that suitable internal candidates have not been overlooked before recruiting begins outside the organization. Thus, the system appears not only to help recruit people and ensure that they stay, but also to provide a firm basis for job-related recruitment and selection procedures.

There are two major components in a job-matching system: *job profiles* and *candidate profiles*. **Job profiles** are elaborate job descriptions and job specifications. **Candidate profiles** contain information regarding the candidate's experience or skills related to specific jobs. These jobs are the same ones described in the job profiles. The candidate profile also lists their job preferences and interests. With these profiles, the organization can identify many more potentially qualified job applicants for specific jobs.

TIMING OF RECRUITMENT PROCEDURES. In markets where recruiting occurs in well-defined cycles (as in college recruiting), organizations have the option of being either early or late entrants into the recruiting process. Assuming that most individuals evaluate job options sequentially, organizations enhance their chances of obtaining high-potential candidates through very early entry into the recruitment process. For example, high technology companies begin the recruitment process by involving high-potential juniors in summer internships or cooperative education programs. Progressive organizations are also bypassing traditional second semester campus interviews and inviting high-potential candidates directly to corporate headquarters early in the senior year. Most major accounting firms have job offers accepted by year-end. Such strategies are designed to induce commitment from top graduates before exposure to competing firms. Organizations that rely on traditional second-semester interviews and long selection processes may find themselves in a less competitive position than their more aggressive recruitment rivals.

HRM IN THE NEWS VIGNETTE
Creating a Competitive Canada

MINIMIZING HIRING RISKS

Overselling in the hiring process probably cost Ottawa software house Cognos Inc. in excess of $180,000.

Estimate Real Costs:

• Damages	$67,000
• Prejudgement interest	9,000
• Legal fees	40,000
• Training expenses and learning curves	15,000
• Original hiring costs	15,000
• Move and relocation to Ottawa	5,000
• Down-time in Cognos management in preparation and testimony	9,000
• Ineffectiveness of Mr. Queen after reassignment	20,000
Total estimated real costs	$180,000

Intangible Costs:

- Damage to corporate image and reputation;
- Effect on staff morale and resulting lower productivity;
- Risk of additional litigation from other employees.

Mr. Queen won $67,000 in damages for negligent misrepresentation; the job for which he left Calgary and came east was never formally approved by Cognos, and was curtailed shortly after his arrival. He was transferred to fill-in jobs and dismissed barely a year later.

Source: Excerpt from an article of the same title by W.R. Gale and J.A.L. Compton in *The Human Resource*, Dec. 89/Jan. 90 Reprinted with permission.

WRONGFUL HIRING VERDICT QUASHED BY APPEAL COURT

The Ontario Court of Appeal has overturned what has become known as the wrongful hiring case. "Employers will be delighted to hear this," lawyer Randall Scott... said ... about the appeal judgement. "It will certainly allow recruiters to sleep a little better at night and I think frankly it will send the message that wrongful hiring is not nearly the hot potato it was perceived to be." However, he added, the decision doesn't mean that employers can make careless statements about a job to prospective staff. "It merely restricts their duty to emphasize the downside when recruiting."

The case created a buzz among human resource managers concerned that their companies could be caught by similar claims of promises unmet. It even led to seminars advising how to avoid such situations.

There are two main reasons for the Court of Appeal's reversal.... The first is that Mr. Queen had an employment contract with Cognos including a clause allowing him to be let go without cause on one month's notice.... The second is that Sean Johnson, the Cognos official directly responsible for hiring Mr. Queen, believed the representation about the company that he made to Mr. Queen—that it was going ahead with the project he was being hired for. Mr. Johnson himself lost his job when that project was curtailed.

Source: Excerpt from a feature article of the same title by M. Gibb-Clark in *The Globe and Mail*, 11 May 1990, Reprinted with permission.

POLICIES REGARDING JOB OFFER ACCEPTANCE. Employers can also influence job applicants' selection decisions through the amount of time they allow individuals to ponder their offer. Giving unlimited time to do so will result in delays by the job seekers because they may not have completed their job search. While potentially advantageous to job seekers, the lack of a deadline places the organization at a distinct disadvantage. Unless job openings are unlimited, the organization cannot extend an offer to a second-choice candidate until a decision is made by the preferred candidate.

The attractiveness of the organization can be enhanced by providing some extras to the job applicant. Some of the more common attractions include career opportunities, reducing job stereotyping, relocation assistance, and child-care assistance.

Expanding Career and Job Opportunities

CAREER OPPORTUNITIES. Career opportunities involve several choices for the organization. First, should the organization have an active policy of promotion from within? Second, should the organization be committed to a training and development program to provide sufficient candidates for internal promotion? If the answers to these questions are "yes," then the organization must identify career ladders consistent with organizational and job requirements, and employee skills and preferences.

An organization may identify several career paths for different groups or types of employees. This concept is based on the premise that an organization cannot afford to recruit applicants for lower level jobs when they already possess those skills necessary for higher level jobs. This actually occurs, however, with many people recruited from college. Although they are essentially overqualified for their first jobs, the organization hires them for more difficult "future" jobs. This approach is partially to blame for the higher turnover rate of new college graduates. It is also a cause for concern regarding legal compliance. Employers may claim that a college degree is necessary for the second or third job. Such a policy can lead to discriminatory barriers for recruitment and promotion.

One way to reduce the possibility of discrimination is for an organization to establish career ladders and career paths. When organizations have career ladders and paths with clearly specified requirements, anchored in sound job analyses, they can present a better legal defence for their recruitment policy. Organizations with clearly defined career ladders may also have an easier time attracting and recruiting qualified job applicants, and have a better chance of keeping employees (career paths are also discussed in Chapter 12).

An attractive way to begin recruitment is to offer temporary career opportunities to individuals, especially those who are less apt to be familiar with organizational life. Two of the most popular temporary opportunities are summer internships for college students and internships for middle-aged women looking for careers.

REDUCING JOB GENDER-TYPING. In Chapter 3, job gender-typing and sex–role stereotyping were discussed in explaining why females and males traditionally occupy the jobs they do. To open up job opportunities, organizations can "de-gender" job titles, and by doing this they can avoid use of the "old boy network" for recruitment and requests for "male only applicants." Although these changes will help increase pools of applicants for many more jobs, especially the top jobs, the increases are likely to be gradual, based upon the progress of the 1980s.

RELOCATION ASSISTANCE. As organizations find employees are more reluctant to relocate, they find it necessary to provide relocation assistance. This assistance can be made available for employees who are promoted or transferred. In recent years, the costs of relocation have soared for both the individual and the organization. Providing low-interest mortgages to employees who have to sell their houses in one town and buy houses in the new town (often with mortgages at much higher interest rates) is one increasingly common form of relocation assistance.

CHILD-CARE ASSISTANCE. Many Canadian employers are providing some kind of child-care services for their employees. The provision of such benefits may cause reductions in turnover, tardiness, and absenteeism, and improvements in recruiting success, morale, productivity, public relations, and product quality. There is a wide spectrum of child-care services available for meeting the needs of working parents. Organizations can:

- *Support existing facilities.* Employers can help lower program costs for participants and, at the same time, improve the delivery of child-care services by contributing funds or products or donating "in-kind" assistance.
- *Set up information and referral systems.* To help eliminate some of the worries of being a working parent, the personnel department can keep a current list of child-care centres, including fee schedules and eligibility requirements.
- *Subsidize employees' child-care costs.* Providing vouchers and "subletting" centre slots are the two most common ways of underwriting child-care expenses. In the former, the employer issues a voucher for use at any participating centre, which then bills the company for the amount of the subsidy. Under the latter arrangement, management reserves a number of slots in a centre and then passes along to employees the savings associated with the group rate.
- *Establish a child-care centre.* Where community services are deficient, management can set up its own child-care program for workers, or even join with other area employers to form a community centre.

Although providing these types of programs is expensive, it is probably less costly than less effective recruitment and increased absenteeism and turnover, which result from not having these programs. However, to help keep costs in line and to provide the most appropriate assistance, the HR department should conduct a careful analysis of the organization's needs for this type of service and a careful review of what is available in the community. In Canada, the provision of child-care service to working mothers is much more prevalent in the health and service industries than in the industrial sector. The results of a number of studies indicate that although such service by the employer aids in attraction and retention of some employees, the reduction of absence and tardiness is not apparent.[25] In the mid-1980s there were an estimated ninety-one worksite child-care centres across Canada, and many employers provided this service for different reasons.[26]

Other forms of benefit include a host of alternative work arrangements, such as flextime, compressed work week, job sharing, and part-time work, all of which are part of an attempt to improve the QWL and are discussed in more detail in Chapter 13.

TRENDS IN RECRUITMENT

Assessing Recruitment Activity

The recruitment activity is supposed to attract the right people at the right time within legal limits so that both people and organizations select each other in their best short-run and long-run interests. Recruitment is not just concerned with attracting people, but rather with attracting those whose PIPs will most likely be matched by the needs of the organization, and who have the SKAs to perform adequately. It is only by matching PIPs and SKAs with the organization's needs that the recruitment activity will result in productive long-term employees.

Job performance and turnover are benefit criteria for recruitment and their value could be assessed. Another benefit criterion by which to assess recruiting is legal compliance. Job applicants must be recruited fairly and without discrimination. During the entry and post-entry stages, they must also receive fair opportunities to be matched to appropriate jobs and to perform to their maximum abilities. Thus, the value of the costs saved (benefits gained) from not paying fines should be assessed (as it should be for selection).

In addition to assessing each benefit criterion of recruitment, each method or source of recruitment can be evaluated or costed out. For example, for each method, such as radio advertising or employee referrals, the cost per applicant and cost per hire can be determined. One can determine the value of the benefit criteria for each method, such as the average length of time the newly hired employee stays and the average level of performance of each employee. All the costs and benefits of each method can then be compared.

HRM DYNAMICS
Recruitment Profiles of Selected Canadian Organizations

Air Canada

Like most other large corporations, Air Canada tries to promote from within in order to provide career opportunities to its employees. A standard "Position Vacancy Advice" form describing the minimum job requirements is posted for a two-week period. Any interested employee is required to advise the direct supervisor, who normally is required to submit a recommendation to the HR department. Based on the applications and recommentations, the HR department decides who will proceed to an interview. When the candidate is not found internally, external sources are used, primarily through advertisement. In the last campaign to hire 600 flight attendants, over 20,000 applications were received.

Canadian Pacific Rail (CPR)

CPR typically forecasts its job vacancies annually, through its HR planning. Its HR department will then receive the applications and, depending upon the position, will decide how to go about filling it. Typically, however, recruitment is from within. Promotions and transfers are done through a computer matching system. The company will check the files to see if there are any internally qualified candidates. The latter will be notified and if they wish may participate in an interview. CP Rail also has an excellent job posting program called "The Aspire—Hire Program," which has been in place since 1974. It consists of posting various job openings and encouraging employees to apply by sending a résumé. For the past few years the company has been attempting to implement an affirmative action program for minorities and, most specifically, the handicapped.

Hewlett Packard (HP) Canada

HP Canada strongly supports internal recruitment. Many of the vacant positions are filled by employee transfers. Occasionally, the company resorts to an advertising campaign, on-campus recruitment, or the services of a professional private employment agency. In favouring internal sources, HP has a policy that all employees are eligible to apply to a posted job as long as they have been working in their present job for six months (for an entry-level position), twelve months (most other positions), or eighteen months (management positions). For an employee referral, the company provides a symbolic award in the form of either a dinner for two (value of $80) or a calculator of the same value. According to company statistics, these recruitment policies are very satisfactory; the turnover rate is 2 percent lower than the average in the same type of industry.

On the basis of this comparison, some methods may be used more, some dropped, or some just modified to reduce their costs. Recruiting sources can be assessed in a similar way.

Many organizations receive unsolicited employment applications every year. In order to maintain their image, they normally acknowledge these applications, and if they wish to retain the information for future use, they must develop a tracking system. Data on applicants is important for employment equity records and for controlling the recruitment function. The monitoring of all these functions is managed through a computerized tracking system. About half of the firms that responded to a survey conducted by the Association of Human Resource Systems Professionals in 1987 reported having such a system.

Computer
Applications

According to a recent writing, this number is definitely higher today since more than sixty packaged applicant-tracking systems are available on the market.[27]

Along with applicant tracking there are systems that track requisitions, maintain skills inventories of existing employees, control internal job posting, and monitor special populations with the view of generating reports to the government in compliance with legal requirements.

S U M M A R Y

Recruiting is a major activity in an organization's program to manage its human resources. After HR needs have been established and job requirements have been identified through job analysis, a program of recruitment can be established to produce a pool of potentially qualified job applicants. These applicants can be obtained from internal or external sources.

For recruiting to be effective, it must not only consider the needs of the organization, but those of society and the individual. Society's needs are most explicitly defined by various federal and provincial regulations in the name of equal employment opportunity. The needs of individuals figure prominently in two aspects of recruiting: attracting candidates and retaining desirable employees. The legal commitments and obligations that influence an organization's recruitment activity most significantly are those associated with affirmative action programs.

Once legal considerations are established, the organization must recruit a sufficient number of potentially qualified applicants so that the individuals selected are adequately matched to the job. This matching will help ensure that the individuals will perform effectively and not leave the organization. Organizations can attract and retain these job applicants by numerous methods and through various sources. Although some methods and sources are more effective than others, the ones chosen are often necessarily determined by the type of applicant sought.

If the traditional sources and methods fail to produce a sufficient number of potentially qualified applicants, organizations can make employment seem more desirable and feasible for the applicant. This can be done by providing child-care facilities, by reducing gender–job and sex–role stereotyping, and by providing other conditions that support a high QWL.

P O S T S C R I P T

In 1992–93, when the present text was written, a very few "lucky" companies were recruiting. As the jobless rate hit a six-year high, often the vocabulary used in organizations was that of "de-hiring," "downsizing," "rightsizing," and the like. Consequently, much of the discussion in this chapter may seem to be less relevant. This means that for most jobs, almost any source of recruitment will likely generate a huge turnout of job applicants. For example, when Lotto–Quebec advertised the need to staff 850 positions in its new casino operation, 150,000 people applied. These are the realities of the market. Nevertheless, if we look to the horizon, it is evident that serious shortages of some skills will be evident and companies cannot afford to be fooled by present conditions and be complacent. In the next decade, nearly two-thirds of all new jobs created will require at least a high school diploma and 40 percent of these jobs will require more than 16 years of training. This was also echoed by the recently released study produced by Michael Porter, a Harvard economist, who warns Canadians that their economic competitiveness is at stake. Thus one imminent trend in ensuring the availability of qualified candidates in the future will be the focusing on long-term training.

Yet in the midst of high unemployment, statistics are sounding a new alarm. They indicate an emerging shortage of the skilled and semi-skilled workers most needed in the new age of global competition. A recent survey of 437 organizations concluded that almost 60 percent of them already have difficulties in recruiting four categories: managers and supervisors, professionals, technical and technical support employees, and skilled trades. Although many companies expressed concern about this shortage, very few have acted on their concern.[28] For every company breaking new ground with strategic management changes aimed at recruiting, maintaining, and developing the kinds of employees needed to help the organization achieve a competitive edge, there is another clinging to conventional methods (increased pay, enhanced benefits, automation, or capital investment). The latter make up 60 percent of the 1,500 firms surveyed.

Because of the labour shortages predicted for the last half of the 1990s, and because of the major shift in the profile of these new employees (80 percent will be made up of women, visible minorities, and immigrants), attracting them by traditional methods (an ad in the newspaper for instance) will no longer work. According to a recent report, employers will have to be more creative and proactive in their approach. Some of the new methods may include:

- Advertising in the ethnic press media,
- Utilizing mail and catalogue inserts,
- Hosting an open house at the potential employees' place or region,
- Seeking out handicapped employees,
- Maintaining the current workforce beyond traditional retirement and seeking older employees,
- Making better use of part-time employees.[29]

Moreover, the traditional match between workers' SKAs and organizational demands is giving way to considering workers' PIPs. The more the workforce becomes educated, the more the emphasis will be placed on this type of match, because change and flexibility will be the relevant "buzz-words" in future organizations. From day one of being hired, the emphasis will be on the potential of the newly hired to be promoted, to be transferred or to learn new skills as required by the organization. If once we talked about an expert with limited skills, today we talk more and more about multi-skilled workers. What employers are looking for more and more in their recruitment of new people is those who can diversify, welcome responsibilities, and prepare to zig-zag laterally before moving up.

In many cases, technology itself will dictate this trend. Imagine the traditional manager who has been used to being assisted by a secretary. A growing number of young executives today choose to organize their work without a secretary. This means that they type their own letters and keep their own appointments by carrying electronic agendas, which can easily be accessed and changed. These executives are not doing it because they do not like to be assisted; they do so because they have learned that with full use of computers as a primary management tool, they can have access to various networks and online outside sources instantly. Consequently, they find that they can improve their own competitive edge by having hands-on experience.

Ultimately, one of the best ways to attract good candidates is for the company to maintain a good reputation. Thus, although GM, IBM, and other blue chip companies are currently reducing the workforce and laying off many employees, early indications are that these companies are doing it in the most civilized manner, with real care and assistance for the employees that are let go. Consequently, their behaviour will not tarnish their reputation in the future. Other companies should take note of this example.

REVIEW AND ANALYSIS QUESTIONS

1. What contemporary challenges do organizations face in recruiting job applicants? Do these challenges vary according to the state of the economy?
2. What are the purposes of recruitment and how do those purposes affect other organizational activities?
3. Just-in-time inventory management is a concept that was highly utilized in Japan; it enables manufacturers to assemble products from parts that are delivered as needed rather than kept in inventory, which is costly. Could this concept be applied to the recruitment function and the management of human resources?
4. Are you aware of recent legal developments pertaining to employment equity that are not covered in the text? What are they?
5. Do you know of any large Canadian organization that has successfully implemented an employment equity program (in the spirit of the law)? What are the principles of its success? Elaborate.
6. Why do some organizations use external searches, whereas others use internal searches?
7. Is there a "best" method for recruiting potentially qualified applicants? Give examples to substantiate your answer.
8. How can organizations increase their attractiveness to potential job applicants? What can they do to increase the chances that applicants will stay once hired?
9. Imagine that you are an HR professional in charge of recruiting clerical employees from a labour pool consisting of a large percentage of single parents. What programs might you consider implementing in order to attract qualified single parents to work for your organization? Outline the content of these programs and the rationale for them. (P.S. Keep in mind the relevant legal constraints.)

CASE STUDY

THE PROMISE

Stan Fryer, project leader at General Instruments (GI), knew that today would be one of those proverbial Mondays that managers so often fear. Stan's boss and group manager, Marguerite Albrecht, had left town on business the previous Friday and would not return until the following week. GI, a defense contractor, employs nearly 500 engineers, and designs and manufactures a number of electronic navigation systems. Recruiting qualified engineers has been difficult because of the competitive market in Metropolitan Toronto and the fairly substantial cost-of-living increase for anyone relocating to the area.

Stan's immediate problem this morning concerned a new engineer recruit, June Harrison, a single 23-year-old systems engineer hired three weeks ago upon graduation from the University of Calgary. Much to Stan's surprise, June had submitted her letter of resignation, stating personal reasons as the cause for her departure. In addition to the letter of resignation, Stan also had a memo from June's supervisor, Lou Snider, describing the events leading up to June's resignation.

It seemed, as well as Stan could reconstruct these events, that June was expecting overtime in this week's paycheque because of the extra hours she had put in over the previous three weeks. Lou Snider, however, had neglected to file the proper payroll paperwork so that June could receive her overtime in the current pay period. This did not surprise Stan, given Lou's prior history of not getting the job done in other supervisory positions at GI. Apparently, Stans' boss had reprimanded Lou for filing so much overtime for his section, so Lou decided to spread out some of the overtime charges over several pay periods.

What Lou had not realized was that June had finally secured an apartment in downtown Toronto (she had been renting a room in a nearby hotel) and had committed herself to make a three-month payment and deposit from the amount she expected to receive for both the regular and overtime pay. When June realized what was going to happen, she called Marguerite to set up a meeting to discuss how she could cover her housing expense. June remembered that when she was being recruited, Marguerite had told her to contact her if she ever needed anything or had any problems settling into her new job. Marguerite was in a bit of a rush to make a staff meeting, so she agreed to see June early the following day. When June reported to Marguerite's office the next morning, she was understandably upset when the secretary told her that Marguerite had left town on a business trip. She returned to her office and drafted her resignation letter.

As Stan contemplated how to resolve his problem, he recalled the speech Marguerite had given him two years ago when he joined GI. Marguerite made clear her distaste for young engineers who had a tendency to live beyond their means and to count on bonuses and overtime as if they were regular and assured components of their paycheques. Despite this, Stan decided that the company must try to arrange for a loan covering June's housing expenses and, more importantly, to persuade her to reconsider her hasty decision.

No sooner had Stan decided on a course of action when June appeared in his doorway. She had done some thinking over the weekend after talking with another GI project engineer, a temporary employee hired only for the duration of his project. It seemed that temporary employees earned about 20 percent more than comparable permanent employees at GI, although they received considerably fewer benefits such as retirement and health insurance. June made a proposal to Stan: she would retract her resignation letter if GI would permit her, in effect, to quit and be rehired as a temporary project engineer. Otherwise, she planned to leave GI and accept a standing offer she had received from an engineering firm in her home city of Calgary.

As Stan listened, he wondered how Marguerite would handle this situation. In his own mind, June's proposal sounded more like blackmail.

Case Questions

1. What, in your estimation, created this problem?
2. What recruitment practices might improve GI's ability to attract new engineers?
3. Could June's problem have been prevented? How?
4. If you were Stan, what would you do?

NOTES

1. "Employer Recruitment Practices," *Personnel*, May 1988, 63–65; and B. Schneider and N. Schmitt, *Staffing Organizations*, 2nd ed. (Glenview, Ill., Scott, Foresman, 1986).

2. Information is based on the authors' discussion with Mr. R. Szawlowski, former Manager, Manpower Planning and Development, Pratt & Whitney, Canada. See also R. Szawlowski, "Training and Development in High Technology Industry: Present and Future Trends," *Canadian Readings in Personnel and Human Resource Management*, ed. S.L. Dolan and R.S. Schuler (St. Paul, Minn.: West Publishing Co., 1987), 302–11.

3. *The Employment Law Report*, 1989, 61.

4. H.C. Jain "Employment Equity: Issues and Policies," *Proceedings of the Human Rights and Employment Interdisciplinary Perspectives Conference*, Ottawa 1991: 525–52.

5. J.D. Leck and D.M. Saunders, "Canada's Employment Equity Act: Effects on Employee Selection," *Working Paper #91–10–25*, McGill University, Faculty of Management, 1991.

6. Employment and Immigration Canada, *Report*, Ottawa, 1989, 3

7. Canada, *Employment Equity Act*, Section 4.

8. H.C. Jain, "Human Rights: Issues in Employment," in *Human Resource Management in Canada*, 1983, 50,012. Other cases are cited in the same text, which was revised in 1989, section 50,042.

9. L.R. Sayles and G. Strauss, *Managing Human Resources* (Englewood Cliffs, N.J.: Prentice–Hall, 1977), 147.

10. See A. Patton, "When Executives Bail Out to Move Up," *Business Week*, 13 September 1982, 13, 15, 17, and 19. For a review of the costs of relocation, see H.Z. Levine, "Relocation Practices," *Personnel*, January–February 1982, 4–10; and the entire issue of *Personnel Administrator*, April 1984.

11. M. Axmith and B. Moses, "Career Planning and Relocation Counselling: An Emerging Personnel Function," in *Canadian Readings in Personnel and Human Resource Management*, ed. S.L. Dolan and R.S. Schuler (St. Paul, Minn.: West Publishing Co., 1987), 431–37.

12. "Recruiting and Selection Procedures," in *Personnel Policies Forum, Survey No. 146* (Washington D.C.: BNA, 1988); see also T. Rendero, "Consensus," *Personnel*, September–October 1980, 5.

13. A. Halcrow, "Employees Are Your Best Recruiters," *Personnel Journal*, November 1988, 42–49.

14. C. Green, "Sun Life dangles $1,000 Bonus in Search for Staff," *The Financial Post*, 27 March 1989, 4.

15. S. Arnott, "Recruiting bonus wins mixed support," *The Financial Post*, 22 March 1989, 9.

16. A. Hasan and S. Gera, "Aspects of Job Search in Canada," *Discussion Paper No. 156* (Ottawa: Economic Council of Canada, 1980).

17. S. Magun, "The Placement Activity of the Canadian Employment Agency," *Industrial Relations/Relations Industrielles* 38, 1 (1983): 72–94.

18. L. Millan, "Executive Search Market Mushrooms," *This Week in Business*, 4 November 1989, 18.

19. M. Gibb-Clark, "Managers Urged to Take the High Road, Though It May Be the Long Way Around," *The Globe and Mail*, 25 February 1988, B7.

20. See P. Donohue, "Light and Dark on the Hiring Scene," *Human Resource Management in Canada* (Current Matter, February 1984), 168.

21. "Temporary Help Becoming Permanent Fixture," *Bulletin to Management*, 9 June 1988, 183.

22. A.E. Marshall, "Recruiting Alumni on College Campuses," *Personnel Journal*, April 1982, 264–66.

23. For the Toronto area the average cost is closer to $5,000. See M. Gibb-Clark, "Recruiting companies taking a hard look at advertising," *The Globe and Mail*, 8 May 1989, B30; and D. Marty, "Career Advertising," *The Globe and Mail*, 12 June 1989, B10.

24. For a discussion of the realistic job review or preview, see J.P. Wanous, *Organizational Entry* (Reading, Mass.: Addison–Wesley, 1980); M.D. Hakel, "Employment Interviewing," in *Personnel Management,* ed. K.M. Rowland and G.R. Ferris (Boston: Allyn and Bacon, 1982), 153–54; R.R. Reily et al., "The Effects of Realistic Previews: A Study and Discussion of the Literature," *Personnel Psychology* 34 (1981): 823–34. and R.D. Arvey and J.G. Campion, "The Employment Interview: A Summary and Review of the Recent Literature," *Personnel Psychology* 35 (1982): 281–322.

25. S.L. Dolan, "Working Mothers' Absenteeism: Does Workplace Day-Care Make a Difference?" in *Effective Management Research and Applications* (Proceedings of the Eastern Academy of Management), ed. D. Vredenbourgh and R.S. Schuler (Pittsburgh: Eastern Academy of Management, 1983), 48–51.

26. R. Wright, "Work-Site Day Care in Canada," Feature Report in *Human Resource Management in Canada*, 985, 5,421–5,431.

27. S.E. Forrer and Z.B. Leibowitz, *Using Computers in Human Resources* (San Francisco: Jossey–Bass Publishers, 1991), 24.

28. From a survey conducted by The Hudson Institute of Canada and Towers Perrin Management Consultants, entitled "Workforce 2000." Results were cited by J. Purdie, "Skills Shortage Challenges Management," *The Financial Post*, 11 November 1991,

29. Based on feature article by D. Perry, "The New Recruiting Realities," in *Human Resource Management in Canada*, July 1990, 25,547.

CHAPTER SIX

SELECTION AND ORIENTATION

KEYNOTE ADDRESS

Peter Broadhurst
Vice-President Employee Relations, Litton Systems Canada Ltd.

Challenges to Staffing People in Organizations

At Litton Systems Canada we compete in global markets; our management is measured on global financial criteria, in particular return on capital utilized (ROCU); and we access the global labour market for our talent and skill requirements. These three global realities and the fact that we are subject to Canadian federal and provincial laws and regulations drive our approach to selection and orientation of our people.

The market in which we operate demands that our costs be globally competitive. This has spurred the transition from being predominantly a manufacturing operation to that of a total capability technology-driven company in both the avionics product and systems engineering fields.

The recent recession led to a significant downsizing of some operations. The large associated Canadian-legislated severance costs, which could otherwise have been deployed in new R&D and capital investments, have led to management caution in hiring full-time staff. In future this activity will be regarded in the same light as a "sinking fund," with funding provisions for severance being included in the financial statements.

This situation also drives the company back to its original philosophy of examining everything we do against a "make or buy" discipline, or in the case of human resources "hire or buy." As a result we are transitioning from a classical hierarchical structure, through matrix management, to what is now referred to as a "shamrock configuration."

In this tripartite structure, the full-time professionals, technicians, and managers who are the source of our "core competencies" and are essential to the identity of the organization form the primary group. A second group are consultants and suppliers in various disciplines, services, and products that we retain or purchase on an as-required basis. The third group comprises a flexible pool of part-time and temporary help that are hired in order to handle the fluctuating workloads and special situations.

In our company the human resource function has had to extend its charter to participating in the "hire or buy" process, and then to obtain the appropriate resources from both the global and local labour market in a cost-effective manner.

It is apparent with the present state of the Canadian labour market that Litton is not unique in this respect and that this approach is not only applicable to avionics. With the decimation of both middle-management and staff positions, it is also apparent that many of our selection and orientation processes are based on success criteria that are no longer appropriate to the new structures. The factors outlined above have in general blurred the previously used job descriptions and job competencies to the stage where they require complete revision.

This presents the opportunity to initiate a systems approach to a personnel system built around the concept of "behavioural dimensions" rather than the previous system of performance management derived from management by objectives. Organizing subsystems and programs within subsystems around behaviour dimensions, and basing them on the concept that past and present behaviour predicts future behaviour, leads to more accurate assessment. Behaviour is obtained from different sources such as interviews and direct observation, and is related to the behaviour required on the job. This provides a reasonable prediction of future job-related behaviour. It is possible to apply a content validity strategy to the development of interviewing, assessment, and appraisal programs and thus meet employment equity and human rights requirements.

To sum up, the major issues in selection and orientation are:

- The radical changes in structure and business approach that nullify many existing selection systems;

- The necessity for a selection system to rapidly reflect the new requirements. The behavioural approach allows rapid and valid correlation of new jobs and candidate performance prediction within the available lead times of corporate change;

- A system must meet the Canadian legislative requirements. Our experience with behavioural systems has encouraged us to conclude that this is the right approach;

- The selection and orientation of a variety of full-time, associate, and temporary human resources that will be a feature of competitive companies in the 1990s;

- The selection and orientation function is a primary business management contributor to competitiveness and should be staffed appropriately with high calibre professionals.

• • •

As indicated by the Keynote Address, companies such as Litton Systems Canada are revising the philosophy underlying their selection and orientation systems in order to become more competitive in a global market economy. Some of the changes introduced by Litton are quite radical; they are aimed at cost reduction and increased efficiency in utilizing human resources on the one hand, and complying with the various legislative acts on the other hand. A key strategy is the "make or buy" question. While previously this approach was applicable to products or goods, we now witness an extension of it to human resources. The implications of this approach might be far reaching. However, in order to place this in the proper context, other approaches to selection and orientation need to be elaborated. Consequently, this chapter will present both a traditional and a more complex approach to devising a selection and orientation policy and translating it into action.

• • •

INTRODUCTION TO SELECTION AND ORIENTATION

Selection is the process of gathering legal information about job applicants in order to determine who should be hired for an available position in an organization. **Orientation** and **placement** are concerned with ensuring that job and organizational characteristics match individual SKAs, thereby increasing the likelihood that an individual will become a content and productive long-term employee. Traditionally, selection and orientation have primarily been concerned with evaluating and matching employee SKAs with the demands of the job; currently, however, there is an additional emphasis on matching employees' preferences with job and organizational characteristics. Thus, this chapter is concerned with both matches since it is consistent with our emphasis on serving the individuals as well as the organization. Such a perspective leads to an effective selection and orientation process.

Both the HR department and the line managers play an important role in the selection and orientation activity. Line managers help identify the need for staffing, assist with the job analysis, evaluate employee performance, and assist in inducting new hires to the job. HR departments, however, are responsible for gathering information, sometimes through reference checks, testing and other means, and for arranging interviews between job applicants and line managers. These responsibilities are often assigned to them for several reasons:

- Applicants have only one place to go to apply for a job and have a better chance of being considered for a greater variety of jobs.
- Outside sources of applicants can clear employment issues through one central location.
- Line managers can concentrate on their operating responsibilities; this is especially helpful during peak hiring periods.
- Hiring is done by specialists trained in staffing techniques and, consequently, selection decisions are better.
- With increased government laws and regulations pertaining to selection, it is important to have someone in the organization who is knowledgable about them. HR managers often assume this responsibility, which serves them during the selection and hiring process.

Purposes and Importance of Selection and Orientation

Selection and placement procedures provide the very essence of an organization—its human resources. In addition, effective selection and orientation means attaining several specific purposes, including:

- Contributing to the organization's bottom-line goals. For example, in a study of budget analysts, the dollar value of the productivity of the superior performers (top 15 percent) was $23,000 per year greater than that of low performers (bottom 15 percent). In another study of computer programmers, the dollar value difference was $20,000 per year;[1]
- Ensuring that an organization's financial investment in employees pays off. For example, hiring an assistant professor with a starting salary of $45,000 and 30 percent more in benefits along with annual cost-of-living adjustments (COLAs) of about $1,000 per year, will cost a university approximately $375,000 in six years, before a final decision regarding tenure will be considered;
- Helping fulfil hiring goals and quotas specified in affirmative action programs;
- Minimizing litigations with people who claim to be rejected on discriminatory bases;
- Helping to hire and place job applicants in the best interest of the organization and the individual.

In order to serve these purposes effectively, selection and orientation activities must be integrated with several other HR activities.

Selection and Orientation Relationships and Influences

As illustrated in Exhibit 6.1, selection and orientation decisions begin with a pool of potentially qualified job applicants, an analysis of the qualities of the jobs that are open,

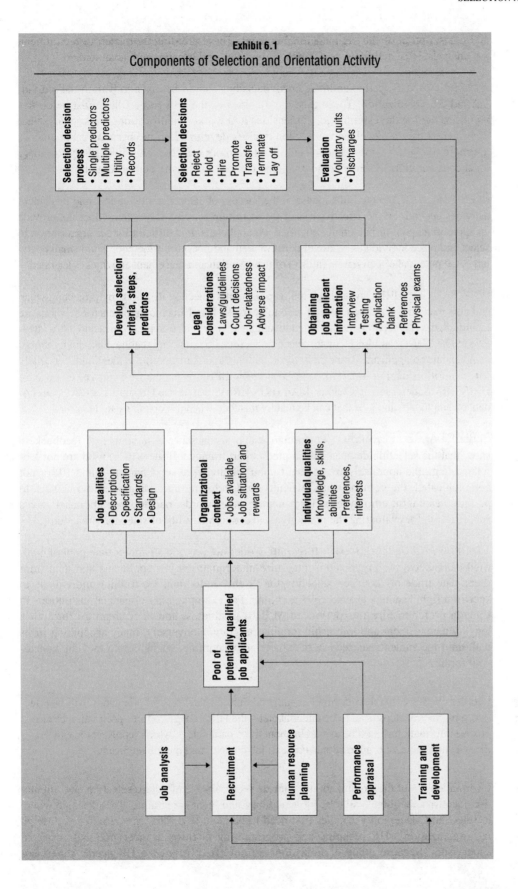

Exhibit 6.1
Components of Selection and Orientation Activity

and a description of the organizational context. These are directly related to recruitment, job analysis, HRP activities, performance appraisal, and training and development.

JOB ANALYSIS. Selection and placement decisions should be made to benefit the individual and the organization. To do this, the qualities of the jobs to be filled must be clearly identified. When the essential job dimensions and worker qualifications are known, selection devices can be developed. Selection devices developed on the basis of a job analysis are more likely to be job-related—and therefore more effective and more likely to satisfy legal considerations because content validity can be more easily demonstrated.

RECRUITMENT. As noted in Chapter 5, the success of selection, orientation, and placement activities depends on the effectiveness of the recruiting activity. If recruiting does not provide an appropriate pool of potentially qualified job applicants, it is difficult for the organization to select and place individuals who will perform well and not quit. If the pool is too small or too large, the potential effectiveness (utility) of the selection and placement activities is lessened.

HR PLANNING. HRP can facilitate the organization's selection decisions by projecting when and how many of such decisions will need to be made. If staffing requirements for new jobs are identified, the HR department may need to anticipate new selection procedures and job-relatedness studies. HRP can also facilitate selection decisions by ensuring that the maximum number of potential job applicants (especially those within the organization) are identified (especially for promotion decisions). This can be done with the use of an extensive, up-to-date HRIS/HRMS, described in Chapter 4. An HRIS/HRMS can be used to store extensive banks of data on employees and jobs that can be readily matched when job openings are identified.

PERFORMANCE APPRAISAL. Performance appraisals serve as a source of feedback to show that the selection devices indeed predict performance. If the criteria used are not job-related (e.g., the appraisals are not built upon job analysis, see Chapters 9 and 10) or not communicated, the company has difficulty in developing and using selection devices to predict meaningful employee performance. In other words, performance appraisal serves as a criterion for evaluating the predictive and economic utility of selection procedures.

TRAINING AND DEVELOPMENT. If recruiting does not provide an appropriate pool of qualified candidates, the organization may hire underqualified job applicants and then train them. The trade-off between selecting the "right" individual vs. training individuals to "perform right" centres around costs and time. For example, many financial institutions in Canada prefer to hire inexperienced M.B.A. graduates, and have them go through a lengthy management and internship training program. Conversely, many accounting firms wait until the students succeed in the chartered accounting exams before they are considered for hire.

SELECTION AND ORIENTATION INFORMATION

In order to ensure that the information gathered during selection and orientation will be effective, a number of steps need to be undertaken by the HR manager. More specifically, clear and precise information should be available about three parameters, which represent the essence of the selection process: organizational context, job context, and the job applicant.

The Organizational Context

Information about the organizational context necessary for effective selection and orientation identifies the jobs available, job situations, and legal constraints. To determine whom to select and place, job vacancies first need to be identified. This can be initiated through the organization's HR planning and programming or through direct requisitions from supervisors. Because many organizations do not effectively plan HR needs, supervisor requisitions often become the major source of information about job openings. However, with some forecasts of managerial and professional shortages by the mid 1990s, more organizations are beginning to systematically program for their HR needs.

Managerial succession programs are evidence of this systematic effort. Without effective HRP, job availability is often not determined until vacancies exist. Consequently, recruitment, selection, and placement may be undertaken without awareness of the jobs that are open, or performed so quickly that a thorough recruitment and selection process is not possible.

Job performance may be determined only in part by the individual. Such organizational characteristics as compensation policies, group pressures, management philosophy, and quality of supervision also determine an individual's level of performance. In fact, there are many job situations in which employee performance is really determined by the pace of the machines more than by any qualities of the employee. Because these aspects of the organization and job situation are so important, they must be accounted for in selection and placement procedures. These organizational characteristics should also be conveyed to job applicants in order for them to determine if the characteristics match their PIPs. For example, two jobs may require the same technical skills. But if one is isolated and the other is part of a larger group, the selection process for the job in the larger group may need to be designed to select people with good interpersonal skills. The selection process for the isolated job might be designed to select people with a low preference for affiliation. The job situation not only influences employee performance but also determines job rewards.

In more prescriptive terms, here are some concrete hints for the practising HR manager:

- Ensure that top management is in agreement to hire and that the budget, if relevant, has been approved and allocated.
- Ensure that you fully understand the requisition form filled out by the supervisor.
- Plan and document the hiring process, particularly where systematic programming (as in the case of requisitions) is absent. Although this is time costly, both recruitment and selection are more thorough.
- Give all candidates an accurate picture of employment conditions and other pertinent information.
- Make the offer of employment in writing, including all verbal commitments and unusual or unique details. Include a clause indicating that this is the whole contract between the parties and that no oral assurances are binding.
- Verify that all legal constraints pertaining to employment equity have been observed.

In order to choose a job realistically, job applicants must know the conditions under which the job is to be performed. For example, it is important for both the applicant and the organization to know the physical conditions that the applicant may confront on the job. Other aspects are time pressures under which the work is performed, the hours of work, and where the work is performed.

The Job Context

In order to do the above, many HR experts suggest providing a copy of the job analysis (described in Chapter 3) to all candidates. Information about job requirements or demands and specifications is obtained from it. This information is needed to match individual SKAs, with job demands. In addition to obtaining job analysis information, job design information should also be provided so that the qualities or characteristics of the job are known. This is critical in helping applicants determine if their interest would be satisfied by the characteristics. To further aid the applicants in choosing jobs and in performing well once hired, standards of performance and other job-related expectations (e.g., absenteeism) should be obtained from the job analysis and conveyed to the applicants.

The Job Applicant

An estimated 50 percent of pertinent information about an applicant's chance to succeed comes directly from the candidate. The specific types of information often obtained about an individual are SKAs, and PIPs. This information, in conjunction with that obtained about the organization and job, is the basis for predicting how successfully an applicant will perform in a future job. Therefore, these pieces of information are often called **predictors**.

Gathering valid and reliable information from job applicants in order for it to be used as a predictor is not easy. In many cases multiple techniques are used to verify the accuracy of the information obtained.

MAKING A SELECTION DECISION

The Concept of Success (Criteria) in Selection

It is important that the criteria selected are critical to the job the organization wants to fill, that is, that they are **job related**. For example, if someone wants to hire a secretary, the reference point should be what an *excellent* secretary is doing. The same applies to any other position. The reference point, or the criterion, is a set of behaviours that represent a very successful job holder. Because very rarely, if ever, job success consists of a single behaviour, it is necessary to identify the range of behaviours that constitute success. A successful manager needs to do a number of things in order to be called a "good manager"; similarly, a successful teacher needs, for instance, to have good knowledge of the material, possess good communication skills, be firm and fair with the students, arrive at class on time, etc. The message is clear: "success" is made up of multiple behaviours that should be clearly identified and measured. Establishing the exact criteria and their relative importance is critical to developing valid predictors and having a valid selection process.

The exact criteria are also important because they help determine the type of information that should be obtained from the job applicants and, to some extent, the method used to gather that information. For example, if absenteeism is an appropriate criterion, a check of references on employment history or a preference test may be used. If quantity of performance is identified as a criterion, a written test measuring an applicant's SKAs may be used.

It should be remembered that the basis for determining the appropriate, relevant, and important criteria is the job analysis, as described in Chapter 3. Exhibit 6.2 shows the selection plan matrix for the position of corporate loan assistant. It identifies the SKAs that are necessary to perform the assistant's job. Since those job dimensions were identified as the essence of the job, they essentially represent the job criteria. Notice that these criteria are behaviours rather than outcomes such as quantity of output or absenteeism. To make a selection decision in this case, then, one must determine whether the SKAs identified as necessary to perform specified behaviours (job dimensions criteria) are present or absent in the applicant. The methods (predictors) by which each skill or behaviour is to be measured are indicated in the matrix in Exhibit 6.2. These measures become the predictors of the applicant's future performance in each job dimension.

Obviously, then, careful attention and consideration must be given to what is meant by "success" on a job. We often disagree about the definition of success on the job (i.e., who is a good manager? a good worker? a good programmer?). Not only might we disagree about the definition of success, but we may also disagree about the standard instruments that are available to measure it. The term "criteria" for the HR specialist means "the evaluation norms" that are used to measure such things as performance, aptitudes, or skills. The type of criterion against which a selection device is validated can vary greatly. At one end of the spectrum are direct measures of output (number of traders, number of grievances, volume of sales) and, at the other end, some companies are using the results of the performance appraisal as a criterion, hence direct output measures are nonexistent for many jobs.

PROBLEMS IN MEASURING JOB SUCCESS. In the HRM literature, two types of criteria are often mentioned: an *ultimate criterion* and an *actual criterion*. The ultimate criterion is a theoretical construct or abstract idea that can never actually be measured. It represents a

Exhibit 6.2
Selection Plan Matrix

FOR: _____ CORPORATE LOAN ASSISTANT _____   DATE: _____

Practices, Procedures, and Tests Used in Selection

1	2		3	4	5	6	7	8	9	10	11	12	13
Coding		Short Title	R = Rank		SAF					DAI	BI/REF		PAF
A	B												
		Knowledges/Skills											
MQ		1. Communication	R		X					X	X		X
MQ		2. Math			X					X	X		X
MQ		3. Writing			X					X	X		X
MQ		4. Reading			X					X	X		X
MQ		5. Researching			X					X	X		X
MQ		6. Organizing	R		X					X	X		X
MQ		7. Listening	R		X					X	X		X
MQ		8. Social skills			X					X	X		X
MT	B	9. Sales	R		X					X	X		X
MQ		10. Interpret	R		X					X	X		X
WT		11. Bank policy											X
MT	C	12. Bank services	R		X					X	X		X
WT		13. Computer											X
WT		14. Credit report											X

MQ = Minimum qualification. MT = May be trained or acquired on the job (desirable). Preference may be given to those who possess this knowledge/skill. When used on a physical characteristic, MT means a reasonable accommodation can be made. WT = Will be trained or acquired on the job because it can be learned in a brief orientation, i.e., 8 h or less. Not evaluated in the selection process. MQ/MT = Lower level is minimum qualification; higher level may be trained or acquired on the job (desirable). MQ/WT = Lower level is minimum qualification; higher level will be trained or acquired on the job. WT part is not measured in the selection process. MT/WT = Lower level may be trained or acquired on the job; higher level will be trained or acquired on the job. WT part is not measured in the selection process. R = Rank. Applicants may be ranked by their level of work skills. This is differentiating among those who possess more and who will probably perform the duties better. Not all the differentiating knowledges, skills, physical characteristics, and "other characteristics" are ranked. SAF = Supplemental application form. WKT = Written knowledge test. ST = Skills test. PCD = Physical capability demonstration. SOI = Structured oral interview. DAI = Departmental appointment interview. BI/REF = Background investigation/Reference check. ME = Medical examination. PAF = Performance appraisal form.

Source: Biddle & Associates, Inc. Reproduced with permission.

complete set of ideal factors that constitute a successful person. The actual criterion is the measurable, referring to real factors that are used to determine or measure success. For example, some organizations use the periodic results of a performance appraisal, or the number of days the individual was absent.

The relationships between the ultimate and the actual criteria can be expressed in terms of two problems: deficiency and contamination. Exhibit 6.3 shows the degree of overlap between the ultimate and actual criteria. The circles represent the conceptual content of each type of criterion. The true and valid elements of job success are described in the shaded area (the relevance).

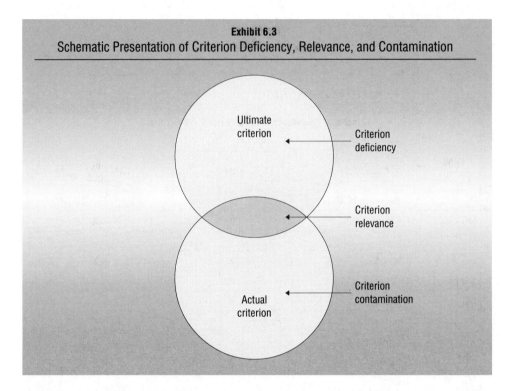

Exhibit 6.3
Schematic Presentation of Criterion Deficiency, Relevance, and Contamination

Criterion deficiency is the degree to which the actual criterion fails to overlap the ultimate criterion (i.e., we fail to include an important job dimension in the overall success on the job). For example, a company omits considering "ability to manage time" in the recent hiring of an executive, or fails to recognize the "ability to play part in a team." There is always some degree of deficiency in the actual criteria used by organizations, but research shows that failing to conduct thorough job analysis increases the chance for neglecting to define important job dimensions.

Criterion contamination refers to the actual criteria that, in fact, are unrelated to the ultimate criteria (e.g., How good is the coffee prepared by the secretary?). Contamination consists normally of two parts. One part, called *bias*, is the extent to which the actual criterion systematically measures something other than what the job is supposed to ultimately entail. For example, if performance appraisal ratings are used as the criterion, bias can be introduced when the particular supervisor who performed the assessment is either too lenient or too demanding. This might result in an evaluation that reflects more the supervisor's personality and standards rather than the actual performance of a given job holder (more on these problems is found in Chapter 9). Unfortunately, the world of work is plagued with biases, and attempts should be made to minimize them. The second part, called *error*, is the extent to which the actual criteria are not related to anything at all. For example, often volume of sales is used as a criterion to assess the performance of real estate agents, when it is fairly well known that their performance is affected by market conditions. Consequently, should the volume of sales be retained as a measure of success, it should be corrected by employing "an adjusted volume of sales."

Managers in many organizations are often puzzled by the difficulties in predicting an applicant's success in a future job. The process of making the selection decision is not a simple one. For companies with a poor record of success in staffing, the problem probably relates to the fact that they either avoid, duck, or neglect defining in behavioural terms or in outcome terms what exactly it is that they wish the candidate to do on the job. Thus, the first step in the process of improving the selection decision is to refine the measure of job success.

What the organization wants is a predictor or set of predictors that will enable it to anticipate how a job applicant will perform according to the job performance criteria. The job-relatedness of a predictor is determined by how accurately it indicates whether the applicant, if hired, will perform successfully in the cited area.

Selection decisions are generally made on the basis of a job applicant's predictor scores. Typically, selection decisions are made using scores from several predictors that are administered to the job applicant sequentially or in steps. Consequently, selection decisions are also made in steps.

STEPS IN THE SELECTION DECISION. The information on which a selection is based is generally gathered in steps or stages. A typical example of the steps in selection used by HR managers is shown in Exhibit 6.4. The order of the steps reflects the common practice (norm), but it may vary according to the type of position and the type of organization. Nonetheless, it should be noted that many organizations decide on the sequence of the steps based on convenience of screening and the number of applicants.

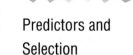

Predictors and Selection

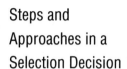

Steps and Approaches in a Selection Decision

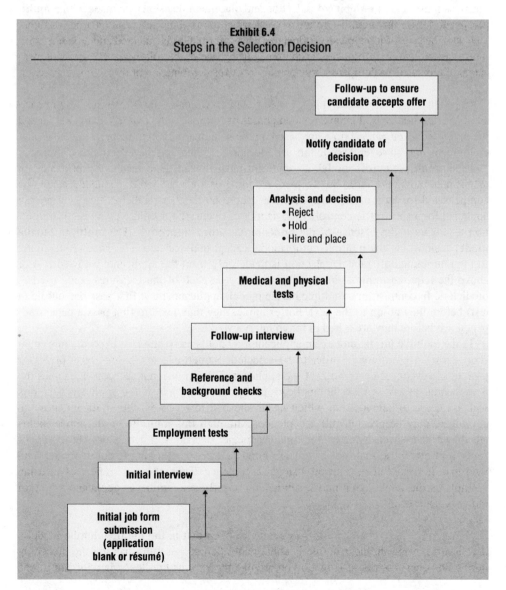

Exhibit 6.4
Steps in the Selection Decision

- Follow-up to ensure candidate accepts offer
- Notify candidate of decision
- Analysis and decision
  - Reject
  - Hold
  - Hire and place
- Medical and physical tests
- Follow-up interview
- Reference and background checks
- Employment tests
- Initial interview
- Initial job form submission (application blank or résumé)

Before arranging these steps the HR manager needs to decide which approach he or she will be using in making the selection decision. Two approaches are commonly used: the single predictor approach, and the multiple predictor approach.

THE SINGLE PREDICTOR APPROACH   When HR managers use only one piece of information or one method for selecting an applicant, they are taking the **single predictor approach.** Single predictors are used by many organizations to select employees, especially when they can be readily validated. This occurs most frequently when a single predictor captures the essence (or the major dimension) of the job, thereby making it easy to validate. But for the vast majority of jobs, a single predictor cannot be used, nor can a single dimension. Many jobs, as stated above, can be fully described only with several job dimensions (duties). For such jobs, several predictors, such as written tests and application blanks, are used in making the selection and placement decisions.

THE MULTIPLE PREDICTORS APPROACH.   When several sources of information are combined, as illustrated in Exhibit 6.4, selection and placement decisions are made with a **multiple predictors approach**. There are several ways to combine information from different sources. The type of job typically influences what information is gathered and how it is combined. Generally, the information is combined using one of the following: (1) a noncompensatory approach, (2) a compensatory approach, or (3) a combination of these two approaches.

Noncompensatory Approach to Multiple Predictors.   Two major models are used in making selection decisions based upon a noncompensatory approach: the *multiple cutoff model* and the *multiple hurdle model*. Both are based on the idea that the job to be performed has several dimensions, so several predictors are appropriate in making the selection decision.

In the **multiple cutoff model,** an applicant must exceed fixed levels of proficiency on *all* the predictors in order to be accepted. A failing or low score on the predictor cannot be compensated for by a higher than necessary score on another predictor. For example, an applicant for an air traffic controller job cannot compensate for failure on a visual recognition test. This is the essence of the **noncompensatory approach.** The **multiple hurdle model** is similar to the multiple cutoff model except that decisions are made sequentially. In the multiple cutoff model, selection is made only from the applicants who score at or above the required minimal levels of proficiency on each of the measures being used as predictors. In contrast, in a multiple hurdle model, applicants must first pass one hurdle (a test) before they go on to the next. For example, they may need to first pass a paper-and-pencil test before they are asked in for an interview.

In the multiple hurdle model, an applicant may not need to attain or exceed a minimum score on each predictor in order to be selected. Sometimes low scores on a predictor prompt a provisional acceptance of the applicant. This provisional acceptance enables the organization to assess how the applicant performs on the job. If the applicant performs well on those dimensions on which he or she had low scores, the applicant, now an employee, may be granted full acceptance. Although this multiple hurdle model helps ensure a higher success rate for the final acceptance decisions, it necessitates hiring applicants who otherwise may not have been hired (e.g., under a multiple cutoff model) and who may not make it beyond provisional acceptance. Thus, there is some cost in using multiple hurdles, although it may result in a more sufficient number of applicants who turn out to be successful.

Common Pitfalls in the Multiple Hurdle Model.   Given that in the multiple hurdle model a decision regarding the next hurdle is contingent upon successfully passing the preceding hurdle, the question arises: How do you arrange the various hurdles? Many organizations sequence them according to comfort and convenience considerations, though convenience does not necessarily reflect the validity of the hurdle. Ideally, hurdles should be sequenced in terms of their relative validity (the more important should be first, and the least important should be placed last). Imagine, for example, a hospital that wishes to hire a cook. Following the successful passing of several hurdles, which included application blanks, interviews, and even simulation, the physical examination (which is the last hurdle) reveals that the candidate has tuberculosis, (i.e., a communicable disease), and cannot work in the kitchen. In cases like this, the proper approach would be to deduce from the criteria the most important requirements for the job, and schedule the hurdles in this order. Consequently, physical health (bona fide) will emerge first. Therefore, it is highly recommended for an employer using a multiple hurdle approach to consider the sequence of the various hurdles not as a function of convenience, but rather of validity.

Compensatory Approach to Multiple Predictors. **Both** of the previous models assume that doing well on one predictor cannot compensate for doing poorly on another one. In situations where this assumption is not applicable, the multiple regression approach is used. This is a **compensatory approach** that assumes that good performance on one predictor can compensate for poor performance on another. A low score on ability, for example, can be compensated for by a high score on motivation. Based on this assumption, a statistical analysis of multiple regression can then be used to combine predictors of job performance.

Combined Approach to Multiple Predictors. **Many** organizations use the combined approach, often beginning with recruitment. This approach may use aspects of both the noncompensatory and compensatory approaches. Generally, the multiple cutoff approach (or part of it) is used first: "You have to get through the door before we'll interview you." Once in the interview, the compensatory approach applies. For example, an organization may establish one minimum requirement—an undergraduate degree in accounting or a high grade-point average—in order to be hired. If this condition is met, other characteristics are negotiable. Thus, when organizations decide to use multiple predictors they need to assess the characteristics of the jobs to determine the appropriate number of predictors and the extent to which predictor scores can compensate for each other.

Until there is a legal challenge, the employer does not have to demonstrate validity or defend the predictors used. Nonetheless, it might prove to be most cost effective for an organization to use only valid predictors and to make sure that each one meets the bottom-line criterion discussed in the previous chapter. In addition to demonstrating the job relatedness of the selection procedures used, employers also should be able to show that nonjob-related procedures and information did not enter into the decision process.

The quality and effectiveness of selection and placement decisions depend upon the organization hiring as many applicants as possible who are good performers. This, in turn, leads to an increase in overall organizational productivity. When an organization makes selection and placement decisions based on predictors (and criteria) that are valid and reliable, employees succeed in their jobs. The meaning of reliability and validity is discussed in the following section.

CONSIDERATIONS IN CHOOSING SELECTION INSTRUMENTS

Reliability

Reliability is the *consistency* or *stability* of a selection instrument (i.e., a predictor or a criterion). This means that the instrument used (be it the results of a written test, or impressions obtained during an interview) should yield the same estimate on repeated uses under identical conditions. In the HR literature, there are references to two types of reliability: test–retest and internal consistency.

TEST–RETEST RELIABILITY. The simplest way to assess a measuring device's reliability is to measure something at two points in time and compare the scores. This is known as **test–retest reliability**. For example, we can administer an intelligence test to a group of applicants three months before the hiring, and again a month before the decision. The two sets of scores are then correlated, and the coefficient that results is called the **coefficient of stability** or the **correlation coefficient** (because it reflects the stability of the test over time). The higher the coefficient of stability the more reliable the measure. As a rule of thumb, stability coefficients around +.70 and higher are professionally accepted.

INTERNAL CONSISTENCY RELIABILITY. **Internal consistency reliability** refers to the extent to which the selection instrument has a homogenous content. It concerns the degree to which the different items on the instrument (a test for example) are measuring the same thing. Because psychological tests are widely used in selection decisions (see next section), an examination of the different ways to assess the test internal consistency is briefly discussed here.

One common method is called *split-half* reliability. During the scoring of the test, items or questions are divided or split in half. Thus, for each person, two scores are computed and these scores are then correlated. If the test is internally consistent, the correlation coefficient is usually high. A closely related technique for assessing internal consistency reliability is to compute a coefficient called Cronbach alpha. Conceptually, each item of a test is thought to be a mini-test in itself and is correlated with the response to every other item. This generates a matrix of inter-item correlations, and all are averaged to get a composite measure of the item similarity or homogeneity of the test. Both reliability coefficients are very popular in HR research.

Validity

Validity refers to how accurately a measure assesses an attribute. Validity is distinguished from reliability in the sense that it refers to the accuracy and precision of measurement. Moreover, while reliability is inherent in a test (or any other selection instrument), validity depends on the use of it. Validity concerns the appropriateness of using a given measuring device for drawing inferences about the criteria. For example, a given test may be highly valid for predicting an employee's direct performance, but totally invalid for predicting attendance. In this case, it would be appropriate to use the predictor for making inferences about direct performance only, but not to predict the employee's absenteeism.

Several types of validity are discussed in HR texts, of which four types are particularly relevant in selection and placement decisions: (a) empirical or criterion-related, (2) content, (3) construct, and (4) differential. Although all of these validities are important, the strategies used to collect the information to demonstrate them are significantly different. Employers should be familiar with them all, so that they can demonstrate the validity of their predictors in defense against adverse impact charges.

EMPIRICAL OR CRITERION-RELATED VALIDITY. As its name suggests, **empirical validity**, or **criterion-related validity**, refers to how much a predictor relates to a criterion (measure of job success). There are two types of empirical validation strategies—*concurrent* and *predictive*—as shown in Exhibit 6.5.

Concurrent Validity. **Concurrent validation** determines the relationship between a predictor and a job criterion score for all employees participating in the study at the same time. For example, to determine the concurrent validity of the correlation between years of experience and job performance of first-line supervisors, HR managers can collect information about each supervisor's years of experience on the job and latest overall performance appraisal scores. All supervisors in the study would have to be working in similar jobs, gen-

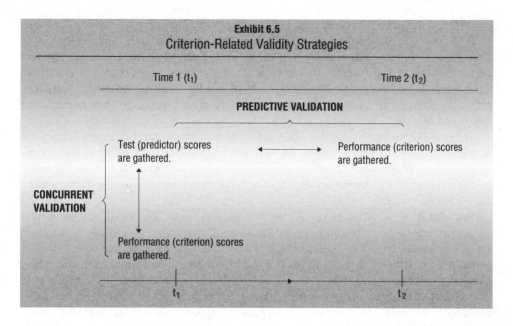

Exhibit 6.5
Criterion-Related Validity Strategies

Time 1 (t₁)   Time 2 (t₂)

PREDICTIVE VALIDATION

Test (predictor) scores are gathered.   Performance (criterion) scores are gathered.

CONCURRENT VALIDATION

Performance (criterion) scores are gathered.

t₁   t₂

erally in the same job family. Then a correlation would be computed. If the correlation is high, it means that supervisors with more experience are better performers, and vice versa. In concurrent validity, there is no time interval between collecting the predictor and the criterion data, since the two are assessed at the same time (*concurrently*). Normally, this is done for deciding if years of experience for applicants to a supervisory position will be a valid predictor in making a selection decision. This validation strategy is simpler, quicker, and less expensive to use than the predictive validity strategy. However, it is less accurate, hence results obtained for already working employees may not be completely relevant for predicting the success of new applicants who have not yet worked for the firm.

Predictive Validity. The steps in **predictive validation** are similar, except that the predictor is measured some time before the criterion is measured, as shown in Exhibit 6.5. Thus, the predictive validity of a test (predictor) is determined by measuring an existing group of applicants on a predictor, and waiting to gather their criterion measure later on. In order to test the empirical validity, all of a random sample of applicants must be hired regardless of their score on the predictor. Otherwise, we cannot find out if those that were already rejected have had the chance to succeed on the job. In the second step of the predictive validation process, a measure of the criterion (performance) needs to be obtained. This is done later on (normally after six months or a year). Again, at that time the correlation coefficient is computed. If it is found that those who initially score higher on the predictor also score higher on the criterion, the validity of the measure is empirically demonstrated. The next time the process need not be repeated, since knowledge about the validity of the instrument can be repeatedly used to select these types of applicants. It should be revised, however, from time to time if the job content changes; in that case other predictors may need to be used. Because this procedure is expensive, most organizations tend to employ the concurrent validation strategy.

In both concurrent and predictive validity, predictor scores are correlated with criterion data. The resulting correlation is referred to as the validity coefficient. The correlation is important because it describes the covariation (linkages) between two measures. A job applicant who passes a welding test, for example, should be able to perform successfully as a welder if the test is valid; an HRM student who performed extremely well in an HRM class, should possess good knowledge about HRM.

It is important to note that there is a range of validity. The degree of validity for a particular measure is indicated by the magnitude of the correlation coefficient, which ranges from –1 or +1 (most valid) to 0 (least valid). In fact, –1 and +1 show perfect validity (perfectly correlated), and 0 shows the absence of validity (perfectly uncorrelated). Perfect validity comes in two forms: **Perfectly positive validity** (+1) means the two variables move in the same direction; **perfectly negative validity** (–1) means they move in the opposite direction.

The **correlation coefficient** discussed here measures the extent or degree of linear relationship between two sets of values, for example, scores on a test (predictor) and performance scores. Illustrations of several linear relationships with validities of +1, –1, and 0 can be represented by plotting actual data of test–criterion relationship on **scattergrams** as shown in Exhibit 6.6.

But what do these values of validity mean in the real world? Perfect validity means that future performance on the job is perfectly predictable from a job applicant's score on selection tests. If the test lacked validity, it would be impossible to predict on the basis of test scores whether one job applicant would be a better performer than the other. Generally, most tests used by organizations have less than perfect validity. That is, tests are not perfect predictors of performance. However, as long as a test has some validity, it is useful to the organization because it can indicate which applicants are most likely to be the best performers.

On many occasions employers are not able to present empirical data for empirical validity determination. Consequently, other methods of validation are necessary. The most common are content and construct validity.

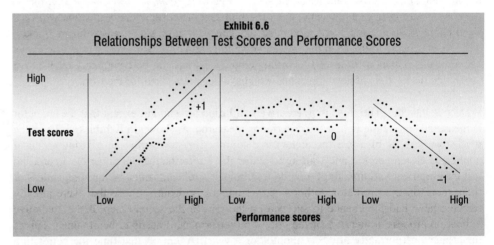

Exhibit 6.6
Relationships Between Test Scores and Performance Scores

CONTENT VALIDITY. **Content validity** differs from empirical validity in that it estimates or judges the relevance of a predictor as an indicator of performance without collecting actual performance information. In essence, job-relatedness here is an estimation or judgment. The administration of a typing test (actually a job sample test if used for typists) as a selection device for hiring typists is a classic example of a predictor judged to have content validity. Notice that in this case the predictor is a skill related to a task that is actually part of the job. Content validity thus refers to predictors that measure SKAs related to those required on the actual job. Thus, to demonstrate content validity it is necessary to know the duties of the actual job and the individual SKAs needed to perform those duties. Unlike criterion-related validity, no statistical correlation is involved in assessing content validity. Rather, experts in the field provide the assessment of relevance.

In order for the experts to develop an appropriate test, they must be familiar with the domain of job behaviour, which needs to be first specified by the organization. Clearly then, job analysis is a critical element in the validation process. It should be regarded as the starting point and the thread that ties together any basic selection and validation study. All in all, the major steps in any validation process are displayed in Exhibit 6.7.

CONSTRUCT VALIDITY. Instead of showing a direct relationship between test results or other selection information (e.g., education or experience levels) and job criteria, selection methods seek to measure (often by tests) the degree to which an applicant possesses abilities and aptitudes ("psychological traits") that are deemed necessary job criteria. These underlying psychological traits are called constructs and include, among many others, intelligence, leadership ability, verbal ability, interpersonal sensitivity, and analytical ability (essentially, the "other category" of applicant information). Constructs deemed necessary for doing well on the job are inferred from job behaviours and activities (duties) indicated in the job analysis. **Construct validity** requires demonstrating that a relationship exists between a selection procedure or test (a measure of the construct) and the psychological trait (construct) it seeks to measure. For example, does a university exam that consists of a case study really measure the extent to which students possess analytical ability? In order to demonstrate construct validity, one would need data showing that high scorers on the test actually analyze more difficult material and are better thinkers than low scorers on the test. If the test is being used in management training, for example, it should also be

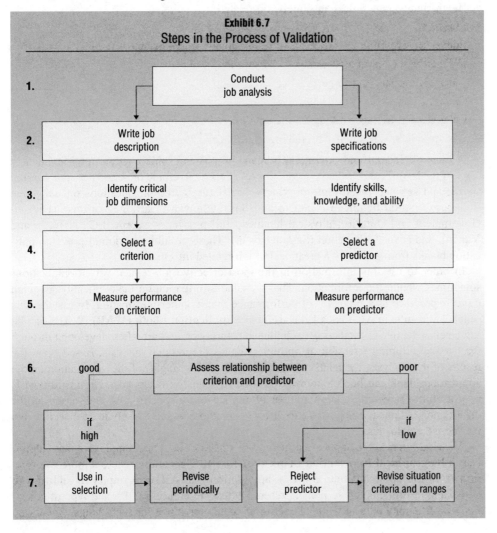

Exhibit 6.7
Steps in the Process of Validation

1. Conduct job analysis

2. Write job description | Write job specifications

3. Identify critical job dimensions | Identify skills, knowledge, and ability

4. Select a criterion | Select a predictor

5. Measure performance on criterion | Measure performance on predictor

6. Assess relationship between criterion and predictor — good / poor

if high | if low

7. Use in selection → Revise periodically | Reject predictor → Revise situation criteria and ranges

necessary to show that analytical ability is related to the duties shown in the job description.

All in all we see that choosing the right candidate and the appropriate device is not a simple process. There are many technical factors that need to be considered in improving the selection decision, of which the choice of predictors is critical.

SELECTION INSTRUMENTS

Application Blanks and Bio Data

Based on the assumption that past behaviour is a good predictor of future behaviour (or performance), the **application blank** seeks information about the applicant's background and present status. These forms are often also called biographical information (or bio data) or résumés. Usually this information is used as an initial or pre-employment screen to decide if the candidate meets the minimum job requirements. Although application blanks formerly requested a great deal of information, legal constraints have reduced the requests substantially.

Information that generally should not be requested in an application blank or an interview because of the difficulty in demonstrating job-relatedness or because it is discriminatory includes:

* The name of a clergy as a reference;
* Whether one has children and who will care for them;
* Height and weight, unless absolutely job-related;
* Marital status;
* Education level or degree (except for professionals where licence is required);
* Conviction record, unless strongly related to job;
* Nature of military discharge;
* Credit history;
* Relatives and friends working for the employer;
* Age, colour, sex, religion, national origin, or race.

Almost all federal and provincial human rights acts prohibit questioning about: age (except for N.W.T. and Yukon), colour, creed or religion; ethnic or national origin; marital status; and sex and race. Some provincial legislatures prohibit questions on: language (Quebec); mental handicap (Ontario and Saskatchewan); pardoned offense (Federal Government and Ontario); physical handicap (all provinces except B.C., N.W.T., and Yukon); and sexual orientation (Saskatchewan). These prohibitions do not prevent application blanks from gathering a great deal of job-related information.

In order to use this information in the most effective job-related way, organizations sometimes weight the information. That is, some information on the application is given more importance as a predictor of performance than is other information. In essence this procedure results in what is called a **weighted application blank (WAB)**. WABs can be extremely effective in predicting such things as turnover, and are often developed through the use of multiple regression or multiple stepwise regression analysis. Based upon the results of the analysis, the relative importance (thus, the weight) of the information on the application blank can be determined and used in selection decisions.[2] The instrument is very useful in screening a large number of applicants for specific jobs and, based on the information obtained, it is possible to differentiate those who are likely to be effective and ineffective employees.

As an addition to the application blank, or even as a substitute, employers may administer a **biographical information blank (BIB)**. A BIB generally requests more information from the applicant than does an application blank. For example, in addition to requesting information about name, present address, references, skills, and type of education, the BIB may request the applicant to indicate preference for such things as working split shifts, being transferred, working on weekends, or working alone. Exactly which items are asked should be a reflection of the nature of the job. If the job does require split shift working, the BIB should include questions regarding preference for split shifts, since the answers may be a good predictor of turnover. Other information often gathered in a BIB is an applicant's work history and pre-work history. For example, an applicant may be asked to indicate whether he or she worked while in high school or had a car in high school. This information, along with other biographical background information, is gathered on the assumption that past behaviours and experiences may be important predictors of future behaviours and experiences, particularly job performance. Using these data for selection assumes behavioural consistency. That is to say: past behaviour is the best indicator of future behaviour.

RESEARCH ON APPLICATION BLANKS/BIOGRAPHICAL DATA QUESTIONNAIRES. Research shows that if the application blank or biographical data questionnaire is carefully constructed, it could be a very useful tool for predicting job success. The literature is filled with evidence of the relatively high validity of this method. While the predictive validity is extremely impressive, it is also worth noting that the application blank method is fair to members of all racial groups.

Other issues relevant to this type of predictor relate to the honesty of the people responding to the questions. The limited information we have on these issues suggests that most people don't lie. However, people seem to be more honest when they think their answers will be verified. It is therefore important to avoid questions that cannot be verified. For example, an application for a secretarial job at the Toronto Symphony Orchestra should not include the question: Do you like classical music? Questions like this lead quite naturally to responses that are perceived by the candidate to be socially desirable by the organization.

A second issue is the stability of the application over time. Most studies show validity decay. Changes in applicant pools, job market conditions, and the job themselves cause the stability (validity) of the information to fluctuate. Therefore a periodic check and revision of items is desired.

In sum, research shows that relative to other selection procedures, questionnaires for biographical data are among the most valid. One researcher notes: "If they gave an Academy Award for the most consistently valid predictors used to forecast job performance, biographical information (as a general class) would be the winner."[3] However, surveys indicate that although most organizations use application blanks, fewer than a third of the larger employers bother to validate them, thereby running the risk of potential discrimination.[4]

Reference Checks

Another way of gathering information is by reference verification. Although listed as the fourth step in the selection process, it may be done earlier. While reference verification is widely practised, its use has raised some legal concerns because it could lead to discriminatory practices. For example, there was a settlement accepted by the Canadian Human Rights Commission against an employment agency in Halifax that had failed to refer a fully trained woman to a job vacancy for an orderly because the employer had specified it wanted a man.[5]

On the other hand, employers should be free to discriminate among job applicants, especially when seeking performance-related information about them. That liberty for the organization often leads to infringement of an individual's privacy. The conflict between liberty and privacy promises to remain a central issue in HR management for the next several years. Consequently, it is getting more difficult to obtain information because of the potential for defamation of character suits. Former employers are becoming "street smart" and are limiting the type of information they give out on departing employees.

If the HR manager conducts the reference check, there are several things that he or she should do to ascertain valid and reliable information:

- Ask the referee who else could comment on the candidate; perhaps someone who can give another point-of-view.
- Ask the referee to compare the candidate with other people he or she has supervised.
- Check with other referees especially to clarify some negative point provided.
- Be prudent, especially if the referee is lukewarm rather than negative; it means that more proving is needed.
- Be forceful if the referee is ducking some questions. For example: On a scale of 1 to 10, how would you rate Mr. Dolan compared to other subordinates?
- Verify whether the candidate will be eligible for rehire by the company; the answer to this question is both the bottom line and the last word in a reference check.

The HR manager should not:
- Use leading questions, such as: She is a good manager, isn't she?
- Forget the obvious such as dates and times.
- Describe the position until the check is completed.
- Allow the referee to focus exclusively on the positives; probing is always needed.
- Focus exclusively on task-related questions. It is important to also get comments about behaviours such as commitment, sense of urgency, attention to details, etc.
- Allow the use of personal relationships as referees. The latter tends not to reveal negative points.

RESEARCH ON REFERENCE CHECKS AND RECOMMENDATIONS. Research has demonstrated that the references listed by the candidate may not be as valid as those obtained from a former employer, peers, and subordinates. Further, some of the most reliable information can be obtained during face-to-face interviews, by observing whether the nonverbal responses coincide with what is being said.[6] Most studies indicate that few employers consider written references alone a reliable source of data. Only references from former immediate supervisors who have recently observed the applicant in a work situation seem to be accurate predictors of the applicant's success in a new job.

The Selection Interview

The interview remains one of the most popular methods of obtaining information. However, while it appears to be a good procedure for gathering factual background information, it is not a particularly good procedure for making assessments because it is too subjective.[7] Nevertheless, employers continue to use the interview for both data gathering and decision making, despite the pressure by agencies such as the various federal and provincial commissions on human rights to use more objective methods of gathering information, i.e., methods or procedures that are more precise and reliable. Such agencies are concerned with interviews because their results can be unreliable (e.g., two people interviewing the same applicant come up with different findings and conclusions), and because they can be used to obtain discriminatory information.

A case in point is *Segrave vs. Zellers (1975)*, where the complainant alleged that he was refused employment because of his sex and marital status. The applicant was interviewed by Zellers' female personnel officer who told him that there were only women in the position he applied for. And further, in the preliminary interview he was rejected for further processing on grounds of his "undesirable marital status." The board of inquiry in Ontario found that Zellers had discriminated against Segrave on both sex and marital status grounds and ordered the company to remedy the hiring practices.[8]

There are a number of reasons for HR professionals' and other managers' insistence on using interviews inspite of their inherent problems: (1) they like to get a personal "feel" for the candidate, (2) they like to have the opportunity to sell the job (and even the organization), and (3) they like to have the opportunity to entertain the candidate's questions. Many managers swear by this method.

Because interviews are used so frequently, it is important to discuss them in more detail and see how they can be used more reliably and in a job-related context. In general, information obtained from interviews is more likely to be job related if the prohibitions listed above for application blanks are observed. Many human rights commissions have published a kit containing "A Guide to Screening & Selection in Employment"; there one can find the list of questions that can and cannot be asked during the interview.[9]

The interview is important at two points in the selection process: the beginning and the end. The way the interview is conducted depends on the type of job being filled. In the case of middle- and upper-level managerial and executive jobs, individuals often submit résumés to organizations (by mail or through a placement or job search firm). An initial interview is made over the phone if the organization wants to gather more information from the applicant. For lower-level management and nonmanagement jobs, an individual may see a job advertised in the newspaper or posted on the organization's bulletin board and fill out an application. Then the initial interview may follow.

Frequently, several individuals interview the applicant, especially for middle- or upper-level managerial or executive positions. Often these interviewers ask for in-depth information about motivation, attitudes, and experience. These interviews are for the purpose of making assessments, not just gathering information. Even the initial interview has an assessment aspect, because a reject/pass decision could be made at that stage. Therefore, both interview stages are crucial.

TYPES OF INTERVIEWS. Interviews can be categorized according to the techniques and format used. One common interview is the **depth interview**. The interviewer has only a general outline of topics to be covered and often pursues them in a rather *unstructured* or nonpatterned way. The interviewees may be allowed to expand on any question they like. Because the quality of this interview depends on the skill of the interviewer, which is difficult to guarantee, organizations often use a **patterned or structured interview**. This interview, in order to ensure consistency, actually resembles an oral questionnaire. But because it is structured, validation studies indicate that the patterned interview can be quite useful in predicting job success.

As indicated above, several individuals may interview an applicant. This is called a **panel interview**, and because of its cost, is usually reserved for managerial job applicants. Another type of interview that may be used for certain types of managerial job applicants is the **stress interview**. The types of jobs (managerial or nonmanagerial) for which applicants would be subjected to a stress interview are those in which it is important to remain calm and composed under pressure. In the stress interview, the applicant may be intentionally annoyed, embarrassed, or frustrated by the interviewer to see how the applicant reacts. Although this may be a particularly good format for certain types of jobs, such as those found in law enforcement and the military, it appears to be less useful (less job-related) for most organizational jobs.

The final form of interview is the **behavioural description interview**. It is based on the assumption that past behaviour is the best predictor of future performance and consequently it requires candidates to give specific examples of how they have solved problems or performed job duties in the past. Here are sample questions from this type of interview:

- Tell me about the last time you had a good idea and had to persuade your superiors to accept it.

- Tell me about a time when you aided an employee in understanding a difficult policy.
- Describe a time when you implemented a procedure to help make your job run more smoothly.[10]

Regardless of the interview format and technique used, there are several problems that can adversely affect interviews. An awareness of them can help reduce their likelihood of occurrence. HR managers can play a key role by making sure that the people doing the interviewing are aware of these problems.

COMMON INTERVIEW PROBLEMS.   There are several problems that interviewers often encounter. They relate to the interview as a procedure for gathering information as well as for assessing that information.

- Managers (as interviewers) do not seek applicant information on all the important dimensions needed for successful job performance (or success in meeting other criteria). Often the interviewers do not have a complete description of the job being filled or an accurate appraisal of its critical requirements. In addition, the interviewer often does not know the conditions under which the job is performed. Nevertheless, for performance and legal reasons, it is important that all the information obtained be job-related.
- Especially when there are several interviewers, managers overlap in their coverage of some job-related questions and miss others entirely. In fact, it may happen that an applicant has not had four interviews but one interview four times.
- Managers may make "snap" judgments early in the interview. Consequently they block out further potentially useful information. Research has found that most interviewers make a decision within the first four to five minutes of an interview. In the remainder of the interview, they search for cues and clues to substantiate the impressions they formed at the initial phase of the interview.
- Managers permit one trait or job-related attribute to influence their evaluation of the remaining qualities of an applicant. This process, called the **halo effect**, occurs when an interviewer judges an applicant's entire potential for job performance on the basis of one characteristic, such as how well the applicant dresses or talks. The halo effect may lead to poor and discriminatory (illegal) choices by the interviewer; it may also affect the choices made by the job applicant: the interviewer becomes the symbol for the company, and yet he or she represents a sample size of only one. Nevertheless, the applicant often places more importance on his or her estimate of the company representative than on judgments based on the company literature.
- Managers have not organized the various selection elements into a system. Key references may not be checked before the intensive interviews, resulting in interviews with unqualified applicants. Occasionally, applicants are treated differently, some given certain tests and others not. This may be a result of lack of clarity on who was to do what. Regardless, it results in unfair and ineffective selection practices.
- Information from interviews with an applicant is not integrated and discussed in a systematic manner.
- If several interviewers share information on an applicant, they may do so in a very haphazard manner. They may not identify job-related information or seek to examine any conflicting information. This casual approach to decision making may save time and confrontation—but only in the short run. In the long run, everyone in the organization will pay for poor hiring decisions.
- Managers' judgments are often affected by pressure to fill the position. As a result, they lower their standards. If this leads to a bad decision, the manager who made the decision can always make an excuse. Managers may also hire an applicant because of low

price (salary demands). HR managers can reduce this possibility by not revealing salary demands to the line managers responsible for hiring. The best philosophy is to select the best person for the job first and then to be concerned with the cost.

- Managers' judgments regarding an applicant are often affected by the available applicants. Two concepts—**contrast effects** and **order effects**—are important here. First, a good person looks better in contrast to a group of average or below-average people (contrast effect). An average person looks below-average or poor in contrast to a group of good or excellent people. Second, there are two important order effects—first impression and last impression. At times a first impression (**primacy effect**) is important and lasting; the first person may become the standard used to evaluate the quality of all the other people. But an interviewer, especially at the end of a long day of interviewing, may be more likely to remember the last person better than many of the other people (**recency effect**). Applicants should be aware and take advantage of these effects. Ideally, they should try to get an interview in the middle of an interviewer's schedule, but this is not always possible.

OVERCOMING POTENTIAL INTERVIEW PROBLEMS. There are several ways to overcome the above problems. The methods suggested below are essentially ways to increase the validity and reliability of the interview (increase its job-relatedness, the scope of qualifications measured, and the consistency and objectivity of the information gathered).

- *Gather only job-related information.* That is, use only information from job-related questions as predictors of future performance. This requires that a job analysis be done on the positions to be filled and, if possible, validation of the predictors being used. Increasing job-relatedness can be facilitated by structuring the interview and using multiple interviewers. This procedure increases the validity in part by increasing the reliability of the interview results.
- *Use past behaviour to predict future behaviour.* Essentially, concentrate on getting information about the applicant's past job behaviour. This background information can be obtained conveniently in the initial interview. It is most useful to obtain specific examples of performance-related experiences and the events surrounding those examples.
- *Coordinate the initial interview and succeeding interviews with each other and with other information-gathering procedures.* Job-related information should be combined in an objective, systematic manner. The coordination and systematic combination of information can aid in reducing quick decisions, bias, and the use of stereotypes in selection. Also assisting in this reduction is the final step.
- *Involve several managers in interviewing and in the final decision.* Although the final decision may be made by only one person, several should be involved in gathering the information and assessing its merits.

NONVERBAL CUES IN INTERVIEWS. Another important aspect of the interview is the nonverbal component, information communicated without words. Things like body movements, gestures, firmness of handshake, eye contact, and physical appearance are all nonverbal cues. Often interviewers put more importance on the nonverbal cues than on the verbal. It has been estimated that, at most, only 30 to 35 percent of the meaning conveyed in a message is verbal; the remainder is nonverbal. Similarly, in terms of attitudes or feelings, one estimate is that merely 7 percent of what is communicated is verbal, while nonverbal factors account for the remaining 93 percent.[11] Therefore, it is important to be aware of nonverbal cues. "In fact, one of the reasons that nonverbal cues are so powerful is that in most cases interviewers are not aware of them as possible causal agents of impression formation."[12]

Written Selection Tests

Written testing is another important procedure for gathering, transmitting, and assessing information about an applicant. In Canada, it is estimated that approximately one-third of all employers use tests to obtain information on job candidates.[13] The most common types of written tests measure ability (cognitive, mechanical, and psychomotor), personality, interest and preferences, and honesty.

The validity and reliability of written tests are of utmost importance for both the organization and the job applicant. Validity and reliability help ensure that an applicant will perform at a certain level. They also help provide the job applicant with a sense of fairness and legality in the selection procedure. While an invalid test that rejects people on all the grounds specified by the federal and provincial human rights acts is prohibited (same grounds as those specified for the application blank), test validity as it relates to discrimination has not yet received as much attention in Canada as it has in the U.S.A. There, since the 1960s, no component of staffing has generated more controversy and criticism than the use of written paper-and-pencil testing. The problems centre around questions of test fairness (or cultural bias), validity, and test item characteristics such as vagueness and irrelevancy.

A major problem for many Canadian companies may arise one day. Many of the tests currently used in Canada were developed in the U.S.A. and validated with different groups of workers. An examination of the catalogue of psychological tests offered by the Corporation of Psychological Research, for example, reveals that less than 10 percent of all the tests offered were properly validated in Canada. If this estimate is correct, a serious potential problem relating to discrimination exists. In one such case, the Supreme Court of Canada ruled that CN Rail must cease using the Bennett Mechanical Comprehension Test because it had an adverse impact on hiring of women for entry-level blue-collar jobs.

While it is essential for each organization to use its own staff to validate the tests it uses, there is no need for it to develop its own tests since it may become too costly. The HR manager can select from over 1,000 tests that are commercially available. Most of them are distributed by a few management consulting firms that will be ready to adapt, and/or further develop the tests to accommodate the organization's needs. It should also be noted that, although many tests typically used for employment decisions are valid predictors of job criteria such as performance, for many jobs in a variety of organizations they should not be used exclusively. The best approach will be to use a test (or a battery of tests) in conjunction with other selection procedures (bio data, interviews, simulations, etc.). Nonetheless, it is useful to understand which tests are the most frequently used in selection.

TYPES OF TESTS. Tests can be classified on the basis of information sought regarding the applicant's personal characteristics and habits. These include aptitude, achievement (or proficiency), and preference, interest, and personality tests.

Aptitude tests measure the potential of individuals to perform. Measures of general aptitude, often referred to as general intelligence tests, include the Wechsler Adult Intelligence Scale and the Stanford–Binet test. These tests are primarily used to predict academic success in a traditional setting. Several multidimensional aptitude tests were developed for organizations including: Differential Aptitude Tests, the Flanagan Aptitude Classification Test, the General Aptitude Test Battery, and the Employee Aptitude Survey. Because they are standardized, they are not specific to any particular job. Yet they are reliable and general enough to be used in many job situations, especially for indicating the contribution that more specific tests can make.

Another group of aptitude tests, called **psychomotor tests**, evaluate a combination of mental and physical aptitudes. Two of the more widely used psychomotor tests are the MacQuarrie Test for Mechanical Ability and the O'Connor Finger and Tweezer Dexterity Test. The MacQuarrie Test measures skills in tracing, tapping, dotting, copying, locating, arranging blocks, and pursuing. This test seems to be a valid predictor for success as an aviation mechanic or stenographer. The O'Connor Test is a valid predictor for power sewing machine operators, dental students, and other occupations requiring manipulative skills. Typical problems from a standardized Test of Mechanical Comprehension are illustrated in Exhibit 6.8.

A final group of aptitude tests relates to personal and interpersonal competence. One **personal competence test**, the Career Maturity Inventory, measures whether individuals know how to make appropriate and timely decisions for themselves and whether they really put forth the effort to do so. It includes five competence tests related to problems, planning, occupational information, self-knowledge, and goal selection. The better the score on these five competency tests, the more likely an individual is to make career decisions resulting in higher satisfaction and performance.

Interpersonal competence tests measure social intelligence. These tests include aspects of intelligence related to social information and nonverbal information, which is involved in human interactions where awareness of attention, perceptions, thoughts, desires, feelings, moods, emotions, intentions, and actions of other persons and of ourselves is important.

Achievement tests predict an individual's performance on the basis of what he or she knows. Validation is required for any test used by an organization, but validating achievement tests is a rather straightforward process. The achievement tests almost become samples of the job to be performed. However, hiring on the basis of achievement tests may exclude applicants who have not had equal access to the opportunities needed to acquire the skills. It should also be noted that some achievement tests are less job-related than others.

Exhibit 6.8
Sample Problems in a Typical Mechanical Comprehension Test

Look at Sample X on this page. It shows two men carrying a weighted object on a plank, and it asks, "Which man carries more weight?" Because the object is closer to man "B" than to man "A," man "B" is shouldering more weight, so blacken the circle under "B" on your answer sheet. Now look at Sample Y and answer it yourself. Fill in the circle under the correct answer on your answer sheet.

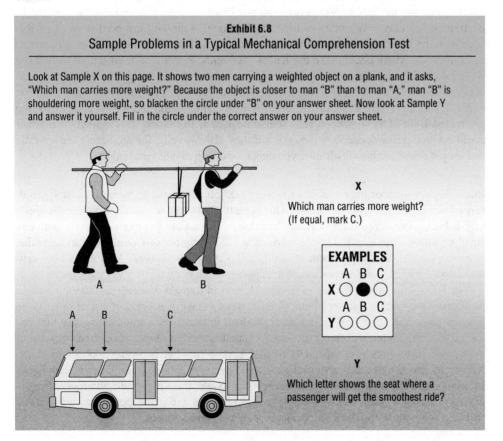

X
Which man carries more weight?
(If equal, mark C.)

EXAMPLES

	A	B	C
X	○	●	○
Y	○	○	○

Y
Which letter shows the seat where a passenger will get the smoothest ride?

Paper-and-pencil achievement tests tend to be less job-related because they measure the applicant's knowledge of facts and principles—not the actual use of them. For example, you could take a paper-and-pencil test measuring your knowledge of tennis and pass with flying colours and yet play the game very poorly. Although this is a serious drawback to these tests, they continue to be used in many areas because of their wide-spread acceptance. For example, admission to the legal profession is through the bar exam, and the medical profession is entered through medical boards. Paper-and-pencil tests are used in these cases because they are related to or are assumed to be related to performance in the actual job. Job-relatedness can be, of course, a necessary legal defence for the use of paper-and-pencil tests (as well as all other tests).

Recognition tests are often used in advertising and modelling. The applicants bring to the job interview portfolios of their work and/or samples of the work they have done. However, portfolios contain no clues to the conditions or circumstances under which they were done. Some organizations may insist on seeing written samples from school work for jobs where written expression may be important. Recognition tests are really examples of past behaviour.

Preference tests and personality tests are distinguished from other types of tests by having no right or wrong answers. Several common multidimensional tests of personality are the Edwards Personal Preference Schedule, the California Psychological Inventory, the Gordon Personal Profile, the Thurstone Temperament Survey, the Guilford–Zimmerman Temperament Survey, and the Minnesota Multiphasic Personality Inventory. At present, the utility of personality tests for selection for most jobs appears limited. They may be useful, however, for placement and career counselling after a selection decision has been made. Orientation and career decisions can thus be facilitated by **interest tests**. Two major interest tests are the Strong Vocational Interest Blank and the Kuder Preference Records. Both are essentially inventories of interests. Although generally not predictive of performance on the job, they can predict which occupation will be more in tune with an individual's interests. Many people take the Kuder Preference Records in high school to find out what jobs or occupations might match their interests. Records are grouped into ten vocational categories—outdoor, musical, computational, scientific, persuasive, artistic, literary, musical, social service, and clerical. Specific jobs can be identified within each of the ten groupings. Both of these interest tests should be used with caution. It is unlikely that either could predict performance in a job, nor are they always valid for predicting the specific type of job one will choose within a vocational or occupational grouping.

Other Categories of Tests

Increasing numbers of organizations routinely ask job applicants to submit to a **polygraph test** as part of the selection procedure. This is particularly true in situations where the applicant is being considered for a fiduciary position or has access to pharmaceuticals or to any small consumer item that has resale value. The U.S. Chamber of Commerce estimates that employees steal $40 billion worth of goods and services every year. Also it has been estimated that between 7 and 10 percent of job applicants are not who they say they are![14]

The information about the use of polygraph tests in Canada is sketchy. Although there is no federal law forcing job applicants or employees to take a polygraph test in order to be hired or promoted, many companies may ask them to sign a release indicating that they are taking the test voluntarily. Generally, the job applicant or employee should be prepared to answer questions honestly, especially as they pertain to what is on the application blank. Refusal to answer questions about religion, sexual activity, politics, and other nonjob issues is appropriate. The test-taker may, however, want to take this up with the employer after the exam. Typically, organizations hire polygraph examiners and place them in an office away from the company with which the applicant is seeking employment.

The use of polygraph testing has been challenged on several grounds, both psychometric and ethical. On psychometric grounds, people question both the validity and reliability of the readings. The polygraph does not measure lies, but variations in a person's breathing, blood pressure, and pulse. With this information, a trained operator interprets the responses. Given that the average length of training for an operator is usually six to eight weeks, opponents of polygraph use question the proficiency of these operators. Low interoperator reliability in interpreting results may be the greatest drawback to using this instrument as a selection device. A second problem relates to its constitutionality and the invasion of privacy of those tested.

As a result of those concerns, twelve states (in the U.S.A.) recently passed laws banning the use of polygraph tests for employment purposes. Nineteen states have laws about licensing requirements for operators. In Canada, a Royal Commission inquiring into the Metropolitan Toronto Police practices concluded that some of the deficiencies of the polygraph were that it is crude and many of the operators are unskilled in its use as a scientific instrument. Justice Monard, who headed the Commission, was amazed to observe the naive and dogmatic pronouncements by the polygraph operators and called for legislative control in this field. As of today, there are only limited legislative efforts in this regard.

Because of the costs and complications involved in using polygraph tests, companies are beginning to use paper-and-pencil **honesty tests** to predict which individuals are likely to lie or steal. The theory behind the honesty test is that attitudes are accurate predictors of behaviour: a thief believes everybody steals, thinks he or she is normal, and will accept dishonest behaviour. A thief will probably enjoy stories of successful crimes and might answer yes to the question: Have you ever been so entertained by the cleverness of a crook that you hoped he or she would get away with it? Other sample questions in a typical honesty test may include:

- Would you tell your boss if you knew of another employee stealing from the company?
- Is it all right to borrow company equipment to use at home if the property is always returned?
- Have you ever wished you were more physically attractive?

Honesty tests are legal, less costly than the polygraph, easier to score, and almost anybody can administer them. Given that honesty tests are a spin-off of the polygraph, however, they suffer the same criticism, especially with regard to their validity and reliability. Very little research has been conducted on the validity and reliability of these paper-and-pencil tests, and the little information that is known is anecdotal in nature. For example, one retail chain indicated that employee theft was cut by 28 percent after the Reid Report (a popular honesty test) was put into use.

Work simulations, which are often called **work sample tests**, require applicants to complete verbal or physical activities under structured supervision and standard conditions. Work sample tests are frequently given to applicants for secretarial jobs. Applicants may be asked to type a letter in the office where they would be working. There is still some artificiality in work sample tests, however, because the selection process itself tends to promote some anxiety and tension. Nevertheless, work samples are used rather extensively because of their applicability and validity.

Work Simulations

Anxiety and tension may not be artificial for certain jobs, such as a managerial job under time pressure. Therefore, a work sample test referred to as the **in-basket exercise** has been created for that type of job. Its objective is to create a realistic situation that will elicit typical on-the-job behaviours. Situations and problems encountered in the job are written on individual sheets of paper and set in the in-basket. The problems or situations described to the applicant involve different groups of people—peers, subordinates, and those outside the organization. The applicant is asked to arrange the papers by priority, and occasionally may need to write an action response. The applicant is usually given a set time limit to take the test but is often interrupted by phone calls meant to create more tension and pressure.

Other work sample tests used in managerial selection are the **leaderless group discussion** (LGD) and **business games**. In the LGD a group of individuals are asked to sit around and discuss a topic for a given period of time. IBM uses an LGD in which each individual makes a five-minute presentation of a candidate for promotion (generally a fictitious person) and then defends this candidate in a group discussion. Business games are living cases. That is, individuals must make decisions and live with them as they would in the in-basket exercise. Because in-basket exercises, LGDs, and business games all tend to be useful in managerial selection, they are often all used together in an assessment centre.

Assessment Centre

In an **assessment centre**, job applicants or current employees are evaluated on how well they might perform in a managerial or higher-level position. Over 20,000 North American companies use this method, and its use grows each year because of its validity in predicting which job applicants will turn out to be successful. In Canada, some of the organizations that regularly use assessment centres include: the Federal Public Service Commission, Ontario-Hydro, and Northern Telecom, to name a few.

An assessment centre is usually attended by six to twelve people chosen by the organization to undergo training. The centre is usually run by the organization for one to three days, and normally off the premises. The performance of attendees is usually evaluated by managers in the organization who are trained assessors. An excellent example of the use of an assessment centre is General Motors' Manufacturing Supervisors Assessment Program. The purpose of the Assessment Program, and the exercises and tests, is to help determine potential promotability of applicants to the first-line supervisory positions.

The General Motors Assessment Program measures eight areas of qualification identified through job analyses and other research as being essential to good performance in manufacturing supervision. These are: (1) organizing and planning, (2) analyzing, (3) decision making, (4) controlling, (5) oral communications, (6) interpersonal relations, (7) influencing, and (8) flexibility. The Program also provides an overall evaluation of each candidate's qualifications.

The Program content includes a wide range of evaluation techniques, such as group problems, interviews, in-baskets, tests, interesting videotape exercises, and questionnaires. These are designed to simulate the situations and problems that manufacturing supervisors regularly encounter on their jobs. As candidates go through these exercises, their performance is observed by a specially trained team of assessors drawn from the local management group. The assessors then meet after the candidates have finished the program to discuss the candidates and prepare evaluations of them, based on the combined judgments of all the assessors, in the areas of performance listed above.

Composite performance in the exercises and tests is often used to determine an assessment centre attendee's future promotability and the organization's HRP requirements and training needs, as well as to make current selection and placement decisions. The composite performance evaluation is generally shared with the attendee, who in turn can use this information for his or her own personal career planning purposes.

COMPARING ASSESSMENT CENTRES TO TRADITIONAL SELECTION METHODS.

Assessment centres (ACs) represent one pole of the sample vs. sign distinction in selection. Thus, in discussing these centres, balance should be maintained by reviewing the success of traditional selection methods. How well do ACs compete, for example, with personality inventories, ability tests, internal staff assessments, and the like? Conventional wisdom suggests that the AC compares very favourably indeed: support for this position was originally based on a review of twenty-two studies that demonstrated the preferential predictive strength of the AC approach.[15] However, it should be noted that a number of discordant voices regarding the preferential status of AC techniques have also been heard, especially in light of the major costs associated with them compared to their effectiveness. For example, one study found that AC ratings were indeed substantially more valid than interview ratings and even paper-and-pencil ability tests administered by the centres themselves, but the statistical difference did not necessarily translate into an economically significant return on the greater investment in AC technique.[16] In conclusion, it is clear that the comparison of AC and traditional means seems far from straightforward. The conventional wisdom that ACs may be more valid is true, but the economic benefits are not always evident. In this light, arguments for the integration of AC techniques with well-formulated, traditional methods take on an added weight. The form and the content of these hybrids remain an avenue for future exploration and analysis.[17]

Perhaps the biggest issues to hit the employment scene in recent years are illegal drug use and medical conditions at the workplace. Not only have these become important factors in the screening process but in the employment community at large. The issues have become concerns to both employers and employees, and many of the arguments at play in general terms also affect the screening issue. For this reason, we will look at these issues in somewhat more detail.

Medical and Physical Parameters

DRUG TESTING. What are the origins of the illicit drug use problem? The main issues are both economic and legal. The U.S. National Institute on Drug Abuse (NIDA) reports that "10 million current users of illicit drugs are employed, costing their employers $26 billion annually in higher health care costs and lost productivity."[18] Although NIDA says little empirical data links drug use to performance problems on the job nationwide, studies within the Postal Service indicate that this group is absent 50 percent more often than other employees. In 1991, an estimated 2.5 million Canadians used illicit drugs on a regular basis.[19] Since drug use is reaching epidemic proportions, many employers advocate the use of drug testing to protect themselves and the public they serve.

There are conflicting views on drug testing issues, because against the advantages that such tests may yield, there is the issue of the personal privacy clearly provided by the Charter of Rights and Freedoms of the Canadian constitution. Generally, employer initiatives that require individuals to submit to drug testing are seen as threats to the personal privacy of the employee.

A recent survey shows that most Canadians favour mandatory drug testing.[20] However, as a result of civil liberties associations' pressures to maintain employee privacy, the federal government has not legislated, as of today, a law permitting such testing. Two recent events, however, represent the first serious attempts by companies to introduce drug testing. The first is the attempt to force top managers in the Toronto-Dominion Bank to submit to drug testing (see HRM in the News Vignette). The second was the announcement in March 1990 by the government that it wanted to introduce drug testing for the 250,000 transportation workers.

Both of these issues were attacked by unions as well as civil liberty groups. Maxwell Yalden, Chief Commissioner of the Canadian Human Rights Commission (CHRC), stated the following key points in a speech to a Commons committee:

- A positive drug test says nothing meaningful about a person's ability to do the job.
- Drug tests done at worksites, rather than in laboratories, may not be highly accurate.
- A special committee of the Ontario section of the Canadian Bar Association recommended a legislative ban on all pre-employment and post-employment drug testing.

• Mandatory random drug testing would be an invasion of privacy.

Consequently, the federal policy states that the use of "positive" results from drug testing to disqualify an applicant from employment considerations may be discriminatory on prohibited grounds.

AIDS. Even more controversial is the issue of AIDS (Acquired Immune Deficiency Syndrome) and employment. Many companies are currently struggling to develop a clear policy. Only a few Canadian organizations have chosen to address the issue, and policies developed mostly consist of educational programs or referring the entire matter to their employee assistance programs. The policy with regard to selection and staffing has not been fully dealt with.

The issues at stake consist of addressing the following: employee rights vs. company liabilities, and the right to privacy vs. the right to know. These controversies are fuelled by public debate that presently borders on hysteria. Advocates of testing cite historical precedence in support of their position. Earlier widespread concern over tuberculosis and syphilis resulted in rational testing policies, and in both cases testing began before cures were found. Opponents of testing cite an unreasonable breach of privacy as their major argument.

From a legal perspective, a few arbitration awards and the policy of the CHRC provide the framework for company policy. The CHRC recognized three occupational situations that could justify treating an employee with an HIV (human immuno-deficiency virus) different from other employees:

1. When the employee is supposed to carry out invasive procedures;
2. When the employee is required to travel to countries where AIDS carriers are barred;
3. When a sudden deterioration of brain or central nervous system functions would compromise public safety.

PHYSICAL EXAMINATIONS AND GENETIC SCREENING. The physical or medical examination is often one of the final steps in the selection process. While many employers give common physical exams to all job applicants, special exams may be given to only a subset of applicants. For example, production job applicants may receive X-ray exams of the back while office job applicants may not. Physical exams, however, should only be used to screen out applicants when the results of the exam indicate that job performance would be adversely affected.

HRM IN THE NEWS VIGNETTE

TD Drug Testing Starts at the Top

About 250 top Toronto-Dominion Bank executives are being asked to submit to drug tests in a program that could be extended to all the bank's employees. "It was not my idea, but the reason that we're doing it is that we want to set an example to employees and to the community," says TD chairman Richard Thomson, who, along with president Robin Korthals, plans to take the urine test. "We've had a good response. Most people were overwhelmingly in favour of it."

"It is a criminal offence to take drugs, and employers have a right to protect themselves," Korthals says. Most Canadian companies do not test employees for fear they will face court challenges. The bank's 250 top executives received private letters asking them to voluntarily submit to the tests as part of their annual medical checkups. If an executive is found to have a drug problem, the bank will help rehabilitation.

Source: S. Horvitch, *The Financial Post*, 8 January 1990, 3. Reprinted with permission.

Some examinations are mandated by government regulations. If any of the following conditions exist in the workplace or during the work process, specific regulations may be referred to for the required testing:

- Respirator use;
- Commercial diving;
- Occupational noise levels above 85 decibels;
- Exposure to lead, asbestos, arsenic, vinyl chloride, coke oven emissions, cotton dust, ethylene oxide, etc.[21]

Physical exams can be used in conjunction with physical ability tests to help ensure that proper job accommodation is made and to provide a record for the employer in order to prevent employees from making workers' compensation claims for pre-existing injuries. The physical abilities that are included in standard tests include such things as dynamic strength, trunk strength, and static strength.

Ensuring that physical ability tests are job related is important, especially where tests produce adverse results. Through the process of attempting to demonstrate the job-relatedness of physical ability tests, such as those for dynamic strength, potentially nonjob-related tests (previously assumed to be job related) may be identified and either modified or replaced. This process may also suggest job modifications that can provide more equal employment opportunity, especially for women and for handicapped individuals (reasonable accommodation here is a necessity anyway), and at the same time maintain the integrity of the job.

Misuse of the physical ability test is illustrated in the following example. The case involved the firing of an experienced waitress on the first day on the job because she had a limp. The British Columbia Council of Human Rights awarded the waitress $2,000 in compensation for the humiliation and mental anguish she suffered and found the operator of Sam's Restaurant guilty of discrimination on the basis of physical handicap. The waitress in this case had more than eleven years of experience. She used a built-up shoe and walked with a limp as a result of polio she had contracted as a child. This handicap, however, did not prevent her from providing good service.

A more recent use of the physical exam is to screen applicants based upon their genetic make-up. **Genetic screening**, as it is called, is based upon the premise that some individuals may be more sensitive than others to workplace elements such as chemicals. The screening is done on the basis of an analysis of an applicant's blood sample, or urine analysis. With approximately 55,000 chemicals in use in industry presently and 800 added yearly, the benefits of genetic testing to millions of Canadian workers exposed to those chemicals daily are most apparent. Both employees and job applicants should be told about their genetic susceptibility so they can decide whether they want to work in this type of environment. However, some legal as well as ethical questions must be asked: Should companies be permitted to select employees according to their inherited probability of contracting occupational illness? Who should bear the cost of adapting workplaces for the employees most susceptible?

Presently there are no laws that deal with genetic testing in the workplace. Genetic screening is still a relatively new issue, but will most likely grow in use in the 1990s. David Bennett, the national representative for Workplace Health and Safety of the Canadian Labour Congress predicts that "companies will employ genetic screening to reduce costs; rather than cleaning up polluted workplaces, they will search for genetically super-resistant workers, shades of George Orwell circa 2004."[22] Recent research, however, suggests that genetic screening can be used more appropriately for placement decisions rather than selection.[23] If all applicants are shown to have equal sensitivity to a workplace chemical, genetic screening information may be used for workplace modification.

ORIENTATION

Orienting and Socializing New Employees

Orientation is the HR activity that introduces new employees to the organization, to their tasks, and to other people the new hire will be working with. In general, orientation is part of the placement process, which also interfaces with the socialization process. The latter provides information about the norms and the organizational culture, which facilitates effective functioning. In an organizational setting, people learn the values, expected behaviours, and social knowledge required to assume an organizational role. A poor orientation process increases a new employee's stress and may be a contributing factor for the new hire to decide not to stay in the organization.

The major purposes of orientation and socialization include:

* *Reduction of start-up costs.* It is expected that a new recruit will be less efficient for a period of time. This period can be substantially reduced with proper orientation.
* *Reduction of stress and anxiety.* A new employee is keen on doing the right things and needs to prove himself or herself, so a perception of not performing up to standards will inevitably cause stress. Another stress results from the attempt to be accepted by other members of the work group. Effective orientation will alert the new employee to what is expected of him or her in the initial period, thereby reducing stress.
* *Reduction in employee turnover.* If the new hire perceives himself or herself to be ineffective or unwanted, they may choose to deal with the negative feeling by looking for another job elsewhere. Proper orientation may reduce turnover rates.
* *Time saving for supervisors and co-workers.* New employees will initially need assistance from both colleagues and superiors to become efficient in their job. The time spent with new recruits can be reduced where orientation is well conducted.

It is important to remember that new employees can represent unparalleled opportunities to the organization. However, much of the enthusiasm, creativity, and commitment is often lost due to poor orientation and ineffective guidance during the socialization process. The goal of the HR department, therefore, is to develop an orientation system that will complement their recruitment and selection efforts aimed at obtaining a successful candidate who will remain motivated and committed to the organization.

Duration, Scope, and Content of an Orientation Program

There are hundreds of different orientation programs used in Canadian firms. They vary in content, scope, and duration. Some companies, such as Hewlett Packard (HP), program the orientation over a twelve-month period. Their program is very detailed and can provide a good example to other companies. Excerpts from the HP orientation program are provided in Exhibit 6.9.

HP orientation program consists of five phases, each of which is targeted at different objectives for the new hire:

Phase I: *Getting Started* starts at day one or even before arrival. New employees receive the information necessary to begin a comfortable transition into the new HP job environment.

Phase II: *Gaining Perspective* continues for the first month. New employees gain a perspective of their manager's expectations and their department's purpose, direction, and relationship with other departments.

Phase III: *Gathering Basics* continues during the second and third months. New employees gather the essence of their duties and, purpose, and gain a conceptual overview of HP's organizational philosophies and purposes.

Phase IV: *Building Integration* covers the fourth to sixth months. New employees gain an in-depth understanding of HP's philosophies and processes, and how their role is integrated with these; they also gain an understanding of the performance evaluation process and how to participate in the creation of their developmental plan.

Phase V: *Charting a Course* lasts from the seventh to the twelve month. New employees gain the knowledge, skills, and access to resources necessary to chart their course of continuous development.

Other companies spend substantially less time on orientation programs. On the average a program may last from a mere two hours to a full day, but it is usually conducted within a week of an employee's initial employment date. At VIA Rail, for example, the orientation session lasts five full weeks and is given by a permanent team of trainers who are assigned to orient the newcomer to the different operations.

Exhibit 6.9
HP Orientation Framework

	PERSONNEL	MANAGER	NEW EMPLOYEE
PHASE ONE Pre-arrival	• T & D keeps guides updated • Personnel sends pre-arrival package to new employee • Personnel delivers Manager's and Employee's Guides to manager	• Receives Manager's and Employee's Guides from Area Personnel • Selects orientation mentor for new employee	• Receives pre-arrival information
First Day/First Week	• Personnel meets with new employee and completes a benefits session and reviews Orientation Process.	• Welcomes new employee and discuss the Employee's Guide • Completes First-Day Checklist	• Meets with T & D • Meets with manager • Meets work group and tours facility
PHASE TWO First Month	• Personnel contacts new employee about progress	• Meets with new employee about Phase Two exercise discussions (2–3 meetings, 1/2 hour)	• Completes Phase Two exercises in Employee's Guide and has meetings with manager
PHASE THREE Second and Third Month	• Personnel coordinates New Employee Orientation Program (NEO)	• Makes sure that new employee is learning job responsibilities • Ensures employee participates in NEO program	• Attends New Employee Orientation Program
PHASE FOUR Fourth to Sixth Month	• Personnel ensures all employees attend the NEO • Personnel calls manager for Orientation Process feedback • Feedback evaluations to T & D	• Formulates development plan with new employees • conducts six-month performance evaluation • Gives Orientation Process feedback to Orientation Coordinator	• Works with manager on development plan • Completes Orientation Content Review and Orientation Evaluation Form
PHASE FIVE Seventh to Twelfth Month		• Reviews development plan progress • Helps new employee with access to resources • Conducts twelve-month performance evaluation	• Works on development plan

Source: Reproduced with permission of Hewlett Packard (Canada) Ltd.

The scope and content of the orientation programs vary as well. Habitual topics during the orientation session cover the following five themes:

1. Introduction to the company,
2. Review of important policies and procedures,
3. Overview of benefits,
4. Overview of services,
5. Question period.

Some companies prepare a folder with basic facts about the firm, its products and services, its profitability portfolio and its major clients. Other firms conduct the orientation via a standard video prepared for this occasion. But one of the best approaches is to use audio-visual techniques to accompany verbal presentations.

In the vast majority of cases, the HR department develops and coordinates the orientation program. However, the supervisor plays a key role in it since he or she is expected to know the company policies and practices. In order to ensure that important information is not omitted by supervisors, the HR department prepares a standardized check list that should be adhered to during an orientation session.

Job Assignments

The important socializing aspects of job assignments are the characteristics of the initial job, the nature of early experiences on the job, and the first supervisor. The initial job often determines the new employee's future success. The more challenge and responsibility the job offers, the more likely it is that an employee will be successful with the organization. A challenging (but not overwhelming) job assignment implies that the organization values the employee and believes that he or she can do well. Many times organizations give new employees simple jobs or rotate them through departments to give them a feeling for different jobs. But employees may interpret these practices to mean that the organization does not yet trust their abilities or loyalties.

Experience in a new job and with a new supervisor helps prepare new employees for the acquisition of the appropriate values, norms, attitudes, and behaviours. Supervisors can serve as role models and set expectations. The positive influence that the supervisor's expectations can have on the new employee is referred to as the **Pygmalion effect**. If the supervisor believes that the new employee will do well, he or she is more apt to live up to these expectations.

The key to individual success in the first job assignment is the way the organization (via the direct supervisor) deals with success and failure. Employees will develop positive feelings toward the organization if they are not punished for initial failure; are given clear feedback on their achievements and shortcomings; are provided an explanation for why they are succeeding or failing; and if they find out that they can count on their supervisors to provide instrumental guidelines in case of failure. It is therefore important to alert line managers to the impact of their initial behaviour on the ultimate success of their new employees.

TRENDS IN SELECTION AND ORIENTATION

Assessing Selection and Orientation

Selection and orientation decisions and processes can be assessed using a number of different criteria, some of which are objective and some of which are more subjective in nature. Objectively, HR managers can use tangible approaches, such as the utility of various selection instruments and their relative costs, as well as the turnover rate amongst the newly hired. Subjectively, the HR manager can conduct surveys measuring new employees' satisfaction with work, the extent to which they feel their skills and abilities are being used, and, generally, the degree of their involvement in the job and in the organization. A detailed illustration of the use of utility and cost analyses is provided in Chapter 18 (i.e., "staffing example").[24]

In addition to comparing the costs and benefits of alternative selection and placement procedures, organizations should also compare the costs and benefits of techniques other than selection and placement to obtain increases in job performance and employee retention. In part, the costs and benefits of alternatives versus those of selection and placement will be influenced by other basic criteria.

In evaluating alternatives to selection and placement, it is important to consider the impact these alternatives will have on HRM activities. For example, if an organization is considering dropping its selection and placement procedures, the state of its training and development activity should be considered. If an organization is considering changing the design of its jobs, the PIPs and SKAs of its current employees should be considered. These considerations, in addition to the cost–benefit determinations, are important in a total utility assessment because they represent a **feasibility assessment**. Some alternatives may be more cost-effective to use than selection and placement procedures, but they may not be feasible. For example, it may not be feasible to increase the complexity of jobs, because top management will not remove the assembly-line technology.

Organizations also need to predict the extent to which the hired candidates will stay in the organization. Retaining good people is critical for all organizations. In some instances, organizations are unable to retain good employees because their selection system does not incorporate such issues as over-qualification for a job. For example, a candidate with a Ph.D. in English Literature, who happens to possess good typing skills, will not be likely to remain in a low-level secretary–typist position. If the organization does not provide career opportunities beyond the entry position, such a candidate will seek other employment. Hiring *overqualified* candidates can be as detrimental to the organization as hiring *underqualified* ones.

EXIT INTERVIEWS. One way of finding out why new employees leave shortly after being hired is through an exit interview. This information can provide a good measure of the efficiency of the recruitment and selection process and can lead to improvements in the hiring of future applicants.

The success or failure of the exit interview depends largely on who conducts it. The exit interview should not be conducted by the departing employee's immediate supervisor. Rather, a member of the HR department or another manager who is sufficiently objective should assume the responsibility for it. At the end of the interview, the interviewer should prepare a report with some recommendations as per remedies pertaining to the selection process.

Computer Applications

Computer applications in selection are growing tremendously, especially with regard to testing. Instead of using various manuals for written tests, most commercial tests are becoming computerized. This reduces the time it takes to administer the tests and it also increases the reliability and validity of the testing process in general. Computerized tests have a number of advantages over traditional paper-and-pencil instruments. They include:

1. Fewer potential errors during the coding and transcription of the manual results (i.e., such errors are virtually eliminated);
2. Fewer possibilities of "faking" results, since computerized tests are substantially more valid and reliable;
3. Reduced dependence on external consultants due to in-house testing by HR staff;
4. More standardized scores across applicants and, consequently, improved opportunities for employment equity; one standard condition, such as time limits that are imposed for many aptitude tests, is being meticulously monitored by the computer itself;
5. Instant results; this facilitates quicker decisions (applicants also benefit from fast feedback on their performance on the tests);

6. Enhanced playfulness; the new generation of applicants who are computer literate enjoy taking the computerized tests; it is less stressful for them;

7. Norms for the company could be accumulated over time, and used with more precision after a while in correcting the cut-off scores on the tests.

As a result of these developments, testing in the industry is currently in the middle of a revolution. Fewer and fewer organizations use the traditional paper-and-pencil forms. In addition to simple tests, many more sophisticated tests including simulations can be used via computers. For additional information on this last point, see Chapter 11.

HRM DYNAMICS
Orientation Profiles of Selected Canadian Firms

Allergan Canada

Allergan Canada is a pharmaceutical company that specializes in eye-care products and is based in Markham, Ontario. Orientation is conducted by the HR recruiter and consists of two stages: the first stage takes three hours and is conducted at the board room. It involves a welcome speech and briefing about the company. This is supplemented by brochures with information about benefits, rules and regulations, company philosophy, pension plans, health insurance, vision- and dental-care plan, and the savings program. Finally, films are shown about the company and its different divisions as well as the company's main products. The second stage is a follow-up that takes place two to four weeks after the initial phase.

Elliot Marr and Company

Elliott Marr and Company is a small food distribution firm located in London, Ontario. The orientation program lasts two days. It includes a formatted checklist to ensure that all items are covered. In the first day the HR department along with the employee's supervisor present the company and the job, and deal with everything else that the employee wishes to discuss. On the second day the employee is shown a video tape, "The Oshawa Story," which describes the company's history.

Jostens Canada Ltd.

Jostens Canada Ltd. is a producer of school photographs, ring, and yearbooks. It has plants in Winnipeg, Montreal, and Sherbrooke and sales and marketing in Mississauga, Ontario. Because of the decentralized operations, each manager is responsible for his or her employee's orientation. Because the company is committed to the philosophy of Total Quality Involvement Process (TQIP), the core of the orientation program is to introduce each new employee to this process. Consequently, the bulk of the orientation involves an awareness training process. The rest is left to the immediate supervisor.

SUMMARY

This chapter has assumed that an essential goal of selection and orientation is to place the right person in the right job in order to serve the short- and long-term interests of both the organization and the individual. This means that organizations should make selection and placement decisions based on information about an individual's motivation and the rewards of the job and organization, as well as an individual's abilities and the demands of the job. Only by considering both matches can the major purposes of selection and placement be attained.

Selection, placement, and orientation decisions therefore require a great deal of information. There are many ways by which organizations can gather this information. It can be done through interviews, application blanks, references, and numerous paper-and-pencil and job sample tests. The methods used to gather selection information should depend on the type of information needed and the validity and reliability of the methods. Determining the type of job information to be sought is a function of the difficulty in demonstrating its job-relatedness. This, in turn may be a function of both the type of information sought and the method used.

In the process of gathering information, however, the organization must be aware of several legal considerations. Failure to do so may not only result in lawsuits, but also decisions to hire less than the best qualified job applicant. Legal considerations are also important when the organization actually combines the information gathered to make the final selection and placement decision. The best way for organizations to help ensure they are making appropriate selection decisions, with respect to employment equity considerations, is for their HR managers to stay abreast of pertinent legal developments and to implement fair and affirmative HR policies and practices.

Organizations obtain qualified employees by using valid selection instruments. Within this parameter, organizations can continue to improve their selection and placement decisions by identifying and utilizing more job-related predictors. This should all be done within a cost–benefit framework to help ensure that, if two predictors are equally job-related, the less costly one should be used.

Another way to help enhance the effectiveness of an organization's selection and placement decisions is to engage in effective orientation and socialization of employees, since this can help reduce turnover or other possible negative behaviours. Most individuals do not know about the values, norms, attitudes, and behaviours that an organization expects of its members. Orientation, in essence, attempts to provide the individual with the information he or she needs to fit into the organization. Most organizations use many methods in their efforts to socialize new employees (and even old employees), including the initial job assignment, the manner of recruitment and selection, and the formal orientation program.

After selection and orientation, organizations must monitor the performance of new employees. This is critical for the overall success of the organization and for the assessment of the selection and orientation methods and procedures.

P O S T S C R I P T

One of the most controversial issues in the selection of employees involves the dilemma between respecting employees' rights to an equal opportunity in obtaining jobs and an employer's rights to choose whomever it likes, regardless of legal requirements. Without a doubt, this debate is less relevant for public organizations that have a moral and financial obligation to respect the will of society. Nonetheless, the problem applies to many small entrepreneurial firms that wish to hand pick their employees based on their own criteria. Many entrepreneurs strongly hold the view that selecting an employee is a matter of chemistry, an art and not necessarily a scientific method. Furthermore, although they are aware of employment equity legislation, they view it as limiting their choice to select anybody that they really like. Naturally, an employer would like to hire an employee who will be loyal and committed to the organization for a long time. Against such convictions, there is the legislation that forces the employer to adhere to a strict code of equity in hiring and even to affirmative action programs. Whose right is violated? Is there a conflict between the right of society and the right of the employer? The answer is not easy.

Any conflicts in the selection of employees are apparent during the selection interview. Managers claim repeatedly that without the interview they cannot make a final decision; they need to have "a feel" for the candidate. On the other hand, it is fairly well known that interviews, even when conducted by professional interviewers, are highly biased and subjective. In fact, some researchers believe that if employment equity is to be strictly enforced, the employment interview should be eliminated altogether as a means of making a selection decision. Moreover, the same people assert that all the information that can be obtained during the interview can be obtained in a more valid and reliable way, using other selection instruments.

Obviously, this controversy reflects societal concerns. It does not look as if a fool-proof nondiscriminatory instrument is readily available. Consequently, although undesired, some discriminatory practices will always be evident in the selection process. (Remember, however, that some practices are legal and some are illegal.) We as a society and as employers are all better off if we use valid means that predict performance to the extent that it is possible.

REVIEW AND ANALYSIS QUESTIONS

1. What is the notion of "success" (criteria) in selection? What are some typical problems associated with it and how can they be minimized?
2. A frequent saying in organizations is: "Well, Joe was a selection mistake—We shouldn't have hired him in the first place." What are the short- and long-term consequences of these so-called "selection mistakes?"
3. Why does a selection instrument need to be reliable?
4. Successful selection and placement decisions are often dependent on other HR activities. Identify these activities and explain their relationships to selection and placement.
5. Under what conditions is a multiple hurdle selection procedure more appropriate than a compensatory procedure?
6. How can an application blank be improved as a predictor in selection?
7. Given that the selection interview is plagued with problems and biases, why is it still the most popular selection device?
8. Why are drugs and genetic testing controversial?
9. What are some advantages of the assessment centre as a method for selecting managers? What are its drawbacks?
10. Why is proper orientation important for organizations?
11. Examine an application form used by a company and comment on the legality, reliability, and validity of the items/questions.

CASE STUDY

USE, MISUSE, OR ABUSE OF TESTS

Like many other industries, Maritime Employers' Association (MEA) has been confronted with the problems deriving from technological changes. While most work in the different ports under its jurisdiction has been done in the past primarily through the use of manual labour, the drive to become more competitive forced the Association to mechanize its operations. Yet, MEA knew that the decision to use new technology was not going to be without difficulties. Apart from the obvious problems pertaining to securing financing to purchase the new equipment, there was the problem of what to do with its current labour force and the union.

As a responsible employer, MEA wanted to ensure that changes in technology would benefit the existing workforce. On the other hand, MEA was aware of the fact that the "new operators" would require quite different skills, knowledge, and effort than those currently possessed by most of its longshoremen employees. Consequently, with a view to complying with a collective agreement, MEA looked for a solution that would meet the company's needs and also minimize the impact on existing employees' job security. Part of the solution involved a two-tiered strategy:

1. First, the company will attempt to train all tenured employees; then employees will be tested. Those who succeed will stay, and the other employees will be de-hired in the most civilized manner.

2. MEA also employs about 400 nontenured employees, who have been with the company for a period ranging from three months to two years. All of these employees will be tested, specifically about their aptitude pertaining to the use of new equipment. Those who pass the test will proceed to training and will become part of the regular workforce. Conversely, those who fail the test will be instantly terminated.

While attending an executive development seminar, Peter Gray, VP human resources for MEA, learned of a battery of tests used by the New Jersey Port authorities for selecting longshoremen. He contacted his old friend Roy Lepage (they had graduated together from the same M.B.A. program), and asked him to obtain a copy of the test. After obtaining the battery of tests and after a short discussion of the "presumed changes in the job description for machine operators," Peter concluded: "This battery of tests is exactly what we need; we need to find out if the employees have the right aptitude pertaining to memory, vision, and manual dexterity, and the proper personality and attitudes. It looks like it will be the best solution to our problem." He instructed Roy to obtain copyright permission from the test developers and then to proceed to translate it into French, because many of MEA's employees would need the test administered in this language. "When you are ready," added Peter, "give me a buzz and we shall arrange to schedule the test."

Lepage, who was also the president of his small management consulting firm, was very glad to be retained as a consultant in this project. Although he had never acquired formal training in industrial or organizational psychology, his firm, Personnel Testing Inc., had made arrangements with a number of test developers to market and use their products in Canada. Over the years, he believed he had acquired lots of experience. In addition to translation, the mandate signed with MEA called for the administration, scoring, and production of an individual report and recommendation for each employee tested.

On what turned out to be "Black Tuesday—Grim Week," the first contingency of 100 MEA employees were summoned to a huge hangar that was transformed into a testing place. The remainder of the employees were scheduled for successive days. No explanation was provided, except that the company wished to learn more about employees' potential and therefore each would participate in taking a battery of tests. The vast majority of these employees had never participated in this or any similar type of exercise.

Because Roy was going out of town for the first two testing days, he sent his administrative assistant to provide instructions and supervise the testing. Joanne had just been hired as an administrative assistant, and this was her first important task. She read the instructions provided to her by Roy, but was unable to reply to employees' questions about the different components of the tests. Some testees complained about the poor lighting in the hangar, others were cold, still others did not have a comfortable desk on which to write, and others simply did not understand what to do and why. Under mounting pressure, Joanne decided that although the instructions called for fixed time limits for some components of the test, she would compensate the testees by granting a few extra minutes to those who needed it: "I'm new on the job, and I feel that because I can't answer your questions, the least that I can do is to give you some extra time." No such extra time was granted to other employees in subsequent days.

In order to compile the results and make recommendations, Roy decided to combine the scores on the five parts of the test; after dividing the total by five he was able to generate a single score, ranging between 0 and 100. Because many good university graduate programs use a cutoff score of 70 to denote a passing grade, he also decided to apply the same criterion in making his personal recommendation.

Upon receiving the test results, Peter Gray sent 121 letters to nontenured employees, informing them that due to their failure on the test, the company would no longer require their services. A copy with the list of de-hired employees was mailed to the longshoremen's union. Upon receiving the news, the union filed an injunction with the superior court, alleging Misuse of tests and gross discrimination.

Case Questions

1. If you were a consultant for the union, what arguments would you be using pertaining to reliability and validity problems in this case?

2. Could the company have avoided the charge? How?

3. What steps should a company like MEA take when developing and implementing an HRM program to resolve the problem of "new technology?"

4. How would you have computed the results if you had been in Roy's place?

NOTES

1. For a description of these results and calculation of dollar costs and benefits, see F.L. Schmidt and J.E. Hunter, J.E., "Research Findings in Personnel Selection: Myths Meet Realities in the 1980s," in *Public Personnel Administration: Policies and Procedures for Personnel* (New York: Prentice–Hall, 1981); see also F.L. Schmidt, J.E. Hunter, and K. Pearlman, "Assessing the Economic Impact of Personnel Programs on Productivity," *Personnel Psychology*, Summer 1982, 238–348.

2. D.G. Lawrence et al., "Design and Use of Weighted Application Blanks," *Personnel Administrator*, March 1982, 47–53, 101.

3. P.M. Muchinsky, *Psychology Applied to Work*, (Homewood, Ill.: The Dorsey Press, 1983) 4th ed., 124.

4. G.T. Milkovich and W.F. Glueck, *Personnel: Human Resource Management (A Diagnostic Approach),* 4th ed. (Plano, Tex.: Business Publications, Inc., 1985), 301.

5. H. Jain, "Human Rights: Issues in Employment," *Human Resource Management in Canada*, 1989, 50, 025.

6. R. Deland, "Recruitment: Reference Checking Methods," *Personnel Journal*, June 1983, 460.

7. For an excellent discussion of interviewing, see M.D. Hakel, "Employment Interviewing," *Personnel Management*, ed. K.M. Rowland and G.R. Ferris (Boston: Allyn and Bacon, 1982), 129–55; *Interview Guide for Supervisors* (Washington, D.C.: College and University Personnel Association, 1981); R.D. Arvey and J.E. Campion, "The Employment Interview: A Summary and Review of Recent Literature," *Personnel Psychology* 35 (1982): 281–322; and T. Janz, "The Selection Interview: The Received Wisdom versus Recent Research," in *Canadian Readings in Personnel and Human Resource Management*, ed. S.L. Dolan and R.S. Schuler (St. Paul, Minn.: West Publishing Co., 1987), 154–61.

8. Jain, *Op. Cit.* p. 50,028

9. To obtain the kit, write to: The Canadian Human Rights Commission, 400–90 Sparks St., Ottawa, Ontario K1A 1E1, or contact the regional office. Interesting guidance is also provided in J.M. Jenks and B.L. Zevnik, "ABCs of Job Interviewing (Shooting the Rapids)," the *Harvard Business Review*, July/August 1989, 42.

10. The behavioural description interview was developed by Dr. Tom Janz, formerly with the University of Calgary. The sample questions are borrowed from: T. Janz, L. Hellervik, and D.C. Gilmore, *Behavior Description Interviewing* (Boston: Allyn and Bacon Inc., 1986), 178–85.

11. J.D. Hatfield and R.D. Gatewood, "Nonverbal Cues in the Selection Interview," *Personnel Administrator*, January 1978,

12. Hatfield and Gatewood, "Nonverbal Cues," 37.

13. S. Cornshow, "The Status of Employment Testing in Canada: A Review and Evaluation of Theory and Professional Practice," *Canadian Psychology* 27 (1986): 183–95.

14. "Personal Business," *Business Week* 27 July 1981, 85–86. The extent of polygraph usage is demonstrated by fact that in the U.S.A. 50 percent of all retail firms, and 20 percent of all corporations and many banks use the polygraph tests; see *U.S.A. Today*, February 1981, 16.

15. W.C. Byham, "Application of the Assessment Center Method," in *Applying the Assessment Center Method*, ed. J.L. Moses and W.C. Byham (New York: Pergamon, 1977).

16. A. Tziner and S.L. Dolan, "Validity of an Assessment Center for Identifying Future Female Officers in the Military," *Journal of Applied Psychology* 67 (1982): 728–36.

17. For more information on the status of the assessment centre, see S.L. Dolan and A. Tziner, "The Assessment Center Revisited: Critical Evaluation of Philosophy, Theory, Instruments and Practices," in *Empowerment in the Workplace and Classroom* (Proceedings of the Twenty-Eighth Annual Meeting of the Eastern Academy of Management), ed. A.M. Herd and W.P. Ferris (Hartford, Conn: EAM, 1991): 170–73.

18. B.L. Thompson, "A Surprising Ally in the Drug Wars," *Training*, November 1990.

19. P. Buchignany, "White collar drug abuse: these dope addicts wear shirts and ties. They run banks, law offices, and multinational corporations," *The Montreal Gazette*, 7 July 1991, A5.

20. A 20 September 1989 poll conducted for *The Financial Post* revealed that (1) a majority of Canadians think companies should require their employees to undergo drug tests, and (2) 66 percent of those questioned favoured mandatory drug testing.

21. Title 29, Code of Federal Regulations, (Supply and Services Canada, Ottawa, 1989).

22. Cited in S. Yanchinski, "Employees under a microscope," *The Globe and Mail*, 3 January 1990, D3.

23. S.L. Dolan and B. Bannister, "Emerging Issues in Employment Testing," in *Psychologie du travail et nouveaux milieux de travail*, ed. A. Laroque et al. (Montréal: Presses de l'Université de Québec, 1987), 490–99.

24. For more information about utility and costs of selection procedures, see W.F. Cascio, *Costing Human Resources: The Financial Impact of Behavior in Organizations*, 2nd ed. (Boston: Kent Publishing, 1987), 195–220.

CHAPTER SEVEN

DIRECT COMPENSATION

KEYNOTE ADDRESS
Ronald M. Kirshner
President, Ivanhoe Inc.

Compensation Practices: An Integral Part of Human
Resource Management

Ivanhoe Inc. is a Montreal-based, commercial real estate development, investment, and management company with assets of $1.5 billion. The company, with offices in Quebec and Ontario, has 200 employees, with 10 percent classified as senior management, 52 percent professional, managerial and supervisory, and 38 percent support. Our type of business requires a wide variety of disciplines and employee characteristics.

The organizational philosophy, flowing from our management philosophy, has much to do with how we manage our people. We have taken a client approach, with the recognition that we have both external and internal customers, and have established business units that recognize the distinctiveness of each business and of their particular clients. This has allowed us to push responsibility, authority, and accountability downward in the organization. We stress the necessity of teamwork, the value of the individual, and the importance of internal and external communication. Our planning process, from corporate strategic plans to business plans to annual budgets and action plans, establishes HR requirements. The group and individual objectives forming part of the plans flow into our performance management system.

Because our compensation strategy fits into our overall HR management and planning, we have taken the following route:

- Our senior management collectively established an overall corporate benchmark profile, weighting the inherent essential and important functions and traits of Ivanhoe.
- Using position descriptions and questionnaires, individual tasks and functions were measured by task forces of employees and subsequently compared to the benchmark profile using a computer-driven model. The usual data cleansing, error elimination, gender equity, and relative position ranking tests were incorporated to establish each position's final point count and to group jobs of equal value.

- Compensation surveys of our own and other industries are used to establish medians for each of our fourteen job levels.
- We have incentive plans for our senior and operating management personnel. Payouts are based on budget attainment, long-term return and individual contribution, with each component weighted based on job level. Profit-sharing plans are in place for other employees based on their performance rating and the attainment of budget.
- Senior people have a choice from a menu of items, with the maximum dollar value based upon a percentage of salary established by job level.
- We attempt to fit our benefit programs to our employee profile and are working on pension plan changes, based on surveys of employees' perceived needs.
- Our policies concerning automobile, vacation, and office space are often reviewed to best fit our people needs.

Our compensation philosophy for the nonsenior levels is to pay at the median for each job level, while recognizing the relative contribution of each individual by their placement within their job-level salary range. Direct compensation for the senior staff is targeted at 5 percent below median but with the potential for bonuses and other forms of incentives to produce above average income. We conduct "global" compensation surveys in order to comparatively measure our total remuneration.

Much of my time is invested in HR matters, since people at all levels are the key to the success or failure of a business. In Ivanhoe, the orientation of the relatively small population is toward action, decision making, and management. It is a great place to work but a difficult group to manage. We have used the theory and science of compensation and benefits to build a framework that fits our company. One finds, however, that individuals seldom fall at a mathematical median, and don't really care if they do or not. The art of managing individuals within the established framework is really what the HR profession is all about.

• • •

Given the trend toward global competition, companies are struggling to attract, retain, and motivate employees within their labour market. Thus, compensation becomes a significant and timely HR tool to carry out this task. However, there should be an important link between salary and wage cost on the one hand and productivity and the competitiveness of the firm on the other. The Keynote Address by the president of Ivanhoe Inc. points out the careful attention paid by the company to ensure that the compensation strategy fits into the overall HR policy, which in return is contingent on broad corporate business plans. However, because Canadian wage costs are among the highest in the world today, competition in the global market becomes very difficult. A related issue, which raises another important point in compensation, pertains to the effects of minimum wage laws on unskilled labour and on the company's total labour costs. Some evidence suggests that although the legislative policies are well intentioned, they may actually reduce opportunities for employment. Equally important are the legal considerations affecting total compensation, particularly regarding pay for different jobs.

• • •

TOTAL COMPENSATION

This chapter discusses a number of issues critical to the notion of direct compensation. They are:

1. How wage and salary levels for jobs are determined;

2. The different methods used to establish job worth and to conduct job evaluation;

3. Some of the most pertinent issues in salary administration, including market surveys, issues in equity, and pay secrecy;

4. The legal considerations in direct compensation;

5. What performance-based pay systems are, and some advantages and disadvantages in using them;

The compensation function is the activity by which organizations evaluate the contributions of employees in order to distribute direct and indirect monetary and nonmonetary rewards within legal regulations and the organization's ability to pay. As Exhibit 7.1 shows, there are two categories of **direct compensation**: the *basic wage* and *performance-based pay*. **Indirect compensation**, which will be discussed in Chapter 8, consists of *federal and provincial protection programs*, *pay for time not worked*, and *employee services*

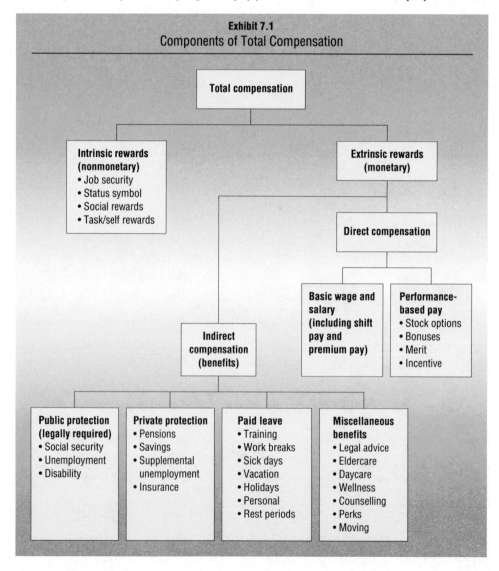

Exhibit 7.1
Components of Total Compensation

Total compensation

Intrinsic rewards (nonmonetary)
• Job security
• Status symbol
• Social rewards
• Task/self rewards

Extrinsic rewards (monetary)

Direct compensation

Indirect compensation (benefits)

Basic wage and salary (including shift pay and premium pay)

Performance-based pay
• Stock options
• Bonuses
• Merit
• Incentive

Public protection (legally required)
• Social security
• Unemployment
• Disability

Private protection
• Pensions
• Savings
• Supplemental unemployment
• Insurance

Paid leave
• Training
• Work breaks
• Sick days
• Vacation
• Holidays
• Personal
• Rest periods

Miscellaneous benefits
• Legal advice
• Eldercare
• Daycare
• Wellness
• Counselling
• Perks
• Moving

and perquisites. **Total compensation** is the total value of all direct and indirect payments to the employee.

Compensation is important because it serves several major purposes:

* *To attract potential job applicants.* The total compensation program can help assure that pay is sufficient to attract the right people at the right time for the right jobs. In this regard, compensation works in conjunction with the recruitment and selection efforts.
* *To retain good employees.* Unless the total compensation program is perceived as internally equitable and externally competitive, good employees (those that the organization wishes to retain) are likely to leave whenever other opportunities present themselves.
* *To motivate employees.* Total compensation can help produce a motivated workforce by tying rewards to performance; this is the core of performance-based pay.
* *To administer pay within legal regulations.* Because there are several legal regulations relevant to total compensation, organizations must be aware of them and avoid violations in their pay programs.
* *To facilitate organizational strategic objectives.* To create a very rewarding and supportive climate and to attract the best applicants an organization can design an attractive total compensation package. As a result, organizational objectives such as rapid growth, survival, or innovation can be more readily achieved.
* *To gain a competitive edge by controlling labour costs.* Compensation represents a significant portion of the total operating budgets for most organizations; depending on the industry, labour costs can vary from 10 to 80 percent of total costs. In order to gain a competitive advantage, an organization may choose to relocate to an area where labour is "cheaper." For instance, many companies are moving to regions where anti-union sentiments run high or the minimum wage is lower, thus reducing labour costs.

The ability that compensation has to attract, retain, and motivate individuals is related to the importance people place on money. Money is able to satisfy many employee needs. Because compensation, in both direct and indirect forms, has the potential to satisfy the various needs of different individuals, it can take on varying degrees of importance.

However, employees are often willing to join an organization and perform well in it for reasons other than just the money. They are often motivated by the nonmonetary rewards that an organization may offer, for example, job status and prestige, job security, safety, job responsibility, and variety. As shown in Exhibit 7.2, these are all status symbols, social rewards, or task–self rewards. Although these mainly intangible rewards can be critical, the two chapters on direct and indirect compensation focus primarily on monetary rewards, which are usually regarded as the major part of compensation in most organizations.

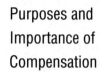

Purposes and Importance of Compensation

Compensation, being one of the most important HR activities to individuals, as well as organizations, has an extensive set of relationships with other HR activities. First, for its success, it relies on certain HR activities such as job analysis and performance appraisal for input in determining total compensation; second, it influences other HR activities such as recruitment, selection, union–management relations, and HRP.

Compensation Relationships and Influences

JOB ANALYSIS. Compensation is integrally related to job analysis. The job evaluation process, which determines the relative worth of jobs, is based in large measure on how the job is described in the formal job description. Job evaluation and job analysis influence the basic compensation structure for the organization, including job classes and individual and job wage rates.

Exhibit 7.2
Organizational Rewards

MONETARY REWARDS, INCLUDING FRINGE BENEFITS		STATUS SYMBOLS	SOCIAL REWARDS	FROM THE TASK– SELF REWARDS
Pay	Theatre and sports tickets	Office size and location	Friendly greetings	Interesting work
Pay raise	Recreation facilities	Office with window	Informal recognition	Sense of achievement
Stock options	Reserved company parking	Carpeting	Praise	Job of more importance
Profit sharing		Drapes	Smile	Job variety
Bonus plans	Work breaks	Paintings	Evaluative feedback	Job-performance feedback
Christmas bonus	Sabbatical leaves	Watches	Compliments	Self-recognition
Provision and use of company facilities	Club memberships and privileges	Rings	Nonverbal signals	Self-praise
Deferred compensation, including other tax shelters	Discount purchase privileges	Formal awards/ recognition	Pat on the back	Opportunities to schedule own work
Pay and time-off for attending work-related training programs and seminars	Personal loans at favourable rates	Wall plaque	Invitations to coffee/lunch	Working hours
Medical plan, including free physical examinations	Free legal advice		After-hours social gatherings	Participation in new organizational ventures
Company auto	Free personal financial planning advice			Choice of geographical location
Pension contributions	Free home protection—theft insurance			Autonomy in job
Product discount plans	Burglar alarms and personal protection			
Vacation trips	Moving expenses			
	Home purchase assistance			

HRP AND STRATEGIC PLANNING. Compensation is normally integrated into the organization's strategic planning. Here is an example that illustrates this point. A manufacturer of a line of technology-based products developed a strategic vision of itself as a leader in new technologies. Since accomplishing this could have disrupted the current business (located in Ontario), the company decided to acquire small entrepreneurial companies in British Columbia. The parent company quickly realized that these smaller companies required different management styles and a different pay system. Therefore, the managers' base salaries in these small companies were set significantly lower than those in the parent company, but the potential size of their annual bonus was four times greater![1]

RECRUITMENT AND SELECTION. Employees differ in the value they attribute to pay. If HR departments can determine how important pay is to individuals, they can recruit people to fill specific jobs with specific pay policy options. It appears that in order to attract and retain even the best applicants, maximum pay levels (i.e., the most competitive) need not be offered. Individuals make job choice decisions on the basis of several factors, including the location of the organization, its reputation as a place to work, what friends think of the company, as well as the nature of the job and the pay level offered. Consequently, rather than taking the job that simply pays the most, individuals often take the job that satisfies as many of these factors as possible.

PERFORMANCE APPRAISAL. The relationship between compensation and performance appraisal is perhaps the most important for individuals in the organization. Especially where performance-based pay exists, the results of the performance evaluation are significant. Without the ability to measure performance in a reliable and valid way, linking such an important reward as pay to the results may lead to diminished motivation and lowered performance. Where promotions are available as some type of reward for performance, the performance evaluation system can have added significance.

LABOUR RELATIONS. Wage levels and individual wage determinations can be influenced greatly by the existence of a union. A union's influence includes not only wage gains but also wage "givebacks." As well, a union can play an important role in the job evaluation process and may determine the type of pay plan an organization will have. More discussion on these issues is provided in Chapter 16.

A summary of these relationships, along with a list of administrative and contemporary issues, is given in Exhibit 7.3. Also shown are several aspects of the environment that influence an organization's total compensation process and hence its ability to attract, retain, and motivate employees for productivity, legal compliance, and QWL improvements. Since the legal environment and the labour market are so critical, they are presented in detail here and will be discussed further in the next chapter.

As with many of the other HR activities discussed before, there are several provincial and federal laws and court rulings, as well as human rights commission and tribunal decisions, that affect the total compensation of employees under federal jurisdiction.

Legal Considerations in Compensation

THE CANADIAN LABOUR CODE (PART III). The Canada Labour Code (also known as the Canada Labour Act) is the most comprehensive law regulating several aspects of compensation and affecting all employees under federal jurisdiction. It regulates the minimum wage, overtime pay, minimum age, and documentation of hours worked. The Code states that overtime must be paid at a rate of at least 1-1/2 times normal pay for any hour that exceeds 40 hours in a week. It also sets a minimum wage, though trainees and apprentices employed by the federal government are exempt from this provision. All provinces have similar legislation that regulates the overtime pay, minimum age, and documentation of hours worked. Several provincial laws also influence the hours that employees can work. All provinces have minimum-wage laws covering employees not covered by federal minimum-wage laws. The minimum wage varied in 1993 from $4.75 per hour in Newfoundland to $6.24 per hour in the Yukon Territory. The laws covering minimum vacation pay also differ among provinces. The required minimums are the lowest in British Columbia (2 percent of annual pay); most other provinces enforce a minimum of 4 percent or more.

The Code, along with the Canada Labour Standards Regulations (SOR/72–7), contains provisions for allowable hours of work. Employees may not work more than 48 hours in a week except in cases of an emergency. The Code also requires that employers keep detailed records on hours worked, pay rates, amount of overtime, deductions and additions to pay, and various miscellaneous information related to compensation. The relevant compensation records must be kept for at least thirty-six months after the work has been performed and should be available for inspection at any time.

Certain categories of employees are exempt from the Code (or certain provisions of it, for example, the hours-of-work provision). The employee exemption is based on responsibilities, duties, and type of compensation. Generally, executives, administrators, and professionals are **exempt employees**, not only from the overtime requirements of the Code (i.e., they may not be paid overtime for work beyond 40 hours per week), but also from the minimum wage. These individuals would normally be paid on a salary basis (bi-

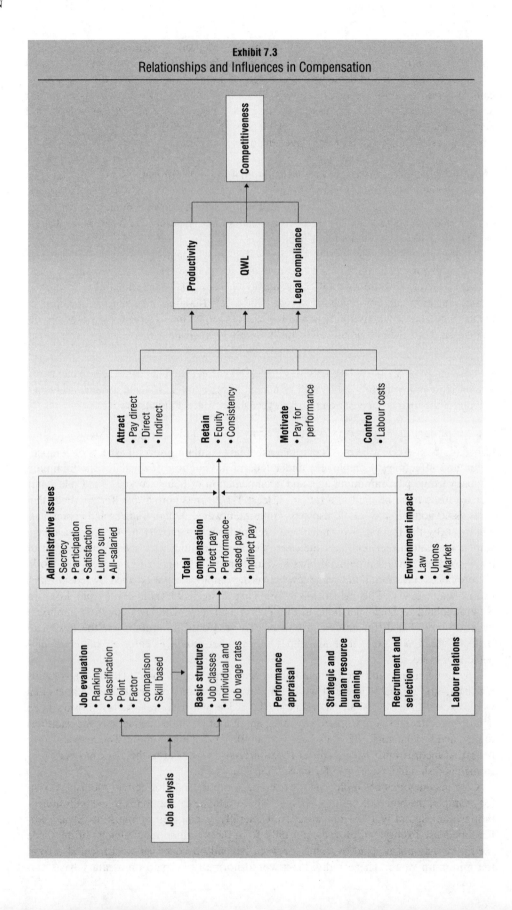

Exhibit 7.3
Relationships and Influences in Compensation

weekly or monthly). Hourly or daily wages earners are usually **nonexempt employees**. This distinction, however, is changing rapidly, so it is difficult to generalize whether or not salaried or piecework employees are exempt.

Because compensation laws vary from province to province and are constantly changing, HR managers are well advised to keep continuously informed in respect to them. Most of these laws are normally enforced by the provincial Ministry of Labour, and updated information could be obtained by contacting them directly.

Finally, an Act to amend the Canada Labour Code and the Financial Administration Act (Bill C–34) was proclaimed on March 1, 1985. Substantial changes were made to provisions of the Code regarding maternity leave, child-care leave, bereavement leave, sick leave, and reinstatement. Also, provisions concerning sexual harassment were added. Other changes related to compensation included holiday pay entitlements, penalties for employers who do not comply with provisions of the law (up to $100,000), and minimum wage exemptions (for trainees).

PAY EQUITY LAWS.   Several federal and provincial equity laws dating back to the 1960s influence the individual wage determination. For example, the discriminatory practice of establishing or maintaining differences in wages between males and females employed in the same establishment and performing work of equal value (as defined in the Canadian Human Rights Act and the Equal Wages Guidelines) is prohibited by the Canadian Labour Code. Inspectors appointed by the Minister of Labour may file complaints with the CHRC if they have reason to believe the prohibition is not being observed. Similar statutes have been enacted by most provinces. These Acts require that companies found guilty of pay discrimination must make up for past discrepancies. Nevertheless, as will be discussed later, the comparable pay concept is very difficult to demonstrate.

Although the various pay equity acts are meant to ensure that employees doing the same work and with comparable seniority, performance, and background are paid the same, regardless of sex, age, national origin, religion, etc., as specified in the various human rights acts, evidence suggests that employees are still being paid differentially on the basis of their gender. On a national scale, although the proportion of women in the labour force has increased dramatically, their earnings in Canada are about 70 percent of those of men.[1]

There are several possible reasons for the wage discrepancies. One is outright sexual discrimination. Another is that women may work in jobs that are valued less (based on job evaluation results) than those performed by men. This has given rise to the idea of **comparable worth**, and the demand for equal pay for jobs of comparable value. Given that most pay equity acts provide legal coverage only when men and women are performing the same job, it is very difficult to enforce comparable worth if there are differences in performance, seniority, or other conditions. Nonetheless, the evidence suggests that many employers attempt to comply with the provisions of the laws; the gap in wages for men and women has narrowed since the early 1980s.

The Quebec Human Rights Commission has recommended that the province enact a pay equity law that would require all employers to eliminate wage differences based on gender, race, or physical disabilities within four years. This would reduce the current 35 percent gap between men's and women's wages to 15 percent.[3]

COMPARABLE WORTH ISSUES.   Comparable worth is likely to be a significant compensation issue in the years to come. The heart of the comparable worth theory is the contention that, while the "true worth" of jobs may be similar, some jobs (often held by women) are paid at a lower rate than others (often held by men). The resulting differences in pay are disproportionate to the differences in the "true worth" of jobs, and therefore amount to wage discrimination. According to comparable worth advocates, legal protection should be provided in these cases.

Pay equity legislation was instituted in a number of provinces (as well as in the federal government). Given that this legislation is recent (except for Quebec and Manitoba), the legal test has been very limited thus far. In one case, the Ste. Anne de Bellevue Veterans Hospital near Montreal had to increase a woman's salary by $10,000 and pay $14,262 in back wages for past discrimination. In another case, *Beatrice Harwatiuk vs. Pasqua Hospital (1983)*, a job evaluation in a Saskatchewan hospital failed to support differential pay for male- and female-dominated jobs.

Because Ontario's pay equity legislation is one of the most recent (1987) and most comprehensive, it is presented in slightly more detail. The legislation is designed to redress systemic gender discrimination in compensation for work performed by employees in female-dominated job classes. In a nutshell, the primary objective is to require employers to ensure compensation equity between males and females where the work performed is equally valuable in terms of skill, effort, responsibility, and working conditions, even where the jobs being compared are different in nature and content. The legislation requires public and private sector employers who have 100 or more employees to determine whether pay equity exists for each female job class and to develop and post a pay equity plan before the mandatory posting date (varies from two to five years depending on the size and complexity of the firm). To a certain extent, the development of pay equity plans is tied to the collective bargaining system, since employers must bargain with unions in developing a remedial plan for each bargaining unit. To secure compliance, the legislation has been complaint-driven and wide-ranging powers were vested with the Pay Equity Office and the Hearing Tribunal, which form part of the Pay Equity Commission.[4]

Environmental Impact and Policy Implications

UNIONS. Unions and employee associations have had a major impact on wage structures, wage levels, and individual wage determinations, even in companies that are not organized. Union action influences every phase of compensation, from the early stages of job analysis and job evaluation to the final determination of specific wage rates and the selection of the criteria used to set those roles. Although unions generally do not conduct job evaluation programs, in many instances they do help design, negotiate, or modify com-pany programs. Even if union interests are not completely served in the job evaluation process, they can be served at the bargaining table. In fact, serving the interests of members at the bargaining table puts job evaluation into perspective for the union as well as the management.

Since 1980, the trend toward higher pay and benefit demands by unions has slowed dramatically. This has been due in large part to two general recessions and the serious financial difficulties faced by organizations in their quest to survive. In fact, conditions have become so severe in several industries that workers have actually voted to take *pay cuts* in order to prevent layoffs as a consequence of *take-back negotiations* between the union and management. For example, in 1992 workers at Stone-Consolidated Inc. in Bathurst, Nova Scotia, were forced into major concessions, including a 20 percent wage rollback in order to keep the plant from shutting down. Similarly, unionized workers at General Motors in Oshawa agreed to reduce overtime and to changes pertaining to seniority in order to keep two assembly plants open.

THE MARKET. Both union and management base final wage rates and levels on far more than the results of job evaluation and wage surveys, although both often rely on wage surveys. The surveys provide data on wage rates for comparable work in other sections of the industry, and wages paid in the locality or the relevant labour market. Organizations need to be aware that paying what the market will bear and paying women and minorities less because they will accept it just to land a job are not acceptable excuses for wage discrimination.

In addition to the market wage levels, other criteria for wage determination are labour market conditions (the number of people out of work and looking for work), the past history of the organization's wage structure, fringe benefits, indexes of productivity, company profit figures or turnover data, and the Consumer Price Index, which helps determine cost-of-living increases.

The market impact is used both directly and indirectly in the determination of wage rates. Directly, the market provides comparisons against which organizations can establish pay rates for benchmark jobs. The rates for these jobs in turn are used to establish pay rates for all other jobs. When used indirectly, organizations first perform a job evaluation on their existing jobs, then establish pay grades and classes (or families), and then study the market to see what other organizations are paying. Whether used directly or indirectly, however, the market rates are generally not the ones used by an organization. The final rates generally represent a composite of market-rate information and answers to pay policy questions such as: "Does the organization want to be a pay leader?" and "For what does the organization want to pay: job content, seniority, performance, or cost of living?" These usually are the central issues in basic wage determination for most organizations.

FREE TRADE. According to many sources, the free trade agreement with the U.S.A. has caused multiple hardships to Canadian firms. Cost of production and competition for skilled labour are advantageous in the U.S.A. and, consequently, they result in layoffs and a decline in sales for many Canadian firms. This has been primarily due to the lower wages paid by U.S. manufacturers. Not only are the salaries lower, but U.S. real estate is also more affordable. For example, an acre in Ohio would cost between $7,500 and $22,500, whereas in Toronto it would cost $500,000. There is a strong fear among Canadian manufacturers that the situation will become worse with the new free trade agreement that includes Mexico. All in all, the free trade agreements have put pressure on government, businesses, and unions to lower salary expectations in order to remain competitive.[5]

There are four principal determinants of wages that represent most activities in many compensation departments: (1) determination of the value/worth of jobs through job evaluation processes, (2) determination of job classes, (3) establishment of pay structure, and (4) individual wage determinations.

PRINCIPAL DETERMINANTS OF WAGES

Job Evaluation

Job evaluation is the foundation for a sound compensation program. Its purpose is to establish a relative value for each job in an organization and to assign a rate or range of pay for those jobs. Additionally, job evaluation is concerned with the establishment of **internal equity** among the different jobs in the organization. The amount paid for a job could be decided on the basis of a manager's impression of what the job should pay or is worth, but to help ensure internal equity, more formal methods are often used. **Job evaluation** is defined as the process of comparing jobs by the use of formal and systematic procedures to determine their relative worth within the organization. After jobs are formally evaluated, they are grouped into classes or grades. Within each class, jobs are then arranged in order of importance, and ranges of pay are established with the aid of wage surveys.

Although organizations generally compensate individuals on the basis of their job performance and personal contributions, organizations implicitly recognize job-related contributions by assigning pay in accordance with the difficulty and importance of jobs. Most organizations use some type of formal job evaluation or informal comparison of job content to determine the relative worth of job-related contributions. It is usually only in the formal job evaluation process, however, that job-related contributions are explicitly specified.

Prior to the establishment of a job evaluation system, the company needs to decide whether to use a single plan or multiple plans. Traditionally, job evaluation plans have varied depending on the job family (e.g., clerical, skilled craft, professional). The premise of this approach is that the work content within each of the job families is too diverse to be captured by one plan. Thus, proponents of multiple plans contend that these are necessary to capture the unique job characteristics of a job family. On the other hand, advocates of comparable worth and pay equity prefer the use of a single pay plan. Their argument is based on the assumption that there are universal compensable factors that relate to *all* jobs. Only when jobs are evaluated using the same criteria can the relative value of *all* jobs be determined. When separate plans are used, it is much easier to discriminate against specific classes of jobs. Consequently, in order to prevent this from happening, universal factors must be utilized.

There are four essential steps in the job evaluation process. The first step is a thorough job analysis (see Chapter 3). This provides information about the job's duties and responsibilities and about employee requirements for successful performance of the job.

The second step is deciding what the organization is paying for—that is, determining which factors will be used to evaluate jobs (although not all methods of job evaluation explicitly use factors). The factors are like yardsticks used to measure the relative importance of jobs. Since these factors help determine what jobs are worth (jobs and not people at this point), they are called **compensable factors**. The factors used by organizations vary widely, but they all presumably reflect job-related contributions. Accountability, know-how, problem-solving ability, and physical demands are examples of these factors. The factors chosen should:

- Represent all of the major aspects of job content for which the company is willing to pay (compensable factors), typically skill, effort, responsibility, and working conditions;
- Avoid excessive overlap or duplication;
- Be definable and measurable;
- Be easily understood by employees and administrators;
- Not be excessively costly to install or administer;
- be selected with legal considerations in mind.

After compensable factors are determined, their relative importance must be defined. This is reflected by the differential points or degrees (weights) assigned to each of the compensable factors. The weights assigned to the factors are usually determined by the employer's judgment of the relative importance of the factors to the organization. An illustration of differential factor weighting is provided in Exhibit 7.4.

Exhibit 7.4
Sample of Point Rating Method

COMPENSABLE FACTOR	FIRST DEGREE	SECOND DEGREE	THIRD DEGREE	FOURTH DEGREE	FIFTH DEGREE
1. Job knowledge	50	100	150	200	
2. Problem solving	50	100	150	205	260
3. Impact	60	120	180	240	
4. Working conditions	10	30	50		
5. Supervision needed	25	50	75	100	

The third step is to design a system for evaluating jobs according to the compensable factors chosen in the second step. There are many basic methods of job evaluation that organizations can adapt to their own needs. Several of these are discussed below.

RANKING METHOD. Job analysis information can be used to construct a hierarchy or ladder of jobs that reflects their relative difficulty or value to the organization. This is the core of the ranking method. Although any number of compensable factors could be used to evaluate jobs, the job analyst often considers the whole job on the basis of just one factor, such as difficulty or value.

This is the least specific job evaluation method. However, it is convenient when there are only a few jobs to evaluate and when one person is familiar with them all. As the number of jobs increases, and the likelihood that one individual will be familiar with them all declines, detailed job analysis information becomes more important and ranking is often done by committee. When a large number of jobs is to be ranked, key or benchmark jobs are used for comparison.

One difficulty with the ranking method is that it is only effective when all jobs are different from one another. Often it is difficult to make fine distinctions between similar jobs, and thus disagreements arise. Because of these difficulties, ranking is generally adopted only by small organizations.

JOB CLASSIFICATION METHOD. The job classification method is similar to the ranking method, except that classes or grades are established and the jobs are then placed into the classes. Jobs are usually evaluated on the basis of the whole job, either using one factor, such as difficulty, or an intuitive summary of factors. Again, job analysis information is useful in the classification and benchmark jobs are frequently established for each class. Within each class or grade there is no further ranking of the jobs.

Although many organizations use job classification, the largest organization to use this method has been the Canadian Public Service, which is gradually replacing it with more sophisticated methods. It is also commonly used for managerial and engineering/scientific jobs in the private sector.

One advantage of this method is that it can be applied to a large number and wide variety of jobs. As the number and variety of jobs in an organization increase, however, the classification of jobs tends to become more subjective. This is particularly true when an organization has a large number of plant or office locations, and thus jobs with the same title may differ in content. Because it is difficult to evaluate each job separately in such cases, the job title becomes a more important guide to job classification than job content.

A major disadvantage of the job classification method is that the basis of the job evaluations is either one factor or an intuitive summary of many factors. The problem with using one factor, such as difficulty (skill), is that it may not apply to all jobs. Some jobs may require a great deal of skill, but others may require a great deal of responsibility. This does not mean that jobs requiring much responsibility should be placed in a lower classification than jobs requiring much skill. Perhaps both factors could be considered together. Jobs should be evaluated and classified on the basis of all factors valued by the organization. However, this balancing of the compensable factors to determine the relative equality of jobs often causes misunderstandings with the employees and the labour leaders. To deal with this disadvantage, many organizations use more quantifiable methods of evaluation.

POINT RATING AND POINT FACTOR METHOD. The most widely used method of job evaluation is the **point rating and point factor** method, which consists of assigning point values to previously determined compensable factors and adding them to arrive at a total. There are several advantages to the point rating method:

1. The point rating method is widely used throughout industry, permitting comparisons on a similar basis with other firms.
2. The point rating method is relatively simple to understand. It is the simplest of the quantitative methods of job evaluation.

Methods and Techniques in Job Evaluation

3. The point values for each job are easily converted to job and wage classes with a minimum of confusion and distortion.

4. A well-conceived point rating method has considerable stability. It is applicable to a wide range of jobs over an extended period of time. The greatest assets here are consistency, uniformity, and widespread applicability.

5. The point rating method is a definitive approach requiring several separate and distinct judgment decisions.

The limitations of the point rating method are few. Point rating is relatively high in cost, difficult to administer, generates lobbying for reclassification, and generates inequity in the transfer from point to monetary value. But an especially critical problem is the assumption that all jobs can be described with the same compensable factors. Many organizations avoid this by developing separate point rating methods for different groups of employees. In Exhibit 7.4 there are five compensable factors used by one organization to evaluate the jobs in supervisory, nonsupervisory, and clerical categories. Exhibit 7.4 also describes what is associated by degree (relative weight) and points. Some factors are more important than others, as shown by the different point values. The HR department determines which degree of a compensable factor is appropriate for the job, and then the points assigned to each degree of each factor represented in the job are totalled. Levels of compensation are determined on the basis of the point totals.

As with other job evaluation plans, the point rating method incorporates the potential subjectivity of the job analyst. It therefore has the potential for wage discrimination. *Bias* or *subjectivity* can enter: (1) in the selection of the compensable factors, (2) in the relative weights (degrees) assigned to factors, and (3) in the assignment of degrees to the jobs being evaluated. What is at stake here is equal pay and job comparability. In order to make sure its point rating evaluation system is free from potential bias and is implemented as objectively as possible, an organization may solicit the input of the job incumbent, the supervisor, and job evaluation experts as well as its HR department.

THE CLASSIFICATION POINT SYSTEM. This method, developed by Towers Perrin Company, combines the point rating methods with the job classification method. The advantages of this hybrid approach are:

- It establishes internal equity among positions through a point rating method.
- It allows a direct comparison to the market on a job family basis through the classification approach.
- It minimizes senior management involvement in the evaluation process.
- It lends itself to decentralization while ensuring the overall consistency of the evaluators.
- It can readily be explained to employees.
- It is relatively easy to implement.

The backbone of the process consists of selecting a number of compensable factors that are particular to the organization. Each factor is subdivided into a series of degrees, the number and definitions of which are determined through consensus. Then, benchmark positions are selected from all major occupational groups and key responsibilities levels are evaluated. In the next stage, job evaluation guidecharts are prepared for each job family. Finally, a multiple regression analysis is conducted to statistically correlate the unweighted evaluation results and market values of benchmark positions and to assess their relationship. Once the factor weights and point scales are finalized, the relative value, or ranking, of all positions (and all job family levels) is established. Total point scores provide both overall position ranking and relative ranking within each job family. The final factor weighting reflects internal value systems and external market practices.

HAY PLAN. This is one of the most widely used job evaluation systems in the world. Like the Towers Perrin method, it combines the best characteristics of point evaluation and factor comparison methods, except that it utilizes only three general factors, as shown in Exhibit 7.5. This method, generally known as the **Hay Plan**, is a widely used method for evaluating managerial and executive positions. The three factors, **problem solving**, **know-how**, and **accountability** are used because they are assumed to be the most important and universal aspects of managerial and executive positions. For all practical purposes there are eight factors: two subfactors in problem-solving, three in know-how, and three in accountability. In deriving the final point profile for any job, however, only the three major factors are assigned point values.

FACTOR-COMPARISON METHOD. The point rating method, regardless of the number of factors and degrees of each factor, derives a point total for each job. Several very different types of jobs can have the same total points. After the total points are determined, jobs are priced—often according to groups or classes, much as they would be using the job classification method. The **factor-comparison method** avoids this step between point totalling and pricing by assigning dollar values to factors and comparing the amounts directly to the pay for benchmark jobs. In short, factor-comparison is similar to point rating in that both use compensable factors. But the point rating method uses degrees and points for each factor to measure jobs, whereas factor-comparison uses benchmark jobs and monetary values on factors.

Exhibit 7.5
Hay Plan Compensable Factors

MENTAL ACTIVITY (PROBLEM SOLVING)	KNOW-HOW	ACCOUNTABILITY
The amount of original, self-starting thought required by the job for analysis, evaluation, creation, reasoning, and arriving at conclusions Mental activity has two dimensions: • The degree of freedom with which the thinking process is used to achieve job objectives without the guidance of standards, precedents, or direction from others • The type of mental activity involved; the complexity, abstractness, or originality of thought required Mental activity is expressed as a percentage of know-how for the obvious reason that people think with what they know. The percentage judged to be correct for a job is applied to the know-how point value; the result is the point value given to mental activity.	The sum total of all knowledge and skills, however acquired, needed for satisfactory job performance (evaluates the job, not the person) Know-how has three dimensions: • The amount of practical, specialized, or technical knowledge required • Breadth of management, or the ability to make many activities and functions work well together; the job of company president, for example, has greater breadth than that of a department supervisor • Requirement for skill in motivating people Using a chart, a number can be assigned to the level of know-how needed in a job. This number—or point value—indicates the relative importance of know-how in the job being evaluated.	The measured effect of the job on company goals Accountability has three dimensions: • Freedom to act, or relative presence of personal or procedural control and guidance, determined by answering the question, "How much freedom has the job holder to act independently?"; for example, a plant manager has more freedom than a supervisor under his or her control • Dollar magnitude, a measure of the sales, budget, dollar value of purchases, value added, or any other significant annual dollar figure related to the job • Impact of the job on dollar magnitude, a determination of whether the job has a primary effect on end results or has instead a sharing, contributory, or remote effect Accountability is given a point value independent of the other two factors.

Note: The total evaluation of any job is arrived at by adding the points (not shown here) for know-how, mental activity, and accountability.

The "prices," or wage rates, for the benchmark jobs are determined by the market. Although this is a quick method by which to set wage rates, it has the potential to perpetuate the traditional pay differentials between jobs, because it is against these jobs that the wage rates for other jobs are determined. Moreover, the process of determining the rates of other jobs is really in the hands of the wage and salary analyst who can be subjective, thereby furthering the potential for wage discrimination. It has therefore come under attack from the job comparability advocates who claim it allows or causes pay discrimination.[6] Only about 10 percent of employers that do formal job evaluation use the factor-comparison method. The complexity of the explanation demonstrates why.

SKILL-BASED EVALUATION. Whereas previously mentioned job evaluation plans "pay for the job," **skill-based evaluation** is based on the idea of "paying for the person." This type of evaluation is concerned with the skills of the employees and, therefore, incorporates training programs to facilitate skill acquisition by employees. The idea of paying for the person, or at least the person–job combination rather than just the job, is not new. Many professional organizations have been doing this for a long time, e.g., universities, law offices, and research and development labs. What is new, however, is paying for the person in blue-collar jobs. One of the more visible examples of skill-based evaluation for blue-collar jobs is Shell Sarnia in Ontario. Its plan is based on the starting rate given to all new employees. After coming on board, employees are advanced one pay grade for each job they learn. People can be trained for jobs in any order and at any price. Members of each employee's team ensure that the jobs are taught correctly, and they determine when the employee has mastered a job. Employees reach the top pay grade in the plant after learning all jobs.

Common Discriminatory Aspects in Job Evaluation Methods

The following represents a brief assessment of the tendency to bias and discrimination with some of the methods mentioned above:

- *Ranking Methods*: Jobs usually performed by women are often perceived to have low social status and may, therefore, be undercompensated.
- *Classification Methods*: Job families, such as clerical and secretarial, which consist almost completely of women, are often allotted low wage rates. Generally, in the classification system, no mechanisms exist for comparison with other job families, so the wage range for classes of undervalued incumbents remains lower than the range set for other classifications. This discriminatory aspect of evaluation is validated and becomes systematic when compensation rates are based on labour-market pay data. The undervalued remain undervalued.
- *Point Factor Methods*: Wage scales are normally adjusted to reflect both labour market rates and the subjective assessment of raters as to the relative importance of the job. For example, the total point score can be adjusted to fit the pay data, so that while some jobs might be allowed a certain dollar amount per point, jobs with a tendency to be undervalued, as are many women's jobs, could be assigned less than that, regardless of the necessary skill, effort, and responsibility factors for the job.
- *Factor-Comparison Methods*: A high degree of subjectivity is present in the selection of benchmark jobs, in the definition of worth, and in the determination of the degree or involvement of each compensable factor. As with other systems, worth is in part determined by external pay rates, rather than in terms of contribution to the organization;

A number of discriminatory aspects are common to all systems of job evaluation (except skill-based systems). For example, many factors are based on men's jobs and are weighted accordingly. Moreover, since most of those involved with devising pay structures for "women's jobs" have little understanding of or direct experience with the work, many of these jobs are undervalued. Consequently, the following guidelines could be used in order to reduce biases in job evaluation systems:

1. Ensure that those associated with the analysis and evaluation of jobs are aware of and understand the issues concerning women's jobs and the possible discriminatory aspects of systems.
2. Ensure that the actual job content, and not the person doing the job, is analyzed and evaluated.
3. Conduct comprehensive and structured job analyses to screen factors, job families, and benchmarks for discriminatory aspects.
4. Ensure that factors associated with work usually done by women, such as manual dexterity, accuracy, continuous routine, and concentration, are weighted on a comparable basis with factors associated with jobs usually done by men.
5. Discuss all aspects of work usually done by women with incumbents to determine previously unrecognized or undervalued factors, such as physical and mental effort and skill, responsibility, and varied working conditions.
6. Ensure that where more than one evaluation system is established for different types of jobs, discriminatory aspects are not present.
7. Maintain records of job analyses, the definitions and weighting of factors, the scores for each job, and the reasons for rating decisions.
8. Inform all involved employees of job evaluation procedures.[7]

A new system of job evaluation that is supposed to be "bias free" has been recently introduced to Canadian organizations. This computerized system is called JEBOR (Job Evaluation by Operations Research). Companies such as Gulf Canada, Olympia and York, and Epton Industries, Inc. have been experimenting with it. Unlike other systems, JEBOR's evaluations are made only by employees—superiors, peers, or subordinates—with direct knowledge of the jobs being rated. Using a computer's user-friendly language, JEBOR can be tailored to the company's own values and, if equity philosophies are part of this culture, the system accounts for them during the compilation of the ranking data.

Once the job evaluations are conducted, and before salaries are determined, job classes or job families are created, based on the results of the job evaluation. Determining **job classes** or **job families** means grouping together all jobs that are similar in value; for example, grouping all clerical-type jobs together or grouping all managerial jobs together. The jobs within the same class may be quite different, but they should be roughly comparable in value to the organization. All jobs in each class are assigned one salary or range of salaries.

Determining Job Classes

One reason for grouping jobs into classes is efficiency of salary administration. Also, it can be hard to justify the small differences in pay that might exist between jobs if job classes are not created. Finally, small errors that occur in the evaluation of the jobs can be eliminated in the classification process. On the other hand, employees can find fault with the classification results if their jobs are grouped with jobs they feel are less important. Additionally, the jobs that are grouped together may be dissimilar when there are too few classes of jobs. Using only a few classes is most appropriate when many of the jobs are of similar value.

Once jobs are evaluated and job classes are determined, wage rates or ranges need to be established. Although job classes are determined for the purpose of establishing wage rates, job classes are often based on wage rates that already exist. This practice may seem

Establishing the Pay Structure

somewhat backwards, but it is common in organizations. Most organizations have firmly established pay schedules, and thus need to determine job classes only when many new jobs are introduced or if the organization has never really had a sound job analysis program. Newly established organizations are likely to be small, and would therefore price their jobs based on surveys of what other organizations are paying.

WAGE AND SALARY SURVEYS. Wage surveys can be used to develop compensation levels, wage structures, and even payment plans (the amount and kind of direct and indirect compensation). Whereas job evaluation helps ensure internal equity, wage surveys provide information to help ensure external equity. Both types of equity are important if an organization is to be successful in attracting, retaining, and motivating employees. In addition, survey results can also indicate the compensation philosophies of competing organizations. For example, a large electronics company may have a policy of paying 15 percent above the market rate (the average of all rates for essentially the same job in an area); a large service organization may choose to pay the market rate; a large bank may decide to pay 5 percent less than the market rate.

Most organizations use wage surveys extensively. Separate surveys are published for different occupational groupings; thus, many larger organizations subscribe to several surveys. For example, there are surveys for clerical workers, professional workers, managers, and executives. Separate surveys are conducted not only because there are such wide differences in skill levels, but also because labour markets are so different. An organization surveying clerical workers may need only to survey companies within a ten-mile radius, whereas a survey of managerial salaries may cover the entire country.

A sample of the results of a survey for management compensation in Canada for 1991 is provided in Exhibit 7.6. This survey indicates that the average salary increase of executives in 1991 over the previous year was 6.3 percent. Furthermore, the same survey found the average bonus to be around $10,040, which corresponds to approximately 13 percent of the mean salary.[8]

Similar results were reported in a survey conducted by the Conference Board of Canada for 1990. Average increases of job salary ranges were 5.2 percent; however,

Exhibit 7.6
Executive Compensation for Canada (1991) by Position

POSITION	% INCREASE	MEAN SALARY (in thousands)
Sales and Marketing		
Top management (sales and marketing)	6.5	107.3
Top management (sales)	6.3	80.6
Director of sales (Division level)	6.3	67.7
Accounting and Finance		
Top management (finance)	8.9	100.6
Corporate comptroller	7.3	74.1
Human Resources		
Senior executive		
Manager (compensation	5.9	87.8
and benefits)	5.8	72.4

Source: MLH + Inc. (1991 Survey).

outstanding performers averaged 8 percent. The average incentive/bonus or profit sharing payment, as a percentage of salary, ranged from 4.6 percent for clerical and support staff to 19.4 percent for the executive group.[9] There were also slight differences by region, as indicated in Exhibit 7.7.

Once the survey data are collected, the organization must decide how to use them. It could use only the average wage and salary levels from all the companies in the survey to determine its own levels, or it could weight the wage and salary levels of companies by the number of employees. Another option would be to use the wage and salary ranges from all the companies to determine its own wage and salary ranges. After selecting the wage and salary information it wants, the organization develops a grade structure with pay rates for job categories.

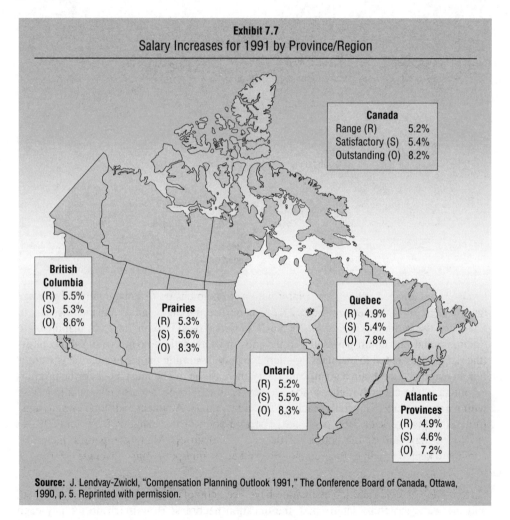

Exhibit 7.7
Salary Increases for 1991 by Province/Region

Canada
Range (R)	5.2%
Satisfactory (S)	5.4%
Outstanding (O)	8.2%

British Columbia
(R)	5.5%
(S)	5.3%
(O)	8.6%

Prairies
(R)	5.3%
(S)	5.6%
(O)	8.3%

Quebec
(R)	4.9%
(S)	5.4%
(O)	7.8%

Ontario
(R)	5.2%
(S)	5.5%
(O)	8.3%

Atlantic Provinces
(R)	4.9%
(S)	4.6%
(O)	7.2%

Source: J. Lendvay-Zwickl, "Compensation Planning Outlook 1991," The Conference Board of Canada, Ottawa, 1990, p. 5. Reprinted with permission.

GRADE STRUCTURE. A typical example of a grade structure is shown in Exhibit 7.8. This grade structure is based on job evaluation points associated with a point-factor evaluation. The boxes shown are associated with a range of job evaluation points (the job class) and the range of pay grades. In essence, these **pay grades** are the job families or classes. Consequently, there may be several different jobs within one box that are very similar in job evaluation points.

As illustrated, the boxes ascend from left to right. This reflects the increase of worth and the associated higher pay levels (shown on the vertical axis) for more valued jobs. The pay

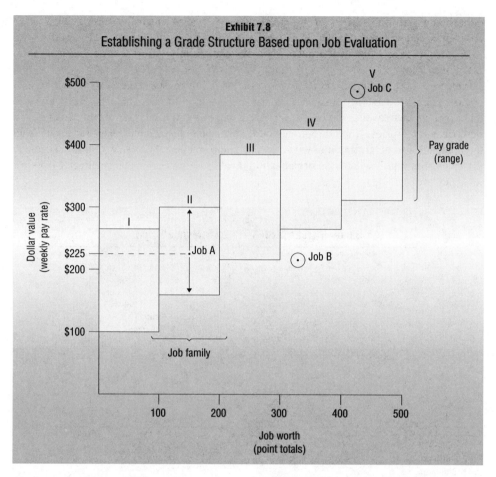

Exhibit 7.8
Establishing a Grade Structure Based upon Job Evaluation

levels are established using market information (to help ensure external equity). The wage rate for each job is then determined by locating or determining its grade and moving over to a point on the vertical axis, as done for Job A in Grade II, in Exhibit 7.8. Note that there are minimum and maximum pay limits to the jobs in each grade. Staying within those limits (the range) is essential to maintaining internal equity, assuming the job evaluation is valid.[10] For an employee to obtain a significant salary increase he or she must move, or be promoted, into a job in the next higher grade. However, an employee can also receive a pay raise within a given grade. Generally, each job has a rate range. As illustrated, Job A has a range from $150 per week to $300 per week. The mid-point of this range is $225. Initially, an employee may start at the bottom of the range and go up. Many companies, however, attempt to keep the bulk of their employees paid at the mid-point range (average salary).

Individual Wage Determination

Once the job analysis and job evaluation have been completed, the job classes established, and the wage structure determined, the question becomes: How much do we pay each individual? For example, consider Maya and John, both of whom work on the same job. If the rate range were $2,500 to $3,500 per month, Maya might be paid $3,000 and John $2,750. What might account for the pay differential? Although performance contribution would be an appropriate explanation, personal factors such as seniority, gender, age, size of family, experience, and appearance also have been found to influence individual wages. Age and seniority, in fact, are frequently perceived to be rather important factors. In certain cases, variables such as an employee's potential and his or her negotiating skills and leverages also play a role in determining compensation levels.

In actuality, individual wage determinations are often based on both personal contributions and performance. Thus, age and seniority, as well as performance, may influence Maya's and John's pay. However, many managers would argue that pay differences based on performance are more equitable than those based on such personal contributions as seniority. Unions, on the other hand, regard seniority as a "sacred cow." They believe that seniority should be the critical factor in determining pay rate for a number of reasons: (1) rewarding seniority means recognizing experience: assuming a maturity curve for many jobs, the argument is that the senior people in the organization contribute the most; (2) it may be seen as recognition for past performance; and (3) it is a recognition of an employee's loyalty to the organization. Many Japanese companies, for example, reward seniority more than performance for similar reasons.

Performance-based pay systems relate pay to performance. The extent of the relationship and the method of measurement are used to differentiate the two major types of performance-based pay systems: *incentive pay plans* and *merit pay plans*. In **incentive pay plans** performance is often, but not always, measured by standards of productivity and direct indexes of individuals', groups', or organizations' output. By contrast, **merit pay plans** generally use less direct measures of performance, such as rankings or ratings made by supervisors.

> **PERFORMANCE-BASED PAY SYSTEMS**

The major portion of an individual's compensation under a performance-based system is from incentive pay. Since the level of compensation varies with performance, the level of an individual's compensation can vary greatly. Traditionally, incentive pay plans have used only money as a reward. More recently, such nonmonetary rewards as praise, participation, and feedback are also being tied to performance. Merit pay plans affect a relatively small percentage of an individual's total salary because merit pay is generally used only to move an individual's compensation within a rate range, and this adjustment is made only once a year.

Many people are rewarded through a blended incentive/merit pay system, although there are firms that use merit only. Consequently, much of the compensation people receive is primarily not related to performance, but rather to the results of the job evaluation and steps in rate ranges. In either case, performance-based pay plans can motivate workers to perform at high levels. This is, in large part, the objective of performance-based pay systems.

Studies have shown that individual incentive plans can improve performance an average of almost 30 percent in comparison to nonperformance-based pay plans. Group incentive plans can increase performance by 15 to 20 percent.[11] These figures are impressive, given that other HR programs, such as goal setting, participation plans, and job enrichment, have less of an impact on productivity. If pay is going to influence employee performance, two sets of conditions must exist. One describes the employee's perspective and the other describes the organization's perspective. For the employee, the following are important:

> **Objectives of Performance-Based Pay**

- The employee must perceive a close relationship between performance and pay. In other words, pay must be perceived as contingent upon performance.
- Pay must be important or of high value to the employee.
- The employee must be able to perform (i.e., have the ability and know what is expected).
- The employee must not be placed in jeopardy or conflict by working for the extra pay. For example, he or she must not fear physical injuries, rate cutting, job insecurity, or ridicule from co-workers.
- Performance measurement must be fair. If performance evaluations are viewed as biased, many employees will not be motivated by pay.

In order that these conditions exist for the employee, the organization must do its part:

* There must be a high level of trust between the organization and the employees.
* The employee must understand how the pay program works.
* The employee must be able to control the performance on which the pay is based.
* The performance appraisal system must be free from potential bias.
* Managers must be trained in giving feedback.
* The amount of money set aside for merit or incentive pay must be sufficiently large to make extra effort worthwhile.
* The job evaluation must be valid so that the overall salary relationships are equitable.

Different performance-based pay plans are more appropriate under different conditions. Knowing which conditions currently exist in an organization is critical for successfully using performance-based pay plans. A list of plans to choose from and their key features are shown in Exhibit 7.9. Some of these pay plans, and their strengths and weaknesses, will be discussed in more detail in this chapter as well as in the next one.

Prevalence of Performance-Based Pay in Canada

All surveys indicate that the 1990s will see a more extensive use of performance-based pay in Canada. Global competition is forcing Canadian employers to make corporate and individual performance a top priority. Companies will attempt to reduce fixed costs whenever possible; payroll is a natural target. Additionally, Canadian employers will be prepared to take a greater stake in the success of the business by accepting higher risks in return for higher reward.

Surveys conducted by the Conference Board of Canada in 1990 show that 35 percent of companies offer stock options or have stock grant plans in place, especially for their executives; 27 percent have a stock option purchase plan in effect; and the majority of companies surveyed indicate broad-based eligibility. The same survey shows that amongst the companies surveyed, 22 percent provide profit-sharing plans that are open to most employees. Individual cash bonus plans (in addition to, and *not* including, merit or regular pay increases) are present in 61 percent of responding organizations. Although the majority of annual bonus plans are aimed at executives, an increasing number of organizations (28 percent) make them available to other employees as well. Finally, the same survey revealed that productivity gainsharing plans are in existence in 6 percent of the firms surveyed and another 4 percent have pay-for-knowledge or skill-based pay plans.[12]

Similarly interesting results emerged from a recent survey conducted by the Wyatt Company. Exhibit 7.10 highlights the trends in incentive-based pay. Except for 1986/1987, there was at least a 10 percent net growth rate in the use of incentive compensation amongst the survey participants from 1985/6 to 1989/1990. Over 80 percent of respondents (companies totalling 300,000 employees) offered an incentive/bonus plan.[13] Cash plans are generally used in Canada to accomplish short-term objectives, while stock-based plans are being used to accomplish long-term objectives.

What is surfacing is the importance of diversifying plans and the benchmarks used to evaluate performance. The Wyatt report states that the most popular incentives in Canada are those that consider *before tax profitability*, and those that rely on individual performance rather than objectives and productivity measures. Consequently, employers are beginning to structure their incentive plans to reflect their corporate culture, objectives, and financial capabilities.

INCENTIVE PAY PLANS

Until the mid 1980s, most incentive plans in Canada were either piecework or standard hour plans.[14] In general, there is a great deal of variation in the type of incentives used, depending on the type of industry or even the region. For example, a significant percent-

Exhibit 7.9
Key Features of Performance-Based Pay Plans (Incentive and Bonus Plans)

	STOCK OPTION	STOCK GRANT	STOCK PURCHASE	PROFIT SHARING	CASH BONUS	PRODUCTIVITY GAINSHARING
Definition	employee buys company stock at fixed price within specified time	employee awarded stock at no cost; 3 types: -restricted -phantom -performance share/unit	employee purchases company stock with own funds on voluntary basis; a company contribution is common	employee receives share of company profits (cash or deferred)	employee receives cash bonus based on performance	employee receives share of group gain in productivity
Performance indicator(s)	stock price	stock price, company financial results	stock price	company financial results	individual company and/or business unit financial results	productivity gains
Incidence (current/planned)	43% of firms (67% of those with publicly traded shares)	13% of firms	39% of firms (61% of those with publicly traded shares)	27% of respondents	78% have management plans; 18% non-management	16% of respondents
Objectives	(1) motivation, long-term; (2) shareholder identification; (3)competitive compensation	(1) motivation, long-term; (2) shareholder identification; (3)competitive compensation	(1) shareholder identification; (2) entrepreneurial spirit; (3) motivation, long-term	(1) motivation, short-term; (2) productivity improvement; (3) competitive compensation	(1) motivation, short-term; (2) competitive compensation; (3) productivity improvement	(1) productivity improvement;(2) motivation, short-term; (3) entrepreneurial spirit
Success in meeting objectives	44% highly successful; 40% moderately successful; 16% not successful	57% highly successful; 37% moderately successful; 6% not successful	54% highly successful; 29% moderately successful;17% not successful	63% highly successful; 30% moderately successful; 7% not successful	65% highly successful; 31% moderately successful; 4% not successful	83% highly successful; 17% moderately successful; 0% not successful
Eligibility	executives: 97%; sr. management: 67%; mid. management: 28%; lower levels: low	executives: 100%; sr. management: 52%; mid. management: 24%; lower levels: very few	most available to all employees	substantial number are broad-based	primarily for employees at higher levels, but some (20%) for non-management	primarily for lower levels (clerical, production)
Strengths	employee and shareholder interests same	not stock price dependent, flexible	universal eligibility, helps company identification	employees share in company success in tangible way	promotes increased teamwork	promotes increased teamwork
Weaknesses	dependent on stock price performance	restricted eligibility	weak link to individual performance	little unionized employee participation	finding right performance measuring rods	lack of union participation

Source: P.L. Booth "Playing for Performance: The Growing Use of Incentives and Bonus Plans," in Report 22–8, (Ottawa: Conference Board of Canada,1987), 35. Reprinted with permission.

Exhibit 7.10
Trends in Incentive Plan Types in Canada

	% GROWTH RATE				
	1985-1986	1986-1987	1987-1988	1988-1989	1989-1990
Annual Cash Incentive/Bonus Plan	12%	2%	10%	10%	11%
Intermediate/Long-Term Cash Incentive/Bonus Plan	(-22)	100	25	0	50
Performance Units	0	(–43)	0	0	17
Phantom Shares	33	100	(-20)	0	0
Stock Options	21	26	14	16	3
Stock Appreciation Rights	50	0	50	33	33
Restricted Stock Grants	0	0	20	25	0
Stock Purchase/Low Interest Loan Plan	20	21	18	15	4
Gain sharing	0	0	20	33	25
Profit Sharing	7	8	3	12	13
Other	25	0	13	11	13
Cash Plan Subtotal	8	6	9	10	13
Stock Based Plan Subtotal	21	17	14	16	4
Net Growth Rate	12	9	11	12	10

Source: Wyatt Company, *1990 Survey of Canadian Incentive Compensation Plans*, 8. Used with permission.

age of the employees in the textile, clothing, cigar, and steel industries are covered by incentive plans, whereas fewer in the service industry are covered. Almost no public employees are paid under incentive plans. Broadly speaking, it is more likely that incentive plans will be used if labour costs are high, the market is cost-competitive, technology is not advanced, and one employee's output is relatively independent of another's. These factors also may influence the specific type of plan used. The easiest way to discuss the plans is by the level at which they are applied: individual, group, or organization. Each type of plan is generally unique to a specific level.

Individual Incentive Plans

THE PIECEWORK PLAN. Piecework is the most common type of incentive pay plan. Under the **piecework plan**, employees are guaranteed a standard pay rate for each unit of output. The pay rate per unit is frequently determined by the time-and-motion studies of standard output and the current base pay of the job. For example, if the base pay of a job is $45 per day and the employee can produce, at a normal rate, 45 units a day, the piece rate may be established at $1 per unit. The "normal" rate is usually more than what the time-and-motion studies indicate, because it is supposed to represent 100-percent efficiency. The final rate will be adjusted to reflect the bargaining power of the employees, the economic conditions of the organization and community, and what the competition is paying.

STANDARD HOUR PLAN. The second-most-used incentive is the **standard hour plan**, which is essentially a piecework plan, except that standards are denominated in time per unit of output rather than money per unit. Tasks are broken down by the amount of time it takes to complete them. This can be determined by historical records, time-and-motion studies, or a combination of both. The time to perform each task then becomes a "standard time."

MEASURED DAY WORK. **Measured day work plans** play down the connection between rates and standards. Again, formal production standards are established and employee performance is judged against these standards. But with measured day work, the typical standards are less precise. For example, standards may be determined by the results of a rating or ranking procedure rather than by an objective index, such as units produced.

SALES INCENTIVE PLANS. All the incentive plans discussed thus far share an important characteristic: they are usually applied to blue-collar employees and only in some cases to office employees. **Sales incentive plans** apply to salespeople and managers, who generally receive their pay in the form of **commissions**. About two-thirds of all salespeople are paid a base salary plus commission. In real estate sales, however, almost 75 percent of the people are paid straight commissions. Although these data are old, it has been suggested that only 22 percent of all other salespeople are paid straight commissions and only 11 percent of all salespeople work without some guaranteed minimum pay.[15] Similar trends concerning salespeople exist today.

MANAGERIAL INCENTIVE PLANS. Incentive plans for managers generally take the form of cash bonuses for good performance by the department, division, or organization as a whole. Other forms of compensation that can be used as managerial incentives are *stock options* and *performance shares*. A **stock option** is an opportunity for a manager to buy an organization's stock at a later date but at a price established when the option is granted. The idea behind this is that managers will work harder to increase their performance and the profitability of the company (thus increasing the price of the company's stock) if they can share in the long-term profits. If the market price of the stock increases over time, managers can use their options to buy the stock at a lower price and therefore realize financial gain. Moreover, governments also recognize stock option purchases as boosts to the economy. To encourage this trend the province of Quebec, for example, is granting employees tax deductions for purchasing shares of companies they work for. **Performance shares** provide a very close connection between individual performance (as reflected in company profitability) and rewards. This is because the manager or executive is rewarded only if established goals are met. The goals are usually stated in terms of earnings per share (EPS). If the EPS goal is met, the manager receives shares of stock directly. Usually the manager receives cash (called bonus units), as well as stock, in order to pay the taxes on the equity (stock) reward. Receipt of just the shares, however, is usually a substantial reward in itself.

   Here are two recent examples of the use of managerial incentives. In the first case, the Siemens company offers its managers a starting salary of $60,000, but salary raises for excellent performers can be as much as 30 percent a year.[16] In the second case, the newly hired president of Air Canada has been granted options to acquire 400,000 shares in the airline, at an exercise price of $7.35.[17]

   The current trend in managerial incentive plans is toward long-term options. This strategy contains many advantages for both the company and the individual:

- It provides executives with a means of accumulating capital at comparatively favourable tax rates.
- It minimizes the potential impact of the plan on earnings.
- It provides favourable tax treatment for the company (and in many cases for the employee).
- It minimizes the potential negative cash flow and the dilution of earnings.
- It motivates managers to maximize the future growth and profitability of the company.
- It retains outstanding executives and attracts others from the outside labour market.

Exhibit 7.11 illustrates the advantages of long-term incentives over other plans in terms of impact on attraction, retention, and motivation.

Exhibit 7.11
Effectiveness of Executive Compensation Components

COMPONENT	ATTRACTION	RETENTION	MOTIVATION
Base Salary	High	High	Moderate
Benefits	Low	Moderate	Low
Short-Term Incentives	Low	Moderate	Low
Long-Term Incentives	High	Moderate	High
Perquisites	Moderate	High	Moderate

SUGGESTION SYSTEMS. **Suggestion systems**, which reward employees for money-saving or money-producing suggestions, are important because they are used so extensively. Approximately 80 percent of North America's 500 largest corporations have suggestion systems. These are also important because they can result in gains of substantial sums of money. Some organizations allow employees as much as 30 percent of the savings of the first year after implementation. Since the inception of Eastman Kodak's suggestion system, over 1.8 million suggestions have been made and approximately 30 percent have been accepted. As much as $2 million per year has been awarded to Kodak employees for their suggestions. IBM Canada paid out $680,000 in awards for savings totalling $2.5 million, and the Treasury Board of Canada awarded $250,000 in 1983 for savings of almost $11.5 million.[18]

Nevertheless, suggestion systems generally do not have a very favourable reputation, often because individual awards are too small. Also, employees sometimes never learn the results of their suggestions, and companies often save much more than they acknowledge and pay the individual for. In some cases, an individual's suggestion is at first ignored, but is later put into operation by management—with no reward to the employee. This creates hostility, resentment, and distrust between management and employees. The suggestion box itself, in these cases, may become an object of ridicule and games.

Although most suggestion systems are designed to elicit and reward individual suggestions, some systems are designed for groups of employees. One such system is part of the Scanlon Plan, which is discussed in the section on organization-wide incentives. The suggestion system is unique because it is designed to increase the number of good ideas rather than the output of products.

WHY DO INDIVIDUAL INCENTIVES WORK? For incentives to work, principles of **positive reinforcement** need to be present. Accordingly, employees need to know how well they are meeting specific goals and how rewards are tied to improvements:

> To establish a positive reinforcement program, the employer must define the behavioral requirements of the work to be done and evaluate how well it is being done. Job performance goals must be formulated in measurable terms, such as the meeting of deadlines, quality levels, and volume. Once these are established, employees must be provided with timely data on their goal performance.[19]

One of the basic premises of positive reinforcement is the belief that behaviour can be understood and modified by its consequences. In fact, all incentive systems are based on this premise: performance is elicited because of the consequence of receiving rewards. In many organizations the rewards for behaving well are not monetary.

In order for positive reinforcement to effectively elicit the repetition of desired behaviour/performance, several conditions must be met. The parameters of effective reinforcement in compensation (PERC) include:

1. *Nature of the reinforcer.* Only praise that is valued by the employee is effective.
2. *Time of the reinforcer.* Only reinforcers that immediately follow the desired behaviour are effective. A response such as: You did a good job, so I will recommend a pay raise in the next year's budget, is an example of an ineffective reinforcer.
3. *Magnitude of the reinforcer.* Only reinforcers that have sufficient magnitude and are strongly tied to the desired behaviour are effective.
4. *Specificity of the reinforcer.* Only reinforcers that are very specific and clearly understood by the employee are effective. Vague and nonspecific feedback such as: "You did a good job" may not be an effective positive reinforcer.
5. *Routineness of the reinforcer.* Reinforcers that superiors use repetitively lose their effect over time. People get used to them and eventually take for granted the anticipated reward. An annual Christmas bonus is an example of a reinforcer that loses its effect over time.
6. *Schedule of the reinforcer.* Most rewards could be classified into one of two groups: continuous or partial reinforcement. Continuous reinforcement is administered every time a desired behaviour occurs. For example, a manager could praise (or pay) employees every time they perform properly. Partial reinforcement is administered at specific intervals (not every time a desired performance is exhibited). Research has shown that partial reinforcement elicits slower learning but leads to stronger, more permanent retention.

As organizations become more complex, a growing number of jobs become interdependent in terms of the sequencing of actions or operations; in other words, the jobs that precede and follow them affect their performance. Other jobs are part of a joint effort that is necessary to achieve results. In either case, measurement of individual performance is difficult at best. Individual incentives are not appropriate under these conditions because they fail to reward cooperation. Group incentives offer a viable option.

Group Incentive Plans

Most group incentive plans are adaptations of individual plans. The standard hour and performance sharing plans are frequently used, but in group applications base rates are paid for a group standard output and group performance above this standard determines the premium for the individuals in the group. However, for group incentive systems to effectively motivate performance, several conditions must be present:

- Group performance measures (i.e., standards and goals) must exist.
- Group members must believe that they can achieve these objectives through effective performance.
- Organizational culture must be supportive of group collaboration and cooperation.

Organization-Wide Incentive Plans

Because many organizations need high levels of cooperation among their employees, they use some form of incentive on an organization-wide basis. Many Canadian firms use either plant-wide bonus plans or profit-sharing arrangements.[20]

Under these systems, employees receive, as a bonus, a percentage of their base wage if the organization reaches a set goal. Employees receiving the same base wage or salary rate will therefore receive the same incentive. **Profit-sharing plans** are often not considered a form of incentive compensation because individual employees have only partial and indirect control over organizational profits. However, since the extent of employee control over performance in a profit-sharing plan is a matter of degree rather than kind, profit-sharing plans are included here as an organization-wide incentive.

PROFIT-SHARING PLANS. Many profit-sharing plans are registered with the Department of National Revenue to comply with current tax laws. There are two major types of profit-sharing plans that organizations can use.

Cash plans provide for payment of profit shares at regular intervals, typically monthly or yearly. The percentage of profits distributed ranges from 8 to 75 percent. If profits are not realized by the company, no cash payments are made to employees. For this reason, many profit-sharing plans are also called "gain sharing." Gain sharing leads to enhanced productivity and subsequently creates additional profits in which all parties share.

Wage–dividend plans (a special type of cash plan) set the percentage of profits paid to employees according to the amount of dividends paid to stockholders. It is assumed that these plans increase understanding between employees and stockholders and are often perceived as more fair to employees than regular cash plans.

Although these two types of profit-sharing plans are the most common, organizations continue to develop new ones to fit their own unique situation. One such plan has been developed by IPSCO Steel of Regina. IPSCO asks profit-sharing participants to put anywhere from $200 to $500 of their own money into the plan through payroll deductions. The employees' money is then put together with the profit-sharing pool to buy IPSCO shares on the open market. The $200 contributor gets two-fifths of the shares allotted to a $500 contributor. Those eligible can also shield their share purchase in a group registered retirement savings plan so that they can benefit from immediate tax deductions.

Profit sharing within Canadian corporations is growing fast. In the mid 1950s there were 2,000 registered plans. By the mid-1970s there were 8,000 plans, and by the mid-1980s, over 25,000.[21] Companies such as IPSCO Steel, Dominion Envelope, Supreme Aluminum Industries, DOFASCO, and Canadian Tire Co. are only a few to use this system. Yet, while virtually all of the American plans are system-wide (i.e., involve all employees), over 95 percent of Canadian profit-sharing plans limit participation to senior executives. Several studies conducted in the U.S.A. have concluded that on all financial measures, the profit-sharing companies out-performed the nonprofit-sharing companies.

THE SCANLON PLAN. The **Scanlon Plan** represents as much a philosophy of management–employee relations as it does a company-wide incentive system. It emphasizes employer–employee participation in the operations and profitability of the company. The Scanlon Plan is adaptable to different companies and changing needs, and is used in unionized as well as nonunionized plants.

The Scanlon Plan reflects the fact that efficiency of operations depends on company-wide cooperation and that bonus incentives encourage cooperation. The bonus is determined on the basis of savings in labour costs, which are measured by comparing the payroll to the sales value of production on a monthly or bimonthly basis. Previous months' ratios of payroll to sales value of production help establish expected labour costs. Savings in labour costs are then shared by employees (75 percent) and the employer (25 percent). Because all employees share in the savings, one group does not gain at the expense of another. Each employee's bonus is determined by converting the bonus fund to a percentage of the total payroll and then applying this percentage to the employee's pay for the month. In The Canadian Valve and Hydrant Manufacturing Co., for example, the ratio of payroll costs to net sales revenue was dramatically improved after a Scanlon-type plan was introduced.

Although Scanlon Plans can be successful, their real incentive value can be short-lived. This can occur if employees feel they can no longer work smarter or harder and, therefore, feel they cannot improve upon previous months' payroll-to-sales-value-of-production ratios. At this point, employee performance levels off and the Scanlon Plan loses its incentive value. This problem, however, is greatly minimized where work methods and products are always changing. Under these conditions employees are more likely to feel they can always find better ways to work.

As previously mentioned, the survey conducted in 1990 by the Conference Board of Canada shows that outstanding clerical and support staff received an average 8 percent merit increase while executives received 8.7 percent. Of all companies surveyed, 59 percent claimed they would be using merit only for salary increases in 1991.[22] To effectively use merit pay plans it is necessary to determine the size of merit pay raises, the times at which they are to be given, and the relationship between merit pay increments and position in the salary range.

A typical merit pay plan is shown in Exhibit 7.12. The pay increments depend not only on employee performance, but also on employee position on the salary range. The lower the position on the range (the first quarter is the lowest), the larger the percentage of the merit raise.

Merit Pay Guidelines

It is important to monitor the *number* of people in each quarter. Although the percentage size of merit increases is greater in the lower quarters, the absolute size of the increases is often larger in the upper quarters. The more people in the upper quarters, the larger the budget necessary for merit increases. Therefore, the compensation manager must monitor the line managers, who may attempt to push their employees to the top of the ranges in each job as a way to offer more rewards. The compensation manager ends up playing the role of police officer, especially in a highly centralized operation. Unpleasant as it may be, this role is necessary for budget purposes and to ensure equity for all employees in the organization. Employees who perform equally well on the same job generally should not be paid different salaries and given different merit increases.

Exhibit 7.12
Sample Merit Pay Plan

Performance Rating	CURRENT POSITION IN SALARY RANGE			
	First Quarter	Second Quarter	Third Quarter	Fourth Quarter
Truly outstanding	13–14% increase	11–12% increase	9–10% increase	6–8% increase
Above average	11–12% increase	9–10% increase	7–8% increase	6% increase or less
Good	9–10% increase	7–8% increase	6% increase or less	delay increase
Satisfactory	6–8% increase	6% increase or less	delay increase	no increase
Unsatisfactory	no increase	no increase	no increase	no increase

Many large organizations grant **cost-of-living adjustments** (COLAs) or general (nonperformance related) increases to their employees, especially firms in which unions have written COLAs into their contracts. Neither COLAs nor general increases are based on performance, yet they can account for the lion's share of money available for compensation increases. And where unionized workers have COLA guarantees, the pressures are great to provide the same benefits to nonunion, often white-collar, employees.

Merit vs. Cost-of-Living Adjustments

Many organizations would rather eliminate their COLAs in favour of merit pay plans, primarily because COLAs are often rather expensive and have no relationship to performance. In addition, COLAs often take some salary control out of the hands of the organization and the compensation manager. Since most COLAs are tied to the Consumer Price Index (CPI), salaries increase arbitrarily as the CPI goes up. And the greater the COLA budget, the smaller the pot for merit increases. Some argue that because merit increases must be substantial to work effectively, the issue in times of high inflation becomes whether to use the entire salary budget for COLAs or for merit increases. Yet the incentive value of merit raises tends to be modest in even the best economic circumstances. This is due to the relatively small size of the average merit increase, and to the relatively small differences (in absolute dollars) between getting the top increase and the lowest increase. Consequently, organizations look to incentive pay plans when they desire more motivational value from their compensation dollar.

ADMINISTRATIVE ISSUES IN PERFORMANCE-BASED PAY

Although performance-based pay plans are capable of substantially improving productivity, there are often many obstacles in design and implementation that limit their potential effectiveness.

Obstacles in the design and implementation of performance-based pay plans can be grouped into three general categories: (1) difficulties in specifying and measuring job performance; (2) problems in identifying valued rewards (pay being just one of many rewards); and (3) difficulties in linking rewards to job performance. These problems are presented in more detail in Exhibit 7.13 along with their implications for management.

Exhibit 7.13
Obstacles to the Design of Effective Reward Systems and their Implications for Management

OBSTACLES	CAUSES	IMPLICATION FOR MANAGEMENT
A. Difficulties in specifying and measuring performance	1. Changes in the nature of work • Increase in service-oriented jobs • Increase in white-collar, managerial, and professional jobs • Increases in the interdependencies and complexity of work 2. Multi-dimensional nature of work • Single-item measures of performance are often inadequate • In many jobs today, multiple criteria are necessary to assess performance 3. Technological developments • Technological developments often result in new and untested methods of work • Machine-paced jobs permit little variation in performance 4. Lack of supervisory training • Use of untrained, inexperienced supervisors in the evaluation process • Perceptual biases 5. The manager's value system • Lack of interest in or inability to differentiate among high and low performers • Failure to see long-range outcomes of differential rewarding	1. Develop techniques for specifying desirable behaviours and clarifying the objectives of the organization. 2. Utilize evaluation procedures that recognize the multi-dimensional nature of performance 3. Develop a reliable and valid performance appraisal system based on results and/or behavioural standards 4. Train supervisors to use the performance appraisal system appropriately and to understand potential sources of bias 5. Clearly define long-term consequences of performance-contingent and non-contingent reward practices

	Exhibit 7.13 (continued)	
OBSTACLES	**CAUSES**	**IMPLICATION FOR MANAGEMENT**

B. Problems in identifying valued rewards	1. Choice of rewards
	  • Choosing a reward that is not reinforcing
	
	2. Utilizing rewards of insufficient size or magnitude
	  • Lack of resources
	  • Company policy
	
	3. Poor timing of rewards
	  • Size of organization: bureaucracy
	  • Standardization/formalization of feedback mechanisms
	  • Complexity of feedback system
		1. Make managers aware of the effects of rewards on employee performance and satisfaction
		
		2. Train managers to identify rewards for their subordinates
		
		3. Administer rewards of sufficient magnitude
		
		4. Administer rewards as quickly after desirable responses as possible

C. Difficulties in linking rewards to performance	1. Failure to create appropriate contingencies between rewards and performance
	  • Lack of knowledge, skill, experience
	  • Belief system
	  • Difficulty in administration
	
	2. Creating inappropriate contingencies
	  • Rewarding behaviour that does not increase performance
	  • Rewarding behaviour A, but hoping for B
	
	3. Nullifying intended contingencies
	  • Using improper performance appraisal instrument
	  • Improper use of performance appraisal instrument
	  • Failure to use information obtained
	  • Inconsistently applied
	
	4. Employee opposition
	  • Individually: mistrust, lack of fairness, inequity
	  • Socially: restrictions due to fear of loss of work
	  • Outside intervention: union
		1. Train manager to establish appropriate contingencies between rewards and performance
		
		2. Use information obtained from appraisals of employee performance as basis for reward allocation decisions
		
		3. Administer the reward system consistently across employees
		
		4. Obtain employee participation in the design and administration of the pay plan

Source: Reprinted by permission from P.M. Podsakoff, C.N. Greene, and J.M. McFillen, "Obstacles to the Effective Use of Reward Systems," in *Readings in Personnel and Human Resource Management*, 2nd ed., ed. R.S. Schuler and S.A. Youngblood (St. Paul, Minn.: West Publishing Co., 1984). Copyright © 1984 by West Publishing Company. All rights reserved.

In order to reward job performance one must first specify what it is, then determine the relationships between levels of job performance and rewards, and then accurately measure job performance. Doing this is often difficult due to the changing nature of work, its multidimensional nature, technological developments, lack of supervisory training, and the manager's value system.

A second set of obstacles applies to the selection of appropriate monetary as well as nonmonetary rewards. Other rewards may have more motivational value than pay, especially for employees whose pay increments may be largely consumed by increased taxes. Consequently, it is important for the manager to learn which kind of rewards are valued by the employees and contingently to administer those that are most reinforcing.

Obstacles to Performance-Based Pay Plan Effectiveness

The third set of obstacles relates to the difficulties in linking rewards to job performance. It can be difficult, for example, to create appropriate contingencies or accurate performance appraisal measures. In addition employee opposition is sometimes a major obstacle in successfully implementing performance-based pay, especially incentive plans. This is due to a number of beliefs held by employees, such as:

- Incentive plans result in work speed-up.
- Rates are cut if earnings under the plan increase too much.
- Incentive plans encourage competition among workers and the discharge of slow workers.
- Incentive plans result in unemployment by "working yourself out of a job."
- Incentive plans break down crafts by reducing skill requirements through methods study.
- Workers don't get their share of increased productivity.
- Incentive plans are too complex.
- Standards are set unfairly.
- Industrial engineers are out to rob workers.
- Earnings fluctuate, making it difficult to budget household expenditures and even to obtain home mortgages.
- Incentive plans are used to avoid a deserved pay increase.
- Incentive plans increase the strain on workers and may impair their health.
- Incentive plans increase the frequency of methods changes.
- Incentive plans ask workers to do more than a fair day's work.
- Incentive plans imply a lack of trust in workers by management.

All in all, many of the stereotypical beliefs emerge from a lack of trust in management. This has immediate implications for the establishment of the rates and standards that incentive systems are based upon. Workers may put on elaborate charades for the benefit of time-study engineers doing work measurement (described in Chapter 3). To further complicate matters, the engineers (who know that workers might try to be misleading) will incorporate into their data estimates of how inaccurate the measures are. This combination of scientific observation measurement and educated guessing can result in inaccurate or unfair rates, which reduce the incentive value of the system, the profitability of the company, or both.

Auditing the Merit Pay System

Critical to the success of any merit pay system is that it be administered so as to maintain integrity. This suggests that merit pay be administered accurately and fairly across employees and divisions/units in a company. That is, it is important for all employees to know that all merit raises are being determined in the same way, regardless of the supervisor, and that the determination is based on an accurate measure of job performance. While ensuring accuracy of appraisals may be effectively addressed by a behavioural-based performance appraisal method, such as BARS or BOS (see Chapter 9), ensuring fair and consistent administration (within the pay structure) is done through the use of *compa-ratios* and *performance ratios*.

Compa-ratios and performance ratios used together can highlight pay and job performance relationships by individual employee, by salary grade, by level in the organization, or by department or division in the company. The **compa-ratio** is the measure of an individual's salary in relationship to the mid-point of the range for a salary grade. This ratio is determined by dividing an individual's salary by the mid-point of the salary range and multiplying by 100. A ratio of 110, for example, means that the individual is being paid 10 percent over mid-point. Assuming a normal distribution of job performance and experience levels, the average compa-ratio in any department or division should be close to 100. Ratios higher than 100 may suggest leniency, and therefore inaccuracy in a supervisor's appraisals and ratios less than 100 may suggest the opposite. Differential ratios across departments or divisions may indicate inconsistent merit pay administration.

Similar conclusions can be drawn from the use of **performance ratios**, which indicate where the performance rating of any employee stands relative to the other employees. This is done by determining the mid-point of a performance range and dividing that into each employee's performance rating and multiplying that figure by 100. This process can be facilitated by using a performance appraisal method with points rather than rankings. Most performance appraisal methods discussed earlier in the chapter, except the ranking approach, can thus be used in determining performance ratios. Again, assuming normal performance distributions, the average performance ratio for a department or division should be close to 100. Variations from 100 may suggest unfair and inconsistent merit pay practices.

Employee participation can take place at two critical points in performance-based pay plans: (1) the design stage, and (2) the administration stage.

Participation in Performance-Based Pay Plans

DESIGN STAGE PARTICIPATION. Many pay plans are designed by top management and installed in a fairly authoritative fashion. It appears, however, that employees can not only design pay plans, but design them more effectively. That is, employees can be responsible when designing a pay plan and they are more likely to understand and accept a plan that they have helped to design. Participation in plan design also helps reduce the resistance that accompanies almost any change in an organization. As a consequence, employees are more motivated to increase performance.

ADMINISTRATION PARTICIPATION. As indicated before, employees can responsibly determine when and if other workers should receive pay increases. This also appears to be true for individuals determining their *own* pay increases. An example in a U.S. company (Friedman Jacobs) illustrates this point. Friedman decided to allow his employees to set their own wages based on their perception of their performance. This radical approach apparently has worked well. Instead of an all-out raid on the company coffers, the employees displayed responsible behaviour. They set their wages slightly higher than the scale of the union to which they belonged and apparently find their pay quite satisfactory. When one appliance serviceman who was receiving considerably less than his co-workers was asked why he did not insist on equal pay, he replied, "I don't want to work that hard."

There are several contemporary issues in wage and salary administration, three of which have particular importance: (1) what are the advantages and disadvantages of **pay secrecy**? (2) what is needed for employees to be satisfied with their pay? and (3) Should all employees be salaried? Other administration issues are addressed in the next chapter.

CONTEMPORARY ISSUES IN WAGE AND SALARY ADMINISTRATION

Ask anyone who works for a living how much money he or she makes, and you are likely to encounter responses ranging from evasion to outright hostility. Such responses, however, should not be surprising. According to organizational etiquette, it is generally considered gauche to ask others their salaries. Nevertheless, some companies practise open salary administration because they feel it is the right thing to do. For example, the Polaroid Corporation has established a pay-level structure for its exempt salaried employees and, in keeping with its policy of openness, involves those employees in making salary decisions. Employees are also involved in the job evaluation process to get a broad understanding of

Pay Secrecy

the process by which job value is established. A small-scale survey among ten large Canadian firms found half proclaimed to have an open salary policy, although the understanding of the meaning of open salary varied from one respondent to another (i.e. full vs. partial disclosure).[23] Recently, however, as can be seen in the HRM in the News Vignette, the Ontario Securities Commission moved to keep individual executives' pay secret.

PROS AND CONS OF OPEN SALARY POLICY. The most commonly stated reason for keeping pay secret is that it helps reduce unfavourable pay comparisons. Studies show that this is not supported by any evidence; on the contrary, employees do compare their salaries to those of peers, subordinates, and supervisors. Worse is that employees have a tendency to overestimate the pay of peers and subordinates and to underestimate the pay of their superiors, which may well result in dissatisfaction with their own pay. This is the prime cause of their developing a feeling of inequity. According to proponents of the theory of inequity, secrecy may result in high costs to employers due to the fact that a dissatisfied employee will put in less effort in order to achieve a perceived equity in the organization. On the other hand, disclosure of pay must force the organization to have a clear policy or rationale for pay; absence of such rationale may lead to an even greater feeling of inequity and to further losses to the organization. Consequently, organizations that have a clear and systematic compensation policy might benefit from having an open salary policy, while those that lack such a policy might be better off by keeping salaries undisclosed.

HRM IN THE NEWS VIGNETTE
OSC Proposal Would Keep Individual Executives' Pay Secret

The salary of individual executives would remain largely hidden from investors under pay-disclosure proposals introduced yesterday by the Ontario Securities Commission.

...OSC chairman Robert Wright said his organization believes the pay of a public company's five highest-paid executives should be disclosed in one aggregate or collective amount.

An individual executive will be singled out only if he or she earns more than 40% of the total compensation of the five highest paid people. The proposals are a milder version of U.S. Securities and Exchange Commission regulations, which require companies to reveal each individual senior executive's salary.

...Lawyer Philip Anisman called the proposals an improvement over the current system, but said they don't go far enough. Companies must now disclose the aggregate compensation paid to all executives who have a "policy-making function," a group that could be of virtually any size.

...Wright said the proposals balance the need and right of investors to be informed about pay levels against executives' right to privacy. When the Commission asked in its bulletin last year whether disclosure requirements for executive pay should be expanded to include individuals, opinion was overwhelmingly against.

Wright said the OSC believes disclosure for individuals could promote competition between companies "with the potential of creating round after round of compensation increases." He said the current system in Ontario isn't working because it doesn't allow shareholders to assess the link between compensation and corporate performance, and whether one executive is taking a disproportionate piece of the salary pie.

Wright said the disclosure proposal has been discussed with other provincial securities regulators and will be formally presented at an April meeting of the Canadian Securities Administrators. The proposal would then have to be approved by the Ontario government, something he hoped would be done by the end of the year.

Source: Excerpt from a feature article of the same title by R. Carrick, Canadian Press, reprinted in *The Montreal Gazette*, Business Section, 4 March 1992, C1. Reprinted with permission of Canadian Press News Limited.

If organizations want to minimize absenteeism and turnover through compensation, they must make sure that employees are satisfied with their pay. And since motivation to perform is not always a function of overall satisfaction with pay, it is necessary to know the specific facets of pay satisfaction. With this knowledge organizations can develop pay practices that are more likely to result in satisfaction. Perhaps the three major determinants of satisfaction with pay are pay equity, pay level, and pay administration practices.

Satisfaction with Pay

PAY EQUITY. Pay equity refers to what people feel they deserve to be paid in relation to what others deserve to be paid. The tendency is for people to determine what they and others deserve to be paid by comparing what they give to the organization with what they get out of the organization. In comparing themselves with others, people may decide whether or not they are being paid fairly, that is, what they deserve in relation to what others deserve. If they regard this comparison as fair or equitable, they are more likely to be satisfied. If they see this comparison as unfair, they are likely to be dissatisfied and be motivated to engage in behaviours that will restore equity (or reduce inequity). These behaviours may include: (1) decreasing own inputs (tardiness, absenteeism), (2) decreasing own outcomes (e.g., if on a piece-rate system, concentrating on quality not quantity), (3) acting on the "other" (sabotage, vandalism), or (4) leaving the field (transfer or resignation). Consequently, a sound compensation system should reflect three types of equity: (a) external equity—corresponds to the market wage rates; (b) internal equity—corresponds to the value of the job; and (c) personal equity—where comparison, for an employee, reflects performance.

A current issue in pay equity deals with top-executive compensation: Are they paid too much? In the U.S.A. and Canada, it is estimated that, on the average, top executives earn twelve to eighteen times as much as the lowest-paid employee. As a point of interest, Japan's top level earns only six times as much. And for further contrast, in Romania during the communist regime, the gap was closer to that of the U.S.A. and Canada (1:18), while the former Soviet Union experienced a gap of 1:40. It has been suggested that this excessive gap generated a high level of dissatisfaction, not only among workers but also among the general public.

PAY LEVEL. Pay level is an important determinant of the perceived amount of pay. People compare actual pay to what they feel should be received. The result of the comparison is satisfaction with pay if the "should" level of pay equals the actual level of pay. Pay dissatisfaction results if the actual level is less than the "should."

PAY ADMINISTRATION PRACTICES. If the employer is to attract new employees and keep them satisfied with their pay, the wages and salaries offered should approximate the wages and salaries paid to other employees in comparable organizations (i.e., **external equity** must exist). Also, the pricing of jobs can enhance pay satisfaction when it is perceived not to neglect a philosophy of equal work or equal pay for jobs of comparable worth. The worth of jobs must be evaluated according to the factors considered most important by the employees and the organization (so internal equity exists).

Furthermore, pay-for-performance systems must be accompanied by a method for accurately measuring the performance of employees, and must be open enough so that these employees can clearly see the performance–pay relationship. Compensation rates and pay structures should be continually reviewed and updated/revised if necessary. Over time the content of a job may change, thus distorting the relationship between its actual worth and its evaluated worth.

Finally, employees must perceive that the organization is looking out for their interests as well as its own. An atmosphere of *trust* and *consistency* must exist. Without this, pay satisfaction will probably be low, and pay administration will become a target for complaints, regardless of the real issues.

All-Salaried Workforce

Although there is some evidence that all employees prefer to be on salary rather than to be paid on an hourly basis, most organizations distinguish between their employees by method of pay. That is, salary status is usually reserved (along with a parking space) for management, and the nonmanagement employees (except clerical workers) are paid on an hourly basis.

Nevertheless, some organizations have put all their employees on salary. IBM had, until recently, an all-salaried workforce since the 1930s. The all-salary concept shows a general respect for the entire workforce, which is treated as mature and responsible. The policy therefore establishes an atmosphere of trust and respect. Though there is little hard evidence to support the effectiveness of the all-salaried concept, it appears to be a practical way to increase productivity and QWL, two measures by which one can assess total compensation.

TRENDS IN DIRECT COMPENSATION

Assessing Direct Compensation

In assessing how effectively an organization administers its compensation program, the following major purposes of total compensation must be kept in mind:

- Attracting potentially qualified employees,
- Motivating employees,
- Retaining qualified employees,
- Administering pay within legal constraints,
- Facilitating organizational strategic objectives and controlling labour costs.

In order to attain these purposes, employees generally need to be satisfied with their pay. This means that the organization's pay levels should be extremely competitive, that employees should perceive internal pay equity, and that the compensation program should be properly administered. It also means that compensation practices must adhere to the various provincial and federal wage and hour laws, including comparable worth considerations. Consequently, an organization's total compensation program can be assessed by comparing its pay levels with other organizations, by analyzing the validity of its job evaluation method, by measuring employee perceptions of pay equity and performance–pay linkages, and by determining individual pay levels within jobs and across jobs.

Attracting, motivating, and retaining employees are worthy purposes of total compensation and can facilitate organizational objectives. Attaining them at a lower, rather than higher, cost can also facilitate an organization's strategic objectives. This can be done by replacing nondeductible pay expenditures (expensive perquisites such as cars and club memberships) with deductible pay expenditures, such as contributions to employee stock ownership plans. This replacement, of course, must be done with consideration for the differential impact of alternative pay expenditures on attracting, motivating, and retaining employees. These differentials can increase the effectiveness of the total compensation dollar.

Regardless of organizational conditions, performance-based pay plans can be assessed on the basis of three criteria: (1) the relationship between performance and pay—that is, the time between performance and the administration of the pay; (2) how well the plan minimizes the perceived negative consequences of good performance, such as social ostracism; and (3) whether it contributes to the perception that rewards other than pay (such as cooperation and recognition) also stem from good performance. The more it minimizes the perceived negative consequences and the more it contributes to the perception that other good rewards are also tied to performance, the more motivating the plan is likely to be.

Computers have virtually revolutionized salary administrators' jobs, enabling them to handle such time consuming tasks as salary structure development, merit budgeting, and survey analysis more quickly and accurately than ever before. More recently, its impact has been felt in the area of job evaluation.

Unquestionably, computer-aided job evaluation (CAJE) systems speed up evaluations and improve the objectivity and consistency of the evaluation process. They can also help make it more difficult to manipulate the process and, thus, help to limit political battles.

Designing a CAJE system and collecting data are probably the most critical aspects of the system. The typical method involves the use of structured, or close-ended, questionnaires in which employees are given multiple-choice questions or asked to provide specific quantitative data. Generally, all data can be fed directly into the computer, either through an optical scanner, batch processing, or manual inputting. Data validation routines and audit reports are standard features of all systems. The statistical checking routines simply look at the reasonability of responses from a single incumbent or cross-check responses from all incumbents in a given job family or organizational hierarchy.

Computer Applications

HRM DYNAMICS
Direct Compensation Profiles in Selected Canadian Organizations

Du Pont Canada

In 1989 the company decided to restrict employees' salary raises and to introduce a bonus scheme based on a performance-sharing plan. The total payout to the 4 000 employees reached $14 million. Payout was based on the company's return on equity. The formula employed was a 4 percent recoup on a 16 percent return on equity. However, no cash was awarded if the return was less than 11 percent. At the same time, a ceiling maximum bonus of 10 percent of income was set for instances when the company would achieve a 28 percent return on equity. There are, however, two negative byproducts for this scheme: (a) emphasis on return on equity may provide incentives for short-term gains, but may sacrifice long-term objectives, and (b) spectacular employees may receive smaller payouts than they deserve.

E.D. Smith and Sons

The company has an elaborate suggestion savings plan. In 1989 $1.5 million in savings were translated to a minimum of $1,850 per employee and up to $3 500. Over half of the 260 employees participate in the program, which requires them to set aside an hour a week to work on these ideas/suggestions.

Royal Bank

The Royal Bank has several different performance-based pay systems. Some are paid organization-wide and others are linked to individual performance. Two such examples include: (a) the Quality Performance Incentive program (QPI), which covers all employees. If the bank meets its planned level of strategic financial performance, every eligible employee receives a bonus. Each year a pool of funds is created for this purpose. The degree to which the bank achieves its business objectives determines the size of the pool; (b) the Royal Performance Incentive, which recognizes excellent employees. Every quarter, directors and managers choose employees who have excelled in sales, service, and participation. In addition to symbolic monetary rewards, about 400 top performers and their spouses are invited to spend a week aboard a luxurious cruise liner. Per employee cost of this reward is reported to exceed $5,000.

Automating job evaluations requires a statistical model. The one most often used is derived from multiple regression analysis or through direct mapping. In regression analysis, data collected from benchmark jobs are analyzed and regressed against a dependent variable—either market rates, current pay, current midpoints, or evaluation points.

CAJE simplifies the maintenance and administration of the system. Because all non-benchmark jobs can be simulated through the model to determine their relative value to the organization, it eliminates the necessity of having evaluation committees. Many CAJE systems currently available offer additional administrative features, including integrated software for maintaining employee records, survey data, and salary structure information; analytical capabilities for regression analysis; graphics packages; and software that creates job descriptions and organizational charts from the data in the structured questionnaire.

Despite the advantages of CAJE, there are a few words of caution. It is rather expensive and its implementation requires a major effort. Additionally, human judgment is still necessary, particularly in cleaning up the data and in reviewing and approving the final model and resulting evaluations. As such, CAJE is not a stand-alone product, but should be considered as part of the fully integrated salary management program.

Hay Management Consultants has developed a number of computer-assisted job evaluation and measurement tools. The *HayXpert Quick Evaluation Database (QED Chart)* software allows organizations to provide added support to job evaluation committees. For those not using committees, *QED Comparison* is designed to assist line managers in evaluating jobs.

Computers are an essential tool in helping the organization maintain internal and external equity. Many compensation analysts are becoming experts in the use of *Lotus 1-2-3* or other spreadsheet programs. This enables them to project the effect of pay increases on their total labour costs.

Recent sources suggest that there are approximately sixty packaged software solutions created to help compensation managers with their various responsibilities.[24] In addition to performing job evaluations, as suggested before, there are systems that interface salary surveys and help price jobs according to the market; others facilitate the development of salary structures, costing out various scenarios; and still other programs help budget and allocate increases according to alternative criteria and track the results in terms of compra-ratios and other statistics. Finally, because executive compensation presents a special challenge to many firms, there are systems to track stock options, bonuses, and various forms of deferred compensation.

SUMMARY

In the world marketplace of today, companies realize that in order to attain a competitive edge they need to attract, retain, and motivate the best employees that they can find. Compensation becomes a significant and timely HR tool to carry out this task. This chapter focuses on direct compensation, which has two components: the basic wage and performance-based pay. As with many other HR activities, there are several federal and provincial laws that affect total compensation. One important issue regarding legal compliance is the comparable worth or the "true value" of a job.

There are four principal determinants of basic wage: (1) the value/worth of jobs as established through the job evaluation process, which is concerned with achieving internal equity among the different jobs; (2) the determination of job classes; (3) the establishment of a pay structure through wage and salary surveys, which provide information that helps ensure external equity; and (4) the individual wage determination, which is often based on both performance and personal contributions.

There are two major types of performance-based pay systems: incentive pay plans and merit pay plans. Incentive plans can be applied at three levels: the individual, the group, and the organization. Performance-based plans are gaining popularity in the private sector, because they are perceived to be the best approach for rewarding the "star performers." The success of many incentive plans depends on the circumstances under which they are implemented. For example, an incentive pay plan requires an effective performance appraisal program: the more objective the measures of job performance, the more value incentive plans have. Also, the parameters of effective reinforcement in compensation need to be satisfied. They include the nature, time, magnitude, specificity, routineness, and schedule of the reinforcer.

The basis of merit pay plans is to reward performance with merit salary increases. Effective use of merit pay plans necessitates the determination of the size of the merit pay raises, the times at which they are to be given, and the relationship between merit pay increments and position in the salary range. Many large organizations grant COLAs to their employees; firms would rather use merit plans because COLAs are often expensive and have no relationship to performance.

The choice of performance-based pay plan must be determined by several factors. These include the level at which job performance (individual, group, or organization) can be measured accurately, the extent of cooperation needed between groups, and the level of trust between management and nonmanagement. Several plans can be used together to reward different groups of employees for good job performance. However, there may be limits on a specific organization's use of performance-based pay, such as management's desire to have performance-based pay, management's commitment to take the time to design and implement one or several systems, the extent to which employees really influence the output, and the degree of trust in the organization.

Most organizations are not able to provide the full incentive value of pay. Nevertheless, more and more organizations are attempting to remove the obstacles to incentive plans by allowing a great deal of employee participation in the design, implementation, and administration of performance-based pay plans, which provides employees with a clear understanding of these plans. This also gives employees opportunities to appeal pay decisions and provides rewards as soon as possible after the job performance. Some contemporary issues in wage and salary administration are pay secrecy, employees' satisfaction with pay, and the option of having an all-salaried workforce.

P O S T S C R I P T

In this postscript we wish to briefly discuss two concerns: the first pertains to the possibility of extending performance-based pay to nontraditional industries, including the public sector; the second is a warning against using it as a panacea for poor productivity.

Without doubt, the pay-for-performance plan is a hot topic in corporate Canada. It seems that the need for incentive plans is here to stay. It is to be hoped that positive results will help spread the message to the public sector as well. Currently, only a few public sector organizations that experience economic pressures similar to those of the private sector utilize incentive programs. Traditionally, this sector has looked for innovations in other HR functions rather than compensation. This is the principal reason why this sector is not able to attract, retain, and motivate "top performers." With minor exceptions, a common belief held by the public is that a public employee has significantly less ambition, less drive, and fewer capabilities than his or her counterpart in the private sector. Via introduction of a pay-for-performance scheme, perhaps such stereotypes could be changed and the sector would become altogether more productive. Yet government, municipal, and other public sector agencies resist the pressure to introduce such plans, using as a pretext the need to adhere to principles of equality. The recent experience of the largest public employers in the world (i.e., the former communist and socialist countries) just provides further proof of the inefficiencies of large bureaucracies. Thus, the idea of promoting entrepreneurship by rewarding industrious employees is intriguing. Imagine the teacher (or group of teachers) in the public high school who would receive a bonus based on a student's score in national exams; imagine the clerk in a department of revenue who would retain a percentage of sums recovered from tax evaders; imagine the crown attorney who would get a merit raise based on the number of convictions. Evidently, there might be drawbacks to some of these suggestions, but will the public sector follow the examples set in the private sector?

Let us examine some of the potential problems for two examples cited above. In the case of crown attorneys, we feel that the motive behind conviction should be to serve justice, not to get a raise. The main reason for crown attorneys to do their job properly and effectively is to serve justice. Introducing merit raises based on the number of convictions might push some to commit certain "irregularities" that would compromise the proper functioning of the justice system.

Merit pay has been established for teachers in some states in the U.S.A., but the results are mixed. Problems with it include funding and developing evaluation systems. Also, merit pay is often part of a "career ladder" program that rewards teachers for self-improvement, not for improved student performance. As a result, instruction and curriculum have improved, but there is no evidence that merit pay has had an impact on the students. Furthermore, teachers have complained that reviews were subjective and bad teachers "just cleaned up their act" during the evaluation. Perhaps the biggest obstacle, though, is the conflict between merit pay and the teaching culture, which often depends on teamwork. To get around merit pay's problems, some states are opting to reward improved performance for whole schools with lump sums that can be used for nearly any purpose.[25]

Tough economic times like those that characterized the early 1990s force companies to trim personnel and be more innovative in rewarding the remaining staff, which must now share greater responsibility. Pay for performance seems to be the direction chosen to achieve that goal of retaining and motivating these "survivors." However, these programs are often poorly conceived and omit examination of how and why they should be structured in terms of individual and corporate objectives. From the outset, it should be clear that incentive plans introduce a degree of entrepreneurial risk-taking behaviour that requires open lines of communication to support it. Otherwise long-term motivation may vanish. Research has clearly indicated that although financial rewards are effective in providing short-term motivation, in order to meet the long-term objectives they must be combined with appropriate intrinsic rewards. Thus, in order to affect the bottom line, direct compensation strategies must be complemented with indirect compensation and must be aligned with other HR functions, such as training and development, career planning, and, most importantly, effective performance appraisal systems.

REVIEW AND ANALYSIS QUESTIONS

1. Explain why there is a critical link between job analysis and compensation.
2. What is the issue of comparable worth and how is it related to compensation?
3. What are the principal determinants of wages?
4. Compare and contrast any two *different* job evaluation methods.
5. What factors contribute to whether employees will be satisfied with their pay?
6. Suppose that you go to the same barber or restaurant on a regular basis. Based on the principles/parameters of effective reinforcement, how would you develop a tipping policy with the aim of eliciting the best service over time? Elaborate.
7. What is the difference between a merit pay plan and an incentive pay plan?
8. What conditions are necessary for effective implementation of performance-based pay systems? Under what conditions are group incentive pay plans more appropriate than individual ones?

9. Describe a performance-based pay system that you have experienced. Did the system work? If not why not?

10. Assume that you are a manager of a small bookstore where all seven employees rotate tasks. A major problem is that at times items in the store cannot be easily found; additionally the cash does not always balance. Design a compensation program to address these problems.

CASE STUDY

DOUBLE BLOW IN ONE MEETING: WHAT NEXT?

This is just one more boring Monday morning, thought Mike Hammer as he entered the monthly supervisory meeting. Mike was late this morning, due to the fact that he had had to stop at the bank and arrange credit for the new car he had just purchased for his wife. Mike had been a supervisor at the McMillan Bloedel paper mill near Vancouver for the past fifteen years. While going to his seat, Mike got a copy of the agenda and quickly glanced through it. At first, nothing struck him as unusual: Item 1 - discussion on productivity improvements; Item 2 - production and scheduling; Item 3 - off-shore competition; and Item 4 - annual bonus. Mike was very excited about the annual bonus. He had been planning for some time to use the extra money to replace his wife's old Chevrolet; they had been talking about it for several years, but something else always came up and the money was gone. This time, thought Mike, she really deserves it. An important birthday was coming, and it would be a perfect surprise.

To his surprise, the meeting began with Item 4. Rumours had been circulating for a while that the company would not be giving the bonus this year, and Mike thought that the presence of Maria van Burke would put an end to this rumour. Although the size of the bonus varied, the company had always paid it. It had become part of the compensation package. Nonetheless, Mike noticed that the tone of the discussion was very heated. "No way those guys in our shift will make more money than us," said Bill Clifton, a colleague whom Mike had great respect for. It had taken him a few more minutes to grasp the double blow: he had learned that for the first time in the company's history, not only had all supervisory personnel salaries been frozen, but there was not going to be any bonus this year. Additionally, it was revealed by Bill that such a decision would result in most of the foremen having less take-home cash that their subordinates.

"You are absolutely right," exclaimed Budd Sampson from the other corner of the room. "Nowadays it is better to be a unionized worker in this company than a manager. At least as a worker you are paid for overtime and can make a lot more money," he added angrily. Maria van Burke, VP Human Resources, who was at the meeting, replied: "Guys, you know that this company has always treated you fairly. We also attempted to maintain a healthy pay difference between you and your subordinates. This year, unfortunately, profit is substantially down, and the company decided to freeze pay raises to its exempt employees. This is done across the board, including myself and the president. Naturally, during this difficult period we cannot afford to pay you a bonus. You know that in the past we were very generous when we made money. As for your subordinates, we are really stuck. The collective agreement with local 101, signed last year, provides for an automatic COLA adjustment and 5 percent additional raise for most jobs. It is also true that the contract with the union provides for overtime pay at a rate of 1-1/2 times the normal rate. But this is only temporary, and I am certain that the situation will be corrected in the future."

Added Bill Wong, a recently promoted supervisor: "You know, my subordinates laugh at me constantly. They have good reason to suggest that there are really no incentives to become a supervisor in this company. We have more responsibility, we work more hours, and our final pay in dollars and cents is now substantially lower than many of theirs. With the fact that we are also losing the bonus, I find it extremely demoralizing."

The meeting ended without any particular solution. Everyone felt deeply distressed. Mike thought about how to break the news to his wife. He also thought about the steps he needed to take to cancel the car order. As far as work was concerned, it was agreed that the president would be asked to attend the next group meeting and Maria was supposed to prepare a plan addressing the situation.

Case Questions

Assume the role of Maria van Burke (VP Human Resources).

1. What are the major problems in the case?

2. What will be your principal points for addressing the situation?

Assume the role of Mike Hammer (supervisor).

1. What did you do wrong. Why?
2. What will you say to your subordinates who aspire to become supervisors?

NOTES

1. R.M. Tomasko, "Focusing Company Reward Systems to Help Achieve Business Objectives," *Management Review*, October 1982, 8–12.

2. "Women, a Force to be Reckoned with in Canadian Economy," *The Globe and Mail*, 15 July, 1985, B7 and M.C. Lortie, "Les femmes gagnent toujours moins que les hommes mais l'écart se rétrécit," *La Presse*, 14 April 1993, C2

3. F. Bula, "Pass Law to Guarantee Pay Equity: Rights Commission," *The Montreal Gazette*, 7 March 1992.

4. For more information, see N. Agarwal, "Pay Equity in Context," *Human Resource Management in Canada*, March 1988, 50,521–50,526; J.N. Tascona, "Towards Equity: An Analysis of Ontario's Pay Equity Legislation," *ibid.*, 50,527–50,533; and D. Sclauzero, "An Employer Response: Toward Pay Equity at Ontario Hydro," *ibid.*, 50,535–50,538.

5. "Giving Up, Moving Out," *MacLean's*, 18 March 1991, 37–38.

6. *An Approach to Bias-Free Job Evaluation Procedures*, Office of the Deputy Premier, Ontario Women's Directorate (undated).

7. Ibid., addendum. Used with permission of the Ontario Women's Directorate.

8. Results of a survey conducted by MLH+ Inc. in 1991.

9. J. Lendvay-Zwickl, "Compensation Planning Outlook 1991," (Ottawa: Conference Board of Canada, 1990),

10. For a discussion on the validity of job evaluation systems, see T.A. Mahoney, "Compensating for Work," in *Personnel Management*, ed. K.M. Rowland and G.R. Ferris (Boston: Allyn & Bacon, 1982), 257–58.

11. See: E.E. Lawler, "The Strategic Design of Reward System," in *Readings in Personnel and Human Resource Management*, 2nd ed., ed. R.S. Schuler and S.A. Youngblood (St. Paul, Minn.: West Publishing Co., 1984), 253–59; and R. Kanungo, "Reward Management: A New Look," in *Canadian Readings in Personnel and Human Resource Management*, ed. S.L. Dolan and R.S. Schuler (St. Paul, Minn.: West Publishing Co., 1987), 261–76.

12. Lendvay-Zwickl, "Compensation Planning Outlook 1991," 6.

13. Wyatt Company, *1990 Survey of Canadian Incentive Compensation Plans*,

14. D. Nightingale, "Profit Sharing: New Nectar for the Worker Bees," *The Canadian Business Review*, Spring 1984, 11–14.

15. "Compensating Field Representatives," *Studies in Personnel Policy 202* (New York: National Industrial Conference Board, 1966).

16. C. Delvalle, S.D. Atcheson, and Ula Lecia Konrad, "Merit Pay for Teachers," *Business Week*, 9 March 1992, 38–39.

17. *The Financial Post*, 9 March 1992.

18. W. Carr, "Communicating with ESP," (Current Matters/New Ideas) *Human Resources Management in Canada*, 1985, 5,342.

19. W.J. Kearney, "Pay for Performance? Not Always," *MSU Business Topics*, Spring 1979, 6. Reprinted by permission of the publisher. Division of Research, Graduate School of Business Administration, Michigan State University.

20. See W. Lilley," A Compensation Special: More Money," in *Canadian Business*, April 1985, 48–57; about profit sharing in Canada, see: D. Nightingale, "Profit Sharing: New Nectar for the Worker Bees," *The Canadian Business Review* 2, 1 (1984): 11–14..

21. Nightingale, "Profit Sharing," 13.

22. Lendvay-Zwinkl, "Compensation Planning Outlook 1991,"

23. A. Laplante, "Abolishing Pay Secrecy: An Inexpensive Way to Gain Employee Satisfaction and Increase Motivation" (Unpublished paper prepared for a course in personnel administration, Montreal, McGill University, November 1988).

24. S.E. Forrer and Z.B. Leibowitz, *Using Computers in Human Resources* (San Francisco: Jossey–Bass Publishers, 1991), 19.

25. C. Delvalle, S.D. Atcheson, and Ula Lecia Konrad, "Merit Pay for Teachers," *Business Week*, 9 March 1992, 38–39.

CHAPTER EIGHT

INDIRECT COMPENSATION

KEYNOTE ADDRESS

Kenneth S. Benson
Vice-President Personnel and Administration, Canadian Pacific Limited

The Importance of Indirect Compensation

Canadian Pacific Limited (CP) was incorporated in 1881.... At present the businesses that CP directly and through subsidiaries and associated companies operates, in Canada and internationally, are: railways, ocean shipping, and trucking; the exploration, development and production of oil, gas, coal, and other minerals; the manufacture and sale of forest products; the development and management of real estate and hotels; the provision of telecommunication services; the manufacture and sale of industrial products; and the provision of waste management services. CP and its subsidiaries employ approximately 78,000 people, the majority of whom reside in Canada.

In the 1980s CP initiated the complete revision of its direct and indirect compensation programs. The objective was to design and implement leading-edge programs that would help define the people and the organization as it enters the twenty-first century.

The process began with the establishment of a base salary program related to appropriate comparator companies and relative compensation positionings. This was followed by the implementation of a new variable compensation program, consisting of a short-term plan that provides for the payment of cash bonuses on the achievement of annual targets and two long-term plans: one is a stock option program and the other a performance unit plan designed for those very senior executives whose decisions mould the future of the corporation over time. The objectives of the two long-term variable plans are to link the participants' interests with those of the shareholders; to relate financial rewards to the achievement of performance goals; to promote the long-term profitability of the corporation; and to foster an entrepreneurial spirit among participants.

The revised direct compensation program, though of major proportion, represented only about one-third of the total objective. Activities were therefore directed to the equally large and important task of designing and, where necessary, modifying new and revised indirect compensation programs, often referred to simply as "benefits programs." Again the objective was to design and implement indirect compensation programs that could be contemporary, be cost effective, and contribute to the achievement of strategic goals. The then-current indirect compensation program was clearly inappropriate, having been developed from a bottom-up process that related to negotiated settlements with unions representing the large blue-collar workforce. The indirect plans were demotivational for existing employees, inhibited the engagement of new employees, and lacked overall credibility.

In an environment of rapid change, management recognized that establishing a flexible indirect compensation program would be in the best interest of both CP and its employees. A full, cafeteria-style flexible benefits program was established, with plans tailored to employees' individual needs and preferences in the area of health, dental, life, dependent life, accidental death and dismemberment, and short- and long-term disability insurance.

The corporation's pension plan was a defined benefit plan. It had not kept up with developments and innovations, as had most other major Canadian corporate pension plans. Pension amendments included provisions for early retirement, portability, participation by part-time employees, earlier vesting, formal indexation, and improved disability provisions....

The indirect benefits afforded to CP's executive employees were clearly noncompetitive. New or revised executive medical, financial counselling, and automobile plans were established, as was change in control protection. Coinciding with legislation limiting the amounts that may be provided by registered pension plans, amendments were implemented to reduce levels of employee contribution; pay pensions in excess of the cap imposed under the Income Tax Act; pay certain bonuses from short-term compensation plans as pensionable earnings; to enhance retirement pension benefits for executives who joined the plan in mid-career; and provide certain security for the payment of pension obligations.

Contemporary and effective indirect compensation programs are essential to companies' continued existence and long-term success as they compete in rapidly changing global economies. It is paramount that relevant indirect compensation programs be available when required to retain and attract the quantity and calibre of employees needed to operate the businesses of the twenty-first century.

Increasingly, in both the U.S.A. and in Canada, shareholders, investors, the media, and the public express dissatisfaction with the quantum of compensation, particularly for executive levels. Much of the criticism relates to a limited number of primarily U.S. companies. All corporate programs must be cost effective, and effective indirect compensation programs must be viewed as a necessary and proper ongoing cost of business. Indirect compensation programs most assuredly contribute to the bottom line, both on a short- term and on a long-term basis.

Communication is a vital ingredient of indirect compensation programs. Failure to properly and repeatedly provide clear and relevant information about the terms, provisions, and benefits of indirect compensation plans will significantly affect their impact, acceptance, and cost effectiveness to the corporation. Well-designed communication programs will return a significantly greater value to the corporation than the cost represented thereby.

Historic or noncontemporary indirect compensation programs will be totally inadequate for surviving and successful Canadian businesses to deal with the frequency and magnitude of future challenges. Today, let alone tomorrow, the most respected and established of Canadian businesses is having to re-evaluate and restructure its organization, businesses, markets, and customers. The economic and social conditions are changing fundamentally and unpredictably, all at a time when capable, imaginative, and motivated executives and employees must achieve financial success for today while planning for and establishing strategic goals and objectives for the future. Contemporary and effective indirect compensation plans are important, needed ingredients in any corporation's strategic plan and are fundamental to its ability to survive and prosper.

• • •

As can be seen in the Keynote Address, indirect compensation is an important segment of a company's strategic HR plan today. Indirect compensation represents a significant portion of the total compensation package. In some cases, these costs may equal and even exceed those of direct compensation. But, on the average, indirect compensation costs tend to total 30 to 40 percent of direct compensation. The rising costs of benefits have led over the years to a search for new ways to render these benefits more effective (i.e., meet the compensation objectives). The diversity and flexibility in benefits packages is one way of achieving this goal. Another way is by introducing all sorts of avant-garde benefits packages that reflect a company's social responsibility to society at large, as well as to selected employees. IBM Canada, for example, once awarded 80 percent of the administrative cost of adopting a child. Other companies are also exploring some unique avenues in benefit pay plans.

• • •

INDIRECT COMPENSATION

Many employees are vitally concerned about indirect compensation. After all, parts of this form of compensation are tax free. As the cost of indirect compensation grows in proportion to the total payroll cost, employers are becoming more interested in choosing only benefits that are cost effective (i.e., those that employees really value). Consequently, benefits-pay and administrative issues become a dynamic and vital HR activity.

The terms "fringe benefits" and "benefits-pay" are used by many corporations to denote indirect compensation. **Indirect compensation** is defined as those rewards provided by the organization to employees for their membership and/or participation (attendance) in the organization. Indirect compensation can be divided into three categories:

* Protection programs (public and private),
* Pay for time not worked (on-the-job and off-the-job),
* Employee services and perquisites.

Although some of these rewards are mandated by federal and provincial governments and therefore must be administered within the boundaries of laws and regulations, many others are provided voluntarily by organizations to varying degrees. Because such rewards are so diverse and employees' preferences are so varied, indirect compensation is not always valued or seen as a reward by all employees. On the other hand, when companies are sensitive to this issue and make an attempt to match rewards with employee preferences, the purposes of indirect compensation are more easily achieved.

Purposes and Importance of Indirect Compensation

GOALS OF INDIRECT COMPENSATION.   Because indirect compensation is part of the total compensation package, it shares many of the purposes of the latter, which were discussed in Chapter 7. More specifically, the following goals should be an integral part of the compensation plan:

* *Attraction.* Benefits should be *appealing* to the employees in order to attract qualified people. This involves two aspects: (1) benefits alone promote a desire to want to produce, and (2) benefits can influence people into believing that this is a good company to work for.
* *Retention.* Benefits should also provide a means to retain desirable members. People who are satisfied in a company will be less likely to consider leaving. Certain types of benefits can provide an incentive to produce and dedication to the company.
* *Cost control.* Keeping the above factors in mind, one major point is control of costs. If the productivity level does not justify the current costs of the benefits, then an evaluation of the total benefits package is necessary. For example, insurance companies assist in reducing the costs of health benefits by providing standard benefits packages to companies having twenty employees or less. By grouping together the claims experience of small companies, risk is reduced and this prevents penalizing one company for having a year with heavier insurance claims.

In addition to the principal goals already listed, organizations seek to: (1) increase employee morale, (2) reduce turnover, (3) increase job satisfaction, (4) motivate employees, and (5) enhance the organization's image among employees.

While most companies are aware of these objectives, using indirect compensation as a *motivator* is a recent discovery. In order for it to work, however, the reward should correspond to an individual's needs at that time. An example of this would be an employer who promotes further education by subsidizing the education costs, providing bonuses for passing grades, or providing a facility where learning can take place.

The importance of benefits is that they provide a competitive advantage to the employer and assist in reducing environmental stressors that may affect an employee's performance. Many benefits are tax deductible for employers, thus there is an added incentive to include these in the overall benefits package.

For indirect compensation to foster the desired result, it must be carefully planned with the employees' needs at the top of the list. One way of keeping abreast of these needs is through a survey. Surveys may include many aspects of the benefits package, but the most important questions are:

- Which benefits do you value the most? Why?
- How could we improve our benefits package to suit your personal needs?

The desired result is an atmosphere in which the employee can focus his or her concentration on the job. This involves many facets because of the differences in individual needs. Dedication in designing the benefits package is a must for success. The HR team has to satisfy their clients, the employees of the company. Through benefits, we can provide a team that is not only resourceful but has the knowledge to do a quality job.

A word of caution should be added here. Many employees do not regard indirect compensation as rewards but as conditions (entitlements) of employment. They think of benefits as safeguards provided by the organization as part of its larger social responsibility:

> *Workers have an expanding sense of what is due them as rights of employment. From pension, health care, long vacations, to a high standard of living, the perception by workers of what constitutes their rights is inexorably being enlarged. Concomitant with this spiralling sense of rights has been a declining sense of responsibility.*[1]

COSTS OF INDIRECT COMPENSATION. According to a survey published by Toronto-based Peat Marwick Stevenson & Kellogg, in 1989 organizations across Canada spent on benefits an average of 33.5 percent of gross payroll (including vacation time and statutory holidays).[2]

Clearly, they are expensive, but an employer has no choice but to provide the legally required benefits: unemployment insurance, workers' compensation, and Canada/Quebec Pension Plan. The typical annual cost per employee is illustrated in Exhibit 8.1. For calculating the costs, it has been assumed that the employee works in Ontario in the manufacturing sector and earns $40,000 per year; coverage includes spouse and children.

Exhibit 8.1
Annual Benefits Cost per Employee

BENEFIT PLAN	COST
Legally required benefits (Canada Pension Plan, unemployment insurance, Ontario health payroll tax, and workers' compensation)	$4,900
Medical and dental benefits	800
Pension plan	2,700
Vacation and holidays	3,800
Miscellaneous benefits (group life, accident, weekly indemnity, long-term disability, employee assistance program, lunches, parking, etc.)	2,800
TOTAL	$15,000

Group health-care costs have risen by 10 to 15 percent for each of the past ten years, and some plan sponsors have responded by increasing deductibles and tightening certain plan provisions. Thus, organizations have to analyze their health plans to see what costs can be reduced. For instance, if an individual has a choice between getting a service for free from the government (diagnostic tests, physiotherapy, psychiatric services) or through the company health plan, employers may consider a lowering their co-insurance contribution for these services.

Cost containment can best be achieved through proper plan design, cost-sharing, and effective communication of the group insurance plan's role in the organization. These proactive approaches will help manage health plan costs as the national health-care system undergoes radical surgery in the coming years.[3]

Relationships and Influences of Indirect Compensation

Although the relationships described in Chapter 7 between compensation in general and other HR activities are also applicable here, it is appropriate to highlight a few of those activities that apply more specifically to indirect compensation. This is particularly the case with staffing (both recruitment and selection), health and safety functions, and training and development.

RECRUITMENT AND SELECTION. As individuals demand more indirect compensation, an organization must offer more to attract a pool of potentially qualified job applicants. Without providing benefits comparable to those offered by others in the same industry or same area, an organization may lose qualified individuals to other employers. Often, however, an individual may not learn of an employer's indirect compensation package until after being recruited. If this is the case, the recruitment policy is not very effective.

Benefits are especially important in attracting executives and professionals. Thus, it is not surprising to find executive want ads that not only include prerequisites for hopeful candidates, but also include information about benefits such as: dental plan, health plan, competitive salary, bonus plan, convenient location, pleasant atmosphere, and diverse and stimulating assignments. A typical ad is provided in Exhibit 8.2.

Exhibit 8.2
Typical Recruiting Advertisement with Specified Benefits

Assistant Accounting Manager

Applications are invited from university graduates with a professional accounting designation for the position of Assistant Accounting Manager in the Accounting Department of Stora Forest Industries Limited.

Applicants must have experience in the areas of cost accounting, sales, general and payroll accounting, as well as specialized knowledge of sales taxes, import/export duties and fixed asset accounting.

A minimum of five years' supervisory experience, preferably in the pulp and paper industry or related industries, together with exposure to highly computerized systems are desirable.

This position offers a full range of benefits common to the pulp and paper industry, including a participatory pension plan and fully paid group life insurance, A.D. & D., major medical health, drug and dental plan, and short- and long-term disability insurance. A full relocation allowance is provided.

Apply in confidence, outlining experience, education, personal data and references, to:

STORA♀ FELDMÜHLE

S.H. (Sam) Wilson
Controller & Manager Accounting
Stora Forest Industries Limited
P.O. Box 59
Port Hawkesbury, Nova Scotia
B0E 2V0

Source: Reproduced by permission of Stora Forest Industries Limited.

Why include these benefits in an ad? Take the case of dental and medical plans. The cost of dental procedures increases on an annual basis according to the Canadian Dental Fee Guide. Dental work is not covered by most government health insurance plans, so company dental insurance provides the coverage. Similarly, health-care costs increase every year. While government medical insurance programs provide basic coverage, any excess is paid for by the user. This is where supplementary health insurance fills the gap.

TRAINING AND DEVELOPMENT. In an age of constant change, employees prefer to work in organizations that help them develop. Acquired skills permit them to chart a career within the organization, but the skills also provide opportunities for mobility and employability in case of job loss. The early 1990s were characterized by huge job losses across the board, and it has been proved that skilled employees can be reintegrated more rapidly. Consequently, while training in most organizations is not considered a benefit but rather a necessity, development programs are often regarded as benefits. Some of the typical non-specific types of training included in this category are:

- Oral and written communication (e.g., telephone techniques and effective business writing),
- Health and safety education,
- Computer training.

Additionally, as will be discussed in Chapter 11, many companies offer subsidies and forms of financial assistance to employees who pursue studies off-site (i.e., in colleges and universities or at professional seminars).

HEALTH AND SAFETY. As health and safety problems in organizations increase, the level of workers' compensation rates also increases. This in turn increases the cost of indirect compensation to organizations. Even if indirect compensation costs do not increase, damage suits against the employer may result in an increase in total compensation costs.

Benefits have existed in Canada since World War I, starting with the establishment of the Workers' Compensation Board in Ontario, but only a small segment of the population could benefit from or rely on these programs. Not until 1927 was a federal/provincial constitutional conflict resolved, enabling the federal government to institute the Old Age Pension (which constitutes the basis for today's pension system). Unemployment policies emerged following the Great Depression and were translated into law in the early 1940s. The post-war economic growth in the 1950s and 1960s led to the development of a network of social programs and benefits legislation. Much of the influence on Canadian benefits laws came from European and British laws, rather than from the U.S.A. Today, Canadian benefits (social and welfare legislation) are considered some of the most progressive in the western hemisphere. Currently, the government is trying to trim the enormous cost of these programs to reduce an increasing national deficit. In the following section, the entire network of legal benefit plans for Canadians will be presented.

Legal Considerations in Indirect Compensation

CANADA/QUEBEC PENSION PLAN. The pension plan system in Canada is based on a three-tiered structure. Each tier is of equal importance for generating retirement income:

Tier 1—Government income security plans

Tier 2—Employer-sponsored retirement plans

Tier 3—Personal retirement savings

The **Canada Pension Plan** (in effect since January 1, 1966) and the Quebec Pension Plan are mandatory for all self-employed persons and all employees in Canada. Both are joint contributory; in 1992, the employer contributed 2.4 percent of a year's maximum pensionable earnings (YMPE), and the employee contributed the same. To receive pension benefits an employee must have been in Canada for a minimum of ten years including the year prior to retirement. The retirement pension, approximately 25 percent of the contributory earnings up to the YMPE, is paid monthly for the contributor's lifetime.

Other benefits include disability, death (survivor's benefits), and portability if one moves to another country. If the contributor becomes disabled, he or she receives a monthly pension based on a fixed nominal amount plus an additional lump sum. In case the contributor does, a maximum of 10 percent of the YMPE is paid in one lump sum to the contributor's estate. This is followed by a monthly pension to the surviving spouse. The amount varies depending on the age of the spouse at the time of death and whether there are dependent children. Furthermore, a set amount is payable monthly to each dependent child. Canada has international agreements with several countries to protect the acquired social security rights of the eligible individual. Benefits are paid regardless of the country of residence after qualification.

In twenty years, Canada's total population is expected to increase by 20 percent and the population of those over age 65 is expected to increase by 70 percent. Since the national debt keeps increasing year after year, many experts worry whether there will be any money left in the government coffers for these seniors. Therefore, individuals currently in their forties should give greater consideration to Tier 3 if they want to be able to enjoy their retirement years. In any case, agreements are already in place for gradual increases in contribution rates to Canada Pension Plan so that contributions go up to 7.6 percent of the YMPE by 2011.[4]

PENSION BENEFITS STANDARDS ACT. This Act regulates pension plans of firms under the jurisdiction of the federal government (such as crown corporations, chartered banks, etc.). In addition, seven provinces (Alberta, Saskatchewan, Ontario, Quebec, Nova Scotia, Newfoundland, and Manitoba) have similar Pension Benefits Acts. The federal Act requires that pension funds be held in trust for members and that the funds not be completely controlled by either the employees or the employer. To accomplish this, a third party, such as a life insurance company, a trust company, or even the government of Canada, is registered as custodian and administrator of the fund.

OLD AGE SECURITY ACT. All Canadians who meet the age and residency requirements are entitled to an old age pension under the Old Age Security Act. Payments are indexed on a quarterly basis to reflect changes in the cost of living. A supplement is available to those who qualify on an income test. Those whose net income before adjustments exceeds $53,215 in 1992 will have to pay back up to 15 percent of their old age security pension. This is the first erosion of the concept of a "universal" old age pension. Recent indications are that the trend will continue.

UNEMPLOYMENT INSURANCE. All workers in insurable employment must pay a weekly premium of $3.00 (for 1991) and the employers must pay $4.20 per $100 of weekly insurable earnings. The maximum weekly contributions for 1993, were $22.35 for the employees and $29.82 for the employers.

There are two types of unemployment insurance payments: regular and special. In order to receive the regular benefits, the applicant must have had an interruption of earnings for at least seven consecutive weeks, and must have worked in insurable employment for a period of at least twenty weeks in the past fifty-two weeks. The weekly benefit rate is based on 57 percent of the claimant's average insurable earnings. The maximum weekly insurable earnings for 1993 was $745.00 of which $447 represents the maximum benefits entitlement. Special benefits are paid to people who are sick, injured, pregnant, or in quarantine. They are paid for a period of up to fifteen weeks. Some recent changes in these benefits include the implementation of parental benefits payable for up to ten weeks over and above the maternity benefits in order to take care of a newborn, or to adopt a child; these benefits may be shared between parents if both are eligible.[5] A recent development in unemployment insurance legislation is that any individual who voluntarily quits his or her job without a valid reason will no longer be eligible for unemployment insurance benefits.

WORKERS' COMPENSATION LAWS.   Workers' compensation legislation gives employees protection for job-related accidents and industrial illnesses. Every province in Canada has its own Workers' Compensation Act. The administration of the Act is the responsibility of provincial Workers' Compensation Boards. Employers are classified into groups depending on the special industrial hazards. Each group of employers collectively pays the cost of compensation for any injured workers employed by the firms in that group. The annual contribution rate from each employer is determined on a pro rata basis according to total annual payroll figures. It is possible for an employer to be charged a higher premium than this pro rata basis due to a higher-than-average accident record compared to other organizations in this group. There is therefore a monetary incentive for enhancing the work environment.

Benefits provided under workers' compensation include: (1) medical care; (2) lump sum death payment to a spouse, and pension to spouse and orphans in case of death; (3) compensation in nonfatal cases, including wage loss for temporary disability; and (4) rehabilitation services.

In British Columbia, New Brunswick, Nova Scotia, Ontario, Quebec and Saskatchewan, benefits are indexed to reflect changes in the cost of living, or in industrial wages, depending on provinces; in the other provinces, periodic improvements are legislated.

PROVINCIAL HOSPITAL AND MEDICAL BENEFITS.   While Canada does not have a national health insurance plan as such, all Canadians are covered through a series of arrangements under the Canada Health Act (1984). Some provinces, such as Manitoba and Quebec, provide a full health plan, while other provinces provide only a minimum coverage. Manitoba finances its health care through a tax that ranges from 0 percent to 2.25 percent of gross payroll depending on the size of the firm; Quebec collects 3.45 percent on all payroll amounts; Ontario's health tax ranges from 0.98 percent to 1.95 percent of payroll, also depending on the size of the firm. Alberta and British Columbia charge premiums that are payable by the resident or an agent (usually the employer). In Alberta, for an employee group of five or more it is mandatory for all employers (in this category) to provide enrollment and collect premiums.

Medical insurance plans cover all services rendered by medical practitioners at home, in the office, or in the hospital. As for prescription drug expenses, British Columbia, Manitoba, and Saskatchewan reimburse 80 percent of these expenses after some fixed annual deductible; Ontario provides prescription drugs to all citizens over age 65 and the plan is billed directly; and the other provinces reimburse most drug expenses for residents age 65 and over.

PRIVATE PROTECTION PROGRAMS

Certain private and public organizations offer private protection programs that are not required by law, although their administration may be regulated by law. The programs provide benefits for health care, income after retirement, and insurance against loss of life and limb.

Retirement Benefits

Approximately 40 percent of all Canadian employees are covered by private pension plans. Most employers contribute to these plans. Pension coverage is most likely to exist for unionized employees. The average firm spends approximately 6.3 percent of its total payroll costs on pension plans.

An employer can choose a pension plan from two types: *contributory* and *noncontributory*. A **contributory plan** is one in which both the employer and the employee make deposits. The advantages of contributory plans include: (1) either a larger benefits fund or a lesser burden on the employer, (2) greater employee interest in and appreciation of the cost of a pension plan, and (3) tax deductible contributions. A **noncontributory pension plan** is funded solely by the employer. Noncontributory plans also have advantages, namely: (1) lower payroll and bookkeeping costs, (2) the possibility of increased employee loyalty with less demand for wages and other benefits, and (3) more autonomy in making plans and investment decisions.

Over the years, two significant problems have developed in the administration of pension plans in many industrial nations. First, some employers go out of business, leaving the pension plan unfunded or only partially funded. Secondly, the gap between yearly benefits paid and contributions keeps widening, and the amount of unfunded liabilities keeps growing. The reason for this growing gap, according to several experts, is because many plans (in both the private and public sectors) were installed over the years where the key decision makers had no understanding of the financial liabilities created by their pension plan. Both these problems have been buffered in Canada through the imposition of expert custodial administration (by virtue of the Pension Benefits Standards Act).

Canadians now draw full pension benefits if they retire at age 65, and 70 percent of benefits if they start drawing them at 60. Those who wait until age 70 can get 130 percent of normal benefits. Revenue Canada limits what employers can pay retirees through a registered pension plan to 2 percent of the employee's annual salary for each year of service (based on the average pay for the three best years) to a maximum of $1,715 per year's service. This means that maximum pension payments of approximately $60,000 a year can be made to an executive who earned $200,000 a year and had 35 years of service. To compensate for this retirement cashflow shortfall, some companies sweeten job offers with an additional benefits package. For example, an employer might offer a yearly supplement of $80,000 for the executive mentioned above. The total pension income would then be 70 percent of the pre-retirement salary.

One survey of 125 Canadian employers found that they have "restructured" their pension plans in recent years. Some of these changes include:

- Once the pension is vested, employees are entitled to receive the company's contributions to the plan, as well as their own, when they change jobs.
- Employers are now adding part-time employees to the pension plans.
- Eight employers surveyed are converting defined benefit plans, which promise a certain level of benefits to the retiree, to money purchase plans, which are riskier but may provide higher returns for the plan member;
- Defined benefit plans comprise 88 percent of the plans in the survey and cover 92 percent of members.
- Twenty-three out of 110 sponsors are considering either replacing or terminating their pension plans; thirteen were thinking of changing to money purchase plans; nine were considering terminating their plans and switching to a group registered retirement savings plan (RRSP); and one was terminating the plan with no replacement.[6]

ALARMING TREND IN PENSION PLANS.   Nickel company Inco Ltd. is taking unusual steps in paying almost half of its 1992 pension contributions with newly issued shares, because it would have been forced to borrow the money needed to pay in cash. The purpose is to conserve cash and strengthen the balance sheet. Pension funds do not usually invest in sponsors' companies because of concerns over conflict of interest. Although most Canadian companies are not expected to imitate Inco, if the current economic conditions continue, they might look at it as a possibility.[7]

Thousands of Canadians have taken advantage of corporate offers of financially alluring early retirement programs. This trend began during the 1981–82 recession and continues today. Employers, many of whom have not fully recovered from the recession, have devised strategies that encourage their older, and usually most highly paid, employees to retire before they reach normal retirement age as a way of reducing operating costs. Among the corporate leaders in the field: Vancouver-based forest products giant MacMillan Bloedel Ltd., with 12,000 employees; Metropolitan Life Insurance Co. of Ottawa with 2,800 employees; Oshawa-based General Motors of Canada Ltd. with 45,000 workers; and Imperial Oil Ltd. of Toronto with a staff of 14,700. They have introduced plans that allow them to save as much as 30 percent of the cost of carrying their older employees through to age 65.

In order to make early retirement plans attractive, companies have to offer a wide variety of inducements. Most of the programs partially compensate older employees for the loss of that portion of the pension they would have received if they had worked until they were 65 years old. Some firms also provide a one-time cash settlement that can be converted, along with the pension, into tax-sheltered (RRSPS), and they allow retirees to retain other benefits, such as life insurance and medical plans.

However, as the HRM in the News Vignette suggests, coercion by employers to entice workers into early retirement might shift the burden to the entire economy and there are doubts as to whether or not the country will be able to support its aging population.

Early Retirement Benefits

HRM IN THE NEWS VIGNETTE

Early Retirement Trend Must Be Reversed: ECC

Employers may have to stop pushing early retirement because the Canadian economy can't afford it, the Economic Council of Canada says.

To help secure Canada's economic future, employers should gradually reverse the "inexorable" pressure for increasingly earlier retirements despite the fact that people are living longer, Harvey Lazur, the council's deputy chairman, recently told the Purchasing Management Association of Canada. "Employers in both the private and public sectors need to begin re-examining the reasons why they create large financial incentives for long-serving employees to retire young."

Lazur said it is hard to gauge the economic impact of Canada's aging population or even determine whether the economy can generate enough income to pay for the extra health and pension costs.

Assuming that the per capita rate of increase in health-care spending is reduced to 1.0 per cent a year (considerably lower that current levels), and public pensions remain at current levels in real terms, the economy might be able to support an older population, he said.

But our ability to support a retired population will depend on Canada's productivity growth, which has shrunk from an average of 2.5 per cent a year in the early 1970s to about 1.25 per cent in the early and late 1980s, he said. Current projections put productivity growth at about 1.0 per cent a year through the 1990s.

If the 1.0 per cent estimate for productivity growth is right, and if that rate continues into the next century, it will be enough to cove the extra costs of pensions and health care for the elderly, he said, but it will leave little money for other pressing needs including the environment, child care and labour force training.

"If Canadian performance were to fall below the Council's projections, then it is certain that there will be strong pressures for cutbacks and a messy economic and political struggle as groups seek to maintain their living standards," said Lazur.

Source: Feature article of the same title by P. Menyasz in *H.R. Reporter*, 14 March 1990. Reprinted with permission.

EARLY RETIREMENT IN SOME CANADIAN FIRMS.   At Imperial Oil employees between the ages of 55 and 65 with a minimum ten years of service are offered a retirement package that includes up to seven additional years of service plus a cash payment to bridge the gap between retirement and federal payments. At Metropolitan Life, employees with twenty years of service are offered a year and a half's pay (either as a lump sum or continued salary) and paid relocation costs. An additional six month's salary is paid if no job was found. Sears offers 10 percent guaranteed service at current pay plus full benefits, including 100 percent medical and dental insurance for life. Inco offers eligible employees an option to increase their pension payments by 12 percent for the life of the pension by foregoing receipt of pension payments for the first year.

LEGAL RESTRICTIONS.   The Canadian government is applying new restrictions on special retirement provisions. Actuarially reduced pensions are for workers who have had thirty years of service or are retired because of permanent disability, unless they are aged 60 or more. Firefighters and police officers are exempt. The reason for the restrictions is to limit the amount of tax-deductible contributions to occupational pension plans, thereby limiting loss in tax revenues.

Insurance Benefits

There are three major types of insurance programs: life, health, and disability. These insurance programs are provided by most organizations at a cost far below what would be charged to employees buying their own insurance. These programs have grown substantially, both in the dollar amount of benefits and in the percentage of employees covered.

LIFE INSURANCE PROGRAMS.   Surveys have shown that the majority of companies provide life insurance coverage for their employees. Benefits tend to equal about two years' income for managerial employees. Nonmanagerial, clerical, and blue-collar employees are generally covered for less than one year's income. After retirement, the benefits may continue, but they are reduced substantially. A majority of the life insurance programs offered by organizations are noncontributory—the employee does not pay premiums. There is, however, also a trend toward providing more coverage, especially coverage to family members. Despite the cost, organizations are doing this to keep up with other organizations.

A similar philosophy supports the popularity of *supplementary health insurance plans*. All Canadian citizens are covered by provincial health-care programs (for basic hospital care and medically required services); the supplemental health insurance plans provide coverage for those services excluded from the provincial plans. They include: private or semi-private rooms in a hospital, ambulance services, extended rehabilitation services in case of lengthy recovery, and other supplementary services.

DENTAL INSURANCE.   Dental insurance is one of the fastest growing additions to benefits packages. Surveys show that 86 percent of the employers participating in the survey offered dental plans. This benefit is rather expensive. In most plans, there is an annual maximum allowable expense and there are limits imposed on special services such as orthodontics.

DISABILITY INSURANCE.   While health insurance programs generally cover short-term absences from work due to sickness, short-term absences due to disability are covered by short-term disability insurance. Longer-term absences are covered by long-term sickness and disability insurance. Both types of insurance generally supplement provincial disability programs, often referred to as workers' compensation. However, short-term disability protection is generally offered by more organizations than is long-term disability protection. Virtually all the organizations surveyed offered short-term paid sick leave plans.

Employers who make available a long-term disability benefit plan usually make a large contribution toward the cost. It ranges from 50 percent to 100 percent, and many plans are noncontributory.[8] It is to the employee's advantage to pay for disability insurance because the benefits received are then not taxable.

At present, both the Quebec and Ontario workers' compensation systems are headed toward disaster, threatening the future ability of these provinces to address injured workers' claims. The systems are breaking down because the net of entitlements has been cast too wide, encouraging exploitation.

A small number of organizations offer employees protection against loss of income and loss of work before retirement. **Supplemental unemployment benefits** (SUB) are for people laid off from work. When SUBS are combined with unemployment compensation benefits, laid-off employees can receive as much as 95 percent of their average income. The size of these benefits makes it easier for employees with many years of service to accept layoffs, thus allowing employees with less service, often younger, to continue working. These programs exist in a limited number of industries, and all are the product of labour–management contracts. SUB plans must be approved by Employment and Immigration Canada, or payments will result in a reduction in unemployment insurance benefits. To avoid this, managers must design SUB plans in line with Unemployment Insurance Canada (UIC) regulations that outline acceptable plan provisions such as duration, funding, vesting, eligibility, and separation payment clauses.

Supplemental Unemployment Benefits

Pay for time not worked is less complex to administer than benefits from protection programs, but it is almost as costly to the organization. Pay for time not worked continues to grow, in both amount and kind. Recently, however, the effects of concessionary bargaining between union and management have meant fewer, not more, paid vacation days and holidays. There are two major categories of pay for time not worked: *off the job* and *on the job*.

PAY FOR TIME NOT WORKED

Payments for time not worked (referred to primarily as off-the-job benefits) constitute a major portion of the total cost of indirect compensation. The most commonly provided off-the-job benefits are vacations, sick leave, holidays, personal days, and statutory holidays.

Specific policies concerning holidays and vacations vary from organization to organization. For example, paid vacation may vary from two weeks per year to four weeks or more. Paid holidays may range from six to thirteen. Some common statutory holidays in Canada are New Year's Day, Good Friday, Victoria Day, Canada Day, Labour Day, Thanksgiving, Christmas, and Boxing Day. A new wave is also to compensate employees for vacation not used. This can be achieved by allowing a carryover of time or pay for this unused vacation. In one example, Dome Petroleum paid its departing president $416,274 for unused vacation time.

Most employers allow their staff to continue accumulating seniority while absent on maternity or parental leave. A survey by Hewitt Associates, as reported in *The Globe and Mail*, found that 95 percent of all employers surveyed allowed seniority rights to continue for pension and vacation purposes.[9]

Off the Job

With increased awareness of the relationship between job stress and coronary heart disease and other physical and mental disabilities, organizations have become more concerned with alleviating stress whenever possible. People who are in good physical condition and exercise regularly can often deal with stress better and suffer fewer negative symptoms. By providing athletic facilities on company premises, organizations are encouraging their employees to be physically fit and to engage in exercise. Paid time for physical fitness is

On the Job

clearly pay for time not worked on the job, but organizations often offer it because of its on-the-job benefits.

EMPLOYEE SERVICES AND PERQUISITES

The final component of indirect compensation is employee services and perquisites (perks). Employers, now more than ever, are being pressured to review their policies concerning perquisites. Most perquisites are reserved for senior management and executives. Recent articles suggest that noncash compensation strategies regarding perquisites now include such unexpected items as: car phones, fitness clubs, weight loss seminars, and seminars for those who are quitting smoking.[10]

Perquisites tend to be largely influenced by fashion and government taxation restrictions. Due to the increasing level of complexity in administering personal finances, financial counselling has become one of the more often requested perquisites. Company cars have always been a popular benefit; however, new tax implications are reducing employee enthusiasm.

Certain industries tend to offer certain plans. For example, financial institutions tend to offer more loans or low interest mortgages to their employees. Exhibit 8.3 compares benefits and perks paid to executives in three economic sectors: industrial organizations, financial institutions, and public service organizations.

Although services and perks represent the smallest percentage of indirect compensation, they are highly rewarding to some employees and necessary to others. Some perks represent an important element in the status system of the organization. Others, such as the provision of day-care services, are a means by which working is made possible.

Surveys by the Conference Board of Canada found that employees regard some perks as most effective for alleviating HR problems. For instance, sabbatical leaves were reported to be "effective" or "very effective" in dealing with recruitment problems (59 percent), retention (69 percent), and morale (57 percent). However, respondents were divided in regard to the effectiveness of benefits when it came to productivity and employee performance. Moreover, sabbaticals were not effective in dealing with absenteeism and tardiness related problems.[11]

PERKS ON THE RISE. Much emphasis is currently focused on *employee fitness* and lifestyle programs. Organizations are benefiting from the positive changes in individuals who are, in turn, increasing their productivity. Child care and elder care are other up-and-coming perks. Growing interest in day care has been largely influenced by the increasing number of women entering the workforce. Although there are many benefits from offering such a program, most research carried out by organizations into this topic does not result in the establishment of facilities, due to the initial capital costs. Nonetheless, organizations that offer on-site day care claim that it reduces transportation schedules, provides peace of mind, and allows close access for greater parental involvement in case of emergency. Employers also benefit from reduced tardiness and increases in commitment and motivation. The reasons for providing elder-care benefits are different. With the greying of the Canadian population, employers are forced to think about ways in which they can assist workers who are caring for elderly relatives. The most common type of employer-provided elder-care assistance is information and referral programs that help link employees with community services that already exist. In addition, some companies are looking into other forms of elder care, such as contributing to the cost of respite care and providing adult day care.[12]

INNOVATIVE PERKS AND BENEFITS. The results of a survey conducted by Hewitt Associates among Canadian employers indicate that creative perks are being offered.[13]

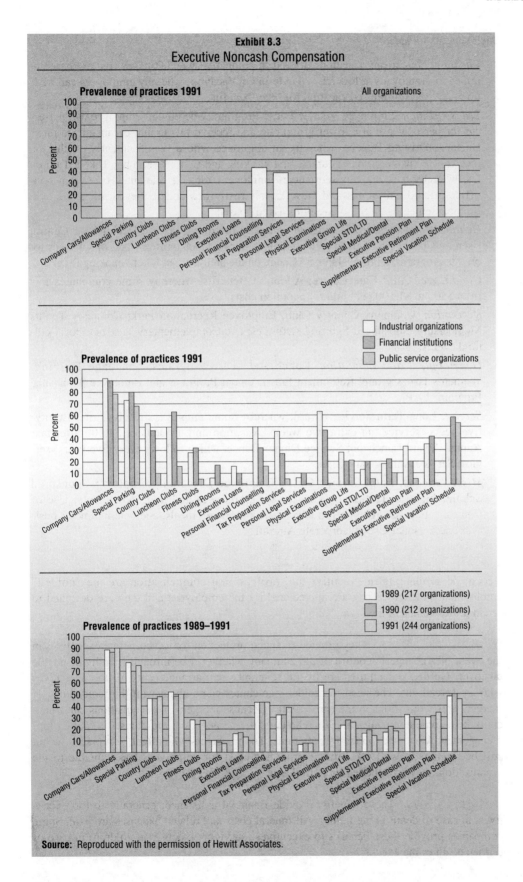

Exhibit 8.3
Executive Noncash Compensation

Source: Reproduced with the permission of Hewitt Associates.

Such benefits include:

1. *Vacations.* Lakefront Vacations offered in company-owned cottages free of charge or rented to employees at low rates; Trade-in Of Vacation, whereby employees can trade up to five days of unused vacation for other benefits;

2. *Transportation.* Employee Vehicle Lease Program, whereby an employee can lease a car for personal use at a lower group rate and receive favourable car insurance rates; Business Driving Benefit, whereby an employee who drives frequently on the job receives defensive driving courses, first aid kits, and first aid training; Take a Taxi on Us, whereby the company reimburses employees for taxi rides they take from non-office-related Christmas and New Year's festivities and if they drink too much. Reimbursement is on a "no questions asked" basis;

3. *Health.* Blood Pressure Testing on company premises; Private Health Care Centre; Exercise Classes either given on the premises during lunch or after work, or subsidies for off-site programs; a Physical Fitness Centre on the premises; and Stop Smoking Program.

4. *Child Care.* Child-Care Centre; Adoption Benefits, whereby some companies pay from $500 to $1,500 per child for adoption costs;

5. *Recreation.* Company Country Club; Employee Recreation Park; Company Tennis Membership; Subsidized Sporting Activities; and Complementary Tickets to local cultural events;

6. *Development and Education.* Lunch and Learn Programs; Language Training; Women's Issues group; Retirement Enhancement Program; and Employee Assistance Program (EAP);

7. *Service.* Long-Term Service Award, whereby some employees receive, after twenty-five years' service, an extra two weeks' vacation and a bonus of $1,500 after tax; Annual Award Luncheon; Service Dinner Dance, which follows every five years' service; Service Anniversary Gifts;

8. *Miscellaneous.* Food Service Costs; Employee Discounts; Employer-Sponsored Scholarships (or Tuition Assistance) for employees and their dependents; Use of Company Expense Accounts to cover personal travel, meals, and entertainment; business and personal Use of Corporate Aircraft.

Golden Employment Practices

Recent developments in executive and professional compensation are the "golden" employment practices. They are appreciated by the employees and they are designed to retain professionals in the organization.

GOLDEN PARACHUTES. They provide financial protection for top corporate executives in the event of a change in control of the company whether it be through friendly or hostile takeover. **Golden parachutes** are liberal severance pay arrangements for top executives who are forced out. The need for golden parachutes came about with the rapid flurry of mergers and acquisitions in the early 1980s. Because mergers and acquisitions can financially help some companies and shareholders, the parachutes were devised to soften top-management resistance to takeover attempts. Top managers who might be replaced would still be financially well off. Similar programs exist for employees less valuable to the organization; they are labelled *tin parachutes.*

GOLDEN COFFINS. These benefits provide financial assistance, generally to top executives, in case of death in the family. All funeral costs and related expenses are paid. Some companies provide these benefits to executives' survivors (spouse or children) in case of sudden death of the executive.

GOLDEN HANDCUFFS. While golden parachutes help executives exit the corporation and golden coffins help the executive or the family in case of death, golden handcuffs provide incentives for the executive to remain a member of the organization. They do it by making it very costly for the executive to leave an organization. Stock options and retirement packages are the most common golden handcuffs. By leaving, the executive forfeits these financially attractive benefits. A wise use of golden handcuffs can help keep valued employees. In a recent example, the Coca-Cola company notified its shareholders that its CEO (Roberto Goizueta) received one million shares of restricted stock under a longstanding program for Coca-Cola executives.[14] However, restricted stock carries limitations on the shareholder's freedom to sell and must be forfeited if the individual leaves the company for reasons other than death, disability, or retirement.

Although organizations tend to view indirect compensation as a reward, recipients do not see it this way. This causes organizations to become concerned with their package of indirect compensation benefits and how they are administered.

The benefits package should be selected on the basis of what is good for both the employee and the employer. Being aware of employee preferences can often help determine what benefits package the employer should offer. Employees may indicate strong preferences for certain benefits over others. The most desired benefit appears to be time off from work in large chunks. Older workers consistently express a desire for increased pension benefits. This is also the case for employees with rising incomes. The existence of diverse preferences argues strongly for benefit flexibility.

When employees can design their own benefits package both they and the company benefit. At least that is the experience at Eatons, Cominco, and several other Canadian companies. Seventy-five percent of Cominco's 1,800 eligible employees have chosen to participate in a flexible benefits program. The company provides a core package of benefits to all employees covering provincial medical plan payment where applicable; extended medical coverage with $500 deductible; life insurance offering one year's salary to the beneficiary; accident, death and dismemberment coverage equal to three times annual salary; short- and long-term disability insurance; vacations; a company pension; and a group RRSP. In addition, each employee can choose, in "cafeteria style," from a variety of optional benefits. Some core benefits can be "sold" back to Cominco to add to the individual's cash account. For instance, if an employee's spouse is covered at work with an extended medical plan, the employee can obtain a credit in flexible dollars for the core medical plan. And, depending on years of service with the company, a maximum of five holidays can be converted to flexible dollars to purchase other benefits. The options include extended medical coverage with $25 deductible; three ranges of dental insurance; life insurance upgraded by six increments, and increased insurance for accidental death, dismemberment, and long-term disability.[15]

With more women entering the workforce, fewer traditional families (where the man is the sole wage earner), and more single parent families, the trend emerges of adjusting benefit plans to accommodate the changing needs of employees. However, it is estimated that only 30 percent of Canadian organizations offer flexible benefit plans to their employees.

When designed effectively, a flexible benefits approach should increase the variety of plans offered to employees without increasing the costs to employers. Many items that can be offered at a relatively low cost improve the employees' outlook, causing them to feel

ADMINISTRATIVE ISSUES IN INDIRECT COMPENSATION

Determining the Benefits Package

Providing Benefit Flexibility

good about the company they work for. There are three common approaches to developing flexible compensation packages:

- *Core plus options.* A general core program is offered to all eligible employees. In addition, an option is granted to either increase or expand coverage and, in some instances, employees may elect to receive cash amounts rather than benefits.
- *Modular approach.* This method allows employees to select a preferred package from various existing modules. These modules are structured in such a way as to satisfy common situations within the workforce.
- *Flexible spending.* This concept functions somewhat like a bank account. In the preceding example where the employee opted out of the core supplementary medical benefit, the firm would "deposit" to the employee's "benefit funding account" an amount equal to the value of the unused benefit. In this way, therefore, the employee receives reimbursement. This plan's main appeal is tax effectiveness because the employee's pre-tax dollars are paying for expenses. This plan is often used in conjunction with the above plans.[16]

Since the main objective of a flexible benefits plan is to ensure harmony between plans offered and employees' needs and to create a more effective means of managing benefit costs, HR managers are advised to seek employees' input through the use of attitude data. Otherwise, the effects of the benefit plans might be counterproductive. For instance, a flexible benefits plan introduced by Liptons was designed for a traditional family where the wife is at home and the family has on average of two children. Not even one employee at Liptons met this description. Consequently, a committee was formed to work jointly with the HR manager to determine the parameters that would render the implementation of the program successful. Unfortunately, Liptons has discovered that the final program has increased costs by 15 to 20 percent over the previous plan. Employees, however, are satisfied with the new plan.[16]

To illustrate the content of cafeteria-style benefits, we can examine those offered by National Bank and Hyundai Canada. National Bank's program includes five parameters:

- Preferential interest rate on loans;
- Preferential interest rate on credit card balances;
- Savings plan—the bank adds 25 percent to the amount that the employee is saving, up to a maximum addition of $1,500;
- Pension plan—50 percent is paid by the employer and 50 percent by the employee;
- The total value of all benefits represents 31.5 percent of the salary.

Hyundai Canada developed a cafeteria-style plan called the Hyundai Plus Program. It was implemented in February 1989. Its main concept is the flexidollar. The company allows its employees an amount of flexidollars equal to 2.5 percent of their annual basic salary. This amount is not taxable, and employees can invest their flexidollars in one or more of the following programs:

- Supplemental health insurance;
- Collective retirement savings: an employee can invest additional money any time during the year, transfer his or her personal retirement savings into the group retirement savings plans, and add his or her spouse to the program;
- Mortgage program: flexidollars can be used to reduce the employee's mortgage.

Communicating the Benefits Package

Providing benefit flexibility is important not only because it gives employees what they want, but also because it makes employees aware of the benefits that they are receiving and, hence, it increases their morale. Many employees are unaware of both the types and the costs of the benefits they are receiving. If employees have no knowledge of their benefits, there is little reason to believe that the organization's indirect compensation program objectives will be attained. Many organizations indicate that they assign a high priority to telling employees about their benefits, although a majority spend only 1 percent of payroll doing this.[18]

Employees may more easily appreciate the cash portion of their compensation, since it is readily visible as a function of their pay schedule. Indirect compensation is not visible, so most employees only realize the benefit once they use the plan. This is evident in corporations where contributions are solely made by the employer. Conversely, benefit plans where employees' contributions are required or which permit flexibility require more employee involvement.

Thus, many of the indirect compensation objectives are not currently attained, probably due to ineffective communication techniques. Almost all organizations use impersonal, passive booklets and brochures to convey benefits information; only a few use more personal, active media, such as slide presentations and regular employee meetings. Communicating the benefits package should not be taken for granted.

For the communications strategy to be effective, employees must fully understand the contents of their benefits package. Today, more organizations understand the importance of communication in ensuring the success of their flexible benefits plans. For example, flex plans can be communicated through videos that set the tone and help the employees understand the concepts by outlining the rationale behind the benefits package. Seminars are most productive for groups of twenty-five to thirty, with an opportunity provided for questions and answers. Before launching a new flexible benefit program, it might be wise for the employer to hire an external communication consultant to help with the implementation process. This seems to ensure better success.[19]

TRENDS IN INDIRECT COMPENSATION

Assessing Indirect Compensation

In view of the continuing escalation of costs, employers are under increased pressure to closely examine every aspect of the cost of their indirect compensation program. From the organization's point of view, a competitive advantage will be most easily enhanced by controlling benefit costs to the maximum extent possible within the constraints imposed by competition. If benefit costs can be reduced relative to those of competitors while maintaining wage levels, increased profitability should result. Alternatively, if some benefit program could be shown to influence productivity, then, all other things being equal, the employer with the comparatively better implementation of that program should experience higher output and achieve a competitive advantage.

Along with this concern for costs, organizations should also consider the effectiveness of the programs that are instituted or retained. Employers should ask themselves:

- What objectives are set for indirect compensation?
- What effects can reasonably be expected from a given program?
- How can indirect compensation help the company become and stay competitive in changing global markets?

Organizations that choose to spend funds on employee benefits should make sure that the effects they desire are accomplished by the programs they provide. For instance, cafeteria-style or flexible benefit plans may offer a solution in catering to young and old workers, since these employees have different needs throughout their careers.

There are also indirect returns to employers from offering indirect compensation: a healthier workforce, the perception that the company is a good place to work, and being seen as a good corporate citizen in the community. Some observers suggest that Royal Bank of Canada has assuredly reached those objectives with its comprehensive benefit program; it has recognized that benefits attract good employees, motivate employee productivity, and reduce employee turnover; its program is proactive in its choice of benefits and shows that the bank cares about its employees.

Employers must also become more aware of their employees' attitudes concerning their indirect compensation packages. For instance, employees tend to undervalue their benefit packages and underestimate the costs incurred by their employers. Also, employee satisfaction with benefits increases with improved coverage and decreases with increased personal cost. It is quite likely that employees who have been with their employers for a long period are in general satisfied with their benefits. Therefore, companies should take steps to ensure that newer employees are aware of the benefits they receive and their monetary value. Thus, organizations must make frequent attempts at benefit communication, particularly aimed at newer employees. IBM has a Speak-Up Program in place allowing its employees to ask questions, voice concerns, complain, make recommendations, or even compliment any of IBM's operations and policies. With this communications program in place, employees generally believe IBM is a good organization to work for.

Computer Applications

With the implementation of an HRIS, data can be manipulated to formulate projections concerning salary structure proposals, compa-ratios, the total cost of selected configurations of

---

HRM DYNAMICS
Benefits Pay Profiles in Selected Canadian Organizations

Canadian Pacific

CP provides its officers, supervisors, and specialists with some special benefits and perks in addition to the ones offered to other employees. The main additions include: extended health-care plan; dental care where the company pays the entire cost of this coverage (up to $800 per year); income protection plan, which includes short-term illness/accident benefits, long-term disability, and regular pension plan; survivors benefits, which include life insurance, personal accident insurance, and a savings plan.

The Montreal Gazette

The Gazette is Montreal's largest English language newspaper and is part of the Southam group. The company offers a wide range of benefits to its permanent employees including: group life insurance, short-term disability, long-term disability, an accidental death and dismemberment plan, travel accident insurance, a dental plan, and extended medical plan, and a joint contributory retirement plan. Some more specific benefits include: purchasing Southam stocks at 95 percent of market value, interest-free loan up to 50 percent of base salary, educational assistance (100 percent coverage), and an EAP.

Marconi Canada

Marconi is one of Canada's leading high-technology electronics firms. In order to remain competitive, it offers its employees a variety of benefits and perks. Some of the most important include: three weeks' vacation following three years of service; a 10 percent joint contributory pension plan; an early retirement package for employees age 55 who have at least ten years of service; and a group benefit program that includes life insurance, survivor income coverage, long-term disability, short-term disability, supplemental health care, dental care, an accidental death and dismemberment insurance plan, and life insurance for dependents.

the benefit package, and the cost of compensation in the future (including indirect compensation) under different rates of inflation. Consequently, with the aid of this technology, organizations can more easily implement and administer a flexible benefit package.

Computer technology can also be applied to analyze the various components of indirect compensation during planning. These include such items as health and dental benefits, vacation time, sick time, pensions, and profit sharing. The emphasis is on planning.

Benefit administration was one of the first HR applications to be computerized. Before the introduction of PCs, packaged benefit systems were available for mainframes and mini-computers only. The cost of using such technologies was high and consequently the systems were more prevalent in larger organizations. In the past seven to eight years, however, numerous computerized systems, especially micro-based ones, have been introduced to meet the more complex needs of corporations.

Benefit plan sponsors are discovering several innovative tools that allow them to get to the heart of pension fund performance. *Attribution analysis* breaks down the rate of return into policy return and active management return. This analysis tool comes in a variety of formats, such as PC-based diskettes, some requiring a modem link with the software of the vendor, others are updated through monthly exchanges of disks. Some systems allow a sponsor to compare fund performance against a customized benchmark. Canadian pension funds are moving toward attribution analysis, but it should be remembered that this type of software may be only suitable for large funds. For example, Frank Russell Canada, a Toronto-based consulting firm, has been marketing a product called *RPA* (*Russel Performance Attribution*), which is a PC-based graphics software package. It was designed for large pension funds, its smallest user being McGill University, with a fund of $488 million. The software costs $24,000 and there is a $6,000 set-up fee.[20]

The *Employee Benefit Software Directory* lists approximately 450 packaged benefit-administration systems that seem to cover every aspect of record keeping, reporting, analysis, and control that could be needed by the benefit function. This fierce competition among software developers has led to improvements in overall product quality and to substantial price reductions.

SUMMARY

Chapters 7 and 8 address the most frequently asked questions in organization orientation programs: "How much do I get paid?" and "How long is my vacation?" Most organizations have been responding to both questions with, "More/longer than ever before." In fact, the growth in indirect compensation has been double that of direct compensation. This doubling has occurred despite the lack of evidence that indirect compensation is really helping attain the purposes of total compensation. Money, job challenge, and opportunities for advancement appear to serve the purposes of compensation as much as, if not more than, pension benefits, disability provisions, and services, particularly for employees aspiring to managerial careers.

This is not to say, however, that employees do not desire indirect benefits. Organizations are offering them at such an increasing rate because employees desire them. However, employees do not always value the specific indirect benefits offered by an organization, nor do all employees know what benefits are offered. Current evidence suggests that employees' lack of awareness of the contents and value of their benefit programs may partially explain why they are not perceived more favourably. For that reason, some organizations solicit direct information about employees' preferences for compensation programs. Also, organizations are becoming more concerned about the communication of their benefit programs. Increased communication and more employee participation in the design and selection of the benefit packages may increase the likelihood that organizations will receive increased gains from providing indirect compensation. However, these gains do not come without a cost.

In order to ensure that an organization is getting the most from its indirect compensation, thorough assessments must be made of what the organization is doing, what other organizations are doing, and what employees prefer to see the organization doing.

P O S T S C R I P T

Many changes will be seen in compensation benefits by the year 2000, as projected by a survey of managers of 300 Canadian benefits plans conducted by Hewitt Associates in November 1988. Exhibit 8.4 portrays the results of this survey. More than two-thirds of the respondents believe that today's average benefit costs of about 35 percent of payroll will increase. The increases stem from many factors: facing cost hikes in publicly funded programs, governments may attempt to shift the burden to private sponsors; inflation has boosted the cost of many benefit plans, particularly for dental and extended health benefits; and prescription drug prices continue to climb.

Exhibit 8.4
Use of Employee Benefits by the Year 2000

	Increased	About the same	Decreased
Flextime	76%	22%	2%
Flexible benefits	85	13	2
Broad-based financial counselling	58	42	0
Mail order prescription drug plans	24	66	10
Group universal life insurance	36	60	4
Homeowner's insurance	46	51	3
Auto insurance	47	49	4
Group legal	47	49	4
Personal liability insurance	33	64	3
Employer-sponsored day care	83	15	2
Elder care benefits	38	59	3
Long-term (nursing home) care coverage	42	56	2
Employee Assistance Plans	75	25	
Dental capitation plans	60	37	3
Defined benefit pension plans	28	30	42
Profit sharing plans	70	28	2
On-site fitness/health facility	65	33	2
Maternity/paternity leave	72	28	
Company stock plans	61	38	1

Source: Hewitt Associates, Toronto 1988. Reprinted with permission.

By the year 2000, a substantial increase will be seen in the following employee benefits: flexible benefits, employer-sponsored day care, employee assistance plans, profit-sharing plans, on-site fitness/health facilities, elder care, and maternity/paternity leave, to name a few.

TOWARD A NEW COMPENSATION PHILOSOPHY. In order to plan appropriate compensation packages, benefit managers will have to analyze the needs of employees, as well as those of the organization. Key elements will include employee involvement and development, performance, and communication. Keeping these elements in mind, the employer will devise new benefit packages. To develop innovative ways of establishing compensation packages, it is necessary to understand the goals of the organization and not just duplicate the offerings of competitors. Successful plans will usually start with one or two pilot projects to test their acceptability; then they will be extended to the entire organization. The objectives, however, must be specific, tangible, and comprehensible. Thus, to be successful in the future the new compensation philosophy will have to combine rewards with business goals.[21]

Labour shortages will result in minorities becoming a source of new workers. Workers in the ranks of part-time, contract, and permanent temporary will continue to grow. The challenges for employers in the future will be to tailor compensation benefits to these new employees and at the same time minimize costs.

EMERGING TECHNOLOGIES IN BENEFITS ADMINISTRATION. Technology is allowing the development of products not possible a few years ago and is finding its place in benefits administration. Marrying retail point-of-sale technology (magnetically encoded identification cards) with health and dental claims administration will speed up claims settlement. The payoff: greater convenience for employees, better service for providers of services, and more attractive prices from plan sponsors.

A competitive market will demand efficiency and low operating costs. Technology will allow further differentiation among products and services, and increased networking, data sharing, and data exchange among organizations. Expert systems will assist pension and benefits professionals to reach more consistent decisions. Closer integration of the administration responsibilities between the supplier and the sponsor will reduce overall cost, and raise service levels and flexibility.[22]

REVIEW AND ANALYSIS QUESTIONS

1. What are the purposes of indirect compensation? How can these purposes best be met?
2. What legislative acts at the federal level have influenced the rate and type of indirect compensation an organization must offer its employees?
3. How are unemployment benefits derived and what is the status of unemployment compensation?
4. Identify and describe the major private protection programs employers offer employees.
5. What are the major types of pay for time not worked and what is their relative cost to organizations?
6. Skim through the business section of a newspaper and report on some innovative perks used by Canadian organizations. Comment on their apparent usefulness.
7. Explain briefly the content and goals of the "golden" employment practices.
8. What are the pro's and con's of flexible benefit programs?
9. Why is it important to communicate benefit programs to employees? How can it be done effectively?
10. How does computer technology facilitate the administration and assessment of indirect compensation?

CASE STUDY

TO BE SICK: RIGHT OR FRINGE?

On 1 December 1992, Metro-Hospital concluded a new sick-pay agreement with the Union. The agreement stated, in part, that all employees with more than three years' service were entitled to ten days' sick leave a year (without proof of medical certificate) and that, at no time, could more than fifteen days be accumulated. Sick pay was full salary for the employee. The contract further stipulated that a doctor's certificate might be requested for sick leave extending for three consecutive days.

In the previous five years (prior to December 1) the average absenteeism due to sickness among the nurses in the hospital was approximately 2.5 days. The work was of such nature that, when a nurse called in sick, someone else had to be found to perform her duties. Thus, under the old contract, no one received sick pay for short-term illnesses, because additional expenses were incurred in hiring replacements for sick employees.

By 1 June 1993, when the new agreement had been in effect six months, some alarming symptoms were noted: the average sick leave taken by the hospital's nurses had jumped to seven days, and in some units, such as Intensive Care and Emergency, it was even higher (an average of nine days).

This worried Tom Watson, the director of human resources for Metro-Hospital. Not only did it cause severe administrative disturbances, such as those entailed by trying to find replacements at the very last minute, but it significantly boosted the deficit in the operating budget for personnel. He called his staff for a special meeting to discuss possible remedies to this situation.

Case Questions

1. What suggestions would you give Tom Watson?
2. How could the hospital ensure that the nurses do not misuse sick leave?
3. Aside from a compensation strategy, what other HR strategies could be considered?

NOTES

1. J. O'Toole, "The Irresponsible Society," in *Working in the 21st Century*, ed. C.S. Sheppard and D.C. Carroll (New York: Wiley, 1980), 156.
2. R.E. Berger and L.T. Smith, "Let Them Have Cash," *Benefits Canada*, February 1991, 35–39.
3. L. Dixon, "Containing Health Care Costs," *Benefits Canada*, February 1991, 24–26.
4. M. Cu-Uy-Gam, "More Executives Considering Early Retirement," *The Financial Post*, 3 May 1990, 14.
5. William M. Mercer, *Benefits Legislation in Canada* 1991.
6. M. Gibb-Clark, "Many firms altering their pension plans," *The Globe and Mail*, 17 December 1990, B4.
7. C. Lakshman, "Stock pension contributions to stay rare," *The Financial Post*, 27 February 1992.
8. *Canadian Benefits Administration Manual* (Toronto: Richard De Boo Publisher, 1990).
9. *The Globe and Mail*, 2 September 1991.
10. W. Lilley, "Perks of the Moment: What's Hot—and What's Not," *Canadian Business*, April 1985, 58; and H. Nizman and A. McKinley, "Employee Benefits: Yesterday, Today and Tomorrow," *The Human Resource*, 4, 6 (Jan./Feb. 1988): 15–19.
11. H. Paris, "The Corporate Response to Workers with Family Responsibilities," *Conference Board of Canada Report 43–89*, (Ottawa: Conference Board of Canada, 1989) 30.
12. One such case is Hallmark Cards. See "Eldercare: Employers Taking Action," *Bulletin to Management*, 20 February 1988, 64.
13. The ensuing discussion is based on *Innovative Benefits*, (Toronto: Hewitt Associates, 1985).

14. *The Globe and Mail*, 20 March 1992.

15. W. Lilley, "A Compensation Special," *Canadian Business*, April 1985, 57.

16. For more information, see G.E. Sutherland, "Demographics Partially Underlies Push Toward Flexible Compensation," *Canadian Human Resource Reporter*, 14 December 1987.

17. "How Liptons Launched Flexible Benefits Program," *The Canadian Human Resource Reporter*, 30 November 1987.

18. W.P. Cooke, "Telling Employees About Benefits," *Human Resource Management in Canada*, 1988, 5 339.

19. "Communication is the Key," *Benefits Canada*, May 1990, 46.

20. L. Bak, "To What Do You Attribute Your Success?" *Benefits Canada*, January 1992, 33.

21. Based on C.T. Walker, "The New Compensation Philosophy," *Benefits Canada*, April 1990, 11–15.

22. Based on H. Ryckman, "A Means to an End," *Benefits Canada*, April 1990, 515–16.

CHAPTER NINE

PERFORMANCE APPRAISAL: METHODS AND PROCEDURES

KEYNOTE ADDRESS

James Whitelaw
Senior Vice-President Human Resources, Air Canada

Employees' Performance and Feedback: The Air Canada Experience

The airline business is service-oriented, people intensive, and highly competitive. Like any company in such a business environment, Air Canada's ability to achieve its mission and goals is highly dependent on the ability of its people and their focus on the achievement of agreed upon goals and objectives.

The basic role and mission of human resources is to build a partnership with line management and employees aimed at the achievement of business results and strategies. One requirement of this partnership is the provision by the HR department of sound, user-friendly HR systems, including an effective performance appraisal process. This key system forms an integral part of the overall HRM system in Air Canada.

The basic purposes of the performance appraisal process are to provide a vehicle for formal feedback and evaluation of employee performance; to assess and act on employee developmental requirements, both short and longer range; and to provide a link and guide to the principle of pay for performance.

No performance assessment can operate without pre-agreed performance criteria on which to base a fair and objective assessment. At Air Canada, we have a system for the establishment of specific improvement objectives and performance standards between boss and subordinates for a particular planning cycle—normally a twelve-month period. This in turn requires discussion on a continuing basis to adjust plans to meet changing conditions.

Annual performance appraisal thus becomes a natural culmination or "stock-taking" based on the achievement of planned results. We have taken some initial steps toward including the comments of an individual's peers and subordinates in his or her performance evaluation, and the results suggest that this effectively broadens the process to provide feedback on leadership skills that is not otherwise readily obtainable.

Another key lesson we have learned is that training on conducting an effective performance appraisal is essential. The results of the process will fall short of employee and company expectations if the manager is uncomfortable with the task, or is limited in the required people interaction skills.

Today's HR practitioner must add value to the organization by enhancing its capability to achieve its business plan and to meet the test of product and service excellence in the marketplace. One of the key ways it can do so is by providing the means for employees to direct their efforts to the right tasks and to receive the feedback and assessment that results in constant improvement.

• • •

As the Keynote Address indicates, performance appraisal at Air Canada is viewed as a strategic HR activity. It helps the employee's developmental plan via the feedback process, as well as through his or her input into the appraisal process; it also serves to align employees' performance to the achievement of the company's business plans. The company also realizes the importance of training managers to conduct and manage the performance appraisal process properly.

Given that appraisals are vital to organizations, are widely used, and represent an amalgamation of data, two chapters are devoted to this topic. This chapter discusses the various aspects related to the gathering of the appraisal information. It also describes the purpose of performance appraisal and its relationship with other HR functions. The next chapter (Chapter 10) discusses using the information, especially the performance appraisal interview. Moreover, it will identify deficiencies in employee performance and develop strategies to remedy them. It will also examine the elements in diagnosing and assessing how effectively an organization is conducting performance appraisals.

• • •

Although employees may learn how well they are performing through informal means, such as comments from co-workers or superiors, **performance appraisal (PA)** is defined here as a formal structural system of measuring, evaluating, and influencing an employee's job-related attributes, behaviours and outcomes, and level of absenteeism, so as to discover how productive the employee is and whether he or she can perform better in the future.

A **performance appraisal system (PAS)** encompasses all of the following factors that can affect the formal, structural system of measuring and evaluating performance:

* The form(s) or the method(s) used to gather the appraisal data;
* The job analysis conducted to identify the proper job elements (criteria) against which to establish standards to be used in examining the appraisal data;
* The assessment of the validity and reliability of the methods used to measure employees' job behaviour and performance;
* The characteristics of the rater and ratee, which may influence the outcome(s) of the interview process;
* The process involved in utilizing the appraisal information for development and evaluation;
* The evaluation of how well the PAS is utilized in relation to stated HR policy and objectives.

In this chapter, the terms **supervisor** and **manager** are generally discarded, because both the appraiser and the appraisee may be managers or supervisors. Thus, the term **superior** or **rater** is used to denote the person doing the appraising, and the term **subordinate** or **ratee** is used to refer to the employee whose performance is appraised. The terms superior and subordinate are used in this chapter only for clarity; they do not imply that the person doing the appraising (the rater) is "better" than the appraisee (ratee) or that the subordinate is "inferior" to the superior.

PERFORMANCE APPRAISAL

Purposes and Importance of PA

As suggested throughout the text, productivity improvement is of concern to all organizations. Although the productivity of most organizations is a function of technological, capital, and *human resources*, many organizations have not sought to increase productivity through improving the performance of their human resources. This is unfortunate because employees generally work at only 60 to 70 percent of their capabilities, with the difference in productivity ratio as high as 3:1 for high vs. low performance.

Employee performance, as discussed in various chapters, includes outcomes (i.e., quality and quantity of outcomes), behaviour (i.e., good attendance, polite treatment of customers), and job-related attributes (i.e., cooperativeness, team playing, loyalty). All these can be measured and evaluated in a variety of ways. However, the choice of appraisal process has a profound effect on how effective the evaluation is.

The utility of using a comprehensive PA, feedback, and goal setting program in a company of 500 employees has been estimated at $5.3 million for one year.[1] During an average week in 1987, 2.9 million workers in Canada were away from their jobs for all or part of the week. As a result of these absences, the full labour potential of people with jobs was reduced by 53.4 million hours or 11 percent.[2] On the average, each employee will miss work anywhere from seven to twelve times a year.[3] In some industries and among some occupations, as discussed in Chapter 1, absenteeism rates run as high as 10 to 20 percent. In one particular example, that of the Bank of Montreal, it has been estimated that in one year, 54,000 hours a week are lost due to absenteeism, which was translated to a direct cost of $18 million per year in salaries alone.[4] These performance-related problems can be identified and dealt with effectively, if sound PA processes are put in place and properly used in the organization.

In addition to having an impact on productivity, an effectively designed PA form serves as a *contract* between the organization and the employee. This contract acts as a control and evaluation system that enables the system to better serve a multitude of purposes, including:

- *Management development*: It provides a framework for future employee development by identifying and preparing individuals for increased responsibilities.
- *Performance measurement*: It establishes the relative value of an individual's contribution to the company and helps evaluate individual accomplishments.
- *Feedback:* It outlines what performance is expected from employees.
- *HR planning*: It audits management talent to evaluate the present supply of human resources for replacement planning.
- *Legal compliance*: It helps to establish the validity of employment decisions made on the basis of performance-based information (also helps to defend management actions such as demotions, transfers, or terminations).
- *Communication*: It provides a format for dialogue between superior and subordinate and improves the understanding of personal goals and careers.
- *Enhanced supervisory understanding of the job*: It forces superiors to be aware of what their subordinates are doing.

Relationships and Influences

As shown in Exhibit 9.1, PA is linked with several other HR activities. Also shown in this exhibit are the rather extensive legal considerations relevant to appraising employee performance.

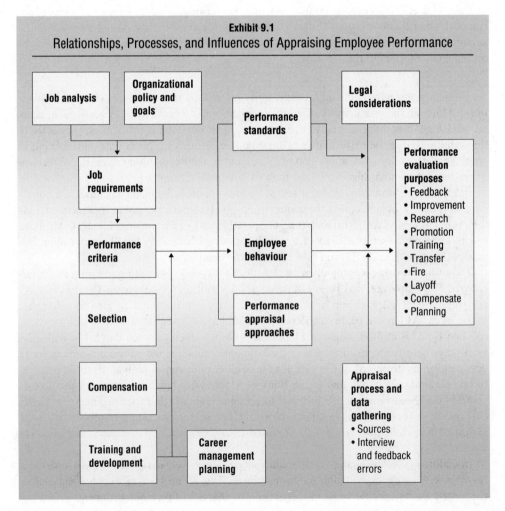

Exhibit 9.1
Relationships, Processes, and Influences of Appraising Employee Performance

JOB ANALYSIS. The foundation of PA is job analysis. If a formal job analysis has not been conducted to establish the validity of the PA form, and thus the job relatedness of an evaluation criterion, the company may be accused of discrimination. In fact, such a case has been submitted recently to arbitration in the Province of Quebec. A group of television producers at Radio-Quebec were denied tenure, after having worked for the company for an average of five years. The decision was made by the administration, based on a PA form that had never been validated (i.e., no formal job descriptions existed for the job of a producer).

SELECTION AND PLACEMENT. PA information is vital for making a number of selection and placement decisions. It helps ensure that only candidates who will perform well are from a large pool of applicants. Second, because empirical validation of a selection test requires the calculation of a correlation between test scores and performance scores, PA results are necessary (as described in Chapter 6). Without them, performance scores cannot be established.

COMPENSATION. One purpose of PA is to motivate employees. PA can be used as a basis upon which to distribute compensation. A valid appraisal is necessary for an organization to provide contingent rewards (that is, those based on performance). PA information can be used in the determination of pay levels as well as pay increments, as discussed in Chapter 7.

TRAINING, DEVELOPMENT, AND CAREER PLANNING. Because employee performance is determined by ability as well as motivation, training can improve it. In order to provide the appropriate training, however, it is necessary to be aware of the employee's current level of performance and any unsatisfactory aspects of performance. It is also necessary to know if the undesirable performance is caused by a lack of ability or motivation, or by the situation. In order to gain this knowledge, PA is necessary. Used in conjunction with job analysis, PA is necessary for implementing effective pre-employment training programs. Thus, assessment of performance can also help the employee make a decision about changes in his or her career. If the employee finds out that, in spite of his training and aptitudes, he or she is unable to turn out a satisfactory performance, a change in career may be sought. This can be done internally (i.e., transfer) or externally (i.e., change to another organization).

Many observers of the Canadian labour scene agree that legal requirements will have a major effect on the development of PASs. The federal government (through the Charter of Rights and Freedoms) and the various federal and provincial human rights laws, require that appraisal procedures be valid. This implies, of course, that any staffing decision should be made based on job-related criteria. Much of the legal context was described in detail in the section dealing with staffing. Unlike the U.S. experience, there is less litigation pertaining to PASs in Canada. Nonetheless, in a number of court cases and arbitration hearings involving layoffs, dismissals, and even promotions, indirect references to PA have been made. One can conclude from the early cases, that whenever arbitrary management decisions are contested, courts and boards of inquiry tend to rule in favour of the employee.

In the case of *Sorel vs. Tomerson Saunders Ltd. (1985)*, Justice Gibbs of the British Columbia Supreme Court ruled that the company cannot dismiss an employee with significant seniority (thirty-seven years of uninterrupted service) "without warning, without notice, and without cause." Sorel was awarded $254,556 in compensation for lost benefits. In the case of *B.L. Means et al. vs. Ontario Hydro (1984)* seven black employees alleged

LEGAL ISSUES IN PA

Establishing Valid Performance Criteria: Case Anecdotes

discrimination in layoffs undertaken by Ontario Hydro. The layoffs were made on the basis of an informal ranking system. Management used "vague" criteria for assessing workers and failed to keep written records of the ranking to support the layoffs. The Board of Inquiry ruled in favour of four of the complainants and concluded that because Ontario Hydro failed to use "objective" criteria, the possibility of racial discrimination was left open.

Another example of an employer's failure to justify its actions occurred in a case involving a fire security company that hired a man of East Indian ancestry to be its assistant controller (*Almeida vs. Chubb Fire Security Division (1984)*). The assistant controller worked for the company for six years. During this time, four new controllers of "Caucasian or white ancestry" were hired, despite the company's usual policy of promoting from within. Shortly after the fourth appointment, the company dismissed the assistant controller, who then filed a complaint with the Ontario Human Rights Commission. The assistant controller alleged that both the failure to promote him and his dismissal were "motivated by a discriminatory bias."

The assistant controller presented evidence that during his early months with the company, his performance was highly regarded by management. About seven months after the assistant controller was hired, the controller left the company. The assistant controller "assumed and discharged many of the controller's responsibilities during the interim period before the appointment of a new controller." His salary was raised in appreciation of his efforts, but he was not promoted to the position of controller. During the term of the new controller, the assistant controller raised his qualifications by obtaining the R.I.A. designation. Over the space of several years, four controllers were hired in succession, and during each interim period, the assistant controller "ably discharged" the duties normally handled by the controller. When the assistant controller did not receive the appointment for the fourth time, his work deteriorated and he "no longer fully cooperated with the incumbent of the controller's position." Approximately eight months later, the assistant controller was dismissed for his *inadequate work performance*.

At the hearing, the Board of Inquiry referred with approval to an American decision that stated that a person complaining of racial discrimination must first establish:

- That he belongs to a racial minority;
- That he applied and was qualified for a job opening;
- That he was rejected; and
- That, after his rejection, the position remained open and the employer continued to seek applicants with the complainant's qualifications.

According to the Board, once the person lodging the complaint has established these facts, the employer, in order to defend himself, must offer reasonable explanation for its actions. In this case, the employer was able to justify itself for not promoting the assistant controller the first time because he did not then have his R.I.A. designation. The employer was also able to justify not promoting the assistant controller when the vacancy occurred for the fourth time. The evidence disclosed that the assistant controller's resentment for being passed over on previous occasions had influenced his attitude and his work had deteriorated. The employer was also able to justify the dismissal of the controller on this ground.

However, the Board did not accept the employer's reasons for not promoting the assistant controller on the other occasions when the controller's post became vacant. The employer claimed that the assistant controller lacked "people skills," and was unable to get along with management. However, the employer did not present evidence to support these claims. Moreover, there was evidence that the company never seriously considered the assistant controller for promotion. For example, the assistant controller's superiors had not been questioned about his work performance.

The Board of Inquiry found the company guilty of discrimination and ordered it to pay damages to the assistant controller. The amount of the damages was based on what the assistant controller's salary would have been if he had been promoted the second time the controller position became vacant to the time the final appointment of controller was made.[5]

When performance criteria are clear, organizations can make hiring, firing, or promotional decisions, for example, without violating the laws. A Board of Inquiry in Ontario dismissed a racial discrimination complaint directed against the Metropolitan Toronto Board of Commissioners of Police. A police constable of East Indian racial origin and a "Sikh by religion" complained that he had been refused reclassification and was ultimately dismissed for race-related reasons. At the hearing, the constable's superiors claimed that the reasons for the refusal to reclassify and the dismissal were based on the facts that the constable was unable to get along with his fellow officers and had broken police rules. The evidence indicated that the reasons for the constable's inability to get along with his fellow officers were not based on their disliking him on racial grounds.

Fellow officers testified that they objected to working with the dismissed constable because he was overbearing, he drove dangerously, he had a hostile manner of dealing with the public, he demonstrated cruelty toward animals, and "would not take direction and advice easily from more experienced officers." Moreover, evidence was presented that on one occasion he wore improper attire in court and on another occasion failed to remain in court in contravention of the rules. The "culmination incident" was the officer's failure to report an accident in which he was involved, and his attempts to deny being involved in it when confronted. The Board of Inquiry, in dismissing the constable's complaint, said that the constable's "problem was not racial. If he had shown reliability and competence in his performance as an officer, he would have been accepted by his fellow officers and would not have had problems in getting along with them. His problem was a personal one rather than a racial one."[6]

Finally, two U.S. cases are worth mentioning since similar cases might occur in the future in Canada. In the first example, *Grove vs. Frostburg National Bank*, the court ruled that the system of evaluating employees was not a merit system, because it was "not organized or structured and was not based on systemic evaluation using pre-determined criteria." The vice-president responsible for pay raises testified that the primary criterion in pay decisions was his "gut feeling" about the individual. This type of practice opens the door to discrimination arising from the superior's personal prejudice. Consequently, the court ruled this practice constituted discrimination, since a male teller was paid more than a female teller doing the same job.[7] By contrast, a minority female employee who claimed that she had been discriminated against when denied promotion and ultimately transferred, lost her case. The appraisal clearly indicated that although she met the minimal job requirements, she constantly needed extra time to complete assigned functions; she also had difficulties involving analytical work. Attempts had been made, and documented, to motivate her through awards, a merit increase, and developmental assignments, all of which failed.[8]

Not only does it make good business sense to use valid PA methods, it may also help avoid the cost of mounting a defence against lawsuits.

Using Valid PA Instruments

Once the criteria are established, forms (instruments) must be used to gather information about the criteria (critical job components). For example, if *quantity of output* is a critical job criterion, having a supervisor comment only on how personable the employee is may lead to an inappropriate appraisal. If this appraisal is used for an employment decision, a *prima facie* case of adverse impact or discrimination may result. Appraisal forms on which the rater indicates by a check mark (✓) his or her evaluation of an employee on things such as leadership, attitude toward people, and loyalty (attributes) are often referred to as **subjective forms**. They are in contrast to appraisals in which the evaluation is done against specifically defined behaviour, level of output, level of specific goal attainment, or number of days absent (behaviour and outcomes). These appraisals are often called **objective forms**. These different forms will be discussed in more detail in the next chapter.

COMMUNICATING PERFORMANCE CRITERIA AND STANDARDS. Once performance criteria and standards have been identified, employees should be told what the standards are. Can you imagine being in a class and not knowing how your grade will be determined? Many employees, unfortunately, indicate that they *do not know* on what basis they are being evaluated. A synthesis of the broad legal guidelines for appraisal systems emerging from the cases reported earlier, as well as from the various charters of human rights, is shown in Exhibit 9.2.

Exhibit 9.2
Prescriptions for Legally Defensible Appraisal Systems

- Procedures for HR decisions must not differ as a function of the race, sex, colour, national origin, marital status, creed, or age of those affected by such decisions.
- Objective-type, nonrated, uncontaminated data should be used whenever available.
- A formal system of review or appeal should be available for appraisal disagreements.
- More than one independent evaluator of performance should be used.
- A formal, standardized system should be used for the HR decisions.
- Evaluators should have ample opportunity to observe ratee performance (if ratings must be made).
- Ratings on traits such as dependability, drive, aptitude, or attitude should be avoided.
- Appraisal data should be empirically validated.
- Specific performance standards should be communicated to employees.
- Raters should be provided with written instructions on how to complete the performance evaluations.
- Employees should be evaluated on specific work dimensions rather than a single overall or global measure.
- Behavioural documentation should be required for extreme ratings (e.g., critical incidents).
- Raters should be trained in conducting the appraisal.
- The content of the appraisal form should be based on a job analysis.
- Employees should be provided with an opportunity to review their appraisals.
- HR decision makers should be familiar with and trained in laws regarding discrimination.

Source: The list has been modified from H.J. Bernardin and W.F. Cascio, "Performance Appraisal and the Law," in *Readings in Personnel and Human Resource Management*, 3rd ed., ed. R.S. Schuler, S.A. Youngblood, and V.L. Huber (St. Paul, Minn.: West Publishing Co., 1988).

PERFORMANCE CRITERIA: WHAT, WHO, AND HOW

Identifying Criteria

In establishing a PAS, decisions regarding *what, who,* and *how* to measure should be made very clearly. Other important decisions centre around the time period for the appraisal and the context in which it will take place.

RELIABILITY AND VALIDITY. The emphasis should be placed on the validity and reliability of the PAS A *reliable* system produces the same appraisal of a subordinate regardless of *who* is doing the appraising at any given point in time. Over time, a reliable PAS should produce the same results from the same rater if the actual performance of the subordinate has not changed. A PAS may be unreliable due to numerous errors in rating, as described in a later section in this chapter.

A *valid* PAS must specify **performance criteria** that are job-related and important, and can easily be determined through job analysis. Employees' contributions to the organization can be evaluated based on the degree to which they perform those activities and attain the results specified in the job analysis. For example, if selling 100 units per month is the only important result of an employee's job, then the PAS should only measure the number of units sold. In this case, there is only one performance criterion. Similarly, if McDonald's decides that the criterion against which it will evaluate the franchise manager is the increase in volume of sales for a specific period, then the manager would see this number as a goal and concentrate on meeting it.

SINGLE OR MULTIPLE CRITERIA. Generally, job analysis identifies several performance criteria that reflect employee contributions. For example, selling 100 units per month may be accompanied by such criteria as "effects of remarks to customers," "consistency in attendance," and even "effects on co-workers." If all these performance criteria are determined to be important by the job analysis, they all should be measured by the PA.

If the form used to appraise performance does not address the job behaviour and results identified in the job analysis, the form is said to be **deficient**. If the form includes appraisal of anything either unimportant, or irrelevant to the job, it is **contaminated**. Many PA forms actually used in organizations measure some employee attributes and behaviour unrelated to the employee's job. These forms are contaminated and, in many cases, also deficient.

WEIGHTING OF CRITERIA. For jobs involving more than one duty, there is another decision to be made. How should these separate aspects of performance be combined into a composite score that will facilitate comparisons of incumbents? One way is to weight each criterion *equally*. This simplest, but most accurate, approach is to use weights generated through job analysis. Individual weights can also be determined for each criterion, relative to its ability to *predict overall performance*. Multiple regression also can be utilized to determine appropriate weights for each job dimension.

STANDARDS. Standards must be identified to evaluate how well employees are performing. By using standards, performance criteria take on a range of values. For example, selling 100 units per month may be defined as excellent performance, and selling eighty units may be defined as average. Organizations often use historical records of employee performance to determine what is possible and to establish what constitutes average or excellent performance. Standards can also be established by time and motion studies and work sampling, as described in Chapter 2. These methods are often used for blue-collar nonmanagerial jobs, but many organizations employ other methods to evaluate how well their managers perform. One of these methods is *management by objectives*, to be discussed shortly. Increasingly, managers are also being evaluated against standards of profitability, revenues and costs, or innovations.

Sources of performance data include supervisors, peers, subordinates, self-appraisal, customers, and computer monitoring. While many of these can be used to gather data, the relevance of each source needs to be considered *prior* to choosing the PA method.

APPRAISAL BY SUPERIORS. The superior is the immediate boss of the subordinate being evaluated. It is assumed that the superior is the one who is most familiar with the job of the subordinate and his or her performance. But there are some drawbacks to appraisal by the superior. They include:

- Since the superior may have reward and punishment power, the subordinate may feel threatened.

Choice of Performance Assessors

- Evaluation is often a one-way process that makes the subordinate feel defensive. Often, little coaching takes place; rather, justification of action prevails.
- The superior may not have the necessary interpersonal skills to give good feedback.
- The superior may have an ethical bias against "playing God."
- The superior, by giving punishments, may alienate the subordinate.

Because of the potential liabilities, organizations may invite other people to share in the appraisal process, even giving the subordinate greater input. Allowing other people to participate in the PA creates a greater "openness" in the PAS, thus helping to enhance the quality of the superior–subordinate relationship.

SELF-APPRAISAL. The use of self-appraisal, particularly through subordinate participation in setting goals, was made popular as an important component of management by objectives. Subordinates who participate in the evaluation process may become more involved and committed to the goals. It appears that subordinate participation may also help clarify employees' roles and reduce role conflict.

Self-appraisals are often effective tools for programs focusing on self-development, personal growth, and goal commitment. On the other hand, self-appraisals are subject to systemic biases and distortions when used for evaluative purposes. These biases and distortions may be important topics of discussion in the PA session between superior and subordinate. In spite of the limitations, there is a clear trend toward self-evaluation, as employers recognize the importance of creating dialogues with the boss. In many companies, self-appraisals are considered in conjunction with superior evaluation and, in the process, the two are compared.[9]

PEER APPRAISAL. Peer appraisals appear to be useful predictors of performance. They are particularly useful when superiors lack access to some aspects of subordinates' performance. However, the validity of peer appraisals is reduced somewhat if the organizational reward system is based on performance and is highly competitive, and if there is a low level of trust among subordinates. They are useful, on the other hand, when teamwork and participation are part of the organizational culture.

APPRAISAL BY SUBORDINATES. Perhaps many of you, particularly as students, have had the chance to evaluate an instructor. How useful do you think this evaluation process is? A significant advantage of appraisal by students is that many instructors are unaware of how they are being perceived by their students. They may not realize that students fail to understand some of their instructions. It is the same in a work setting: subordinates' appraisals can make superiors more aware of their impact on their subordinates. Sometimes, however, subordinates may evaluate their superiors solely on the basis of personality or in respect of their own needs rather than those of the organization. Of course, subordinates may inflate the evaluation of their superiors, particularly if they feel threatened by them and have no anonymity.

APPRAISAL BY CUSTOMERS. Another source of appraisal information comes from customers or clients of the job incumbents. Appraisals by customers are appropriate in a variety of contexts. For example, many service managers for GM dealers in Canada routinely have a customer rate the service employee who dealt with him or her on such features as courtesy, promptness, and being able to explain the problems needing repair. Similarly, many restaurants ask their customers to comment on the quality of the service and other important information. To encourage customers to complete the forms, these restaurants hold periodic promotions such as drawing for a free dinner for two.

COMPUTER MONITORING. A more recent trend in PA is the gathering of performance data by computers. Although this method may be fast and seemingly objective, it has raised a number of critical issues in the management and use of human resources, namely in terms of invasion of an employee's rights to privacy.

Several surveys show that PA is a widely used management tool in North America. A Conference Board of Canada study found that 93 percent of the large and medium-sized companies responding to the survey had appraisal systems.[10]

The majority of managers, although recognizing the importance of appraisal, hate to do it. In fact, if they can avoid it, they would prefer not to do it altogether. For this reason many companies require their managers to conduct an annual formal appraisal. Many HR experts assert that due to the fact that informal appraisal, in the form of feedback and guidance by superiors, is a continual process conducted on a day-to-day and week-to-week basis, there is no need for more frequent formal appraisals. This is especially the case when research indicates that neither managers nor employees have full confidence in the effectiveness of their PAS. One study reports that only 10 percent of HR managers surveyed felt that their PAS is effective, and one senior manager went to the extreme of stating: "I have not seen a PA form which was worth the paper it was printed on."[11]

The above indicates that, while most companies have instituted some formal method of PA, such methods are not automatically effective at attaining their objectives. Often the objectives are not clearly defined, and may even be contradictory. Since a poorly designed and executed PAS can impair performance rather than enhance it, care must be taken in the choice and implementation of details.

Time and Context for the Appraisal

HRM IN THE NEWS VIGNETTE

Turnaround at National Life

Used correctly, frequent appraisals can improve communications and employee productivity throughout your company.

Ross Johnson, a human resources consultant based in Oakville, Ontario, knows first hand the power of regular performance appraisals. As executive vice-president and then president of National Life Insurance Co. of Canada from 1979 to 1989, he implemented company-wide "weekly development interviews" (WDI), to help pilot the company out of an employee productivity crisis. "We had seven levels of management," says Johnson. "Working for National Life was like working for the post office—it was a comfortable home."

Johnson's WDI system required manager and subordinate to meet once a week to review performance. A typical performance-review file included a written job description and a list of personal job-development goals. Managers reviewed the week's events with employees and focused on how their performances advanced progress towards the goals. "The system improved communications overnight," says Johnson. "Managers knew where employees were coming from and employees knew what was in the boss's head."

The system also removed deadwood. Managers knew right away when employees weren't producing, Johnson says. Over 1984 and 1985, National Life reduced the number of employees in head office by 100, and by the time Johnson retired in 1982, he had cut the levels of management from seven to three. Annual new life-premium sales during Johnson's tenure rose from $1 million in 1979 to more than $22 million in 1989.

Source: A. Campbell and J. Dangor, "In Praise of Performance Appraisals," *Small Business*, April 1990. Reprinted with permission.

PA METHODS AND APPROACHES

There are many methods and approaches that can be considered for use by organizations. Some can apply across the board to all job categories, while others might be more appropriate for selected occupations. In order to present the typical methods and approaches used in the industry, they have been classified, for the purpose of clarity, into three grand categories: (1) comparative or norm-referenced approaches, (2) behavioural approaches, and (3) output approaches.

Comparative or Norm-Referenced Approaches

For many types of HR decisions, the fundamental question often is: *who* is the best performer in the group? or *who* should be assigned a specific task? For finding an answer to these types of concerns, comparative or norm-referenced approaches are appropriate.

STRAIGHT RANKING. The first and the most simple of these approaches is the **straight ranking** format, in which a superior lists the subordinates in order, from best to worst, usually on the basis of overall performance. Incumbents can also be ranked with regard to their performance on specific duties, such as attendance, record for meeting deadlines, quality of reports prepared, etc. This type of ranking is useful in small organizations. As the number of incumbents increases, it becomes difficult to discern differences in the performance of all incumbents—particularly average incumbents.

Exhibit 9.3
A Ranking Peer Evaluation Form

Purpose:

This form provides you with an opportunity to assess the performance of your group members. Remember that these evaluations are a factor in your participation grade. Please feel free to comment in detail on the back of this form.

Procedure:

Write each group member's name, including your own, in the spaces provided. Rank each individual in each category. Use a ranking of 1 to 6, where 1 = the best, 2 = second best, and 6 = the worst.

NAME OF GROUP MEMBER	GROUP RESPONSIBILITY A. Does his/her share of the work B. Is prepared for meetings		GROUP INTERACTION C. Contributes to discussions D. Is receptive to constructive criticism		OVERALL EVALUATION E.
	A	B	C	D	E
1.					
2.					
3.					
4.					
5.					
6.					

PLEASE MAKE ADDITIONAL COMMENTS ON THE BACK OF THIS FORM.

SIGNATURE: _____

ALTERNATIVE RANKING. **Alternative ranking** normally takes place in several steps. The first step is to put the best subordinate at the head of the list and the worst subordinate at the bottom, usually on the basis of overall performance. The superior then selects the best and worst from the remaining subordinates. The middle position on the list is the last to be filled. Ranking approaches could be used quite efficiently not only by a single supervisor, but by the subordinates themselves. They could be particularly useful in generating performance data for a group of individuals who perform similar tasks as a team. Exhibit 9.3 shows the forms used by many university professors, which allow students to assess each other's contributions to a team project.

PAIRED COMPARISONS. The **paired comparison method** involves comparing each assessee to every other incumbent, two at a time on a single standard, to determine who is "better." A rank order can be obtained by counting the number of times each individual is selected as the better of a pair. The subordinate with the most favourable count of "being better" is thus ranked in the first place; the subordinate with the second-greatest number of favourable comparisons is ranked second, and so on. An advantage to this approach over traditional ratings is that it overcomes the problem of an "elevation set." That is, it forces the assessor to compare the performance of each incumbent to all other incumbents, one by one.

FORCED DISTRIBUTION METHOD. The **forced distribution method** was designed to overcome a frequent complaint levelled against the various ranking methods, namely, that all of them give each assessee a unique rank and thus do not allow for two (or more) incumbents' performances to be very close to each other. In other words, in many instances it is very hard to "really" differentiate between two employees. The forced distribution method overcomes this problem and incorporates several factors or dimensions (rather than a single factor) into the ranking process. The term "forced distribution" is used because the superior must assign only a certain proportion of subordinates to each of several categories in respect to each factor.

A common forced distribution scale may be divided into five categories, with a fixed percentage of all subordinates in the group falling within each of these categories. Many universities in North America that use a letter-grade system (i.e., A, B, C, etc.) rather than percentages (i.e., a grade mark out of 100) use forced distribution. Typically, the distribution follows a normal "bell-shaped" pattern. An example of forced distribution is shown in Exhibit 9.4.

CONCERNS WITH COMPARATIVE APPROACHES. Regardless of the specific comparative approach, all are based on the assumption that performance is best captured or measured by one criterion: overall performance. Since this single criterion is a global measure and is not anchored in any objective index, such as units sold, the result can be influenced by rater subjectivity. The rankings may lack behavioural specificity and may be subject to legal challenge. Further, in the rank order method, for example, it is not specified how good the "best" is or how bad the "worst" is; the *level* of performance is unclear. This may result in arbitrary ranking. In addition, a major limitation of the paired comparison method is that the number of comparisons becomes too great to perform with large numbers of employees.

Because these methods yield ordinal rather than interval data, managers do not know whether the best performer in a group is actually outstanding, average, or poor, or whether two individuals with adjacent ranks are quite similar or quite different. Using such information for promotion decisions may be inappropriate, because an average performer in one group could actually be excellent in another group, and thus there is the danger that the latter will be promoted simply due to his place in a particular reference group.

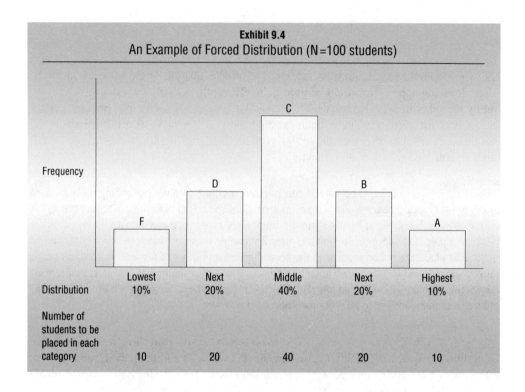

Exhibit 9.4
An Example of Forced Distribution (N=100 students)

Distribution	Lowest 10%	Next 20%	Middle 40%	Next 20%	Highest 10%
Number of students to be placed in each category	10	20	40	20	10

All four comparative methods assume that there are good and bad performers in all groups. You may know from experience, however, of situations where all the people in a group actually perform identically. Forced distribution methods are ineffective in these situations. For one, it is impossible for all employees to be rated "excellent" when applying this approach. Proponents of this method, however, claim that it encourages a healthy competition among employees who know that their level of performance will ultimately be judged against that of their peers. Opponents claim that forced distribution may lead to individualism and noncooperation. Moreover, some claim that the procedure creates artificial distributions among employees.

Ratings and Behavioural Approaches

While in the comparative approaches the superior is forced to assess each incumbent in relation to other incumbents, in the ratings and behavioural approaches, superiors evaluate each incumbent's performance independently in relation to specified criteria. The tendency today is to select behavioural criteria.

NARRATIVE ESSAY. One of the simplest forms for evaluating employees is the **narrative essay**. Using this form, the rater can describe the ratee's strengths and weaknesses and suggest methods for improving performance. Certainly, if these essays are unstructured, they often vary in length and detail; consequently, comparisons within a department or across departments are difficult. Furthermore, the essay form provides only qualitative data. However, including behavioural criteria on the form, such as critical incidents, behavioural checklists, and forced-choice forms enriches the qualitative appraisals. It should also be mentioned that because some supervisors have better written communication skills than others, variation in quality may result. This method should not be used with supervisors who do not have these skills, or do not have the time required to write an essay (often the case of first-line supervisors). Nonetheless, the narrative essay method can be improved by structuring the form, as illustrated in Exhibit 9.5. Notice that in this form the incumbent is required to read the content, thereby forcing the superior to conduct a more responsible job rating.

Exhibit 9.5
Structured Narrative Essay Form

Employee Name:_____

Job Title: _____

Give examples of the employee's effective behaviour:

Give examples of the employee's ineffective behaviour:

What steps have been taken (or will be taken) to modify ineffective behaviour?

Does the incumbent's job description need revision? No   Yes   Explain:

Supervisor's Comments: (additional explanations pertaining to conditions and circumstances of effective and/or ineffective behaviour)

Incumbent's Comments: (additional explanations pertaining to conditions and circumstances of effective and/or ineffective behaviour, or other relevant comments)

(Signing this appraisal does not denote agreement with the rating, only that the incumbent has read it)

------------------------------------   ---------------------------
Incumbent's signature and date   (Supervisor's signature and date)

CONVENTIONAL RATING. The **conventional rating** is the most widely used form of performance evaluation. Conventional forms vary in the number of dimensions of performance they measure. The term *performance* is used advisedly here because many conventional forms use personality characteristics or traits, rather than actual behaviours, as indicators of performance. Frequently used traits are *aggressiveness*, *independence*, *maturity*, and *sense of responsibility,* to name a few. Many conventional forms also use output indicators such as quantity and quality of performance. Conventional forms vary in the number of traits and output indicators they incorporate. They also vary in the range of choices for each dimension and the extent to which each dimension is described. A sample of a conventional rating format is shown in Exhibit 9.6.

Conventional forms are used extensively because they are relatively easy to develop, permit quantitative results that allow comparisons across ratees and departments, and include several dimensions or criteria of performance. But because the rater has complete control in the use of the forms, they are subject to several types of error including leniency, strictness, central tendency, and halo (to be discussed below). Often separate traits or factors are grouped together and the rater is given only one box to check. Another drawback is that the descriptive words often used in such scales may have different meanings to different raters. Terms such as "motivation," "cooperation," and "social skills," are subject to many interpretations, especially when used in conjunction with words such as "outstanding," "average," or "very poor."

In addition to their potential for error, conventional forms are criticized because they cannot be used for developmental as well as evaluative purposes. They fail to tell a subordinate how to improve and they are not useful for the subordinate's career development needs. Consequently, when such forms are actually used, organizations often modify them and add space for short essays so that the appraisal results can be used for developmental as well as evaluative purposes (see Exhibit 9.7 for an illustration).

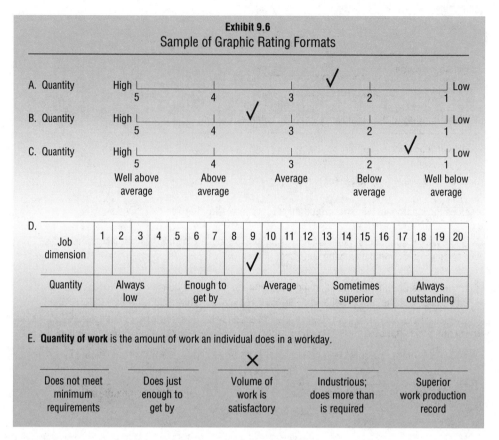

Exhibit 9.6
Sample of Graphic Rating Formats

CRITICAL INCIDENTS. Dissatisfaction with conventional rating scales and with the narrative essay, has led to the development of other types of assessments that place the emphasis on behaviour. The methods vary in scope and structure, but among the most easy to conduct is the **critical incident technique**. Here, the superior observes and records things that subordinates do that are particularly effective or ineffective in accomplishing their jobs. These incidents generally provide descriptions of the ratee's behaviour and the situations in which that behaviour occurred. For example, a negative critical incident for a life insurance salesperson might be "lied to the client when insurance was sold." A positive one might be "responded to a client complaint in a prompt and cordial manner." One advantage of this method is that when the superior then provides feedback to the subordinate, it is based on specific behaviour rather than personal characteristics or traits such as dependability, forcefulness, or loyalty. This feature of the critical incident technique can increase the chances that the subordinate will improve, since he or she learns what in particular is expected.

Proponents of the critical incident technique emphasize its simplicity and behavioural focus. Another advantage is that since performance incidents are recorded throughout the year, the supervisor may not be subject to "recent behaviour" biases. Furthermore, many claim it is more logical to spend a fraction of the time to record the critical incidents than to use more sophisticated and time-consuming methods (which suffer from many errors and biases) just to arrive at the conclusion that most of your employees performed at average capacity. Critical incidents can point out the best and worst performers, and absence of information (incidents) can be attributed to a mediocre performance.

Drawbacks of the critical incident technique include the superior's need to keep records ("little black books") on each subordinate, its nonquantitative nature, the fact that the incidents are not differentiated in terms of their importance to job performance, and the difficulties in comparing subordinates when the incidents recorded for each one are quite

Exhibit 9.7
Conventional Rating Format

NAME		EMPLOYEE NUMBER		EVALUATION DATE	
LOCATION		POSITION		DATE OF LAST REVIEW	

UNSATISFACTORY	MARGINAL	GOOD	VERY GOOD	OUTSTANDING	POINT RATING
1. QUALITY —- Consider accuracy, thoroughness, and neatness of work.					
2	4	6	8	10	
Makes frequent errors. Perform-ance unacceptable.	Instances of care-lessness and errors.	Performance satisfactory. Requires normal supervision.	Consistently above average.	Extremely accurate work. Requires no super-vision under nor-mal circumstances.	
2. QUANTITY —- Consider amount of work accomplished and time required to complete.					
2	4	6	8	10	
Below minimum standards. Unable to complete assigned tasks.	Requires frequent assistance and fol-low-up.	Usually completes assigned workload on schedule.	Output always above normal.	Exceptionally efficient worker. Requires no assis-tance or follow-up.	
3. JOB KNOWLEDGE —- Consider knowledge of job and skill used to accomplish.					
2	4	6	8	10	
Inadequate knowledge of job.	Lacks under-standing of some duties.	Sufficient knowl-edge and skill to perform assigned tasks.	Good understand-ing of job. Functions skillfully.	Complete knowl-edge of job. Implements high degree of skill.	
4. INITIATIVE —- Consider the ability to originate and implement effective actions.					
2	4	6	8	10	
Unable to cope with nonroutine situa-tions.	Needs close guid-ance in most non-routine matters.	Effectively handles unusual situations with occasional assis-tance required.	Self-starter. Shows good judgment in nonroutine situations.	Develops and implements effec-tive solutions for nonroutine situa-tions without assis-tance.	
5. LEADERSHIP —- Consider ability to guide and influence others.					
2	4	6	8	10	
Incapable of self-management.	No evidence of abil-ity to direct others.	Able to guide and direct associates under normal supervision.	Ability to direct and influence others is evident.	Consistently achieves maximum results.	

Exhibit 9.7
Conventional Rating Format (continued)

UNSATISFACTORY	MARGINAL	GOOD	VERY GOOD	OUTSTANDING	POINT RATING
6. COOPERATION — Consider attitude toward job and ability to get along with others.					
2	4	6	8	10	
Fails to adhere to Company regulations or creates undue friction.	Occasionally uncooperative. Has difficulty getting along with some people.	Generally cooperative. Shows active interest in job. Able to work well with others.	Cooperation above average. Tactful in avoiding conflicts.	Consistently cooperative. Willingly assumes responsibility.	
7. RELIABILITY — Consider the employee's ability to perform tasks in a consistent and effective manner.					
2	4	6	8	10	
Cannot be counted on.	Requires frequent monitoring.	Performance usually meets with expectations.	Performance consistently above average.	Exceptionally dependable person.	
8. ADAPTABILITY — Consider the employee's ability to cope with changing environments or job responsibilities.					
2	4	6	8	10	
Totally unable to cope with change.	Experiences difficulty coping with change.	Adjusts reasonably well to change.	Shows high degree of versatility.	Extremely accommodating to any changes.	
9. ATTENDANCE — Consider attendance and punctuality.					
2	4	6	8	10	
Frequent unjustified absences or tardiness.	Absent on several occasions. Tardiness usually justified.	Attendance satisfactory. Tardiness always justified.	Good record of attendance and punctuality.	Not absent or late in past year.	
10. Appearance — Consider appearance as it relates to proper conduct of the job.					
2	4	6	8	10	
Fails to meet minimum requirements.	Usually acceptable. Improvements recommended on occasion.	Generally neat, clean, and presentable.	Always neat and dressed in good taste.	Consistently well-groomed and business-like.	
				TOTAL POINTS	100

SUMMARY RATING—THE OVERALL PERFORMANCE RATING OF THIS EMPLOYEE IS:

UNDER 40	40–59	60–79	80 – 89	90 – 100
UNSATISFACTORY	MARGINAL	GOOD	VERY GOOD	OUTSTANDING

STRENGTHS: _____
_____
_____
_____
_____

AREAS FOR IMPROVEMENT: _____
_____
_____
_____
_____

OVERALL - COMMENTS: _____
_____
_____
_____
_____
_____

_____   _____
SUPERVISOR'S SIGNATURE   (DATE)

To Be Completed by Employee Being Rated

My rating has been fully explained to me

_____   _____
Signature of Employee   Date

I consider this rating to be fair ☐   unfair ☐

I would like to discuss my rating with the Human Resources Department ☐

EMPLOYEE'S COMMENTS: _____
_____

DEPARTMENT MANAGER'S COMMENTS: _____
_____
_____

_____   _____
DEPARTMENT MANAGER'S SIGNATURE   (DATE)

_____   _____
SENIOR MANAGER - HUMAN RESOURCES: (DATE)

different. To overcome some of these drawbacks: (1) supervisors need to be trained in using the method, and (2) pre-determined job-related critical incidents could be established as part of the criteria.

WEIGHTED CHECKLIST. After several critical incidents are gathered from several superiors or expert raters knowledgeable about the job, they can be used to construct **weighted checklists** of incidents. The rater merely has to check the incidents for each subordinate. The form may be designed to include frequency response categories, e.g., "always," "very often," and "infrequently." With this form the rater checks the frequency category for each incident for each subordinate. This method saves the rater time and can yield a summary score. Nevertheless, the rater does not know the relative importance of each incident, thus making it difficult for him or her to provide feedback.

FORCED CHOICE. To reduce the potential for a leniency rating error (rating everybody "high," as will be discussed later on) and to establish a form that allows for a more objective comparison of ratees, the **forced-choice form** was developed. The forced-choice method differs from the weighted checklist because it forces superiors to evaluate each subordinate by choosing which of two items in a pair better describes the subordinate. The two items in a pair are matched to be equal in *desirability* but of differential relevance to job performance or discriminability. The degrees of desirability and discriminability are established by individuals familiar with the jobs. Through use of this format, leniency error is minimized and validity and reliability may be enhanced. Although the forced-choice scale can be very useful, the raters are essentially unaware of how their ratings of subordinates are interpreted. This not only makes feedback difficult, but it also reduces the trust the rater has in the organization. These scales are also expensive to develop, and the cost–benefit relationship is not readily apparent.

BEHAVIOURALLY ANCHORED RATING SCALES. A major breakthrough in utilizing critical incidents to evaluate incumbent performance was the development of **behaviourally anchored rating scales (BARS)**. These scales provide results that subordinates can use to improve performance. They are also designed so that superiors can be more comfortable giving feedback. The first step in the development of a BARS is similar to the critical incident approach where emphasis is placed on collecting incidents that describe effective, average, and ineffective behaviour for each job category. These incidents are then grouped into broad overall categories or dimensions of performance (e.g., administrative ability, interpersonal skills). Each dimension serves as one criterion in evaluating subordinates. Using these categories, another group of individuals lists the critical incidents pertinent to each category.

Exhibit 9.8 shows an example of one such criterion or category, *knowledge of information,* and the critical incidents pertinent to it. The example is taken from VIA Rail, in reference to the job of a telephone sales agent. In the first step, the following job dimensions were identified and served as criteria for BARS:

- Know Via's mission (VIA orientation);
- Interact with computer reservation system (e.g., interpret specific reserVIA information);
- Provide appropriate information to guests (e.g., provide travel information);
- Update train information recording (e.g., prepare train performance information);
- Sell services to guests (e.g., cross-sell additional services);
- Advise guests of service changes (e.g., determine priority of queue);
- Respond to guests' concerns (e.g., focus on concern).[12]

Exhibit 9.8
Sample BARS for One Dimension, Knowledge of Information, for a Telephone Service Agent in *VIA* Rail

Position: **TSA**
Job Dimension: **Scale for Knowledge of Information**

1. Excellent Performance		*Determine guests' needs and provide appropriate and accurate information in an efficient, courteous manner 100% of the time.*
2. Good Performance		*Determine guests' needs and provide appropriate and accurate information in an efficient, courteous manner 95% of the time.*
3. Fair or Average Performance		*Determine guests' needs and provide appropriate and accurate information in an efficient, courteous manner 85% of the time.*
4. Poor Performance		*Determine guests' needs and provide appropriate and accurate information in an efficient, courteous manner 70% of the time.*
5. Unacceptable Performance		*Determine guests' needs and provide appropriate and accurate information in an efficient, courteous manner less than 50% of the time.*

Source: Reproduced with the permission of *VIA* Rail.

In the second step, a numerical value (weight) is assigned for each incident in relation to its contribution to the criterion. A similar process is repeated for the seven job dimensions shown above.

Another example is shown in Exhibit 9.9, where a manager's job dimension entitled "organization of work activities" is illustrated. Note that the format and the scale are slightly different from that illustrated in Exhibit 9.8, but the principles of designing BARS are similar.

Armed with a set of criteria with behaviourally anchored and weighted choices, the superiors rate their subordinates on a form that is relatively unambiguous in meaning, understandable, justifiable, and relatively easy to use. Because most BARS forms use a limited number of performance criteria (in the example above seven are used), many of the critical incidents generated in the job analysis stage may not be used. Thus, the raters may not find appropriate categories to describe the behaviours—the critical incidents—off their subordinates. Similarly, even if the relevant incidents are observed, they may not be worded in exactly the same way on the dimension. Thus, the rater may not be able to match the observed behaviour with the dimension and anchors.

Another concern with BARS is that it is possible for an incumbent to simultaneously display behaviour associated with both high and low performance. For example, the

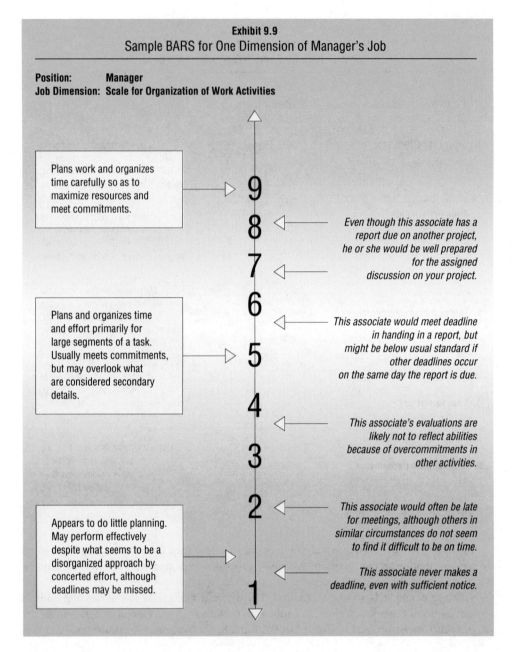

Exhibit 9.9
Sample BARS for One Dimension of Manager's Job

Position: Manager
Job Dimension: Scale for Organization of Work Activities

Plans work and organizes time carefully so as to maximize resources and meet commitments.

9
8
7 — Even though this associate has a report due on another project, he or she would be well prepared for the assigned discussion on your project.

6
5 — This associate would meet deadline in handing in a report, but might be below usual standard if other deadlines occur on the same day the report is due.

Plans and organizes time and effort primarily for large segments of a task. Usually meets commitments, but may overlook what are considered secondary details.

4 — This associate's evaluations are likely not to reflect abilities because of overcommitments in other activities.

3
2 — This associate would often be late for meetings, although others in similar circumstances do not seem to find it difficult to be on time.

Appears to do little planning. May perform effectively despite what seems to be a disorganized approach by concerted effort, although deadlines may be missed.

1 — This associate never makes a deadline, even with sufficient notice.

telephone sales agent may be able to determine guests' needs and provide accurate information in an efficient, courteous manner 100 percent of the time (i.e., excellent performance), but also receive complaints from guests about inappropriate travel information provided (i.e., unacceptable performance). In a situation such as this, it is difficult for the rater to determine whether the overall rating should be high or low.

A procedure that overcomes these and other limitations of the BARS, but retains its advantages, is called the behavioural observation scale (BOS).

BEHAVIOURAL OBSERVATION SCALES. The **behavioural observation scale (BOS)** and the BARS are essentially the same except in the development of the scales or dimensions, the scale format, and scoring procedures. In developing BOSs, experts are not asked what level of performance they illustrate. Instead, they are asked to indicate the *frequency* with which job incumbents engage in the behaviours. Scores are obtained for each behaviour by assigning a numerical value to the frequency judgment. For example, a score of two may be assigned if it is almost always observed. These scores can be summed to get an overall rating. Alternatively, scale items relating to a particular performance dimension can be summed and then multiplied by an importance weight. Behaviour items are eliminated if the observed frequency is too high or too low, because in either case the item does not discriminate well between high and low performers.

Exhibit 9.10 includes examples of effective and ineffective job behaviours and the resulting BOS scales. Note that the examples of ineffective performance are reverse-scored.

Exhibit 9.10
Sample BOS Items for Telephone Sales Agent, Illustrating both Effective and Ineffective Performance

Effective Performance

1. The TSA determines guests' needs and provides information in an accurate, efficient, and courteous manner.

Almost Never				Almost Always
1	2	3	4	5

2. The TSA cross-sells additional services.

Almost Never				Almost Always
1	2	3	4	5

- -

Ineffective Performance

1. The TSA fails to advise guests of service changes.

Almost Never				Almost Always
1	2	3	4	5

2. The TSA interacts with the computer reservation system in interpreting special guest requests.

Almost Never				Almost Always
1	2	3	4	5

Note: On the actual form, the items would neither be grouped nor identified as effective and ineffective performance.

The advantages of the BOS include the following: (1) it is based on a systematic job analysis; (2) its items and behavioural anchors are clearly stated; (3) in contrast to many other PA methods, it allows for employee participation in the development of the dimensions (through the identification of the critical incidents in the job analysis), which facilitates understanding and acceptance; (4) it is useful for performance feedback and improvement, because specific goals can be tied to numerical scores (ratings) on the relevant behavioural anchor (critical incident for the relevant performance criterion or dimension; and (5) the BOS appears to be satisfactory against potential discrimination charges, since its validity and reliability are relatively high.

The limitations of the BOS are connected with some of its advantages, especially the time and cost needed for its development in comparison with forms such as the conventional rating. Furthermore, several dimensions, which are essentially behaviours, may miss the real essence of many jobs, especially managerial and highly routinized ones where the essence of the job may be the actual outputs produced, regardless of the behaviour used to obtain them. When these conditions exist, some argue that a better method is one that is goal-oriented or that measures output. Additionally, the BOS, more than other types of PA scales, requires that the rater be able to observe the incumbent's performance. If the span of control is large, this may be an impossible task.

Output Approaches

While the methods described above focus on job behaviours or processes, output-based appraisals focus on job products. There are four variations of common output-based formats: management by objectives, performance standards, direct index measure, and accomplishments records.

MANAGEMENT BY OBJECTIVES.　**Management by Objectives (MBO)** is probably the most popular method used to evaluate managers. Its popularity appears to result from its congruence with people's values and philosophies, for example, the belief that "it is important to reward people for what they accomplish." MBO is also popular because it can attain greater individual–organizational goal congruence and reduce the likelihood that managers will be working on things unrelated to the objectives and purposes of the organization (goal displacement). The essence of how MBO works can be described in four steps:

Step 1: Establish the goals each subordinate is to attain. In many organizations, superiors and subordinates work together to establish the goals. The goals can refer to desired outcomes, means (activities) for achieving the outcomes, or both.

Step 2: Set a time frame within which the subordinate must meet the objectives. As subordinates perform, they can budget their time by knowing what there is to do, what has been done, and what remains to be done.

Step 3: Compare the actual level of goal attainment against the agreed-on goals. The evaluator explores reasons why the goals were not met or were exceeded. This step helps determine possible training needs. It also alerts the superior to conditions in the organization that may affect a subordinate's performance, but over which the subordinate has no control.

Step 4: Decide on new goals and possible new strategies for achieving goals not previously attained. Subordinates who successfully reach the established goals may be allowed to participate even more in the goal-setting process the next time.

Although the use of goals in evaluating managers is effective in motivating their performance, it is not always possible to capture all the important dimensions of a job in terms of outputs. How the job is done, i.e., job behaviour, may be as critical as the outcomes. For example, it may be detrimental to an organization if a manager meets his or her goal by unethical or illegal means. And even if output measure can capture the essence of the job, there is still the concern about establishing goals that are of equal difficulty for all managers and that are sufficiently difficult to be challenging.

Because MBO is used as more than a PA method (it is also a motivational instrument when employees are involved in the goal setting sessions), it is mandatory to make sure that the objective(s) agreed upon are a function of the employee's SKAs. Otherwise, the implementation of MBO might be counter-productive and demoralizing. The following example will illustrate this concern.

In one case, a large fast-food franchise organization had decided to implement an MBO system for its unit managers. A group of unit managers collectively negotiated a fixed increase in sales in comparison to the previous year's sales in the same unit. Although the unit managers agreed to the fixed objective (and to the financial bonus used as an incentive for attaining this objective), the results after the end of the first year generated ample dissatisfaction and low motivation for many of the managers.

These managers complained that the single criterion (of increased sales) was not within their direct control. Factors such as type of neighbourhood, price of meat, and marketing and advertising in the head office all contributed to the attainment (or nonattainment) of the objective, more than their own effort. This led to random attainment of the objective: some managers exerted much effort but did not attain the objective, and vice versa. A management consultant brought in to resolve the problem suggested replacing the sales criterion with other criteria more intimately linked to individuals' SKAs (management of personnel; neatness of the unit, etc.). This example illustrates that although MBO sounds plausible theoretically, there may be many operational problems in implementing the program.

To help avoid some of the problems encountered in establishing goals in the MBO approach, some organizations have implemented a policy of multiple rating. At Alcan, for example, compensation for the ramification of longer-term objectives in an individual's annual performance appraisal is limited to 50 percent of the employee's annual rating. The other half depends on how the person has carried out his or her principal accountabilities, in other words, his or her overall performance.

PERFORMANCE STANDARDS APPROACH. While similar to MBO, the **performance standards** approach uses more direct measures of performance and is usually applied to non-managerial employees. Standards, like objectives, need to be specific, time bound, conditional, prioritized, and congruent with organizational objectives. Compared to objectives, there are generally more standards, and each is more detailed. Each standard is rated separately and multiplied by an importance weight. As such, this is a compensatory approach to the global evaluation, since high performance in one area can counteract deficiencies in another.

The major advantage of this approach is that it provides clear, unambiguous direction to incumbents regarding desired job outcomes. When exceptional performance is also specified, these scales can motivate the average as well as the exceptional employee.

The disadvantages of these work standards are that they require time, money, and cooperation to develop. As with MBO, the essence of job performance may not be captured entirely by set standards. Consequently, important job behaviours may be ignored in the evaluation process. Additionally, they may also induce undesirable competition among employees to attain their standards.

DIRECT INDEX APPROACH. This approach differs from the other approaches primarily in how performance is measured. The **direct index** approach measures subordinate performance by objective, impersonal criteria, such as productivity, absenteeism, and turnover. For example, a manager's performance may be evaluated by the turnover or absenteeism rate of that manager's employees. For nonmanagers, measures of productivity may be more appropriate. These can be broken down into measures of quality or quantity. Quality measures include scrap rates, customer complaints, and number of defective units or parts produced. Quantity measures include units of output per hour, new customer orders, and sales volume.

ACCOMPLISHMENT RECORDS. A relatively new type of output-based appraisal is called an **accomplishment record.** It is suitable for professionals who claim "my record speaks for itself" or that they cannot write standards for their job because every day is different. With this approach, professionals describe their achievements relative to appropriate job dimensions on an accomplishment record form. The professional's supervisor verifies the accuracy of the accomplishments. Then a team of outside experts evaluates the dossier to determine its overall value. While time consuming and potentially costly, because outside evaluators are used, this approach has been shown to be predictive of job success for lawyers. It also has face validity because professionals believe it is appropriate and valid. A similar process is often used by various universities for the purpose of assessing faculty members for promotion and for making decisions pertaining to the granting of tenure.

BIASES AND OBSTACLES IN PA

Despite the prevalence of PASs, many people are dissatisfied with them. This disillusionment stems from three principal reasons: (1) a variety of organizational problems, (2) several inherent characteristics of the PA processes and the vulnerability of these measures to intentional as well as unforeseen biases on the part of raters and ratees, and (3) erroneous expectations and assumptions concerning the PA process.

The rating process is made more complex because it requires the condensation and analysis of large amounts of information. First, incumbent behaviour or outcomes must be observed. This information must then be aggregated and stored in the rater's short-term memory. Because of long appraisal periods, information must be condensed further and stored in long-term memory. When a judgment needs to be made, information relevant to the category to be rated must be retrieved from memory and a comparison made between observed behaviours and the rater's standards. Finally, a rating must be made based on aggregated data retrieved from memory and any additional information the rater intentionally or unintentionally chooses to include. Ratings at this point may be revised depending on the reaction of the incumbent or higher-level managers. What makes the retrieval and classification even more complex is the variety of attitudes, stereotypes, and values held by raters in addition to circumstantial conditions that might affect decisions (i.e., who is the ratee, what will be the impact of the decision on the ratee's future, etc.). Unfortunately, raters' memories are quite fallible. Consequently, they fall prey to a variety of rating errors, including deviations from the "true" rating an employee deserves and the actual rating assigned.[13]

Organizational Problems

Although many of the organizational problems that represent obstacles to an effective implementation of PASs are described in the next chapter, a few will be mentioned here. The principal organizational obstacle has to do with conflicts arising between the different purposes served by PA, which often result in some employees being dissatisfied with it. For example, listing an employee's weaknesses would be instrumental in detecting training needs, but at the same time it may deter the employee's chances for promotion. Supervisors therefore often find themselves in the difficult position of deciding what information to include or exclude, depending on the potential consequence of the information. As one expert noted, "one appraisal cannot satisfy all organizational needs.[14] Consequently, if organizations wish to avoid such conflicts, they should theoretically consider separate PA processes for different objectives. Since this is not always feasible, many organizations neglect to address these problems.

SUPERIOR–SUBORDINATE RELATIONSHIPS. Important aspects of the superior–subordinate relationship are the personal characteristics of the superior, the characteristics of the superior in relation to those of the subordinate, the superior's knowledge of the subordinate and the job, and the subordinate's knowledge of the job.

There are basically four problems that may arise with the superior. The first is that superiors may not know what employees are doing or may not understand their work well enough to appraise it fairly. This particular problem occurs more frequently when a manager has a large span of control but also when the tasks of the employees are varied and technically complex or changing. The second problem is that, even when superiors understand and know how much work subordinates do, they may not *have* performance standards for evaluating that work. Because of the resulting variability in standards and ratings, subordinates may receive unfair (invalid) evaluations. This unfairness may be particularly obvious when comparing the evaluations of subordinates working for different superiors. The third problem is that superiors may *use* inappropriate standards: they may allow personal values, needs, or biases to replace organizational values and standards. The last major problem related to the superior, although important in itself, is also important because it often leads to some of the errors listed in the next section, particularly the halo and leniency errors: superiors do not like, and where possible resist, making ratings, especially ones that need to be defended or justified in writing. Superiors may consider PAs to be too time-consuming. For example, they may perceive that appraisals take time away from their "real job." It may also be the case that superiors fail to see how PAs reveal meaningful information about the behaviour of people in organizations.

RATEE CHARACTERISTICS. As one might expect, the actual level of performance attained by a ratee has the *most* influence on performance ratings. However, other ratee characteristics also directly affect performance ratings, particularly when performance criteria are not precise. The gender of the ratee and the "gender" of the job interact, so that males receive higher ratings than females in male-dominated jobs but equivalent evaluations in traditionally female jobs. Due to *perceptual congruence*, ratees tend to receive higher ratings from same race raters. Also, managers often associate job tenure with job competency. As a result, they tend to give higher ratings to senior employees. The exception is in public sector organizations that use merit systems, where less senior employees receive higher ratings to advance them up the merit pay system. Age and educational level tend not to affect ratings.

RATER CHARACTERISTICS. The characteristics of the rater exert a more subtle and indirect influence on performance judgments. Limited data suggest that female raters are more lenient than male raters. When performance standards are used, female raters also tend to give more extreme ratings to high and low performers than male raters do. For the average performer, gender of the rater doesn't make a difference. Younger and less experienced raters and those who have received low evaluations themselves rate more strictly than older, more experienced, and/or high performing raters do. Contrary to popular belief, supervisors who have previously held the job in question rate accurately. The personality of the rater may also affect judgment accuracy. Self-confident, less anxious, intelligent, and emotionally stable raters tend to pass a better judgment. [15]

Rater and Ratee Characteristics

When criteria are not clearly specified and there are no incentives associated with conducting an accurate rating, a variety of errors may occur during the evaluation process. Some of the typical and most researched errors are presented in this section.

HALO AND HORN ERROR. The most common error committed by raters occurs when superiors rate an employee or group of subordinates on several dimensions of performance. Frequently, a superior will evaluate a subordinate similarly on all dimensions of performance just on the basis of the evaluation of *one* dimension, the one perhaps perceived as most important. This effect is the *halo error*. The opposite of the halo error is a **horn error**, when a poor rating in one area unjustly affects ratings in other job performance areas, resulting in a poor overall appraisal.

ERROR OF LENIENCY. A second common, and often intentional, error is called **leniency**. In order to avoid potential conflict with subordinates, a manager rates all employees in a particular work group higher than they should be rated objectively. This is particularly likely to happen when there are no organizational sanctions against high ratings, when rewards are not part of a fixed and limited pot, and when dimensional ratings are not required.

Typical Rating Errors

ERROR OF STRICTNESS. At an opposite extreme is the error of **strictness** in which ratees are given unfavourable ratings, regardless of performance level. Inexperienced raters, those with low self-esteem, new superiors who are attempting to impress their own superiors by their standards, or those who use the PAS to "settle accounts," are most likely to rate strictly. Training sessions that include reversal of superior–incumbent roles and confidence building will reduce this error.

The incidence of all three errors mentioned above can be reduced by establishing specific criteria for all performance dimensions, requiring raters to assess each performance dimension separately, and then summing these ratings to attain an overall score. Additionally, raters should receive normative information about their rating patterns.

CENTRAL TENDENCY BIAS. Rather than using extremes in ratings, there is a tendency on the part of many raters to "play it safe"; to evaluate ratees as average, even when performance actually varies. This bias is referred to as the **error of central tendency**. Raters with a large span of control and little opportunity to observe behaviour are likely to rate the majority of incumbents in the middle of the scale rather than too high or too low. Central tendency may also be a bi-product of the rating method. The various ranking formats, and more particularly the forced distribution, require that most employees be rated average.

PRIMACY AND RECENCY EFFECTS. Because the typical appraisal period is six months to a year, it is too difficult to retain in memory all performance-related behaviours of the incumbents. As a cognitive shortcut, raters may fall prey to the **primacy effect** and/or the **recency effect**. They will use initial information to categorize a ratee as either a good or a poor performer. Subsequently, information that supports the initial judgments is amassed, and contradictory information is ignored. Because special attention is paid to information initially collected, this bias is referred to as the *primacy bias*. Although the time span is much shorter, this bias is similar in nature to the "first impression" bias discussed in the selection interview in Chapter 6.

Conversely, a rater may not pay attention to an employee's performance throughout the appraisal period. As the appraisal interview draws near, the rater searches for information cues about the value of performance. Unfortunately recent behaviours or outputs are salient. As a result, recent behaviours are weighted more heavily than they should be. Called the *recency error*, this bias can have serious consequences for a ratee who performs well for six months or a year, but then makes a serious or costly mistake in the last week or two preceding the appraisal. Incumbents and managers can minimize these two errors by documenting ongoing critical events. While time-consuming to complete, these files ensure that information for the entire appraisal period is incorporated into judgments.

CONTRAST EFFECTS. A **contrast effect** occurs when the evaluation or observation of one subordinate's performance is affected unjustly by an earlier evaluation or observation of another ratee's performance. When compared to weak employees, an average employee will appear outstanding; when evaluated against outstanding employees, an average employee will be perceived as a low performer. As with other errors, the solution is to have specific performance criteria established *prior* to the evaluation period.

SPILLOVER EFFECT. The **spillover effect** occurs when past PA ratings, whether good or bad, are allowed to unjustly influence current ratings. It happens most often when new managers are being briefed on current employees by departing managers. Thus the information provided, which is already biased, is being carried on. One solution to the problem is to avoid examining past appraisal records/information prior to the conduct of the assessment; past records, on the other hand, can be consulted in conjunction with current appraisal for the purpose of detecting trends and for giving feedback to the incumbent.

SIMILARITY ERROR. A **similarity error** occurs when raters evaluate more positively those whom they perceive to be similar to themselves. The implicit assumption underlying this error is that they are (or have been) "model" employees, and thus subordinate similarity will most likely reflect good performance.

Even the most valid and reliable appraisal forms cannot be effective when so many extraneous factors impinge on the process. The most serious obstacles to the accuracy and efficacy of PA are the following common assumptions (which should be changed):

Minimizing Appraisal Bias

- The supervisor is not only the best source of information on an employee's performance, but is a sufficient source as well.
- The appraisals must be kept as simple as possible so that they do not interfere with the more important duties of the supervisor.
- Appraisals should be done every six months or once a year.
- The rater can accurately recall each employee's performance over a long period of time.
- Appraisals should always be done on individual performance rather than on work units or groups.
- An overall average level of performance is sufficient information about an employee's performance.
- All raters are motivated to rate accurately.
- The use of a behaviourally based appraisal format will ensure rating validity (and reliability).[16]

But, as suggested above, many of these errors can be minimized, and more realistic assumptions can be made, if the following steps are taken:

- Each performance dimension addresses a single job activity rather than a group of activities.
- The rater can observe the behaviour of the ratee on a regular basis while the job is being accomplished.
- Terms like "average" are not used on a rating scale, since different raters have various reactions to such a term.
- The rater does not have to evaluate large groups of employees.

- Raters are trained to avoid such errors as leniency, strictness, halo, central tendency, and recency of events.
- The dimensions being evaluated are meaningful, clearly stated, and important.

In addition to the above suggestions, it should be re-emphasized that rating accuracy, as well as effectiveness in general, can be improved through careful training. One expert suggests the training to include five basic processes, each requiring a different skill:

- Setting goals and performance standards,
- Observing employee actions and performance,
- Recording the observations,
- Averaging and evaluating the performance,
- Providing feedback to the employees.[17]

TRENDS IN PA

Assessing PA Form Effectiveness

Although the appraisal form or method is just one component, the PAS often centres on that form. Consequently, attention is focused on assessing the available appraisal forms, thus enabling HR managers to choose the best one. While this chapter discusses appraisal form assessment, the next chapter will discuss assessment of PASs.

CRITERIA FOR ASSESSMENT. To determine which appraisal form is best, one must ask the question: "Best for what?" That is, what purpose is the technique supposed to accomplish, or what performance is it supposed to measure? The purposes of PA are generally evaluation and development, but an effective appraisal technique should also be free from error, be reliable, be valid and cost effective, and allow comparisons across subordinates and departments in an organization.

Each of these goals can be used as a criterion. Each form should also be evaluated in terms of its influence on the superior–subordinate relationship. Does the form encourage superiors to watch their subordinates in order to collect valid data for evaluation and developmental purposes? Does it facilitate the appraisal interview (discussed in the next chapter)? All these criteria must be counterbalanced by one other major criterion: economics. The costs of developing and implementing a form must be compared against its benefits or how well it does on the other criteria. This is the essence of the notion of utility.

WHICH FORM IS BEST? Research on this question is limited. It does, however, reinforce the necessity of first identifying the purposes the organization wants to serve with PA. Each form can then be assessed in relation to the following criteria pertaining to usefulness:

- *Developmental*: motivating subordinates to do well, providing feedback, and aiding in HR planning and career development;
- *Evaluational*: promotion, discharge, layoff, pay, and transfer decisions, and therefore, the ability to make comparisons across subordinates and departments;
- *Economic*: cost of development, implementation, and use;
- *Freedom from error*: halo, leniency, and central tendency and the extent of reliability and validity;
- *Interpersonal*: the extent to which superiors can gather useful and valid appraisal data that facilitate the appraisal interview;
- *Practicality*: ease of development and implementation;
- *User acceptance*: the extent to which users find it reliable, valid and useful.

Exhibit 9.11 shows an assessment of the appraisal forms in relation to each of these criteria.

Exhibit 9.11
Evaluation of Performance Appraisal Forms

FORM	CRITERIA FOR EVALUATION						
	Developmental	Evaluative	Economic	Error-Free	Interpersonal	Practical	Accepted
COMPARATIVE NORM-REFERENCE							
Straight Ranking	P	E	E	P	P	G	P
Alternative Ranking	P	E	E	G	P	G	P
Paired Comparison	P	E	E	P	P	G	P
Forced Distribution	P	G	E	E	G	G	P
RATINGS AND BEHAVIOURAL							
Narrative Essay	P	P	E	P	P	P	P
Conventional Rating	P	G	E	P	P	P	P
Critical Incidents	G	P	G	G	G	G	E
Weighted Checklist	G	G	G	G	P	G	E
Forced Choice	P	G	P	E	P	G	P
BARS	G	G	P	G	E	G	E
BOS	G	G	P	G	E	G	G
OUTPUT APPROACHES							
MBO	E	E	P	G	G	G	G
Performance Standards	G	E	P	G	G	E	G
Direct Index	P	E	E	G	G	E	G
Accomplishment	E	E	P	G	G	G	E

Note: P = POOR; G = FAIR TO GOOD; E = VERY GOOD TO EXCELLENT

Without doubt, the use of computers for evaluating the PA results has increased dramatically over the past few years. Not only are many of the rating forms listed in this chapter becoming entirely computerized, but linkages to other HR functions and activities are becoming easier.

Because PA is often related to pay increases, many software programs enable companies to tie these increases to the annual performance rating. For instance, one U.S. firm based in Salt Lake City developed a computer-aided merit increase program that interfaces with its personnel payroll system. The system based merit distribution in each individual PA in relation to other ratings, the wage rate, and the total money available for raises. Combined with the use of graphics software, all statistics and actual distribution of appraisal ratings can be mapped, analyzed, and compared.

Another company, based in Israel, developed a very sophisticated expert system with specific PA applications. The program enables the company to design various ratings formats and to test and validate the dimensions used to assess employees. Based on accumulated data, the system can empirically identify the dimensions that should be given more weight than others when calculating a total score. Furthermore, the system can detect some common errors (biases) committed by certain raters and can correct them by normalizing the results and calculating an adjusted score.

This is only the beginning. It seems that with the introduction of computer technology and the increased facility of using various data banks, the validity and reliability of many

Computer Applications

PASs can be improved. A very interesting and useful possibility is using artificial intelligence techniques in computer-based assessment systems to detect certain unusual factors such as substance abuse and burnout. Work colleagues are sensitive to behaviour changes on the job, and by using them as a source of assessment data, the computerized appraisal tool can give early warning of potential problems for which prompt treatment is most effective.

HRM DYNAMICS
Performance Appraisal Profiles in Selected Canadian Organizations

Bell Canada

In the late 1950s Bell introduced a five-step PAS that was later modified to what was known as the Job Planning and Review Process. The essence of the program is an MBO system jointly developed by supervisor and incumbent. The formal appraisal is prepared once a year and is called a review board. During the review the supervisor presents the written assessment of each subordinate to a panel consisting of peers, bosses, an HR representative, and other management employees. Procedures vary according to departmental preferences and size of the group. Upon completion of the review board process, the completed assessment form becomes the basis for salary adjustments and other HR decisions (training, development, transfers, etc.).

CP Rail

CP Rail employees are evaluated annually, around the time of their birthday. Most appraisal officers receive formal training from the HR officers. Emphasis is placed on legal considerations and how to avoid different types of errors. CP Rail uses two types of forms for each evaluation: (a) a conventional rating form in which the dimensions for appraisal are discussed and mutually selected from a list of factors that appear on the form, including skills, results, knowledge, and personal factors; (b) an accomplishments form in which the rater specifies accomplishments, development plans, and superior's commitment as communicated to the ratee. In addition, an unsatisfactory performance form is completed for all employees who receive an overall rating of "unsatisfactory" on the first form. The HR department ensures high involvement and due proces in preparing and conducting the appraisal interview.

Standard Life

Appraisals are conducted at Standard Life on an annual basis except if certain circumstances require closer scrutiny. Each rater receives a short guide entitled: "The Ethics of Performance Appraisals," where common instructions and pitfalls are indicated. The appraisal forms are semi-structured (open-ended), and the performance requirements are left to the discretion of each manager. The incumbent, however, participates in the process to ensure that the list of job duties performed is complete. For each item, a percentage of job importance is attached, as well as three possible categories: (1) below minimum, (2) 80–100 percent, (3) above 100 percent. In addition, achievements and abilities are being evaluated in a similar manner. As a rule, the rater asks each ratee to first provide a self-rating on each item. Once completed, the supervisor is then required to recommend numerical ratings for each employee. The department head reviews the rating and makes a final decision before it is forwarded to the personnel department.

S U M M A R Y

Appraising employee performance is another important HR activity. This chapter examined PA as a set of processes and procedures consisting of developing reliable and valid standards, criteria, and measures that evolve over time. To ensure the effectiveness of the PA process, HR managers must be concerned with the implementation and monitoring of the multiple aspects of the PAS.

An effective PAS depends upon several components of appraisal, but it must generally serve two purposes: (1) an evaluative role to inform incumbents where they stand, and (2) a developmental role to provide specific information and guidance in order to enable individuals to better perform in the future. Recognition of the important role of the subject in PASs has helped focus attention on such components of appraisal as the superior–subordinate relationship, job qualities, and organizational conditions. Another important component of the PAS is the raters themselves, particularly how they process appraisal information and make evaluation decisions. This is examined in more detail in the next chapter.

Because PA is linked to other HR functions, it is important to understand why PA data are gathered, as well as how this information is used. Legal considerations have also heightened the need for organizations to review this process. Special emphasis is placed on the need for conducting a thorough job analysis as a means of developing job-related performance criteria. In general, the more subjective the PA approach, the more it is vulnerable to legal challenges. Although various methods and approaches have been developed and used by organizations over the years, they have been presented in this chapter under three headings: (1) comparative or norm-referenced approaches, (2) ratings and behavioural approaches, and (3) output approaches. The choice of the best approach is really a function of several criteria, including: the purpose of the PAS (evaluation vs. development), the costs of development and implementation of the system, the degree to which rater errors are minimized, and user acceptance of the system.

Despite the most well-laid plans for PASs, HR professionals are often frustrated by the failure of line managers to consistently apply and use them. A number of obstacles can contribute to rater resistance to a PAS: (a) raters may not have the opportunity to observe a subordinate's performance, (b) raters may not have performance standards, (c) raters as human judges are prone to errors, or (d) raters may view PA as a conflict-producing activity and therefore avoid it. For these reasons and others, it is important to examine not only why and how PA data are gathered but also how they are used.

P O S T S C R I P T

As competitive pressures build and the pitfalls of existing PASs come to light, employers are searching for ways to increase PAS effectiveness. Attempts have been made over the years by many organizations to improve the process by ameliorating the methods and approaches used. In fact, the attempt to de-emphasize the importance of *traits*, and to focus on assessing *behaviours* that are important to the job and the organization has been one fruitful trend. However, this has not been sufficient, so validity and accuracy of the rating process remain problematic, primarily for reasons such as raters' error problems, raters' low motivation to do a good job in performing this task, and a low level of acceptance of PASs by employees. In order to overcome these problems, some innovations are being introduced and are worth further exploration. These include:

1. *Making the proper conduct of the PA by a supervisor a task for which the rater himself or herself will be evaluated.* By recognizing that this is an important part of their job, it is hoped that raters' motivation will increase and will lead to more serious attempts at appraising subordinates. An interesting question for future research might be an

examination of the trade-off between the sophistication of the form used and the degree of rater motivation to do a good job. In fact, many believe that motivation is more important than the tool.

2. *Changing PAs from supervisor-only appraisals to multiple rater and peer-rating systems.* This also better fits the increasingly "flat" organizational structures that are emerging. In order to become more efficient in handling the data administration and scoring required, multiple rater measurement methods are becoming computerized. Thus, much of the administrative and time burdens associated with appraisals is shifted to the computer. Multiple appraisal rating systems are used by a number of companies. Westinghouse, for example, allows an employee to select those persons who will form the evaluation team, and on what criteria the appraisal is to be conducted. Kodak and Walt Disney have used a multiple rater system such as TEAMS (Team Evaluation and Management System) that can immediately identify rater bias toward gender, age, or any other protected group. Some multiple rater evaluation systems are exploring artificial intelligence technologies. For example, at Bell (of Pennsylvania), certain sources of error, such as particular raters or evaluative criteria, are being spotted. Employees therefore have a better knowledge of the reliability of their evaluative measures, and thus they have increased confidence in the PA system.

3. *Correcting obvious biases by measuring the degree of affection that exists between a rater and a ratee.* Some innovative attempts are underway to devise instruments that will point out the "effect of affect" in appraisal, which, if proved valid, can allow organizations to correct biases and obtain a more objective "true score" (evaluation).[18]

4. *Training the raters.* An essential component of an effective PAS is an informed and trained rater. Training may ensure a uniform application of policies and procedures. Raters are taught about the relationships between performance evaluation and developmental activities, and this results in shifting the focus away from compensation.

All in all, the following are some critical questions that should be addressed by each organization prior to implementation and development of an appraisal policy:

- Who are the raters (supervisors, peers, external, etc.)?
- What will be measured (and what will be excluded)? To what extent are the chosen dimensions observable and important?
- What is the primary and secondary purpose of the appraisal (feedback, merit pay, test validation, etc.)?
- What about the confidentiality of the results? Who will have access and when?
- What will be the frequency and the timing of the appraisal? Why (justification)?
- What will be the better type of feedback (absolute vs. relative)?
- How will the PA data be processed and managed (computer vs. manual operation)?
- How can one increase rater motivation and the ability to rate accurately?
- How can one detect and correct "after the fact" biases and errors in the PA process?

REVIEW AND ANALYSIS QUESTIONS

1. What is involved in a PAS? Identify the principal factors.
2. What are the purposes of PAs (identify at least four distinct purposes)?
3. Discuss what points the boards of inquiry have implicated as important in a legally viable PAS.
4. How can PA forms be developed so that supervisory errors in PA can be minimized?
5. What criteria are important in answering the question: "What is the best PA form?"
6. What relationships exist between PA and other HR activities (name at least three)?

7. PA approaches differ according to whether behaviour or results are evaluated. Can you cite organization examples where one approach might be preferred over the other? Explain why.
8. What is the primary difference between the BOS and the BARS?
9. What are some typical "errors" in PA? How can these be minimized?
10. What are some trends or future concerns in PA?

CASE STUDY

ALLEGED DISCRIMINATION IN APPRAISAL

Micheline, Marielle, Louise, and Nicole were surprised to find an internal memo from the director of personnel services inviting them to be present at a formal PA session to be conducted that afternoon. Having worked as temporary producers for Tele-Montreal, Inc. for an average of five years, they did not recall any such session in the past. In fact, none of the other producers in the station were invited to this appraisal. The individual performance interviews were conducted by the director of personnel, the production supervisor, and the director of professional services.

To their surprise and astonishment, they discovered that a decision had been reached based on the results of a recent PA, to demote all of them to the position of assistant producer. Each was given a brief summary of the reasons for this decision and was then asked to sign a statement indicating that she was told of the results of the superior's evaluation. All four left these consecutive hour-long meetings shocked, angry, and helpless.

The next morning the four decided to get together and learn a bit more about the decision and the performance evaluation process in Tele-Montreal, Inc. The following is what they learned from Johana Watson, the personnel director, regarding the new PAS: Tele-Montreal had recently decided to reorganize their operation and to implement a new PAS for all their professional employees. With the help of National Management Consulting, Inc., they had developed a "bias-free" PA policy that included the following elements:

1. Each producer will be assessed on four criteria: creativity, versatility, management of technical material and budgetary resources, and management of human resources.
2. Evaluation will be conducted on an annual basis effective immediately.
3. Evaluation will be carried out by a committee of three supervisors and will be guided by the following rating scale in assessing each dimension:

   • Performance for surpassing the job demands 5 points

   • Performance that satisfactorily meets the job demands 3 points

   • Performance that exhibits average satisfaction of job demands 2 points

   • Performance that is inferior to job demands 1 point

4. A differential weighting is applied for the criteria; creativity, management of human resources and management of technical, material, and budgetary resources will have factors multiplied by four (4) and versatility in the producer program will be multiplied by two (2).

5. The total score compiled for each employee is then interpreted as follows:

Meaning	Score
Nonsatisfactory performance	30 or less
Minimal performance	30–40
Satisfactory performance	40–50
Excellent performance	50 +

According to Watson, "given that this PA procedure has been tested and used by many Canadian organizations to their complete satisfaction, it is probably a very valid procedure. This sophisticated numerical and highly accurate system leads Tele-Montreal, Inc. to believe that in no way can they 'perform poorly' in utilizing this new performance appraisal system."

Upon learning of the new system, the four producers demanded to see the detailed breakdown of their assessment along with those of other producers. Johana Watson agreed and produced the data (Exhibit 9.12). When asked why they had not been given a detailed job description, Watson answered: "Don't tell me that after working as assistant producers for two years and then as producers for three years, you don't know what your job is."

This answer did not satisfy the four, and they filed a formal complaint alleging discrimination (possible sex discrimination) with the Human Rights Commission of Quebec.

Exhibit 9.12
Breakdown of Producer's Performance Appraisal

PRODUCER'S NAME	CREATIVITY	VERSATILITY	MANAGEMENT OF MATERIAL, TECHNICAL, AND BUDGET	HUMAN RESOURCES	TOTAL
Louise	4 x 3 = 12	2 x 3 = 6	4 x 2 = 8	4 x 2 = 8	34
Nicole	4 x 2 = 8	2 x 2 = 4	4 x 2 = 8	4 x 3 = 12	32
Micheline	4 x 1 = 4	2 x 3 = 6	4 x 2 = 8	4 x 2 = 8	26
Marielle	4 x 2 = 8	2 x 4 = 8	4 x 1 = 4	4 x 1 = 4	24
John	4 x 3 = 12	2 x 3 = 6	4 x 3 = 12	4 x 4 = 16	46
André	4 x 4 = 16	2 x 3 = 6	4 x 3 = 12	4 x 3 = 12	46
Marcel	4 x 3 = 12	2 x 4 = 8	4 x 4 = 16	4 x 4 = 16	52
David	4 x 2 = 8	2 x 3 = 6	4 x 4 = 16	4 x 4 = 16	46

Case Questions

1. Put yourself in the position of the human rights investigator. Based on the limited information, decide whether there is any justification to the complainants' charges. In making your decision, focus on the following questions:
   a. Are issues of reliability involved in this case? If so, what sources of error must you consider?
   b. Are issues of validity involved in this case? If so, what sources of error must you consider?
   c. Is the measuring instrument itself an issue here?
   d. Are problems of administration an issue here?
2. Another way to analyze the case is by assigning yourself the role of lawyer for the complainants:
   a. How would you build the case?
   b. What would you emphasize?

NOTES

1. P.M. Podsakoff, M.L. Williams, and W.E. Scott, "Myths of Employee Selection," in *Readings in Personnel and Human Resource Management*, 3rd ed., ed. R.S. Schuler, S.A. Youngblood, and V. Huber (St. Paul, Minn.: West Publishing Co., 1988), 178–92.

2. Statistics Canada, *The Labour Force: Time Loss from Work for Personal Reasons* (Ottawa: 1988).

3. "Absenteeism," *Small Business Report*, April 1985.

4. "Absenteeism Costs Bank $18 Million a Year: Survey," *First Bank News*, February 1983, 2.

5. Excerpts taken from *The Employment Law Report* 6, 6 (June 1985): 45–46. Used with permission of the publisher.

6. Ibid.

7. R.W. Goddard, "Is Your Appraisal System Headed for Court?" *Personnel Journal* 68, 1 (January 1989): 117–18.

8. Ibid., 115.

9. *Wall Street Journal*, 25 June 1985,

10. Cited in M. Gibb-Clark, "Evaluating Work Performance of Employees," *The Globe and Mail*, 22 February 1989, B13.

11. Cited in H. Schwind, "Performance Appraisal: The State of the Art," in *Canadian Readings in Personnel and Human Resource Management*, ed. S.L. Dolan and R.S. Schuler (St. Paul, Minn.: West Publishing Co., 1987), 198.

12. Information for preparation of the BARS examples using VIA Rail was supplied by Sylvie Plante, a McGill University student, as part of a term paper project submitted to Professor Dolan in 1989.

13. For more information, see J.M. Feldman, "Beyond Attribution Theory: Cognitive Process in Performance Appraisal," *Journal of Applied Psychology* 66(1981): 127–48; R.L. Heneman, K.L. Wexley, and M.L. Moore, "Performance Rating Accuracy: A

Critical Review," *Journal of Business Research* 15 (1987): 431–48; and D.R. Ilgen and J.M. Feldman, "Performance Appraisal: A Process Focus," *Research in Organizational Behaviour*, Vol. 5, ed. B.M. Staw and L.L Cummings (Greenwich, Conn.: JAI Press, 1983), 141–97.

14. R. Loo, "Quality Performance Appraisals," *Canadian Manager* 14, 4 (Winter 1989): 25.

15. Unpublished research results supplied by Professor S.L. Dolan.

16. J.H. Bernardin and R.W. Beatty, *Performance Appraisal: Assessing Human Behavior at Work* (Boston: Kent Publishing, 1984), 2–3.

17. S.B. Wehrberg, "Train Supervisors to Measure and Evaluate Performance," *Personnel Journal* 67, 2 (February 1988): 78–79.

18. S.L. Dolan and D. Morin, "The Effect of Affect in Assessing Employees: Universal or Restricted Phenomenon?"(Paper presented at the Third International Congress of Work Values, Carlsbad, Czechoslovakia, July 1992).

CHAPTER TEN

PERFORMANCE APPRAISAL:
APPLICATIONS AND IMPROVEMENTS

KEYNOTE ADDRESS
Pierre Girard
Corporate Vice-President Human Resources, St-Hubert Group

Performance Appraisal: Key to Employee Empowerment
and Commitment

Over the past few years, we have attempted to use different means to increase the commitment and loyalty of our employees toward corporate goals. This challenge is becoming vital given our corporate view, which clearly distinguishes between the "excellent" companies and the others. Simply stated, in the excellent companies employees are "empowered" and consequently fully engaged, while in the other companies employees are simply "doing their job."

St-Hubert Group is a company in the food business. We have grown over the past forty years from fifty to approximately 7,000 employees. We have restaurants in three provinces, and other products distributed across Canada. In order to confront mounting competition, the company has decided to gain its competitive edge by placing the emphasis on quality in our services and products. In order to achieve that, the PAS has been chosen as our primary HR strategy.

We are aware that this is a formidable task, hence, in principle, management and employees alike are attaching great importance to the PAS; it has to be properly used and accepted by everybody in the organization. Moreover, the PA process is becoming even more important as it is recognized that it will be used as a tool to measure and monitor the achievement of corporate goals.

In order to do so, the PA process must be characterized by the following:

- A continuous formal communication process;
- Active joint participation by the rater and the ratee;
- A results-oriented approach.

Thus, the PAS is an integral part of a management philosophy that encourages participation. Often organizations preach about participation but do not deliver the means by which to actually achieve it. In our case, the means chosen to measure and improve the employees' contribution to the organization is a formal communication process between an assessor and an assessee. The extension of this philosophy and its translation into concrete actions is guided by the following:

- It is done in writing.
- It contains specific (measurable) performance indices.
- It requires the rater to attribute precise points to each dimension measured.
- It specifies the frequency with which the evaluation is to be conducted.
- It ensures uniformity in the method of conducting the appraisal.

In order to encourage participation, the ratee must be involved in the PA process; he or she must be forced to think about what he or she wishes to do, and how the task(s) will be carried out. Consequently, both performance objectives and the skills needed for improved performance are jointly established. This process leads to the establishment of a "quasi-contract" between two people. All these various contracts need to ultimately achieve corporate goals where both parties to the contract (managers and subordinates) are accountable.

In sum, the PA is a vital process for all enterprises that wish to commit their human resources to meeting corporate objectives. However, it has to be prescribed in a general organizational philosophy that recognizes and reinforces the performance of each employee. Additionally, it must recognize the employee's needs for training and development. Increasing commitment requires linking two other HR functions to PA. For one, the organization must provide formal and informal opportunities for improving the superior–subordinate relationships. Secondly, top performers need to be recognized and properly compensated. In my view, a process of managing performance that is well structured and supported by well-trained managers is likely to achieve the goals it was set up for—increasing employees' commitment.

• • •

The Keynote Address suggests that there are two important points in utilizing PA information. First, it can be very useful for a company to utilize PA data as part of an attempt to increase employee commitment to the organization. Second, when organizations attempt to develop strategies to improve performance on the basis of PA information, they have to develop specific guidelines and procedures. In the case of St-Hubert Group, the philosophy of joint participation is the vehicle for such drive. Third, PA is not likely to succeed if it operates in a vacuum. It should be administered by well-trained managers and linked to training and development, as well as compensation policies.

This chapter discusses issues and potential solutions associated with providing subordinates with feedback via the PA interview. Also, issues associated with improving performance, including a paradigm for diagnosing causes of performance gaps, are presented. Finally, the overall assessment of the PAS is presented.

• • •

INHERENT CONFLICTS IN PA

Although the PA interview is used to gather additional data, its major use is to feed that data back to the subordinate. On the basis of this feedback, the intended purposes of PA are served. The success of the process depends upon how the appraisal system is designed and how the interview is conducted.

As suggested in the previous chapter, PAs draw poor reviews from employees, employers, and experts alike. Managers seem equally disgruntled over the appraisal process. One study suggested that of all managers surveyed, only 10 percent believe that production actually increases as a result of the appraisal process; the majority of appraisers saw little or no practical value in conducting PA interviews. Whether the feedback they gave was positive or negative, supervisors felt that, at best, the status quo was maintained; moreover, many contended that the only certain outcome of giving negative feedback was so adverse that they preferred not to conduct appraisals at all. The study concluded that managers also feared the organizational consequences of "making waves" with their subordinates.[1]

An understanding of the inherent conflicts in PA is pertinent to the discussion of the design of the system and the conduct of the interview. These conflicts therefore are discussed first. Then, thorough examination is made of methods of improving performance deficiencies.

Differential Focus

One reason that PAs are problematic is that supervisors and incumbents view the process from different perspectives. For the incumbent, the focus is outward, keying on the environmental factors (the supervisor, lack of support, lack of cooperation among co-workers, problems with machinery) that impinge on his or her performance. The supervisor's focus, on the other hand, is on the incumbent and the displayed motivation and ability. These differences in perceptions are often called *actor and observer differences* and can lead to conflict when it comes to identifying the causes of poor performance. This problem is accentuated by the tendency to account for performance in a *self-serving* manner. In order to protect one's ego, an incumbent is likely to attribute the causes of poor performance to external factors and attribute successful performance to one's motivation and ability. Supervisors may respond similarly.

Conflicts in Goals

Goal conflict may also be a problem. From organizational and individual goals come three sets of conflicts. One is between the organization's evaluative and developmental goals. When pursuing the evaluative goal, superiors have to make judgments affecting their subordinates' careers and immediate rewards. Communicating negative judgments can lead to the creation of an adversarial, low-trust relationship between superior and subordinate. This in turn precludes the superior from performing a problem-solving helper role that is essential in serving the developmental goal.

A second set of conflicts arises from the various goals of the individual being evaluated. On the one hand, individuals want valid feedback that gives them information about how to improve and where they stand in the organization. On the other hand, they want to verify their self-image and also obtain valued rewards. In essence, the goals of individuals imply a need for evaluator openness (giving valid feedback for improvement) and also protectiveness (allowing the individual to maintain a positive self-image and obtain rewards).

The third set of conflicts arises between the goals of the individual and the goals of the organization. One conflict is between the organization's evaluation goal and the individual's goal of obtaining rewards. Another conflict is between the organization's developmental goal and the individual's goal of maintaining self-image. The nature of these conflicts is shown in Exhibit 10.1.

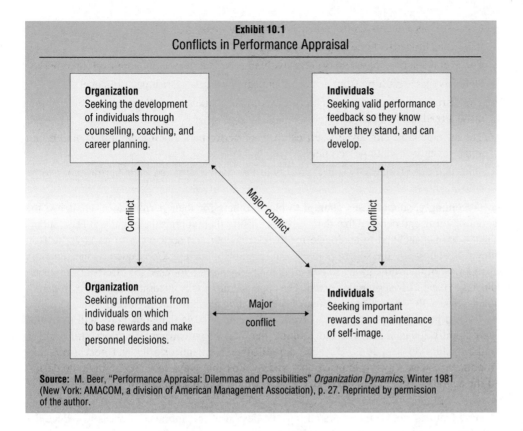

Exhibit 10.1
Conflicts in Performance Appraisal

Organization
Seeking the development of individuals through counselling, coaching, and career planning.

Individuals
Seeking valid performance feedback so they know where they stand, and can develop.

Conflict

Major conflict

Conflict

Organization
Seeking information from individuals on which to base rewards and make personnel decisions.

Major conflict

Individuals
Seeking important rewards and maintenance of self-image.

Source: M. Beer, "Performance Appraisal: Dilemmas and Possibilities" *Organization Dynamics*, Winter 1981 (New York: AMACOM, a division of American Management Association), p. 27. Reprinted by permission of the author.

Consequences of Inherent Conflicts

Several consequences of the inherent conflicts described above are ambivalence, avoidance, defensiveness, and resistance. Ambivalence is a consequence for both the superiors and the subordinates. Superiors are ambivalent because they must act as judge and jury in telling subordinates where they stand, both because the organization demands it and because the subordinates want it. Yet they are uncertain about their judgments and how the subordinates will react upon receiving negative feedback. This feeling is intensified when superiors are not trained in giving feedback. Subordinates are equally ambivalent because they want honest feedback, yet they want to maintain their self-image (that is, they really want only positive feedback) and to receive rewards. Additionally, if they are open with their superiors in identifying undeveloped potential, they risk the chance that the superiors may use this to evaluate them unfavourably.

A consequence of this joint ambivalence is avoidance. Subordinates, to avoid negative feedback, may avoid seeking appraisal data in general and may attempt to play down the importance of PA data. The superiors, meanwhile, avoid giving appraisals by concluding that the subordinates really would rather not know anyway. This process has given rise to the term "vanishing performance appraisal."[2] If organizations both demand that superiors engage in the PA process and that they give negative feedback (to support current and future decisions regarding layoffs, terminations, and demotions), superiors may resort to the **sandwich approach**. Here the superiors squeeze the negative feedback between two pieces of positive feedback. When this is done, subordinates may report never having received negative feedback even though superiors will report giving it.

Subordinates and superiors also become defensive during PAs. The subordinate becomes defensive in responding to negative feedback that threatens his or her self-image and chances for gaining rewards. This is corroborated by the results of a study at General Electric where it was found that:

- Criticism has a negative effect on achievement of goals.
- Praise has little effect one way or the other.
- The average subordinate reacts defensively to criticism during the appraisal interview.
- Defensiveness resulting from critical appraisal produces inferior performance.
- The disruptive effect of repeated criticism on subsequent performance is greater among those already low in self-esteem.
- The average G.E. employee's self-estimate of performance before appraisal placed him at the seventy-seventh percentile.
- Only two out of ninety-two participants in the study estimated their performance to be below average.[3]

Accordingly, subordinates attempt to blame others for their performance, challenge the appraisal form, and demand that their superiors justify their appraisals. Initially at least, subordinates are not inclined to apologize for their behaviour and seek ways to improve; in fact, they resist efforts by the superiors to engage in problem solving. Consequently, the superiors spend most of their time trying to defend their appraisals and to resist the efforts of the subordinates to have their appraisals altered. The appraisal process is uncomfortable for both participants, especially when poor performance and negative feedback are involved.

Even if good performance is involved, and it is inevitable that somebody will be evaluated slightly lower and come out looking like a poor performer, superiors still have to make evaluation decisions. Because appraisals are uncomfortable, yet necessary, it is important to seek ways to improve the process. Possible ways to do so involve the design of the appraisal system and the characteristics of the appraisal interview.

DESIGNING APPRAISALS FOR BETTER RESULTS

Several features can be incorporated into the design of the appraisal process to reduce the problems caused by conflicts inherent in it.

Separate Evaluation and Development

Because many subordinates react defensively to evaluations that are negative, they block out from consideration, at least at that time, ways to improve. Consequently, attempts by superiors to engage in developmental activities such as problem solving are likely to be futile; for problem solving to be effective, subordinates have to be open and the superiors have to play the role of helper, not judge or prosecutor. Thus, if organizations want to serve both the evaluation and development purposes effectively, there should be two appraisal interviews. One interview can focus on evaluation and the other, at a different time of the year, on development.

Use Appropriate Performance Data

A key factor in reducing conflict is to utilize performance data that focus on specific behaviours or goals. Furthermore, these performance expectations need to be clearly communicated to the incumbents prior to the beginning of the appraisal period.

Data that focus on personal attributes or characteristics are likely to prompt more defensiveness because they are more subjective and thus more difficult for the superior to justify. Also, more of the subordinate's self-image is at stake. As shown in the previous chapter, superiors can facilitate specific performance feedback through their selection and use of the appropriate appraisal forms. Specifically, if superiors want to use performance data on behaviours, a critical incident technique or a BOS method would be effective, while performance data on goals would be more effectively displayed using an MBO or work standards approach. Using these appraisal forms allows the supervisors to monitor *what* subordinates are doing, as well as *how* they are doing.

Separate Past, Current, and Potential PAs

It is important to separate the evaluation of present performance from that of potential performance. The current performance of subordinates may have little to do with their potential, yet superiors may unconsciously incorporate evaluations of potential performance into evaluations of current performance. Alternatively, superiors may incorporate past performance into the evaluation of present performance. In either case, the appraisal of current performance is inappropriate, since it amalgamates and confuses past, current, and/or potential performance.

As a result, the appraisal is likely to be viewed as unfair. Consider people with high potential. They may receive a lower evaluation than do their peers who are performing at an equivalent level because their superiors have higher expectations of them. In the same way, adequate performers with low potential may be evaluated in an unfair way simply because they do not have high potential. In the former case the appraisal is unfair to the high-potential employee because performance standards are raised. The latter appraisal is just as unfair to those incumbents who may not be interested in being promoted, yet who perform adequately in their current job.

To minimize the emotionally charged atmosphere that normally surrounds the PA process, managers need to take several steps to ensure that the process is perceived as fair and equitable.

Encourage Procedural Fairness

UPWARD AND RECIPROCAL APPRAISALS. To encourage openness in the PA and to improve superior–subordinate relationships, subordinates can be allowed to engage in appraisal of their superiors as well. Upward appraisal can help put into better balance, if not equalize, the power of the superior vis-à-vis the subordinate. Such a balance is useful in reducing the hierarchical character of the superior–subordinate relationship, which contributes much to the defensiveness and avoidance in the PA.

Organizations and superiors facilitate the upward appraisal process by providing forms for subordinates to use and by engaging in other HR policies and procedures indicative of openness. Such policies and procedures may include allowing employees to participate in deciding their own pay increases, or to be involved in analyzing their own jobs.

SELF-APPRAISAL. This open and power-equalizing approach to PA can be furthered by a policy of self-appraisal. Self-appraisal is likely to provide more information for the superior and result in a more realistic appraisal of the subordinate's performance and a greater acceptance of the final appraisal by both subordinates and superiors.

CONSISTENCY AND OPPORTUNITY TO REBUT TRADITIONAL APPRAISAL. Performance standards should be applied consistently to all incumbents. Allowances should not be made for workers with special problems, nor should high performers be expected to carry more than their own weight. In addition, the process should enable incumbents to challenge or rebut evaluations.

Part of the difficulty in managing the appraisal process is collecting and maintaining information on all incumbents. As the span of control increases in size, this task grows to unmanageable proportions. One way to resolve this problem, while at the same time increasing fairness, is to shift the responsibility for performance record keeping to the incumbent. To carry out this process, incumbents first need training in writing performance standards and in collecting and documenting performance information. In addition, a two-way communication process needs to operate effectively, so that incumbents feel free to renegotiate performance standards that have become obsolete or unattainable due to constraints.

Delegating responsibility offers incumbents several advantages in terms of performance planning, goal setting, and record keeping. First, they are no longer passive participants, reacting to superiors' directives. Second, because it is now their responsibility to identify

Empower Incumbents

performance hurdles and bring them to the attention of their manager, defensiveness is reduced. Third, the supervisor is free from this task, and can concentrate on other important activities such as coaching and managing rather than policing. Finally, the incumbent feels *ownership* of the process.

THE PA INTERVIEW

To further enhance PA effectiveness, several things should be taken into consideration regarding the actual interview.

A supervisor needs to *prepare* for the PA interview. Emphasis should specifically be placed on two issues: the schedule and the gathering of relevant information.

Preparing for the Interview

SCHEDULE IN ADVANCE. A few weeks prior to the scheduled performance review, the manager should *personally* notify the appraisee of the time, date, and place. Having a secretary schedule the interview increases the potential for misunderstandings. Sending a formal notice builds unneeded formality into the process and immediately shrouds the interview in ambiguity and mistrust. Also, in setting up the interview agreement should be reached regarding its purpose and content. For example, will the incumbent have an opportunity to evaluate the performance of the superior, or will the evaluation be one-way? It is also useful, although possibly inconvenient, to select and use a neutral location, so that neither the manager nor the incumbent has a power advantage. Still, the session will be more constructive if both parties have time to do their homework.

GATHER RELEVANT INFORMATION. If subordinates are empowered, advance notice will give them sufficient time to update their performance records and do a self-review. In situations in which employees formally review their own performance, comparisons of self-ratings with ratings by the supervisor can actually be made by each party prior to the session and then used for discussion during the interview.

Furthermore, the manager and the ratee must gather all information that has any bearing on the discussion. Here, critical incident files or behaviour diaries can be reviewed. It is also important to review the employee's job description. An agenda can be developed to allow the ratee to study it and make additions or deletions.

Types of Interviews

There are essentially four major types of interviews: (1) tell and sell, (2) tell and listen, (3) problem-solving, and (4) mixed.

TELL AND SELL. The **tell-and-sell** or directive interview lets subordinates know how well they are doing and sells them on the merits of setting specific goals for improvement if needed. This efficient type of interview is also effective in improving performance, especially for subordinates with little desire for participation. It should be noted though that while this type of interview may be most appropriate in providing evaluation, subordinates may become frustrated in trying to convince their superiors to listen to justifications for their performance levels.

TELL AND LISTEN. The **tell-and-listen** interview follows no rigid format but requires that raters should prepare questions as well as possess questioning and listening skills. The interview provides subordinates with a chance to participate and establish a dialogue with their superiors. The purpose of tell-and-listen interviews is to communicate supervisors' perceptions of subordinates' strengths and weaknesses and let the subordinates respond to those perceptions. The superiors summarize and paraphrase the responses of their subordinates, but generally fail to establish goals for performance improvement. Consequently, the subordinates may feel better but their performance may not change.

PROBLEM SOLVING. Because of the weaknesses of the approaches described above, some raters view the appraisal interview as a forum in which to engage in a **problem-solving interview** strategy with their subordinates. Here, an active and open dialogue is established: perceptions are shared and solutions to problems or differences are presented, discussed, and sought. Goals for improvement are also mutually established. This type of interview is generally more difficult for most superiors to conduct, thus, training in problem solving is usually necessary and beneficial.

MIXED INTERVIEW. The **mixed interview** is a combination of the tell-and-sell and problem-solving interviews. It can be used effectively when raters are trained and when they possess the appropriate skills to carry out the multiple purposes of the interview; namely, to make the transition from one type of interview to the other. As explained earlier, it is desirable to use the tell-and-sell interview for evaluation and the problem-solving one for development, but separate interviews for each purpose may not be feasible. Consequently, a single mixed interview may accomplish both purposes. The interview may begin with the subordinate listening to the superior's appraisal, followed by a participative discussion of what and how performance improvements can be made (problem solving), and conclude with agreed-upon goals for improvement.

A mixed interview may certainly prove to be an effective format by which to structure an interview, but overall interview effectiveness is dependent on more than simply following the format. In addition to the steps to be undertaken prior to the interview, a very important feature is the way in which effective feedback is communicated.

> ## ENHANCING INTERVIEW EFFECTIVENESS

Whether negative or positive, feedback is not always easy to provide. Fortunately, several characteristics of effective feedback have been determined. They include:

1. *Effective feedback is specific rather than general.* Telling someone that he or she is domineering is probably not as useful as saying, "Just now you were not listening to what I said, but I felt I either had to agree with your arguments or face attack from you."

2. *Effective feedback is focused on behaviour rather than on the person.* It is important to refer to what a person does rather than to what that person seems to be. Thus, a superior might say that a person talked more than anyone else at a meeting, rather than saying that he or she is a loudmouth. The former allows for the possibility of change; the latter implies a fixed personality trait.

3. *Effective feedback also takes into account the needs of the receiver.* Feedback can be destructive when it serves only the evaluator's needs and fails to consider those of the person on the receiving end. It should be given to help, not to hurt.

4. *Effective feedback is directed toward behaviour that the receiver can change.* Frustration only increases when people are reminded of shortcomings over which they have no control, or a physical characteristic they can do nothing about. At an extreme, workers may experience *learned helplessness*, in which they give up trying to perform well because they know of no way to perform adequately.

5. *Feedback is most effective when it is solicited rather than imposed.* To get the most benefit, receivers should formulate questions for the evaluator to answer and actively seek feedback.

6. *Effective feedback involves sharing information rather than giving advice.* Thus receivers are free to decide for themselves on the changes to make in accordance with their own needs.

7. *Effective feedback is well timed.* In general, immediate feedback is most useful when it is provided constructively and directed toward recent behaviours.

8. *Effective feedback concerns limited information.* Though an evaluator may have much information, he or she should provide only as much as the receiver can use. Overloading a person with feedback reduces the possibility that he or she will use it effectively. An evaluator who gives more than can be used is more often than not satisfying some personal need, rather than helping the other person.

9. *Effective feedback concerns what is said or done and how—not why.* Telling people what their motivations or intentions are tends to alienate them and contributes to a climate of resentment, suspicion, and distrust; it does not contribute to learning or development. If appropriate for the situation, the evaluator can express uncertainty regarding the receiver's motives or intent, and ask for an explanation. It is not constructive to assume knowledge of why a person says or does something.

10. *Effective feedback is checked to ensure clear communication.* One way of doing this is to have the receiver try to rephrase the feedback, to see if it corresponds to what the evaluator had in mind. No matter what the intent, feedback is often threatening and, thus, subject to considerable distortion or misinterpretation.

Even with the most effective feedback, follow-up is essential to ensure that the behavioural contract negotiated during the interview is fulfilled. Because changing behaviours is hard work, many supervisors tend to neglect follow-up by placing the agreement on the back burner and re-examining it just prior to the next appraisal period. In contrast, effective managers verify that incumbents develop a strategy for improvement, and if results are realized, reinforcement should follow.

ANALYZING PERFORMANCE PROBLEMS

Designing effective PASs, conducting effective interviews, and providing effective feedback will all increase the likelihood of an effective PA. They will not, however, eliminate performance problems. In the best case, an effective PAS may aid organizations in spotting performance problems and in developing strategies to solve them.

Improving performance is a process of identifying performance deficiencies or gaps, understanding their causes, and then developing strategies to remove those deficiencies.

Identifying Performance Gaps

As discussed in the previous chapter, employee job performance is appraised in terms of behaviours, outcomes, and goals. These serve not only to determine performance, but also to identify performance gaps. To do so, however, they are used somewhat differently. For example, suppose that an employee had a performance goal of reducing the scrap rate by 10 percent, but only reduced it by 5 percent; there is a 5 percent performance gap. The discrepancy between actual performance and set goals can be used to spot performance gaps. This method is valid as long as the goals are measurable and are not contradictory.

Another method of identifying performance gaps is by *comparing* subordinates, units, or departments with one another. Organizations with several divisions often measure the overall performance of each one by comparing it with all the others. The divisions that are ranked on the bottom become identified as problem areas, i.e., they have performance gaps. Whether ranking individuals or units, identifying performance gaps by comparisons does not provide an effective diagnosis of the cause of the performance gaps.

The other method by which gaps can be identified is *comparisons over time*. For example, a manager who sold 1,000 compact disks (CDs) last month but only 800 CDs this month appears to have a performance gap. This method also does not identify the cause of the gap. The month during which 1,000 CDs were sold may have been at the peak of the buying season. Or, the month during which only 800 CDs were sold may have been when the employee had to attend an important conference vital to longer-run CD sales.

Before examining the processes used by managers for determining the causes of performance deficiencies, it is useful to discuss determinants of employee performance. Exhibit 10.2 illustrates that an employee's behaviour directly influencing performance is complex because it is affected by diverse variables, experiences, and events. The factors that determine behaviour fall into three major categories: (1) individual variables (i.e., abilities and skills, background variables, and demographic variables); (2) psychological variables (i.e., perception, attitudes, personality, learning, and motivation); and (3) organizational variables (i.e., resources available, leadership, reward system, structure, and job design).

Determining the Causes of Performance Deficiencies

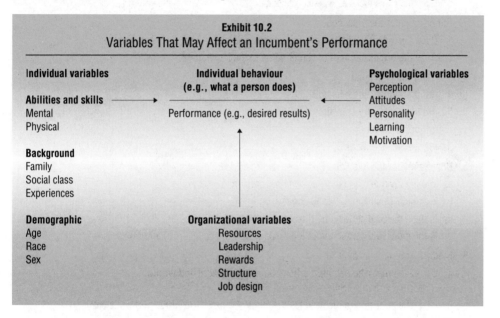

Exhibit 10.2
Variables That May Affect an Incumbent's Performance

Individual variables	Individual behaviour (e.g., what a person does)	Psychological variables
Abilities and skills →	Performance (e.g., desired results) ←	Perception
Mental		Attitudes
Physical		Personality
		Learning
Background		Motivation
Family		
Social class		
Experiences		
Demographic	**Organizational variables**	
Age	Resources	
Race	Leadership	
Sex	Rewards	
	Structure	
	Job design	

The determinants of behaviour identified in Exhibit 10.2 can lead supervisors to ask specific questions regarding the causes of performance deficiencies:

1. Does the employee have the skills and abilities to perform the job?
2. Does the employee have adequate resources to perform the job?
3. Is the employee aware of the performance problem?
4. When and/or under what circumstances did the performance problem surface?
5. What is the reaction of the employee's co-workers to the performance problem?
6. What can the manager *do* to help alleviate the performance problem?
7. Does the employee have the right attitudes/motivation to perform on the job?

A more systematic approach by which to analyze performance deficiencies is shown in Exhibit 10.3. Here the manager can utilize a standard checklist in the process of determining the likely causes for a performance deficiency.

Strategies to improve performance can be categorized into two groups: (1) those implemented to *reduce or control* actual deficiencies, and (2) those implemented to *prevent* actual deficiencies from occurring. Although many strategies are implemented on both bases, they are discussed here under two categories: positive reinforcement strategies and negative behavioural strategies.

STRATEGIES FOR IMPROVING PERFORMANCE

Exhibit 10.3
Checklist for Identifying Performance Problems

Check which of the following factors affecting an individual's performance or behaviour apply to the situation that you are analyzing.

	Yes	No
1. Skills, knowledge, and aptitudes of the individual	—	—
a. does the individual have the skills to do as expected?	—	—
b. Has the individual performed previously as expected?	—	—
2. Personality, interests, and preferences of the individual	—	—
a. Does the individual have the personality or interest to perform as expected?	—	—
b. Does the individual clearly perceive what is actually involved in performing as expected?	—	—
3. Opportunity for the individual	—	—
a. Does the individual have a chance to grow and use valued skills and abilities?	—	—
b. Does the organization offer career paths to the individual?	—	—
4. Goals for the individual	—	—
a. Are there goals established?	—	—
b. Are the goals very specific?	—	—
c. Are the goals clear?	—	—
d. Are the goals difficult?	—	—
5. Uncertainty for the individual	—	—
a. Is the individual certain about what rewards are available?	—	—
b. Is the individual certain about what to do?	—	—
c. Is the individual certain about what others expect?	—	—
d. Is the individual certain about job responsibilities and levels of authority?	—	—
6. Feedback to the individual	—	—
a. Does the employee get information about what is right and wrong (quality or quantity) with performance?	—	—
b. Does the information received tell the employee how to improve performance?	—	—
c. Does the employee get information frequently?	—	—
d. Is there a delay between the time when the employee performs and when he or she receives information on that performance?	—	—
e. Can the information easily be interpreted by the employee?	—	—
7. Consequences to the individual	—	—
a. Is it punishing to do as expected (immediate)?	—	—
b. Is it punishing to do as expected (long-term)?	—	—
c. Do more positive consequences result from taking alternative action (immediate)?	—	—
d. do more positive consequences result from taking alternative action (long-term)?	—	—
e. Are there no apparent consequences of performing as desired?	—	—
f. Are there no positive consequences of performing as desired?	—	—
8. Power for the individual	—	—
a. Can the individual mobilize resources to get the job done?	—	—
b. Can the individual influence others to get them to do what is needed?	—	—
c. Is the individual highly visible to others higher up in the organization?	—	—

Source: Adapted from Robert F. Mager and Peter Pipe, *Analyzing Performance Problems* (Belmont, Calif.: David S. Lake Publishers, (1984). Used with permission.

If subordinates exhibit job behavioural deficiencies, a positive reinforcement strategy may be effective. The positive approach to improvement involves efforts to encourage desirable behaviour by establishing behavioural criteria and setting up reward systems that are contingent upon the successful execution of the desired behaviour. Implementing this strategy requires the development of accurate behavioural measures of performance. This can be done using the critical incident technique to identify critical behaviours of effective and ineffective performance described before. If the organization already uses a behaviour-based appraisal form such as the BARS or the BOS, these can be used instead of the critical incident technique. Use of behavioural criteria should help eliminate many rating errors, thus improving the validity of the appraisals.

Positive Reinforcement Strategies

Once these behavioural criteria are established, subordinates should be made aware of them. Next, goals should be established for each behavioural dimension and rewards specified for goal attainment. To obtain maximum benefit from the goal setting process, the goals should be relatively challenging, specific, clear, and acceptable to the subordinates.

As with all incentive systems, a basic premise of positive reinforcement is that behaviour can be understood and modified by its consequences. That is, performance is elicited because of the consequence of obtaining rewards. In this case, the consequences of behaving well are not monetary rewards, but this need not be the case all the time.

A positive organizational control strategy used specifically to reduce absenteeism is called **earned time**. Earned time is a new approach to the way paid absence is accumulated and used. Under earned time, employees have more of a choice in the way they use their paid off-time. Thus the responsibility for the use of earned time is their own. Accumulating earned time depends on the preferences of each employee. Rather than divide benefits into specific numbers of days for vacation and personal leave, sick leave, or short-term disability, earned time lumps these days into one package. These days can be used for a variety of purposes, including a cash payment at the time of voluntary termination. Earned time is available for use as soon as it is "earned" on the job. Earned time, in effect, is "no-fault absence."

The essence of the program is that the number of earned-time days for which an employee may receive a cash payment is less than the previous total of sick, vacation, jury duty, and all other benefit days combined. For example, the previous combined total may be divided by two, three, or four to get the earned time. And earned times are available to use without having to meet a plethora of special requirements. The program's prime advantages are: (1) reduction in unplanned absences, (2) reduction in employee–supervisory conflict over legitimacy of absences and individual responsibility, and (3) flexibility for use of time to suit individual priorities.

Unlike positive behavioural strategies, which seek to encourage desirable behaviour patterns through systems of reward, negative strategies seek to discourage unwanted behaviour by either punishing it or ignoring it. A negative strategy is used in many organizations because of its ability to achieve relatively immediate results. Punishments can include material consequences, such as a cut in pay, a disciplinary layoff without pay, a demotion, or, ultimately, termination. More common punishments are interpersonal and include oral reprimands and nonverbal cues, such as frowns, grunts, and aggressive body language.

Negative Behavioural Strategies

Punishment (discipline) is an effective management tool for the following reasons:

- It alerts the marginal employee to the fact that his or her low performance is not going to be tolerated and that a change in behaviour is warranted.
- It has vicarious reinforcing power. When one person is punished, it signals other employees regarding expected performance and behavioural conduct.
- If the discipline is viewed as appropriate by other employees, it may increase their motivation, morale, and performance.

While discipline strategies are the most common and most favoured absence control techniques among HR managers, they do have several negative side effects. Extensive use of discipline, for example, leads to an increase in expensive, time-consuming grievances that are stressful to handle.[4]

Because it is the immediate supervisor or manager who plays the major role in administering discipline, to increase its effectiveness the HR department and the organization should:

- Allow managers and supervisors to help select their own employees.
- Educate managers and supervisors about the organization's disciplinary policies and train them to administer these policies.
- Set up standards that are equitable to employees and that can easily and consistently be implemented by managers and supervisors.

By taking these steps, an organization not only reduces the likely negative effects generally associated with discipline, but it helps ensure that employee rights are respected (discussed further in Chapter 15). This is further ensured with the establishment of fair work rules and work policies consistently applied and enforced.

No organization can operate safely and efficiently without *work rules and work policies.* Generally, employers make the rules and policies, supervisors enforce them, and employees follow them. But no employer has a completely free hand to establish any rules or policies he or she wishes. Work rules and policies are really part of the internal discipline system.

Work rules and policies must be reasonably related to appropriate management goals to be effective, and they should also be effectively communicated. The rules and policies designed and enforced must not result in an unfair, adverse impact against any group of employees, and the rules and policies cannot violate acts and court decisions defining employee rights to job security. Furthermore, these rules and policies should embrace the notion of progressive discipline and respect due process (discussed in Chapter 15).

In other words, the rules and policies:

- must apply equally to all employees, regardless of race, religion, national origin, sex, age, or disability;
- must be clearly stated;
- must be enforced objectively;
- should reflect the information necessary to prove equal application and enforcement of work rules.

It pays an organization to be consistent in the enforcement of its rules and policies. It also pays an organization to provide other strategies to reduce undesirable behaviours that influence job performance and absenteeism.

The negative effects of discipline and other negative behavioural strategies can be reduced by incorporating several *hot stove* principles, including:

- *Provide ample and clear warning.* Many organizations have clearly defined steps of disciplinary action. For example, the first offence might elicit an oral warning; the second offence, a written warning; the third offence, a disciplinary layoff; the fourth offence, discharge.
- *Administer the discipline as quickly as possible.* If a long time elapses between the inappropriate behaviour and the negative consequence, the employee may not know what the consequence is for.
- *Administer the same discipline for the same behaviour for everyone, every time.* Discipline has to be administered fairly and consistently.

- *Administer the discipline impersonally*. Discipline should be based on a specific behaviour, not a specific person.[5]

Helping incumbents, especially the problem ones, improve their work performance is a tough job. It is easy to get frustrated and to wonder if you are just spinning your wheels. Even when we want our efforts to work, they sometimes fail. Still, when you conclude that "nothing works," you are really saying that it is no longer worth your time and energy to help the employee improve. This conclusion should not be made in haste because the organization has already invested a great deal of time and money in the selection, and possibly training, of the problem employee. However, some situations require a more dramatic intervention, if for instance:

When Nothing Else Works

- Performance actually deteriorates;
- There is only marginal improvement in the problem behaviour, which is still causing the organization to lose money or reducing the morale of other employees;
- Drastic changes in behaviour occur immediately following the intervention, but it is gradually regressing to the previous condition.

If, after repeated warnings and counselling, performance does not improve, then four last recourses are available:

1. *Transferring*. Sometimes there just is not a good match between the employee and the job. If the employee has useful skills and abilities, it may be beneficial to transfer him or her. The underlying assumption, of course, is that the employee's skill deficiency in the current job would have little or no impact on performance in the new position.
2. *Restructuring*. Sometimes performance suffers because the employee finds his or her particular job (or job environment) unpleasant or stressful. For these situations, the solution may be in redesigning the job, rather than replacing the incumbent. (More can be found on this option in Chapter 13.)
3. *Neutralizing*. Neutralizing a problem employee involves restructuring that employee's job in such a way that his or her areas of needed improvement have as little impact as possible. Because group morale may suffer when an ineffective employee is given special treatment, *neutralizing should be avoided* whenever possible. However, it is a fact of organizational life that neutralizing may be practical when the firing process is time-consuming and cumbersome or when an employee is close to retirement. In neutralizing the employee, a manager should not harass the employee, hoping that he or she will quit or transfer, but instead should assign the employee noncritical tasks in which he or she can be productive.
4. *De-hiring*. While HR policies vary across organizations and industries, de-hiring (i.e., firing) is generally warranted for dishonesty, chronic absenteeism, substance abuse (on the job), gross negligence, and insubordination. Unfortunately, de-hiring, even for legitimate reasons, is an unpleasant task. In addition to administrative hassles, documentation, and other paperwork involved, supervisors often feel guilty about being the "bad guy." And the thought of sitting down with an employee and delivering the bad news makes most supervisors anxious. As a result, they continue to put off the firing and justify it by saying that they won't be able to find a better replacement. Still, when one considers the consequences of errors, drunkenness, and accidents on the job, de-hiring may be cost effective.

Employee
Assistance
Programs

Employee assistance programs (EAPs) are designed specifically to assist those with chronic personal problems that hinder their job performance and attendance. They are often used with employees who are alcoholics, have drug dependency problems, suffer from stress-related illnesses, or have severe domestic problems. Since these problems may be, in part, caused by the job, many Canadian employers are taking the lead in establishing EAPs to help affected workers.

PREVALENCE OF EAPs. According to numerous sources, there has been a robust growth of EAPs in Canada over the last two decades, although there is no clear agreement as to their exact number. According to one source, roughly 10 percent of the Canadian workforce is covered by this type of program. In an interview published in *Employee Assistance Quarterly*, it has been estimated that 15 percent of Canadian workplaces have EAPs, affiliation with EAPs, or affiliation with EAP consortia.[6] In a survey conducted in Ontario by the Addiction Research Foundation, out of a sample of worksites with fifty or more employees, it was found that 16.1 percent of the worksites had EAPs; these worksites comprised some 710,000 employees, who constituted 27.3 percent of all the employees whose worksites were surveyed. The study also established that approximately 53 percent of the worksites with over 500 employees had EAPs, while only 6 percent of the worksites with fifty to ninety-nine employees had EAPs. Furthermore, government, health, and education services were found to be more likely to have EAPs, whereas the construction and retail trade sectors were found to be under-represented.[7]

While EAPs are increasing for a number of reasons, the principal one relates to "problem" performance. *The Financial Post* reported for 1988 that 65 to 80 percent of employee terminations were due to personal factors rather than technical ones.[8] As a result of a considerable rise in the incidence of mental and emotional difficulties (e.g., divorce, substance abuse, single parenthood, stress, depression) within the workforce, many companies have come to realize that instituting an EAP may serve the interests of both management and employees.

Some of the reasons for the increased interest and popularity of these programs over the last twenty years include: federal and/or provincial legislation, endorsement by organized labour (Canadian Labour Congress), realization by businesses that EAPs can be used as cost saving and productivity enhancement tools, a growing appreciation that a genuine people orientation in the workplace is intimately related to corporate success, and, finally, the increasing complexity of our society.

SCOPE AND PURPOSES OF EAPs. It is important to note that EAPs developed with different purposes in mind will have different goals and definitions of success. Nonetheless, some of the advantages expected to be gained through implementation of EAPs are:

- Demonstrating a caring attitude to employees;
- Helping troubled employees constructively;
- Promoting wellness;
- Reducing health risks;
- Monitoring and improving the quality of life of both employees and their families;
- Improving employee morale;
- Containing health-care costs;
- Improving productivity and profits;
- Reducing withdrawal behaviours (i.e., accidents, tardiness, absenteeism, and turnover);
- Reducing grievances and arbitration cases;
- Limiting employer liability;

- Enabling better decisions to be made;
- Resolving management problems.

These advantages can be categorized as either "beneficial to the employee" (e.g., reducing health risks, promoting wellness, improving quality of life), or "beneficial to the employer" (e.g., improving productivity and profits, resolving management problems, limiting employer liability). Some advantages apply to both parties (e.g., improving employee morale, helping troubled employees constructively, etc.).

The literature on EAPs suggests that, as this fairly new support system for workers has developed, its purpose has been shifting somewhat from programs for improving productivity to a more comprehensive employer benefit. These changes have profound implications for the way EAPs are organized, staffed, and designed to function.

WHO USES EAPs? A survey aimed at determining the differences between users and nonusers of EAPs noted the following:

1. *Demographics of nonusers:* Employees who did not utilize EAPs were (a) from middle and upper management and professional occupations (73 percent), (b) 50 years of age or older (61 percent), (c) males (42 percent), and (d) those suffering from high job stress (79 percent).

2. *Perceptions of nonusers*: The nonusers expressed the following attitudes, beliefs, and/or feelings: (a) denial of a problem or of a need for services (11 percent), (b) feeling of self-reliance (10 percent), (c) belief that EAP use would devaluate them (7 percent), (d) belief that their EAP was for others (6 percent), (e) fear that their EAP was not confidential (6 percent), (f) lack of information about their EAP (6 percent), (g) resistance to change (5 percent), (h) perception of supervisors as unsupportive of EAP use (5 percent), and (i) concern about their job security (5 percent).

3. *Perceptions of users*: The EAP users expressed the following attitudes, beliefs, and/or feelings: (a) confidence in the services provided by the EAP (20 percent), (b) openness to change (10 percent), (c) desire to seek services because of peer referral (10 percent), (d) perception of the EAP as free and convenient (7 percent), (e) belief that supervisors support EAP use (6 percent), (f) belief that EAP use is an alternative to job loss (5 percent), and (g) perception of a need for help (5 percent).[9]

ASSESSING EAPs. It has been argued that a program needs to be assessed for its cost-effectiveness and efficiency, and the results of this exercise should be made known to all members of the organization. Case records and office records should be designed to facilitate data retrieval. Evaluation instruments must be developed and implemented as the program begins. The evaluation should gather data relating to work performance and should contain control groups. However, conducting a proper evaluation amounts sometimes to a "mission impossible" because of the confidentiality issues intrinsic in such programs. In such cases, an adequate evaluation can be achieved using a third party. At any rate, there are those who believe that no one should ever risk compromising the confidentiality of EAPs for statistical data.

At least four areas are regarded as problematic when examining the various EAP evaluation programs:

1. *Staffing*: Most program administrators are not trained to carry out a proper evaluation procedure.

2. *Preparation*: Very few programs include an evaluation phase as part of the initial planning process.

3. *Standardization*: Because of the lack of standardized measures and definitions it is almost impossible to compare one program with another. Success is not a tangible concept.

4. *Data collection*: For most organizations the available data are less than adequate for conducting a meaningful evaluation.

In today's competitive business environment, questions of economic benefit often arise. While statistical and clinical significance are of critical importance for EAP researchers, decision makers within a company may be most interested in financial significance. Therefore, the most common and basic question being raised by many groups is: "Does an EAP save the company money?" Answers to this key question can be obtained through the following methods:

1. *Cost-containment activities*: These activities are used to reduce expenditures or control rising costs. Typically, they do not focus on long-term issues. Cost-containment is a response to providing services with limited resources, which operates on the premises that there is waste in the system and that by mandating maximum amounts of funding to be spent, costs can be controlled. Areas where cost-containment strategies are used include: prepaid services, claims/utilization review, use of preferred providers, use of outpatient as opposed to inpatient care, increasing deductibles, mandated length of stay, and case management.

2. *Cost-offset or cost-impact analysis*: These types of analysis are used to identify areas where cost savings occur as a result of providing a service. They do not compare models nor is a dollar estimate of the savings required. They seek to demonstrate that there is an economic return when EAPs are available because of reductions in illness, unemployment, legal problems, etc. Cost-offset or cost-impact analysis strategies include: showing the percentage reduction in absenteeism after referral by the EAP, and following areas that are not directly and easily converted into dollars on a balance sheet, e.g., legal problems, productivity, and employee morale.

3. *Cost-effectiveness analysis*: This is used to calculate the cost of obtaining some desired outcome. The analysis will typically provide a ratio of the cost of obtaining a result divided by the number of desired outcomes (not necessarily expressed in dollars). It can compare different ways of achieving the same objective. It has been argued that this technique is more appropriate for measuring less accessible results. Also, it may be even more useful to organizations evaluating whether to have an EAP or, if this decision has already been made, evaluating what type of program would be most useful (contract or in-house). This type of analysis is conducted prior to making the final decision and is known as ex-ante cost-effectiveness analysis. An example of cost-effectiveness analysis is comparing inpatient and outpatient programs by dividing the real costs of each by the number of improved clients.

4. *Cost-benefit analysis*: This is used to compare the tangible and intangible benefits of a program with its costs (directly and indirectly). It requires consideration of all long-term and related benefits and costs. It can be used to compare very different programs. Cost–benefit analysis is applied more often in technical and industrial areas than in human service fields. An example of the issues considered is a comparison of an employee hypertension screening program with an alcoholism treatment program.

OUTCOMES AND STATISTICS. The following outcomes and statistics characterize the trends in EAPs. The data show a divergence in estimates concerning return on investment, although the balance is positive according to all accounts. Outcomes reported include:

• "A good EAP has a very favourable cost–benefit ratio—usually at least $3 saved for each $1 invested."[10]

- "Of a large number of U.S companies consulted, the minimum saving claimed from the operation of EAPs—arising from decreases in absence levels and increases in job performance, was $3 for every $1 spent."[11]

- The National Institute on Alcohol Abuse and Alcoholism conservatively calculates a $5.78 return on every $1 invested in an EAP.

- Consulting companies promise large increases in worker productivity savings of up to $8 for each $1 spent with external EAPs.

- "The economic benefit in terms of return per dollar invested in EAPs is quite significant, with a range for 6:1 to as high as 16:1."[12]

Some researchers report that the mere presence of an EAP has been associated with:

- 30 to 60 percent fewer employee accidents, with 40 to 80 percent reductions in on- and off-site accidents;

- 33 to 52 percent decrease in number of sick days or disability units;

- 43 to 50 percent reduction in absenteeism;

- 50 to 75 percent of treated alcoholic employees remaining abstinent for six to twelve months;

- 79 percent decrease in grievances.[13]

Actual performance savings have been reported for the following Canadian companies:

- Babcock and Wilcox Canada reduced employee absences for 950 employees from an average of twenty-two days to twelve days as a result of an EAP. Their reported savings were $400,000

- As a result of their EAP, Warner–Lambert Canada Ltd. estimates savings of between $180,000 and $200,000 per year. Reduced absenteeism accounted for 80 percent of the savings, while 20 percent was due to group insurance savings and reduced loss of production due to accidents. For every $1 spent on the EAP, they report a $7 to $10 saving.

- CanCare-Canada EAP Services Corporation reports the following in their brochure:
  - On average, employees with emotional problems annually cost employers $1,622 each.
  - 65 percent of all terminations are related to emotional problems.
  - The rate of return of employees to satisfactory levels of job performance has been identified at 60 to 70 percent.
  - A 68 percent decline in sickness and disability cases has occurred over a five-year period.
  - Alcohol-related accidents have been reduced by 85 percent.
  - Experience shows that compared to their co-workers, troubled employees have: two to four times the absenteeism rate, six times the accident rate, three times the sickness benefits.

- General Motors Canada Ltd. in its first year on an EAP reported savings of $81,000 in absentee costs and sickness and accident benefits for 104 employees. General Motors reported a return of $5 for every dollar invested in their program. They have had over 10,000 employees go through their program and the study found that they were saving $3,700 a year for each employee, for a total annual saving of $37 million. General Motors reported a 40 percent drop in absenteeism as well as a 50 percent drop in accidents and disciplinary problems after instituting an EAP.

To change the habits of chronically absent employees, some companies have devised a counselling program that stresses problem-solving and goal-setting techniques. This

Counselling and
Performance
Enhancement

approach focuses on the 5 to 10 percent of the workforce that has a history of absenteeism. Before beginning the actual counselling with individual employees, supervisors should:

- Identify the consistently worst offenders. Make a list of all employees who have a record of repeated absences, regardless of the presumed legitimacy or the underlying reasons for missing work.
- Centralize the absenteeism data. Records and information should be accumulated, analyzed, and maintained in one central location.
- Collect long-term data. Absenteeism records on individuals should be kept for a sufficiently long period to show that a clear pattern exists.

Once the decision is made to meet with an employee, supervisors should:

- Examine the attendance record with the employee.
- Be sure the employee is aware of the severity of the problem, as well as the organization's attendance standards.
- Prepare a brief, accurate memo at the session's end outlining the problem, noting the reasons given by the employee, and specifying whether or not the employee responded with a desire to improve.

If the first session has not produced a significant change, a second counselling session should be scheduled. Participants in this session should include the worker's supervisor, the employee, a union representative (if applicable), and higher management officials. An upper-level manager should be present to ensure that *due process* protection is provided for the employee. Results of the second counselling session should be documented.

If the employee shows no improvement after the second session, another session can be held, which also should include a high-level manager. At this stage it should be made clear that the responsibility for meeting the expected standard of attendance, and thereby continuing employment, rests with the employee. The employee should be allowed to take off a day with pay in order to decide whether he or she wishes to resign or to commit to a long-term program of positive improvement. If there is no sign of improvement after this step, it may be necessary to discharge the employee.

Whether or not employee counselling is an appropriate remedy depends upon an analysis of the behavioural determinants. This is also true for the other strategies. For example, if the undesirable performance is caused by a lack of positive reinforcement for desirable behaviour, attaching supervisory praise, organizational recognition, or monetary compensation to these behaviours may produce better results than counselling. If employees are not performing well due to a lack of information about their progress, increased feedback or the establishment of goals may be appropriate.

There are a variety of counselling and performance enhancement programs used by Canadian firms. The HRM in the News Vignette shows the role of the supervisor in reacting to employees' problems on the job. One should note the careful attention that should be paid when undertaking "sensitive yet firm" actions to remedy the situation. Another example of instituting a performance enhancement program is that of the Royal Victoria Hospital, one of the largest in the Montreal region. The experience of this organization is illustrated later on in the chapter.

TRENDS IN PA AND PERFORMANCE IMPROVEMENT

The purposes of PA are both evaluative and developmental. That is, appraisal information is used as input for making evaluation decisions, such as: (1) salary increases or decreases, (2) demotions, (3) layoffs, (4) promotions/transfers, and (5) terminations. Information is also used as input for developmental purposes including: (1) spotting training needs, (2) motivating employees to improve, (3) providing feedback, (4) counselling employees, and (5) spotting performance deficiencies. Although all organizations may not want to use PA for both of these purposes, all should be concerned with the legal requirements they must

HRM IN THE NEWS VIGNETTE

Handling Employees with Problems

The best way to deal with employees struggling with personal problems is to focus on job performance. Here are some guidelines:

- Some signals an employee may be having personal problems: emotional outbursts, a sudden decline in work performance, frequent absences and tardiness, or a sharp change in attitude.

- Take immediate action. Talk to the employee in private and keep it confidential. Be friendly, and sympathetic, but also make it clear you're the supervisor. Your role is to help employees do their best work and meet your organization's needs. Try to identify the issues causing the distress, but leave diagnosis to professional counsellors.

- Listen. Accept a troubled employee's feelings as facts; don't dismiss emotions with a comment like: "It's silly to feel that way." Don't assume talking and listening alone will fix problems. Troubled people improve by learning why their lives aren't working, and that's where professional help is needed.

- Give two messages to troubled employees: (1) This company wants to be supportive so you can get help; and (2) We still expect you to meet job performance standards. The second message is harsh. But it may be the only way to make sure employees know how important it is to solve the problem.

- You may have to do some counselling yourself if the employee's problems stem from work, such as problems with co-workers, reorganizations, layoffs, salary freezes, or job dissatisfaction. In such cases, listen to the employee's concerns with empathy and patience.

- If the employee won't acknowledge the problem, keep focusing on job performance. Cite specific instances when the employee did not meet standards.

- If the problem seems to involve a personality clash between two co-workers, try basic conflict resolution. Talk to each employee separately in a neutral place. Learn their perspectives. Then bring them together. Show them where they agree. Ask them what each could do to meet on middle ground.

- When employees cry or become emotionally unravelled at work, offer them some privacy so they won't "lose face" in front of co-workers. Acknowledge their emotions by saying you understand that what happened is upsetting them. If this is a first-time occurrence, you might suggest a long break or going home early. But don't budge on your standards.

Source: Feature article by P. Ancona, reprinted in the Management section of *The Montreal Gazette* 9 September 1991. Reproduced by permission of Scripps Howard News Service.

---

meet. When PA is used to serve evaluation and developmental purposes and to meet the legal requirements, it is affecting the bottom-line goals of the organization.

An important message of this chapter is that when subordinates are empowered and responsible for their behaviour, performance management becomes easier. An extension of this philosophy is self-management, which requires employees to manage their own behaviour. Other significant trends include the linkage between PA and performance management and the overall assessment of the PAS.

Self-management is a relatively new approach to resolving performance discrepancies, which teaches people to exercise control over their own behaviour. Self-management begins by having people assess their *own* problems and set specific, but individual, goals in relation to those problems. Once goals are set, the employees discuss ways in which the environment facilitates or hinders goal attainment. The challenge here is to develop strategies that eliminate blocks to performance success. In other words, self-management teaches people to observe their own behaviour, compare their outputs to their goals, and administer their own reinforcement to sustain goal commitment and performance.[14]

Self-Management

The power of self-management in organizations is only beginning to be recognized. In a recent study, twenty unionized government employees with habitual attendance problems identified and learned to overcome personal obstacles to regular attendance. During eight 30-minute one-on-one sessions, they identified the reasons for using sick leave, the conditions that elicited and maintained the problem behaviour, and, more importantly, identified specific coping strategies. This completed the self-assessment phase of the program. Next, distinct goals were set to increase attendance by a specified amount over a specific time period. These were coupled with the development of individual day-by-day strategies to help attain the long-term goal. The employees were then taught to record their own attendance, the reason for missing work, and the steps that were to be followed to get to work. Finally, they identified powerful rewards and punishments that could be self-administered. The results showed a 13 percent improvement for these employees in comparison to others with similar problems. A follow-up study showed that the improvement in attendance persisted for over a year.[15]

While a self-management strategy has been proved effective in resolving the problem of chronic absenteeism, its usefulness in remedying other performance problems remains to be seen.

Performance Management and PA

The challenge for the future lies in the capacity of organizations to move beyond PA as a primary focus of performance improvement activities to what is called "performance management." Successful performance management depends on four classical activities: directing behaviour, energizing and gaining commitment to action, controlling behaviour, and rewarding desired behaviour.[16] Although some conceptual differences can be made among them, in practice all four activities are closely related. For example, although some key rewards are not administered until the end of the cycle, the prospect of receiving them is a primary energizing factor. Similarly, the appraisal process supplies some of the information required for feedback in the controlling process.

DIRECTING. Because employees cannot give equal attention to every facet of work behaviour, it is necessary to alert them to those areas that provide the biggest payoff for the organization. Furthermore, in a good performance management program, the superior is able to focus on the identification of individual responsibilities and the specific job behaviours associated with fulfilling these responsibilities. The main thrust of directing is addressing very clearly the issues of *what* and *how*.

ENERGIZING. Two factors are linked to high performance motivation: (1) goal setting, and (2) participation. Thus, a performance management system that provides for these factors has a greater likelihood of eliciting a commitment from employees to maintain motivation over time.

CONTROLLING. This activity is most often associated with performance management because it encompasses the PA process. However, it should be mentioned that by exclusively focusing on narrow measurable aspects of performance, organizations may lose sight of the global direction they should pursue. In other words, most PASs are being evaluated in the short term, yet a strategic long-term view should be considered as well. Too often managers push themselves to the limit to obtain annual impressive results, just to find out that at the end of the process they become ill (mentally or physically), and obviously will not be in a position to maintain the same level of performance in the future. Thus, controlling should include a long-term diagnosis alongside the traditional periodic appraisals.

REWARDING. This is the final element in the performance management process. One of the "hottest" items on the agenda of most compensation specialists is "pay for performance" systems. In spite of their popularity, organizations realize that most plans fall short of this objective. The principal reason for the failure of the plan is the limited budget allocated to "merit pay." Other reasons were discussed in Chapter 7.

Finally, it should be recognized that a successful performance management program is an ongoing process, and that constant fine tuning in the four elements mentioned above is necessary.

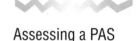

Assessing a PAS

Before assessing specific aspects of an organization's PAS, it may be useful to perform an overall assessment. It will quickly suggest how well the PAS is doing and may provide an added stimulus for a more specific assessment.

HR managers could ask members of the organization, both managers and nonmanagers, about specific aspects of the PAS, but this would be very time-consuming. An alternative is for both supervisors and subordinates to respond to a questionnaire such as the one shown in Exhibit 10.4. As indicated in the scoring of the questionnaire, there are the subcategories (A, B, C) and that sum to form an overall PAS assessment score. The three subcategories correspond to the major purposes of appraisal: Categories A and B assess the developmental purpose, and Category C assesses the evaluation purpose. Note that the assessment of the evaluation purpose includes the administrative features of appraisal, that is, whether PA records are maintained and how accessible they are. These features also facilitate the developmental purpose of PA.

By using this overall PAS assessment questionnaire, the organization can determine how effective, in general, its PAS is. Scores of 9 or 10 in each subcategory suggest the PAS serves its purpose well, while scores of 4 to 8 suggest average service, and scores of 2 or 3 suggest it does not serve its purpose well. Totalling the scores on the three subcategories results in an overall assessment of how well the purposes of appraisal are being attained. Scores of 26–30 suggest quite well, scores of 21–25, good, 11–20, average, and less than 11, quite poorly. Because of the breakdown of the forms, scores that indicate there is room for improvement (e.g., average scores or less) also highlight specific areas to be assessed in depth.

SPECIFIC PAS ASSESSMENT. The specific assessment of an organization's PAS requires the examination of several aspects of the entire system. Answers to the following questions can provide an assessment of the specific components:

- What purpose does the organization want its PAS to serve?
- Do the appraisal forms really elicit the information needed to serve these purposes? Are these forms compatible with the jobs for which they are being used, that is, are they job-related? Are the forms based upon behaviours or outcomes that might be included in a critical incidents job analysis?
- Are the appraisal forms designed to minimize errors and ensure consistency?
- Are the appraisal processes effective? For example, are the appraisal interviews done effectively? Are goals established? Are they developed jointly? Do superiors and subordinates accept the appraisal process?
- Are superiors relatively free from task interference in doing performance appraisal? And, are superiors rewarded for conducting objective and thorough appraisals?
- Are the appraisals being implemented correctly? What procedures have been set up to ensure this? What supporting materials are available to aid superiors in appraising their subordinates?

Exhibit 10.4
Organizational Performance Appraisal Questionnaire Evaluation

Instructions

Respond to the following six statements by indicating the extent to which you agree (or disagree) that the statements accurately describe performance appraisal in your organization. Some statements refer to your experiences in appraising your subordinates' performance, others refer to your experiences in being appraised yourself. Try to reflect as accurately as you can the current conditions in your organization, based on your experiences.

SA = Strongly Agree	A = Agree	? = Neither Agree nor Disagree	D = Disagree
	SD = Strongly Disagree		

1. I have found my boss's appraisals to be very helpful in guiding my own career development progess. SA A ? D SD

2. The appraisal system we have here is of no use to me in my efforts toward developing my subordinates to the fullest extent of their capabilities. SA A ? D SD

3. Our performance appraisal system generally leaves me even more uncertain about where I stand after my appraisal than before. SA A ? D SD

4. The appraisal system we use is very useful in helping me to clearly communicate to my subordinates exactly where they stand. SA A ? D SD

5. When higher levels of management are making major decisions about management positions and promotions, they have access to and make use of performance appraisal records. SA A ? D SD

6. In making pay, promotion, transfer, and other administrative personnel decisions, I am not able to obtain past performance appraisal records that could help me to make good decisions. SA A ? D SD

Scoring

Use the following grid to determine point scores for each item by transferring your responses onto the grid. Place the number in the box at the bottom of each column, then add pairs of columns as indicated.

		Statement Number					
		1	2	3	4	5	6
Response	SA	5	1	1	5	5	1
	A	4	2	2	4	4	2
	?	3	3	3	3	3	3
	D	2	4	4	2	2	4
	SD	1	5	5	1	1	5

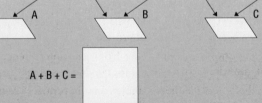

A + B + C =

- Do methods exist for reviewing and evaluating the effectiveness of the total system? Are there goals and objectives for the system? Are there systematic procedures for gathering data to measure how well the goals and objectives are being met?

By addressing these questions and taking corrective action where necessary, an organization's PAS is more likely to serve its purposes and the broader organizational HR goals of productivity, QWL, and legal compliance. An organization just beginning to design a PAS should incorporate the information produced by answering these questions into the initial design and implementation of the PAS.

HRM DYNAMICS
Performance Management in a Selected Canadian Organization

The Initiation of Performance Management at the Royal Victoria Hospital

Montreal's Royal Victoria Hospital initiated a performance management program in in 1988. In order to facilitate the planning, design, and implementation of the program, a full-time training counsellor was hired. As a first step, a needs analysis was carried out, which revealed that poor communication and lack of long-range planning were the principal determinants contributing to performance problems in the hospital. Another paramount concern was the need to develop a more valid and reliable PAS.

The first step in the program was to create management awareness and commitment to support changes in various HR functions, namely job analysis, performance appraisal and training, and to link these to the overall strategy and vision of the hospital. It was also decided to begin the program by concentrating on middle management.

Prior to designing a PAS, a thorough job analysis was conducted. Since strategic planning was one of the program goals, managers were asked to set their own performance objectives that feed into and support departmental and organizational goals. Consequently, a modified MBO approach was developed. The core of the MBO was a focus on **self-management** by middle managers in planning and evaluation whereby incumbents wrote or revised their own job description, set their own objectives, tapped superiors as a resource, and monitored and evaluated their own performance. The motto for the program was: **enabling** rather than **disabling** management.

This phase was followed by extensive training sessions. Managers were encouraged to adapt their own tools of performance management to suit their particular situations and needs. They were also taught how to set objectives, how to follow them up, and how to monitor success and incorporate changes as they occurred.

The next phase involved training the managers in conducting appraisal interviews, and in providing continual and timely feedback and constructive criticism to their subordinates. Training made use of films such as "Can you Spare a Moment?" and "Managing Problem People," both with John Cleese of Monty Python fame, as well as role-playing and role-modelling. Because managers in the public sector have limited control over pay decisions, training in the PA process focused primarily on developmental objectives

Currently, the Hospital is implementing its PAS. Recently, it expanded the training to senior management. The training for the latter revolves around the need for greater strategic planning and the support they may provide to the maintenance and further development of the performance management system.

Computer Applications

Some assessors are turning to computers to help them prepare for the appraisal interview. In one such case, a U.S.-based firm in Palo Alto, California, developed a program called *Performance Mentor*. Role-playing with the computer prior to the actual conduct of the appraisal interview may decrease managers' anxiety because it gives them guidance on how to prepare for the review. More particularly, this program has been found useful for inexperienced managers, because it helps them through the process in a very short time.[17]

S U M M A R Y

In this chapter two critical components of utilizing the PA data were discussed: feeding back the data to the subordinate via the PA interview, and spotting performance deficiencies and developing strategies for improvement.

It was suggested that, in providing effective feedback to subordinates, superiors should use the appropriate and specific performance data, that the purposes of evaluation and development should be served separately, that current and potential PA discussions should be separated, and that there should be upward or reciprocal appraisals. The effectiveness of the PA interview session in providing feedback can also be enhanced if the appraisals are conducted in a legally defensible way. To do this, the organization and the HR department must conduct evaluations on all employees, using only objective judgments whenever possible and letting subordinates review their appraisals and records.

Programs for spotting and correcting performance deficiencies were identified. Such programs begin with a determination of the causes. When these deficiencies are traced to employee motivation rather than ability, several programs designed either to control or prevent these behaviours can be developed and implemented. Emphasis has been placed on traditional strategies, which include the application of various systems of reinforcements. Additionally, two contemporary strategies have been described: EAPs, and performance enhancement programs.

The assessment of the entire PAS and specific components of it can increase its effectiveness. Such assessments are necessary to help determine how well the evaluational and developmental purposes are being met and if the legal considerations are being observed. On the basis of such assessments, revisions in current appraisal methods can be made and more effective strategies for improving performance can be developed and implemented. Once done, an organization has a much better basis upon which to make other HR decisions, particularly those associated with compensation and training and development.

P O S T S C R I P T

Competitiveness, international or domestic, is becoming increasingly critical to the success of Canadian business. A key element in it is managing the performance of the workforce. Many leading Canadian corporations view the PA as one of the most important tools in the management arsenal. According to Theodore F. Brophy, former chairman of GTE, an appraisal system complements the emergent strategic planning emphasis in all areas of the corporation."[18] However, establishing the linkage between PA and an organization's strategy is not easy. Decisions must be made regarding how tight and complete the linkage will be. For example, will appraisal practices be standardized across organizational units, or will each unit be free to develop its own system? Standardization allows comparison across units but may not provide the flexibility needed in large, diverse organizations.

Another issue is the security of the information. Questions need to be answered regarding who will have access to performance-related information and how that information will be stored (in a centralized system or in individual files). This is even a more problematic issue in the context of EAPs. How does the firm maintain confidentiality? Many EAPs do not have credible mechanisms (and policies) to keep all information strictly confidential. Hence organizations need to have, at least for the purpose of control, some statistics regarding users and the success rates of the counselling. Finding a formula that will satisfy the criterion of confidentiality and at the same time provide some control for the employer is highly problematic. Some organizations insist on having more professional information regarding the general nature of an employee's problems and a prognosis regarding success. It is generally acknowledged that the doubts of employees regarding the confidentiality of the system might result in an EAP being underused and subsequently becoming a failure.

These are two issues that require companies to make decisions pertaining to their PA system and processes. They exemplify the depth of probing needed to link appraisal processes to a corporation's strategic plan.

REVIEW AND ANALYSIS QUESTIONS

1. What are the inherent conflicts in a PAS? How can such conflicts be reduced?
2. What considerations are there in designing an effective PAS?
3. Suppose you have decided that an employee is not "working out" and must be fired. What PA approach would you use to support this decision? Why?
4. Identify and discuss the features of several different types of PA interviews.
5. What characteristics of the interview are likely to enhance and facilitate the effectiveness of PA?
6. What characteristics of feedback and goals inhibit acceptable levels of individual performance?
7. With what causes are performance deficiencies associated, and what are the respective strategies used to correct those performance deficits?
8. Briefly explain "positive reinforcement strategy" and provide an example of its use to improve performance.
9. Are negative behavioural strategies effective for remedying performance problems? What are their drawbacks?
10. What are the main features of EAPs? How can an organization measure their effectiveness?
11. What are the advantages of self-management for the organization? For the employee?

CASE STUDY

THE PAIN OF PERFORMANCE APPRAISAL

Joe Miller sat at his desk, looking over the appraisal form he had just completed on Bill Cox, one of his insurance underwriters. Bill was on his way to Joe's office for their annual review session. Joe dreaded these appraisal meetings, even when he did not have to confront employees with negative feedback.

Two years earlier, Standard Insurance Company, which had experienced very rapid growth, had decided to implement a formal appraisal system. All supervisors had been presented with the new appraisal form, which included five different subcategories, in addition to an overall rating.

Supervisors were asked to rate employees on each dimension using a scale from 1 (unacceptable) to 5 (exceptional). They were also advised to maintain a file on each employee into which they could drop notes on specific incidents of good or poor performance during the year to use as documentation when completing the appraisal form. They were told they could only give an overall rating of 1 or 5 if they had "substantial" documentation to back it up. Joe had never given one of these ratings because he was not diligent about recording specific incidents for each employee. He believed it was just too time-consuming to write up all the documentation necessary to justify such a rating. There were several employees in his department who deserved a 5 rating in Joe's opinion, but so far no one had complained about not receiving one.

Bill was one of Joe's exceptional workers. Joe had three or four specific examples of exceptional performance in Bill's file, but looking over the form he could not clearly identify the category in which they belonged. "Oh well," Joe said to himself, "I'll just give him 3s and 4s. I don't have to justify those, and Bill has never complained before." One of the categories was "Analyzing Work Materials." Joe had never understood what that meant or whether it was relevant for the job of insurance underwriter. He had checked 3 (satisfactory) for Bill, as he did on all the evaluations. He understood the meaning of the other categories—Quality of Work, Quantity of Work, Improving Work Methods, and Relationships with Co-workers—although he was confused as to what a 3 or a 4 indicated about each category.

Bill knocked on Joe's door and came in. Joe looked up and smiled. "Hi Bill. Sit down. Let's get through this thing so we can get back to work, OK?"

Case Questions

1. What problems do you see with the appraisal system Joe is using?
2. What are Bill's likely reactions to being told by Joe that he has scored 3s and 4s even though he is one of Joe's exceptional workers?
3. What suggestions do you have for improving the appraisal system?
4. What suggestions do you have for improving Joe?

NOTES

1. N. Napier and G. Latham, "Outcome Expectancies of People Who Conduct Appraisals," *Personnel Psychology* 39 (1986): 827–39.

2. For a discussion of the vanishing performance appraisal and other career issues, see D.T. Hall, *Careers in Organizations* (Glenview, Ill.: Scott, Foresman and Company, 1976).

3. H.H. Meyer, E. Kay, and J.R.P. French, Jr., "Split Roles in Performance Appraisal," *Harvard Business Review*, January–February 1965, 125.

4. G. Johns, "Did You Go to Work Today?" *Montreal Business Report* 4th Quarter (1980): 52–56; G. Johns, "Understanding and Managing Absence from Work," in *Canadian Readings in Personnel and Human Resource Management*, ed. S.L. Dolan and R.S. Schuler (St. Paul, Minn.: West Publishing Co., 1987), 324–36.

5. For an excellent discussion of the application of discipline in organizations, see R.D. Arvey and J.M. Ivancevich, "Punishment in Organizations: A Review, Propositions and Research Suggestions," *Academy of Management Review 5 (1980): 123–32;* W.C. Hamner and D.W. Organ, *Organizational Behaviour: An Applied Psychological Approach* (Dallas, Tex.: Business Publications, Inc., 1978), 73–88; R.J. Hart "Crime and Punishment in the Army," *Journal of Personality and Social Psychology* 36 (1978): 1456–71; J.P. Muczyk, E.B. Schwartz, and E.P. Smith, *First and Second Level Supervision* (Indianapolis, Ind.: Bobbs–Merrill, 1980); H.P. Sims, Jr., "Further Thought on Punishment in Organizations," *Academy of Management Review* 5 (1980): 133–38; R.J. House and M.L. Baetz, "Leadership: Some Empirical Generalizations and New Research Directions," in *Research in Organizational Behaviour*, Vol. 2, ed. B. Staw (Greenwich, Conn.: JAI Press, 1980); and G.R. Oldham, "The Motivational Strategies Used by Supervisors: Relationships to Effectiveness Indicators," *Organizational Behaviour and Human Performance 15* (1976): 66–86. Additional considerations in dealing with performance problems are presented in Chapter 15 on Employee Rights, especially the use of termination as a way of correcting gaps.

6. J. Santa-Barbara, "Characteristics of Some EAP Models and Their Consequences," *EAP Digest*, July–August and September–October 1984; L. Stennett-Brewer, "Interview: Anthea Steward—A Comparison of Canadian and U.S. EAPs," *Employee Assistance Quarterly* 2, 1 (1986): 87–97.

7. S. MacDonald and S. Dooley, *Ontario Worksites with 50 or More Employees: The Nature and Extent of EAPs, Programs and Worksite Characteristic* (London, Ont.: Addiction Research Foundation, University of Western Ontario, 1989).

8. W. Shepell, "Does Your EAP Pass the Scrutiny Test: Guidelines for Selecting an Employee Assistance Program," *Human Resource Professional*, 6 September 1989, 7–8.

9. A.C. Browne, "Employee Drug and Alcohol Use Estimates: Assessment Styles and Issues," *Employee Assistance Quarterly* 3, 3-4 (1988): 265–78.

10. T.R. Cowan, "Drugs and the Workplace: To Drug Test or Not to Test?" *Public Personnel Management* 16, 4 (1987): 313–22.

11. "Whitbread's Employee Counselling Programme," *Industrial Relations Review and Report*, 25 April 1989, 11–14.

12. R.P. Maiden, "Employee Assistance Programs: Issues for Social-Work Practice," *social Casework: The Journal of Contemporary Social Work* 68, 8 (1987): 503–6.

13. J.M. Jerrell and J.F. Rightmyer, "Evaluating Employee Assistance Programs: A Review of Methods, Outcomes, and Future Directions," *Evaluation and Program Planning* 5 (1982): 255–67.

14. C. Frayne and G. Latham, "Application of Social Learning Theory to Employee Self-Management of Attendance," *Journal of Applied Psychology* 72 (1987): 387–92; G. Latham and C. Frayne, "Self Management, Training for Increasing Job Attendance: A Follow Up and Replication," *Journal of Applied Psychology* 74 (1989): 411–16; and P. Karoly Pand F. Kafner, *Self Management and Behavior Change: From Theory to Practice (*New York: Pergamon Press, 1986).

15. Latham and Frayne, "Self Management," 411–16.

16. W.J. Heisler, W.D. Jones, and P.O. Benham, *Managing Human Resources Issues* (San Francisco: Jossey–Bass, 1988), Chapter 8.

17. P. Lewis, "Job performance set (Performance Mentor) aids managers: Bosses told how to handle interviews," *The Vancouver Sun*, 2 May 1990, D2.

18. Cited in R.S. Schuler and V.L. Huber, *Personnel and Human Resource Management*, 4th ed. (St. Paul, Minn.: West Publishing Co., 1990), 254.

CHAPTER ELEVEN

TRAINING AND DEVELOPMENT

KEYNOTE ADDRESS

E.R. (Rony) Israel
General Manager, Skill Dynamics Canada™
An IBM Canada Company

Education 2000: A Vision of Human Resource Performance

Our future view of HR performance is important in that, first, it will allow us to define our "destination" so that we can validate or fine-tune strategies and investments that we are making today. Second, we can define the dependencies that the education function will have on other functions. Third, the future vision will suggest starter projects where partnerships with other institutions, such as universities and colleges, can create "deliverables" that will help us reach our ultimate goal. Finally, this view provides an excellent basis for discussions with other leading companies with which we share ideas and trends in education and training.

WORKFORCE CHALLENGES

Demographic trends indicate labour shortages in major global job markets, increased world urbanization, and changing values in workforce participants. Corporate competitiveness and an accelerated pace of technological change abound. These will result in a shortage of high-tech skills and in increased obsolescence. "Information anxiety" is becoming a huge challenge for employees.

The work environment of the next decade will increasingly be characterized by flexibility in work locations and schedules, diversity among the workers and their skills, and complexity as a result of rapidly changing skill requirements and information overload.

Formal education in companies will change. It will become multisensory, transferable, and modular; it will be distributed so that "the right person can attend the right course at the right time." At IBM Canada, education is a $60 million a year business, which means it must be designed, developed, and delivered in creative new ways, managed by what we call a "systems approach to education" to ensure the highest levels of quality.

INSTRUCTION DEVELOPMENT

Automated design models (expert systems) will allow subject matter experts to develop courses without the intervention of an instructional design professional. This will greatly shorten the development cycle for new modules.

The following summarizes expected changes in formal education and training in industry:

- Planning will be done by skills rather than by jobs.
- Instruction will be provided in modules rather than in courses.
- Development of courseware will be automated with expert systems.
- Testing will be embedded and continuous rather than being an explicit event.
- Digital modules will be more easily translated for cultural and language differences.
- Instruction will be multisensory.
- The network will provide access to worldwide libraries of instruction modules rather than limiting users to local catalogues.
- Education will be truly distributed rather than under the central control of someone other than the learner.
- Employees will be able to initiate necessary education experiences themselves.

EDUCATION DELIVERY

Multimedia workstations will move with an employee and deliver education on a "just in time" basis. Most education will be delivered individually rather than in groups. Where group learning is important, multimedia classrooms will be used. Often, they will be connected electronically, allowing students in different locations to participate simultaneously in a "class." Satellite connections will become commonplace. Multimedia workstations will provide text, sound, graphics, and still and moving images, while accepting input from a keyboard, a writing tablet, or a natural language. Portable workstations will be self-powered and untethered so that employees may use them in a variety of locations.

By the year 2000, the major countries will be interconnected by an integrated services digital network for the transmission of instruction modules between countries. Digital video interactive technology will form the basis for instruction modules, and computer animation will allow for the creation of interactive modules without the large investment of human actors, sets, and photography.

PERFORMANCE/LEARNING SUPPORT SYSTEMS

In the decade to come, these methods of learning can only be delivered electronically by what we call a performance/learning support system (P/LSS). A P/LSS enhances individual employee and organization performance and learning with a minimum of human intervention. The components are integrated at the employee's workstation and correspond to the job structure and work environment. The system, as depicted in Exhibit 11.1, consists of several components including, but not limited to, interactive training, databases, expert systems, help facilities, and applications and productivity software.

By the company providing access to such a P/LSS, employees are able to learn exactly what they need to while

doing their particular job. As a result, the need for formal education and training in the traditional sense is reduced. We focus on learning experiences as opposed to education events. We leverage the capability of less experienced or less knowledgeable employees and, potentially, dramatically improve their productivity and performance.

The education function in industry must lead in the development of P/LSSs since it possesses the skills required to ensure that these systems truly enhance learning while they help employees get the job done. Education has a key role to play in enhancing the performance capabilities of human resources.

Over time, formal education will become only one element of the P/LSSs that must be created so that employees can truly live up to their performance potential.

ASSUMPTIONS VS. REALITY

Historically, whenever a corporation has encountered a performance deficiency with an individual employee or group of employees, formal education or training has frequently been assumed to be the appropriate response to that performance need.

Education and training, given the way they are currently provided, rarely produce competent employees by

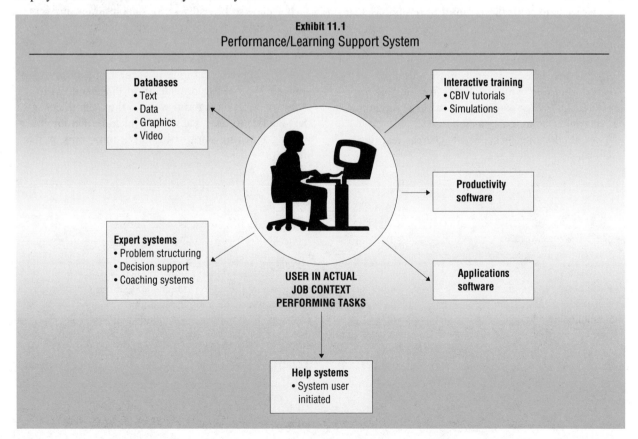

Exhibit 11.1
Performance/Learning Support System

Databases
- Text
- Data
- Graphics
- Video

Interactive training
- CBIV tutorials
- Simulations

Productivity software

Expert systems
- Problem structuring
- Decision support
- Coaching systems

Applications software

USER IN ACTUAL JOB CONTEXT PERFORMING TASKS

Help systems
- System user initiated

themselves, rarely match the precise needs of an individual learner, either in timing or in content, and rarely integrate into the actual job or work situation. In fact, while instructional designers will readily agree that people learn best by "doing," they will generally default and revert to creating educational experiences that assume that employees must "know" certain materials before they are able to "do" the job.

As a result, corporate education and training programs have been treated as events; events that happen at a particular period in time, usually independent of the particular job situation.

These events were created for a number of historically justifiable reasons. There may have been too many employees to train using the apprenticeship method. Or, several employees had to be prepared in advance to be able to do a common job. Or, the event was viewed as a way to introduce sudden changes such as new methods of operation, new products, or new strategies. The group might be viewed as being homogeneous, and therefore a single approach, i.e., a structured event, would be more appropriate. Lastly, the use of linear media, such as lectures and audio or video tapes, dictates a single approach to the educational event.

However, education and training, offered as events, are inconsistent with the notion of continuous learning…a notion that we believe to be so important to the continual enhancement of employee performance.

IBM, and no doubt many other companies, has traditionally run its education function under a set of assumptions that we must begin to question in our search for a "better way." Some of those assumptions can be contrasted to reality as follows:

- Formal education is an event whereas learning is a process,
- We say formal education is "competency based," when in fact we usually transfer information,
- We treat groups to be trained as homogeneous groups, when in fact they have always been heterogeneous, and are becoming increasingly more so,
- We assume that experts must structure education for the learners (employees), when in fact it is the employees who control what they learn,
- We assume that the employees must "know" before they can "do," when employees are perfectly capable of assessing their capability throughout the learning process,
- We assume that "knowing" is equal to "doing," when in fact employees must practise to gain proficiency,
- We provide consistent methodologies and programs for developing and delivering instruction that result in inconsistent performance because we are working with a heterogeneous set of employees,
- We assume that post-training support will be in place, when in fact post-training support, if it even exists, is usually inadequate,
- We assume that the jobs we are training people to do are static in nature, when in fact most of these jobs are changing at an ever-increasing rate.

If we are to be really serious about impacting on the performance of employees, we must shift our focus from "instruction" to "learning" and to the performance enhancement that goes hand-in-hand with improved learning. This learning can occur from a variety of sources. We need to provide all of those sources to the employee, in a thoughtful way, so they can select what best applies to their individual situation, thereby maximizing learning and, ultimately, enhancing performance.

• • •

Education 2000 is a very ambitious, innovative approach to training in the future. The Keynote Address draws scenarios and writes prescriptions for altering education systems in order to satisfy the needs of dynamic organizations. Because IBM has always been a leader in the field of training and development, the message should be taken seriously. Nonetheless, in order to appreciate IBM's newer approach, one needs first to understand the more traditional approach to training and development.

In this age training and development are vital for any organization's success. Consequently, organizations will invest more in them in the years ahead. Some will spend money without getting the proper return on their investment, while others will do a more professional job of analyzing, implementing, and assessing their programs. Nonetheless, the task of training and developing employees does not reside with the organization alone. Governments, educational institutions, and labour will have to pitch in to make the labour force more skilled and qualified for future performance needs. Indeed, research shows that countries with a national strategic approach to training and development will have a competitive edge over those that leave these initiatives to organizations alone.

Canada suffered from poor economic performance in the 1980s and early 1990s, as evidenced by high structural unemployment, a declining balance in merchandise trade, and low productivity growth. Illiteracy and skill shortages are believed to be the underlying causes of Canada's lack of competitiveness. The balance of the 1990s will be characterized by even stiffer competition in the wake of liberalized trade agreements and increasing global competition. Ironically, neither the Canadian government nor Canadian businesses have learned a lesson: they have been skimping on the training and development of their employees. The federal government, while paying lip service to the importance of education and training, also cut back drastically on transfer payments to the provinces for education.[1]

According to a Statistics Canada survey conducted in 1987, Canadian companies spent 1.3 billion on training in that year. This represented 0.24 percent of the total output of the economy that year and is only about half the level invested in training by U.S. private sector companies (Canada ranks even lower in comparison to Japan and many other European nations). A more recent survey, conducted in 1991 by the Canadian Labour Market and Productivity Centre, revealed that on average each employed Canadian received fourteen hours of annual training, which translates to approximately two days per year. A 1989 Conference Board of Canada report indicates that the trend in training is to spend more money on executives and managers' training than on other categories of employees. In fact, three times more than the $80 average spent to train nonmanagement personnel is spent on executive and management training. Although other studies have reported slightly higher figures, Canada is still lagging far behind Japan, where a typical worker receives six to eight days of training and a beginning manager as much as ten weeks in the first year of work.

In the not too distant future companies will be forced to invest substantially more in training and development, given the fast obsolescence of knowledge and the accelerated introduction of new technologies in the workplace. This will require an awareness of how to use the many training and development techniques and programs.

•　•　•

TRAINING AND DEVELOPMENT

What is Training and Development?

Employee **training and development** are learning-based activities that attempt to improve an employee's current or future performance by increasing his or her ability to perform through the improvement of SKAs. An employee's performance could be illustrated by the following formula:

$$P = f \text{ (skills, knowledge, attitudes, situation)}$$

where performance (P) is a function (f) of SKAs and the situation.

Training is sought when a performance deficiency can be attributed to the employee's SKAs. While it must be remembered that performance could also be affected by situational factors (e.g., technology, quality of supervision, etc.), these simple questions could aid organizations in determining performance deficiencies:

- Skills—Is the employee *able* to do the job?
- Knowledge—Does the employee *know* how to do the job?
- Attitudes—Does the employee *want* (is he or she motivated) to do the job?

Although all training and development programs are designed to address one (or a combination) of these questions, sometimes training and development are treated as two separate concepts. In this case, *training* usually refers to improving skills needed to perform better in the *current* job, and *development* refers to improving knowledge of jobs in the *future*. Nonetheless, both approaches are concerned with improving the employee's ability to perform. Because many programs help to improve SKAs for current and future jobs, training and development are treated in this chapter together.

From an organizational perspective, training and development consists of providing learning experiences for improving individual performance through changes in SKAs. In a broad sense it includes experiences intended to:

- Evoke new insights,
- Update skills,
- Prepare people for career changes,
- Rectify skill and knowledge deficiencies,
- Improve employees' attitudes toward the job and the organization.

Purposes and Importance of Training and Development

As noted, a major purpose of training and development is to remove the performance deficiencies, whether current or anticipated, that cause employees to perform at less than desired levels. Training for performance improvements is particularly important to organizations with stagnant or declining rates of productivity. Training is also important to organizations that are rapidly incorporating new technologies and consequently increasing the likelihood of employee obsolescence. For example, IBM Canada budgeted nearly $40 million in 1990 for training and retraining its personnel; much of this was related to dealing with obsolescence and upgrading skills for dealing with clients. The company also spent $14 million training customers to use its products.[3]

On the other hand, an advisory council on adjustment to Canada–U.S. free trade reported that three-quarters of the companies in the private sector spend nothing on training and development. Those that do not train sometimes piggyback onto other organizations that do.[4] Clearly, large discrepancies exist in how Canadian corporations view the importance of training and development. In contrast, in order to ensure that all companies invest in training and development, each company in France is required by law to invest 1.3 percent of its salary base in this area. Large French companies must spend considerably more than others, since their expenditures raise the national average to 2.5 percent of gross salary, which is about five times the Canadian expenditure.

Training and development can also increase employees' level of commitment to the organization and improve their perceptions that it is a good place to work. This can result in less turnover and absenteeism, thus increasing the organization's productivity. Moreover, when an organization helps employees build skills that are transferable from job to job, this can result in gains during periods of expansion and development as well as periods of personnel reductions and downsizing. In both cases, current employees may obtain preference in career promotions and/or have more job security.

As shown in Exhibit 11.2, training and development involves a large number of procedures and processes that are related to many other HR activities, namely HR planning, job analysis, performance appraisal (PA), recruitment and selection, career management and planning, and compensation.

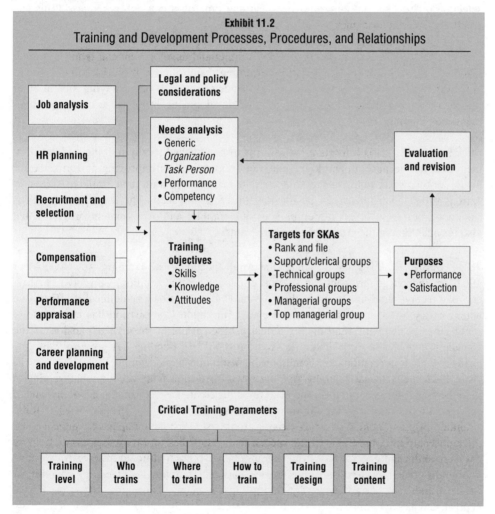

Exhibit 11.2
Training and Development Processes, Procedures, and Relationships

HR PLANNING. As a result of changing technology, organizations are finding it increasingly difficult to fill some of their HR needs with already-trained employees. Consequently, they are finding it more and more necessary to do their own training and to develop talent from within the organization. HR planning helps formalize this necessity and articulates management's concern for effectively utilizing its human resources now and in the future.

JOB ANALYSIS AND PA. Whereas planning establishes the general context within which training and development takes place, job analysis and PA help identify specific training and developmental needs. Appraisal may reveal certain performance deficiencies, which in turn may lead to the design of a training program to alleviate the deficiency. Moreover, the preparation of a multiskilled workforce can give the organization the flexibility to redesign jobs and assign people to them.

RECRUITMENT AND SELECTION. Needed skills can be acquired from outside the organization through recruitment or cultivated from inside through training. When organizations recruit from the outside, not only do they incur extra costs, but also reduce promotional options that could serve as incentives for current employees. Consequently, many organizations have instituted training and development programs to enhance skills for both current and future jobs. Finally, training and development can be integrated with the selection process so that an employee's learning time on a new job is reduced. This can result in increased efficiency.

CAREER MANAGEMENT AND PLANNING. Training and development can reduce turnover when it enables people to acquire skills permitting them to move from one job to another. However, well-trained individuals can also decide to move to better paying jobs in other organizations. For these reasons, training and development is related to career management and planning.

COMPENSATION. It is important for rewards to be attached to any training and development activity, because an employee may not be interested in improving performance for his or her own sake. For instance, to encourage managers to train their employees, organizations often reward them for performing this function well. The use of incentives is important, not only for getting employees into training and development programs, but also for maintaining the effects of these programs.

Legal and Policy Issues in Training and Development

THE FEDERAL GOVERNMENT. Under the Adult Occupational Training Act (AOTA) of 1967, the federal government can support employer-centred training. Currently, employers may receive funding for up to three years. Under the broad guidelines of affirmative action policy, the Canada Employment and Immigration Commission has been steadily increasing the level of funding for industry-based training through expansion of the Canada Manpower Industry Training Program (CMITP). Funding has grown in absolute terms as well as in relation to expenditures on institution-based training.

In 1982, the National Training Act was established to provide occupational training to help the labour force better meet the need for skills created by a changing economy, and to increase the earning and employment potential of individual workers. The National Training Program includes courses ranging from basic skill development to language and apprenticeship training. Some of the special features of the Act promote not only training for trade skills and general industrial training, but also nontraditional training for women. Within the context of these subsidy schemes, particular emphasis is placed by government on the training of certain disadvantaged groups: women, visible minorities, the handicapped, and native peoples.

Employment and Immigration Canada administers the bulk of training-related programs offered by the federal government. One of the most important programs is the *Canadian Jobs Strategy* (CJS), which was unveiled during the summer of 1985 and focused on long-term training and development, but has since changed its focus and scope. As of 1992, the objectives of the program are as follows:

- *Employability Improvement (focus on individuals).* The objective is to achieve improved employability and facilitate the successful integration into appropriate employment of select individuals who require assistance in overcoming existing or anticipated labour market barriers through the provision of counselling assistance, training and work experience, mobility assistance and related services, and income support.

- *Labour Market Adjustment (focus on employers)*. The objective is to induce more employers, particularly in key adjustment situations, to assume their primary responsibility for effectively meeting changing skill needs in their workplace by negotiating partnership arrangements directed toward their adoption of human resource planning (including employment equity), workplace-based training, and other related adjustment measures.
- *Community Development (focus on communities)*. The objective is to support the development of local employment opportunities and to assist communities facing severe labour market problems in effectively organizing their resources to assess local problems and opportunities, establish realistic objectives, formulate and manage appropriate plans, and implement strategies that are critical to the success of their plans and that promise significant labour market impacts.

THE PROVINCIAL GOVERNMENTS. Many provincial governments have also developed policies and programs to upgrade the employability of the labour force via training. The responsibility for that falls to different ministries, some of which are more important than others. A brief mention of some programs include:

Alberta. A few such programs are available through the Department of Career Development and Employment, including: the Alberta Training Program, Alberta Youth Employment and Training Program, Post-Secondary Internship and Training, and the Youth Experience and Training Program.

British Columbia. The bulk of these programs is administered by the Ministry of Advanced Education and Job Training; three programs are available: Training Investment Program, Training Opportunity Program, and Provincial Upgrading and Retraining Program.

New Brunswick. The Employment Development Branch of the Department of Labour has a program labelled: Opportunity Corps/Community Corps. The aim of the program is to provide work experience and skill development within the public sector for social assistance recipients.

Nova Scotia. The Nova Scotia Training and Employment Program is a two-part program set up to create employment opportunities for unskilled workers in resource-based industries and small businesses through structured on-the-job training. It provides financial assistance to employers who are training employees on the job and who are facing low productivity during the initial employment/training period. The program applies to lower-level skills, not to high technology. The program is administered by the Department of Advanced Education and Job Training.

Ontario. The Ministry of Skills Development is offering a number of programs. In October 1986, the government launched a five-year, $500 million workplace training initiative called Ontario's Training Strategy. Its objectives range from improved access to training for under-represented groups to upgrading and modernizing the skills of the current workforce. The programs complement existing federal initiatives. The overall goal is to create a climate in which both employers and employees see training as a normal, ongoing feature of business. In addition, the Training Consulting Service provides advice to firms on how to create competitive training strategies for their workers. Offices are located at all community colleges and satellite campuses in the province. The other components of the strategy, Ontario Training Trust Funds, Trades Updating, and Access to Training, resemble the programs offered by the federal government.

Quebec. The government of Quebec has a number of programs related to training. Through the Ministry of Manpower, it is offering a program designed to assist small- and medium-sized companies experiencing training and retraining, technological, or economic changes. Another program, labelled on-the-job training, provides recipients of social aid benefits with practical experience by way of relevant training outside production, either on the job or in the classroom. Under the Canada–Quebec Accord, a special support program for women is also sponsored by the Ministry. It includes initiation to nontraditional occupations, access to technological careers, and upgrading of professional skills.

Saskatchewan. The Ministry of Human Resources, Labour and Employment is offering the Native Career Development Program to find meaningful employment opportunities for natives.

Manitoba. The Manitoba Training and Development Program was set up to provide help to three categories of job seekers: (1) young people—for their career start; (2) new immigrants with technical and professional skills—for the recognition of skills acquired outside of Canada; and (3) single parents—for training that will free them from the social assistance program.

Newfoundland. In 1986 an agreement was reached between the federal government and the government of Newfoundland that facilitated the establishment of numerous programs aimed at promoting training and development. Some of these programs focused on helping post-secondary and graduate students find jobs in their field of study; other programs focused on facilitating access to seasonal workers.

The Training and Development Process

Although training can be conducted for a variety of reasons and can use a number of different media, most experts agree that training effectiveness is enhanced if it follows a sequence of phases from the initial needs assessment to the ultimate evaluation phase. Exhibit 11.3 shows a typical three-phase model applicable to any training program: (1) the *assessment phase*, which determines the training and development needs of the organization, (2) the *implementation phase* (actual training and development), in which certain programs and learning methods are used to impart new SKAs, and (3) the *evaluation phase*.

DETERMINING TRAINING NEEDS

Too often organizations decide to embark on a training program because someone in the organization has heard a program is offered by a competitor, or because a "training kit" has been advertised and successfully marketed, or simply because a smart consultant is making a plea for the use of any surplus training budget before it is cut off the following year. As with any other management program, some training techniques seem to have been *à la mode*, which is unfortunately the sole reason for their adaptation and use in organizations. Because training is so vital (and costly) to organizations, the criteria for selection and implementation of a program should be based on "real needs" rather than other considerations.

The first step in establishing a viable training program is assessment of needs. This provides information on where training is needed, what the content of the training should be, and who within the organization needs training in certain kinds of SKAs.

Of the three common methods of needs assessment available, *performance analysis*, *competency analysis*, and a *generic method*, the latter is the oldest and the most popular and will therefore be described in detail. Nonetheless, a brief presentation of the other two methods will follow. The generic method identifies three levels of needs analysis: organizational, operational or task-related, and individual.

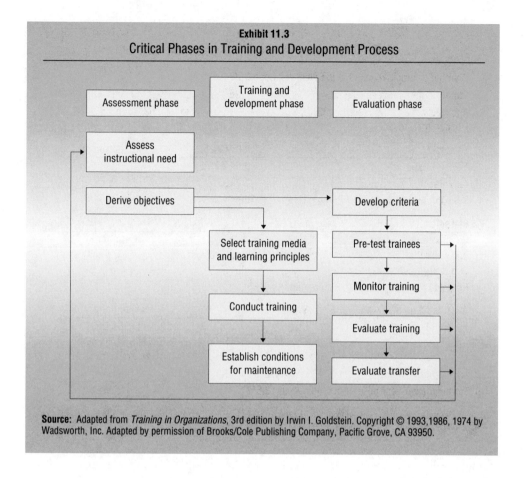

Exhibit 11.3
Critical Phases in Training and Development Process

Assessment phase | Training and development phase | Evaluation phase

Assess instructional need

Derive objectives → Develop criteria

Select training media and learning principles | Pre-test trainees

Conduct training | Monitor training

Establish conditions for maintenance | Evaluate training

Evaluate transfer

Source: Adapted from *Training in Organizations*, 3rd edition by Irwin I. Goldstein. Copyright © 1993, 1986, 1974 by Wadsworth, Inc. Adapted by permission of Brooks/Cole Publishing Company, Pacific Grove, CA 93950.

The analysis begins with an examination of the short-term and long-term objectives of the organization as a whole, and the trends likely to affect these objectives. The organizational needs analysis also consists of HR analysis, analysis of efficiency indices, and analysis of the organizational climate.

HR analysis translates the organization's objectives into the demand for human resources, skills required, and programs needed for supplying these skills and human resources. Training and development programs play a vital role in matching the supply of human resources and skills with the demand. Exhibit 11.4 shows a hypothetical analysis. All in all, there are nine parameters included in the analysis. The difference between parameters 1 and 2 shows the pressing need to train a new employee; parameter 3 shows that two employees are likely to retire soon and their replacements need to be trained; parameters 4 and 5 show that nine employees have some or serious performance-related problems (i.e., if we combine the "questionable" and the "unsatisfactory" categories) and further analysis should be done to find out if the latter can be improved by training; parameter 6 suggests that lack of job skills prevents employees from being transferred to other jobs in the company; parameters 7 and 8 suggest that, given the company policy, external recruitment needs to be undertaken and all new recruits will have to spend about twelve to sixteen weeks in training; and finally, parameter 9 indicates that due to past turnover patterns, five new employees will need to be trained within the next two-year period.

An analysis of efficiency indices provides information on the current efficiency of work groups and the organization. Indices that can be used include costs of labour, quantity of

Analysis at the Organizational Level

Exhibit 11.4
A Human Resource Analysis: Hypothetical Case

1. Number of employees in the job classification: 37
2. Number of employees needed: 38
3. Age levels:

Age levels:	29	33	45	47	50	51	53	55	59
No. per age group:	2	8	7	10	3	2	2	1	2

Factors	Satisfactory	Questionable	Unsatisfactory
4. Skill	32	2	3
5. Knowledge	33	3	1

6. Skill and knowledge for other jobs within the company:

Classification	Number	Jobs
No other jobs	35	none
One other job	1	Job Z, Dept. Y
Two or more other jobs	1	Job Z, Dept. Y; Job A, Dept. B

7. Potential replacements and training time:

Outside company	Within company	Training time
0	1	Less than 1 week
0	1	3 weeks to 6 weeks
10	0	12 weeks to 16 weeks

8. Training time on job for novice: 12 to 16 weeks
9. Turnover (two-year period): 5 employees: 13.5%

Source: Example taken and modified from K.N. Wexley and G.P. Latham, *Developing and Training Human Resources in Organizations* (New York: Harper Collins, 1991), 40 table.

output, quality of output, waste, equipment use, and repairs. The organization can determine standards for these indices and then analyze them to evaluate the general effectiveness of training programs and to locate training and development needs for groups within the organization.

Analysis of the organizational climate is often used to describe the quality of the climate and how the employees feel about various aspects of work. Like the analysis of efficiency indices, it can help identify congruencies, or incongruencies, between employees' perceptions of the job environment and their own needs and aspirations. Sometimes, when significant gaps are discovered and when it affects a large number of employees, it may call for training and development efforts. It is widely recognized that antagonistic attitudes on the part of employees affect their direct behaviour and certainly indirect performance in the form of low commitment, absenteeism, and low morale. Thus changing perceptions and fostering more commitment through training can be effective.

An organizational climate survey typically uses a questionnaire. Some of the more known climate questionnaires are those developed by the University of Michigan, Institute for Social Research, called Survey of Organizations; other popular measures include the Minnesota Satisfaction Questionnaires, the Porter and Lawler Job Attitudes, and the Smith, Kendall & Hulin Satisfaction Questionnaire.[5]

The use of organizational surveys is well-illustrated by a survey conducted for Air Canada in 1991. The results show wide differences among categories of employees with regard to twenty different climate dimensions including:

- Directions and goals
- Work organization
- Operating efficiency
- Performance appraisal
- Training and development
- Rewards and recognitions

- Management effectiveness
- Management and supervisory style
- Involvement and participation
- Respect and fairness
- Teamwork work relations
- Communication
- Performance orientation

- Benefits
- Job security
- Job satisfaction
- Employee commitment
- Company image
- Customer service orientation
- Competitive position

Results show that significant differences exist among the employee groups across the dimensions studied. For example, management and technical support rated areas such as reward and recognition very low; pilots, on the other hand, were more concerned about the company's ability to compete; and flight attendants signalled significant negative results in PA and reward recognition.[6] In addition to measures of attitude, other indicators of the quality of the organizational climate include data on absenteeism, turnover, grievances, productivity, suggestions, and accidents.

In order to comply with numerous federal and provincial equity laws, organizations also need to conduct *demographic studies* to determine the training needs of specific populations of workers. Some Canadian companies are engaged in training programs that encourage women and minorities to assume skills in areas where, traditionally, they are underrepresented. For example, Hydro-Quebec is attempting to upgrade by training an increasing proportion of females in the technical and engineering group, which traditionally has been dominated by males. Similar programs are in place in Canadian National, where an attempt is being made to bring more women into various supervisory levels.

Another aspect of demographic analysis pertains to the fact that different groups have different training needs. For example, first-line supervisors need more technical training (e.g., record keeping, written communications), while mid-level managers rate HRM courses as most important for meeting their needs, and upper-level managers require more strategic and conceptual training (e.g., goal setting, planning skills). Moreover, in a study of male and female managers, male managers were found to need training in listening, verbal skills, nonverbal communication, empathy, and sensitivity; women managers, on the other hand, needed training in assertiveness, confidence building, public speaking, and dealing with male peers and subordinates.[7]

Analysis at the Task Level

As important as organizational analysis, and perhaps often neglected, is task needs analysis. Because the organizational needs analysis is too broad to identify detailed training needs for specific jobs, it is necessary to conduct a *task-level analysis*. Essentially, this analysis provides information concerning the tasks to be performed on each job (i.e., the basic information contained in job descriptions), the skills necessary to perform those tasks (from the job specifications or qualifications), and the minimum acceptable standards of performance. These three pieces of information may be gathered independently from current employees, personnel files, or supervisory personnel. Exhibit 11.5 depicts the process of task needs analysis.

From job description, the analysis proceeds to extract the observable behaviours that are involved in performing a job. A task listing for a gas attendant might include:

1. Fills up gas according to customer instructions,
2. Checks oil,
3. Collects money (cash or credit charges),
4. Checks tire pressure,
5. Washes windows and wipes dirt,
6. Gives directions.

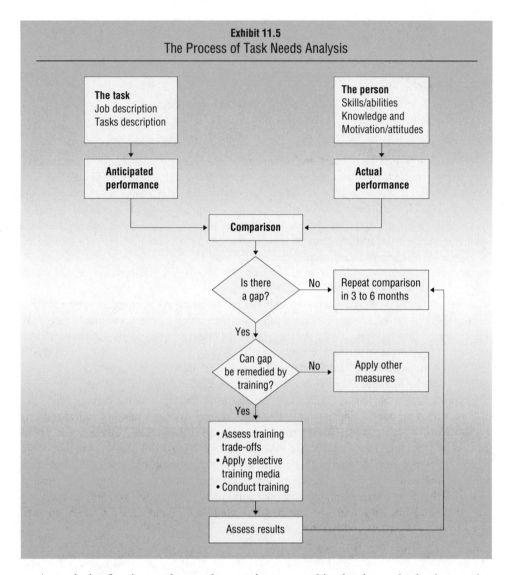

Exhibit 11.5
The Process of Task Needs Analysis

An analysis of various tasks may be most instrumental in charting and selecting a training plan. Using a few criteria, a *training trade-offs* chart can be designed, by replying independently to the following questions for each and every task:

a. What is the frequency of the task?

b. What is the importance of the task to the organization (in terms of added value as well as possible repercussions due to poor performance)?

c. How difficult is it to learn the task?

Without doubt, training efforts should be directed more selectively toward tasks that are frequent, important, and relatively difficult to learn. Other combinations may exist which guide the trainer in terms of selection of a training media, time, and other considerations. In the case of the gas attendant, an owner of a gas station will be better off by training a new hire more intensively in handling money, since this meets the more important criteria. Other tasks should receive less attention.

Analysis at the Person Level

Person analysis focuses on the individual and addresses the question: who needs training of what kind? The analysis can be accomplished in two different ways. Employee performance discrepancies may be identified either by comparing actual performance with the minimum acceptable standards or by comparing an evaluation of employee proficiency on each required skill dimension with the proficiency level required for each skill. Notice that the first method is based on the actual, current job performance of an employee; therefore, it can be used to determine training and development needs for the current job. The second method, on the other hand, can be used to identify training and development needs for future jobs.

A relevant training question for the first method is: will the employee be able to do the job assigned? For the second method, the relevant question is: will this employee or new job applicant do some job he or she has yet to do? Both these questions have important implications for equal employment opportunity and affirmative action. To ensure employment equity and affirmative action, the basis for the above answers must be a validated set of measures that will enable the organization to determine current performance and potential performance, as described in Chapter 9.

An increasingly used technique to gather information in person needs analysis is self-assessment. It can elicit from the individual an appraisal of training needs for his or her present job or those necessary for desired future jobs. Because this step requires a systematic attempt to identify the individual's strengths and weaknesses, using the self-assessment information in conjunction with the PA information enhances the validity of the diagnosis.

Although it somewhat resembles the task and person analysis, this method revolves around the concept of deficiency, which has been defined as skill mastery minus initial skill repertory.[8] Consequently, two types of deficiencies may be found in organizations: skill deficiency, which can be remedied through training, and execution deficiency, which may arise from poor supervision (i.e., inadequate feedback about performance, poor management of reinforcements) or from other interruptions preventing performance. Training may be appropriate for the first situation.

Performance Analysis

In order to pinpoint the cause of most performance problems and to decide if it can be corrected via training, performance analysis should be focused upon five issues: work context, worker, worker behaviour, work results, and feedback about results. The following example illustrates the typical queries a trainer must ask:

1. Is the work context clear to the performer? Do people know *when* they need to perform?
2. Are workers physically and mentally able to perform?
3. Do workers know *what* to do? Do they possess the skills? Are necessary resources—money, time, and equipment—available?
4. Are workers rewarded for performance?
5. Do workers get feedback about their performance? Is poor performance criticized? Is good performance praised?[9]

Competency Analysis

This method focuses upon opportunities for improvement. Trainers identify how they think workers *should* perform and then provide necessary instruction to enable them to acquire the needed skills. Training needs, according to this approach, could be divided into three categories: repetitive, short-term, and long-term.

Repetitive programs are offered on a regular basis, for instance, an induction program to each new employee. Often, new employees lack knowledge about the organization's culture, rules, and unique methods of doing things. An orientation program is designed to fill the repetitive needs for all new employees. Other programs are short-term in nature, for example, training people to use a new machine purchased by the organization. Finally, there are the long-term needs. These consist of, for example, developing a curriculum to be used systematically in the long term. Such is the case of developmental job assignments or stages in a program for career assessment and development. Another example is Bell Canada, which set up an objective to match each position with a training program that would help employees take a more systematic approach to improving their skill base.[10]

Successful implementation of training and development programs depends upon selecting the appropriate media for the right workers under the right conditions. Needs analysis helps to identify the key parameters in these considerations. In more specific terms, the following questions can guide the HR manager or a training director in implementing a program:

- Who participates in the program?
- Who trains?
- What media are used to train?
- What should be the level of learning?
- Where will the program be conducted?

Training Considerations: Who? What? Where?

WHO PARTICIPATES IN TRAINING? Generally, training and development programs are designed specifically to teach particular skills because, in most instances, only one target audience is in attendance. There are, however, times when training two or more target audiences simultaneously may be helpful. For example, rank-and-file employees and their supervisors may effectively learn about a new work process or machine together, so that they have a common understanding about the new process and their respective roles. Bringing several target audiences together may also facilitate group processes, such as problem solving and decision making, and help them develop skills useful in quality circle projects and semi-autonomous work groups.

An important decision is also *how many* employees are to be trained simultaneously. Some conditions are more favourable for using an on-the-job approach, as is the case for one or two employees. On the other hand, if large numbers of individuals need to be trained in a short period of time, then other media may be more cost effective.

WHO TRAINS? Training and development programs may be taught by one of several people:

- Immediate supervisors;
- Co-workers, as in buddy systems;
- Members of the HR staff, such as training directors;
- Specialists in other parts of the company;
- Outside consultants;
- Industrial associations;
- Faculty members at universities.

The selection of a trainer often depends upon where the program is held and which skill is being taught. For example, basic job skills are usually taught by members of the organization, namely the supervisors or co-workers, whereas other skills such as interpersonal and conceptual, integrative skills for management, and the like are often taught by university professors or outside consultants. However, large organizations, such as McDonald's, IBM, Xerox, and Air Canada, which have large numbers of employees, allow their training departments to oversee a variety of programs, including upgrading management skills.

A concern with using immediate supervisors or co-workers as trainers is that while they may perform very well, they may not have the proper training skills. It is possible that they will teach workers their own shortcuts rather than the correct procedures. Consequently, if supervisors or co-workers are to be used as trainers, they should be taught how to conduct training sessions and they should be given sufficient time on the job to work with the trainees.

WHAT MEDIA? There are several methods of delivering training information. In many colleges and universities, the basic ones are lectures, lecture–discussion combinations, case discussions, and some self-programmed instruction. These are also the methods used in many training and development programs. The decision of *what* media to select is closely related to *what* to teach. Although the choice of media depends to some extent on the trainer's preferences, much research has been conducted in this area and it is evident that some delivery methods are more appropriate than others for a particular kind of learning. Also, the available budget is normally taken into consideration. In general, media that incorporate more principles of learning and require repetition and exercises are also more expensive.

The common media used in training and their advantages and disadvantages will be discussed later on in the chapter. However, it should be noted that often a combination of techniques is used in order to obtain the best results. For example, some retail stores are training their department managers to use a videotape–behaviour modelling combination. First, the management trainees view a videotape of a manager (really an actor) behaving in an ideal way. Then, the managers are given a chance to "model" the behaviour of the actor on the videotape. Some large transportation companies use similar methods to conduct safety training for their truck drivers (e.g., Montreal-based Provost Transport). In brief, the rule of thumb in selecting training media is: the more active the trainee is within the selected media, the higher the retention rate.

WHAT LEVEL OF LEARNING? In addition to selecting the proper media, training programs must have a content that is congruent with the types of skills being taught. There are three levels at which needed skills can be learned. At the lowest level, the employee or potential employee must develop *fundamental knowledge,* which means developing a basic understanding of the field and becoming acquainted with the language, concepts, and relationships involved in it. The goal of the next-highest level is *skill development,* or acquiring the ability to perform in a particular skill area. The highest level aims for increased *operational proficiency*, which means obtaining additional experience and improving skills that have already been developed.

Another way to classify the level of learning is by grouping the various learning objectives into three categories that correspond to the skills and abilities that are being increased by the training.

- *Basic skills:* Many organizations are increasingly concerned about basic skills, which include grammar, math, safety, reading, listening, and writing. These skills are often missing in new employees and they are also missing in many executives who have been around a long time.
- *Interpersonal skills:* These include skills in communications, human relations, leadership, and negotiation. Also included here are skills related to legal considerations, and even organizational and time-use skills. Perhaps nowhere is the demand for these types of skills greater than at the level of first-line supervisors, although such skills are integral at all levels of management. Moreover, the development of such skills is important for employees who interface with the public (e.g., receptionists, sales people).
- *Conceptual integrative skills:* Strategic and operational planning, organizational design, and policy skills are normally needed by top management. Because of the complexities and changing environments, management needs to develop skills that will enable better decision making when responding to these changes. Nowadays, emphasis on creativity, ability to empower subordinates, and entrepreneurship is the core of such skills.

WHERE IS THE TRAINING CONDUCTED? A final consideration in implementing a training program is the location. This decision may be constrained by the type of learning that is to occur, the level of learning desired, as well as cost and time considerations. Nonetheless, there are two basic options: *on-site* and *off-site.*

Typically, the basic job skills and grammar skills are taught on the site. Much of the conceptual and integrative skills training is done off the site. The term **on the job** often refers to on-site locations, and **off the job** refers to off-site locations.

Optimizing Trainee Learning

Even when the training media are appropriate, learning may not take place if the training does not take into consideration an optimal utilization of learning principles that will facilitate training. Steps need to be taken prior, during, and after training to increase self-efficacy and retention of knowledge.

BEFORE TRAINING. When large numbers of trainees are involved, an attempt should be made to classify them into homogeneous groups in terms of learning capacity and preferred style of learning. By applying this principle, one can make the most of individual differences; this system is already being used in many elementary and secondary school systems and results are very encouraging. Although the objectives of the training are similar whether or not groups are classified, the homogeneity of the group enables the trainers to use different methods and a different pace of learning, and consequently to achieve better results. There are a number of criteria by which trainees can be grouped: style of learning (i.e., concrete vs. abstract), level of learning, pace of learning, etc. Many commercial tests/measures permit such classifications.

One of the most recent developments with reference to building congruencies between training content and individual differences is the Aptitude-Treatment Interaction (ATI). The idea is to fit each trainee with the most appropriate model of instruction based on the trainee's aptitude level. An aptitude refers to any characteristic that may affect the trainee's capability to learn.[11]

Another issue to be considered is the *trainability* of the employees selected to attend a program. Since a critical factor in the training success is the motivation and ability to learn of the trainee, both should be assessed prior to training. If employees are *motivated to change* and acquire different behaviours, training is likely to be easier and more successful. In order to obtain information about trainability, self-assessment measures along with opinions of supervisors can be used. An excellent research result pertaining to screening tests was reported by two British researchers. They found these tests are quite useful for predicting an untrained applicant's subsequent success in training and job performance. Typical trainability tests include the following process:

First, using a standardized form of instruction and demonstration, the instructor teaches the applicant a task;

Second, the applicant is asked to perform the task without assistance;

Finally, the instructor records the applicant's performance by noting errors on a standardized error checklist (prepared and different for each trade), and by making a rating of the applicant's likely performance in training (usually on a 5-point scale).[12]

Prior to launching a training program, a trainer needs to consider how information will be presented and what types of environmental arrangements he or she will undertake to facilitate learning. Research has demonstrated that learning will be enhanced if task instructions are clear and precise. This includes giving clear instructions and establishing appropriate behavioural expectations. Statements of training expectations should be specific, and conditions under which performance is or is not expected should be identified, along with the behaviour to be demonstrated. In other words, the objectives of the training, including performance expectations, should be communicated to and understood by the trainees. A good training objective might include the following characteristics:

- It should use terminology and language commonly understood by the trainees (not only the trainer).
- It should specify the behavioural outcome expected following the training and/or after some time in the transfer situation.
- It should include the minimal level of accepted performance.
- It should include the conditions upon which performance (after training) will be measured.

To set the stage for desired performance, it is also useful to specify, up front, the reward that will be given for performing as desired. A trainee is more likely to be motivated if he or she knows that successful performance can lead to positive reinforcement (e.g., promotion, pay raise, recognition) or can prevent the administration of negative reinforcement (i.e., firing, criticism).[13]

Moreover, desired behaviour will be enhanced if principles of *behavioural modelling* are used. Behavioural modelling is a visual demonstration of desired behaviour. The model can be a supervisor, co-worker, or subject area expert and the demonstration can be live or videotaped. What is important is to show employees what needs to be done prior to their performance. The effectiveness of the modelling process can also be improved by sequencing behaviours from the least to the most difficult. For example, some social work agencies train new social workers by showing them how to deal with minor case problems, and gradually the second and third modelled performances deal with more severe cases. Although controversial, some research suggests that the inclusion of a negative model (showing incorrect performance) along with a positive model (showing the right performance) appears to facilitate transfer of learning to other situations.[14]

DURING TRAINING. Research shows that adult learning can be enhanced if several factors are considered during the training. First, trainees perform better if they are *actively involved* in the learning process. Participation may be direct (hands on) or indirect (role-plays and simulations). Through active participation, trainees stay more alert and are more likely to be confident.

Regardless of individual differences, whether a trainee is learning a new skill or acquiring knowledge of a given topic, the person should be given the *opportunity to practise* what is being taught. Practice is also essential after the individual has been successfully trained. It is almost impossible to find a successful professional tennis player or piano player who does not practise several hours every day. An important consideration in designing learning practice is whether to divide the practice period into segments or plan one continuous period. This dilemma is often labelled *massed vs. distributed practice*. For example, professors of business administration often hesitate between giving their students short case studies to be discussed for about thirty minutes at the end of each class, or allocating two to three sessions of approximately six to nine hours to discuss a more comprehensive case. The answer to this dilemma is not simple and depends upon the nature of the task being taught. Nonetheless, it seems that distributed practice is more effective for learning motor skills. Many companies prefer massed training because they are eager to "get it over with" and have the trainees back on production as soon as possible. This, however, may not be in the company's interest in the long run, because, in order to gain mastery, some tasks require distributed practices.

Goal setting can also accelerate learning, particularly when it is accompanied by knowledge of result. Individuals generally perform better and learn more quickly when they have goals, particularly specific and appropriately challenging ones. Goals that are too easy or too difficult have little motivational value. It is only when people consider themselves capable of reaching the goal that they really become motivated. The motivational value of goal setting may also increase when employees participate in the goal-setting process. When the manager or trainer and the employee work together to set goals, the employee's unique strengths and weaknesses can be identified. Then, aspects of the training and development program can be tailored to that specific employee, which may increase the effectiveness of the training program.

While goal setting clearly affects a trainee's motivation, so also do the expectations of the trainer. Research has demonstrated that expectations are often self-fulfilling prophecies, so that the higher the expectations, the better the trainee's performance. The self-fulfilling prophecy is also known as the **Pygmalion Effect**. Legend has it that Pygmalion fell in love with a statue, and in answer to his prayer it was given life. Pygmalion's fondest wish, his expectation, came true.

In order for trainees to master new concepts and acquire new skills, they must receive accurate diagnostic feedback about their performance. In order for feedback to be instrumental in training it must be specific, timely, behaviourally and not personally based, and practical. This is the core of principles of reinforcement similar to the one explained in the chapter on incentive-based compensation. This feedback, which is also called **knowledge of results**, must be managed effectively. An effective trainer:

- Gives the feedback as soon as possible after the trainee's behaviour;
- Ensures that the relationship between behaviour and feedback is evident;
- Ensures that the amount and specificity of feedback are proportional to the stage of learning of the trainee (i.e., too much feedback at one time or too early in the process can be confusing);
- Should attempt to use positive feedback as much as possible, since research indicates that it is perceived and recalled more accurately than negative feedback;
- Should attempt to use a variety of reinforcers as part of the feedback. Repeating the same praise or identical comments may lose its effect over time. So, a good trainer needs to be creative in choosing and applying feedback.

Finally, an important consideration aimed at optimizing learning involves the organization and content of the material. Material is more easily learned when it is *factual and meaningful* to the trainees. The following suggestions enhance the meaningful structure of the material:

- Begin training by providing an overview of goals, methodology, forms of evaluation, etc.
- Present examples and vocabulary using concepts familiar to the trainees.
- Present the material in a logical order. The logic can be deductive, inductive or linear, but the sequence should be explained to the trainees at the outset.

AFTER TRAINING.   Once training has been completed, it is important to set up a mechanism to monitor whether new behaviours are being used. All too often, participants who do want to change their current behaviour get back to work and slip into the old patterns. This greatly decreases the effectiveness of the training program. One serious mistake in designing training and development programs is the failure to provide definite systems, policies and/or follow-up programs to ensure the learners' effective use of their newly acquired SKAs on the job. As a result, what an employee learns in a training program may never be tried in the actual job situation. Or, if the newly learned behaviour is tried, it may quickly be extinguished due to lack of support. It is therefore important that provisions be made in training programs for the positive *transfer* to the job *of the behaviours learned* in training. There are three ways to do this. One is to have conditions in the training program identical to those in the job situation. The second is to teach principles for applying the behaviours learned in the training program to the job situation, and the third is the contract plan.

The **contract plan** works in this way. Near the end of a training program, each participant drafts a statement indicating which aspects of the program he or she feels will have the most beneficial effect back on the job and then agrees to apply those aspects. Each participant is also asked to give another participant from the program a copy of the contract; this individual then agrees to check up on the participant's progress every few weeks.

A number of other strategies can also be considered to ensure that new behaviours are maintained. *Developing learning points* is one such strategy where key behaviours, particularly those that are not obvious and serve as cognitive cues back on the job, are summarized and handed to the trainee. To ensure that the trainee applies these behaviours, some rewards should be placed in the job situation. These **reinforcements** in the form of praise, financial reward, or otherwise, must be tied to performance. Furthermore, because trainers cannot always be around to reinforce new behaviours, other people, such as supervisors or co-workers, must be trained in monitoring and reinforcing the changes. Supervisors should also be told to be patient and tolerate certain initial errors without discouraging a trainee, since noninstrumental criticism will constitute no incentive for the trainee to continue to display new behaviour. It is also useful to *set specific goals* for subsequent performance. These goals should be realistic so as to be perceived as attainable by the trainee. Without goals, trainees have little basis for judging how they are doing.

A knowledge of the principles of learning, the four categories of skills needed by individuals in organizations, and the methods of training available and their advantages and disadvantages provide the necessary information to select the training programs that are most appropriate for specific organizations. Program selection is based on the answers to three questions:

Selecting a Program

- What skills do the employees need to learn?
- At what level do these skills need to be learned?
- What training and development programs are most appropriate for the required skills and level?

SKILLS NEEDED. The answers to the first two questions are determined from the needs analyses. For example, if there are performance deficiencies among the supervisory and rank-and-file employees, most of the training should be aimed at increasing technical skills; on the other hand, the primary need of middle-management employees would be interpersonal skills, and top-level managers would most be in need of conceptual or managerial and administrative skills. These matches between type of employee and the predominant type of skill training needed are useful training guides for current and future jobs. Knowledge of these matches can be used to facilitate employee career development and the organization's planning regarding training and development programs.

LEVEL NEEDED. To use these matches for the benefit of the individual and the organization, it is still necessary to know the appropriate level of skill training: increased operational proficiency, skill development, or fundamental knowledge. The results of the job and person needs analyses determine the necessary level, particularly for current job training. The levels required for future job training depend on the organizational needs analysis, as well as task and person needs analyses.

PROGRAM NEEDED. The final step is to determine which program is most appropriate to teach the targeted skills at the level needed. A guide for this determination is shown in Exhibit 11.6. For example, apprenticeship training is appropriate for those who need to increase their operational proficiency in basic technical skills, whereas the case discussion method is appropriate for conceptual or managerial and administrative skill training at all three levels.

Naturally, the criteria for selection mentioned above omitted discussion of cost considerations. These will be discussed in the next section. Nor does the appropriate selection guarantee the success of a training effort, because other factors are involved, such as the effective use of the principles of learning, the skills of the trainers, and the systematic and supportive organizational policies for the training and development efforts.

Exhibit 11.6
Selecting a Training and Development Program

		Skills Required		
		Basic Skills	Interpersonal Skills	Conceptual Integrative Skills
Level of Skill Required	Fundamental Knowledge	job rotation multiple management apprenticeship training job instruction training	role-playing sensitivity training formal courses	job rotation multiple management simulation case discussion
	Skill Development	job rotation multiple management simulation supervisory assistance	role-playing sensitivity training job rotation multiple management simulation	job rotation multiple management simulation case discussion
	Operational Efficiency	job rotation multiple management apprenticeship training job instruction training simulation internship and assistantship supervisory assistance	role-playing job rotation multiple management apprenticeship training job instruction training simulation	job rotation multiple management simulation case discussion

Source: Adapted from T.J. Von der Embose, "Choosing a Management Development Program: A Decision Model," *Personnel Journal*, Oct. 1973, 911. Reprinted with permission of *Personnel Journal*, Costa Mesa, Calif. All rights reserved.

TRAINING PROGRAMS: METHODS AND MEDIA

A multitude of training programs, methods, and media are available. Decisions also need to be made regarding where the training will take place. A common approach to classify training programs is according to the locale: on-site or off-site. This decision may be constrained by the type of learning that is to occur (basic, technical, interpersonal, or conceptual), as well as by cost and time considerations.

In general, *on-site* programs are divided into two categories: *on-the-job* and *off-the-job*. On-the-job training is often developed and implemented by the organization, but some training and development is informal. On-the-job training is used by organizations because it provides "hands-on" learning experience that facilitates learning transfer and because it can fit into the organization's flow of activities. Separate areas for training and development are thus unnecessary, and employees can begin to make a contribution to the organization while still in training. On-the-job training programs, however, are not without their disadvantages. For example, have you ever been waited on by a trainee in a restaurant? Or have you ever had to wait in line a particularly long time because the bank was "breaking in" several teller trainees? On-the-job programs may result not only in customer dissatisfaction, but also in damage to equipment, costly errors, and frustration for both the trainer (most likely a co-worker or supervisor) and the trainee. The disadvantages of on-site training can be minimized by making the training as systematic and complete as possible.

Another option is for the training to be on the site but off the job. This is appropriate for required after-hours training and for implementing training that requires maintaining contacts with various work units. It is also appropriate for voluntary after-hours training and for programs to update employees' skills while allowing them to attend to their regular duties.

An obvious advantage of *off-site* training is that it enables the trainee to acquire skills and knowledge away from the regular job pressures. Companies operate off-site training in training centres, hotels, conference centres, university facilities, or resort areas. By going off the site, the potential for making an error or damaging equipment is minimized. Off-site training is appropriate when complex skills need to be mastered. Another benefit of off-site training is the use of competent outside resource people. There are, however, a number of disadvantages. First, the costs are normally higher than for on-site training. There is also the potential concern over transfer of knowledge to the workplace. As research has shown, the more dissimilar the training environment is from the actual work environment, the more likely it is that trainees will not be able to apply knowledge learned to their jobs.

The following sections describe the common media used in both on-site and off-site training. The respective advantages and disadvantages of these different media and methods are summarized in Exhibit 11.7.

Exhibit 11.7
A Summary of the Advantages and Disadvantages of the On-Site and
Off-Site Job Training Programs

	ADVANTAGES	DISADVANTAGES
On-Site Methods		
On the Job		
Job Instruction Training	Facilitates transfer of learning No need for separate facilities	Interferes with performance May damage equipment
Apprenticeship	No interference with real job performance Provides extensive training	Takes a long time Expensive May not be related to job
Internship/Assistantship	Facilitates transfer of learning Gives exposure to real job	Not really a full job Learning is vicarious
Job Rotation	Exposure to many jobs Real learning	No sense of real responsibility Too short to stay on the job
Coaching/Mentoring	Facilitates improvements Real on-the-job constant feedback	Highly dependent on coach's style Very informal
Off the Job		
Programmed Instruction	Provides for individualized learning Faster learning	Time consuming Expensive
Videotapes	Conveys systematic information Rich in stimuli	Costly to develop No feedback is provided
Interactive Video/Computer-Based Instruction	Stores large amount of information Self-paced learning	Extremely costly to develop Requires expensive equipment
Off-Site Methods		
Lecture/Formal Course	Inexpensive Meaningfulness of organization	Requires good verbal skills Not always job related Limited feedback
Conference/Panel	Inexpensive Stimulating	Not always organized material
Case Studies	Stimulates discussion and practice Enables feedback	Limited experience
Simulation	Helps transfer Creates lifelike situations	Cannot always duplicate work
Role-Play	Good for interpersonal skills	Not always meaningful

On-Site Methods

ON-THE-JOB MEDIA. **Job instruction training (JIT)** was developed as a guide for giving on-the-job skill training to white- and blue-collar employees as well as technicians. Since JIT is a technique rather than a program, it can be adapted to training efforts for all employees in off-the-job as well as on-the-job programs. JIT consists of four steps: (1) careful selection and preparation of the trainer and the trainee for the learning experience to follow; (2) a full explanation and demonstration by the trainer of the job to be done by the trainee; (3) a trial on-the-job performance by the trainee; and (4) a thorough feedback session between the trainer and trainee to discuss the trainee's performance and the job requirements.

Another medium that is very useful for organizations that employ skilled tradespeople, such as plumbers, electronics technicians, and carpenters, is **apprenticeship training**. In fact this method is mandatory for admission to many of the skilled trades. To be really effective, the on- and off-the-job components of the apprenticeship program must be well integrated and appropriately planned, recognize individual differences in learning rates and abilities, and be flexible enough to meet the changing demands and technology of the trades. Countries such as Germany use this training method to a large extent and are able to meet the labour demand. In Canada, as portrayed in the HRM in the News Vignette, shortages of skilled workers are attributed to a culture that does not make use of the apprenticeship method. Apprenticeship programs last anywhere from two to five years and they combine on-the-job instruction with a minimum number of hours per year to be spent in classroom and shop instruction.

HRM IN THE NEWS VIGNETTE

Siemens Group Gears Up for Rapid Expansion but Canadian Skills Training Cannot Meet the Challenge

At a time when company after company is closing factories and firing workers, the Siemens group has a different problem: finding trained workers to help it meet its intended sales expansion. Siemens AG of Munich, an electronics and electrical manufacturer, already is the world's 24th largest company, with 1990 revenue of $39 billion and quadruple that in North America by the year 2000.

...A major handicap to fulfilling its sales goal, said William Waite, president and CEO in Canada, is the wrong-headed attitude towards apprenticeship training in Canada. Only 31% of Canadian businesses offer apprenticeship training.

Michael Porter, in his recent study on Canadian competitiveness, issued a similar warning. Apprenticeship training is being neglected, Porter maintained, and must be expanded and updated if this country is to hold its own in the world markets.

Waite, who has spent his whole career at Siemens, said he is worried the Canadian subsidiaries will have problems finding enough trained recruits for the planned expansion.... To test his thesis, he commissioned a study comparing Canada's apprentice training with Germany's, whose quality he said is recognized worldwide. The paper concluded that Canada is indeed lagging: 4% of workers in Germany benefit from such training, for example, compared with 0.8% here.

Apprenticeship courses combine on-the-job instruction with formal education at the college level. In Germany, they are considered a career opportunity and thus attract students straight from high school. Canadians, on the other hand, often drift into such training as a last resort, when their jobs have dried up. "These are people who have not been successful," he said.

Waite put part of the blame on the educational system, which varies by province and thus lacks what he termed a common concept. He also faulted politicians for not doing more to promote training. "The same politicians that wrote the advertisement: 'Join our forces, save our country,' in the 40s, should be saying today: 'Become an apprentice so we can position our country in North America better."

Source: Excerpts from Alan D. Gray, "Begging for Skilled Workers," in This Week in Business Section of *The Montreal Gazette*, 9 December 1991, 3. Reprinted with permission.

Somewhat less formalized and extensive than apprenticeship training are the internship and assistantship programs. **Internships** are often part of an agreement between schools and colleges and local organizations. As with apprenticeship training, individuals earn while they learn, but at a rate less than that paid to full-time employees or master craft-workers. The internships, however, function not only as a source of training but also as a source of exposure to job and organizational conditions. Students in internship programs are often able to see the application of ideas taught in the classroom more readily than students without any work experience.

Assistantships involve full-time employment and expose an individual to a wide range of jobs. However, since the individual only assists other workers, the learning experience is often vicarious. This disadvantage can be eliminated through the use of job or position rotation.

Job rotation programs are used to train and expose employees to a variety of jobs and decision-making situations. Although job rotation does provide employee exposure, the extent of training and long-term benefits it provides may be overstated. This is because the employees are not in a single job long enough to learn very much, and are not motivated to work seriously because they know the situation is temporary and that they will move on to another position in the near future.

Two different approaches to on-the-job training are **coaching** and **mentoring**. They are the most informal programs of training. They include day-to-day coaching and counselling of workers on how to do the job and how to get along in the organization. The effectiveness of coaching depends in part on whether the supervisor creates feelings of mutual confidence, provides opportunities for growth to employees, and effectively delegates tasks. Mentoring is related to coaching with the exception that the role of a mentor is assumed by an established employee who takes on the role of guiding and developing a less experienced worker or "protégé." The concept dates back to Greek mythology: Odysseus asked his friend Mentor to teach his son Telemachus what could be learned from books as well as from the ways of the world. Although mentoring is an informal process where both people are interested in maintaining a relationship, some organizations have recently decided to adopt a policy of matching up mentors and protégés. It has been suggested that the rise in popularity of mentoring derives from the fact that more and more women seek promotions to managerial positions and require more refined cues from a mentor about entering and succeeding in a male-dominated milieu.[15]

OFF-THE-JOB MEDIA. New technologies have rapidly increased the options available to organizations that want to provide on-site training. The two predominant auto-instructional methods are linear programming and branch programming, both of which are types of **programmed instruction (PI)**. In each, the learning material is broken down into "frames." Each frame represents a small component of the entire subject to be learned, and each frame must be learned successfully before going on to the next. To facilitate the learning process, feedback about the correctness of the response to a frame is provided immediately. The successful use of PI requires that the skills and tasks to be learned be broken down into appropriate frames. Once this is done, the probability of an individual learning by PI is high because it allows individuals to determine their own learning pace and to get immediate and impersonal feedback. Nevertheless, there are many skills and tasks that are impossible to break down into appropriate frames. Also, PI is very expensive to develop. It is estimated that one hour of PI requires fifty hours of development work. Consequently, for this approach to be cost effective, it requires conditions in which "canned" programs (i.e., word- and data-based tutorials) are used or large numbers of employees are to be trained.

Videotapes can be used on the site or off the site and have generally replaced films as the visual medium of choice for organizational training. At its most basic level, video training includes taped instruction that can be stopped and started at any point in time. Because videotapes are less expensive than traditional training films their popularity has increased rapidly in recent years. An advantage of videotape is that instruction can be standardized. For companies that are spread out geographically, this can be a most effective medium. For example, both Pizza Hut and McDonald's use videotapes to introduce their franchisers to new products or ways to improve customer service.

Computer-based training (CBT) and **interactive video training (IVT)** combine the best features of PI with some of the attributes of videotape. Interactive video programs show a short video and narrative presentation and then require the trainee to respond to it. Usually the video is attached to a personal computer (PC) and the learner responds to the video cues by using the keyboard or by touching the screen. This multi-media package provides for true individualized learning. It is also very entertaining and thus helps maintain trainee motivation.

On the downside, development and equipment costs associated with IVT are high. Hardware alone can cost between $6,000 and $12,000, and master disks cost between $2,000 and $5,000. For sophisticated programs, more than 500 hours can be spent on developing one hour of interactive video training, with costs running as high as $150,000. Approximately 2,000 employees of Canada Post received PC training between 1989 and 1991 using CBT workstations with IVT. Because of a price tag of around $20,000 per workstation, the company has decided to rent the hardware for its Ottawa, Montreal, and Toronto offices. Compact disk technology is already enhancing interactive training to new heights. In a prototype system, TV-type eyepieces built into a helmet generate realistic, three-dimensional displays in front of the trainee. Integrating touch-simulating gloves with helmet electronics will allow courseware developers to realistically model tactile experiences that range from driving a car to removing a cancerous lesion.

Computer-based training, which preceded IVT, shares many of the features of the latter but is less expensive to develop. Hundreds of software programs are commercially available to train people in how to use various types of software or even in how to use a computer. Both Apple and IBM have developed a course on how to use their computers. CBT also teaches how to use other popular programs such as word processing programs (e.g., *WordPerfect*), statistical analyses (e.g., *SPSS, SAS*), utilities programs (e.g., *Norton Utilities, PC Tools*), database management programs (e.g., *Lotus 1-2-3, dBase*) and many more. The popularity of CBT in industry stems in part from the fact that it can reduce costs by cutting down on trainee travel and training time. Moreover, it is estimated that CBT increases retention of training content by 80 percent.[16]

Off-Site Methods

Many training programs use the *lecture/formal course* method, because it efficiently conveys large amounts of information to large groups of people in one sitting. Although the method is used by more than 83 percent of all organizations, it has been frequently criticized for its numerous drawbacks.[17] It perpetuates the authority structure of traditional organizations and hinders performance because the learning process is not self-controlled. Except in the area of cognitive knowledge and conceptual principles, there is probably limited transfer of useful material from the lecture to the actual skills and abilities required to do the job. The high verbal and symbolic requirements of the lecture method may be threatening to people with low verbal or symbolic experience or aptitude. Also, the lecture method does not permit training based on individual differences in ability, interests, and personality. For these reasons survey after survey of training directors in large companies shows that lecture is the least effective for attaining training success. Nonetheless, in relative terms, the accumulated research suggests that lecture is more effective for knowledge acquisition than for skills or attitude change. With the increase of organizational size and geographic disparity, many institutions use taped lectures and distribute them to different locales. Recorded lectures are significantly less expensive that a full production of a video or a film. Many universities' continuing education programs adhere to this method in providing televised courses for credit. This eliminates the need for a student to commute from far away in order to attend a lecture at the university. Taped lectures are available in libraries for students who missed a class. A university in the U.S.A. has decided to take an innovative approach to meet the needs of commuters. Adelphi University offers a two-year M.B.A. program on the Long Island Railroad. Classroom cars are equipped to meet learning conditions and classes last an average of about an hour.[18]

The *conference/panel* method is similar to the lecture/course method except that more people are involved and thus the method makes learning more dynamic. As with the lecture method, it is more effective for fostering change in knowledge. A *case study* is a narrative description of a situation, real or fictitious, prepared for instructional purposes. Most case studies are written, and are a proved stimulation for trainees, especially in a small group setting. People become engaged in the case, receive comments and feedback from peers, and have the opportunity to apply their conceptual and theoretical knowledge. Case study drawbacks include the fact that experience is very limited and does not always resemble the job situation. Moreover, in order to facilitate learning, a very experienced trainer needs to guide the trainees through the analysis.

Simulations and role-play are the final media to be discussed here. **Simulation** presents participants with situations that are similar to actual job conditions. It is used to train both managers and nonmanagers. A common training technique for nonmanagers is the *vestibule method*, which simulates the environment of the individual's actual job. Since the environment is not real, and generally safer and less hectic than the actual environment, adjustment from the simulated training environment to the actual environment may be difficult. Because of this, some organizations prefer to do the training in the actual job environment. But the arguments for using the simulated environment are compelling: it reduces the possibility of the customer dissatisfaction that can result from on-the-job training, it can reduce the frustration of the trainee, and it may save the organization a great deal of money because fewer training accidents occur.

An increasingly popular simulation technique for managers is the **assessment centre method**. The assessment centre was discussed in Chapter 6 as a device for selecting managers. However, certain aspects of assessment centres, such as the management games and in-basket exercises, are excellent for training and need not be utilized only for selection purposes. Assessment centres are also especially useful for identifying potential training needs. Whether used for training or selection, assessment centres appear to be a valid way to make employment decisions.

Management or business games, which are another type of simulation, almost always entail various degrees of competition between teams of trainees. In contrast, **in-basket exercises** are more solitary. The trainee sits at a desk and works through a pile of papers that would be found in the in-basket of a typical manager, prioritizing, recommending solutions to any problems, and taking any immediate action necessary according to what is contained in the papers. Although the in-basket method tends to be an enjoyable, challenging exercise, the extent to which it improves a manager's ability depends in part on what takes place after the trainee has gone through the exercise. The debriefing and analysis of what happened and what should have happened should help the trainee learn how to perform like a manager. Without the debriefing and analysis, however, the opportunity for improvement may be drastically reduced; the trainee has no expertise in deciding what to transfer from the game or exercise to the job.

Whereas the simulation exercises may be useful for developing conceptual and problem-solving skills, there are three types of process-oriented training that are used by organizations to develop their managers' "interpersonal insights"—awareness of self and of others—for changing attitudes and for practice in human relations skills, such as leadership or the interview. **Role-playing** is such a method. It focuses on emotional (i.e., human relations) issues rather than on factual ones. The essence of role-playing is to create a realistic situation and then have the trainees assume various personalities in the situation. The usefulness of role-playing depends heavily on the extent to which the trainees really "get into" their parts. If you have done any role-playing, you know how difficult this can be and how much easier it is to just read the part. But when the trainee does get into the role, the result is a greater sensitivity to the feelings and insights presented by it.

FACILITATING EMPLOYEES' FUTURE PERFORMANCE

Employees' development in many organizations is considered to be an integral part of career planning. Chapter 12 discusses this topic in detail. Over the past twenty years, development efforts were focused on management and professional employees, given that they were viewed as the most critical human resource in an organization. A variety of formal and informal programs were developed to cater to this population. Only recently are companies beginning to realize that in order to match their long-term strategic objectives, other categories of employees need to be included. Thus, programs such as management development, sensitivity training, and team building are not exclusively reserved for top management. This stems from the realization that skills that are not necessarily task related, such as negotiating, memory improvement, listening, and customer service, might benefit the organization in the long run. By investing in such development programs, firms admit that individuals, not just technology, make things happen. While employee development is distinguished from regular training, it should be mentioned that results should be monitored, although the mechanisms, the time frame, and the targets are somewhat different.

Senior managers and trainers who do not favour developmental programs usually claim that they cannot see any tangible return on investment. This is due to the fact that results are often vague and seldom transfer into on-the-job behaviours. Consequently, employees' and corporate development programs are often called "soft-skills training." According to one expert, this view is rapidly changing for two principal reasons:

- The dramatic growth of service-based industries requires extreme sensitivity and polished human relations skills in dealing with customers. The banking, retailing, and insurance industries are having severe problems recruiting and retaining employees. The quality of most new service workers is often poor because many are simply illiterate. Front-line customer service employees experience a vicious cycle: poorly skilled employees give inadequate service, and irate customers take it out on service workers who cannot tolerate the abuse and ultimately quit.

- For manufacturing industries the rationale is different. As technology and automation increase and fewer managers are needed, employees must be more independent or self-managed with some help from colleagues. Thus, the need for improved decision-making skills and relations with others becomes paramount. Programs that teach workers how to operate in self-managed teams or to help them learn leadership are scant.[19]

Formal training in soft skills is much more difficult than technical or other types of training. Where chances of success for technical training, assuming that the program is well designed, can reach 90 percent or even 100 percent, teaching skills such as leadership, interpersonal communication, problem solving, and consultative sales can be called a success if 20 percent of the employees use the techniques they were taught. The remaining 80 percent may try to apply them a few more times, but eventually they revert to old patterns.[20] Regardless of these constraints, a variety of employee development methods are used in organizations.

Formal Training and Development Programs for Potential Performance

T-groups and human relations training were very popular straight-training programs in the 1960s and the 1970s. Both are considered more related to individual development than to formal organization development (except when carried on as integral parts of an organizational development program). *T-group training* has also been called sensitivity training, encounter group, marathon group, and laboratory training, and has been popularized and introduced to industry by the National Training Laboratory (NTL) in the U.S.A. It heavily emphasizes principles of group dynamics and is geared toward developing skills for learning about oneself and others by observing and participating in group situations. Individuals in an unstructured group exchange thoughts and feelings on the "here-and-now" rather than the "there-and-then." Although the experience of being in a sensitivity group often gives individuals insight into how and why they, and others, feel and act the way they do, critics claim that these results may not be beneficial because they are not transferable to the job and, in addition, some participants finish these sessions psychologically injured. *Human relations training* is aimed at "humanizing" the employee, that is, to be more attuned to "people problems." This school of thought stemmed from the well-known Hawthorn studies.

Transactional analysis started in the 1950s and became popular in the 1960s with the publication of the book by T.A. Harris, *I'm OK—You're OK*. It is based on a theory in which behavioural transactions between people falls into three categories representing three ego states: parent, adult, and child. Through a process known as structural analysis, people are taught how to analyze transactions they have with others. Incongruence in the transaction may cause a person to feel he or she is "not OK," and vice versa; congruency makes a person feel "OK." The core of the training is to analyze transactions between participants by using this scheme and to point out behaviours that will reduce incongruence.

Team building training was first used in management and executive development programs. However, nowadays there is a proliferation of the use of teams, so the training has been enlarged to include many other categories of employees. Committees, task forces, blue ribbon panels, quality circles, joint union–management leadership teams, action committees, and self-managed work teams: they are the buzzwords for the 1990s and are all targets for this approach. Although the goal of team building is very clear, the process of achieving it through training is not at all evident. According to one expert there are ten key flaws in designing training to establish a team concept:

- Confusing team building with teamwork: team training is focused on an effort to make people feel good about each other; teamwork, on the other hand, is a method to ensure that the group performs according to standards, even if interpersonal relations and personality conflicts occur;
- Viewing teams as if they are "closed systems": training often fails to go beyond a specific team and show the relationships to the larger organization;
- Not using a systematic model to plan team development: a reference model that explains how a successful team might excel is needed;
- Starting team training without assessing team needs;
- Sending team members to team training individually rather than collectively;
- Treating team building as a Japanese management technique;
- Assuming that teams are all basically alike;
- Counting on training alone to develop effective teams; follow-up and other policies need to be used to reinforce the training;
- Treating team building as a program rather than a process;
- Not holding teams accountable for using what they learn in team training.[21]

EXECUTIVE DEVELOPMENT. Executive development encompasses many of the techniques mentioned above along with more traditional training programs. Due to intense worldwide competition, executives must carry the burden of making their organizations achieve higher standards of productivity, quality, and effectiveness in order to survive. Executive development is a continual education process designed to help senior management become more competitive in specific, tangible, and measurable ways. The content of the program is tailored to the unique challenges of each particular firm, but high priority is placed on developing leadership skills, becoming customer/market driven, formulating and implementing strategy, and engineering and managing change. Prior to development of a curriculum, a systematic needs assessment is conducted, normally through in-depth interviews with senior executives. A recent survey found that out of twelve learning methods used in executive development programs, using outside experts as faculty emerged as the single most important learning method to be used in the 1990s.[22]

TRENDS IN TRAINING AND DEVELOPMENT

"This training and development stuff is all good, but it's my boss who really needs it." (Middle- and lower-level managers)

"If top management would only show active support of the program, it would be a certain success." (The staff training specialist)

"Management development? Active support? Why, I'm doing that all the time." (Top management)[23]

Problems and Pitfalls in Training and Development

As shown by these three quotations, misperceptions and the tendency to assign blame and responsibility to others are common in discussion about training in organizations. These attitudes are partially responsible for the lack of success of some training efforts. But there are other reasons for failure as well, including:

- Performing hasty and shallow needs analyses and thus failing to define what the real training needs are and who should receive the training;
- Substituting training for selection and relying too heavily on the "magic" of training to increase the ability of individuals who lack the capability;
- Limiting the training and development effort to formal courses and ignoring all other methods;
- Lumping together all training and development needs and thus failing to implement programs appropriate for different needs;
- Failing to give consistent attention to the entire training and development effort;
- Failing to provide for practical application and organizational support systems for the newly learned behaviours.

Observers of the Canadian scene note that, in addition to these general problems, many Canadian training programs have unique pitfalls, including the low priority given to management training and the scarcity of skilled trainers (many executives in charge of training have very limited experience).[24]

Assessment of training and development programs is a necessary and useful activity, though in practice it is often not conducted. However, without an evaluation of results, it is impossible to conclude if the training and development program has met its objectives.

Assessing Training and Development Programs

ASSESSMENT CRITERIA. Assessment involves determining what data and criteria are relevant for a valid evaluation. Options from which to gather data include changes in productivity, interviews, tests, PA results, attitude surveys, and cost savings and benefit gains, to name a few.

Regardless of the method, assessing the effectiveness of any training or development program entails answering the following questions:

- Did change occur?
- Is the change due to training?
- Is the change positively related to the achievement of organizational goals?
- Will similar changes occur with new participants in the same training program?

While different evaluation methods have been proposed through the years, most training experts agree that they should include at least four components:

- *Reaction to training*: How do participants feel about the training program? This is the most commonly used, but can be the most misleading (i.e., no evidence of change is apparent).
- *Learning*: To what extent have trainees learned what was taught? Did they acquire the respective knowledge and skills targeted by the training, and can they demonstrate appropriate behaviour?
- *Behaviour*: What on-the-job changes in behaviour occurred because of attendance at the training program? Can trainees now do things they could not do before?
- *Results*: To what extent have tangible results in terms of productivity occurred? (i.e., productivity in a broad sense: attendance, quality improvements, cost savings, response time, etc.)?

The choice of criteria hinges on the level at which the training evaluation is to be conducted. For example, a short attitude survey could be used to assess the response of trainees to a course. However, such a survey would not provide information regarding learning, behaviour, and results. In fact, when learning has been stressful or difficult, the trainees' reaction may even be negative.

If the objective is to assess knowledge, then paper-and-pencil tests can be used. Additionally, it is possible to analyze the content of responses to such training exercises as in-basket tests, role-play, or case analyses. While this may indicate that learning has occurred, it will not reveal whether learning has been transferred to the job. In order to assess behaviour or performance change, output measures, supervisory evaluations, and employee attitude surveys provide better information.

In addition to determining the appropriate criteria by which to evaluate the program, the HR manager must select an **evaluation design**. Evaluation designs are important because they help the HR manager determine if improvements have been made and if the training program caused the improvements. In addition to aiding in the evaluation of training programs, evaluation designs can: (1) aid in evaluating any personnel and HR program aimed at improving productivity and QWL, and (2) aid in evaluating the effectiveness of any personnel and HR activity. Combining the data collection tools (i.e., organizational surveys) with knowledge of evaluation designs can prove essential for demonstrating the effectiveness of HRM and any of its programs and activities to the rest of the organization.

Evaluation Designs

There are three major classes of evaluation design: pre-experimental, quasi-experimental, and experimental. Although it is preferable to use the experimental design that is the most rigorous, a variety of organizational constraints make this impractical. Therefore, HR managers often utilize the moderately rigorous quasi-experimental design, and even when quasi-experimental designs are feasible, most evaluations rely on the pre-experimental design. The latter is used because it is easier and quicker, but, unfortunately, it is a very poor one for most purposes. All three classes of evaluation design are shown in Exhibit 11.8, which conveys how programs can be evaluated using these designs and what is required.

The better designs in Exhibit 11.8 make use of a control group. A control group consists of employees who are not trained, but who are measured. Using such a design provides the data for comparisons. Panel A shows the most common design used in organizations today. It is also the poorest in judging training effectiveness, since we do not know the base line in knowledge or skills for people who entered training. Panel B is an improved design, since here we have some information about the initial SKAs of trainees prior to training. Yet even if change results after training, we cannot attribute it to the training activities in this design. Panel C, which shows post-measure design with control, may not require a pre-measure, but one has to be very careful in comparing two very similar groups if conclusions about change and causality are to be drawn. Panel D is a full pre–post with control procedure. Evidence for training effectiveness is inferred when pre–post changes are greater for the trained than the untrained. This is, however, a rather costly procedure. Finally, Panels E and F provide for time series design without a control group (E) and with a control group (F). They provide for collection of several initial measurements of critical SKAs, and follow the change after train-

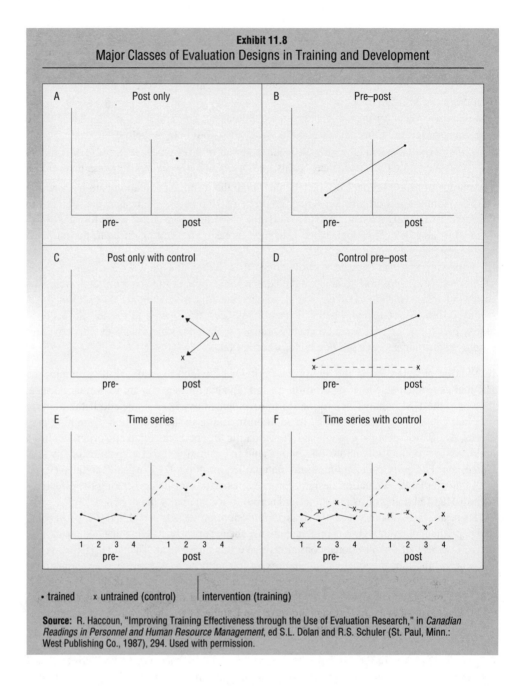

Exhibit 11.8
Major Classes of Evaluation Designs in Training and Development

A   Post only

B   Pre–post

C   Post only with control

D   Control pre–post

E   Time series

F   Time series with control

• trained   x untrained (control) | intervention (training)

Source: R. Haccoun, "Improving Training Effectiveness through the Use of Evaluation Research," in *Canadian Readings in Personnel and Human Resource Management*, ed S.L. Dolan and R.S. Schuler (St. Paul, Minn.: West Publishing Co., 1987), 294. Used with permission.

ing for a while. The trend that emerges from the data provides important estimates of the stability of both pre-training and post-training measurements. It helps eliminate unnecessary training where experience alone improves SKAs over time (i.e., maturity curve). It could also provide estimates as to the retention rate of the newly acquired SKAs. For these, and other reasons, many experts believe that multiple measures seem to be the best since they minimize the so-called measurement and intervention interaction effects.

Many of these design considerations would also apply to measuring the effectiveness of employee development programs, although the latter are different in two areas: *focus and formality*. While training programs are set primarily to meet the organization's needs, development focuses on the individual employee's needs. Consequently, measurement of changes in needs can be sought.

Computers can be used to support a multitude of training and development functions. In the majority of cases where computers are used, the HR unit is responsible for the training.

APPLICATIONS IN TRAINING. One of the most readily available training applications is CBT. As suggested before, CBT systems are very effective training tools, but unfortunately they are being under-used in industry, even among Fortune 500 companies.[25] There is no doubt that CBT will be more frequently used in the future. Naturally, high-tech industries make full use of CBT. Exhibit 11.9 and 11.10 show a typical example of an initial training needs analysis form used by IMS Canada, an international marketing research company (a division of Dunn and Bradstreet). The form was developed for implementing a training curriculum in the use of PCs.

APPLICATIONS IN DEVELOPMENT. Two major applications are used in development: *leadership diagnosis and training*, and *business simulations*. Numerous software programs on the market help managers understand their leadership style. Some examples include: (1) Thoughtware's *Management Diagnosis Series*, which helps to identify personal management skills and interpersonal style. In its training series, the software contains programs teaching managers to lead, motivate, set goals, manage time and stress, as well as conduct effective meetings; (2) the *ACUMEN* series from Human Synergetics combines self assessment with group feedback in reference to such dimensions as problem-solving skills, leadership skills, conflict resolution, and team building; (3) *ExecuGROV* is designed to assess training and development needs and includes planning guides; (4) a recent comprehensive program called *Dimensions of Leadership* targets diagnosis at the following critical dimensions:[26]

1. Managing interpersonal business relationships:
   Energizing and empowering others,
   Building and managing teams,
   Interpersonal flexibility;
2. Achieving business results:
   Planning and implementing skills,
   Decision making,
   Strategic thinking,
   Business knowledge,
   Results orientation;
3. Influencing others and building information networks:
   Building information networks,
   Influencing others.

It should be remembered, however, that leadership training cannot be exclusively based on electronic workbooks. In order for training to be effective, it needs to be combined with actual workshops and group dynamics.

Interactive computer programs are ideal for training employees to react quickly to changing environments. These programs address the need for managers to improve their decision-making techniques in a series of business simulations. As more and more simulations are becoming available, many companies are conducting on-site training. There are hundreds of simulations and business games on the market ranging from very sophisticated games that include the entire array of managerial work, including marketing, finance, production, human resources, etc., to very focused simulations (i.e., one area or field). The following is a list of computerized business simulations listed in one manual:

- *MacManager* has been developed by Harvard Associates, Inc. Players make decisions by reading news bulletins and play against each other. Up to nine players can be includ-

Exhibit 11.9
Personal Computing Training Needs Analysis Worksheet

Name: _____ Department: _____ Local: _____ Location: _____

Curriculum areas	JULY – SEPTEMBER 1991			OCTOBER – DECEMBER 1991			JANUARY – MARCH 1992			APRIL – JUNE 1992		
	Priority	Employee(s)	Course title	Priority	Employee(s)	Course title	Priority	Employee(s)	Course title	Priority	Employee(s)	Course title
1 Introductory skills												
2 Spreadsheets												
3 Database												
4 Word processing												
5 Telecommunications												
6 General												

Priorities: 1 Critical needs   2 Skills enhancement   3 Career enhancement

Signature _____

ed in the game. The winner is the trainee who has the greatest profit or is the last to be forced into closure or bankruptcy.

- *Strategic Management Game* allows one or two players to make business decisions from start-up through expansion.
- Reality Technologie's *Business Strategist* presents a series of what-if questions and allows the user to test plans of action in a simulated business throughout different industries.
- *DECIDE* (Decision Exercises through Computer/Instructor Designed Environment) requires managers to make decisions about issues such as R&D, scheduling, price, purchasing, marketing, etc. Trainees who work in teams make strategic decisions. During the two-day game period, each team's decision is fed into the computer and instant feedback shows the profit of each team ("company"). Feedback includes income statements, balance sheets, manufacturing reports, marketing reports, cash flow information, and so forth.[27]

HRM DYNAMICS
Training and Development in Selected Canadian Organizations

Air Canada

Training is a continuous process for flight attendants at Air Canada. The In-Flight Service Training Division has developed a highly sophisticated methodology for training cabin personnel. The methodology employs several media including: lectures on such topics as evacuation procedures, "service par excellence," interpersonal skills, and dress and grooming guidelines. However, by far the most important instruction technique is a series of simulation exercises practised in realistic "mock-ups" of aircraft interiors. Very often these practice sessions are unexpectedly interrupted by simulating emergencies, from drunk or ill passengers to major equipment failures. All in all Air Canada finds these training media to be very effective.

Bell Canada

Bell Canada is one of the top Canadian organizations in terms of investment in training and development. For example, in the Quebec region the training centre grew from seven employees in the 1970s to fifty-four full-time trainers in the late 1980s. The company offers a variety of on-site and off-site training opportunities. Over the years the training resource centre has become so successful that the company sells training modules to outside customers. The choice of media varies from one sector to another. Approximately half of the preferred media involves lectures, with documents prepared internally. The other half involves computer simulations. Each training program at Bell Canada is guided by a policy called "MR TOP training plan," which is an acronym derived from Material (needed), Resources, Time (frame), Objectives, and Procedure.

Canadian Marconi

Marconi operates seven divisions; eight trainers are assigned each to a specific division. Needs analysis is conducted on a weekly basis where managers and trainers discuss different situations and events and jointly decide if problems can be remedied by training. Then, a more formal task analysis is conducted and the resource department prepares a cost–benefit projection for upper management. This forecasts the cost of training and the related savings in today's dollars. Most training is given on site (on the job or off the job) by senior technicians, supervisors, or professional trainers. Only occasionally does the company hire an outside consultant. The principal methods of training are lecture and coaching.

SUMMARY

Changing technology, global competition, and the rapid obsolescence of skills and knowledge are putting pressure on organizations to train and develop their employees effectively. This requires careful attention to the three principal phases of training and development: assessment of needs, program development, and implementation and evaluation of the entire process. Weak links in this sequence will obviously limit the effectiveness of training and development programs.

In setting up training programs, a number of criteria should be considered, especially a response to the questions of: who? what? and where? A variety of training methods and media is at the disposal of the training and development directors, but their selection should be based on appropriateness to the training objectives and their relative costs. Regardless of the method chosen, the training content should be designed to optimize learning. To achieve that, proper use of reinforcers during and after training should be thought of. Evaluation of training program effectiveness should not be neglected. It requires a commitment by the company to engage in a rigorous, preferably experimental, design for program evaluation. Though similar to predictive validation designs, experimental designs are more costly to implement both in terms of time and money. Quasi-experimental designs and the use of existing PA information can enable the HR manager or the training director to effectively evaluate training and development decisions.

POSTSCRIPT

The notion of training and development in organizations is changing rapidly. In addition to companies understanding the need to ensure that their workforce is capable of performing productively at present, they are beginning to realize that training and development is important as a strategic approach by which to achieve a competitive edge in the future. Headlines, such as "Executive Development as a Competitive Weapon"[28] or "Training Considered Key to Competing,"[29] are found more and more frequently in the pages of newspapers and business journals. We live in a period in which employees, managers, and organizations are turning to training as a solution to productivity issues. Although the general trend is encouraging, it might also be dangerous, because training is regarded as a panacea for all problems. In fact, a more careful examination (at the strategic level) may suggest that some specific training programs may meet the short- and medium-range needs of organizations, but it is the emphasis on broader education and development efforts that may be instrumental in meeting their long-term needs. Consequently, companies should also share their experience and general wisdom in addressing wider societal problems affecting the labour force, such as illiteracy, emerging changes in gender roles, and the general level of education. All are factors that will impact on the organization at one time or another.

Apart from more philosophical concerns, there is the issue of top management's attitude toward training. CEOs' views of training and development "de facto" are somewhat ambivalent. On the one hand there is wide recognition of its importance, and on the other there are not always clear signals that companies are willing to "put their money where their mouth is." Only a few companies in Canada assign significant budgets to training and development. It has also been noticed that even among them, training is regarded as a "necessary evil," therefore representing a cost to the business. While at the outset this is true, the more advanced companies view training and development from the perspective of investment rather than cost.

In attributing importance to a concept, semantic interpretations are very indicative; they denote a change in philosophy and a real commitment to training and development. Perhaps training modules could be conceived in the future to help bring about this evolution in thinking.

REVIEW AND ANALYSIS QUESTIONS

1. What are some common objectives for all training? Which is the most difficult to attain? Why?
2. How do companies decide whether to invest in training? What factors would influence them not to invest in training?
3. Based on your own experience, what benefits did your employer (former or present) receive by training you? Elaborate.
4. What legal considerations influence training and development decisions?
5. What are some relevant considerations when selecting a particular training medium? What are the major drawbacks of using the formal course/lecture method in training?
6. What are some design principles that can enhance the learning that takes place in training programs?
7. Why do organizations often overlook or lack proper evaluation of employee training programs?
8. Suppose that you are a first-line supervisor experiencing a low-performance problem with one of your subordinates. What indicators would you need to decide whether this reflects a selection mistake or merely the need for training? Can you illustrate this dilemma with an example from your present or past work experience?
9. Can you distinguish between formal and informal employee development programs? Illustrate the differences by providing a few examples.
10. Describe a training evaluation design that includes a control group. Explain the advantages of such a design.

CASE STUDY

A TRAINING MISDIAGNOSIS OR MISTAKE?

Sue Campbell, the training representative for the regional office of a large service organization, had been very excited about the new training program. The Personnel Department at headquarters had informed her six months before that it had purchased a speed-reading training program from a reputable firm, and statistics showed that the program had indeed proved to be very effective in other companies.

Sue knew that most individuals in the regional office were faced, on a daily basis, with a sizeable amount of incoming correspondence, including internal memoranda, announcements of new and revised policies and procedures, reports of federal legislation, and letters from customers. So, a course in speed reading should certainly have helped most employees.

The headquarters office had flown regional training representatives in for a special session on how to conduct the speed-reading program. Sue had, therefore, begun the program in her regional office with great confidence. She led five groups (thirty employees each) through the program, which consisted of nine two-hour sessions. Sessions were conducted in the on-site training facilities. Altogether, 1,200 employees in the organization participated in the training, at an approximate cost to the company of $110 per participant (including training materials and time away from work). The program was very well received by the participants, and speed tests administered before and after training showed that, on average, reading speed increased 250 percent with no loss of comprehension.

A couple of months after the last session, Sue informally asked a couple of employees who had gone through the training if they were applying the speed-reading principles in their work and maintaining their reading speed. They said they were not using it at work but did practise their new skill with their off-the-job reading. Sue checked with several other participants and heard the same story. Although they were applying what they had learned in their personal reading and for school courses, they were not using it on the job. When Sue asked them about all the reading material that crossed their desks daily, the typical response was: "I never read those memos and policy announcements anyway!" Sue was concerned about this information but did not know what to do with it.

Case Questions

1. Did Sue really waste valuable training funds?
2. Should Sue now start a program to get the employees to read the memos and policy announcements?
3. How could Sue have avoided the situation she now faces?
4. Should organizations provide training programs to help improve employee skills that can be used off the job?

NOTES

1. Information is based on P. Lush, "Poor economic performance and training linked," *The Globe and Mail*, 1 March 1990, B3.
2. Cited in J. DeSouza, "Training: The Key Human Resources Issues for the 1990s," in *Human Resource Management in Canada*, 1990, 30,512.
3. M. Gibb-Clark, "IBM budgets millions for its employees' skill training," *The Globe and Mail*, 24 January 1990, B1 and B4.
4. M. Gibb-Clark, "Most companies refuse to spend a cent in training," *The Globe and Mail*, 30 October 1989, B3.
5. For more information about the measures and their structure, validity, and reliability, see J.C. Taylor and D.G. Bowers, *Survey of Organizations* (Ann Arbor, Mich.: The University of Michigan ISR, 1967); D.J. Weiss et al., *Manual for the Minnesota Satisfaction Questionnaire*, The University of Minnesota IR Center, 1967); C.P. Smith, M. Kendall, and C.L. Hulin, *The Measurement of Satisfaction in Work and Retirement* (Chicago: Rand McNally, 1969); and L.W. Porter and E.E. Lawler III, *Managerial Attitudes and Performance* (Homewood, Ill.: Irwin, 1968).
6. "Survey Focus: Who said What: 1991 Employee Survey Results—Breakdown by Workgroup," *Horizons*, 30 October 1991, 3.
7. Cited in R. S. Schuler and V. L. Huber, *Personnel and Human Resource Management*, 4th ed. (St. Paul, Minn.: West Publishing Co., 1990), 377.
8. T. Gilbert, "Praxeonomy: A Systematic Approach to Identifying Training Needs," *Management of Personnel Quarterly* 20 (1967): 30–38.
9. Illustration based on text found in W.J. Rothwell and H.C. Kazanas, *Strategic Human Resources Planning and Management* (Englewood Cliffs, N.J.: Prentice–Hall, 1988), 300.
10. *Bell News*, 11 February 1991, 5.
11. For more information on ATI, see D.F. Lohman and R.E. Snow, "Toward a Theory of Cognitive Aptitude for Learning from Instruction," *Journal of Educational Psychology* 76 (1984): 347–76.
12. I.T. Robertson and S. Downs, "Work-Sample Tests of Trainability: A Metha-Analysis," *Journal of Applied Psychology* 74 (1989): 402–7; and I.T. Robertson and S. Downs, "Learning and the Prediction of Performance: Development of Trainability Testing in the U.K.," *Journal of Applied Psychology* 64 (1979): 42–50.
13. V.L. Huber, "A Comparison of Goal Setting and Pay as Learning Incentives," *Psychological Reports* 56 (1985): 223–35.
14. T.T. Baldwin and J.K. Ford, "Transfer of Training: A Review and Direction for Future Research," *Personnel Psychology* 41 (1988): 63–105.
15. R.A. Noe, "Women and Mentoring: A Review and Research Agenda," *Academy of Management Review* 13 (1988): 65–78.
16. R. Neff, "Videos are Starring in More and More Training Programs," *Business Week*, 7 September 1987, 108.
17. *Training, The Magazine of Human Resources Development*, October 1988.
18. A.S. Edson, "Commuting to an M.B.A.," *Scene Magazine*, September 1979, 64–65.
19. J.C. Georges, "The Hard Reality of Soft-Skills Training," *Personnel Journal*, April 1989, 41–45.
20. Ibid., 43.
21. G.E. Huszczo, "Training for Team Building," *Training and Development Journal*, February 1990, 37–43.
22. J.F. Bolt, "Executive Development as a Competitive Weapon," *Training and Development Journal*, July 1989, 71–76.
23. R.J. House, "Experiential Learning: A Social Learning Theory Analysis," in *Management Evaluation*, ed. R.D. Freedman, C. Cooper, and S.A. Stumpf (London: John Wiley and Sons, 1982), 9–10.
24. R. Rajsic, "Organized Learning: Training That Pays," *Human Resource Management in Canada* (Feature Report: Training), October 1985, 5,434.
25. G.J. Dickelman, "Designing and Managing Computer-Based Training for Human Resource Development," in S.E. Forrer and Z.B. Leibowitz, *Using Computers in Human Resources* (San Francisco: Jossey–Bass Publishers, 1991), 140.
26. Cited in J. Rocco, "Computers Track High-Potential Managers," *HR Magazine*, August 1991, 66.
27. Excerpts from Forrer and Leibowitz, *Using Computers*, 98–99.
28. J.F. Bolt, "Executive Development as a Competitive Weapon," *Training and Development Journal*, July 1989, 71.
29. M. Gibb-Clark, "Training Considered Key to Competing," *The Globe and Mail*, 18 January 1990, B1.

CHAPTER TWELVE

CAREER MANAGEMENT AND PLANNING

KEYNOTE ADDRESS
John E. Cleghorn
President and Chief Operating Officer, Royal Bank of Canada
Career Management and Planning at Royal Bank

It used to be that career management meant waiting for the company to tell you what's best for your career. You joined an organization and allowed—even expected—your employer to totally manage where and how your career path would lead.

Times have changed. Careers are no longer looked upon as clear and simple "escalator rides" up through the ranks. Now all employees must take active part in managing and planning their career development. Ultimately, career choices are the individual's responsibility—not the company's.

Businesses are far different than they were even twenty years ago. I know Royal Bank has dramatically shifted from the way we used to be when I first joined in 1974. We have flattened our hierarchy, decentralized authority, and are seeking out nontraditional business opportunities. Our goal is to continue to evolve as Canada's top financial services enterprise, offering clients a complete range of services.

This shift in focus has also led to the creation of a whole new range of jobs. And because there are more job choices available, individuals must take the initiative to make their interests known to the company and to indicate how they would like to see their career unfold. "The boss" cannot be expected to know everything about every job available in an organization, and most are not mind readers either.

Today's marketplace is tougher than ever. Customers have increasingly sophisticated needs. They expect more from us. To set ourselves apart, we know that our biggest advantages stem from our people. We need them to be innovative, creative, and to thrive on challenges. But this does not happen by saying so. They must be supported with specialized training at every stage of their career—from orientation programs for new employees, to advanced professional development for more senior staff....

There is no doubt that in our complex world, career management is more challenging both from a company's and an individual's perspective. As the nature of work and types of career choices continue to evolve, companies and their employees must look increasingly to future needs and patterns rather than focus on past practices and traditional career paths.

The first step in implementing a successful career management process is effective communication. No matter where they work, or the job they perform, all Royal Bank employees are informed about our policies and commitment to career development. We believe they also have a right to know where we are going as an organization, and what careers are available to them.

To make this happen, we provide our staff with a number of planning resources that help them map out personal career strategies. Recently, we produced a video that presents the facts about career planning and the various roles and responsibilities of the employee, the manager, and the bank. We also provide employees with a number of informative self-help booklets. These include a planning workbook for individuals to assess their strengths, weaknesses, and interests; detailed guides with background information on both management and nonmanagement jobs; plus an informative book that details our many learning resources available to help enhance a person's professionalism.

We continue to look for other ways to inform our people about career choices. Things like employee career fairs, detailed charts of management positions, and job posting are being more widely used across the bank.

Another key to career management is performance feedback and coaching. A very valuable person who can provide this information is an employee's manager. Each year our managers meet formally one-on-one with their staff to discuss performance and other matters. But this cannot be the sole source or opportunity for feedback and coaching. Employees should seek out feedback from their manager, colleagues, and even clients on an ongoing basis. Fully understanding your strengths and weaknesses is crucial as you set career objectives and pursue a personal development plan.

Our employees also have access to a human resource counsellor who can provide additional career planning information, plus insights into the challenges and opportunities in different parts of the bank.

Career management is no longer a one-way process. All of this support is designed to encourage our people to take the initiative and responsibility for their career development: to understand our business strategies, the work involved in implementing them, and how their skills can best be applied and developed to support the bank's goals. At the same time, it is essential for individuals to have a clear appreciation of their personal goals.

Perhaps one of the most challenging and rewarding tasks any one of us can undertake is an exploration of what we really want to accomplish in our lives and careers. This means taking a close look at what we stand for, the kinds of things we enjoy doing, the skills we have to offer, and getting our priorities between work and personal goals straight.

It takes courage for people to examine their lives and work patterns and assess them against their dreams and aspirations. And it takes commitment to pursue dreams by working hard to accomplish the many routine day-to-day tasks that must be completed to eventually realize them.

Let's face it, you only go around once in life. So, make your own decisions and take responsibility for pursuing a career that you want and are good at. Those who do, stand a much better chance of fulfilling a happy and rewarding career.

·   ·   ·

The Keynote Address by the president and COO of Royal Bank of Canada shows the relative importance that this company attributes to career planning and development. Whereas not many years ago only few companies paid serious attention to career planning and development, the field is growing in importance as a legitimate HR activity. Individuals, as well as organizations, realize that "the ball game is changing" and the onus on developing careers and providing opportunities for such development is a joint responsibility. In the case of Royal Bank, emphasis is placed on communicating the bank's policies pertaining to careers and providing the means for managers and employees to engage in this activity.

·   ·   ·

CAREER MANAGEMENT AND PLANNING

What Does "Career" Mean?

Many scholars define career as a sequence of work activities and positions and associated attitudes and reactions experienced over a person's lifetime. The two themes in this definition are work and time, along which the career provides a "moving perspective" on the unfolding interaction between an individual and the society or organizations in which that individual works.

A useful way to understand the concept of career is to separate the individual component from the organizational or public component. As for the individual component, some critical benchmarks are used in professional circles to denote fast track progress in one's career. On the other hand, lack of promotion over an expected period, or the nongranting of tenure in certain jobs, indicates a barrier to career and many employees see this as a failure. Although these benchmarks are informal and vary according to professional categories and organizational culture, they are associated with common norms. For instance, the time it takes an employee to reach tenure or to be promoted are typical benchmark examples. Yet, research indicates that very fast career trackers, and very slow ones, develop a variety of stress-related symptoms.

From the organizational perspective, career is equated with the employee's achievements, salary history, recognition by various clients, and the like. Many organizations use such information to identify their "star" performers and groom them to undertake even more responsible positions. However, this type of analysis lacks information pertaining to the real reasons for the career track; it does not answer the question of why the pattern developed in a particular way.

Yet in another perspective, career simply implies work-related experiences. Within this definition, neither success nor failure is implied. A person can remain in the same job, acquire and develop new skills, and have a successful career without getting promoted. Or people can build a career by moving among various jobs in different fields and organizations. This modern concept of career encompasses not only traditional work experiences, but also the diversity of career alternatives, individual choices, and individual experiences. This contemporary view of career is based on four assumptions: (1) that career success or failure is normally determined by the individual rather than by others (i.e., employers, colleagues, etc.), (2) that no absolute yardsticks for evaluating career are available given its subjective nature and its multiple linkages to an individual's needs, (3) that a complete understanding of an individual's career requires examination of both its subjective and objective aspects, and (4) that a career includes broader aspects than mere work for pay; volunteer work, housework, and political activities are also an important part of a career.

This chapter will concentrate on issues pertaining to *career planning*, which is the individual's lifelong process of establishing personal career objectives and acting in a manner intended to bring them about. It will also concentrate on *career management*, which is the process of deciding what work opportunities to accept or reject. It should be noted that, while career planning is the sole responsibility of the individual, career management is a responsibility shared by the individual and the organization. Individuals decide what they want to do; managers, who represent the organization, decide what opportunities to offer and what development activities are necessary prerequisites to qualify for them. In this regard career planning is blended with HRP, although the two processes are complementary rather than substitutes or synonyms.

Purposes and Importance of Career Management and Planning

Career planning is simply the process of formulating meaningful goals for what we want to achieve in our working lives. Without these goals, there is a risk that employees will allow themselves to drift. While it is true that, in many instances, our career may be shaped by accident, fate, or decisions made by others, it is also true that, even in these cases, at some point individuals pause and reflect upon their wishes, needs, and future outlook at work. Research suggests that when individuals do not take charge of their career, they often end up dissatisfied with it. Thus, setting goals and following advice and counselling enables individuals to take control of their own career development. Often, the role of catalyst is assumed by organizations. Many employers conclude that helping employees make career decisions will eventually lead to more satisfaction and loyalty in the organization. Thus, many organizations include the development of career policies, paths, and procedures that assist employees in realizing their goals in their career management programs.

From an individual perspective, the foundation of successful career planning boils down to self-assessment of needs, wishes, and desires with realistic expectations of talents, skills, motivation, and other pertinent characteristics. Thus, it is essential for employees, and especially the skilled ones, to be able to articulate their strengths, skills and values, which is imperative for setting realistic goals. The next step involves the assessment of the opportunities available within their organization.

From an organizational perspective, it becomes imperative to provide employees the opportunity to follow a career path and to successfully manage it. While it is widely recognized that organizations experiencing growth provide more career opportunities to their employees, many come to realize that in the 1990s, plans need to be devised for generating opportunities even for organizations experiencing downsizing. As we will see later on in the chapter, the decline in organizational growth is forcing firms to be more creative in developing and managing careers. Without this creativity, organizations may lose some of their best employees, who will seek to develop elsewhere.

In the past, career planning and development were confined to high school or college students. Today, many organizations offer guidance and counselling to employees who wish to develop a career. According to some experts, a number of forces have converged to stimulate the popularity of career activities in organizations, including:

- Spillover effects of the affirmative action and equity laws that were extended from women and minorities to many other categories of employees;
- An increasing number of two-career couples, making career planning necessary to permit more balance between work and home;
- Greater employee concern for quality of life, and the higher aspirations of a better-educated workforce;
- A growing need for career planning among the baby-boom generation in order to avoid career plateauing and obsolescence;
- The need to cope with an economy that alternates between near depression and very slow growth.

All of these forces make it beneficial to both the employee and the employer to develop a strategy for long-term utilization and development of the employee's talent in the organization. As shown in Exhibit 12.1, career management and planning relate to a number of HR activities discussed so far.

JOB ANALYSIS. Whereas HRP helps establish the general context within which career management and planning take place, job analysis helps identify specific SKAs that may be needed for the career path. For example, in the U.S. Air Force, job analysis data have been used to identify jobs between which individuals can be transferred with minimal retraining. In planning their own careers, employees can use job analysis information to plot career paths and make maximum use of their past experience in moving to different, more challenging jobs.

It is important to remember, however, that while the possibilities of individual development in organizations could be very stimulating and beneficial to both the employee and the organization, they can also be dangerous in that the organization may not be able to meet the expectations of the employee. Moreover, often jobs are described in narrow terms

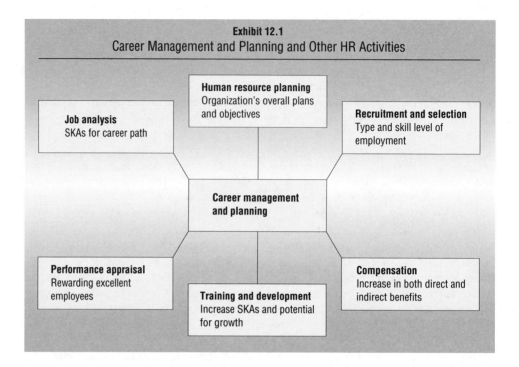

Exhibit 12.1
Career Management and Planning and Other HR Activities

Human resource planning
Organization's overall plans and objectives

Job analysis
SKAs for career path

Recruitment and selection
Type and skill level of employment

Career management and planning

Performance appraisal
Rewarding excellent employees

Compensation
Increase in both direct and indirect benefits

Training and development
Increase SKAs and potential for growth

and thus limit career progress. Furthermore, given the rapid change in technology and organizational needs, some experts believe that it becomes increasingly important to not only define jobs in broader terms (i.e., narrative job descriptions), but to also allow for periodic changes in the definitions and descriptions of jobs.[1]

HR PLANNING. The determination of the organization's career management and planning needs, often depends on its HRP requirements. These requirements, as discussed in Chapter 4, are derived from the organization's overall plans and objectives, its projected HR needs (by skill, type, and number), and the anticipated supply of human resources to fill these needs. As a result of changing technology, changes in the workforce and work habits, and human rights charters, organizations are finding it increasingly difficult to develop and maintain a coherent career management plan. On the other hand, other types of legislation, such as employment equity policies, make HRP mandatory and enable better career management simply by complying with the law.

RECRUITMENT AND SELECTION. Often career management and planning depend on the type and skill level of the employee. All in all, it is fairly well known that professional employees (i.e., those with higher levels of education and skills) are more concerned about careers. Thus, organizations that employ these types of individuals need to meet their career expectations and, consequently, career management is becoming more significant as part of these organizations' HR policies and activities.

COMPENSATION. While most organizations provide better compensation for individuals who progress within a traditional career path, the organization needs to develop a system of rewarding the development of lateral and diagonal career paths in order to encourage such moves. Otherwise, the culture will support only traditional vertical promotion paths.

PERFORMANCE APPRAISAL. Career management involves the rewarding of excellent employees, at least in the case of the more traditional vertical promotions. Thus, valid and reliable policies and techniques are imperative for sound career management from an organizational perspective. At times a close examination of "performance gaps" may lead an employer to the conclusion that an employee might be better off (for himself or herself and for the company) being transferred or doing a different type of work. This case is classic for employees who have reached a plateau in their current career path and seek other opportunities.

Appraisal can also be used as an employee development tool that places the supervisor in a supportive, reinforcing role. The PA session gives the supervisor and the employee an opportunity to discuss the employee's long-term career goals and plans. On the basis of past performance, the supervisor can give the employee short-term, specific suggestions on how to improve performance in ways that will help the employee achieve longer-term career goals.

TRAINING AND DEVELOPMENT. Once career goals are set, employees may seek to participate in a variety of training programs to increase their SKAs and to facilitate the opportunities to grow and realize their career goals. Research indicates that individuals who are committed to their careers and have engaged in career planning seem to respond better to training.[2]

Exhibit 12.2 shows some typical career and planning challenges confronted by individuals and organizations. The remainder of the chapter will elaborate on the many parameters identified there.

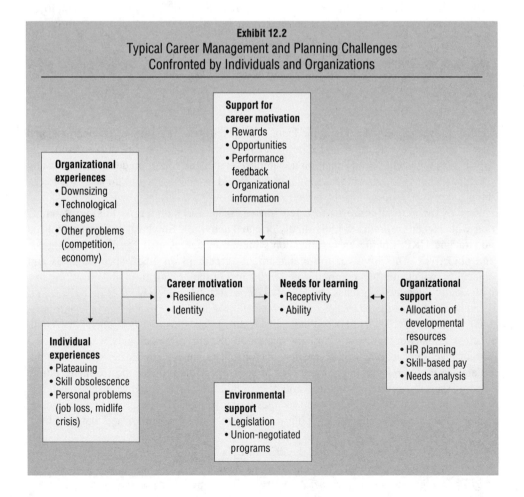

Exhibit 12.2
Typical Career Management and Planning Challenges
Confronted by Individuals and Organizations

Support for career motivation
• Rewards
• Opportunities
• Performance feedback
• Organizational information

Organizational experiences
• Downsizing
• Technological changes
• Other problems (competition, economy)

Career motivation
• Resilience
• Identity

Needs for learning
• Receptivity
• Ability

Organizational support
• Allocation of developmental resources
• HR planning
• Skill-based pay
• Needs analysis

Individual experiences
• Plateauing
• Skill obsolescence
• Personal problems (job loss, midlife crisis)

Environmental support
• Legislation
• Union-negotiated programs

Legal and Policy Issues in Career Management and Planning

Legal and policy considerations are relevant to some limited aspects of career management and planning. One such aspect is discrimination by being excluded from counselling or from promotion. This would be considered illegal. While no human rights tribunal has yet ruled on the discriminatory impact of such events, by and large, relevant legislation does cover this type of HR responsibility. Employees from protected groups can file complaints with human rights commissions if they are differentially prohibited from receiving any career planning programs.[3]

An important case was recently reported in the U.S.A. and it may have future implications in Canada, since discrimination issues in the two countries are similar. The case revolved around Janella Sue Martin who sued Texaco Inc. (the third-largest oil company in North America) for alleged sex discrimination in denying her a promotion. Martin, who at the age of 42 was Texaco's western regional credit supervisor, was denied a promotion although she moved to her current work location based on the promise that she would be promoted whenever a credit manager job became vacant. Instead, the job was awarded to a man. Six years after the time she filed the suit, on 2 October 1991, a jury awarded her $2.7 million in compensatory damages and $15 million in punitive damages. The total sum awarded by the jury was believed, at the time, to be the largest sum ever awarded in a sex discrimination case. While the company is appealing the verdict, the lesson to future employers is clear. To quote Rod Horad, the foreman for the jury: "We wanted to set an example against Texaco; I think they had better open up their eyes to discrimination.[4]

Employment equity concerns initially focused on recruitment and selection. During the next decades, however, emphasis is likely to shift to those individuals already employed by the organization. Providing career opportunities for women and visible minorities is particularly important. Already companies are realizing that in order to help women and minorities advance they must develop programs to break the "glass ceiling" that has blocked career advancement for these individuals. Many companies are working hard to change this situation.

CAREER PLANNING NEEDS AND GOALS

Change is ever present. Trends in the labour force, shifts in the nature of occupations, and new directions in educational programs not only occur rapidly, but can sometimes be subtle or even deceptive. Information about these matters all too often deals with facts and conditions as they *were*, whereas in reality we should be encouraged to think of what conditions *may be like* in the future, as well as what we ourselves *may become*.

One of the current concerns in career management and planning is linking organization-wide career programs to individually oriented activities. Emphasis is therefore placed on strategic HRP; linking an organization's human resources to its basic business goals and objectives. This involves top-management agreement on clear, specific goals and objectives, which are then communicated to the rest of the organization, thus resulting in a realistically integrated business and HR plan (see Exhibit 12.3).

An employer needs to make a number of choices in this regard. First, the employer needs to determine if outsiders will compete with insiders in filling positions. A common practice in many organizations is to give priority to the employees already working up to a certain level, and to turn to the external market only if inside candidates are not found. Related to these considerations are issues of secrecy: is the promotion or transfer policy open or secret? An open promotion policy commits the organization to disclosing information about available positions and enables employees to choose those for which they wish to be considered. In a closed policy, employees are simply informed that they have been selected.

Another choice revolves around the criteria by which employees will be selected for promotion. The two widely used standards, as depicted in Chapter 9, are *seniority* and *merit*, but other factors might operate as well. Companies that practise nepotism or use other criteria unrelated to employees' performance or pre-established procedures, usually generate sarcastic and antagonistic feelings their employees. Thus, it is be unwise to use the latter, since the entire credibility of the career management program might be questioned.

Exhibit 12.3
Career Planning at Royal Bank of Canada

A PARTNERSHIP BETWEEN YOU AND THE ORGANIZATION

Effective career planning requires the combined efforts of you, your manager, and Human Resources.

YOUR ROLE

Assume the initiative by:

- assessing yourself,
- asking for and listening to feedback,
- seeking information about career options,
- setting personal goals,
- communicating your aspirations and interests as well as any changes in your

personal status (i.e. mobility, education and training),
- using education and training opportunities,
- following through on developmental plans.

YOUR MANAGER'S ROLE

Your manager will provide coaching and feedback on your performance, strengths and areas for improvement. He/she will:

THE HUMAN RESOURCE COUNSELLOR'S ROLE

- provide exposure and growth opportunities consistent with your goals and the organization's,
- evaluate progress on developmental plans,

- supplement career information provided by the Bank with his/her personal knowledge of specific jobs and careers.

He or she will provide information/insight on career opportunities, the competition for them, the requirements to be effective as well as confirm the Bank's view of you—your strengths, development needs, and future

prospects. In addition, the HR Counsellor can encourage you to develop challenging goals—to develop professionally and to achieve balance in your personal life.

Source: " A Guide to Taking Charge," *Planning Your Career*, Royal Bank of Canada, 1991, 8. Reprinted with permission of Royal Bank of Canada.

From an individual perspective, career motivation includes being resilient in the face of change; having insight into one's self and the environment; and identifying with one's job, organization, and/or profession. Looking at these elements in slightly more detail can prove useful. *Career resilience* really means how resistant employees are to career barriers or disruptions that affect their work. During economic recessionary periods, resiliency can be tested, as organizations do not grow and are even involved in downsizing. Naturally career is affected. People with high career resilience consider themselves competent enough to control their responses to what happens to them; they respond to obstacles and unpredictable events by reframing their ideas and repositioning their energies to allow them to move ahead anyway. Career counselling, either independent or organizationally supported, is one of the tools that could be used to reposition a career. *Career insight* refers to the extent that individuals are realistic about themselves and their careers and how accurately they relate these perceptions to their career goals. An honest examination

Developing Career Motivation

of strengths and weaknesses can provide an individual with a realistic view of himself or herself (see Exhibit 12.4). *Career identity* reflects employees' career goals, whether they would like to advance in the company or achieve advancements elsewhere, and if they should assume a proactive role or simply wait for it to happen.

The purposes of developing an employee's potential are numerous. Although development usually is concerned with the improvement of intellectual or emotional abilities, other HR goals could be met during the developmental process, such as:

Exhibit 12.4
Summary Checklist of Royal Bank of Canada

If your answer is "yes" to most of the following questions, then you are ready to start mapping out some concrete goals and developmental plans toward their achievement.

BASED ON MY SELF-ASSESSMENT, RESEARCH AND DISCUSSIONS WITH OTHERS, DO I NOW HAVE A CLEARER UNDERSTANDING OF:

Yes/No

- my most important/satisfying values, working conditions, skills and weaknesses? _____
- the jobs/areas which could be a good match for me? _____
- the organization in general? _____
- how I am perceived (potential and otherwise) by others in the bank? _____
- the direction I would like my career to take (job enrichment, upward advancement, lateral/downward assignment, other…)? _____
- what I need to do to enhance my ability to reach my goals (i.e., education, skills development, exposure to certain assignments…)? _____
- the trade-offs I need to make to reach my goals (i.e., financial, mobility, education)? _____

Source: "A Guide to Taking Charge," *Planning Your Career*, Royal Bank of Canada, 1991, 21. Reprinted with permission of Royal Bank of Canada.

Developing Employee Potential

- Enhancing an employee's job satisfaction and QWL;
- Helping an employee discover new interests and potential that have been underutilized;
- Increasing the job-performance effectiveness of the employee;
- Preventing an employee's SKAs from becoming obsolete;
- Sustaining an employee's enthusiasm to avoid burnout.

Employee development depends in many instances on the relationships and attitudes that the employee maintains with the immediate supervisor. By concentrating on the individual's goals and potential, a manager can significantly affect that employee's development. In this sense, almost all managers have an informally assigned responsibility to contribute to employee development, a responsibility that has been labelled the *mentoring function*. Mentoring is a relationship between a junior and a senior colleague that is viewed by the junior as positively contributing to his or her development.

Two types of functions contribute to the development of the junior person: first, a range of career advancement activities (i.e., sponsorship, coaching, exposure and visibility, protection, and challenging work assignments) and, second, a range of personal support activities that help the junior member to develop a sense of personal identity (i.e., role modelling, counselling, acceptance and confirmation, and friendship).

Employee development is much broader than the acquisition of a specific skill. Therefore, a number of conditions are critical for employee development: an organizational philosophy which promotes development and is well supported by top management, and a real understanding of the interrelated nature of development.

Top-management back-up is central in facilitating development; opportunities are in fact created by top management. Delegating decision-making responsibilities to lower-level positions to develop young employees, cultivating a climate that provides opportunities for frequent and open communication between people at different hierarchical levels, and the reward system for mentors are all desirable functions of top-management philosophy. If top management is not committed to employee development, the latter is not likely to happen.

A relationship exists between employee development efforts and other HR activities such as selection, placement, compensation, and appraisal. Neglect of any of these HR functions inhibits development efforts throughout the organization. However, development is not a substitute for proper selection or placement. If a person is chosen to perform in a job that he or she is unable to do (lack of skills or knowledge), no amount of development will change that. Therefore, improper placement can seldom be rectified by development.

Facilitating Employee Development

HRM IN THE NEWS VIGNETTE

Ten Sure Ways To Derail Your Career

Almost every organization has its own story about a fast-tracking executive whose career suddenly went off the rails. How does it happen? Why does it happen? And, more importantly, how can a manager prevent it from happening to him or her?

In a report entitled "Off the Track: Why and How Successful Executives Get Derailed," researchers Morgan McCall and Mike Lombardo of the Centre for Creative Leadership have outlined the ten fatal flaws most likely to show a fast-tracker into the ditch.

1. **Inability to admit business performance problems:** Not surprisingly, a manager who shows that he or she can't deliver the goods is in trouble. This can include profit, production or quality problems. Even more important, if the manager fails to admit the problem, by covering it up, or trying to blame it on others, he or she creates the impression he or she can't—or is unwilling to—change, thus stalling his or her career.

2. **Insensitivity to others:** The most frequent cause for derailment of fast-track executives is insensitivity to others. Some managers are so focused on their work that they are abrasive to others. A bulldog attitude may help a young professional get ahead. When that person becomes a manager, however, the same attitude may push others away and reduce his or her effectiveness.

3. **Cold or arrogant attitude:** Some managers are so brilliant that they become arrogant, intimidating others with their knowledge. Descriptive of such managers is this remark: "He made others feel stupid...wouldn't listen, had all the answers, wouldn't give you the time of day unless you were brilliant too."

4. **Betrayal of trust:** Not the same thing as dishonesty, breach of trust is committed by making promises that can't be kept, holding back important information, or sharing information that someone else trusted you to keep confidential. A manager who isn't trusted by colleagues is heading for trouble.

5. **Over-managing:** This also is known as micro-management. Some managers never learn to delegate. As long as they can control all the work they are responsible for, their career hums along. However, at a certain level in the organization, managers cease to do the work themselves, and have to trust that others will do it. Some never make this transition, never learning to delegate or build a team beneath them.

6. **Overly ambitious:** Some managers spend more time thinking about how to position

themselves for the next job than about how to successfully build this one. They move from apparent success to apparent success, leaving a trail of bruised bodies behind them. Often their successors have a significant rebuilding job to do after they have gone on to the next position. Eventually, this gets known in the organization.

7. **Failing to staff effectively:** Common problems include staffing with people who are clones of themselves instead of picking those who have complementary skills, or staffing with weak people who won't speak up when things seem to be going wrong.

8. **Inability to think strategically:** Preoccupation with detail and technical questions keeps some executives from grasping the bigger picture. Some managers find it more comfortable to spend time on technical questions. A senior manager who can't think strategically is in a precarious position.

9. **Inability to adapt to a boss with a different style:** There is a saying that most managers are hired on ability and fired on fit. High among the "lack of fit" issues is failure to adapt to the style of a new boss. Some managers can adjust. Those who can't are in a dead-end and better start looking elsewhere.

10. **Over-dependence on a mentor or advocate:** Sometimes managers stay with a single advocate or mentor too long. When the mentor falls from favour, so do they. Even if the mentor remains in power, some people will question the executive's ability to make independent judgements. Can she stand alone, or does she need the mentor as a crutch?

The manager who reviews his or her own performance from time to time in the light of these ten "career derailers" can help himself or herself stay on the main track and avoid dead-ending their own career.

Source: Peter Larson, "Ten Sure Ways to Derail Your Career," Business Section of *The Montreal Gazette*, 18 November 1991, 4. Used with permission.

Careers and the Meaning of Work

A common attitude held by a growing number of employees is that work should bring satisfaction and pleasure in addition to monetary rewards. Yet, when people reach a dead end in their career, for whatever reason, their attitude toward work shifts dramatically. At this juncture people begin to ask themselves: how is this job good for me? instead of asking: how can I do a good job? It is important to realize that changes in attitude toward work diminish employees' motivation and, in addition to their personal suffering, the organization also suffers diminishing returns.

Few will contest the fact that work in Western civilization has become increasingly important. In fact many experts believe that it is the single most important place to which individuals turn to receive rewards and gratification. Since we spend a great part of our active life at work, what we do there spills over into our general happiness with life. While it is recognized that most people work to achieve personally derived ends, the means and the magnitude of these multiple ends are very important.

The other side of the coin refers to the prestige attributed to an occupation—what other people think about it is usually based on facts such as the money earned, the education required, and the degree of control over human and capital resources. Thus, it is important to study occupations before choosing a job because occupation also has a lot to do with the life one will lead.

CAREER MANAGEMENT AND DEVELOPMENT

Often ten twenty, even thirty years down the road, individuals begin to realize, for various reasons, that they no longer enjoy going to work; they either find their job too stressful, boring, or repetitive. Sometimes other organizational realities will also leave the individual jobless. In order to prepare for either situation employees are better off if they engage in continued career management planning. But the task of providing these services remains the prime responsibility of the employer.

There are two different strategies of career management planning available for organizational use: one centred on *individual planning needs* and the other centred on *organizational HR planning needs*. Individual career planning centres on people's plans for satisfying their personal needs for growth and development. Organizational career planning focuses on jobs and constructing career paths that provide for the logical progression of people between jobs. Exhibit 12.5 provides an example of career development activities. Although it does not provide a complete list of possible career planning programs, it illustrates many of them on the continuum between the individual-centred and the organization-centred.

Exhibit 12.5 **Career Development Activities**						
ORGANIZATION-CENTRED CAREER PLANNING		MUTUAL FOCUS MANAGER-ASSISTED CAREER PLANNING			EMPLOYEE-CENTRED CAREER PLANNING	
Corporate succession planning	Corporate talent inventories	Development assessment centres (with feedback)	Manager–employee career discussions (includes separate training for managers)	Corporate seminars on organizational career	Company-run career planning workshops	Self-directed workbooks and tape cassettes

Studies have often indicated that career choices are influenced by four individual traits: *interests, self-identity, personality,* and *social background.* Consequently, there are many manuals, textbooks, and even video cassettes that can help individuals diagnose their own career potential. Paper-and-pencil psychological tests, often provided by the organization, can help individuals focus on their vocational interests and preferences. Personality and self-identity inventories are available for planning workshops and seminars, where employees are given guidelines and helpful hints on such topics as: "how to plan your career," or "how to be more assertive in your career planning." In these workshops/seminars, employees learn how to better present themselves (prepare for an interview, prepare a résumé, etc.), how to be more forceful in communicating their career goals, and how to assess different career paths and make choices. The content of such workshops varies from company to company.

Many companies do not apply their career programs across the board, but rather only to individuals who wish to more systematically diagnose their self-image or personal need for power, affiliation, or achievement. Such inventories could provide useful information if properly done. The biggest problem with "public" vs. "self-made" inventories lies in interpreting the results. Interpretation requires understanding of the psychometric characteristics of the paper-and-pencil tests (especially with regard to validity and reliability, see Chapter 6) and should not be left to the novice. Therefore, many organizations provide career counselling by an HR specialist (sometimes coupled with outside career specialists).

On the other hand, many organizations still hold the belief that career is an individual's responsibility and not that of the organization. This philosophy seems to be at the heart of a career management program prepared by the Society of Management Accountants of Canada for use by CMAs. The program instructs members in the ways and means by which to make it in the profession and in the organization. It teaches the members how to take charge of their own career.[5]

Individual-Centred Career Planning

While the above suggests that career planning may lead to tangible results, there are those who hold the belief that, in the final count, career is more a matter of luck than planning. An article profiling three individuals who made it to the top in different fields explored their respective career paths. Although this was not explicitly stated, one was left with the impression that these employees' paths to the top were characterized in large part by chance rather than planning. In fact, one of the three plainly states that a career plan never existed.[6]

The organizational career planning activity is similar to the individual appraisal activity. The major difference is that career planning by the organization is aimed directly to meet its specific HRP goals. For this reason, many organizations devise programs ranging from job progression paths (clear policy communicated to the employees) to career accommodation in the form of retirement or early retirement.

Organization-Centred Career Planning

Career progression paths represent "ladders" that each employee can climb to advance in certain organizational units. For example, the essence of Sears' Job Progression program is the identification of job demands. Sears uses the Hay Plan to analyze jobs on three basic dimensions: know-how, problem solving, and accountability. Because these dimensions require different employee skills, a rational sequence of job assignments consists of jobs with different dimensions (e.g., sales, accounting, budget, etc.). Consequently, Sears can use its program to identify rational paths to target jobs (those that represent the end of employees' paths); to classify paths according to speed and level of development attained; and to justify and identify lateral and downward moves.

Career paths are not always linear, nor do they always have to move up the organizational structure. In fact, many professional and technical employees (such as engineers and scientists) become part of what is called *The Dual Career Ladder*. Those who want to proceed in their technical–professional jobs are given the opportunity (although the career paths are very narrow) and those who wish to advance, usually move into management. The dual career, therefore, provides opportunities for either the management ladder or the technical ladder.

In order to enable organizations to better plan career pathing and career accommodation, many of them use computerized data banks containing information on the career histories, skill inventories, and career preferences of employees. Taking career opportunities into consideration, individuals may be identified for positions that are consistent with their career goals. The Canadian Armed Forces is using such a talent inventory at some of its divisions, and Canadian National has been experimenting with various talent inventories with the aim of using them in their Succession Planning Program.

Other Canadian companies utilize a variety of HR procedures to encourage formal career management and planning. For instance, Ontario Hydro, determined to increase job rotation, has undertaken aggressive communication of its career development program and rewards managers for effective employee career development by including that function in the managers' performance reviews.[7] Imperial Oil offers management employees a career centre where they can assess their goals, pick up information on company courses, and discuss how their aspirations fit with the organization's goals. When Imperial merged with Texaco Canada, employees were given the chance to fill out a questionnaire specifying which positions in the new organization they were interested in. This resulted in 79 percent of employees getting their first choice; 93 percent got one of their three top choices.

Succession Planning

Succession planning is one of the elements of organization-centred career planning, which involves HRP for the top positions in the organization. This process basically identifies top managers and grooms them to become the next generation of leaders, or, in other words, identifies replacement strength for critical positions. However, this can be a very sensitive issue, since it involves the relinquishing of power. Scheduling is often also a conflict; for instance, an employee cannot move up to fill a new position because no one else is readily available to assume his or her place. Any number of such unforeseen circumstances can obstruct the orderly movement of people in an organization, and it is important that the HR planner recognize this and be ready to change plans on short notice. In most organizations, however, top management develops its own succession method so that it fits with the particular culture.

As a result of this succession planning process, there has been renewed interest in the assessment and development of management potential. This is also the result of today's flat-structured organizations, where senior leadership is more critical than ever, but where fewer senior slots are available. Today's employees are better educated and therefore represent better choices, increasing the need for good methods to identify the high-potential candidates.

Additionally, as a result of the flattening of many organizations, an emerging need is to increase the value attached to alternatives to promotion: lateral or horizontal moves, temporary assignments, downward moves, and early and phased retirement. It is quite clear that these moves are active ways to free up the organization and the individual by opening up creative new options. The difficulty is that the culture of most organizations still views career progression only in terms of vertical promotion, and thus changes need to follow in order to attach value to these alternatives.

The core of succession planning, however, is the review of key positions and the incumbent, and the development of a list of back-up candidates. One by-product of succession planning in recent years has been out-placement or other similar activities that *facilitate exit*. With promotion opportunities becoming scarcer as growth slows and layers of managerial positions are diluted, it is in the organization's best interest to help individuals search for alternative careers outside the organization. Although this involves the loss of important managers, blocking advancement and/or forcing managers to do the same things repeatedly might turn out to be more counter-productive in the long run.

The Canadian government recognized this problem and in 1971 created a program entitled Interchange Canada. With the dual objectives of enhancing employees' development and creating new opportunities for employee mobility, the program arranges for private sector managers to spend up to three years on temporary assignments with the federal government, and vice versa. Between 1990 and 1992, more than 1,085 managers benefited from this service.

Dual Careers

Family and work are both important institutions from which individuals can draw gratification. However, they might be in conflict when it comes to career plans for married couples. All in all, work is overtaking marriage and family as a central focus of Canadian lives, according to a Statistics Canada report.[8] There is a strong indication that marriage does not play as positive a role for women as for men, since in many ways marriage limits women's opportunities, while enhancing those of men. This is particularly true once there are children in the family.

Rapid and inevitable changes in the labour force mirror today's complex array of marital and family situations. The number of households with two paycheques is certainly on the rise. This is partially due to the need to increase the household revenues in order to maintain a reasonable standard of living, but it is also due to the relative increase of female professionals entering the labour force with the intention of developing a career.

The term "dual career" has two meanings: (1) traditionally "dual-career family" refers to the type of family structure in which the husband and wife pursue active careers and a family life simultaneously. A distinction should be made between *dual career* family and *dual earner* family. The first tends to emphasize occupation as a primary source of personal fulfilment while the second merely reflects a desire to increase revenues; (2) recently, however, dual career also means *moonlighting* or pursuing two or more careers simultaneously.

DUAL-CAREER FAMILY.   A dual-career family experiences several dilemmas in itsdaily life:

* *Role overload* occurs when spouses have to deal with two major roles, career and household; this results in major strains, especially for wives who normally end up assuming most of the burden of the household and children;
* *Identity dilemma* caused by confusion between culturally prescribed roles and acquired ones;
* *Role-cycling dilemma* caused by conflicts in the career development between the members of the family unit or between work demands and family responsibilities.

A great many dual-career couples postpone childbearing or opt for no children in order to minimize such conflicts. They are popularly called DINKS (Double Income No Kids). One such famous couple is economist Marie-Josée Drouin (Director of the Hudson Institute) and Charles Dutoit (Conductor of the Montreal Symphony Orchestra). Many researchers point to the widening economic gaps between childless households (dual career) and traditional families with children, and foresee the emergence of a child-free society as a function of the dual-career family phenomenon.

DUAL CAREERS OR MOONLIGHTING.   A study published in 1983 by the federal government suggests that an estimated 250,000 Canadians have multiple careers. The number has most likely tripled since then. For some occupations, it is almost expected to find people engaged in more than one career. For instance, many university professors of business are actively engaged in consulting; many high-tech professionals, such as computer analysts, programmers, statisticians, etc., provide private consulting services after their regular working hours. While no formal study is available to accurately describe the magnitude of this practice, it is evident that it is on the rise. Moonlighters are motivated by either the need to make more money or by an intrinsic desire for achievement. But regardless of the motives, studies report that moonlighters do not sacrifice performance nor their personal health by engaging in a dual-career pattern. One researcher shows that nonmoonlighters are not better off than moonlighters in terms of physical health, job stress, social support, absenteeism, anticipated turnover, and job performance. Moreover, moonlighters seem to have higher job satisfaction and more commitment and participation in voluntary organizations than nonmoonlighters.[9] One thing that moonlighters learn is how to use their time effectively. Certainly, moonlighters who are also part of dual-career families face similar, if not more severe, dilemmas of the kind discussed above.

IMPLEMENTING CAREER PLANNING PROGRAMS

There is no precise method for choosing an occupation. Although individuals are urged to choose wisely and carefully, the selection process is not always logical and rational. In fact, many choose their occupation by accident or by default, given certain conditions and circumstances at the time. Most experts believe that individuals begin to think about occupations from a very narrow base and can only name ten to twelve occupations that they know something about. The reality is that thousands of occupations exist, many of which can be found in the *Canadian Classification and Dictionary of Occupations* and the *Dictionary of Occupational Titles*. Since these are available in most universities and public libraries, it would be interesting to browse through it in order to obtain an idea about the range and diversity of occupations.

While choosing a career individuals should explore their abilities, values, and interests. They should identify the abilities, interests, skills, and characteristics they presently possess and those they would like to develop more fully. Finally, it is of utmost importance to assess and understand one's own image.

Many commercial inventories and assessments are available for self-assessment. Typical questions include asking the person to express his or her degree of agreement or disagreement (on a five-point scale) with a series of statements. A small sample from such inventories includes:

- I would rather work alone than as part of a team.
- I feel bored if I don't have a large number of assignments to do.
- I like to get recognition for work well done.
- Job security is very important for me.
- I am affected by other people's opinions of my work.
- I am happiest when I have complete freedom to do my work as I want.

While conducting such assessments, it should be kept in mind that needs and occupations will most likely change in the future. Because changes will be affected by a variety of factors, most of them unforeseeable, choosing an occupation must be guided by the idea that the selection is based on incomplete information. In an attempt to reduce some of the ambiguity surrounding career choice, people are advised to consult forecasts by labour experts and to be alert to magazine and newspaper articles concerning trends and changes in the family of occupations that the individual is interested in pursuing.

Finally, a clear plan is needed. In order to have realistic plans, an examination of the ideal career choice and the practical one should be made. The closer the ideal is to the real, the less the personal conflict. Thus, career choice is often a compromise between ideals and the realities that must be faced. Changes in career choices over time reflect this compromise procedure. Yet, it should also be clear that career development is a lifelong process of continuing adjustment by working adults. Exhibit 12.6 shows the personal career development plan used by Royal Bank of Canada. To facilitate the career development plan, an employee completes a series of inventories in which working conditions, values, skills, and abilities and areas of interest are assessed.

Taking Stock of Abilities, Values, and Working Conditions

The most researched and best documented theory of career orientation is *Holland's Theory of Career Types*.[10] Holland's theory deals with factors influencing career choices and is based on the concept of congruence, or the fit between the individual and the environment. According to him, people search for environments that will let them exercise their skills and abilities, express their attitudes, problems, and roles. Consequently, Holland claims that six personality types are good predictors of career aspiration and choice:

Holland's Theory of Career Types

- *Conventional*: This is perhaps the most dominant career type found in business occupations. These people are usually well organized, like to play with data and numerical facts, like clear objectives, and cannot tolerate ambiguous situations. They are described as conforming, orderly, efficient, and practical. The less flattering description would include unimaginative, inhibited, and inflexible. Accountants typically fit into this conventional orientation.
- *Artistic:* This type is the most dissimilar to the conventional type. These people prefer musical, artistic, literary, and dramatic vocations. They see themselves as imaginative, intuitive, impulsive, introspective, and independent. They have higher verbal rather than mathematical aptitudes. Their negative descriptions could include being emotional and disorganized.
- *Realistic:* This type of person is described as genuine, stable, and practical as well as shy, uninsightful, and conforming. These people usually have mechanical abilities and are likely to feel comfortable in semi-skilled or crafts positions (e.g., plumbers, assembly-

line workers) that present consistent task requirements and few social demands, such as negotiating and persuading.

- *Social:* The social type is the near opposite of the realistic type. This person prefers activities that involve informing, helping, or developing others and works in a well-ordered and systematic work environment. This person, besides being social, is also described as tactful, friendly, understanding, and helpful. The less positive descriptions would include dominating and manipulative. The social type works in occupations such as nursing and teaching, marketing, sales, and training and development.

Exhibit 12.6
Personal Development Plan at Royal Bank of Canada

MY PERSONAL DEVELOPMENT PLAN

NAME: DATE:

MY MOST IMPORTANT	EXISTING JOB		ACTION STEPS
Working conditions	Present	Missing	Ways I can enrich my current job
1.			
2.			
3.			
4.			
5.			
Values			
1.			
2.			
3.			
4.			
5.			
Skills and Abilities			Publications/events I want to investigate
1.			
2.			
3.			
4.			
5.			
Possible Areas of Interest			People I want to talk to
1.			
2.			
3.			
4.			
5.			

Exhibit 12.6 (continued)

MY MISSION/PRIORITY GOALS

What I want to accomplish/contribute over the next 6 months, 2 years, 3 years,...

Goals	By When
1.	
2.	
3.	
4.	
5.	

Job Considerations

In my current/future jobs, I would like to do/avoid doing:

_____

_____

_____

_____

Personal Considerations

To achieve my mission/goals, I must consider some potential barriers/trade-offs (i.e., geographic location, mobility, dual career, children,...):

_____

_____

_____

_____

Developmental Plans

To achieve my mission/goals, I am committed to (i.e., take certain courses, acquire new skills, accept certain assignments,...):

_____

_____

_____

_____

Source: "A Guide to Taking Charge," *Planning Your Career*, Royal Bank of Canada, 1991. Reprinted with permission of Royal Bank of Canada.

- *Enterprising:* This type is similar to the social type in that he or she also likes to work with people. The main difference is that the enterprising type prefers to lead and control others (as opposed to helping or understanding) in order to obtain certain organizational goals. This type is self-confident, ambitious, energetic, and talkative. The less positive descriptions would include domineering, power hungry, and impulsive.
- *Investigative:* This type is the near opposite of the enterprising type and prefers activities involving observation and analyzing phenomena in order to develop knowledge and understanding. These people are described as complicated, original, and independent as

well as disorderly, impractical, and impulsive; biologists, sociologists, and mathematicians are usually this type. Within business organizations, this type is found in research and development positions and staff positions that require complex analysis with little need to persuade and convince others.

An individual may not necessarily be one type but rather a combination of two or three types. Those who represent a mixture of two or more types, according to Holland, might be more prone to situational influences and the job will choose them rather than them choosing the job.

Stages of Career Development

Most career development models suggest that careers include various stages. Career stages are predictable sequences of events that apply to most people independent of the specific type of job they have. A knowledge of career stage can help individuals and organizations understand the typical issues and events across the life span. We will briefly examine five career stages.

Stage I: Preparation for Work. This first stage extends from birth to approximately 25 years of age. The major tasks during this stage are developing an initial occupational choice and following an educational curriculum that will assist in implementing that choice. Overall, an occupational self-image is developed during the life stages of childhood, adolescence, and early adulthood.

Stage II: Organizational Entry. Selecting a job and an organization are the major focus of the occupational entry stage. One of the major issues during this stage is *reality shock.* Individuals may have unrealistically high expectations and find that many entry-level jobs are not particularly challenging, at least initially. This stage usually occurs between the ages of 18 and 25.

Stage III: The Early Career. The essential task of the early career stage is becoming established in one's career and organization. Two periods are encompassed by this stage: fitting into the adult world and struggling for success in one's chosen field. Individuals are usually between 25 and 40 years of age when they undergo this stage.

Stage IV: The Mid-Career. The mid-career stage (age 40 to 55) begins with the midlife transition between early and middle adulthood. Characteristic of the mid-career is the reassessment of the lifestyle that governed the early career. A new life structure is forged that may or may not be in keeping with the previous structure. Employees typically review the goals that they have attained and consider how many additional goals they can achieve in the future. Possible career-stage issues include obsolescence and plateauing.

Stage V: The Late Career. The final career stage, the late career, involves continued productivity and eventual preparation for disengagement from worklife. Although very little research has been directed toward the late career, it is known that a negative bias against older individuals exists in many companies.

CAREER PROBLEMS

As the workforce ages and as many more organizations today face downsizing trends, some important HRM challenges become apparent: retaining and rewarding employees with critical skills, creating career paths to help senior employees break out of plateaus, and retraining senior employees whose skills have become outdated. Consequently, new policies to avoid career plateaus and skill obsolescence will have to be developed.

Career Plateaus

Career plateau is defined as a point beyond which the probability of advancement is quite low. Employees who reach this stage could be divided into two categories: *solid citizens,* who continue to perform well in spite of limited promotion opportunities, and *deadwood* employees, whose performance levels have deteriorated below acceptable levels.[11] Many experts note that labelling an employee as not promotable could be very risky, since he or she will be excluded from any career development opportunities and thus will fall into a vicious cycle of skill deterioration and career stagnation. In other words, solid citizens could be turned into corporate deadwood.

A number of approaches could be used to combat career plateauing. Early intervention appears to be an important element. It could be based on systematic performance reviews to determine appropriate career interventions before both performance and employee confidence deteriorate. HR policies that combine systematic appraisal and succession planning with career counselling and a wide range of training and development options are required to avoid career plateauing.

Alternatively, organizations can use lateral movement as a systematic part of career development, where employees will be moved from one functional area to another even if their expertise in the new area is more limited. For example, in response to the problem of plateauing among its employees, Canada Mortgage and Housing Corporation (CMHC) initiated various policies and programs. The goal of these was to orient the definition of career success more toward employee initiative and contribution to the organization, rather than toward fast-tracking one's way to the top. In addition to providing a variety of training sessions, the company held a workshop on plateauing. It gave employees the chance to explore their plateau problems and it resulted in an understanding that this phenomenon is not necessarily an end to satisfying and challenging work. In more concrete terms, it also resulted in more employees going after lateral moves and taking advantage of training opportunities that would prepare them for special assignments.[12]

Mid-career and senior employees are also vulnerable to skill obsolescence. This results from a combination of job changes as well as personal changes. Obsolescence can occur when opportunities for training fail to keep pace with changing job requirements. Similarly, skill obsolescence may be the result of employees falling behind in their abilities to use new techniques. According to a number of studies, older workers are particularly vulnerable to skill obsolescence simply because they have longer work histories, during which skills and knowledge can become dated.

Skill Obsolescence

Strategies for combatting skill obsolescence include skill maintenance and retraining. Just as in career plateau problems, interventions in the career cycle might be effective at an early stage, when both management and employee view investments in retraining as likely to yield a high payback. Other strategies include the creation of new roles for senior workers and provision for economic incentives for early retirement.

EVOLUTION IN CAREER PLANNING. This section provides an overview of evolving trends in career planning, beginning with a look at how popular (or unpopular) career planning was two decades ago, and what the current situation is. In 1972, a management consulting firm conducted a survey of manpower planning practices among the fifty-three largest and most progressive Canadian companies. The results revealed that career planning was uncommon, and in those companies that did offer career planning and guidance, it was a relatively new process.[13] Only five companies actually had career counsellors and/or guidance. In 1977, another survey reported that moderate career planning plans existed in large firms but none were found in the medium-sized organizations. The researchers concluded that "Canadian business...does not feel high levels of responsibility toward its employees or potential employees beyond the traditional limits of providing jobs and financial security."[14]

TRENDS IN CAREER MANAGEMENT AND PLANNING

Contemporary Trends

It appears that by 1985, career management and planning had become more widespread, but rather than carrying out full-scale career planning policies and programs, organizations were engaged in it primarily as a result of a perception of social responsibility or legal requirements, or if they had no other choice, due to projected skills shortages. In a ten-year study of approximately 1,900 North American medium-sized and large organizations, it was found that employees felt that the real opportunity for advancement had significantly declined between 1977 and 1987.[15] In another study conducted at the same time, it was learned that fewer Canadian employees, compared to their American counterparts, felt that their employers offered them an opportunity for individual growth and development.[16]

A 1988 survey of management and executive development expenditures and policies of Canadian organizations found that career management and planning assistance varied widely among sectors. On the other hand, close to 60 percent of the responding organizations reported on publishing training and development calendars aimed at pointing out to the employees the sort of development programs that they encouraged. The onus, however, for taking advantage of the programs resided with the employees. Only a small sample of managers were singled out by the companies and sent to attend developmental courses.[17]

INTER-ORGANIZATIONAL CAREER. An interesting trend was been revealed in a Time/CNN poll conducted in August of 1989. Employers were seen as being less loyal to their employees than ten years previously, and vice versa. This means that as employees pursue their individual career plans, they may be more likely to hop from a job in one organization to a job in another organization.[18]

The above trends point to the fact that perceptions about careers, and therefore career planning, have changed. Careers no longer involve an upward move; single careers have been replaced in some cases by multi-careers, where individual career paths pass through various fields of work and various organizations. Individuals have become more involved in planning their own careers. Finally, career success is no longer defined simply in terms of money, advancement, and prestige; for some, personal growth is now seen as the key to career success.[19]

WOMEN IN EXECUTIVE POSITIONS. It is rare to find women at the top of the largest Canadian corporations. While an increasing number of women are employed, they are still underrepresented in powerful management positions. Nonetheless, companies have tried to cut back on the travel, relocation, and long hours that can exclude many women with families. On the other hand, the advancement of women into middle management is well documented.

Why is it taking so long for women to reach the top positions in corporate Canada? According to several leading business analysts, there are many reasons for the impasse, ranging from male managers' discomfort with female executives, to the pressures of balancing work and family concerns. "Mention women in management and the instant association in the minds of most men (and women) is: Women have babies. The conclusion follows naturally that women can't be counted on to make a full-time, open minded commitment to their careers," says Felice Schwartz, founder and president of Catalyst, a research organization that studies work–family issues. Ms. Schwartz contends it costs companies more money to employ women managers than men. "Given a man and a woman of equal abilities and motivation, investing in a woman is undeniably riskier.[20] The implication is that women are more likely to interrupt their careers, or forego them altogether, to pursue motherhood. In fact, it has been estimated by one large industrial company that turnover for top managerial women is approximately 2.5 times greater than for their male counterparts.[21] These perspectives can dissuade corporate decision makers from spending the time, money, and effort on grooming women for top spots in their corporations, and are a major factor contributing to the glass ceiling.

In order to project a more equitable image, some organizations may have an influential "queen bee"—a female executive who enjoys being the only woman at the top, and does her best to thwart the advancement of other women. Additional factors that may contribute to the slow growth rate of women to top positions in management include the cultural belief by many Canadians that the male's job is more important than their spouse's and that it is the male's duty to be the major contributor to household income.

How to crack the ceiling? Until recently, the dominant approach has been to focus on the individual developing a "winning style" to succeed in a "man's world." This has been only partially successful. The more long-term approach is the idea that it is management's responsibility to assure that the workplace offers no barriers to women's day-to-day activities or advancement. Several strategies can be used to increase awareness of problems concerning discriminatory attitudes and practices. Managers can be trained to work and manage in a diverse workforce; managers can be held accountable for improving utilization of women in upper management; management can provide opportunities for women to gain experience, knowledge, and exposure as well as career planning; mentoring programs can be encouraged to achieve this goal.

There are many yardsticks for measuring how well career plans or strategies have worked. From an individual perspective, the assessment includes answering the following questions:

Assessing Career Management and Planning Programs and Policies

- *Consistency with values and interests*: How well has the career been attuned to the individual's needs, interests, and values?
- *Consistency with organizational demands:* How well has the career strategy helped the individual realize his or her potential in the organization?
- *Consistency in occupational demands:* How well has the career strategy helped the individual realize his or her potential in the occupation?
- *Consistency with environmental demands:* How well has the strategy helped the individual seize opportunities presented by the environment and avoid problems or threats posed by it?
- *Appropriateness given resources available:* To what extent has the career strategy been appropriate, given time and money available to the individual?
- *Acceptability of risk:* To what extent does the career strategy fit the preferences of significant others, including peers and family members?
- *Appropriateness of time horizon:* How well has the career strategy matched up to individual goals over time?
- *Workability:* How well has the career strategy satisfied individual career objectives? [22]

While there is no universal way to assess the effectiveness of an organization's career management program, a useful means to conduct an audit can be by answering some questions on a strategic level. These might include:

- *Career management policy*: What policies facilitate career planning and control in the organization? Are the policies effective and is there follow-up in assessing success? What is the range of formal career plans in the organization (e.g., succession plans, workshops, counselling, etc.)?
- *Career management structure:* Are there any structures in the organization that can accommodate employee assessment, counselling, and multiple promotion systems? To what extent are these structures permanent?
- *Leadership:* Are the leaders of the organization supportive of its role in providing opportunities for development and careers for its employees? How can this culture be sustained?
- *Reward systems:* Are the reward systems in the organization compatible with employees' career planning? Are employees encouraged and rewarded when new skills are acquired? Is it easier for some occupations to be remunerated than others?

By considering these questions, companies can begin to identify areas that may require more attention. Of course, no organization can offer unlimited opportunities for development and growth, but a genuine attempt by the organization to develop a policy that supports individual careers will be beneficial in the short and long term.

HRM DYNAMICS
Career Profiles in Selected Canadian Organizations

Bell Canada

Bell Canada has been known for its emphasis on the career growth of its employees. The company offers ample growth opportunities to new recruits, both personally and professionally. Bell is known to be a company that constantly looks to the future and its recruitment brochure is suitably entitled: Looking to the Future—Bell University and College Recruiting. When a graduate reaches a management level, he or she works with the support of an experienced supervisor who is responsible for the employee's professional development plan. This is done in conjunction with an HR consultant, if required, and also by regular reviews and feedback sessions.

Canadian Imperial Bank of Commerce (CIBC)

CIBC, one of Canada's leading financial institutions, introduced a career planning program in the early 1990s. Each employee receives the *Career Planning Handbook*, which provides detailed information about the objectives and content of the program. The handbook takes the employees through a step-by-step approach to carefully assess and plan their career in CIBC. It begins with self-assessment and concludes with the setting of goals and monitoring of achievement. Other sections in the guide include: how to take stock and analyze career history; how to analyze accomplishments; how to self-investigate work style and preferences; how to assess general skills; how to test and clarify values; how to assess career/life choices; how to conduct reality testing by, among other things, soliciting feedback from others; and, how to conduct an opportunity search, including finding out about other jobs. Because the program is in its initial phase, it is too early to assess its success.

Royal Bank of Canada

Royal Bank is Canada's largest bank. It defines career planning as the "process of assessing skills and abilities, evaluating opportunities for growth, and pursuing a development plan to achieve the best possible match between an individual's goals and the bank's needs." Accordingly, Royal Bank provides all of its employees with a number of planning resources that help them map out personal career strategies. These include a planning workbook for individuals to assess their strengths, weaknesses, and interests; detailed guides with background information on management and nonmanagement jobs; plus an informative book that outlines the bank's many available learning resources to help enhance a person's professionalism. Career development is also part of an annual performance review, at which time the employee's needs are identified and programs to match them are recommended. Royal Bank's training and development commitment is one of the biggest in Canada. From 1987 through 1991, the bank spent more than $308 million on employee training and development. The 1992 budget exceeds $80 million.

Computer Applications

There seems to be an ever-increasing growth in software applications for employee development and career planning. Interestingly enough, although there is growing awareness within business circles of the importance of career development, most computer technology applications have been developed in academia or community agency settings. Specifically, career development programs are addressed to manage the following processes:[23]

1. *Self-assessment* of reality checking, goal setting, and action planning. This process can be managed easily with a computer.

2. *Complex assessment* of career interests, skills, and values. The on-line delivery and rapid processing of instruments, such as the Holland Self-Directed Search and others, resolves a major problem: assessment checking and scoring; moreover, information can be easily stored and presented for analysis.

3. *Exploration of database.* Computers are used to explore information pertaining to the fit between employees and the organization. Computer-based systems provide rapid, easy access to job databases. Furthermore, they can store extensive information on job descriptions, competency profiles, organizational characteristics, turnover rates, and so on.

Out of a list of career development software that is organizationally focused, Forrer and Leibowitz describe three: (1) *Career Point*, which guides employees through a comprehensive career development process that includes assessment of career interests, skills, and work values; (2) *Matching*, which is based on the Work Style Preference inventory and measures, in addition to individual work interests, also the requirements of jobs; (3) *The Career Planning Center*, which helps employees plan their career through customized organization-based information. The program provides employees with confidential access to job openings, skill profiles, job descriptions, job families, career paths, training-course descriptions, and organizational goal statements.[24]

S U M M A R Y

Career management and planning is becoming an important HR activity. This chapter examined career management and planning from two perspectives: individual and organizational. From an individual point of view, career means making the right decision about vocational choice, deciding about vocational development, and "making it" in the workplace through advancement, promotions, and the ability to satisfy personal goals and objectives. The chapter discussed the main steps in assessing career choices, in setting objectives, and in charting a plan to manage them. From an organizational point of view, information is provided about programs designed to create opportunities for career advancement. The programs were described as being individually centred and organizationally centred. In addition, the chapter reviewed two of the main contemporary problems affecting careers, namely career plateauing and skill obsolescence. Several ideas about ways to deal with these problems were presented.

While career planning as an HR area is expanding, so are computer-assisted programs designed to facilitate its management. Nonetheless, in spite of the considerable investment in developing such tools, only a few have been successfully implemented.

HRM IN THE NEWS VIGNETTE

The Boomer Bust: Will This Generation Ever Have It So Good Again?
Welcome to the Age of Diminished Expectations

Hugh Munro spent eight years at Southam Business Information and Communications Group Inc., working his way up from salesperson to publisher of two directories and an electronic information service with $1.75 M in sales. One day in November, 1990, he arrived at work to find his staff gone and a trio of executives awaiting him with a settlement package.

Munro and his friends are part of the elite group of baby boomers who in the last decade were obsessed with upward mobility. No other generation entered the workforce with more impressive academic credentials or higher expectations. The economy of the 1980s created employment for one million new managerial and professional workers, whose numbers increased from 2.6 million to 3.6 million (40%).

With little excess in the blue-collar occupations, employers cut white-collar people. Middle managers account for 80% of recent layoffs.

Source: Abstract based on a feature article of the same title by Rona Maynard in *Report on Business Magazine* 7, 9 (March 1991): 28–31. Reprinted with permission.

P O S T S C R I P T

As the workforce becomes more educated, employees place rising expectations on their respective organizations, especially with regard to opportunities for growth and development. While career plateauing does not necessarily affect job performance adversely, it certainly leads to low organizational commitment. Thus, whereas interorganizational mobility has been encouraged in the past, today it is viewed differently. Companies in high-tech industries, for example, realize the enormous costs associated with a loss of skilled professionals who, in many cases, join competitors. The company is not only losing a skilled worker, but the competitor is gaining a competitive edge due to the importation of "know how" with the new recruit. Organizations, therefore, are more often caught in a catch twenty-two situation than in the past: on the one hand they recognize the need to satisfy and maintain their skilled employees by providing them with opportunities to grow and develop a career, while on the other hand the opportunities to do so are becoming more and more restricted, since many organizations are experiencing very slow growth or even decline.

Consequently, HR professionals are faced with the challenge of designing programs to minimize the career plateau phenomenon. This will require imaginative ideas and strategic decisions affecting other HR activities. One tendency that seems to be emerging is lateral and/or diagonal career tracks. Such an option will become successful only if it coincides with cultural changes that reflect a new definition of what career is. The odds are against innovations since research shows that even without plateauing, individuals who stay with a single company throughout their career tend to be less satisfied than those who switch jobs.[25] Employers, then, will have to realize that if they do not develop career planning programs, they may be adversely affected. But the investment in developing such programs should not be seen as a panacea for performance- or retention-related problems. Rather, career management and planning should be synchronized with the changing needs of the firm's environments and changes in the workforce.

Although this chapter emphasized career management and planning for a traditional type of employee, a few words should be added about future concerns. In the future attention should be paid to nontraditional employees and to nontraditional career paths. For example, with the rise of the dual-career family, more research is needed in understanding how companies can accommodate individuals (mostly women) who go in and out of the labour force. Additional attention should be paid to those who enter the labour force late in life. Finally, organizations and their respective HR managers may wish to understand career planning and management as a broader aspect of "life planning," since the two are not really separate.[26]

R E V I E W   A N D   A N A L Y S I S   Q U E S T I O N S

1. In what ways is career management and planning related to other HR activities in the organization?
2. What are some factors that will/have influence(ed) your choice of occupation? Why?
3. What are some strategies an individual may select in exploring occupational choices?
4. Elaborate on some problems confronted by a manager who is managing subordinates at different career stages.
5. Comment on Holland's theory of career types. Does it apply to you?
6. The organizational entry stage of career development suggests that reality shock is a fact of organizational life. What can HR managers do to lessen reality shock?
7. Distinguish between individual-centred career planning and organization-centred career planning.
8. What is succession planning? Why are companies engaged in it?

9. What are some typical problems facing women who seek to advance to executive positions?
10. Given the prolonged state of economic recession in the 1990's, will traditional career planning ever be the same? Comment.

CASE STUDY

RETIRED ON THE JOB: CAREER BURNOUT OR WHAT?

George Wilson, the newly appointed manager of Benlux Corporation's Production Control and Methods Improvement Division, faced a rather perplexing HR problem. One of the long-time employees of his division, Tim Norton, was not performing his job properly. In questioning subordinates, Wilson learned that Norton had not performed any real or substantial work for years. Furthermore, his current job actions were a source of embarrassment to the entire division. "Hangover Tim" Norton was observed to arrive at work approximately 45 minutes late each morning and proceed to begin the workday by attempting to recover from the previous evening's outing with his "Scotch friends." Norton's method of recovery appeared to involve: (1) reading the paper for about an hour while smoking and drinking coffee; (2) "office hopping" with his coffee cup in order to visit and interact with his many friends who were employed within the division; (3) a two-hour, three-martini lunch break; and (4) an afternoon nap while secluded back in his office. Wilson had expected the employees of his division to resent Norton's behaviour and obvious poor or nonperformance. Thus, he was quite surprised when he learned that Norton was almost universally liked and considered somewhat of a folk hero among nonsupervisory employees. Therefore, Wilson decided to thoroughly investigate Norton's case before taking any type of action against him.

From company records, Wilson learned that Norton had been employed by Benlux for fifteen years. He had begun his employment with the firm as an internal management specialist. The duties of this position involved both management and nonmanufacturing operations. Initially, Norton had been quite successful in this position. His PAs had routinely cited him for both his ingenuity and complete understanding of the complex production control systems used by the firm. Norton had

been credited with the introduction of new work procedures that lessened both worker fatigue and industrial accidents. Additionally, several of his suggestions had resulted in substantial improvements in product quality within the manufacturing department. Recognizing this performance excellence, the firm had promoted Norton once and issued to him several cash bonuses during his first seven years of employment.

During his eighth year of employment, Norton had been considered for a supervisory position within the division. Although the company did not have a formal career program, everyone had been surprised when Benlux's top management had finally decided to fill this supervisory vacancy with another employee from the research and development group. Norton had appeared to accept this career setback with some degree of indifference. He still seemed to exhibit the friendly and engaging interpersonal style that had won him many friends within the division. Yet, eight months later, a project he had been assigned to direct seemed to "never get off the ground" because of his failure to exhibit proper levels of leadership and enthusiasm when dealing with other project analysts. Subsequent job assignments had also revealed a substantial deterioration in performance. Norton's failure to consider a variety of relevant variables in his work assignments had resulted in the development of nonusable work methods and production control techniques. Norton's supervisor had noted that Tim appeared to be drinking heavily during this period of time and was said to be experiencing marital difficulties. This pattern of poor performance, tardiness, and alcohol abuse continued to the point where Norton's supervisor was afraid to assign him projects of any real significance. In fact, only routine, noncritical work assignments were given to him, and at times Tim was not given any assignments whatsoever.

Case Questions

1. What are the underlying causes of Norton's performance?
2. Who is responsible for the current state of Norton's performance?
3. Should Norton's first supervisor have taken different action? Which?
4. What should Wilson do now? Should he fire Norton?
5. If you were an HR consultant assigned to remedy the situation, what recommendations would you make?

NOTES

1. Narrative job descriptions are the simplest form of job analysis. In broad terms, the job analyst collects qualitative data from any of the sources of job data.

2. R.A. Noe and N. Schmitt, "The Influence of Trainee Attitude on Training Effectiveness: Test of a Model," *Personnel Psychology*, Autumn 1986, 497–523.

3. S.F. Cronshaw, "Future Directions for Personnel Psychology in Canada," *Canadian Psychology* 29, 1 (1988): 30–43.

4. Quoted in M. Goodman and B. Lorenzo, "Taking Gas at Texaco: Refusing to promote Janella Martin may cost the company millions," *People*, 11 November 1991, 75.

5. J.M. Hewer, ed., "Managing Your Career," *CMA Magazine*, 62, 9 (1988): 17–19.

6. B. Daglish, "The route to the top," *Maclean's*, 103, 36 (1990): 36–37.

7. D. Tayler, "Career Paths in the Face of Restraint," *Canadian Business Review* 14, 2 (1987): 29–30.

8. R. Beaujot, *Report on Marriage and Divorce* (Ottawa: Statistics Canada, 15 November 1988).

9. M. Jamal, "Moonlighting: Personal, Social, and Organizational Consequences," *Human Relations*, November 1986, 977–90.

10. J.L. Holland, *Making Vocational Choices: A Theory of Careers* (Englewood Cliffs, N.J.: Prentice–Hall, 1973).

11. Definitions used by T.P. Ference, J.A. Stoner, and E.K. Warren, "Managing the Career Plateau," *Academy of Management Review*, 2 (1977): 602–12, 977–90.

12. M.A. Archer and B. Lea, "Canada Housing and Mortgage Surmounts Plateauing," *Personnel Journal* 63, 4 (1990): 141–42.

13. Towers, Perrin, Forrester & Crosby, (Montreal: *Corporate Manpower Planning in Canada*, 1972), i–ii.

14. V.V. Murray and D.E. Dimick, *Personnel Administration in Large and Middle-Sized Canadian Businesses*. (Supply and Services Canada: Ottawa, 1977), 77.

15. G. Cook Johnson and R.J. Grey, "Trends in Employee Attitudes: Signs of Diminishing Employee Commitment," *Canadian Business Review* 15, 1 (1988): 20–21.

16. G. Cook Johnson and R.J. Grey, "Trends in Employee Attitudes: Differences between Canadian and American Workers," *Canadian Business Review* 15, 4 (1988): 24–27.

17. M.W. Blue, "Management and Executive Development Expenditures and Policies—1988," *Human Resource Development Centre Report 39–89*, (Ottawa,: Human Resource Development Centre, 1989), 9–11.

18. J. Castro, "Where's the Gung-Ho?" *Time*, 134, 12 (1989): 34–36.

19. D.C. Feldman, *Managing Careers in Organizations* (Glenview, Ill.: Scott Foresman, 1988) 3–4.

20. F. Schwartz, "Don't Write Women Off as Leaders," *Fortune*, 8 June 1987, 185.

21. B. Brophy, "The truth about women managers," *U.S. News and World Report*, 29 December 1986, For more recent information, see G.N. Powsell and L.A. Mainiero, "Cross-Currents in the River of Time: Conceptualizing the Complexities of Women's Careers," *Journal of Management* 18, 2 (June 1992): 215–38; and L.K. Stroh, J.M. Brett, and A.H. Reilly, "All the Right Staff: A Comparison of Female and Male Managers' Career Progress," *Journal of Applied Psychology* 77, 3 (June 1992): 251–60.

22. These questions were inspired by the discussion found in W.J. Rothwell, and H.C. Kazanas, *Strategic Human Resources Planning and Management* (Englewood Cliffs, N.J.: Prentice–Hall, 1988), 272.

23. Derived from information found in S.E. Forrer and Z.B. Leibowitz, *Using Computers in Human Resources* (San Francisco: Jossey–Bass, 1991), Chapter 4.

24. Ibid., 87–91.

25. "Switch Rather than Stew," *Training and Development Journal* 29, 10 (1985):

26. Based on correspondence and suggestions made by Professor Abe Korman (Baruch College, City University of New York), December 1991.

CHAPTER THIRTEEN

CONTEMPORARY FORMS OF MANAGING HUMAN RESOURCES

KEYNOTE ADDRESS

Richard Barton
President and CEO, Xerox Canada

Quality: The Human Connection

The greatest era of change for people since the Industrial Revolution, the 1990s are characterized by a global economy, borderless corporations, and, for working people, a dazzling, but daunting, array of professional choices and challenges. If properly managed and adequately trained and educated, individuals truly have the opportunity to be masters of their destinies.

The key words are "properly" and "adequately"; in Canada we are in a state of evolution in our understanding of what these words mean for the future. The redefinition involves our business leaders and, to the greatest extent, employees themselves. But, the day-to-day responsibility, today and tomorrow, for implementing our understanding of proper management support and adequate employee education rests with HR professionals.

Certainly at Xerox Canada, excellence and quality in managing are the most vital components of our business success. They embody the core values that define our company: a complete dedication to customer satisfaction, and quality as a way of life.

In 1982 Xerox embraced, worldwide, a commitment to Total Quality. We were the first major North American corporation to make this bold leap and we did it through a strategic process we call Leadership Through Quality.

Simply expressed, Leadership Through Quality is both a goal and a process. It dedicates and orients every Xerox employee to fully meeting and exceeding customer requirements.

To enable Leadership Through Quality to function, Xerox Canada is built on an inverted pyramid of people support and empowerment. Xerox management, through all levels, is structured to convey authority, responsibility, and accountability directly to our employees. Our management structure enables people to be involved in decisions about their work and performance. The inverted pyramid gives clear direction and support to employees, but does not allow for over-supervision or over-control. And, most importantly, it gives employees the authority, support, and tools to do what repeated surveys show is very important to them—satisfy the customer.

Xerox has had tremendous success with Leadership Through Quality. We doubled our size in the 1980s. Xerox has earned customer satisfaction unparalleled in our industry, and in 1989 Xerox Canada was awarded the first-ever Gold Award for Quality in the Canada Awards For Business Excellence.

These results are gratifying. But we understand that they are not the end of the journey, they are signposts. We remain absolutely committed to Leadership Through Quality. And Xerox remains equally convinced that in the future quality will depend on people.

Why? In the global marketplace, simply selling products is not a competitive approach for Xerox. Customers want end-to-end answers to complex information-management requirements. Therefore, we must sell business solutions. And solutions do not roll off assembly lines. People make solutions: they are crafted, each one differently, by creative and innovative minds.

People power excellence. They are our bridge to our future. And for Xerox the most important link with quality will always be the human connection.

. . .

The Keynote Address by the president of Xerox Canada shows the emphasis the company places on the strategic importance of quality. While Xerox was a leader in embracing the principles of quality management worldwide, not only in Canada, other Canadian organizations have followed suit. Furthermore, the link between quality and the human connection is unequivocal. Companies that enjoy a superior reputation for quality consistently outperform their competitors on account of their philosophy and management of their human resources.

. . .

The importance of improving productivity and QWL for Canadian workers is evident. For many years Canadian workers and organizations thought that they were shielded from global competition, and, thus, few incentives were created for becoming more productive. The picture has been rapidly changing due to a number of factors:

- The longer cycles of economic recessions,
- The globalization of markets and increased international competitiveness,
- The free trade agreements with the U.S.A. and Mexico (NAFTA).

The pressures for increases in productivity are mounting as companies realize their survival is at stake. For instance, during 1991 and 1992 about 20 percent more bankruptcies were declared than in the previous two years. A record number of companies face the ultimate challenge of survival, which is related to the state of the economy, but is also due to low productivity. This decline in productivity is already influencing the standard of living of Canadians, which seems to be deteriorating by comparison to that of other industrialized countries. If the current trend continues, the present generation will live less well than the previous generation—a first-time occurrence in Canada.

Parallel to the productivity crisis and the decline in the quality of products and services in Canada is the decline in QWL. This comes at a time when the workforce is more educated and demands greater control and involvement in jobs. Employees prefer not to be treated like cogs in a machine. Consequently, innovative approaches to simultaneously augment QWL and productivity are called for. This chapter focuses on changing aspects of the organization meant to improve:

- Employee satisfaction and, consequently, to reduce absenteeism and turnover;
- Job involvement to increase employees' understanding and commitment to their jobs;
- Product or service quality to retain clients, customers, and market share;
- Performance, and, consequently, organizational profitability, competitiveness, and survival.

All these goals call for significant inputs by the HR managers, who are assigned the role of change agents in introducing and supporting innovations in management. In fact, they are responsible for the validation of new schools of thought and they should apply their knowledge and skills to manage change and overcome resistance to it. Their role, therefore, is critical in affecting organizational effectiveness.

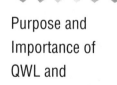

Purpose and Importance of QWL and Productivity

Declining Canadian productivity is increasingly discussed in executive suites and by almost all HR managers. Reversing this decline is a major goal for all organizations. Without it, and given the present intense domestic and international competition, they will not be able to survive. Yet, one of the most perplexing aspects of improving productivity is defining and measuring it. While almost no one challenges productivity's traditional definition, *output divided by input*, there is debate about what output is and what input is. At first glance it appears impossible to measure the output or input of a nursing home, a bank, an orchestra, or many other of the thousands of service and professional organizations. It appears equally impossible to measure the work individual employees do in these types of organizations.

At second glance, however, organizations are discovering that the task is not impossible, just difficult. Measures of productivity have to be tailored to each organization and its goals. In general, **productivity** is defined as measures or indicators of output by an individual, group, or organization in relation to (divided by) inputs or resources used by the individual, group, or organization to create those outputs. Whatever criteria are used, they must be: (1) measurable in some way (valid PA results, quality of outputs, quantity of outputs, etc.); (2) related to the goals of the organization; and (3) relevant to each job.

In the past, attempts to improve productivity concentrated on technological changes, which by and large created a byproduct: the deterioration of the QWL for many employees. In general, people were asked to work faster, to produce more, to spend less time thinking (the task was left to the machine), and to develop their work schedule around the availability of technology. While these approaches seemed to be effective in the short run, we now know they are no longer effective. This has caused the current workforce to seek to exercise more control and discretion and to be involved in all aspects of the work that influences them. Consequently, attempts have been made in the past twenty years to develop a more holistic approach to productivity improvements without sacrificing employees' psychological and physical well-being. The core of this approach revolves around the concept of QWL. Although it is a very commendable, humanistic approach to work organization, QWL is not the ultimate goal of organizations. Their strategic goal is survival, growth, and profit, hence productivity.

Firms' interest in QWL is based on the assumption that improved QWL will result in a healthier, happier, more contented worker who is likely to be more productive.

QWL is complex to define and measure. In this book, it will refer to a process by which all members of the organization, through appropriate and open channels of communication set up for this purpose, have some say in decisions that affect their jobs in particular and their work environment in general, resulting in greater job involvement, and satisfaction and reduced levels of stress and fatigue. In essence, QWL represents an innovative organizational culture or management style in which employees experience feelings of ownership, self-control, responsibility, and self-respect. Generally, in an organization characterized as having a high QWL, industrial democracy is highly encouraged: suggestions, questions, and criticism that might lead to improvement of any kind are welcomed. In such a setting, creative discontent is viewed as a manifestation of constructive caring about the organization rather than destructive griping. Management's encouragement of such feelings of involvement often leads to ideas and actions for upgrading operational effectiveness and efficiency, as well as environmental enhancement. Thus, increased productivity, measured in terms of work quality as well as quantity, is likely to be a natural byproduct.

QWL is a concept and philosophy of work organization that seeks to improve the life of the employee at work. To achieve that, QWL proponents use a number of approaches that range from the very strict and simplistic scientific reorganization of tasks, as advocated by Taylor and his school of thought, to the continuous multidimensional process of change, introduced by the sociotechnical group and the newer systemic and contingency theory proponents.

The QWL concept can be translated into operational terms and applied to the individual organizational context in the form of programs. Some of these are specific and limited in scope, while others seek to bring multiple changes to a wide variety of areas. In order to better understand the place of productivity and QWL programs in organizations, a brief description of their relationships to other HR areas, as well as other work organization theories, is presented.

QWL and productivity programs can be interwoven with several other HR activities and programs. For example, it is possible to base a program such as a pay plan, or a Scanlon Plan, within the firm's compensation activity. Many other examples are shown in Exhibit 13.1 and are further elaborated upon in this chapter.

JOB ANALYSIS. When task change programs are used to improve productivity or QWL, the purposes, duties, and characteristics of jobs are often changed. These changes generate a need for analyses of the new jobs. Although new jobs are most readily created by job enrichment programs, they are also created by task flow changes.

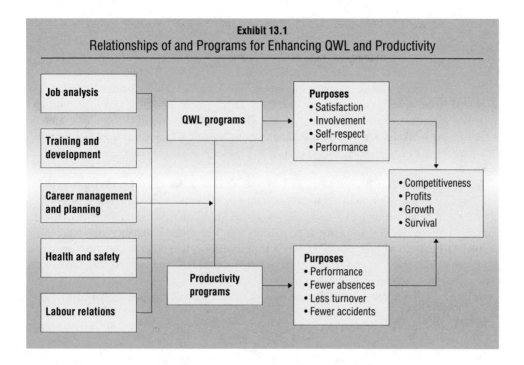

Exhibit 13.1
Relationships of and Programs for Enhancing QWL and Productivity

TRAINING AND DEVELOPMENT. For QWL and productivity programs to work effectively, managers may need to be taught the basics of participative management. Employees also need skill in self-management. Training needs, therefore, will increase, at least during the initiation period of a program.

CAREER MANAGEMENT AND PLANNING. The mere instalment of career plans and the promotion of multiple career tracks might be considered a QWL program. As we have seen in the previous chapter, such programs are likely to increase job satisfaction, and as a direct consequence will reduce absenteeism and turnover.

HEALTH AND SAFETY. Many programs to improve the QWL are also capable of improving occupational health and safety. Consider jobs where workers are likely to have accidents due to the boredom experienced on the job; QWL programs can reduce the boredom and, therefore, reduce the accidents as well. As one consequence of QWL or productivity programs such as job redesign or improved communications, workers become more involved and motivated.

LABOUR RELATIONS. The success of QWL and productivity improvement programs also hinges on employee–management relations. Traditionally structured jobs may need to be redesigned, and in unionized environments these modifications *must* be supported by the union. Thus, unions can play a very important role. While some unions may favour innovations to save jobs, many object to them on the grounds that innovations blur the distinction between the roles of management and labour.

QWL programs were formally introduced in Canada in 1978 through the initiative of the federal government and the QWL Unit of the Employment Relations Branch of Labour Canada. The QWL Unit was advised by E. Trist, an international scholar and pioneer in QWL, who accepted a position at York University in Toronto. The activities of this

Statutory and
Policy Issues in
QWL and
Productivity
Enhancement

organization over the past few years have been quite diverse. Rather than immediately implementing QWL projects, it held a series of workshops across Canada and invited interested academics, managers, trade unionists, and management consultants. The organization produced and widely distributed many writings on QWL, including a newsletter of QWL events, articles about different initiatives, and books of QWL readings. The process appeared to be an effective way to distribute much information on QWL techniques, namely sociotechnical and quality circles. The QWL Unit also provided a steady stream of activities and workshops and provided financial and technical assistance for QWL training and research projects. Finally, this branch developed a network of qualified QWL experts across the country.

Parallel activity has been undertaken by the Treasury Board of Canada since 1975. Experiments in the creation of semi-autonomous work groups were undertaken in 1975 in three federal departments in collaboration with three different public sector unions, despite some hesitations on the part of the latter. These "first generation" experiments were soon followed by a "second generation" series of experiments in two other departments in 1978. Although not always successful, these experiments were highly publicized and other organizations became interested.

The Canadian Labour Market Productivity Centre (CLMPC) was established in 1984. Although the CLMPC is well funded (about $7 million per year), its mission is not very clearly established. It remains unclear whether it will take an active role in promoting innovative work arrangements.

At the provincial level, most activities are less institutionalized. Different provinces set up separate policies regarding QWL and productivity centres. In relative terms, however, Ontario is far more committed to these innovations than the other provinces. In Ontario, the Department of Labour began to research innovative work arrangements in the late 1970s. At the end of 1978, the Government of Ontario created the Ontario Quality of Working Life Centre, which immediately became the best funded and most professionally organized of the QWL organizations in Canada. The Centre's activities include consultation, information services, research and field activities, and educational programs. It also publishes one of the most professional journals on QWL topics: *QWL Focus*. In 1984, the Government of Ontario formed the Ontario Labour Management Study (previously named Quality of Working Life Advisory Committee) to develop recommendations to solve employee and management needs in the private and public sector.

Other provinces have allowed their respective universities and research centres to take the lead in establishing QWL programs. For example, both McGill University and the University of Montreal (H.E.C.) in the Province of Quebec had QWL centres that operated until the late 1980s; in Vancouver, a QWL forum was created under the umbrella of the British Columbia Research Council; in Atlantic Canada, the Institute of Public Affairs at Dalhousie University was founded in 1984 and experimented with implementations of QWL projects in eight organizations. In contrast to the flourishing of QWL government-sponsored activities, only a few provinces established their own centres for researching and monitoring productivity improvements.

Given the financial squeeze in which most governments have found themselves in recent years, many of the aforementioned programs have been discarded or reduced to nonfunctional levels. For example, the Province of Quebec has decided to abolish its Institute for Productivity after only limited years in operation. Similarly, with the election of the Conservative government, the QWL Unit of Labour Canada has also been discontinued.

Trade union support for QWL in Canada has been positive but not universal. It has also been subject to the politics of trade union organizations. While commitments to QWL exist in the official platforms of many major Canadian industrial unions and some public sector unions, it still remains an anathema to some unions, particularly those whose relations with employers are poor or who are strongly ideologically driven.

To understand why traditional approaches to productivity enhancement do not function very well, it is necessary to understand their underlying assumptions and rationales. (It is only fair to mention, however, that these concepts were most effective in the past.) Traditional forms of work organization are characterized by rigidity and a strong centralization of power, which evolved from a number of organizational and behaviourial theories that are still very influential. A brief review of these will provide us with a better understanding of the changes that have since taken place.

APPROACHES TO MANAGING ORGANIZATIONS AND HUMAN RESOURCES

The *classical* approach to work organization is based on three major theories: Taylor's *scientific organization;* Weber's model of *bureaucracy;* and Fayol's concept of *administration.*

Classical Theories

Taylor championed the idea that the best way to execute a task is to divide it into basic elements. Each element should be so simple that any worker with a minimum of training should be able to accomplish it in a fraction of time. Assembly lines, ultra specialization of tasks, and piece-rate compensation have evolved from this approach. Many manufacturing plants, especially in the clothing and automobile industries, still operate on this type of arrangement.

Weber's bureaucratic model brings us hierarchy, lines of authority, and formalized behaviours. Work is to be done routinely, in an impersonal way, within a rigid framework along a fixed set of rules or guidelines. Everything should be planned out, well ahead of time. Nothing should be left to improvisation or to the individual's creativity. This seems to fit the situation of many hospitals and prison systems almost perfectly. Volumes of written instructions, policies, procedures, and organizational charts testify to this fact.

Fayol's theory of management brings us the four classical functions of a competent administrator: *planning, organization, command or direction,* and *control.* From this theory, we also retain the notion of *unity of command,* whereby a subordinate must receive the orders from one and only one supervisor; the distinction between *line* (executive) and *staff* (advisory) authorities; the notion of *span of control,* which determines the number of employees a manager can effectively supervise, and the principle of *specialization of functions* based on the regroupment of similar activities into the same department (e.g., production, finance, marketing, human resources, research and development).

Until today, the underlying philosophy for structuring work in a large number of Canadian establishments has been based on: (1) the worker is used as the need arises; (2) he or she is hired to accomplish a number of specific tasks; and (3) the worker's mandate is to produce a determined output.

In response to the strict and impersonal views of work organization, *behaviourists* offered theories of human needs. The *human relations* school of thought, pioneered by Elton Mayo, proposed that better human relations lead to better output. Efforts to humanize work conditions followed. In this approach, workers are encouraged to identify with the organization and a feeling of pride and belonging is cultivated.

Behavioural Theories

Employee participation in the decision making of the organization seems to be the next logical step in the evolution of work organization. Groups, committees, and ad hoc commissions are instituted. Workers are being given more say and more power, but also more individual responsibility. According to Maslow's Scale of Human Needs, we are trying to satisfy the individual's higher needs of self-esteem, growth, and self-actualization.

Proponents of the behavioural approach also emphasize the importance of groups in facilitating work standards and in contributing to individual performance. However, working with groups requires time, energy, special skills, aptitudes, and leadership. Consequently, only when groups are properly led/managed does productivity increase.

Systems Theories

One of the new system approaches, the *sociotechnical* school of thought, believes that the production, technological, and social systems of work are interdependent. It studies first and foremost the interaction between the individual and his or her work environment. According to this approach, the introduction of new technology may require current work to be redesigned; work redesign in turn has a certain number of social and psychological impacts of its own. Workplace democratization is the trend. Autonomous work groups, multiskills, and employee responsibility are key words. Middle management, status differential, forepersons, and quality control officers are eliminated.

Two other relatively new approaches to work organization are the *systemic approach* and the *contingency theory approach*. The systemic approach takes into consideration the interactions between elements internal to a work system and the environment external to it. The contingency theory approach regards each interaction as a system, and seeks to identify which combination of circumstances and factors is likely to produce the best performance.

CONTEMPORARY FORMS OF QWL PROGRAMS

Why is it that the traditional methods of management do not work today? To find an answer, we need first to examine the inherent characteristics of these approaches, which include:

- The employee is a mere replaceable production factor, hired to perform a number of specific tasks and to produce an assigned amount of a determined product of specified quality.
- Work is divided into simple, specialized tasks. The tasks to be accomplished by each employee are exhaustively and precisely described. There is no room for creativity or autonomous decision making.
- Performance standards are strictly based on time and movement studies. A bonus is awarded if the employee produces above the required standards.
- There is a very clear distinction between the roles of management and those of subordinates.
- The leadership style is competent but authoritarian. Constant and close supervision is the rule.
- Authority is concentrated at the top. Just enough of it is delegated to the subordinate to allow him or her to achieve the assigned responsibilities.
- Communication is vertical, through hierarchy lines.
- Work is regulated by a multiplicity of rules, instructions, and procedure manuals.
- Motivation is based on a system of rewards and punishments.

QWL originated from a concern for productivity and the failure of more traditional systems to account for the full complexity of human behaviour at work. It is based on the principle that the worker is a human being who has needs and expectations that could and should be satisfied, at least in part, by the work environment. The QWL approach is based on the principles of *collaboration* and *mutual respect.*

In more concrete terms, the aims of QWL are to make the job and job environment simpler, easier, safer, healthier, more secure, more interesting, challenging, motivating, and fun to the employee.

How can we achieve these goals? By applying a number of work organization approaches and programs, singly or jointly, to one or several elements, or dimensions of the work system, thereby inducing changes that will lead to an improvement in QWL. The elements of the work system are:

- The *individual* element, meaning the worker with all his or her characteristics;
- The *job* element, meaning the job itself with all its characteristics and requirements;
- The *environmental* element, which is subdivided into *internal* and *external*

environment. The internal environment is the one supportive of the job and immediately surrounding it. In this category; we include the *physical* environment; the *technological* environment, that is, the tools and equipment used; and the *organizational* framework and structures. The external environment is the one external to the workplace; but it is influenced by a number of factors. In this category, we include: family obligations; cultural beliefs; social system of values, rules, and trends; laws and legislation; geographic location, climate, and other natural conditions; and economic circumstances.

- The relationships between the individual, the job, and the environment (both internal and external to the workplace).

An effective QWL program needs to address one or more of the elements listed above. With regard to the individual element, we wish to see a healthier, more content and able worker with growing skills and knowledge that will allow him or her to do well on the job, but also to take on more challenging functions and responsibilities. QWL programs that apply to this group of concerns include: fitness training, stop smoking, weight control, EAPs, career management and planning programs, job-related training programs, and scholarships to further the worker's own education.

With regard to the job element, the idea is to make the job more meaningful, challenging, and fun for the worker. To do that one can enlarge the scope of the job through horizontal loading or job enlargement, and increase the depth of the job through vertical loading or job enrichment. Job rotation is another tool to decrease boredom and teach the employee new skills and new job-related perspectives. One can also act on other job dimensions by increasing the job complexity to encourage the worker to acquire new knowledge and develop new skills, including problem-solving skills. Alternatively, the program can concentrate on increasing job autonomy, giving the worker more freedom to plan and decide on how to accomplish his or her tasks. Work sharing, job sharing, quality circles, semi-autonomous group of production, and the Scanlon Plan are all programs headed in this direction.

With regard to the environment, a distinction should be made between the internal and external environment. With respect to the internal environment, when the aim is to monitor, control, and reduce problems arising from humidity, temperature, noise, lighting, odour, vibrations, and the like, the physical environment is the likely area to change. The technological environment refers to the tools and equipment that may facilitate the task of the worker, but that may also endanger his or her health. Office building sickness syndrome is a well-known malaise thought to be caused by poor ventilation, poor air quality, and the excessive presence of powerful irritants in many construction materials. Lower back pain and loss of hearing are two other frequent complaints.

While there are no widely accepted standards for office ergonomics, efforts are continually made to try to improve physical working conditions. Applied ergonomics have come to mean designing the total environment so as to maximize efficiency, comfort, and health in the relationship between workers and their machines. Although a number of sceptics still dismiss work environment redesign as a cosmetic measure, there is evidence that it can bring a dramatic improvement to employees' QWL and therefore a substantial increase in their performance. After all, productivity is a function of the individual and the environment, and so is job satisfaction and QWL.

The organizational environment includes such factors as management's ideology and style of leadership, company policies and structures, technical support available, information systems adopted and communication systems used, the level of planning or decision-making available to the employee, and the possibilities for lateral mutations and vertical promotions. Measures to reduce status differential, hierarchy layers, and communication obstacles help. Quality circles, semi-autonomous work groups, and the Scanlon Plan will give the workers more say in the decision-making process, but they will make them more responsible for their job and more responsible toward their fellow workers and the company.

The external environment can also be included in the QWL and performance enhancement programs. For instance, family–work balance significantly affects workers' performance, and thus EAPs child care, elder care, dependent care, and the like can be most instrumental.

Economic circumstances are another group of factors beyond the firm's control. Yet even in times of recession, QWL can include a number of policies and programs designed to help the individual climb out of difficult periods. For those who must go, QWL may offer counselling, outplacement, early retirement, termination packages, extended insurance, and supplemental benefits, to name a few. Those who stay can benefit from job sharing; flextime; training and development programs; leaves of absence; and financial support in the form of scholarships, mortgage subsidies, and so on.

Quality Circles

Quality Circles (QCs) are an innovative management concept that has contributed to Japan's dynamic industrial growth. Following forty years of successful experiments there, as well as more recent successes in Europe and in North America, hundreds of Canadian companies have implemented QCs. In fact, QCs became the popular model for Canadian management in the 1980s. Whether the QC is a fad or a permanent addition remains to be seen.

QCs were introduced to Japanese manufacturers in the 1940s by an American, John Deming. In time, based on Deming's teachings on quality control in production, Japan went from being the manufacturer of the poorest quality of finished goods in the world to becoming the world's leader in quality excellence. In the early 1980s, more than 100,000 QCs were reported in Japan, and according to estimates, there were about one million in the early 1990s. Each team submits an average of fifty-five suggestions per year.[1]

QCs are a technique of work organization that considers a company's workforce to be its most valuable resource. This technique organizes workers into groups of eight to ten people that meet on a weekly basis to identify, analyze, and solve problems related to quality, cost, safety, morale, housekeeping, the environment, and other work-related questions in their area. Membership is strictly voluntary and meetings are usually held once a week for an hour. During the group's initial meetings, members are trained in problem-solving techniques borrowed from group dynamics, industrial engineering, and quality control. These techniques include brainstorming, Pareto analysis, cause-and-effect analysis, histograms, control charts, stratification, and scatter diagrams.

Characteristics essential to QCs include:

- The role of the facilitator is the most important aspect of a QC program. He or she must be able to work with people at all levels of the organization, be creative and flexible, and be aware of the political atmosphere of the organization.
- Management must support the QC program. If a union is involved, it also should support the program and its views should be solicited.
- Participation should be voluntary for employees, but management should encourage the establishment of circles.
- Circle members must feel free to work on problems of their own choosing within established limits.
- Facilitators must keep management informed of what the circles are doing and of their progress.
- Quality, not quantity, should be the first consideration.
- A successful program adheres to the concepts and principles of effective QCs. One of the facilitator's most crucial tasks is to see that circles follow correct procedures. If they do not, they become nonproductive and eventually dissolve.

In addition, the development and maintenance of QCs requires :

- Ongoing administration and statistical feedback to ensure that the program can be adjusted as needs change;
- The realization that there will be start-up and maintenance costs that will most likely not be recovered in the early stages of the program.

A few spectacular cases demonstrate that QC programs can benefit companies enormously. At CAMCO, a Canadian-owned subsidiary of General Electric with plants in Hamilton (Ontario) and Montreal (Quebec), impressive improvements in quality and overall plant effectiveness have been reported. Before the implementation of QCs, production costs soared, customer complaints were very numerous, the number of rejects from the assembly line was overwhelming, and employees were bored and generally stressed. Yet, within five years following the implementation of QCs, the following was noted:

- Market share jumped from approximately 25 to 40 percent.
- Service calls for the five-year warranty on appliances were reduced from 11 percent to a mere 1 percent.
- Labour costs were significantly reduced when three roving quality inspectors replaced sixty former inspectors, a quality engineer, and a shop foreperson.[2]

In another case, Thompson Products Division of TRW Canada experimented with QCs in order to reduce its costs and improve product quality. The cost of implementing the program was around $33,000 and the benefits exceeded the costs within a period of six months.

Despite their potential for productivity gains, QCs have not been an unmitigated success. Even in Japan, it is estimated that more than a third of all circles contribute nothing to their organizations. Factors such as over-expectations, lack of systematic organizational support, and a lack of clearly defined organizational objectives prior to establishing QCs, all lead to disappointment and failure.

Semi-Autonomous Work Groups

A semi-autonomous work group is a permanent collection of workers whose objective is to produce a final product. The group has the responsibility to make certain decisions that normally belong to management, such as planning and quality control. It is free to employ means that it considers appropriate to achieve its given objective.

The essence of semi-autonomous work groups is illustrated in Exhibit 13.2. Panel A shows a group of people who, having accepted responsibility for a common goal, are in the process of learning how to use their own resources and abilities. Panel B, in contrast, shows the traditional bureaucratic form of work organization. The striking difference between these two forms points to the simple fact that when responsibility is given to a group of workers to achieve an agreed-upon goal, they must learn to share and allocate all the requirements for control and coordination responsibilities, as well as learn specific skills involved in each of the separate tasks. Given the above characteristics, one can roughly divide the skills required of semi-autonomous groups into six categories:

- Direct job skills,
- Communication and decision-making skills,
- Perceptual skills in extracting information from groups' various environments,
- Work design skills,
- Managerial skills,
- Skills to set and maintain a productive human atmosphere.

HRM IN THE NEWS VIGNETTE

New Forms of Labor–Management Relationship in View of Gaining Competitive Edge

Forging a new relationship between Canadian business and labor in the face of world competition hasn't been easy. Some workforces have embraced change in a spirit of co-operation; in others, the relationship was negotiated under the threat of closing; and in still others, the effort has completely failed.

Nowhere is the change more sweeping than at Shell's chemical plant in Sarnia. For 14 years, teams of workers have run the plant with almost complete autonomy. There are only two job classifications in the whole plant, each team member is able to perform 75 per cent of the jobs there, and 80 per cent of the 150 workers are paid at the top rate of $24.86 an hour.

Shell head office in Calgary retains a veto over crucial decisions, but on many issues, management and labor work out problems together. The decision to switch from an eight-hour to a 12-hour shift, for example, was made by a majority vote of employees and managers.

The plant is represented by the Energy and Chemical Workers Union. Seniority applies only in cases of layoffs. But even in the current recession, which forced Shell to shut a product line that accounted for one-third of production, there have been no layoffs.

Instead, employees have cut overtime to share the work, said union president Peter Kingyens. "I don't think head office in Calgary is a real believer in what we are doing here, but the bottom line is we have the highest profit margin in the company."

Company after company is experimenting with new ways to make better quality products quicker and cheaper. They are trying open communications, work teams, multi-skill job descriptions, just-in-time delivery systems and new quality measurement systems.

In some cases, there isn't much room to negotiate. More than 1,000 tire makers at Uniroyal Goodrich in Kitchener, Ont., were forced to accept major changes in work rules and production schedules to save jobs in a worldwide rationalization of the tire business.

The 400 employees at Phillips Cables in Brockville, Ont., accepted a four-year wage freeze to try to save the plant, as the parent company decides which of five North American sites to close.

Even unions like the Canadian Auto Workers, which is officially opposed to teamwork concepts, are being forced to change. To save a General Motors plant at Ste-Thérèse the union was compelled to accept many changes on the shop floor.

At the CAMI plant in Ingersoll, Ont., the price of union recognition was acceptance of the work teams to build Suzuki and GM subcompacts.

Recently, the CAW quietly agreed to a wage freeze for employees at a Guelph auto parts company.

There have also been plenty of victims and mistakes on the road to greater competitiveness. At Cambridge's Bundy Limited auto parts plant, CAW workers embraced robots, flexible job classifications and raised quality to the point that Ford made Bundy the first Canadian plant to fly its "Quality 1" flag.

But it wasn't enough to save the 250 jobs at the plant. Bundy shut its doors this spring and moved the technology to a new non-union Ohio plant where workers get one-third less money.

At the Simmons Canada mattress plant in Cornwall, new owner-managers slashed warehouse space and radically altered work systems in a bid to make the plant more competitive.

In June the Cornwall plant was one of the first Canadian companies to embrace a new program to improve quality through better communications. But the employees—disturbed by unpredictable shift changes and an ineffective labor-management committee—rebelled. They joined a union and went on strike for two weeks.

Source: Excerpt from a feature article of the same title by B. Hill that appeared in *The Ottawa Citizen*, reproduced in *The Montreal Gazette* 19 November 1991, E5. Reprinted with permission of *The Ottawa Citizen*.

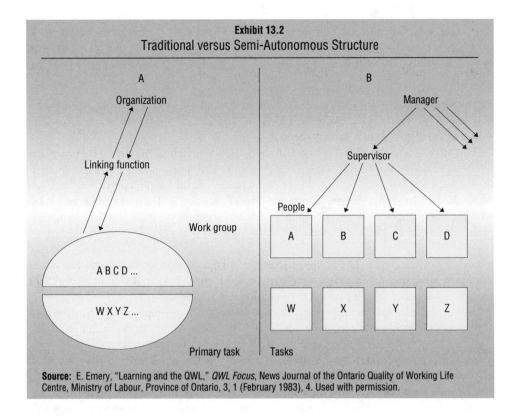

Exhibit 13.2
Traditional versus Semi-Autonomous Structure

Source: E. Emery, "Learning and the QWL," *QWL Focus*, News Journal of the Ontario Quality of Working Life Centre, Ministry of Labour, Province of Ontario, 3, 1 (February 1983), 4. Used with permission.

Volvo was a pioneer in the implementation of the semi-autonomous work group. In 1974, Volvo incorporated such a group into its QWL program in its Kalmar plant. This generated worldwide attention. Now, nearly 20 years after start-up, the venture demonstrates consistent success in terms of production volume, productivity, quality of cars, and other measures.

Whether this experiment is easily transportable to other countries and cultures remains uncertain. Canada has had its share of experiences, many of which were not successful. Nevertheless, two Canadian cases are much talked about. The first is the Refund Services Branch of Air Canada's Finance Department in Winnipeg, where over 50,000 refunds were processed monthly. After altering their structure to self-management teams with greater autonomy in handling refunds for their region, an increase in job satisfaction and morale, as well as a 30 percent increase in job performance, was reported.

In another case, Steinberg Ltd., a large supermarket chain that used to employ over 25,000 people, created semi-autonomous production groups in their frozen-foods distribution centre in Montreal in the late 70s. The results of involving the employees and the unions in the implementation of the program were an increase in morale, 3-1/2 years during which there were no complaints from the stores receiving deliveries, an absence rate of 5 percent as compared to 15 percent prior to the change, and a productivity rate 35 percent higher than the rate prior to the implementation of the program. However, after enjoying a few years of success, the program suffered a few setbacks and was abolished in the mid-1980s.

At National Cash Registers (NCR) there are four assembly lines, each producing one of the basic modules that make up the product. Technology has been adapted in such a way that each line is made up of individual workstations where an assembler installs several components to make an identifiable product. Assemblers at NCR choose their own tools, decide when to change a tool, set their own work pace, and in some cases request alterations to the workstation layout. Assemblers also work under variable hour systems. Managers report that this program has resulted in better quality products and greater employee job satisfaction.

Alternative Work Arrangements

A survey of Canadians' attitudes toward working hours, published by the Conference Board of Canada in 1987, reported that 2.9 million Canadians (nearly 31 percent of the employed labour force) would take a pay cut or trade some of their pay increase for some time off; 5.2 million would reduce, or increase their work time to achieve some flexibility in their schedules. The preferred work pattern is a shorter week. The second choice is to take more time off every year. Early retirement is the third choice. It seems, then, that a majority of working Canadians, especially those aged 25 to 44, would be open to some sort of alternative worktime arrangements.[3]

This may be the decade in which Canadians free themselves from the tyranny of the time clock. Far from representing a decline in the work ethic, alternative work arrangements seem to strengthen it by reducing the stresses caused by the conflicts among job demands, family needs, leisure values, and educational needs. The most frequently used worktime rearrangements are: flextime schedules, compressed work weeks, permanent part-time work and job sharing, and industrial and electronic cottages.

FLEXTIME SCHEDULES. The flextime schedule is popular with organizations because it decreases absenteeism; increases employee morale; fosters better labour–management relations; and encourages a high level of employee participation in decision making, self-control, and in general discretion over the time spent at work. Simply stated, **flextime** is a work schedule that gives employees daily choices in the timing of work and nonwork activities. The work day (or band width) is divided into two time zones: the **core time**, wherein the employee has to physically be at work doing the job, and **flexible time**, wherein the employee may choose when to complete the required number of work hours for that day. Core time and flexible time may be further divided into "beaches," or periods of time.

Let us look at an example. According to a study conducted at the Montreal Assurance-Vie Desjardins headquarters, the work day (band width) would stretch from 7:30 a.m. to 6:00 p.m. From 9:15 a.m. to 11:30 a.m. and from 2:00 p.m. to 3:30 p.m., all workers had to be at their posts and working (core time). Time periods in between these fixed periods were flexible. The flexible beach between 7:30 a.m. and 9:15 a.m. allowed certain workers living in the suburbs to arrive later, say at 9:00 a.m., if they so wished. The other flexible beaches, the one between 11:30 a.m. and 2:00 p.m., and the one between 3:30 p.m. and 6 p.m. provided convenient time off to see a dentist or to pick up the children. According to the company's reports, this flexibility has resulted in a general increase in job satisfaction, a more satisfying integration of work and personal life for the workers, and a decrease in absenteeism and turnover rate at no extra cost to the company. But more coordination in scheduling is needed, and some control mechanism, such as a time clock, is required to keep track of the in and out times of the employees. According to a recent survey by Wyatt (1990), 24 percent of Canadian companies have introduced flexible hours in their work arrangements.[4] Here are some flextime gains in productivity and employee satisfaction reported in the Canadian press:

- Honeywell (Scarborough): 12.5 percent increase in productivity in key punch area;
- Anglo Gibraltar Group (Toronto): 20 percent reduction in absenteeism, 80 percent reduction in overtime pay, 99 percent reduction in lateness, and 25 percent reduction in staff turnover;
- Ashland Oils (Calgary): 25 percent reduction in absenteeism and 20 percent reduction in overtime;
- Canada Trust (London): absenteeism reduced to 1.67 percent per annum.

COMPRESSED WORK WEEKS. An option for employees who want to work fewer than five days is the **compressed work week**. This has been tried out in a number of firms in response to a desire by workers to work more hours per day but fewer days per week, so they may have an extended period of continuous time off to spend with their families or to engage in other activities of their choice.

The Ontario Ministry of Labour published a study on compressed work week schedules as they were applied to a variety of establishments in that province between 1971 to 1973. The results, from management's point of view were: 60 percent of the organizations surveyed reported an increase in productivity; 57 percent, a reduction in absenteeism; 34 percent, a decrease in turnover; 47 percent, an improvement in employee morale; 28 percent, better utilization of equipment and longer production runs; 17 percent, an improvement in scheduling; 6 percent, an improvement in communication; 6 percent, a reduction of overtime; and 3 percent, a reduction in commuting time for the workers. A subsequent and more limited survey in the same province focused on employees' reactions. Although the majority supported the program, many employees indicated that they were more tired following the introduction of the compressed work schedule. Of those surveyed, 50 percent said that their family lives had improved; 25 percent, that their work attitude had improved; and 40 percent reported a decrease in work-related expenses. Productivity and turnover rates improved. It should be noted, however, that there was some difficulty in relating increase of productivity exclusively to the new schedule.[5]

PERMANENT PART-TIME WORK AND JOB SHARING. Traditionally, part-time work has meant filling positions that lasted only for a short time, such as those in retail stores during holiday periods. Now some organizations have designated **permanent part-time (PPT)** positions. These alternative work arrangements are particularly suitable for a growing number of sectors of the labour force, namely women, mothers of young children, dual-income family parents, students, and older workers. Both PPT and job sharing provide the opportunities for employment that these workers may not have otherwise and a certain flexibility to better balance the requirements of work and private life.

A few statistics will give us an idea of the importance of *part-time* employment in Canada. In 1953, part-timers constituted 3.8 percent of the labour force. By 1993, 18.2 percent of all Canadians employed worked thirty hours or less per week. In number, they represented 2.2 million out of a total of 12 million workers in the same year. From 1981 to 1991, part-time employment grew at an average annual rate of 3.2 percent, while full employment's annual rate of growth was .77 percent.[6]

In times of economic downturn, part-time employment and job sharing soften the blow of termination or lay-off. They offer an alternative to outright unemployment to previously full-time workers.

Job sharing is a particular type of part-time work where two employees divide the responsibility of a regular-time job. Both may work half of the job, or one could work more hours than the other. To help avert temporary unemployment, a work-sharing program has been set up by the Canadian Government since 1978. Its budget for 1990 was $30 million.

In a work-sharing program, unemployment insurance would subsidize 57 percent of the full pay for hours not worked, to a maximum of $85 a day. It has a twenty-six week participation limit, and, to be eligible for the program's assistance, firms must operate a minimum of two days a week. In 1989, 1,802 companies and 37,487 employees benefited from the program. In 1990, the numbers were, respectively, 5,800 companies and 110,000 workers.[7]

Job sharing has been used at some branches of Royal Bank since 1985. At one branch in Beloeil (Quebec), twenty positions and forty employees are involved. The reasons for this relatively low participation are: (1) the program has not been actively promoted amongst employees; (2) many employees cannot afford to live at half salary; (3) amongst the forty people involved, all are females who are not the sole earners for their families;

and (4) not all positions can be shared. In order to make the program successful, however, the bank or the employees can terminate the sharing agreement with thirty days' notice, and the individuals involved can return to full-time work if they so desire.

INDUSTRIAL AND ELECTRONIC COTTAGES. Increasingly, individuals are working at home. Scientific personnel can work at home when they have computer terminals linked to the mainframe at their regular office or plant. In essence, the employee's home becomes an **electronic cottage**. The Sun Life Assurance Co. of Canada is one company that decided to experiment with home-work as a response to employee concerns. Although the company does not know if this is cost-effective and it does not appear that home-work will likely become widespread, there are mutual accommodations in this scheme that improve productivity and enhance profitability. Individuals may also take work home that involves assembly, such as small toys, circuit boards, or art objects. After a batch is completed, the worker takes it to the regular plant and turns it in for more parts. In this example, the home becomes an **industrial cottage**. One drawback, however, is the difficulty of protecting the health and safety of the employees at home. Another is ensuring that workers are still paid a fair wage for their work. Provincial and federal laws can also restrict home-work.

Job Design Approaches

Jobs can be designed in many different ways, four of which are discussed here. Other methods of designing jobs are essentially combinations of these four approaches.

SCIENTIFIC. Under the **scientific approach**, job analysts (typically, industrial engineers) take special pains to design jobs so that the tasks performed by employees do not exceed their abilities. The jobs designed by scientific management often result in work being partitioned into small, simple segments. These tasks lend themselves well to time and motion studies and to incentive pay systems, each for the purpose of obtaining high productivity. The scientific approach to job design still is an important part of the many present-day organizational structures previously described in this chapter. The underlying assumption is that workers generally dislike work and are motivated only by economic rewards. Generally, the use of scientific design results in jobs with minimal levels of variety, significance, autonomy, feedback, and identity. Since the jobs are so small, as a result of a high division of labour, they often have a qualitative underload and a narrow purpose. The only reward that employees receive under scientific job design is monetary.

It became evident early on, however, that many workers did not like jobs designed according to the dictates of scientific management. In effect, the person–job relationship had been arranged so that achieving the goals of the organization (high productivity) often meant sacrificing important personal goals (the opportunity for interesting, personally challenging work). Organizations continued to treat the design of the job as inviolate, something not to be changed. Methods were developed to select people who would be satisfied with economic rewards and jobs with simple segments. It is not hard to understand why the success of this strategy was somewhat short-lived. As suggested in the chapter on job analysis, some employees, though by no means all, appear to prefer jobs that include some responsibility and autonomy, as well as good pay. Organizations have responded by designing jobs in other ways to create alternative organizational structures.

INDIVIDUAL CONTEMPORARY. Concerned with the human costs associated with the scientific approach, organizations have begun searching for alternative job design approaches. The **individual contemporary design** strives to achieve high motivation, high quality work performance, increased employee satisfaction, low absenteeism, and low turnover. The latter results when an employee works in an environment in which work is meaningful, there is knowledge of results, and there is responsibility for work outcomes. While there might be different strategies that aim to stimulate core job characteristics, three individual contemporary approaches have become well known: job rotation, job enlargement, and job enrichment.

Job rotation does not change the nature of a specific job, but it often increases the number of duties an employee performs over time. This increases task variety and also may boost job identity and scope of purpose, because the employee is performing several jobs.

Job enlargement differs from rotation by actually adding more duties to a specific job rather than by moving an employee around to experience the duties of several jobs. It is the opposite of the scientific approach, which seeks to reduce the number of duties. It has the potential of increasing skill variety.

Job enrichment involves adding more tasks of a different nature to a job. To distinguish it from job enlargement, which is often referred to as horizontal loading, job enrichment is often referred to as vertical loading. While **horizontal loading** means adding more duties that have the same characteristics, **vertical loading** means creating a job with duties having many different characteristics; for example, job identity, job significance, autonomy, feedback, and skill variety (all the job characteristics shown in Exhibit 13.3). The impact of this job enrichment design, according to Hackman and Oldham, is a significant improvement of the employee's psychological state.

Exhibit 13.3
The Impact of the Core Job Characteristics on an Employee's Psychological State

CORE JOB CHARACTERISTICS	CRITICAL PSYCHOLOGICAL STATES	OUTCOMES
Skill variety Job identity Job significance	Experienced meaningfulness of the work	Less absenteeism Less turnover
Autonomy	Experienced responsibility for outcomes of the work	High internal work motivation
Feedback	Knowledge of the actual results of the work activities	High quality of performance

Source: Adapted from J.R. Hackman and G.R. Oldham, *Work Redesign* (Reading, Mass.: Addison–Wesley, 1980), 77. Reprinted with permission of the publisher.

TEAM CONTEMPORARY.   While the scientific and individual contemporary approaches design jobs for individuals, the **team contemporary approach** designs jobs for teams of individuals. The final designs generally demonstrate a concern for the social needs of individuals as well as the constraints of technology. Here, teams of workers often rotate jobs and may follow the product they are working on from the beginning to the end of the production process. If the product is large, for example an automobile, teams may be designed around sections of the final car. Each group then completes only a section and passes its sub-product to the next team. In the team contemporary design, each worker learns to handle several duties, many requiring different skills. Thus, the group can satisfy needs for achievement and task accomplishment and some needs for social interaction. When faced with decisions, teams generally try to involve all members. If their decisions and behaviours result in greater output, all team members share in the dollar benefits.

Some recent manufacturing innovations draw from this approach for their success. For example, *cellular manufacturing* rearranges the traditional job-shop layout by clustering different machines together and gives work teams a "whole" piece of work to complete.

Zero inventory systems are premised on the assumption that rather than allowing inventory to build up in queues production should stop until the bottleneck or work problem is solved. Workers pitch in to solve the problem rather than wait for solutions.

ERGONOMICS. This approach is concerned with trying to design and shape jobs to fit the physical abilities and characteristics of individuals so that they can better perform the jobs. The **ergonomic approach** is being used by organizations to redesign certain jobs to accommodate women as well as handicapped individuals. Often, this serves equal employment opportunity and affirmative-action objectives. Studies have shown that when jobs are designed along ergonomic principles, worker productivity is greater. A U.S. study done by the National Institute of Occupational Safety and Health (NIOSH) compares two groups of employees working under an incentive pay system. The group working in ergonomically effective jobs was 25 percent more productive than the group working on jobs not designed along ergonomic principles. As one illustration, NIOSH, along with several unions, is also actively involved in redesigning jobs using ergonomic principles to help reduce the incidence and severity of **carpal tunnel syndrome**. This syndrome is characterized by numbness, tingling, soreness, and weakness in the hands and wrists. It is caused or aggravated by jobs requiring repetitive hand motions.

Germany is engaged in considerable work in the area of ergonomics. Germany today is considered to be the world leader in modifying assembly lines and in increasing the workers' job cycle to minimize physical and mental strain and increase productivity. Other countries are following suit. A report in *The Financial Post*, involving two separate examples, illustrates these arguments: in the first study, concerning the airline industry, a 93 percent reduction in errors was recorded when the workplace at an airline computer centre was redesigned. The changes involved the introduction of adjustable work surfaces and chairs; the addition of foot rests and document holders; changes in work area dimensions; and modifications in lighting, colour scheme, noise, air quality, and temperature. When the company added more improvements to an already liberal rest break schedule, "musculoskeletal problems dropped by half and visual fatigue by one-third. Changes in performance were dramatic, with keying speed rising by 37 percent." In a second case, redesign of workstations, combined with work flow modifications and changes in lighting, heat and air quality, produced productivity improvements ranging from 14.7 percent to 17.5 percent, in the Buffalo Organization for Social and Technological Innovation. Ergonomists involved in this research estimated the dollar value of productivity improvements at $4,650 a year for a professional earning $31,600 and $3,042 for a clerical worker earning $17,400. In addition, a study of workplace innovations showed productivity gains of $7,836 per worker over five years when employees were moved from an open environment to workstations with coordinated desks, chairs, and privacy panels.[8]

DESIGN CONSIDERATIONS. Exhibit 13.4 shows some of the advantages and disadvantages to consider in selecting job design.

Employment Security

Employment security is a prevailing concept in Japanese culture. There are signs that with the creation of Japanese manufacturing and distribution centres in North America, the concept is also gaining popularity here. A well-advertised case is that of the San Diego plant for Sony Corporation. When the San Diego plant encountered a sudden decline in sales, and inventories had begun to pile up, production was cut. Consequently, the American managers requested permission from the head office in Japan to begin workforce reductions. To their astonishment, they were denied such permission. When they renewed the request, pointing out that sales were way down and significant losses would soon appear on the bottom line, Akiro Morita, the founder of Sony, replied: "Think of the opportunity." "What opportunity?" the American managers persisted. "We are going to be drowning in

Exhibit 13.4
Some Advantages and Disadvantages of the Four Job Design Approaches

APPROACH	ADVANTAGES	DISADVANTAGES
Scientific	Ensures predictability Provides clarity Fits abilities of many people Can be efficient and productive	May be boring May result in absenteeism, sabotage, and turnover
Individual Contemporary	Satisfies needs for responsibility, growth, and knowledge of results Provides growth opportunity Reduces boredom Increases quality and morale Reduces turnover	Some people prefer routine and predictability May need to pay more since more skills needed Hard to enrich some jobs Not everyone wants to rotate
Team Contemporary	Provides social interaction Provides variety Facilitates social support Reduces absenteeism problem	People may not want interaction Requires training in interpersonal skills Group no better than weakest member
Ergonomic	Accommodates jobs to people Breaks down physical barriers Makes more jobs accessible to more people	May be costly to redesign some jobs Structural characteristics of the organization may make job change impossible.

red ink." "Think of the opportunity," Morita repeated. Then he explained that if employees are kept and supported by the company during difficult times, they will understand the company commitment to them, and in turn they will be loyal and committed to the company. Consequently, there was no layoff. The company absorbed losses for a while until business recovered. In the next few years, the San Diego plant performed very well, in some instances even outperforming the company's plants in Japan.[9]

Other organizations are considering offering employment security. Managers know the multiple consequences of layoffs, including lower morale and loyalty, severance pay, and more. Still, offering employment security might be risky, especially when the organization is already overstaffed or pursuing a strategy of liquidation. While the impetus to the Japanese culture originates from a paternalistic approach, in many Canadian cases employment security is achieved through collective negotiations with unions. Obviously, the impact on employee loyalty is not the same.

Nonetheless, intermediate solutions seem to be on the rise. One such solution involves the setting of a core of full-time employees with job guarantees. This core workforce can be augmented by *contingent or buffer employees*. According to estimates by the Conference Board, approximately one out of every four workers today is actually a contingent worker. They include freelancers and contract workers, temporary office employees, and part-time workers. Because the size of the needed labour force can be quickly reduced to match business needs, the deployment of buffer employees increases staffing flexibility.

And because the latter receive no pensions, vacations, or holiday pay and there is no obligation to train them, they also cost less. And only core employees can be the target for employment security.

As with QWL, productivity improvements can encompass a wide variety of programs. All the programs share an orientation of concern and respect for the employee. Typically, the organization exhibits more openness and willingness to invest in programs that benefit the individual as well as the organization. In this section, four such programs are presented. They include: communicating with employees: organizational surveys, organizational restructuring, automation, and Total Quality Management.

Communicating with Employees: Organizational Surveys

Establishing ways to communicate with employees is considered by the CEOs of many organizations to be one of HRM's top priorities.[10] Improving communications is seen as an effective way to improve both productivity and QWL. It facilitates the transformation of employee ideas into product improvements (as in quality circles) and organizational changes, and at the same time enhances the employee's job involvement, participation, and feeling of self-control. In addition, training programs can be established to improve supervisory communications and the HR department can conduct organizational surveys.

WHAT SURVEYS MEASURE. As discussed in previous chapters, HR data have frequently been used as either measures of job performance itself or as predictors of it. However, the HR manager often has a need for other types of data. For example, in order to develop ways to improve employee job performance, the HR manager needs to measure employees' perceptions of organizational characteristics, including the consequences of job performance, organizational policies, frequency of feedback, job design qualities, task interference characteristics, aspects of goal setting, role conflict and awareness, and supervisory behaviours. It is equally necessary to gather data on the employee's reactions to organizational conditions, QWL, job involvement, and employee stress.

In addition, it is useful to determine the actual or objective qualities (nonreactive measures) of the organizational characteristics. For example, in order to make improvements in job design, it may be necessary to know what the actual job characteristics are that the employees perceive as highly repetitive. This, combined with information about the employees' reactions, can facilitate effective job design changes.

PURPOSES OF AN ORGANIZATIONAL SURVEY. An **organizational survey** serves several purposes. First, it helps determine the effectiveness of HR functions and activities. Second, it measures the quality of the organization's internal environment and, therefore, helps to locate aspects that require improvement. Finally, the survey results help in the development of programs to make the necessary changes, and help to evaluate their effectiveness.

STEPS IN AN ORGANIZATIONAL SURVEY. There are several important steps and issues for the HR manager, or an outside consultant, when conducting an organizational survey. These include planning carefully, collecting the actual data, and ensuring employee participation. These become necessary, however, only after top management has given its support to the survey. As the first step, the HR manager must consider the following:

- Specific employee perceptions and responses that should be measured;
- Methods that will be used to collect the data, including observations, questionnaires, interviews, and personnel records;
- Reliability and validity of the measures to be used;

- People from whom the data will be collected—all employees, managerial employees only, a sample of employees, or only certain departments within the organization;
- Timing of the survey, especially if it is part of a longer-term effort;
- Types of analyses that will be made with the data;
- Specific purposes of the data—for example, to determine reasons for the organization's turnover problem.

This last consideration is important because, by identifying the problem, the HR manager can determine which models or theories will be relevant to the survey. Consequently, the HR manager can decide what data are needed and what statistical techniques will be used to analyze them.

The next step is the actual collection of data. Three things are important here. First, it must be decided who will administer the questionnaire—the line manager, someone from the HR department, or someone from outside the organization. Second, it must be decided where, when, and in what size groups the data will be collected. Both of these considerations are influenced by the method used to gather the data. For example, with a larger group, using a questionnaire is more feasible than conducting individual interviews. Finally, employee participation in the survey must be ensured. This can be done by gathering the data during company time and by providing feedback—for instance, by promising employees that the results of the survey will be made known to them.

The actual feedback process is the third step in the survey. As part of this process, the data are analyzed according to the purposes and problems for which they were collected. The results of the analysis can then be presented by the HR department to the line managers, who in turn discuss the results with their employees. The feedback sessions can be used to develop solutions to any problems that are identified and to evaluate the effectiveness of programs that may already have been implemented on the basis of the results of an earlier survey.

The extent to which employees actually participate in the development of solutions during the feedback process depends on the philosophy of top management. Organizations that are willing to survey their employees to ask how things are going are also usually willing to invite employee participation in developing plans for improvements. It is this willingness that allows organizational surveys to be used most effectively.

A SAMPLE QUESTIONNAIRE. The most common method of obtaining survey data is the paper-and-pencil questionnaire, although more and more organizations resort to direct (online) computer-based surveys. Exhibit 13.5 is a questionnaire asking employees to describe the degree to which they know what is expected of them (role ambiguity) and how much work they face in doing what is expected (job overload). Measures of role ambiguity and job overload have been used extensively in organizational surveys. Now, complete the questionnaire using your experience in a job you hold now or held recently.

Once you have completed the questionnaire, add the numbers you circled in items 1, 2, 3, and 4 and divide the total by 4 in order to obtain a single score. This is your *role* conflict score. The closer it is to 5, the higher the conflict; the closer to 1, the lower the conflict. Now add the remaining numbers you circled and once again divide the total by 4 to determine your *job overload* score. Note that in this case the scale scores were reversed, although the interpretation is similar to the first measure, namely the higher the score the more job overload. This reversal is done deliberately by questionnaire designers in order to minimize problems pertaining to social desirability. You will notice that items in the questionnaire need to meet the criteria of validity and reliability, as was discussed in the chapter on employee staffing.

Next, still considering the job you used for Exhibit 13.5, circle the response in Exhibit 13.6 that measures your overall level of satisfaction in the job. Pay attention to the fact

Exhibit 13.5
Role Ambiguity and Job Overload Questionnaire

These questions deal with different aspects of work. Please indicate how often these aspects appear in your job. *Circle one number per item.*

	VERY OFTEN	FAIRLY OFTEN	SOMETIMES	OCCASIONALLY	RARELY
1. How often do you understand exactly what your job responsibilities are?	1	2	3	4	5
2. How often can you predict what others will expect of you on the job?	1	2	3	4	5
3. How often are your work objectives well defined?	1	2	3	4	5
4. How often are you clear about what others expect of you on the job?	1	2	3	4	5
5. How often does your job require you to work fast?	5	4	3	2	1
6. How often does your job require you to work very hard?	5	4	3	2	1
7. How often does your job leave you with little time to get things done?	5	4	3	2	1
8. How often is there a great deal to be done?	5	4	3	2	1

that the higher the score, the more dissatisfied you are/were with the job. How does your score on satisfaction compare with your scores on role ambiguity and job overload? Are you high on all three, low on all three, or do you have a mixed pattern?

What is the importance of these scores? In most surveys, employees are asked for their perceptions of, and attitudes toward, many aspects of the organization. These surveys generally reveal very definite patterns. Satisfaction, for instance, tends to have a negative relationship with role ambiguity, but one that is consistent with job overload. Role ambiguity and job overload are also frequently related to stress and to employee performance. Therefore, role ambiguity and job overload scores reveal a great deal about an employee.

Organizational Restructuring

Faced with intense competition and rapidly changing environments, organizations are responding by restructuring themselves. Although this is done in a variety of ways, there are a few common themes, namely, an attempt to make the organizations flatter, more democratic, and more capable of adapting to changes. These new structures emphasize different aspects of managing people at work. Exhibit 13.7 compares and contrasts the underlying premises in the new vs. traditional concepts for management.

Some of the most interesting experiments with organizational restructuring include increasing participation schemes and Theory Z management.

Exhibit 13.6
Sample Questions from Job Satisfaction Survey

1. Knowing what you know now, if you had to decide all over again whether to take the type of job you now have, what would you decide?
   I would:

1	2	3
Decide without hesitation to take the same type of job	Have some second thoughts	Decide definitely not to take this type of job

2. If you were free right now to go into any type of job that you wanted, what would your choice be?
   I would:

1	2	3
Take the same type of job as I now have	Take a different type of job	Not want to work

3. If a friend of yours expressed an interest in working at a job like yours, what would your advice be?
   I would:

1	2	3
Strongly recommend it	Have doubts about recommending it	Advise against it

4. All in all, how satisfied would you say you are with your job?

1	2	3
Satisfied	Somewhat satisfied	Not satisfied

Exhibit 13.7
Typical Characteristics of Newer and Traditional Structures

TRADITIONAL	NEW
• Human resources are an extension of machines	• Human resources complement machines and should be developed
• Human potential should be maximized	• Human potential should be optimized
• Human resources are to be controlled externally (supervisors, rules and regulations)	• Human resources are to be controlled internally (self-management, self-discipline)
• Hierarchical structure	• Flat structure
• Autocratic style of management	• Democratic style of management
• Conflicts and rivalry encouraged	• Collaboration; joint effort encouraged
• Alienation	• Empowerment
• No risk (don't rock the boat)	• Innovation, creativity (go and try it)

Source: Translated and adapted from S.L. Dolan and G. Lamoureux, *Initiation à la psychologie du travail* (Montreal: Gaetin Morin, 1990), 427. Used with permission of the authors.

INCREASED PARTICIPATION. While quality circles represent one form of increased employee participation, other structures are being developed as well. One of the first attempts at industrial democracy on a broad scale occurred in West Germany under the name co-determination. It enables workers' representatives to discuss and vote on key management decisions that affect them. Another model of participation is the Israeli kibbutz system, a totally cooperative enterprise.

Canadian firms have mixed results in experimenting with different models (degrees) of participation schemes. Although in theory, these efforts should increase profit and worker satisfaction, in reality this is not always the case. One particular example is that of Tricofil in Saint-Jerome (Quebec). The workers bought the company, restyled it along the lines of a complete self-managed model, and went bankrupt a few years later. Analysis of this case suggests that a number of extraneous conditions need to exist in order for self-management to succeed (i.e., proper market conditions, proper management skills, and a clear vision of goals and responsibilities). On the other hand, a cooperative structure formed at Harpel Printing Industries in Montreal yielded higher employee satisfaction as well as significant productivity gains.

Some interesting formulas for participation have emerged in the past few years and, most likely, similar experiments will be formed in the future. In one example, Normick Perron (in Quebec), each employee with two years' experience can use between 1 percent and 3 percent of wages to buy shares every year. The employer participates by paying for 50 percent of the cost of shares. Between 1969 and 1979 the company's total revenue increased from $8 million with a net profit of 5 percent to $100 million with a net profit of 10 percent. In the case of Tembec Inc., results were even more impressive. After the pulp and paper giant shut its plant in 1973, its 500 workers bought the company with government and local financial assistance. In 1986 the workers sold back their shares to Tembec and profit went from the nominal $0.05 in 1973 to $8.

THEORY Z MANAGEMENT. While participatory systems improve QWL and productivity, they may represent limited changes to the organization itself. **Theory Z management** represents a modification of the more traditional North American management (*Theory A*) that incorporates some of the ideas from traditional Japanese management (*Theory J*). The characteristics of Theory Z, falling between Theory J and Theory A, include:

- Employment of a long-term nature, informally stated;
- Relatively slow promotion and evaluation period;
- Career paths that "wander around" through different functions in the organization;
- Extensive planning and accounting data used for purposes of information and collective decision making rather than for control;
- Decisions made on the basis of sound data and on whether they "fit" the entire organization, rather than just one subpart;
- Sharing of responsibility for making and implementing decisions, although decisions are often guided by one individual.

As with Theory J and Theory A, in practice Theory Z takes many forms. It can be adapted not only to the North American culture, but also to the unique styles and needs of each corporation. This modification of Theory J recognizes the fact that the cultures of Canada and Japan are quite different, so it is really impossible to do in Canada exactly what is done in Japan. In fact, looking at the situational factors that Theory Z recommends leads to a mixed picture:

- Canada has been characterized as a cultural mosaic and its various ethnic groups tend to maintain their cultural identities, a force that works against the uniformity of values in Type Z firms.

- Another factor that would potentially a Type Z firm is the relatively high degree of unionization in Canada. An adversarial union is a competing factor for employees' loyalty.

Despite these factors, a study of the 100 top firms to work for in Canada (published by *The Financial Post*, 1986) shows a number of companies that are considered exemplary of Type Z. Among them are: Canadian Tire Co., Northern Telecom, Four Seasons Hotel, Great West Life Insurance Co., Syncrude, Labatt Breweries, and others. The characteristics of such firms are very similar to those of the Type Z firm, including a strong organizational culture, employment stability, continuity of leadership, as well as promotion from within and a generally high concern for employees.

Recently, however, Theory Z has been on the attack. A recent article suggested that what actually motivates Japanese managers and makes the system work is *Theory F* (fear). The culture does not tolerate failure. The penalty for failure is out, finished. It's a powerful motivator.[11]

Automation

After two decades of decline in the face of low-cost, high-quality imports, industry is beginning to automate at a pace that will soon change the face of Canadian factories and offices. Computer-controlled systems of robots are replacing most humans on plant floors and will produce unprecedented gains in productivity. Automated equipment is also moving into offices. All together these changes will affect millions of jobs during the next ten years.

Since automation is so significant and is likely to be a major contributor to improving productivity, it is critical for HRM to understand it and utilize it to improve productivity and QWL. Automation is especially critical to HRM since it has the potential for changing the nature of so many jobs and creating many new ones. These changes, in turn, will impact on employee recruitment and selection, PA, and training.

PLANT AUTOMATION. Computer-integrated manufacturing (CIM), flexible manufacturing systems (FMS), and computer-aided design and manufacturing (CAD/CAM) will become highly visible in many Canadian factories. In relative terms, however, Canada is lagging behind Japan, Germany, and the U.S.A. in installing CAD/CAM equipment. If Canadian productivity is to be increased, this trend will have to change in the years to come.

OFFICE AUTOMATION. What is happening to the factory is also happening to the office. More and more offices across Canada are becoming automated. The biggest gains in office productivity are predicted to come from automating the jobs of professionals and managers. In late 1985, the Economic Council of Canada conducted its working technology survey, which was designed to explore technological changes and their employment impacts on Canadian industry. Approximately two-thirds of the technological changes reported comprised the introduction of word processors, personal computers, workstations, office networks, and other office applications.

This surge of new technologies, if not carefully implemented, may result in employee resistance due to fear and uncertainty and will be counterproductive. A number of studies concluded that introducing new technologies needs to be carefully planned and executed in order to minimize this resistance.[12] Therefore, HR staff would have to act as facilitators in introducing these new technologies. Ideally, the HR department should be involved in the planning process before a computer system is introduced. The role of the HR officer is to foresee such activities as relocation, counselling, grievances, dealing with health and safety concerns, managing staff redundancies, and meeting new training needs. More often than not, however, the HR department ends up dealing with the aftermath of the decision to automate. This is a *reactive* response; HR strategy should be *proactive* in order to ensure more positive outcomes.

Total Quality Management (TQM)

Companies are rethinking how they manage their business because of the changing conception of their relationship with the customer. Ensuring customer satisfaction by delivering quality products and services is propelling companies into a revolutionary way of managing. The model has three components, which are commonly defined as: *Total, Quality, and Management*. They are imperative to the implementation of successful customer satisfaction models. *Total* focuses on the need to involve all aspects of the organization in the orientation toward the customer (both inside and outside the organization). *Quality* means establishing criteria for excellence in customer satisfaction, determining the level of performance necessary, and following up on delivery. *Management* refers to the strategies and practices adopted and managed by the organization to support the quality goals.

The concept of quality has evolved from an emphasis on inspection (at the end of the production process) to developing measures of quality geared toward zero defects. Yet in the early stages of these approaches, the focus was on prevention and little attempt was made to link these efforts to the strategic goals of the organization.[13] This approach worked fairly well in a stabilized world. However, in the 1980s, it proved insufficient as de-regulation and competition intensified. As a result, emerging in North America in very recent years is an increased emphasis on quality and client satisfaction.

Based on research at many leading Canadian companies, the Conference Board of Canada has recognized three major forces that push organizations to adapt TQM approaches:

1. Companies' recognition that, in the face of competition and in an attempt to maintain market share, they need to satisfy their customers;
2. Companies' response to the explicit demands of customers;
3. Companies' reaction to the needs of their employees for a work environment that recognizes individual and group contributions.[14]

TQM requires major changes in the way companies operate. David McCamus, former president and CEO of Xerox Canada, warns organizations that believe conversion to this philosophy will happen instantly; he states: "TQM requires a major shift away from the philosophy—*if I fix it, it is fixed*—to the Japanese belief that—*nothing is ever fixed*." Nonetheless, when the program is properly applied and supported results are extremely encouraging. Exhibit 13.8 shows the benefits accrued by three Canadian companies that were recipients of Canada Awards for Business Excellence in 1989.

TRENDS IN INNOVATIVE FORMS FOR MANAGING HUMAN RESOURCES

Two major trends are described here: (1) assessing improvement programs, and (2) using computer technology to improve QWL and productivity. Issues associated with strategic changes and overcoming resistance to them are the essence of this section.

Assessing Innovative Forms and Improvements

QWL PROGRAMS. As with the other HR activities, assessing the benefits of QWL programs solely on the basis of dollars and cents is almost impossible. Consider the difficulties involved in assessing the dollar value of the benefit of raising the level of employee self-control or satisfaction by 12 percent. It may be difficult to ask, but the question is: do all QWL programs have to be justified on the basis of dollars and cents? Or can they be justified solely on the basis of increasing self-control, satisfaction, involvement, and self-respect (essentially all employee benefits)? These benefits may be measured through systematic and scientific surveys, as discussed hereafter. At the same time, it is important to obtain data on productivity (both quality and quantity) if possible, and to examine the relationship between it and employee satisfaction. In most instances, the two go hand in hand, and thus, QWL programs also provide benefits to the organization, that is, individual performance and productivity gains.

Implementing QWL programs implies change in one or more aspects of the existing work environment. A major obstacle to any change is *resistance*: resistance on the part of

Exhibit 13.8
Benefits Derived from Total Quality Management for Three Canadian Organizations

AMP of Canada, Ltd.

- on-time delivery performance improved from 60 per cent in 1982 to 95 per cent in 1988
- inventory reduced by 23 per cent in last two years
- shipments from stock improved from 60 per cent to 80 per cent, improving the availability of products to customers
- order changes and credit notes issued halved
- market share improved by 5 percentage points
- sales increased 38 per cent (1986–1989)
- stock delivery from parent company reduced from 20 days in 1986 to 4.5 days in 1989
- in 1987, average months of inventory on hand was 2.3 and in 1989 fell to 1.8
- reduction in staff levels from 295 in 1988 to 282 in 1989 as a result of delayering and efficiency improvements
- sales per employee up 13 per cent
- selling, general and administrative expenses for 1989 held to 1988 levels, while sales increased 8.2 per cent

Avco Financial Services Canada Ltd.

- profit has grown from $8.1 million in 1984 to $17.6 million in 1988
- $5.6 million had been saved since 1985 through the company's Quality Teams and Department Quality Savings
- positive comments on President's letters have increased from 67 per cent in 1984 to 95 per cent in 1988
- accounts per employee have increased from 296 in 1984 to 353 in 1988
- positive responses on employee attitude survey have increased from 76 per cent in 1984 to 83 per cent in 1987

B.C. Tel

- in excess of 200 employee quality improvement suggestions adopted, resulting in a net company benefit of more than $3 million
- vendor quality program resulting in approximately three quality-issue reports per day
- customer satisfaction, as measured by an ongoing survey, has shown consistent improvement, with overall responses in the excellent/good category increasing from 82 to 90 per cent
- improvements in employees' opinions of company in the area of company reputation, prospects for future and management receptivity to employees' ideas have, on average, increased 20 per cent since 1984
- maintained leading market share in four main areas despite stiff competition
- projected productivity and growth factors have been exceeded in each of the past four years

Source: C.R. Farquhar and C.G. Johnston, *Total Quality Management: A Competitive Imperative—Lessons from the Quality Winners of the 1989 Canada Awards for Business Excellence,* Report 60–90E (Ottawa: Conference Board of Canada, 1990), 5. Reprinted with permission.

the employee, and resistance on the part of the employer. Consequently, measuring the effects of new programs should take place after a while, otherwise the reactions may simply imply the relative insecurity of experimentation.

Most criteria used to evaluate QWL programs are *subjective* in nature. They are difficult to quantify. For example, how do you measure worker satisfaction? The answers given by the respondents greatly depend upon their mood and their perception at the time they answer the questionnaire. Also, many effects of a QWL program are *not tangible*, at least not immediately. For example, programs to increase the wellness of employees may not lead to a substantial increase in productivity or a significant decrease in absenteeism and turnover immediately. An accurate assessment of QWL programs certainly represents a challenge.

PRODUCTIVITY PROGRAMS.   The process of assessing productivity programs is less complex than that for QWL programs because outcomes are much more measurable. For example, productivity can be assessed by individual job performance, absenteeism, and turnover. Productivity programs at the organizational level can be evaluated in terms of profitability, competitiveness, and survival measures. The difficulty appears to lie in gaining acceptance of the idea that productivity *will* be measured, rather than that it *can* be measured. Once the organization accepts the fact that productivity can be assessed, measures can be established in almost all job categories, and the effects of productivity improvement programs can be assessed. Today even the qualitative aspects of productivity, as we witnessed in the various TQM programs, can be operationalized and assessed.

Computer Applications

Computer technology can affect QWL and productivity improvements in many ways. One way is to gather and store information that can be used to improve working conditions. Similarly, computers can be used to simulate ergonomic environments and aid in the design of jobs. Furthermore, computerized operations tell employees when to do a particular operation in the most efficient and safe manner.

Computer technology can also assist in improving diagnosis and assessment of QWL and productivity improvement programs. Although performance-improvement software is in its infancy, "a sleeper that's about to wake up," according to one expert, HR managers are beginning to discover that the objectivity of computers is ideally suited to a process that has often been plagued by bias, subjectivity, and controversy.[15] Performance diagnosis has been receiving increased attention recently because it builds on the newest innovations in technology, such as expert systems. The software will analyze particular problems and suggest solutions.

Performance-related software is also closely linked to other key HR functions and programs. It is often part of an organization's integrated HRIS, and proposed individual or team bonuses can be analyzed against department budgets, against the last month/quarter of performance, etc.

One area where computer technology is gaining ground is in monitoring attendance. This application is referred to as an "electronic clock." Old mechanical time clocks to punch in and out at worksites have been replaced by computerized time-management systems running on low-cost microcomputers. The advantages of electronic clocks are numerous:

- They reduce hours of manual clerical time required to assemble records, as well as reducing potential errors in recording the data.
- The employee can have instant access to his or her hours worked during the current pay period, outstanding vacation entitlement, scheduled work dates, and attendance history.
- The supervisors are immediately advised of any irregularities and therefore have better control.
- Electronic timeclocks are very useful in facilitating and managing flextime and a compressed work week.

While computer technology may be very useful for improving productivity, it may also generate problems among employees. For example, an investigation in Ontario by a provincial ombudsman resulted in several departments dropping the practice of providing employees with regular statistics on their performance, and thus put an end to the use of electronic monitoring of individual productivity. Most employees view this as a victory.

HRM DYNAMICS
QWL and Productivity Profiles in Selected Canadian Organizationns

B.C. Tel

B.C. Telephone is the second largest telecommunications company in Canada. The QWL initiatives at B.C. Tel are focused around three feedback systems: (1) customer perception feedback, (2) employee feedback, and (3) investor feedback. In order to achieve these goals, B.C. Tel emphasizes human resources policies of participative management style with hundreds of quality action teams working to improve every aspect of the business. For its performance, the company was awarded a Canada Quality Award for Business Excellence in 1989.

Reimer Express Lines

Reimer Express Lines is a transcontinental motor carrier headquartered in Winnipeg. In its attempt to promote continuous quality improvements, the company operates a Quality/Training Office with the aim of developing the notion of excellence in all employees. Since the introduction of the program in 1986, the company has maintained a record of 98 percent on-time performance, reductions in freight damage, and fewer errors altogether. Recognizing employee involvement as a key element in productivity improvement, employees are encouraged to participate through a PAR system (Positive Action Request). Employees who contribute are recognized and awarded various rewards. For its performance, the company was awarded a Canada Quality Award for Business Excellence in 1989.

Xerox Canada

Xerox Canada is a leading supplier of a wide range of advanced document-processing equipment. Today, it employs about 5,000 people. In the presence of unprecedented competition in the 1980s, the company decided to embrace quality as the vehicle to retain market share. A quality policy labelled "Leadership through Quality" was formulated, and was geared toward achieving total customer satisfaction. As a result, dramatic changes to the company's structure, its management style, and culture were undertaken. All in all, the company moved toward a more participatory form of management and employees' empowerment through adherence to principles of responsibility of every Xerox employee. For its performance, the company was awarded a Canada Quality Award for Business Excellence in 1989.

SUMMARY

Faced with increasing international competition, customer demands for quality, as well as changing social and individual values, Canadian companies are confronted with a productivity crisis of major proportions. This has led some companies to implement innovative programs for managing people. Some companies are implementing programs for productivity improvements, while others are enhancing QWL.

This chapter reviews only a few of many programs used by Canadian companies to improve their productivity and QWL. However, not all programs work well in all companies. Wholesale adoption of programs because they are popular or "everyone else is doing them" does not guarantee success. Therefore, it is imperative to carefully diagnose the needs and conditions required to achieve effective results. Once the diagnosis is accomplished, an organization can choose from among several programs, many directly related to their HR activities. For example, a total compensation system could be changed to one that is more performance based, or formulas for group gain-sharing based on the suggestions in this chapter could be applied. Regardless of the particular program, employee involvement in its design, implementation, or both, enhances the chance for success.

Just as there are many programs to improve productivity, there are many innovative ways to improve QWL. Indeed, it is suggested that much of the productivity crisis would be solved if QWL were improved. In solving these problems, organizations may be able to benefit from Japanese or European ideas. One must not forget though that these ideas must be adapted in content and form to Canadian culture.

POSTSCRIPT

Currently, work organization in the majority of Canadian firms remains very heavily influenced by the traditional models for managing people. Yet, the complexity of social, economic, and cultural changes will force many companies to develop more innovative approaches to people management. Due to the globalization of markets and tougher competition, companies will realize that the road to competitiveness requires innovativeness and responsiveness to customers and employees alike.

The labour market no longer has the same demands it had a few years ago. Workers have become better educated. They entertain a different set of expectations. Jobs are no longer a means to earn a reasonable and secure living. Workers now expect jobs to be interesting, meaningful, valorizing, and challenging. There will be a growing demand to participate in decision making. More and more jobs will have to be designed or redesigned to satisfy these demands. Moreover, we live in a period when the separation of work from personal life is becoming more and more difficult: families break up; an increasing proportion of people lives alone; individualism is on the rise; and social institutions, such as schools and religious institutions, no longer provide the same kind of firm, close-knit support they once did. Consequently, the workplace has become, and will be, a place where individuals find an opportunity to interact, to make use of their skills, to contribute to common goals, and to work at tasks that give some meaning to their lives. All in all, the workplace will be an increasingly important place where the worker's needs for affiliation and self-actualization will be fulfilled.

As we have seen in this chapter, companies are already responding by engaging in a variety of new management philosophies and multiple forms of participative management plans. Nonetheless, more radical experiments will be required in the future. HR managers will play an important role in facilitating the entry of these new ideas and their implementation. While no one can predict what kind of creative ideas the future holds, it will be interesting to conclude this chapter by looking at some avant-garde concepts already being used by selected futuristic companies.

TRANSCENDENTAL MEDITATION (TM). Users of TM find it is a great method by which to reduce their stress levels, to become more creative and productive, and to increase their sense of well-being. Research has shown that TM can lower levels of blood pressure, cholesterol and stress hormones, and can reduce the use of alcohol and cigarettes. A Detroit chemical company that has introduced TM to their employees reported a significant increase in sales and profits, and a decrease in absenteeism and the number of sick days.[16]

PRAYER GATHERINGS IN HIGH OFFICES. In response to a spiritual void in the life of many business executives, a number of business leaders have come together to organize early morning prayer sessions and monthly reflection gatherings at exclusive clubs and other chic meeting places. The aim is to take time out to reflect, to pray, to bring spiritual values into focus again, or to listen to the testimonial of a well-known figure, such as Mother Teresa. The result is perhaps more balanced and humane management, and a cluster of clear-minded executives more at peace with their souls. In Montreal, groups of this sort have been reported to include the president of the board of directors for Ouimet–Cordon Bleu, the president of Domtar, and the former president of the (former) insurance company, les Cooperants.[17]

SCENTING THE WORKPLACE WITH SUBLIMINAL FLOWER EXTRACT. In the 1960s it was shown that music (i.e., Muzak) might affect performance. In the 1990s research suggests that people like to linger longer in a room lightly scented with a pleasant smell rather than in a room equipped with a pair of well-worn sneakers. The idea has already been used to increase sales in a number of stores. Would its application make the office environment more pleasant, or make an assembly line more worker-friendly and more productive? The idea is certainly intriguing.[18]

SURPRISE THE BOSS WITH A LIVE GOOSE! A number of companies encourage their workers to be creative and to have fun at work. In a relaxed and casual atmosphere, playfulness and humour are safety valves for performance enhancement and stress reduction. At Stonehaven Productions Inc., executives may bring their babies and pets to high-level meetings. Personal expression is *de rigueur*. Spontaneous surprises are appreciated. Group activities generate togetherness and fun. Outings are sources of stories, memories, and anecdotes that the staff will refer to again and again. The philosophy is: "Companies that play together usually work together much more effectively." When the sales of Stonehaven hit $1 million a few years ago, the employees took the owner out to dinner and surprised him with a live goose and a gold-plated egg—but only after they had paraded through the restaurant.[19]

CONTROLLED LAWLESSNESS. Other companies practise a certain degree of built-in lawlessness by allowing their employees to "bootleg" some of the company's time and equipment to work on their own private projects. The results are creative new products and a loyal team of contented workers. One such success story is the 3M company whose famous yellow Post-it notes were developed in this manner.

REVIEW AND ANALYSIS QUESTIONS

1. Why are companies pressured to engage in productivity and QWL improvement programs?
2. What is the role of HR managers in relation to productivity and QWL improvement programs?
3. Name two traditional approaches to people management. Why are they labelled traditional?
4. What are some fundamental principles in the newer theories in people management?
5. What are the essential characteristics of Quality Circles?
6. What are the essential characteristics of semi-autonomous work groups? What are the required conditions essential for their success?
7. Identify some of the pros and cons of alternative work arrangements.
8. In what ways is the scientific approach to job design different from the individual and team-contemporary approaches?

9. Why are the benefits of QWL programs more difficult to ascertain than those of productivity improvement programs?

10. How are job enrichment programs different from job enlargement programs?

11. What are some major factors to be considered by an HR manager prior to conducting surveys?

12. What is the essence of TQM toward productivity improvement?

13. Describe in your own words how computer technology can be helpful in implementing QWL and productivity improvement programs?

CASE STUDY

IS "QUALITY PLUS" AT PROCTER & WINSTON CANADA RUNNING INTO TROUBLE?

Procter & Winston Canada, a subsidiary of a large multinational corporation headquartered in the U.S.A., is a leading manufacturer of gas turbines. The company employs about 6,000 people, many of whom are skilled workers and engineers. Because of the critical importance of producing high-precision components (the slightest error can lead to a catastrophic air disaster), the company has been trying for years to promote a tradition of technical excellence. In all of its HR activities, emphasis has been placed on strategies that will reinforce this concept. Although the company has enjoyed a substantial market share and has dominated the small gas-turbine engines market, the employment level has risen and fallen in response to changes in the economy and the respective market demands. In fact, during peak demand, about 8,000 employees have worked for the company, while these figures have been as low as 3,500 during periods of low demand. Consequently, layoffs and rehiring have become cyclical events. While HR policies have been directed toward and have revolved around the achievement of technical excellence, the company has not managed to imprint the same culture in the handling of its human resources. People have been hired and laid-off as the need arose, and with each re-hiring, they have been expected to maintain the same level of technical excellence. In addition, the company has been known for its notoriously poor labour relations. Indeed, over the years the company has experienced a number of highly publicized labour conflicts, many of which have led to strikes and lockouts.

One day, upon returning from the head office in the U.S.A., Malcolm White, the president of the Canadian subsidiary, asked his secretary to assemble all the senior executives for an emergency meeting. In the meeting he informed the group that rumours circulating in the head office suggested that competition would increase in the near future because some Japanese companies were about to enter the market. After four hours of intense discussion, the group decided to initiate a proactive action and prepare the company for such eventual competition. It was agreed that management philosophies needed to be changed and perhaps some Japanese management principles needed to be adopted. At the end of the meeting, the president was charged with the mandate to elaborate such a new program.

The next month, again upon returning from the U.S.A., Mr. White informed his executives that a solution had been found. He reported on a visit made to ARMCO, a large U.S. steel producer, that had been using, with a great deal of success, a program called "Quality+." In this program, a cultural change is sought whereby emphasis is placed on employees rather than on the technology alone. Since ARMCO was ready to share this experience with Proctor & Winston, the executives voted unanimously to adopt the plan.

Quality+ (Q+) is based on the belief that quality is a major element of an organization's culture. In order to promote quality, the board decided to involve not only management but also rank and file employees. The core of the implementation program included developing printed material about it and distributing the material to the employees, as well as holding training sessions for all employees on issues such as: quality management, training leaders, team development, problem solving, effective meeting, management presentations, and measurement. The training director was unofficially assigned to oversee the program.

For the initial phases of the implementation, substantial budgets were assigned to the project. With the passage of time, however, budgets were significantly reduced as more and more employees had already completed the training. Top-management commitment to the project was very strong, although few executives were specifically told how to manage the change process.

Initially, many executives participated in steering committees, executive seminars, etc., but at the end of the first year, management's idea of gaining employees' support was to throw parties and encourage all sorts of social gatherings. Toward the end of the first year, the entire concept was perceived by rank and file employees as a joke, hence having a good time did not lead to more involvement. Indeed, in the company's corridors, when Q+ was mentioned, it meant another "party."

Another problem with this implementation involved first-line supervisors and middle managers. On the one hand, they were subjected to constant pressure to deliver parts on time; on the other hand, they were told to change their management style, while guidelines and support for how to do it were not provided (except for the training sessions). It should be remembered that most supervisors were selected for their positions based on their technical expertise and not on their people management skills. This resulted in the following perceptions about the implications of Q+ on their own work:

- An additional workload,
- A threat,
- A new way to cut budget and staff,
- A new reason for grievance from union as well as nonunion employees.

Four years later, the majority of employees view Q+ in a very negative manner. As stated by one foreperson: "Every time Q+ is mentioned I develop a rash; there is so much talk about principles and philosophies and so little practical, no-nonsense guidance; we are overexposed to the philosophy by management but no one has solicited our ideas about it." Unions have also opposed the concept because they view it as another management gimmick. As stated by the local union steward: "We don't need Q+ to elicit quality in performance; we know the job and most of us have proved our responsibility in the production process." Management, on the other hand, is still committed to the concept with the hope that with time, it will "sink in" and a real cultural change will then follow.

Case Questions

1. What seem to be some of the critical problems in this case?
2. How can management obtain a better idea about progress and prospects regarding Q+ at Proctor and Winston?
3. If you were hired as a consultant to remedy the situation, what strategies and tactics would you adopt?

NOTES

1. Union of Japanese Scientists and Engineers (JUSE), *General Principles of Quality Circles* (Paris: Afnor, 1981).
2. Information is based on an interview with M. Brassard (CAMCO), conducted by Lien Bui on March, 1991.
3. P.M. Benimadhu, *Hours of Work: Trends and Attitudes in Canada*, Report 18–87 (Ottawa: Conference Board of Canada, February 1987).
4. G. des Roberts, "Les régimes d'avantages sociaux collectifs sont en progression," *Affaires*, 9 March 1991, 21.
5. G. Robertson, *Selected characteristics of compressed work schedules in Ontario*, Research Branch, Ontario Ministry of Labour, July 1973; and G. Robertson and P. Ferlejowki, *Employee attitudes toward compressed work schedules in Ontario: a case study of 10 firms,* Research Branch, Ontario Ministry of Labour, Aug. 1974.
6. Statistics compiled from Benimadhu, "Hours of work," (endnote 3); "La population active," Statistique Canada, Cat. no. 70–001, B33, Fevrier 1993; "Statistiques chronologiques sur la population active," Statistique Canada, 1991, 60, 62, and, *Quarterly Labour Market and Productivity Review*, Spring 1990, 21.
7. J. Chianello, "Subsidy for job sharing quadruples," *The Financial Post*, 7 January 1991, 10; and "Loi de l'assurance chomage article 13," Bill C-113, 4 April 1993.
8. J. Purdie, "Better offices mean greater productivity," *The Financial Post*, 26 November 1990, 35.
9. G. Mills, "The New Competitors, 69–70, "Employment Security News and Views," *Bulletin to Management*, 1 August 1985, 40.
10. E.F. McDonough, "How much power does HR have, and what can it do to win more?" *Personnel*, January 1986, 18–25. See also S.L. Dolan, "A Survey of the Perceived Effectiveness of Human Resources Management among Vice Presidents of HR Managers in Quebec" (A paper presented at the annual meeting of Canadian Association of Administrative Sciences, Montreal, June 1989).
11. J. Kotkin and Y. Kishimota, "Theory F," *INC. Magazine*, April 1986, 53–60.
12. D.A. Garvin, *Managing Quality: The Strategic and Competitive Edge (*New York: Free Press, 1988).

13. C.R. Farquhar and C.G. Johnston, *Total Quality Management: A Competitive Imperative—Lessons from the Quality Winners of the 1989 Canada Awards for Business Excellence*, Report 60–90E (Ottawa: Conference Board of Canada, October 1990).

14. Ibid., 53.

15. R.B. Frantzreb cited in M. Bowker, "What's hot in speciality software," *Human Resource Executive*, April 1989, 32–35.

16. "Meditating for Success," *Personnel*, January 1989, 5.

17. R. Poupart, "Dieu au pays des affaires," *Affaires plus*, March 1991, 35–37.

18. For more information, see Gilles des Roberts, "Une nouvelle manière de devancer la concurrence: par un nez!" *Finances*, 5 January 1991, 12.

19. J. Zeidenberg, "For fun and profit," *Profit*, November 1990, 37–40.

CHAPTER FOURTEEN

HEALTH AND SAFETY AT WORK

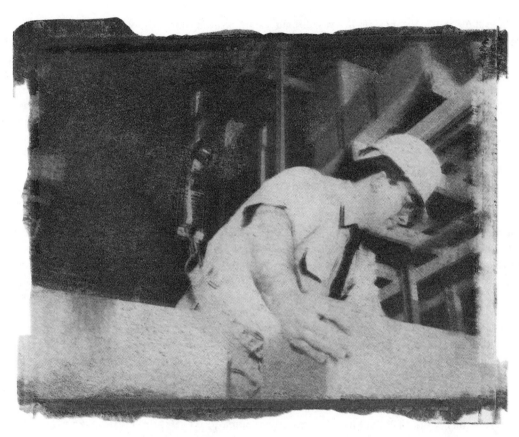

KEYNOTE ADDRESS

Arthur Sawchuk
President and CEO, Du Pont Canada Inc.

Safety and Health at Du Pont Canada Inc.

Protecting the safety and health of employees is a long tradition at Du Pont. In fact, there is a list of safety rules in our archives that dates from our earliest days, nearly 200 years ago. Today, our record in safety and occupational health gives us a great sense of accomplishment. For example, Du Pont Canada employees are about eight times safer than employees in North American industry generally (in terms of the frequency of recordable injuries). This demonstrates that a long-standing intense commitment to safety and health really works. Even so, we have not allowed ourselves to be satisfied with these results. Our goal is no injuries or occupational illness whatsoever. We believe this is attainable and that is what we are striving for.

Du Pont Canada's mission statement begins: "Safety, protection of the environment, concern and care for people, and personal and corporate integrity are the company's highest values and we will not compromise them." It is not mere chance that safety is the first word in that statement.

Over the years, Du Pont has proved that, in addition to the moral obligations to reduce accidents and occupational illness, safety is simply good business. The everyday habits and care that go into making a safe, healthy workplace are part of the pride and satisfaction that employees have in their work. Du Pont has also proved that its determination to work safely—and never to compromise safety standards, whatever the competitive pressures—does not cause extra costs and delays. Just the opposite: it improves productivity and quality, which is directly reflected in bottom-line results.

At Du Pont, employees understand that they bear the major responsibility for their own safety. This is even more important today, as Du Pont completes a decade of restructuring for future growth and globalization. The company has reduced its organizational levels—which ,means less supervision and a more participatory approach to management. With fewer supervisors and managers, there is a greater need for self-management and teamwork. Therefore, the onus is on the individual

to assume more responsibility and work in a team to accomplish common objectives—including excellent safety performance.

Everyone is involved in protecting the safety and health of themselves and co-workers. This does not just happen. Every single employee must be encouraged to "buy in" to the high value that the company assigns to safety and occupational health. And every employee must accept that he or she is responsible for safety at all stages of developing, manufacturing, handling, distributing, using or disposing of the company's products. In the safety effort, managers establish priorities that best meet the needs of individual business operations and achieve corporate safety goals. And the line organization designs safety programs that are geared to each plant or office location. These include monthly safety promotions staged by employee groups, and at one plant, special scratch-and-win lottery tickets that are handed out to employees for using good safety practices and generally showing concern for their co-workers' well-being.

It is also critical that senior managers demonstrate their personal commitment to the safe, healthy workplace. The level of attention and priority that management gives to this issue has a direct influence on employees' safety motivation, knowledge, and performance. For instance, managers are ready to take prompt action when safety or health might be threatened. Du Pont halted a polyethylene operation for several days when an employee found a faulty device that needed to be fixed; the company stopped using a dye in film processing when employees discovered it could be toxic to animals; and when some head office staff were concerned that the marble floors might be slippery, carpet was laid down in walkways and the company paid to have the heels of employees' shoes replaced with non-slip rubber.

Du Pont has found that a safety and health program can be successful only if a company: (1) demonstrates a sincere commitment by senior management; (2)

involves all levels, from the president to the front-line employee; and (3) makes sure the effort is continuous and consistent throughout the organization.

There are three necessary steps in setting up a program: (1) establish firm objectives—just as for other important aspects of a business, such as quality, cost, growth, and return on investment; (2) provide the resources and facilities that will help achieve the objectives—education and training tailored to real situations'; and (3) demand results. At Du Pont, managers are held accountable for their groups' safety performance and this is an important factor in their personal performance appraisals. In other words, how their group performs on safety can directly affect their future careers and compensation. As well, regular impartial audits show if safety and health programs are effective and responding to changing needs.

One of the most important conclusions Du Pont has reached about safety is that it is closely tied to business excellence and people excellence. People want to learn so that they can continuously improve, and they want to personally influence the factors that affect performance, whether it is in productivity, quality, or safety.

●　●　●

The Keynote Address illustrates important aspects of health and safety in the workplace. The issue is a complex one. In order to achieve effective results, such as the excellent record of Du Pont, management needs to have a clear policy and mechanisms in place so as to manage the hazards that might be present each day at work. Furthermore, the case of Du Pont illustrates that when responsibilities for the maintenance of health and safety policy are shared among all employees, and when the organization nourishes the idea of accountability, this may result in an excellent record. It is also a good way of doing business.

●　●　●

HEALTH AND SAFETY AT WORK

With a mandate to be more cost-effective and to play a more significant role in the management of human resources, HR managers can prove their value by concerning themselves with occupational health and safety (OH&S) in their organizations. Indeed, many HR functions and activities are related to OH&S, and its neglect can result in substantial costs to the organization. Thus, the HR manager should develop an awareness of OH&S and develop strategies for improving it.

Occupational health and safety refers to the physiological/physical and sociopsychological conditions of an organization's workforce resulting from the work environment. It encompasses varied responses to a number of compelling influences, the most basic of which is a sense of social and humanitarian responsibility.

Today, health and safety management is a complex activity requiring the expertise of specialists from many disciplines, such as industrial hygiene, occupational medicine, ecology, psychology and safety engineering, to name only a few. Moreover, concerns in health and safety management now reach beyond physical conditions in the workplace to embrace a regard for workers' mental and emotional well-being and a commitment to protecting the surrounding community from pollution and exposure to toxic substances.[1]

Cardiovascular diseases, various forms of cancer, emphysema, sterility, white-lung disease, and actual loss of life or limb are some of the common and traditionally studied occupation-caused physiological and physical maladies. Recently, infections such as hepatitis and AIDS are also included among occupational risk diseases. Sociopsychological conditions that influence the QWL include, among others, stress, burnout, dissatisfaction, withdrawal, procrastination and apathy, not to mention alcoholism, drug use, and other forms of employee escapist behaviour.

Purposes and Importance of Improving Health and Safety

The enormous costs that result from inadequate health and safety conditions, in monetary and human terms, are enough to justify workplace improvement programs. Improving health and safety conditions will reduce these costs and make the work environment better for all employees.

COSTS. Between 1987 and 1991, an average of 800 Canadian workers died, each year as a result of workplace accidents. In an average year, approximately 12.3 million days are spent off work due to occupational injury. In 1982 alone, direct costs of compensation payments to injured workers totalled $1.5 billion, and this amount grew to approximately $3 billion in 1987. It is estimated that indirect costs increase those figures to an alarming $10 billion and $15 billion respectively. In 1986, 586,718 Canadians were injured in work-related accidents that resulted in lost work time. In 1987 this number grew to 602,531, and in 1988 to 617,997. In 1991, this number decreased to 520,547. Recent reports by Statistics Canada show that the total number of days lost each year due to work related injuries and illnesses outnumber the days lost due to labour disputes.[2] Otherwise stated, every six seconds of the working day, an injury occurs in a Canadian organization. Not only has the number of injuries increased over the years, but so has their severity. In a number of provinces, workplace injury severity, as measured by days of work lost per claim, has been greatly increased.

The additional costs associated with organizational stress and low QWL are immense. Alcoholism, often the result of an attempt to cope with job stress and a low QWL, has been estimated to cost organizations and Canadian society in the early 1980s over $21 million a day.[3] Perhaps more difficult to quantify, but just as symptomatic of stress and poor QWL are workers' feelings of lack of meaning and involvement in their work and loss of importance as individuals. Workers are six times more likely to report back troubles if they regard their jobs as unfulfilling and without potential.[4]

HRM IN THE NEWS VIGNETTE

Selected Statistics About Accidents and Injuries

Ontario fatalities up in first quarter of 1991: OFL—Last year, 256 workers died on the job in Ontario and another 480,000 were injured, the Ontario Federation of Labour says. In the first quarter of 1991, 85 workers have been killed and another 100,317 have been injured. The number of deaths this year is up 23 in year-over-year comparisons. On the national scale, Labour Canada estimates that an average of two workers per day lose their lives as a result of accidents on the job.

Source: *COHSN* 6 May 1991. Used with permission.

One fifth of Alta injuries on the job: survey Edmonton, Alta—One in five injuries in Alberta took place at workplaces throughout the province, figures from the Hanna Injury Prevention Project (HIPP) indicate. Injuries on the job represented 20% of the 267 injuries during a study period. Injuries at home made up 31% of the total and recreation accounted for 28%. Looking at gender, females sustained 27.7% of total injuries, with males accounting for the remaining 72.3%. The 21 to 30 age range (at 16.5% of total) and the 31 to 40 year range (at 18.4%) had the highest percentage of accidents.

Source: *COHSN* 23 (18 February 1991): 5. Used with permission.

Workers' compensation injury, illness trends continue in 1989: StatsCan—The number of work-related injuries and illnesses rose only marginally in 1989 compared with 1988, according to Statistics Canada's "Work Injuries 1987–1989 Report." In 1989, Canada witnessed 620,979 illnesses and injuries resulting in lost-time accidents or permanent disability—up about 3,000 from 1988. Data gathered from 11 workers' compensation boards throughout the country were based on claims accepted by individual boards. In line with past trends, sprains and strains, at 42%, were the most frequent injuries....The incidence of contusions, crushing and bruises in 1989 rose 4% to 22%. The last category of cuts, lacerations and punctures remained relatively constant at 12% of injuries, compared with 13% in 1988. The pattern for most frequently injured body parts remained unchanged from 1988 to 1989. The back was injured in 27% of the accepted claims, hand or fingers in 22% of cases and the ankle, foot or toes in 10% of all workers' compensation claims....The report acknowledges that occupational illnesses are currently not well-represented. The difficulty in reporting them stems from whether the illness is recognized in workers' comp legislation, latent for many years, and identified by the coding manual.

Source: *COHSN* 4 March 1991. Used with permission.

BENEFITS. Eliminating harmful conditions in organizations can be very beneficial. A lower incidence of accidents and diseases, a reduced level of occupational stress, and improved QWL result in: (1) more productivity due to fewer lost work days due to absenteeism, (2) more efficiency from workers who are more involved with their jobs, (3) reduced medical and insurance costs, (4) lower workers' compensation rates and direct payments due to fewer claims, (5) greater flexibility and adaptability in the workforce as a result of increased participation and feeling of ownership, and (6) better selection ratios because of the increased attractiveness of the organization as a place to work. As a consequence of these factors companies can increase their profit substantially.

During a national symposium in 1985, the American National Institute for Occupational Safety and Health (NIOSH) and the Association of Schools of Public Health introduced a new vision suggesting that: "unsafe working conditions are no longer tolerable and that clear and understandable steps can be taken to prevent the leading occupational diseases and injuries." [5]

Background on Health and Safety

Historically, Canadian labour unions have been active in urging organizations to improve physical working conditions. They have tended to bargain for OH&S provisions in labour contracts and increasingly request participation on OH&S committees. The labour movement is also an important force behind the initiation of practical research in this area.

Traditionally, an employer's responsibility was to help employees when they were sick and injured. For example, some organizations provide periodic physical examinations, hire a nurse to treat injuries at the worksite, pay an employee's salary during short illnesses, and, in some cases, provide hospitalization benefits. It is now becoming more and more apparent that helping employees stay healthy can prevent unnecessary hardships on both the employees and the organization.[6] The general idea that is evolving is that prevention is better than cure.

A number of factors seem to have focused such attention on OH&S that change is inevitable: social responsibility, the influence of labour unions, and a change of emphasis from compensation to prevention.[7] The working environment affects workers both as people and as part of society in general. Safe, healthy, environmentally sound working conditions must become a priority for any socially responsible employer. They are part of an organization's public image, contribute to positive public relations, and should be reflected in a commitment to employee health and safety that extends beyond economic benefits to the long-term consequences for the worker and his family.

Some of the major developments predicted by the International Labour Organization, for the next decade include: increased awareness and support of OH&S on the part of government, workers and employers; significant improvement in the control of chemical hazards; and improved programs of injury prevention.

Relationships and Influences of Health and Safety at Work

A summary of some of the most important relationships that health and safety activities have with other HR activities is depicted in Exhibit 14.1.

RECRUITMENT AND SELECTION. An organization's ability to provide a safe, healthy, and comfortable work environment may increase its success in attracting and retaining a qualified workforce. When an organization has a high rate of accidents, and therefore a particularly bad reputation for being an unsafe place to work, it will find it more difficult to recruit and select qualified employees.

JOB ANALYSIS AND JOB DESIGN. As described in Chapters 3 and 13, physical job design may have an important impact on performance. Ergonomic problems, stemming from a failure to properly match persons and machines, account for many workplace accidents. Matching the physical abilities of the employee with those required by the job may mean redesigning the job.

LABOUR RELATIONS. One of the major concerns of unions is OH&S. Many union contracts have some type of safety provision(s) complementing the Canadian basic laws regarding health and safety, with particular emphasis on the right to refuse unsafe work. Other clauses include a union/employer pledge of cooperation in the development and operation of safety and health programs, the right to grieve unsafe work, the right to discipline employees for violating safety rules, regulation of crew size, posting rules of safety, and the right of inspection by a joint or union safety committee.

TRAINING. OH&S training is becoming an integral function of HR departments. Because of the complicated web of health and safety laws, companies conduct training sessions for their employees in order to increase compliance. Many companies also conduct safety

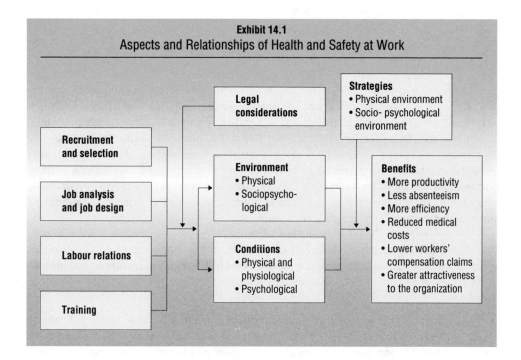

Exhibit 14.1
Aspects and Relationships of Health and Safety at Work

- Recruitment and selection
- Job analysis and job design
- Labour relations
- Training

Legal considerations

Environment
- Physical
- Sociopsychological

Conditions
- Physical and physiological
- Psychological

Strategies
- Physical environment
- Socio- psychological environment

Benefits
- More productivity
- Less absenteeism
- More efficiency
- Reduced medical costs
- Lower workers' compensation claims
- Greater attractiveness to the organization

drills and training to increase awareness of safety features. Other companies engage in "stress workshops" to help their employees to better cope with the sociopsychological work environment.

According to the President and CEO of the Canadian Centre for Occupational Health and Safety: "Occupational health and safety in Canada represents a complex mix of jurisdictions, roles, responsibilities and duties which not only overlap, but at times conflict." [8]

OH&S legislation lies within the federal, provincial, and territorial jurisdictions. Of all of Canada's employed workforce, less than 10 percent are covered by the federal jurisdiction, and slightly more than half of this group are the federal government's own employees. What differentiates Canadian OH&S legislation from that of most other countries is the emphasis it gives to workers' rights. This legislation allows workers to refuse dangerous work, to know about hazardous materials or dangerous conditions in the workplace, and to participate in worksite OH&S committees. These three basic rights of OH&S are of special interest to HR departments.

A HISTORICAL NOTE. The first workers' compensation program was created by Bismarck in the 19th century in an effort to turn aside the progressive reformist movement in Germany. Prior to the enactment of workers' compensation legislation in Canada, the only recourse available to workers injured on the job was to bring a tort action based on the negligence of the employer. Under the common law, the employer had a duty to provide reasonably safe conditions of work, but injured workers were most often discouraged from bringing suit and were left without income or the means of obtaining adequate medical care. In the mid to late 1800s, those who did sue met with a stunning lack of success in their attempts to prove their employer's liability and to recover damages. The inherent unfairness of the situation cried out for reform.

The first act protecting Canadian workers was legislated in 1885. Six years later, Ontario created the first Workmen's Compensation Board, while Quebec established its Workmen's Compensation Commission in 1928.

LEGAL CONSIDERATIONS IN HEALTH AND SAFETY

The Canadian Jurisdictional Framework

Today, OH&S has evolved tremendously in Canada and its provinces. Canada has some of the most advanced legislation in the world.

FEDERAL AND PROVINCIAL JURISDICTIONS. In Canada, there is not one single governmental approach to OH&S law, but rather thirteen somewhat different approaches: ten different provinces, two territories, and the federal government. The Canadian constitution sets the parameters of federal and provincial jurisdiction over workplace health and safety. Under that Act, the federal government's power to legislate is limited to federal government employees and to industries coming under federal jurisdiction. Federally regulated industries include interprovincial railways, communications, pipelines, canals, ferries, shipping, air transport, banks, grain elevators, uranium mines, certain crown corporations, and atomic energy. Generally, the federal government's power is related to areas of national, international, or interprovincial nature.

Each province, on the other hand, has wide regulatory powers over matters within its boundaries relating to the working environment and the employer/employee relationship in the workplace. Thus, each province has its own OH&S legislation with its own unique features, although there are common themes and trends.

Federal Health and Safety Legislation

There are four federal acts of particular significance to OH&S: the Hazardous Products Act, the Transportation of Dangerous Goods Act, the Act underlying the Canadian Centre for Occupational Health and Safety, and an act pertaining to federal government employees, Canada Labour Code, Part II.

THE HAZARDOUS PRODUCTS ACT. This Act has wide application to industry across Canada. Primarily it is directed toward the protection of the consumer. It affects industry in two ways:

1. It prohibits the sale or import of certain specific products: for example, children's furniture painted with material containing more than the acceptable level of lead.
2. It establishes hazard-identification and -labelling requirements applying to the sale or import of specified products. Consumer products must be labelled with respect to the hazards of the chemicals they contain, necessary precautions, and emergency treatment.

Although the Act is directed primarily at consumer safety, it also protects the many small companies that purchase these products from retail outlets for use in the workplace.

THE TRANSPORTATION OF DANGEROUS GOODS ACT. Enacted in 1981, this Act establishes a single legislative authority (Transport Canada) to deal with the handling and movement of hazardous materials by all federally regulated modes of transport in Canada. The aim of the Act is to ensure that dangerous goods are identified, known to the carrier, and classified according to a coding system.

THE CANADIAN CENTRE FOR OCCUPATIONAL HEALTH AND SAFETY ACT. In 1978, a national body was created for the study and cooperative advancement of OH&S. The Canadian Centre, which the Act established, has no regulatory authority; rather it is a forum for the collection of health and safety information from across Canada. The objectives of the Centre are:

1. To promote the concept of a safe working environment,
2. To coordinate research and advisory services,
3. To promote information sharing.

The Centre, located in Hamilton, Ontario, is an autonomous body that does not come under the administration of a governmental department. It is governed by a board composed of representatives from federal and provincial governments, industry, and trade unions.

To date, the main contribution of the Centre has been advisory services in the area of occupational health hazards—particularly chemicals. It has set up an elaborate computer information system and is a useful source of information for all those concerned with OH&S. More than 250 organizations, including governments, now have access to this information system through local terminals and access is also publicly available.

CANADA LABOUR CODE, PART II. Canada Labour Code, Part II, deals in particular with the federal government's employee safety regulations in the workplace and the duties of employers and employees toward the promotion of health and safety. Under this statute, every employer shall ensure that the safety and health of every person employed at work is protected (Section 124). This includes, among other things:

* ensuring that all buildings and structures meet prescribed standards;
* investigating, recording and reporting of all accidents, occupational diseases and other hazardous events;
* posting policies concerning health and safety;
* providing first aid and other health services;
* ensuring that all equipment (fixed and mobile) meets prescribed standards;
* providing safety materials, equipment, devices, and proper clothing;
* ensuring proper maintenance of all equipment;
* ensuring that ventilation, lighting, temperature, humidity, sound, and vibration meet prescribed standards;
* providing instruction, training, and supervision in OH&S;
* ensuring that employees are aware of every known or foreseeable safety hazard;
* ensuring that, in all operations, the government acts in full compliance with the Hazardous Materials Information Review Act.

Each province has its own OH&S legislation. Although these laws vary in content and administrative bodies, during the last decade many of them were reshaped to include the following common characteristics:

Provincial Health and Safety Legislation

* Consolidation of various pieces of legislation into one comprehensive act;
* Changes in the administrative structure, e.g., consolidation under one ministry or the establishment of a separate commission;
* Greater attention paid to occupational health concerns;
* Emphasis on employee involvement through statutory rights;
* Standards and codes referencing so that compliance becomes mandatory;
* More information available regarding employees' general rights and employers responsibilities toward health and safety;
* Mandatory drug testing for certain types of occupations;
* Medical concerns, such as AIDS and work-related stress.

Essentially, three functions are involved in provincial government OH&S administration: legal standard-setting and enforcement, workers' compensation, and accident-prevention education. The various provincial governments control OH&S through the implementation of appropriate laws with the following control mechanisms:

- Incorporating general duty clauses in the legislation; a general duty clause places the overall responsibility for compliance on a specified party.
- Issuing regulations under the authority of the Acts; in general, a wide range of regulations on OH&S matters are specified. Regulations are issued at any time. In some provinces they require only the signature of the lieutenant-governor to become effective; in other provinces certain regulations are subject to public hearings before they can be instituted.
- Setting out statutory rights; these include the right to refuse to work, involvement in joint OH&S committees, and receiving OH&S information.
- Enforcing and inspecting the OH&S procedures; appointed inspectors have the right to enter the workplace and issue orders for remedial corrections where the Act is not being complied with. They can also prosecute those responsible for violations of the Act.
- Referencing standards and codes; in this way compliance becomes mandatory.

These functions are not all integrated under one government agency in all of the provinces, although in British Columbia, for example, they are in fact integrated under The Workers' Compensation Board. In Alberta they all come under the Workers' Health, Safety, and Compensation Ministry. In other provinces (Quebec and New Brunswick), all these functions come under the general policy direction of a commission.

THE RIGHT TO KNOW.   Many provinces are preparing right-to-know legislation that is patterned on a federal–provincial task force act entitled Workplace Hazardous Materials Information System (WHMIS). WHMIS came into effect in 1988 and deals with the labelling of controlled products. Basically, it states that workers dealing with controlled products have the right to know that. More specifically:

- All controlled products must be labelled as such.
- Material safety data sheets listing product name and ingredients, health hazards, disposal procedures, first-aid procedures, etc. must be available to all workers.
- Employers must inform and train their employees in the proper use of these products.

WHMIS, although a federal law, is being applied throughout Canada in cooperation with the provincial workers' compensation/OH&S boards.

Although the legislation is recent, both employers and employees are learning how to cope with its requirements. Employers who tended to avoid implementing proactive safety measures in the past are discovering that avoidance can be very costly. Workers and their representatives are discovering just what their rights are as WHMIS regulations are tested across Canada. For instance, Justice D. Steele of the Ontario Supreme Court awarded $350,000 to a worker who was blinded on a construction site. The case concerned E. Meilleur who was sprayed in the face and eyes with a chemical, Uni-Crete XL, which is used with concrete in sealing the interior of rock excavations. Although Meilleur received workers' compensation payments, the compensation board allowed him to sue the manufacturer and distributor of the product. The case focused on the quality of warning provided by the manufacturers, Uni-Crete Canada and Diamond Shamrock, about the danger of the chemical with which Meilleur was working. Justice Steele found that although the worker was 75 percent responsible for the accident because he failed to wear safety goggles, Uni-Crete Canada was 20 percent responsible, and Diamond Shamrock was 5 percent responsible.

From January 1989 to September 1989, Ministry of Labour inspectors in Ontario wrote 4,395 orders solely related to WHMIS. In Nova Scotia a provincial court judge fined the Aberdeen Regional Hospital of New Glasgow $2,000 for breaching the WHMIS regulations in that province.

HRM IN THE NEWS VIGNETTE
Ruling May Let Cashiers Sit Down on the Job

A ruling handed down this week by the Quebec Workers' Injury Appeal Board could soon see many of the province's 20,000 supermarket cashiers sitting on the job.

Jean-Guy Roy, head of the Commission d'Appel en Matière de Lésions Professionnelles, on Tuesday ordered a Provigo store in Port Cartier to make chairs or stools available for working cashiers.

Céline Lamontagne, vice-president of the Confederation of National Trade Unions, yesterday predicted the decision will have "positive repercussions for the thousands of cashiers who must work standing for several hours."

Two members of the CNTU-affiliated union representing Provigo workers in Port Cartier filed for a complaint against the store in April 1988, demanding access to chairs at their cash registers.

A year later, the Quebec Workers' Health and Safety Board ruled the nature of cashiers' work should allow for chairs or stools. But Provigo appealed the decision by the Commission de la Santé et de la Securité du Travail.

Last March, the CSST revision office took up the cause of the Port Cartier cashiers. Again the supermarket appealed. Roy held six days of public hearings last fall and heard testimony from medical experts before handing down his ruling.

He gave Provigo until June 1 to determine what type of chair or stool it will make available to its cashiers. A CSST inspector will decide by October 1 whether the choice of chair conforms to the conditions listed in the report.

All appeal board decisions are final, CNTU information officer Michel Rioux said.

Source: From a CP article of the same title in *The Montreal Gazette*, 1 March 1991, B12. Reprinted with permission.

One of the most advanced acts concerning OH&S and to right to know and other aspects of OH&S training has recently been promulgated in Ontario. Bill 208, which went into effect on 1 January 1991, encourages the training of both employers and employees regarding OH&S.

THE RIGHT TO REFUSE WORK. A distinctive feature of the reforms that have taken place in most Canadian OH&S legislation is the emphasis placed on a worker's right to refuse unsafe work. Prior to such reforms, every worker had the right, granted in common law, to refuse work that would place him or her in imminent danger. Most existing legislation laid a duty on workers to refuse unsafe work. However, pursuing such rights in common law is usually expensive, difficult, and time-consuming, and it was therefore never a practical option for most workers.

When the right was first introduced into legislation, many employers expressed concern that it would be abused—particularly by the trade unions—and that it would prove to be potentially disruptive to industry. With few exceptions, these fears have so far proved to be unfounded. In practice, work refusals should not occur in an organization with sound communications policies and good safety programs. Those concerned with HRM will need to ensure that company procedures exist to minimize the need for work refusals, and also to deal fairly and efficiently with any refusals that may occur (in compliance with legal procedures).

Generally, the right to refuse work is not dependent on the worker's ability to prove that a hazard exists. In most cases all that is required is "reason to believe" that the work is unsafe. However, in most jurisdictions, this right does not apply to certain types of work. In Ontario, for example, certain workers are specifically excluded—police officers, fire fighters, workers in correctional institutions, workers in hospitals, etc., where the safety of other people would be placed in jeopardy by their refusal. In Quebec, on the other hand, all workers covered by the Act are not permitted the right of refusal where exercise of the right would jeopardize the safety of others or where danger is a normal part of the job.

A study conducted in 1989 showed that 894 cases were reported between 1981 and 1985 and referred to a safety inspector; 98 percent of the cases have involved unionized workers. The 894 cases analyzed were spread among 450 employers and covered nearly all industries. The large majority of these employers, however, experienced only one refusal during the four years analyzed. Seven organizations (three private sector, four public sector) accounted for 31 percent of the refusal that occurred.[9] Several recent examples of refusals are given below:

- Foul air in an Ottawa RCMP building has given workers headaches and sore throats. Consequently, civilian workers refused to go back until things were cleaned up. About 50 workers said that they have no problem with working as long as it isn't being done in the specified location. A similar incident took place when 65 Health and Welfare employees were sent home following complaints of dizziness, headaches, and burning eyes. Union officials suggested carbon monoxide may be seeping into the building from an intake vent located in the parking garage.[10]

- An independent board of inquiry has ordered Emrick Plastics to pay a former spray painter $21,000 after the company refused to move the pregnant worker out of a potentially unsafe area. The worker refused to work in this area and took a leave of absence without pay until after her baby was born. The inquiry board ordered Emrick to pay this sum and justified the employee's refusal to work.[11]

- Fear of crossing picket lines was not a valid reason to refuse work. But truck drivers who have to drive through a picket line could refuse work because of the immediate danger of hurting someone in the picket line. Similarly, inquiry boards ruled that customs officers did not have a valid reason to refuse work due to Indian demonstrations.[12]

JOINT HEALTH AND SAFETY COMMITTEES. The federal government and all the provinces except Nova Scotia and Prince Edward Island have legal provisions requiring the establishment of joint OH&S committees for specified types of workplaces. The overall intent is to place emphasis on the necessary role of workers in establishing OH&S programs and to encourage employers to resolve related problems through their own internal responsibility systems. Government support for joint OH&S committees can be seen in two ways:

1. the statutory provisions with regard to committees and their rights and responsibilities,
2. the way in which joint committees are drawn into the government inspection and enforcement process.

The legal role of joint committees varies among the provinces. In general, Quebec's, Saskatchewan's, and recently, Ontario's, legislation gives joint committees more authority than do the other provinces. Research evidence from preliminary studies indicates that, where cooperation is high, this instrument is effective in reducing occupational injuries and diseases.[13] Nonetheless, many of the committees across industries in Canada have not matured yet. More information will be available when committees in all industries have had more experience.

ACCIDENT REPORTING AND INQUIRIES. In all Canadian jurisdictions, employers are required to report accidents causing injury or occupational diseases to the workers' compensation boards. These requirements are for the purposes of administering compensation and rehabilitation programs. However, most of the jurisdictions also require separate reporting of specified accidents and illnesses to the ministry administering and enforcing OH&S legislation. These report requirements are generally for the purpose of administration and law enforcement.

Reporting provisions differ among the various jurisdictions. Most require immediate notification of accidents that cause fatalities or critical injuries, and explosions that might have caused serious injury or death. In general, the employer must not disturb evidence unless it is necessary to prevent further injury. Some jurisdictions also require the employer to investigate accidents and submit written reports. Notification when an employee has contracted an occupational disease or illness is usually also required.

As Exhibit 14.2 shows, occupational diseases and accidents can pose physical threats to employees' health. Similarly, sociopsychological aspects of the work environment through high stress and low QWL can also generate these health hazards. Traditionally, only the physical environment has received the attention of most companies and OH&S laws. Increasingly, however, companies are admitting to the impact of sociopsychological hazards on OH&S.

WORK HAZARDS

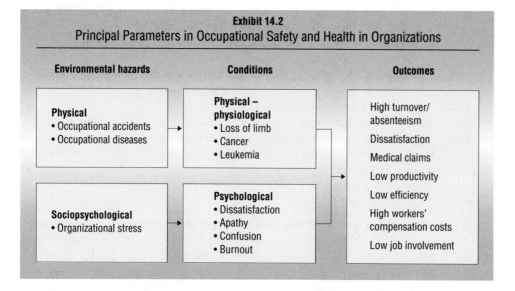

Exhibit 14.2
Principal Parameters in Occupational Safety and Health in Organizations

Environmental hazards	Conditions	Outcomes
Physical • Occupational accidents • Occupational diseases	**Physical – physiological** • Loss of limb • Cancer • Leukemia	High turnover/absenteeism Dissatisfaction Medical claims Low productivity Low efficiency High workers' compensation costs Low job involvement
Sociopsychological • Organizational stress	**Psychological** • Dissatisfaction • Apathy • Confusion • Burnout	

Certain organizations, and even certain departments within the same organization, have higher occupational accident rates than others. Several factors explain this difference.

Factors Affecting Occupational Accidents

ORGANIZATIONAL QUALITIES. Accident rates vary substantially by industry. For example, firms in the construction and manufacturing industries have higher accident rates than firms in services, finance, insurance, and real estate. Small and large organizations (those with fewer than 100 employees and more than 1,000 respectively) have lower rates than medium-sized organizations. This may be because supervisors in small organizations are better able to detect safety hazards and prevent accidents than those in medium-sized organizations. And larger organizations have more resources than medium-sized ones to hire staff specialists who can devote all their efforts to safety and accident prevention.

SAFETY PROGRAMS. Organizations differ in the extent to which they develop techniques, programs, and activities to promote safety and prevent accidents. The effectiveness of these techniques and programs varies according to the type of industry and size of organization. For example, in large chemical firms, greater expenditures for off-the-job safety, medical facilities and staff, safety training, and additional supervision are associated with decreased work-injury costs. On the other hand, work-injury costs can actually increase due to ineffectively applied expenditures for correction of unsafe physical conditions, for safety staff, for employee orientation, and for safety records. As a result, some organizations in the same industry may have higher injury costs per employee than others. And, of course, those organizations that have no safety programs generally have higher injury costs than similar companies that have implemented such programs.

THE UNSAFE EMPLOYEE. Although organizational factors play an important role in occupational safety, many experts point to the employee as the cause of accidents. Accidents depend on the behaviour of the person, the degree of hazard in the work environment, and pure chance. The degree to which the person contributes to the accident is often regarded as an indicator of proneness to accidents. Proneness cannot be considered a stable set of traits that always contributes to accidents. Nevertheless, there are certain psychological and physical characteristics that make some people more susceptible to accidents. For example, employees who are emotionally "low" have more accidents than those who are emotionally "high," and employees who have had fewer accidents have been found to be more optimistic, trusting, and concerned for others. Employees under greater stress are likely to have more accidents than those under less stress, and those with better vision have fewer accidents than those with poorer vision. Older workers are likely to be hurt less than younger workers. People who are quicker in recognizing differences in visual patterns than at making muscular manipulations are less likely to have accidents than those who are just the opposite. Many psychological conditions that may be related to accident proneness—for instance, hostility and emotional immaturity—may be temporary states. Thus, they are difficult to detect until after at least one accident.

Because none of these characteristics are related to accidents in all work environments, and since none are ever-present in employees, selecting and screening job applicants on the basis of accident proneness is difficult. But even if it were possible, aspects of the organization, such as its size, technology, management attitudes, safety programs, and quality of supervision, could still be important contributors to accidents.

Factors Affecting Occupational Diseases

The potential sources of work-related diseases are as distressingly varied as are the ways in which they affect the human organism. Risks for occupational diseases comprise an important part of OH&S. Typical classification of diseases is based on the sources of health risks. Five major categories are often suggested in the literature: chemical, physical, biological, ergonomic, and psychosocial. Additional risk factors may be more related to the individual worker than to the job context. They include: sedentary life pattern (physical inactivity), diet, and work schedules.

CHEMICAL RISKS. Employees are exposed to various chemical risks in their work. Among the risks one can identify: carbon monoxide, lead, dust, and dangerous chemicals. Carbon monoxide, lead, and dust are present in increasingly greater quantities, especially in urban areas.

PHYSICAL RISKS. These include noise, heat, and cold. Noise seems the most pervasive. In Quebec, for instance, regulations state that workers should not be exposed to more than 90db for an eight-hour day in order to conserve the integrity of their hearing function. One study among police officers found that, even though a police cruiser car siren can reach maximum levels of 110db, everyday exposure rarely exceeds 85db.[14] Attempts are being made to move the car siren from the roof to the front hood in order to reduce noise exposure.[15]

BIOLOGICAL RISKS. Employees who come in contact with the public would seem to have more opportunity to meet high-risk individuals with AIDS and hepatitis-B viruses, for example. While these risks are higher for individuals working in the health industry, they may also apply to police officers, who in assisting helpless and injured citizens may come in contact with biological fluids. There is a growing debate about extended general vaccination for hepatitis-B for these types of employees. What seems to be essential in reducing the risk is adequately informing all personnel.

ERGONOMIC RISKS. While injuries to the back are among the most frequent for employees, the fastest growing category of occupational disease includes respiratory illnesses. Cancer, however, tends to receive the most attention, since it is the second leading cause of death in Canada (second only to heart disease). Many of the known causes of cancer are physical and chemical agents in the environment. And because physical and chemical agents are theoretically more controllable than human behaviour, an effort is made to eliminate them from the workplace.

OCCUPATIONAL GROUPS AT RISK. Miners, construction and transportation workers, and blue-collar and lower-level supervisory personnel in manufacturing industries experience the bulk of both occupational disease and injury. The least safe occupations are fire fighting, mining, and law enforcement. In addition, large numbers of petrochemical and oil refinery workers, dye users, textile workers, plastic-industry workers, painters, and industrial chemical workers are also particularly susceptible to some of the most dangerous health hazards.

Occupational diseases are not exclusive to blue-collar workers and manufacturing industries. The "cushy office job" has evolved into a veritable nightmare of physical and psychological ills for white-collar workers in the growing service industries. Among the common ailments are varicose veins, lower back pain, deteriorating eyesight, migraine headaches, hypertension, coronary disorders, respiratory problems, and digestive problems. Situational factors causing these disorders include: (1) too much noise; (2) interior air pollutants such as cigarette smoke and chemical fumes, for example from the copy machine; (3) uncomfortable chairs; (4) poor office design; (5) chemically treated paper; and (6) office technology such as video display terminals (VDTs).

INDIVIDUALS AT RISK. Scientists estimate that approximately 1,600 diseases are caused by genetic defects. Some individuals are more susceptible to a variety of illnesses due to their vulnerable genetic makeup. This assertion, which is difficult to validate, sparked a new controversy surrounding the future role of HR in conducting genetic screening and genetic monitoring.

Theoretically, genetic screening would be used to evaluate the genetic makeup of a given job applicant. This evaluation along with the knowledge of chemicals used could indicate which chemicals could cause disease, such as cancer. By identifying the individual's propensity to contract a given chemically caused disease, companies could: (a) reject the applicant, (b) place the applicant in a work environment away from the hazard, or (c) institute policies (e.g., require protective clothing) to lessen the probability of later disease. At present, there are no laws at either the federal or provincial level specifically governing the use of genetic tests in the workplace.

Although they are not extensively used at present, many large corporations are considering turning to genetic tests in the future. Yet, in no case has the research reported a clear relationship between either possession of a trait or deficiency (which can be measured reliably) and the eventual development of disease. Many who possess the trait or deficiency do not encounter health problems at a later date. Although it may be useful to test the applicants for susceptibility, it would not seem reasonable, advisable, or fair to reject candidates without better estimates of potential risk.

Genetic monitoring may be a better course of action than genetic screening. In monitoring, the focus is on providing ongoing testing to employees exposed to potentially harmful substances so as to detect changes in genetic material that could lead to health risks later on. Monitoring, if used to identify potential toxins, may lead to the transfer of employees that are seemingly vulnerable, and, where possible, rid the workplace of the suspected chemical or agent. This could be extremely beneficial to the worker and the company alike.

MENTAL HEALTH AND LOW QWL

〰   〰

Factors Affecting Mental Health and Well-Being

For many workers, a low QWL is associated with conditions that fail to satisfy important preferences and interests, such as a need for responsibility, challenge, meaningfulness, self-control, recognition, achievement, fairness or justice, security, and certainty. Common organizational conditions causing these preferences and interests to remain unsatisfied include: (1) jobs with low significance, variety, identity, autonomy, feedback, and qualitative underload; (2) high levels of one-way communication and the minimal involvement of employees in decision making; (3) pay systems not based on performance or based on performance that is not objectively measured or under employee control, (4) supervisors, job descriptions, and organizational policies that fail to convey to the employee what is expected and what is rewarded; (5) HR policies and practices that are discriminatory and of low validity; and (6) employment conditions where employees can be dismissed arbitrarily. One particular factor that affects both physical and mental well-being is the work schedule, or more specifically—shift work.

WORK SCHEDULES.   Shift work and irregular schedules represent normal working conditions for numerous workers around the world. Because the human being is essentially diurnal (a day animal), a number of difficulties are associated with shift work. Any disruption in regular biological rhythmic activity (sleep, digestion, body temperature, blood pressure, pulse, etc.) will result in physical and psychological manifestations that will overflow at work as well as in the family and social environment.

Varied work schedules could be grouped into four main categories: permanent regular evening or nighttime work (nighttime security guard); rapidly rotating schedules where one does not have the same hours more than twice in a row (two nights, two evenings, two days, two days' rest, etc.); slow rotating schedules, which are most frequent in North America, where one works one to four weeks on the same shift; and, finally, prolonged states of vigilance (ten- or twelve-hour days; twenty-four-hour duty for interns and residents).

The major problems associated with shift work are sleep disruptions, decreased performance and cognitive abilities, bad nutrition, and abnormal family and social life. Sleep will be particularly affected both in duration and quality. Shift workers have more difficulty falling asleep and then sleep and dream for shorter periods of time and less profoundly. The sympathetic nervous system is overstimulated; fatigue and psychosomatic distress set in. A sleep debt accumulates after a number of days' shift working. Especially in situations where mental and physical activity are very unstable, and the employee alternates between overload and underload, vigilance, reaction time, and performance are greatly diminished. It will take from seven to twelve days for biological rhythms to return to normal after just a few night shifts.[16]

Research pertaining to the effects of shift work, prolonged hours, and lack of sleep on physical performance and cognitive reactions is vast, and yet often contradictory. Cognitive abilities decrease; capacity to execute simple, routine tasks progressively deteriorates, especially in reaction time; while physical performance seems less affected. It seems that such disruptions happen even after one night's lack of regular sleep and become serious after forty-eight hours.

Irregular eating habits closely follow any disruption in working schedules. Meals are irregular and often taken alone, and "fast foods" are more easily accessible on evening and night shifts. Snacking is more prominent, foods are often sweeter and richer in fats; home-cooked meals with the family become rare occasions. Finally, caffeine consumption increases dramatically. The addition of irregular hours, poor food quality, and decreased social atmosphere around meals may result in increased incidence of gastro-intestinal and cardiovascular diseases among shift workers.[17]

The third and most important difficulty associated with irregular working hours is the disruptions that occur in social and family life. The shift worker can easily become isolated from his or her social environment. Today's is a day society: family meals, sports, leisure with friends who work regular hours or on other shifts; rest periods generally occur Saturday and Sunday. Stability, a necessary element for satisfactory family life, no longer exists. Other family members must reorganize their schedules and activities around the shift worker. Days off and holidays may be hard to plan and are therefore almost never an occasion for a family outing. Correlations have been shown between working weekends and family conflicts.[18] Consequently, shift workers spend less time in family and social roles, resulting in decreased quality of family life.

COSTS OF STRESS. Stress and burnout are becoming increasingly important concepts for HR professionals, since there is wider recognition of their effect, both on productivity and on the physical and mental well-being of the employees. HR departments are expected to develop human resources in such a way that significant reductions in accidents, absenteeism, and error rates will occur along with significant increases in morale and in the quality of the product or service. While there is no simple formula to estimate the exact cost of stress in an organization, it is certain that its consequences are very expensive. Here are a few estimates of typical costs and possible benefits pertaining to HR indicators:

Stress and Burnout at Work

- Recent data collected by Angus Reid Research found that 77 percent of migraines (about 2.5 million people in Canada), which in many cases are triggered by stress, resulted in employees having to cease normal activity; 19 percent required absence from work. The resulting annual productivity loss was estimated to be around $500 million.
- Heart disease, associated with stress, is responsible for an annual loss of more than 135 million work days. Psychological or psychosomatic problems contribute to more than 60 percent of long-term employee disability payments and medical bills.
- It is basically accepted that direct and indirect costs of work accidents are staggering. Research completed by the National Safety Council and NIOSH, estimates that 75 to 85 percent of all industrial accidents are caused by the inability to cope with stress, and this costs U.S. industry $32 billion annually.
- Compensation for occupational stress under the Ontario Workers' Compensation Board will produce more than 9,000 claims, costing upwards of $178 million annually, according to a study commissioned by the Employers' Council on Workers' Compensation.

Even if we can argue about the accuracy of the figures illustrated in the above examples, the message is simple: the cost of stress at work in North American organizations is huge. Therefore, any program that aims to address these issues and to reduce costs will be generally beneficial.

WHAT IS STRESS? Stress has been looked at in a variety of ways. Some regard it in terms of stimuli (such as environmental conditions thought to be stressful); others define it in response terms (notably the late Hans Selye, of the University of Montreal). Selye has been often referred to as the "father of stress," because he was the first researcher since the 1930s to observe that the body reacts to various stressors in the same physiological and biological manner. He labelled this phenomenon the "General Adaptation Syndrome" (GAS); the end result of this syndrome is "wear and tear" to the body. Another researcher who concentrated on the hormonal reaction to stress was Cannon, who, like Selye, experimented with animals and discovered a particular response to stress that he termed the "fight or flight" response. In both cases, the body reacts to stress instantaneously. Cannon and Selye's concepts of stress received only partial recognition by social and behavioral scientists; they were criticized for the methodology they used and the subjects they chose for their experiments (i.e., research was conducted in controlled laboratory settings and animals were used for the experiments). Thus, criticism was levelled against the generalization of the findings, especially in its suggestions that the same mechanisms apply to human stress. What distinguishes human stress from animal stress is the cognitive processes, both in perceiving threats and in reacting to them.

Over the years, models and concepts applied to human stress evolved in their definition and scope to account for what is now believed to be a far more complex phenomenon. Today, most organizational stress researchers define stress as the entire process of perceiving and interpreting the environment compared with the capability to respond to it. Under this definition, stress is present when the work environment poses (or is perceived to pose) a threat to the individual, either in the form of excessive demands or in the form of insufficient stimulation to meet his or her needs. Therefore, the definition of "misfit" seems to have the widest acceptance in organizational research. Nevertheless, while a general consensus regarding the generic concept of stress exists, literature dealing with occupational and organizational stress is diverse. Consequently, different models and various operational definitions hinder efforts to compare and contrast research findings.

SOURCES OF STRESS. In general, occupational stress models have focused on several categories of job stressors. Among them: role problems (conflicts and ambiguities), job content demands (workload and responsibility), work organization (lack of participation, number of hours worked), professional perspectives (career ambiguities, skill underutilization), and physical environment (noise, temperature, safety).

One interesting way to classify sources of stress is according to their origin: *job context* (extrinsic) origin or *job content* (intrinsic) origin. Some suggest that extrinsic stressors have linear relationships with adverse consequences, whereas intrinsic stressors have curvilinear relationships. The implications are very important. In so far as the extrinsic stressors are concerned, they may have an additive and cumulative effect; that is to say, some role conflict, added to poor working conditions and to a strong feeling of pay inequity may cause stress (an adverse consequence), which is otherwise nonexistent if each stressor is regarded alone. Similarly, a low level of extrinsic stressors may have no negative effect. By way of contrast, the relationships between intrinsic stressors and some consequences are more complex; here, in either the case of over-stimulation (i.e., too much responsibility) or under-stimulation (i.e., not enough responsibility) adverse consequences may manifest themselves. Naturally, the severity of the stress consequence is moderated by the degree of social support and by the personality of the job incumbent.[19]

Consequences of Job Stress

Numerous indicators denote the adverse consequences of stress on employees' health. An indicator of affective–emotional reaction that has become popular in recent years, especially for professional employees involved in the health-care industry, is the concept of "burnout." Job burnout, according to some, is a special type of organizational stress that occurs when people work in situations in which they have little control over the quality of their performance, but feel personally responsible for their success or lack of it; others view burnout as the culmination of long-term stress and the tedium of prolonged mental and emotional stress. Its main characteristics are physical, mental, and emotional exhaustion that make the employee unable to cope with work demands. Burnout is a progressive state that starts as feelings of inadequacy and develops to a condition in which physical and mental function deteriorates. People most susceptible to burnout are those who are excessively committed to their jobs, work too long and too intensely, and have little control over their lives. It has been found in all professions, in all walks of life, and at all job levels. However, among different occupations the high-risk categories include police officers, prison guards, nurses, social workers, and teachers.

Other psychological manifestations, more traditional in nature, include symptoms such as depression, anxiety, irritability, and somatic complaints. Moreover, it has been found that behavioural symptoms such as smoking and escapist drinking are linked to job demands. In terms of physiological consequences, research shows an increase in catecholamine output (adrenalin and noradrenaline), in steroid output, and in blood pressure, all precursors to peptic ulcers and cardiovascular diseases. It is worth noting that in recent research hypertension has been found to be specifically correlated with intrinsic stress, which leads to a conclusion that stress is present even among employees who are content with their work.[20] Thus, people may become victims of high responsibility and other intrinsic dimensions of their work.

Cases of stressed-out people at work these days are innumerable. One example is that of a 32-year-old lawyer who "freaked out" and plunged a sharp pencil into the back of his own hand several times. He was taken to the hospital to begin treatment for stress-related illness. Stress has become a hot topic in law offices, which has forced the Canadian Bar Insurance Association to greatly increase its disability payouts. In 1990, stress prompted 15 percent of lawyers' disability claims.[21]

IS STRESS/BURNOUT A COMPENSABLE DISEASE?   A real dilemma exists for many workers' compensation boards across Canada pertaining to admissibility of mental disorders resulting from occupational stress and burnout. As there are no clear guidelines in this regard, compensation board decisions are taken on the merit of each case presented to them. However, the number of cases that have been recognized is on the increase. The critical dilemma dealt with by these tribunals mirrors the theoretical arguments found in academic research on the diagnosis of stress and burnout, namely: (1) how valid is the diagnosis of burnout, and what is the level of confidence in its measuring device (i.e., issues of construct and predictive validity)? and (2) assuming that a case of burnout has been established, what are the plausible causes of and/or antecedents to it? Customarily, employers subscribe to the thesis that weaknesses in an individual's personality and/or other personal attributes are the prime causes of the manifested condition, while unions and other employee associations argue the contrary; namely, that the psychological and affective work environment are the provoking agents. Occupational stress researchers are attempting to provide answers to these questions.

Prevention may represent, in the minds of many, doing an everyday task, either with cumbersome equipment (e.g., heavy, ugly, hot, ill-fitting goggles) or changing the procedure from what seemed simple to something complicated. In order to change the mentality of individuals toward prevention, a program could start with a simple, low-cost, easily implemented improvement (e.g,. basic information on the importance of systematic hand washing in the protection against infectious diseases, followed by the distribution of disposable gloves), even if it may not be first on the priority list.

PROACTIVE PROMOTION OF OH&S.   The following indicators might be considered as guidelines for a proactive OH&S program:

- Top administrators should assume the leadership role. If top administration only pays lip service to OH&S, the rank-and-file employees will follow their lead and disregard the policies.
- Individual and/or unit responsibility should be clearly assigned, to ensure that the objectives will be accomplished.

OH&S
STRATEGIES FOR
IMPROVEMENT

General Health
and Safety
Prevention

- All causes for accidents and occupational illnesses should be identified and either eliminated or controlled in order to prevent a recurrence.
- An essential part of any OH&S program is a good, carefully designed training program.
- Managers at all levels should use an accident/illness record system to identify patterns of accidents or health problems that could otherwise be overlooked. This could be expanded to include rate and frequency of exposure of employees to hazardous materials in order to isolate high-risk situations (especially hazardous chemicals).
- The organization should continually encourage on-the-job awareness and acceptance of safety responsibilities on the part of the employees.

THE KEY ROLE OF PARTICIPATION. In the development and ongoing process of health and safety prevention, commitment and motivation must first be demonstrated by management. No program, ideal as it may be, will ever work if supervisors or management personnel do not believe in it.[22] They must be the impetus behind any action toward prevention, integrating program objectives and realization as part of the organizational perspective.

Furthermore, it is imperative that all levels of management and workers participate in the development and structure of any health and safety program. The identification of risks in events and in how things are being done (not how they should be done in the regulations) requires the insight of the rank-and-file personnel. Moreover, when OH&S specialists propose solutions and/or modifications in procedures, before policies are permanently established and implemented they must assess the feasibility, acceptance, and real chance of implementation by the employees. Research indicates that new safety techniques and procedures, which seem ideal on paper or in the lab, will never work if they are not used, either because they are cumbersome, nonrealistic, or simply not liked.

In addition, safety committees should be established and managers must give proper instructions, goals, and target dates to these committees, so that members know their mandate and management's expectations. Promotions and awards can be used as incentives.

THE KEY ROLE OF TRAINING. Although several strategies can be taken by organizations to help employees become safety aware, training plays a key role. Training should take place whenever a new employee joins the company, a worker gets a new job, or a new process is added. Before any task is carried out, it should be subject to a job-safety analysis.

The Quebec Workers' Compensation Commission recently signed an agreement with the province's Department of Higher Education and Science to integrate health- and safety-related issues into all of the vocational training programs given at the secondary school and college levels. There is every indication that, if young people are made aware of the importance of prevention early on, they will be less liable to suffer an injury when they begin to work.[23]

The HR department can be instrumental in accident prevention by assisting supervisors in their training efforts and by implementing safety motivation programs. For example, many organizations display signs indicating the number of days or hours worked without an accident, or display posters saying "Safety First." In safety contests, prizes or awards are given to individuals or departments with the best safety record. These programs seem to work best when employees are already safety conscious and when the physical conditions of the work environment provide no extreme safety hazards.

COMBINING PARTICIPATION AND TRAINING VIA JOINT OH&S COMMITTEES. Many organizations have institutionalized joint labour–management OH&S committees, in order to enhance the effectiveness of their strategy to promote health and safety in the workplace. However, in order for these committees to be effective, all members require sound training based on a formal needs assessment for the training content.[24] A report published by the

Ontario Advisory Council on Joint Health and Safety Committees highlights two benefits reported for companies whose committee members were adequately trained: (1) training improves communication links with the workplace; and (2) it strengthens commitment by senior management to OH&S; the more management knows about it the greater the likelihood of their commitment.[25]

Exhibit 14.3 shows a typical example of integrated OH&S policy principles as practised at United Technologies; Pratt & Whitney Canada adheres to this policy.

Exhibit 14.3
Environmental, Health, and Safety Policy Principles at United Technologies

---

1. Accountability

Operating unit management accountable for meeting the business plan is also responsible for the development and implementation of management systems to ensure adherence to all applicable laws, regulations, and these Policy Principles. Clearly defined authority shall be delegated within the units to carry out these responsibilities.

2. Organization

Operating unit management accountable for meeting the business plan is also responsible for developing organizations commensurate with the inherent risks faced by the unit. Management will appoint individuals in both the safety and environmental protection functions (or one individual for both, where an integrated safety and environmental function exists) to coordinate the overall actions of the unit and to support line management. The organization shall involve line management, establish accountability, and provide a system for developing and implementing action plans.

3. Property Transactions

Environmental and safety site assessments will be performed and incorporated into the business evaluation of any potential acquisition, divestiture, joint venture, or leasing of real property to assure adequate consideration is given to environmental and safety risks.

4. Environmental Protection Management

Environmental protection management systems will identify, evaluate, and control the environmental impact of operations. Major areas requiring effective management include, but are not limited to:

• air quality protection
• community noise protection
• soil and water resources protection
• waste management
• waste reduction

5. Industrial Hygiene Management

Industrial hygiene management systems will identify, evaluate, and control potential health hazards caused by chemical, physical, biological, and ergonomic conditions such as, but not limited to, solvents, vapors, gases, noise, radiation, fume, and musculoskeletal stresses. Major elements of an effective management system include:

• workplace assessments
• industrial hygiene monitoring
• work practices
• engineering controls
• personal protective equipment
• medical services
• records retention

6. Safety Management

Safety management systems will prevent or control exposure of employees to physical harm or injury. Major areas of effective safety management may include, but are not limited to:

• confined space entry
• electrical safety
• elevated work
• energized equipment
• fire/loss prevention
• injury compensation management
• machine guarding
• materials handling
• motor vehicle safety
• protective equipment

7. Annual Planning and Process/Facility Project Review

Procedures will exist to ensure that safety, industrial hygiene, and environmental impacts and risks are reviewed and incorporated into the annual business planning process and into proposed process and facility projects.

8. Communications

Mechanisms will be established to facilitate communications among all employees to ensure receipt of information necessary to perform their functions and enhance general awareness of safety and environmental issues.

9. Education and Training

Employees will be provided the necessary education and training to enable them to perform their work in a safe and environmentally sound manner.

Exhibit 14.3 (continued)

10. Comprehensive Evaluations

Each operation will conduct ongoing comprehensive safety, industrial hygiene, and environmental evaluations and significant findings shall be communicated to operating unit management accountable for meeting the business plan. Deficiencies identified by these evaluations shall be corrected in a timely manner.

11. Hazardous Materials

Procedures will promote the use of non-hazardous materials. If hazardous materials are used, procedures are necessary to minimize and control their use and to ensure the avoidance or reduction of potential health, safety, and environmental risks.

12. Accident Investigation

Procedures will exist to investigate thoroughly accidents causing significant personal injury/illness, property damage, environmental damage, or business interruption, and to take measures preventing their recurrence.

13. Emergency Response Planning

Each permanent location will have an emergency response plan incorporating employee training and drills. The plan shall be coordinated and shared with local emergency response authorities.

14. Facility and Equipment Maintenance

Clearly assigned resources and defined responsibilities will be established to ensure that maintenance of facilities and operating equipment is performed to minimize the risk to human health and the environment.

Source: United Technologies Human and Natural Resource Protection Policy and Policy Principles. Used with permission.

Accident Control and Prevention

One of the first steps in improving accident and disease control in the physical work environment is the use of records. These can be used to assess where the organization is in terms of current incidence of accidents and diseases, in essence forming a base line against which to compare and evaluate other specific strategies for workplace improvements. Because the process of gathering such data creates an awareness of health and safety problems, it could be regarded as a strategy for workplace improvement as well as a process that helps determine the effectiveness of other strategies.

INCIDENCE RATE. The most explicit index of industrial safety is the **incidence rate**. It is calculated by the following formula:

$$\text{Incidence rate} = \frac{\text{Number of recordable injuries and illnesses} \times 1 \text{ million}}{\text{Number of employee exposure hours}}$$

Suppose an organization has ten recorded injuries and illnesses for its 500 employees. The incidence rate, assuming a forty-hour work week and a fifty-work-week year, is:

$$\frac{10 \times 1,000,000}{500 \times 40 \times 50} = 10$$

SEVERITY RATE. Strategies will vary depending on whether an organization is experiencing numerous minor safety problems or one or two major problems. The **severity rate** reflects the hours actually lost due to injury or illness. It recognizes that not all injuries and illnesses are equal. Four categories have been established: deaths, permanent total disabilities, permanent partial disabilities, and temporary total disabilities. The severity rate is calculated by this formula:

$$\text{Severity rate} = \frac{\text{Total hours charged} \times 1 \text{ million}}{\text{Number of employee hours worked}}$$

An organization with the same number of injuries and illnesses as another but with more deaths would have a higher severity rate.

FREQUENCY RATE. While similar to the incidence rate, the **frequency rate** reflects the number of injuries and illnesses per million hours worked, rather than per year:

$$\text{Frequency rate} = \frac{\text{Number of disabling injuries} \times 1 \text{ million}}{\text{Number of employee hours worked}}$$

STRATEGIES TO CONTROL ACCIDENTS.   Designing the work environment to minimize the likelihood of accidents is perhaps the best way to prevent accidents and improve safety. Among the safety features that can be designed into the physical environment are guards on machines, handrails in stairways, safety goggles and helmets, warning lights, self-correcting mechanisms, and automatic shutoffs. The extent to which these features will actually reduce accidents depends on employee acceptance and use. For example, eye injuries will be reduced by safety goggles only if employees wear the goggles correctly. The effectiveness of any safety regulation depends on how the regulation is implemented and whether it is complied with. If employees are involved in the decision to make some physical change to improve safety, they are more likely to accept the change.

Pratt & Whitney Canada implemented a five-year Health & Safety Action plan in an attempt to reduce work-related accidents. The direct cost of accidents to the company in 1990 was in excess of $4 million. The objective of the program is to educate the workers on safety measures and ensure that "each employee will give safety the same priority as is now given to productivity and product quality." [26]

Another way to alter the work environment, and to improve safety, is to make the job itself more comfortable and less fatiguing. This approach, generally referred to as ergonomics, considers changes in the job environment in conjunction with the physical and physiological capabilities and limitations of the employees. As a result, employees are less likely to make mistakes due to fatigue.

Whereas ergonomics focuses on the physical and physiological, another approach focuses on the psychological. Job redesign can also help prevent accidents by increasing employee motivation and reducing boredom. The result may be increased alertness and fewer accidents.

LOWERING FREQUENCIES OF BACK INJURIES.   There seem to be two research directions aimed toward the prevention of back pain: individual and organizational. The first, and more conventional one, is directed at improving physical fitness: exercise and stronger, more flexible back muscles mean less injuries. A number of physical fitness programs have been initiated to achieve that.

Specific Health-Risk Prevention

An organizational approach for reducing back pain and injuries involves a thorough examination of the work environment. Increasingly, a number of studies show that improving ergonomic factors at work significantly decreases lower back pain. A most impressive study in this area involved the redesign of the police patrol car. The research efforts are interesting for a number of reasons:

- Objectives included not only redesign of the seat for better ergonomic position of the back, but also a complete analysis of body motions within the vehicle in accordance with the varied tasks to be performed.

- A participative approach included ergonomists, engineers, driving instructors, car manufacturers, OH&S specialists, police administrators, and officers with and without back injuries.

- Analysis was made of both driver and passenger seating arrangements, communication systems, administrative tasks and proper layout of movable items (stick, walkie-talkie, firearms, flashlight, etc.), fixed equipment (radio, emergency equipment, protective screen, eventual computer, etc.), and wearable equipment (clothes, bullet-proof vest, all gear worn at the waist).

Consensus was reached on the necessity for comfort, safety, space management, and injury prevention. The seat must be comfortable, sufficiently high, and offer good support to back, sides, and head. It must be adjustable and adaptable to the height and weight of the driver. It should be firm, durable, and not lose its shape, and, finally, should be adapted to the equipment worn at the belt. Efforts must be made to make the patrol car more effective and safe when it serves as an "office." These include proper lighting, writing surfaces, and storage space. Finally, space management must be considered in order to prevent disturbing the driver and to diminish clutter and bruises.[27]

Sometimes, changes in the psychosocial work environment can also be instrumental in reducing the frequency of back injuries. There are indications that psychosocial factors related to work organization and job satisfaction are correlated with lower back pain. Correlations between worker participation, decision latitude, autonomy, and frequency of back pain were reported. More on the psychological factors of the work environment is presented in the next section.

A series of studies are currently underway in Quebec in search of a remedy for the most chronic job injury, the back. Called the Evaluation and Re-education Program for Workers with Chronic Back Disorders, the program combines the principles of patient education with exercise, diet information, and psychological counselling. It is possible that the study will confirm what many medical experts have long suspected, that education may be the key to preventing back pain from recurring. This aspect of a patient's treatment generally covers information about anatomy, good posture, and how to safely perform daily activities. Preliminary results show that 67 percent of participants have either returned to work or are preparing to do so.[28]

REDUCING RISKS DUE TO LEAD AND TOXIC CHEMICALS. Adequate information concerning all hazardous materials must be provided, and training on proper prevention procedures must be applied. Many organizations prepare manuals and safety data sheets of all hazardous substances. The manuals contain information on general and specific risks, prevention procedures, and proper storage and elimination. Information and training are often provided through a system whereby first members of OH&S committees are approached, and then they in turn extend the training, through OH&S representatives, to all personnel directly involved.

Environment Canada has published a guidebook that includes data sheets for numerous hazardous substances. For each chemical, one can find detailed description and properties, information on risk to health and fire and reactivity hazard, emergency intervention, protective gear, first aid, transport cautions, and environmental protection and elimination. Moreover, the Canadian Chemists Association has published a handbook that contains safety procedures, information on the proper handling of equipment and toxic and dangerous substances, and emergency procedures applying to workers in laboratories. In addition, suggestions have been made that as an equally important prevention measure, logbooks and records be kept on employees' rate and frequency of exposure.

Both Canada and the U.S.A. are now studying portable instrumentation for immediate, on-site identification and analysis of toxic substances in water, soil, and air. Moreover, the Environmental Emergency Technology Division of Environment Canada has developed a remote control analytical system to assist in the response to spills of highly toxic and volatile chemicals without endangering the lives of response personnel.

A number of guides contain information and instructions on the development of standard operating safety procedures. For example: set up a work plan, prepare for action; describe hazards and evaluate risks; describe requirements for surveillance program (key resources); delineate work areas and ascribe specific functions; choose appropriate protective equipment; control access; set up decontamination and emergency medical care and training procedures.[29]

REDUCING THE RISKS DUE TO AIDS AND HEPATITIS-B. There is a growing debate about the need for extended general vaccination for hepatitis-B for all workers closely associated with high-risk populations. Costs for such an operation are staggering and, for these reasons, a number of researchers do not recommend it. This does not exclude post-exposition vaccination for employees after specific high-risk exposure. Training programs, which include clear, appropriate, and thorough information on contamination risks and protection procedures, should be mandatory for all employees in organizations where the risk is high. This is an easy, inexpensive way to protect employees against biological health risks. Adequate and simple prevention procedures are most effective. Proper and careful handling of biological samples, thorough hand-washing, and wearing disposable gloves are among the measures that are effective against infectious diseases.

A similar approach should be applied to the prevention of AIDS in the workplace. This is an increased concern for employees in the health-care industry as well as prison guards, police officers, and other workers who may be in contact with carriers of HIV. Emphasis should be placed on prevention and education. An ongoing prevention program implemented with the help of local community health services has been successful in providing proper information and diffusing anxiety for the police personnel of the greater Montreal area, and could serve as an example of an efficient prevention program. Two physicians, specialized in OH&S visited each police station, and through a series of conferences informed personnel of all contamination risks and taught everyone proper protection procedures. The prevention program for police officers that is being set up in Montreal by the local union–management OH&S association for municipal affairs includes a module on biological risks.

GENERAL TRENDS. There seem to be four major trends associated with stress management. The first is training and assisting employees to cope with stress. In such training, participants are usually asked to describe how they have reacted during certain specific stress situations. Examples include strategies such as finding a compromise, making a plan of action, taking action to get rid of the problem, playing racketball to get rid of anger, reading a book, thinking about something else, etc.

The second includes programs oriented toward developing and strengthening personal resources. Two types of approaches are employed: behavioural and cognitive. The behavioural programs are the most numerous and include physical fitness, biofeedback, and relaxation techniques. Cognitive approaches usually include such topics as priority restructuring, goal setting, self-worth development, time management, etc.

The use of social support represents the third orientation in stress management. Programs that focus on the development of personal communication skills often represent unique occasions for individuals to create a social support network. Worthy of mention is the fact that, in some organizations, Employee Assistance Programs (EAPs) are often responsible for this type of stress management. EAPs, however, are more often developed for intervention after the fact (i.e., in helping workers with psychological problems, alcoholism, drug-related problems or post-traumatic events) rather than before the fact, which would emphasize prevention.

A more recent and innovative tendency in stress management is to develop programs centred on changing the stressor at its source. A fairly recent American study in the private sector revealed that 27 percent of all organizations with more than fifty employees offered stress management programs, 81 percent of which had some concerns about modifying the work organization.[30]

Because a heavy workload is the number one cause of burnout in many occupations, programs designed to alleviate this include: providing assistance, curtailing overtime, providing training in time management and organization, helping an employee develop outside interests, and making sure that the employee is taking time off to engage in leisure activities. All these are possible solutions to this complex problem.

Managing and Reducing Stress at Work

Tandem Computers Inc., a manufacturer of mainframe computers, confronted the burnout problem by implementing sabbaticals. It was found that the employees almost always returned to work invigorated.[31]

Other examples include setting up a support group or system to develop self-awareness, encouraging senior employees to assume the role of mentors in counselling, and guiding aspiring subordinates.

IMPROVING WORK SCHEDULES.   A number of principles can be deduced from the literature reviewed on irregular work schedules. Although elimination of shift schedules from many jobs is impossible, studies on human adaptation to disturbances of biological rhythms yield interesting suggestions for improving the work situation. The shorter the shift-work period (two or three days), the better the body adapts. One should ideally try to design work schedules with a maximum of three consecutive night shifts, or at least increase the rest period immediately after, in order to decrease the ensuing sleep debt. Moreover, studies have shown that direction of shift work has an impact on bodily rhythmic functions. It is much easier to rest and adapt following a day-evening-night rotation than the inverse direction, night-evening-day. Work schedule planners could easily consider these principles.

Moreover, in order to remedy the negative impact of shift work on diet and health, some organizations hire a nutritionist to guide shift workers and promote better eating habits. A number of easily applicable guidelines include: plan daily meals in order to balance nutrition; take the main meal in the middle of the day, not in the middle of the shift, and reduce caloric intake during the evening and night; increase water and fibre consumption, reduce fats, sugar, and caffeine; include daily relaxation periods to help digestion and promote sleep.

EMPLOYEE WELLNESS PROGRAMS.   Health can be considered as a continuum, with wellness being logically opposite to sickness or illness. Traditionally, medicine concentrated on treating the illness, but with the recent attention being paid to prevention, the focus is shifting to wellness. This has been recognized by an increasing number of organizations that offer employees *wellness programs*. Such a program encompasses all facets of employees' lives, including physical fitness (see next section), mental health, spiritual balance, and economic well being. In the vast majority of cases, it is the HR department that coordinates the various facets of the program. Exhibit 14.4 shows the components of a corporate wellness program. It is important to realize that these components overlap and that elements of one program should be consistent with another. For example, smoking cessation may be offered in conjunction with a program of physical exercise and lifestyle counselling. A 1984 survey of Ontario companies with more than fifty employees indicated that one in three companies offered at least one type of wellness program.[32]

PHYSICAL FITNESS PROGRAMS.   Two forms physical fitness programs are developing among Canadian corporations: in-house and out-of-house. For the *in-house* programs, facilities are located on site where the employees can work-out on their own, or participate in an exercise class. Some companies have facilities with elaborate settings, numerous staff members and advanced equipment, whereas other companies have to operate on a much smaller scale.

Northern Telecom decided to build an extensive in-house facility for both blue- and white-collar employees. Air Canada also has an in-house physical fitness program consisting of a weight training room and low impact aerobic classes, which are taught by qualified instructors five days a week. Other examples include Sun Life Insurance and Canadian National Railway. However, their facilities are temporary and not quite as extensive. It is perhaps worth mentioning that in Japan, for example, fitness programs are incorporated into the regular work day.

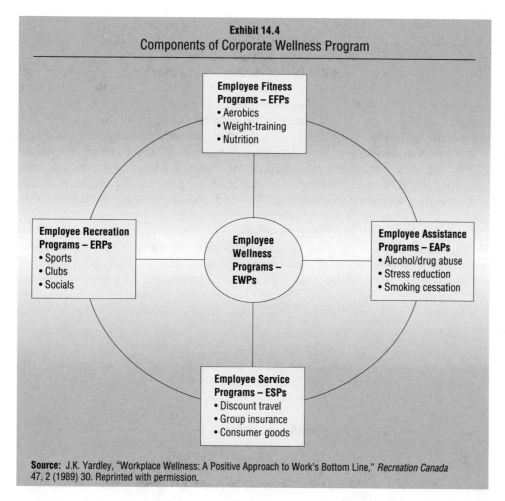

Exhibit 14.4
Components of Corporate Wellness Program

Employee Fitness Programs – EFPs
• Aerobics
• Weight-training
• Nutrition

Employee Recreation Programs – ERPs
• Sports
• Clubs
• Socials

Employee Wellness Programs – EWPs

Employee Assistance Programs – EAPs
• Alcohol/drug abuse
• Stress reduction
• Smoking cessation

Employee Service Programs – ESPs
• Discount travel
• Group insurance
• Consumer goods

Source: J.K. Yardley, "Workplace Wellness: A Positive Approach to Work's Bottom Line," *Recreation Canada* 47, 2 (1989) 30. Reprinted with permission.

Due to lack of space or facilities, many employers are willing to support their employees by subsidizing a portion of their membership fees to a fitness program. Companies such as Royal Bank and Domtar pay between $100 and $200 per employee. Additionally, there are companies that contract for existing out-of-house programs. For instance, sixty-one companies in Quebec are involved with the YMCA's corporate fitness and lifestyle program. Among them: Alcan, Bank of Montreal, Bell Canada, Standard Life, and Tilden. For them, contracting out is less expensive than doing it themselves.

The discussion thus far reveals that prevention in health and safety is still in its infancy, even though legal incentives have been there for more than a decade. Yet, both researchers and practitioners point to the urgency and importance of developing health and safety programs. A number of specialists argue in favour of concentrating prevention efforts at the organizational rather than individual level. In a recent special issue, the International Journal of Health Services called attention to a number of innovations that have taken place in organizations. It included experiments with the democratization of the workplace, but also concluded that there are still urgent steps to be undertaken to change work structure and increase employee participation and control in decision making pertaining to health and safety issues.[33]

In the past few years, the American National Institute for Occupational Safety and Health (NIOSH) proposed a number of national strategies for the prevention of the ten leading work-related diseases and injuries. Among these ten are: musculoskeletal injuries, severe occupational traumatic injuries, occupational cardiovascular diseases, and psycho-

TRENDS IN HEALTH AND SAFETY AT WORK

Emerging Concerns

logical disorders. In each strategy, emphasis was placed on job design, surveillance of risk factors and health disorders, the need for information, and education and training for all levels of employees as well as for continued scientific research.

The principal emerging trend in OH&S focuses on the greater participation and responsibility of workers in health and safety decisions, including those that will alter the work environment. Employers realize that promotion of employee health and safety does not only mean looking for causes of accidents and illnesses and repairing damages, but must include prevention by changing work organization and helping employees anticipate, rather than react to, hazards. This also means changing traditional management philosophies. Traditionally, management's resistance to increasing worker participation in decision-making was based upon economic considerations, primarily the values associated with efficiency. Moreover, workers' rights in health and safety were seen as both irrelevant to the reduction of the frequency and severity of accident rates and the incidence of industrial disease, and an infringement upon management rights and prerogatives. However, there are growing signs that indicate a strong correlation between productivity and worker involvement; joint management–worker cooperation has strong positive effects on health and safety records. "Employee empowerment" is a new buzzword in work organizations, but it is up to management to take the initiative and provide the opportunities for the development of health and safety promotion where employees have more input.

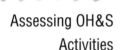

Assessing OH&S Activities

The effectiveness of OH&S measures can be assessed using the outcome data associated with health and safety as depicted in Exhibit 14.5. However, assessing the improvement brought about by strategies targeted at reducing accidents differs from evaluating those targeted at preventing and treating occupational diseases. Moreover, strategies oriented toward the physical work environment are different from those targeted at the sociopsy-

Exhibit 14.5
Prototype Model and Corresponding Remedies for Occupational Health and Safety at Work

ENVIRONMENTAL RISKS	CONDITIONS	REMEDIES	OUTCOMES
Accidents	Loss of limb Back Injuries Death	Ergonomics Safety committee Training Monitoring Protective gear	Turnover/absenteeism Dissatisfaction
Diseases			
• Chemical origins	Hearing impairment Vision problems Skin conditions	Genetic screening Monitoring exposure Assistance programs	Medical costs
• Biological origins	Hepatitis B AIDS Contagious diseases	Monitoring exposure Assistance programs	Workers' comp. costs
• Physical origins	Heart conditions Ulcers Hearing impairment	Ergonomics	Lack of involvement
• Organizational origins	Back injuries Burnout Fatigue	Altering policies Improving work schedules Ergonomics	Poor performance
• Psychological origins	Burnout	Stress management	Suicide

chological work environment. Exhibit 14.5 provides an overview for the risks–conditions–remedies–outcomes scenarios. Some examples of typical variables are identified in each category. Also, the remedies listed are not necessarily mutually exclusive and the outcomes might be linked to all environmental risks. Nonetheless, the exhibit provides a synopsis for this chapter.

Effectiveness is often measured by the effect a specific strategy has on employee absenteeism and turnover, medical claims and workers' compensation rates, costs, performance, and overall efficiency. The effect can also be seen in a change in the accident rate or the incidence of specific diseases. Relative effectiveness can be measured by determining the cost of the program and its relative benefits. For example, it is suggested that the cost of improving ergonomic factors (e.g., seats and comfort in police cars) will be easily offset by the benefits. Since ergonomic changes are relatively within the direct control of the employer, ergonomics may be the most effective remedy for many environmental risks. Similarly, training costs for prevention programs and publicity campaigns can be monitored and compared to outcomes within a specified time frame.

Computer Applications

Employees' right-to-know legislation has prompted dozens of software programs that assist organizations in monitoring inventories of dangerous chemicals, printing information on the safety of materials, tracking the safety training given to workers, creating reports required by different levels of governments, and tracking accidents and exposure to chemicals.

One program created by the Canadian Centre for Occupational Health and Safety currently enjoys one of the highest subscription rates for CD-ROM products anywhere. Over 3,500 employers and unions subscribed in 1989. The disks, which can be accessed by any personal computer, contain instant information about various OH&S issues. Series A1 contains approximately 60,000 material safety data sheets along with information on pure chemicals, natural substances, mixtures that result from industrial processes, products registered in Canada, and various other databases on pest control products, maximum residue limits in foods, and parasitic and predatory insect releases. Series A2 lists information on pure chemicals (as in Series A1), and includes the NIOSH registry of toxic effects of chemical substances, regulatory information on the transportation of dangerous goods, and information on chemicals of environmental concern. Series B1 is a must for professionals in OH&S, because it includes directories of recent Canadian studies in the field, and Canadian organizations and individuals involved in it; Canadian facts and figures on safety documents and occupational health fatalities; summaries of cases from jurisdictions across Canada; and a summary of OH&S legislation in Canada. Also included is an international bibliographic database created by the international centre in Geneva on research into the prevention of occupational risks. The last disk, series B2, contains information on noise-level measurements in actual work situations, nonionized radiation measurements of specific types of equipment, and a bibliographic database of international health and safety documents created by NIOSH.

The advantage of using a CD-ROM disk is that access to information is immediate and convenient, while it occupies a minimum amount of office space. Each of the CD-ROMs listed above contains up to the equivalent of 300,000 pages of information. The information retrieved is accurate and up to date (disks are issued quarterly), and can be printed or stored at the convenience of the user.

Additionally, numerous programs are available for evaluating lifestyle factors (such as diet, exercise, and smoking), using them to determine the seriousness of key health risks. Some of these programs also provide counselling for lowering those risks. An innovative program for diagnosing stress and burnout at work has been recently developed by a Montreal-based firm. *SDI* (Stress Diagnosis Inventory) aids the occupational health

HRM DYNAMICS
Health and Safety Profiles in Selected Canadian Organizations

Air Canada

All health and safety procedures at Air Canada are based upon the "Loss Control Program." The backbone of the program is elaborate training that lasts up to two-and-a-half years, where a different course is given at least once a month. Management 123 involves, for example, training in modules for which progression is made from Level 1 through Level 3. Level 1—contains an orientation of company policy and practices, where to find who's who in the company, and safety techniques; Level 2—emphasizes prevention rather than reaction; and Level 3—refines, focuses on implementation. Other components of OH&S in Air Canada focus on prevention via the use of (a) human factor engineering (ergonomics), for example in designing the cockpit; (b) safety and health committees, which also certify personnel following training as prepared to do the job. For example, a sheet metal worker must know perfectly the tools and material he or she uses as well as the procedures in case of accident; and (c) risk/hazard analysis.

Bell Canada

Bell's OH&S policy is summarized in a manual that gets updated from time to time. A special team of researchers updates the information, which ranges from baby car seats to AIDS. This manual is used by all managers in regular monthly meetings. Approximately one hour is devoted to OH&S, normally covering three subtopics. Often group participation is encouraged, and guest speakers or a video clip are presented. Recently there was a competitive game organized that drew high participation. It lasted a year and included preparation, studies, meetings, and finally a show-down in front of a camera and a large audience. It was made up of over 700 questions on health and safety at work and in the home environment.

Matrox

Matrox is a leading manufacturer of printed circuit boards. Presently it employs 600 people and is located near Montreal. Matrox introduces its OH&S policy during the employee's initiation. Those who will be handling dangerous or toxic materials will be given special training on these items. The company also has prepared a series of documents pertaining to special areas, along with providing safety equipment such as goggles and gloves. But the cornerstone of the company's policy is its pride in providing unique facilities installed on site, which are part of their wellness program. Rarely are these available for companies of its size. The facilities include: a pool, aerobics classes, a soccer field, and a baseball field.

professional in diagnosing both individuals and groups at risk, and also suggests some key areas for intervention. The program has been used on several occasions for guiding the Quebec Workers' Compensation Appeal Board in determining cases of burnout.[34]

SUMMARY

The field of OH&S is gaining increased recognition. Employers are becoming more aware of the cost of ill health and the benefits of having a healthy workforce. The federal and provincial governments, through a complex web of laws, make it more necessary for employers to be concerned with employee health and safety. Even with the use of modern technology, hazards always exist. The current concern is primarily with occupational accidents and diseases caused by the physical environment, but organizations can choose to guard employee health by improving the workers' sociopsychological environment as well. Though many of the latter efforts are voluntary, the government may prescribe (in the near future) regulations for sociopsychological conditions. Thus, it pays organizations to be concerned with both aspects of the work environment now. Effective programs for both environments can significantly improve both employee health and the effectiveness of the organization.

When adoption of improvement programs is being considered, it is important to involve the employees. As with many QWL programs being implemented, worker involvement in improving health and safety is not only a good idea, but is likely desired by the employees.

It is important to distinguish between the two types of environment: the physical and the sociopsychological. Each has its unique components. Hence, while some improvement strategies may work well for one part of the work environment, they will not work in others. A careful diagnosis is required before programs are selected and implemented. The bottom line from a HR perspective is that these programs can reduce costs in the form of insurance premiums, workers' compensation, litigation, and productivity loss due to disability, accident, absenteeism, turnover, and even death.

P O S T S C R I P T

In an era of increasing economic pressure, many corporate executives are preoccupied with major operational problems such as meeting production and delivery schedules, maintaining budgets, and meeting customer expectations. In the past, health and safety issues were not treated in the same manner as other production issues. This, however, is rapidly changing. For one thing, governments, through a web of legislation, force organizations to comply. No one wants to have another "Bhopal." Moreover, executives are beginning to understand that genuine concern for OH&S is also good business: they can attract more qualified workers and can ensure that morale and productivity will be sustained.

However, if for many years emphasis in OH&S has been placed on the physical work environment (at the expense of the psychological one), increases in the incidence of substance abuse, significant increases in employee stress and burnout, and the advent of a new public health crisis in the form of AIDS represent the major new issues to management.

Complicating these issues are a series of legal decisions (court, tribunal, arbitration, and workers' compensation) that suggest an expanded scope of responsibility for organizations as they attempt to develop policies and procedures to contend with these issues What is clear is that HR managers will play a key role in helping their organizations confront these issues. Neglecting to do so will increase the firm's vulnerability to damaging and expensive litigation resulting from improper handling of both old and emerging OH&S issues.

R E V I E W   A N D   A N A L Y S I S   Q U E S T I O N S

1. Why are organizations concerned with OH&S issues?
2. How are physical hazards distinct from sociopsychological ones?
3. Name some key factors that may affect occupational accidents.
4. What are the key factors affecting occupational diseases?
5. Is there such a thing as an unsafe worker? Assuming that accident-prone workers exist, how can HR functions address this problem?
6. Identify and describe the potential causes for (a) stress at work, and (b) burnout.

7. What steps are necessary to develop a strategy for improving an organization's health and safety record?

8. Identify your sources of stress as a student. Identify the possible health consequences of excessive stress. What strategies can you use to better cope with these stressors and reduce the unhealthy consequences?

9. Discuss the principles of stress management in an organization.

CASE STUDY

STRESS MANAGEMENT AT METROPOLITAN HOSPITAL

A stress management program was carried out over a one-year period at Metropolitan Hospital. The initial impetus for the project was widespread complaints from the nurses about feeling stressed, overworked, lonely, and subject to unexpected changes in policies and procedures. Top administrators sought help in dealing with these problems from a local management consulting firm (MDS Management, Inc.) that had previously intervened in another hospital.

The initial stage of the project consisted of diagnosing the causes and consequences of stress experienced at the hospital. Understanding the sources was seen as a necessary prelude to developing an appropriate plan for managing it. The consultants developed a questionnaire to collect data from a sample of 300 nurses representing different wards of the hospital. The questionnaire included items about various organizational stressors, including both ongoing, recurrent stressors and those associated with recent changes. It also included questions about the nurses' use of stress-management techniques, such as exercise, nutritional planning, and the available support systems. The questionnaire ended with items about experienced strain symptoms (e.g., irritability, sleep difficulty, and changes in eating and drinking patterns) and longer-term effects (e.g., health problems, dissatisfaction, and decreased work effectiveness). In addition, the consultants wanted to see the personnel files of the nurses who participated in the study. Absenteeism records for the previous twelve months, as well as PA data were recorded.

Analysis showed that many of the changing events and ongoing working conditions were significantly related to nurses' levels of strain and to longer-term stress effects. Among the most stressful organizational events were major and frequent changes in instructions, policies, and procedures; numerous unexpected crises and deadlines; and sudden increases in the activity level or pace of work. The ongoing working conditions contributing most to stress included quantitative work overload, feedback only when performance was unsatisfactory, lack of confidence in administration, and role conflict and ambiguity. The nurses reported little if any use of stress-management techniques to help them cope with these stressors. Only 20 percent engaged in regular physical exercise, and surprisingly, 60 percent had marginally or poorly balanced diets. The most commonly reported health problems included tension headaches, diarrhea or constipation, common colds, backaches, and depression.

Based on the diagnostic data, senior administrators, with the help of the consultants, implemented several organizational improvements. In order to reduce work overload and role ambiguity, positions were analyzed in terms of work distribution, job requirements, and performance standards. This resulted in more balanced workloads and clearer job descriptions. Hospital administrators also began working with wards to define job expectations and to provide ongoing performance feedback. The nurses were given training in how to better organize their workload and time and in how to more effectively seek social support on a continuing basis.

In order to reduce the stress caused by organizational changes, senior administrators spent more time informing and educating the nurses about forthcoming changes. Top management also held information meetings with ward head nurses on a quarterly basis in order to clear up misunderstandings, misinterpretations, and rumors. While the above changes were aimed at reducing organizational stressors, additional measures helped individual nurses identify and cope with stress more effectively. The hospital instituted yearly physical examinations to detect stress-related problems, and trained nurses to identify stress symptoms and problems, both in themselves and their peers. In addition the hospital developed an exercise club and various sports activities and offered weekly yoga classes. It also created a training program combining nutritional awareness with techniques for coping with tension headaches and backaches.

And, as an alternative to doughnuts, fresh fruit was made available in all meetings and training sessions.

Initial reactions to the stress management program were positive, and the hospital is currently assessing the longer-term effects of the intervention. The total cost for the one-year trial period was estimated at $150,000.

Case Question

Provide a detailed case analysis based on the ideas presented in this chapter.

NOTES

1. W. French, *Human Resource Management*, 2nd ed. (Boston: Houghton Mifflin, 1990),. 620.

2. "Work Injuries 1989-1991," Statistics Canada, Cat. No. 72–208, 5, 19.

3. *Special Report on Alcohol Statistics* (Ottawa: Minister of National Health and Welfare Canada, and the Minister of Supply and Services Canada, 1981).

4. W. Gifford-Jones, "Back Aches Wreak Havoc within Office Absenteeism," *The Montreal Gazette*, 3 March 1992.,

5. J.D. Millar, "Summary of 'Proposed national strategies for the prevention of leading work-related diseases and injuries, part 1,'" *American Journal of Industrial Medicine* 13 (1988): 223–40.

6. M.I. Jacobson, S.L. Yenney, and J.C. Bisgard, "An organizational perspective on worksite health promotion," *Occupational Medicine: State of the Art Reviews* 5, 4 (1990): 653–65.

7. S.J. Matthias, R. May, and T.L. Guidotti, "Occupational health and safety: a future unlike the present," *Occupational Medicine: State of the Art Reviews* 4, 1 (1989): 177–90.

8. G. Atherley, "Occupational Health and Safety: Acts, Actors, and Actions," in *Canadian Readings In Personnel and Human Resource Management*, ed. S.L. Dolan and R.S. Schuler (St. Paul, Minn.: West Publishing Co., 1987), 391.

9. S. Skiadas, P. Gariepy, and U. Finotti, "Occupational Health and Safety" (Unpublished paper, Montreal, McGill University, April 1991), 12.

10. *COHSN* 13, 16 (23 April 1990):

11. *COHSN*, 13, 45 (12 November 1990):

12. H. Goldblatt, S. Price, and J. Sack, eds. "Fear of crossing picket line did not justify refusal to work," *Health & Safety Law* 3, 1 (1987): 1–4; C. Deacon, H. Goldblatt, and S. Price, eds. "Customs employees refuse to work because of demonstration—no actual danger, says Federal Board," *Health & Safety Law* 5, 3 (1989): 1–4.

13. G.K. Bryce and P. Manga, "The Effectiveness of Health and Safety Committees," *Relations Industrielles/Industrial Relations* 40, 2 (1985): 257–83.

14. M. Tremblay and G. Tougas, *Policier patrouilleur, Sureté du Québec: risques à la santé* (Montréal: Département de santé communautaire, Hôpital Saint-Luc, mai 1989);

15. Based on an interview with P.H. Shafer, Senior Environmental H&S Advisor, RCMP, conducted in Montreal, 13 August 1991.

16. J. Rutenfranz et al., "Biomedical and psychosocial aspects of shift work: a review," *Scandinavian Journal of Work Environment and Health* 3 (1977): 165–82.

17. M. Jamal and S.M Jamal, "Work and non-work experiences of employees on fixed and rotating shifts: an empirical assessment," *Journal of Vocational Behaviour* 20 (1982): 282–93.

18 B. Shamir, "Work schedules and the perceived conflict between work and non-work," *Working paper No. 3* (Jerusalem: Hebrew University, Pertelsmann Program, 1982).

19. For more information, see S.L.Dolan and D Balkin, "A Contingency Model Of Occupational Stress," *The International Journal of Management* 4, 3 (September 1987): 328–40.

20. M.R. Van Ameringen, A. Arsennault, and S.L. Dolan, "Intrinsic Job Stress as Predictor of Diastolic Blood Pressure among Female Hospital Workers," *Journal of Occupational Medicine* 30, 2 (1988): 93–97.

21. M. Crowford, "High anxiety sets in," *The Financial Post*, 17 October 1991, 12.

22. W. Pardy, "Back from the brink: how to revive your OH&S program," *Occupational Health and Safety*, Canada 6, 6 (1990): 46–52.

23. Quebec Health and Safety Commission, "Quebec Occupational Health and Safety Plan: 1979–1988 (A Ten-Year Statistical and Financial Overview," (CSST 1989): 8–36.

24. For more information, see D.N. Robertson, "Identifying Joint Health and Safety Committee Training Needs," in *Human Resource Management in Canada*, March 1990: 60, 511–60, 512.

25. Study conducted by the Advisory Council on Occupational Health and Occupational Safety, Eighth Annual Report, 1 April 1985–31 March 1986.

26. Letter of the president, L.D. Caplan, to employees, 22 February 1991.

27. M.M. Coté et al., *Design d'habitacle d'auto-patrouille et prévention des lombalgies: rapport de recherche*, (Montréal: Quebec Research Institute on Occupational Health and Safety (IRSST), December 1990); and M.M. Coté, B. Hoshizaki, and M.A. Dalzell, *Auto-patrouille et maux de dos chez les policiers du Québec: étude/bilan de connaissances* (Montréal: IRSST, June 1989).

28. S. Hirshorn, "Taking care of your back," *Protect Yourself*, March 1991, 33–38.

29 Environment Canada, *Guide pour les déversements de produits dangereux* (Ottawa: Service de la protection de l'environnement, 1985).

30 J.E. Fielding, "Worksite stress management: national survey results," *Journal of Occupational Medicine* 21, 12 (1989): 990–95.

31. "Sabbaticals relieve employee burnout," *Small Business Report* 12, 12 (1987): 80.

32. A planners guide to fitness in the workplace Ontario Ministry of Tourism and Recreation, 1984.

33 J.V. Johnson, "Collective control: strategies for survival in the workplace," *International Journal of Health Services* 19, 3 (1989): 469–80.

34. More information can be obtained by writing to MDS Management Inc., P.O. Box 116, C.S.L. Montreal, P.Q. Canada H4V 2Y3.

CHAPTER FIFTEEN

EMPLOYEE RIGHTS

KEYNOTE ADDRESS

Bob Swenor
Senior Vice-President Corporate Administration, Dofasco Inc.

Beyond Enlightened Labour Relations

"Our Product is Steel, Our Strength is People." In Canada, that venerable no-nonsense motto is a contender for the country's most familiar corporate slogan. For nearly twenty-three years now it has been heard in more than 1,000 radio commercials and mentioned in print on countless occasions. Unlike most company slogans, Dofasco's acknowledges its employees as much as its product, reflecting the company's long-standing awareness of employee relations. Indeed, Dofasco, the largest nonunionized steel company in the world today, has gained a reputation as an innovator in labour relations as well as technology and there are few companies that can match its track record where employees' morale is concerned.

The average term of employment is more than eighteen years and the turnover rate averages just 3 percent. An industry average for a company Dofasco's size is about 8 percent. Absenteeism hovers at 4.8 percent— again below the average. Both figures are enviable.

While the statistics put employee satisfaction in a useful context, they do not quite prepare an outsider for the degree of goodwill employees profess for the company. Without a nudge or a wink, they speak respectfully if not glowingly, of their relationship with the company, creating an impression of the enterprise that is not perfect, but more often than not, embarrassingly virtuous.

Dofasco's efforts in employee relations are not a recent invention. Formally, they go back to the Depression, when Clifton Sherman and his brother and co-founder Frank A. Sherman introduced profit sharing. Introduced in 1938, the profit-sharing plan was the product of a four-year management search that involved canvassing more than 200 profit-sharing plans, mostly in the U.S.A. About the same time, the Shermans created an employee suggestion program, a massive Christmas Party, an annual picnic, a company magazine, a recreation program, an open-door policy for handling complaints, and implemented a gradual change in the powers of foremen, who previously could hire and fire at will.

What the founding fathers were really attending to was attitude from top to bottom, and to make sure everyone caught the flavour of their efforts, they wrote an industrial prescription with advice to "Consider employees at all times as human beings and respect their feelings" and "Develop their confidence by being logical and fair." The crux of their approach was the Golden Rule: "Treat others as you would like to be treated yourself." Around Dofasco today, over fifty years later, those words are considered the essential fibre of Dofasco's employee relations and no one seems prepared to let any dust settle on the old tenet.

We have been called both old-fashioned and paternalistic and while some people around here take offence at that, I do not; I do not see looking after people in a fatherly or friendly fashion as a bad thing. Our founders had the foresight to see that people should be treated well, that they are our most valuable asset, and that they need to be recognized as such. The Shermans recognized that employees' contribution required a tangible show of faith, and profit sharing symbolized Dofasco's willingness to involve employees more directly in the company welfare. Today the profit-sharing plan is a kind of industrial epoxy at Dofasco, with every employee who has worked two years or more, from chairman to labourer, receiving an equal share of the Fund, which is sustained annually by steelmaking profits. Another way Dofasco recognizes employees' contribution is a suggestion system that rewards up to $50,000—the amount depending on how much money the suggestion saves the company.

In lieu of the grievance process, a fixture in unionized firms, Dofasco's open-door policy lets any employee appeal a supervisor's decision to a more senior level—all the way to the chairman if necessary. Although there are not many appeals, most complaints are resolved at a much earlier stage if somebody really is not happy; they know we will listen.

Another familiar chestnut in Dofasco's public image is its annual Christmas party—one of the biggest events of its kind. Each December about 35,000 employees and family members attend it. Familiar as well in the company's public profile is the *Dofasco Illustrated News*, a handsome four-colour publication, launched in the 1930s, published several times per year and widely distributed—even beyond Canada. It contains articles of general interest as well as news about the company. Another publication, the *News'n Views*, shares news of promotions, retirements, births, and deaths as well as chatty updates on the goings-on of more than fifty employee clubs, as well as information on technological and marketplace changes.

At the company's 100-acre recreation park on the outskirts of Hamilton, employees and their families enjoy one of the most impressive company-sponsored recreation centres in North America—a facility chock-full of skating rinks, tennis courts, baseball diamonds, miniature golf, a driving range, nature trails, and other amenities that could be the envy of many communities. Similarly, Dofasco's medical centre is a recognized industrial model complete with ergonomists, physiotherapists, audiologists, and full medical staff and facilities including physicians and an operating room.

The company prepares men and women approaching retirement with planning courses, as well as a ten-week vacation that is a supplement to the maximum eight weeks already given veteran employees. Perhaps nothing mirrors the success of employee–management relations at Dofasco as much as the company's retirees. They are pleased with a continuing esprit de corps that is kindled in picnics, outings, and weekly socials as well as events such as the Christmas party.

. . .

As can be seen in the Keynote Address, employee rights at Dofasco are not mere labour relations, but encompass a variety of HR activities including benefits, grievance procedures, profit sharing, and general care for employees and even retirees. Although Dofasco has often been labelled "a paternalistic company," it does not find this offensive; it feels its management approach is genuinely employee-oriented. The fact that the company has managed to remain nonunionized is a direct indication that it truly lives up to its motto.

Employee rights are becoming a very prominent issue in HRM. Some managers, however, view them as a mechanism by which employees can second-guess management decisions; others believe the currently increasing rights are ushering in an age of employee control of the organization; unions and many employees, however, view these rights as a means to ensure that management decisions are made on a sound, justifiable basis and that employees are protected from arbitrary and vindictive actions. Obviously, these views are in sharp contrast. It is unlikely that the differences will be resolved soon, so the HR manager should understand all positions. The HR manager must have an understanding of the current legal considerations regarding employee rights, and develop strategies for organizations to use in addressing these rights.

This chapter follows the conventional distinction found in research and practice and discusses employee rights in terms of two major headings: job security and rights on the job. After defining employee rights and their increasing importance in HRM, major legislation, court rulings, and some arbitration decisions that have created the present legal climate affecting these rights are reviewed.

The major issue in job security is the erosion of the traditional doctrine of an arbitrary termination. Significant on-the-job issues involve privacy rights and access to employee records, cooperative acceptance in regard to various forms of harassment, and notification and assistance concerning plant or office closing. Employer success in ensuring employee rights in both areas depends upon establishing effective organizational communication as well as setting clear policies for grievances, progressive discipline, privacy, and a safe work environment.

. . .

EMPLOYEE RIGHTS

Although much of the current discussion of employee rights addresses the right of employers to "terminate arbitrarily," employee rights cover much more, including the right to a job under almost any conditions, and also the right to fair, just, and respectful treatment while on the job.

Within these two broad areas of employee rights are several more specific issues, including: freedom from sexual harassment; the right to notification of plant closing; due process treatment in discharge cases; freedom from discriminatory treatment based on sex, marital status, race, religion, or national origin; and the right to have personal records remain confidential. While some of these rights are protected by law or collective bargaining agreements, others are not. This leaves the majority of the nonunionized workforce unprotected.

Employee rights are defined here as those rights desired by employees regarding the security of their jobs and the treatment administered by their employer while on the job, irrespective of whether or not those rights are currently protected by law or collective bargaining agreements. As these rights become recognized by employers, the extent of management rights, that is, the prerogatives management has in dealing with its workforce, diminish. Thus, employee rights have a significant impact on HR activities. Concern for employee rights demands a careful balance between management rights and employee rights.

Purposes and Importance of Employee Rights

The discussion of recruitment and selection in Chapters 5 and 6 focused on the methods of attracting and placing job applicants into organizations; attention is now directed toward the considerations involved in establishing and maintaining relationships with the job applicants who are hired. Previous chapters have stressed the importance of making sure employees (new and old) are informed about what is expected of them and what opportunities are available in the organization. This chapter stresses issues of fairness with respect to employee–employer relationships. This, after all, is the thrust of employee rights.

Treating employees fairly and with respect is important to organizations. Where there is legal protection of employee rights, violations can result in penalties and fines. The violation of employee rights that do not have explicit statutory protection, that is, rights for which no acts (or collective agreements) are in place, is also becoming costly to organizations. Such is the case for the protection given by the courts and arbitrators against wrongful dismissal. For example, a complainant's dismissal was ruled unjust when she was dismissed on the grounds of unsatisfactory job performance. The adjudicator decided that the complainant's twelve years of service with the employer should be recognized and that the company should pay her severance accordingly (eight months' pay rather than the seven weeks she had received).[1]

In another example, the Supreme Court of Ontario ruled that a car dealership must pay a former employee $93,940 plus 15 percent interest from the time of his "callous summary dismissal." Robert Eyers took a holiday from his position as general sales manager for City Buick Pontiac Cadillac Limited after suffering a heart attack in June 1982. Incorrectly assuming he was permanently disabled, the company stopped paying Eyers' salary in August while he was still away and without informing him. Upon his return, Eyers was pronounced fully recovered and fit for work by his doctors. Shortly after contacting his employer in mid-September, Eyers received what looked like a termination letter. It stated: "Due to the economic climate, the position of General Sales Manager…no longer exists and will not be created until such time as the economy brightens up." He was offered a position as Cadillac sales manager at a salary of $14,000. During the trial, the company professed concern about Eyers' health and his fitness to cope with a more stressful position. Supreme Court Justice Joseph Potts deemed the health concern to be a "smoke-screen." Potts asked: "What is the difference between telling a person 'you're fired'…a senior man in the company…and telling him 'the job you had before is no longer there'?" Eyers was an eight-year employee earning $40,000 a year plus fringe benefits and bonus. The judge ruled he should not have been required to accept the new job offer to mitigate his damages: "He would likely have been fired from his new position." Under normal circumstances appropriate notice for an eight-year employee is one year, said Potts, but because of the lack of courtesy with which Eyers was treated and the fact that he was not even informed when he was taken off the payroll, Potts ruled that the period of notice for which Eyers should be compensated was seventeen months.[2] A more recent case is illustrated in the HRM in the News Vignette.

HRM IN THE NEWS VIGNETTE

Montreal Trust Ordered to Pay $437,000 Over Firing

A nine-year court case sparked by a squabble over $1,615.40 ended yesterday with a labour court ordering Montreal Trust to pay former employee Mark Moore $437,000 for unjust dismissal. The award cannot be appealed.

Moore was manager of Montreal Trust's real-estate branch in Notre Dame de Grâce until December 1982 when he was fired.

Moore's dismissal followed his attempts to put together a class action suit with other real-estate managers to fight what Moore felt were illegal deductions by Montreal Trust from his weekly paycheque.

Montreal Trust had seized Moore's $403.85 base salary after he refused to put up additional collateral for $13,000 he owed the company in advances. Moore claimed that the company's demands for collateral violated his contract.

When Moore sued, Montreal Trust immediately repaid him the $1,615.40 and then demanded his resignation. When he refused, the company fired him.

After four court hearings, the Quebec Court of Appeal finally awarded Moore his job back on 1988. The Supreme Court refused in January 1989 to hear Montreal Trust's appeal.

Soon after Montreal Trust was forced to rehire him on Oct. 12, 1988, Moore filed three more suits, again alleging that the company was underpaying him. He also sued for contempt of court and for compensation for the years 1983–1988.

During the hearing before the labour court,

Moore testified that on his first day back he was followed by a private detective. He said he drove through Westmount streets with the detective following. When he entered a dead-end street, the detective backed up and fled, but Moore took his licence number.

Moore also testified that Montreal Trust had paid kickbacks to a city housing employee. He told the court that Montreal Trust paid $19,737 through a beauty salon to Raymond Leclerc, former sales coordinator for what is now the Societé d'habitation et de développement de Montréal—a city housing agency. Leclerc was charged last March with breach of trust and receiving secret commissions in 1988 from Montreal Trust.

Then, on Oct. 11, 1990, Montreal Trust fired Moore again—for disloyalty. The labour court yesterday awarded him $437,000 including interest to compensate for lost income from 1983 to 1988.

"Needless to say I'm very happy," Moore said. "After nine years of litigation it's a pleasure to see the little guy can still win. I'm going to have to pay a big legal bill and my lawyer tells me that I cannot recover my legal fees from Montreal Trust."

Moore is still contesting his second dismissal. The case is to be heard in labour court Dec. 13.

Source: Feature article by W. Marsden, *The Montreal Gazette*, 17 October 1991, A1 and A2. Used with permission.

Employee rights are related to other HR activities. The relationships shown in Exhibit 15.1 are some of the most important.

Relationships to Employee Rights

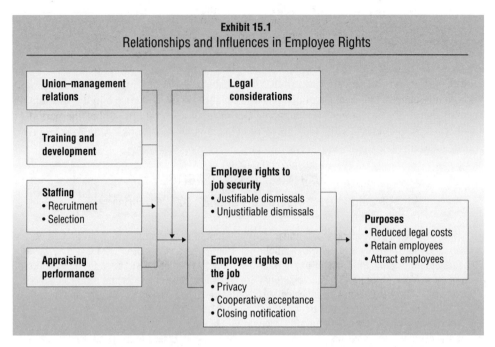

Exhibit 15.1
Relationships and Influences in Employee Rights

- Union–management relations
- Training and development
- Staffing
  - Recruitment
  - Selection
- Appraising performance

- Legal considerations

Employee rights to job security
- Justifiable dismissals
- Unjustifiable dismissals

Employee rights on the job
- Privacy
- Cooperative acceptance
- Closing notification

Purposes
- Reduced legal costs
- Retain employees
- Attract employees

APPRAISING PERFORMANCE. Supervisors often use poor employee performance as grounds for dismissal. However, when asked by the court to show evidence in these cases, supervisors and HR managers are often unable to produce it. Often, records of employee performance are either not accurately maintained or are inaccurately used. Sometimes employees are not informed when they are performing inadequately, or given a chance to respond to charges of poor performance, nor are they given an opportunity to improve (lack of due process). Because employees are winning "unjustifiable dismissal" suits, organizations are likely to intensify efforts to train supervisors and managers to conduct valid appraisals, to maintain accurate HR records, and to establish grievance procedures to ensure due process protection.

TRAINING AND DEVELOPMENT. Supervisors are more likely to unjustifiably dismiss employees as well as to commit sexual harassment offences if they have not received effective training on these issues than if they have received such training. Consequently, a frequently suggested approach to the issue of sexual harassment is to develop an organizational policy and train all the supervisors and managers in that policy.

UNION–MANAGEMENT RELATIONS. Where unions exist, employee job security rights are generally protected by a union–management contract. Because only about one-third of the labour force is unionized, many employees are left without this protection. Nevertheless, if job security becomes a major issue, it may stimulate union organizational activity.

LEGAL CONSIDERATIONS IN EMPLOYEE RIGHTS

Employee rights comprise a web of legal considerations, so this section is much larger than similar sections in previous chapters. After discussing the legal issues surrounding employee rights, HR strategies that can facilitate employer recognition of these rights are discussed.

Employee Rights to Job Security

If neither a collective agreement nor a specific statute governs an employee dismissal, the common law rules of the master and servant relationship apply. Such is the case in the majority of dismissals in Canada, but each termination is judged according to the common law of each province.

In Canada, the notion of "cause for dismissal" has progressed significantly over time. In the past, terminating employees for misconduct, neglect, and disobedience was done almost automatically, but now the employee's behaviour must constitute a serious breach of his or her contractual obligations to merit such action. The Canadian employment situation, through common law precedents, has tended to become a "lifetime" contract. Most employees are hired under an implied contract; others, generally those in management, have written contracts. Implied contracts usually have no established time frames. In many cases of wrongful dismissal, the employee claims that employment under this "implied contract" was terminated without "just cause." Since employment is considered a contract, termination without cause is considered a breach of that contract. A small mistake in the performance of the job, for instance, will not justify summary dismissal, since the courts consider employees fallible human beings. The fault or misconduct must amount to the repudiation of the contract.

In addition, Canadian jurisdictions prohibit dismissal on certain specific grounds. For example, dismissal for union activity is unlawful in all provinces as well as in federal government jurisdictions. Dismissal for pregnancy and wage garnishment have been the object of a statutory ban in several provinces. According to one expert, however, these legislative interventions do not provide a higher degree of job security to nonunionized workers, because of their limited scope.[3]

JUST CAUSE FOR DISMISSAL. Cause for dismissal according to common law includes any act by the employee that could have serious negative effects on the operation, reputation, or management of the firm. This could include, for example, fraud, drunkenness, dishonesty, forgery, insubordination, continuous absenteeism, or refusal to obey reasonable orders. The onus for proving the existence of "just cause" is on the employer.

In any case, the protection offered to employees under Canadian common law remains very limited for a number of reasons: (1) provided that lawful notice is given of the intent, an employer can dismiss an employee without cause; the majority of the Canadian workforce receives only the statutory notice (one or two months); and (2) the remedies available to dismissed workers under common law are very limited. For instance, the dismissed person can only obtain damages that amount to the wages he or she would have earned during the notice period. Reinstatement is not provided for through common law, except in very special cases.[4] Also, traditionally, the employer does not have to respect the requirements of "fair dismissal," and is not obliged to communicate the reasons for discharge or to provide the employee with an opportunity to explain his or her actions.

In one case, the Manitoba Court of Queen's Bench ruled that an owner/employer of an auto service station and his son must jointly pay a former employee $1,000 for slander after firing him in public without cause.[5] Although an employer may think he or she has just cause, the court could very well rule against him or her. Often, chronic lateness or absenteeism is *cause* for dismissal. But, even in this case, *just cause* is not always easy to establish. For instance, in the case of an assistant manager of a co-op who was terminated as a result of alleged lateness, the court found that, given his eight years' standing, the leisurely atmosphere of the workplace, and the absence of any written warning, lateness did not constitute a "just cause." All in all, in the case of chronic absences or tardiness, courts are inclined to accept dismissal only when it constitutes willful disobedience of an employer's reasonable orders. Thus, an employer who wishes to justify dismissal should be prepared to show that absenteeism or tardiness resulted from *intentional misconduct* rather than misunderstanding.[6]

STATUTORY PROTECTION AGAINST WRONGFUL DISMISSAL. To date, few Canadian jurisdictions have enacted general statutes to protect employees against wrongful dismissal. Nova Scotia was the first to draft such legislation. Under this legislation, a dismissed employee can approach the Director of Labour Standards, who first attempts to conciliate. If agreement is not reached, he or she has the authority to issue a binding decision (unless either side appeals to the Labour Standards Tribunal). The Director may require the reinstatement of the employee. Protection under this Act, however, only covers employees with at least ten years of service with the same employer.

Section 61.5 of the Canadian Labour Code covers federal employees who are not part of any collective agreement and who have completed twelve months of continuous employment. When an employee files a complaint for unjust dismissal with Labour Canada, an inspector will attempt to settle the problem. The Minister of Labour may appoint an adjudicator who will determine whether or not the complainant was wrongfully dismissed. Extensive remedial powers are given to the adjudicator, including the authority to reinstate the complainant in his or her former job.

In 1979 the province of Quebec enacted the Act Respecting Labour Standards. Similar to the previously mentioned provisions, it enables employees (with five years' uninterrupted service with the same employer) to engage an arbitrator appointed by the Commission of Labour Standards. This arbitrator also has extensive remedial powers.

CONSTRUCTIVE DISMISSAL AND REASONABLE NOTICE. Once an employee is hired, neither party can unilaterally change the terms of the hiring contract, unless both willingly agree. If, as a result of a change in employment status, the employee resigns, this may be considered constructive dismissal. Examples of changes in employment status that could lead to constructive dismissal include:

- A change in job function,
- A reduction in salary or benefits,
- A change in reporting relationships,
- A demotion,
- Reassignment to a new job or location.

If there is no cause, an employee can be terminated by giving reasonable notice. Apart from the statutory minimum notice periods, no time frames for "reasonable notice" have been established by law. Over the years, reasonable notice has been decided by judges after hearing each case individually. It would appear, however, that the courts take the following into consideration: length of service, age, availability of similar employment, experience and training, level of responsibility, degree of specialization, and method of recruitment.[7] For instance, the British Columbia Supreme Court recently ruled that a handicapped employee should receive longer termination notice than someone who is not handicapped. The paraplegic won an additional two months on his wrongful dismissal because his disability made the search for a new job all the more difficult.

GROUP TERMINATION. In recent years there has been considerable publicity concerning technological change, plant closure, and the removal of branch plants. Their effects have been described as *group termination* or *massive layoffs*. The federal government and some provinces have introduced special legislative measures to help cushion the disruption caused by the sudden release of large numbers of employees, many with highly specialized skills.

The **Canada Labour Code** provides that, where fifty or more employees in an industrial establishment are terminated within a period not exceeding four weeks, the employer must, in addition to any notice required to be given to employees, give notice in writing to the Minister of Labour at least sixteen weeks before the date of termination, and copies to other groups, such as the Canada Employment and Immigration Commission and any trade unions involved. Furthermore, the employer must cooperate with the government and the unions in helping workers find new jobs.

DAMAGES. When an employer terminates an individual's employment, it is understood that either reasonable notice will be given or an amount equal to the employee's salary for the notice period will be paid. Should the employee sue for more compensation and win, this amount is considered damages. However, to be entitled to damages, the employee must have suffered a loss (of income, for example). In awarding damages, the courts apparently also consider such things as benefits and commissions, but only those that the employee would have been entitled to during the notice period. Bonuses might also be considered if the employee's bonus formed part of his or her total compensation. Other awards for damages have included moving expenses incurred in accepting a new job in a new location, reasonable telephone charges, and professional dues.

Since the late 1970s, judges have been awarding damages for "mental distress or suffering" in many cases. Mental distress can result from factors ranging anywhere from the manner in which the termination was handled or the suddenness of the termination, to loss of reputation, seniority, or status. A classic example of this is the case of *Pilon vs. Peugeot of Canada*. Pilon, after seventeen years with Peugeot, was summarily dismissed. He obtained another position within days, but he became physically ill. He sued his former company. The judge, in assessing the merits of the case, found that Peugeot did not live up to the implied contract. Pilon was awarded $7,500 for mental distress brought on by the nature and suddenness of termination.

JOB SECURITY UNDER COLLECTIVE AGREEMENTS. The greatest achievement of many collective bargaining agreements in Canada regarding job security has been the removal of management's authority to terminate any employee without cause and/or due notice. Moreover, job security is enhanced under collective agreements by the regulation of the two specific situations under which employees could be terminated: job redundancy and employees' failure to meet obligations. Under the management rights provisions of most collective bargaining agreements, an employer may cut the workforce due to automation and/or other causes of job redundancies, but cannot lay off whomever he or she chooses (as is the case under common law). Rather, criteria set by the collective agreement must be respected.

Furthermore, although the employer can dismiss a nonsatisfactory employee, nearly all collective agreements limit this to "just cause." The disputes arising from the application of the collective agreement are normally referred to grievance arbitration for adjudication. The expression "just cause" is left purposely vague and provides the arbitrator with high flexibility in his or her judgments. Despite this flexibility, the emerging general trend points to the fair treatment of employees at all times.

Employee rights on the job include privacy and access to employment records, cooperative acceptance (i.e., freedom from harassment), the right to a safe environment, and special plant closing arrangements.

RIGHTS TO PRIVACY AND ACCESS TO GOVERNMENT RECORDS. Since the early 1980s when Bill C–43 was introduced, Canadians have had the right of public access to government records. Additionally, Canadians are protected by privacy clauses, which essentially represent a refinement of Part IV of the Canadian Human Rights Act, and the rights that enable the court to examine any government record and determine whether to order its production in litigation.

The central principle of the Access of Information Act contained in Bill C–43 is that the public is entitled to obtain government records (unless if they are specified as exempt). Further, the Act provides for judicial review of governmental decisions to deny access to particular records. A major departure from the philosophy of disclosure is the exemption relating to personal information. Section 19 of Bill C–43 prohibits disclosure of "any

Employee Rights on the Job

record" that "contains personal information" unless the individual in question has consented to the disclosure or the information is "publicly available."

RIGHTS TO COOPERATIVE ACCEPTANCE. Cooperative acceptance refers to the right of employees to be treated fairly and with respect regardless of race, sex, national origin, physical disability, age, or religion while on the job (as well as to obtain a job and maintain job security). Not only does this mean that employees have the right not to be discriminated against in employment practices and decisions, but it also means that employees have the right to be free of any type of harassment, including sexual.

All provincial legislatures and the federal government prohibit discrimination in employment on the basis of gender. Yet sexual harassment has become a serious and growing problem in the workplace. Several Human Rights Commissions report a continuing increase in the number of sexual harassment complaints.

Amendments to the Canada Labour Code (effective since 1985) have made it mandatory for employers under federal jurisdiction to develop and issue sexual harassment policies, and provide a redress mechanism for victims. Employer responsibility has been clearly indicated in various cases. For example, in *Kotyk vs. Canada and Immigration (1983)*, the tribunal found that the manager of a Canada Employment Centre made unwanted sexual advances to two complainants, Ms. Kotyk and Ms. Allary, who were his subordinates. In addition to finding the manager liable for sexual harassment, the tribunal also found his employer liable because of a lack of policy regarding sexual harassment and lack of clear instructions to their supervisory personnel regarding such matters.

A case in Saskatchewan echoes, on a provincial level, this notion of employer responsibility. Chief Commissioner of the Saskatchewan Human Rights Commission, Ron Kzuzewiski, commented that "It is the employer's responsibility to ensure a nondiscriminatory environment", and warned that those "who try to ignore sexual harassment in the workplace will be responsible for the discriminatory results."[8]

In earlier cases, employers were found liable for sexual harassment because the harassers were either the owners or directors of the corporation. Today, the majority of courts and tribunals across Canada hold the employer responsible for sexual harassment committed by any of its personnel.

RIGHTS TO A SAFE AND HEALTHY ENVIRONMENT. As discussed in Chapter 14, health and safety issues at work are a growing concern in Canada. The various federal and provincial laws require labelling and warning signs in areas where hazardous materials are used or stored. Some provinces invoke legislation enabling workers to refuse dangerous work.

A marked emphasis on the right to a pollution-free environment is spreading among Canadian firms. Some companies have taken proactive measures against substances in the work environment that, until recently, were not considered to be harmful. Other organizations attempt to reduce the stress induced by unhealthy sociopsychological conditions in the work environment.

RIGHTS TO A SMOKE-FREE WORK ENVIRONMENT. Boeing Canada was a leader in imposing a ban on smoking at work. Since then, a growing number of companies have followed suit. However, legislation dealing with workplace smoking is fragmentary at best. The issue is dealt with on a case-by-case basis, since the underlying question has become whether or not the smoker has enforceable rights.

Evidence indicates that workplace smoke does present a real health hazard for passive smokers, in addition to being a health hazard to the active smoker. It is estimated that the annual costs associated with tobacco smoking in the workplace (in the U.S.A.) range from $12 billion to almost $48 billion.[9]

PLANT CLOSING ARRANGEMENTS. The federal government and some provincial ones have shown their concern for terminated employees by passing legislation requiring employers to establish committees to assist those affected by staff reduction. Their role is to help employees affected by large-scale terminations find other employment. In addition, the various governments have special branches designed to assist employers and employees affected by a group reduction.

On the federal level there is the Industrial Adjustment Service (IAS), which is a branch of the Canada Employment and Immigration Commission. It acts as a catalyst to bring employers and workers together to discuss changes in the workplace, to formulate adjustment measures to alleviate the problems that change can bring, and to monitor and evaluate the implementation of plans developed.

The service offers technical advice, guidance, and financial incentives wherever there is a technological or economic problem affecting workers. Several reasons for layoffs may be identified, and the efforts or recommendations of the service will be tailored to the specific situation. Causes of layoffs include: plant expansion, contraction, closure or relocation, technological change, industrial slowdown, manpower planning, or labour instability.

Employment and Immigration Canada, through the IAS, may provide financial incentives to assist in the implementation of the negotiated agreements. The federal contribution is usually 50 percent of the cost. A committee made up of members from the company, the union (or representative of the employees), and an impartial chairperson is supported by a representative of the provincial Ministry of Labour and an IAS consultant.

While there may be industrial relations implications in the consultant process (for example, the recognition of seniority and transfer provisions in the collective agreement), the IAS is not intended to carry out any industrial relations functions that may interfere with the normal collective bargaining process. IAS will terminate all discussions with management and labour when a dispute is in progress or when bargaining is taking place.

The Ontario government established its Plant Closure Review and Employment Adjustment Branch in 1980 to support the government's initiative on layoffs and plant closures. This branch's mandate is:

- To become aware of any announced or impending plant closure or major reduction of operations as soon as possible;
- To make contact with companies considering closure, and also contact the employee representatives or unions, as required;
- To obtain information about the closures and advise the government on the possibility of maintaining the operation;
- Where the closure is unavoidable, to attempt to resolve any disagreements concerning termination rights and benefits and recommend the mediation services of the Ministry of Labour, as required;
- To coordinate the involvement of the Ministries of Colleges and Universities, Intergovernmental Affairs, Industry and Trade, and Community and Social Services on a particular closure situation. This ensures that available Ontario government programs are effectively focused on the needs of those affected by the closure.

The provincial branch works closely with the Industrial Adjustments Service Branch of the Canada Employment and Immigration Commission. The Ministry of Labour is a financial contributor to manpower adjustment committees in layoff situations.

Because of several legal and humanitarian considerations, it is important that organizations develop and implement strategies for recognizing employee rights. Effectively implementing other HR activities discussed in this book is one general way to help ensure that many

STRATEGIES FOR EMPLOYEE RIGHTS

of the legally sanctioned employee rights are recognized. In addition, organizations can implement specific programs, including employee privacy policies, EAPs, outplacement activities, and sexual harassment prevention training.

Employer Strategies for Employee Job Security Rights

In addition to adhering to the applicable job security laws, employers should ensure fair and legal termination by communicating expectations and prohibitions, establishing grievance procedures and due process, and following progressive discipline procedures.

COMMUNICATE EXPECTATIONS AND PROHIBITIONS. Although ignorance of rules is generally no excuse in society at large, it does apply in employment settings. Generally, employees may be disciplined only for conduct not in accordance with what they know or reasonably understand is prohibited or required. Employers must ensure that performance expectations are conveyed to employees along with information about what is prohibited. Employers can do this by issuing written policy statements, job descriptions, and performance criteria. Written standards should also exist for promotions.

SET CLEAR TERMINATION CLAUSES IN THE EMPLOYMENT CONTRACT. The general principle applicable to contracts of employment of indefinite duration is that, in the absence of cause, the contract can only be terminated properly upon reasonable notice or payment in lieu thereof. Thus, an employment contract can contain clauses that benefit both parties. Common clauses that benefit employers include: confidentiality agreements, restrictive covenants, prohibition against moonlighting, patent assignments and invention ownership, severability clauses, and exclusive understanding.

Other clauses that could be negotiated to work to the advantage of the employer or the employee, include: terms of dismissal, golden handcuff clauses, golden parachute clauses, and definition of duties.

The purpose of a termination clause is to determine beforehand what the appropriate period of notice shall be. The following factors should also be kept in mind when preparing an employment contract:

- Termination clauses should be strictly adhered to by the employer or they may not be enforceable against the employee. Termination clauses should be reasonable, otherwise courts will bend over backwards if they regard them as unfair or invalid. In determining reasonableness the court will look at all the other provisions of the contract and the surrounding circumstances.
- Before drafting a restrictive covenant clause (e.g., noncompetition or nonsolicitation), determine what legitimate interests of the employer require protection.
- It is recommended to insert into the employment contract a clause that specifically provides for severance.
- Do not over-reach in a liquidated damages clause, otherwise it may become a penalty clause.

TREAT EMPLOYEES EQUALLY. If the employer discharges one employee for five unexcused absences, then another employee with five unexcused absences must also be discharged. Periodic training can help ensure that discharge policies are communicated and administered consistently by all supervisors.

GRIEVANCE PROCEDURES AND DUE PROCESS. Not only should grievance procedures be established to ensure due process for employees, they should also be administered consistently and fairly. For example, evidence should be available to the employee and the employer, and both parties should have the right to call witnesses and to refuse to testify against themselves. Furthermore, these grievance procedures should be clearly stated as company policy and communicated as such to employees. A typical grievance policy is shown in Exhibit 15.2.

Exhibit 15.2
A Typical Grievance Procedure

With good working relations it is to be expected that supervisory personnel and department heads will recognize and work to resolve employee problems and dissatisfactions at their first appearance and, therefore, that this appeal procedure should have limited usage.

Step 1: Discuss the problem or dissatisfaction with your supervisor who will attempt to resolve it in accordance with established personnel policies within *two working days*, unless there are extenuating circumstances.

Step 2: Should the problem remain unresolved, your supervisor will endeavor to make an appointment for you to discuss the matter with your department head within the next *three working days*.

Step 3: Should the problem continue to remain unresolved, the employee should present the problem or dissatisfaction in writing (see attached form) and forward it to the director, employee relations, who will either schedule a meeting with all interested parties, or will present a recommendation within *five working days* for a resolution of the problem based upon personnel policies and practices.

Most matters of employee concern should be resolved at the conclusion of Step. 3. However, for that unusual problem which may not have been resolved to the employee's satisfaction, the employee may request that the matter be brought to the attention of administration for consideration and decision. An administrative decision will be rendered and communicated in writing to all interested parties within *ten working days*. This decision will be final and binding.

Source: Thomasine Rendero, "Consensus: Grievance Procedure for Nonunionized Employees," *Personnel*, January–February 1980, 7. Reprinted by permission of the publisher. © 1980 American Management Association, New York. All rights reserved.

ESTABLISH PROGRESSIVE DISCIPLINE PROCEDURES.   A formal grievance policy should be accompanied by a progressive discipline policy. For most violations of company rules, firing should be the last step in a carefully regulated system of escalating discipline, often called **progressive discipline.** Maintaining accurate records during all phases of this process is crucial for building a valid justifiable cause for disciplinary discharge. As discussed in Chapter 8, the steps possible in progressive discipline procedures include:

- *Warning* may be oral at first, but should be written and signed by the employee, and a copy should be kept in the personnel files. Valid personnel files, along with a progressive discipline policy for discharge, can be the best defence, according to several cases regarding discharge for excessive absenteeism (see, for example, *Henry vs. Unique Envelope Inc. (1985), Ontario).*

- *Reprimand* is official, in writing, and placed in the employee's file.

- *Suspension* can be as short as part of a day, or as long as several months without pay, depending on the seriousness of the employee's offence and the circumstances.

- *Disciplinary transfer* may take the pressure off a situation that might explode into violence, or one in which personality conflict is a part of the disciplinary problem.

- *Demotion* can be a reasonable answer to problems of incompetence, or an alternative to layoff for economic reasons.

- *Discharge* is the last resort, used only when all else has failed, although it might be a reasonable immediate response to violence, theft, or falsification of records. But firing can be exceedingly painful, even if it is justified and well planned. Thus, some organizations carefully diagnose performance deficiencies prior to termination and occasionally reassign employees to different parts of the organization or trade top-level managers to other organizations.

An optional additional step in progressive discipline is the "last chance agreement." Before resorting to firing, an employer may be willing to grant an employee one more chance, but only with several stipulations. For example, instead of suspending or terminating an employee for excessive absenteeism, the employer may grant the employee one final fixed time period in which to improve.

Taking all these steps does not ensure that the problem will be solved—termination may still be necessary. The following advice may help in performing this difficult task:

- The termination interview should be brief. Normally, a 10–15 minute meeting is sufficient. A longer meeting increases the opportunity for the company representative (in this case, you) to make a mistake. Some mistakes can be costly.
- It is best to conduct the termination meeting in that person's office or in some office other than your own. If conducted in your office, you may be trapped into a lengthy harangue by a disgruntled individual who is using you to vent hostility, anger, and frustration.
- Many individuals hear very little after they understand they have lost their job. This is understandable. They often begin to think of their future [or] the anxiety and stress of having no job, and there is a strong concern about their family, especially if the individual is the chief wage earner in the family.

It is a good idea to role-play with someone before you actually do the termination. It is better yet if you can videotape the role-play(s). Practice can help iron out the bugs and discomfort and make the actual termination meeting easier and less cumbersome.[10]

STRUCTURING A SETTLEMENT.   The essential point in termination is to conclude a quick and quiet settlement. Thus, the HR manager must convey the settlement proposal in such a way that the employee perceives it as fair. If litigation is to be avoided, a good understanding of the employee's work history and terms and conditions of employment is essential. In the settlement offer, the following could be considered:

- *Income tax*: In many cases spreading severance payments over two taxation years might benefit the employee and put less financial strain on the employer. Also, a portion of the retirement allowance can be deducted from income and rolled into an RRSP or RPP.
- *Form of severance pay*: Consideration should be given to offering the employee either a *lump sum*, or *continued monthly salary* for a fixed period, or combination of the two.
- *Treatment of benefits*: Continuation of benefits (or some of them) tends to alleviate some employee concern over ongoing financial cost.
- *Relocation counselling*: Relocation counselling is being offered more and more especially to managerial and professional employees. Offering to pay for such services often results in smoother settlements.

Employer Strategies for Employee Rights on the Job

In order to protect employee rights on the job, employers must develop effective policies, procedures, and programs in regard to privacy and records access; cooperative acceptance and sexual harassment; and plant or office closing.

EMPLOYEE PRIVACY RIGHTS AND RECORDS ACCESS.   Concern for the privacy of personnel records and employee access to personnel files has only been emphasized since the early 1980s. As discussed previously, privacy legislation generally does not cover private employer–employee relationships. Nevertheless, many organizations are moving ahead on their own to establish policies and rules governing employee privacy and access rights. Early efforts in this area produced only a definition of employee privacy. Today, however, a significant number of companies have written policies regarding the privacy of personnel records. In addition, many provide employees with access to records containing information about themselves.

Employer concerns about employee privacy rights are also influencing pre-employment screening and the use of polygraph tests. Pre-hiring practices are being examined to ensure that only job-related information is collected, because collecting nonjob information is now considered an unjustified intrusion into the private lives of job applicants. Similar opinions are becoming widespread on the use of polygraph test results in selection and placement decisions.

EMPLOYEE RIGHTS TO COOPERATIVE ACCEPTANCE. While many issues are associated with employee rights to cooperative acceptance, sexual harassment has recently come to the fore as a concern for many employees and employers. Though this is being focused on here, race, age, disability, national origin, and religion should not be considered to be less significant.

What was perhaps once regarded by some people as good-natured fun between supervisors (or managers) and employees may today constitute sexual harassment, according to various human rights guidelines. Because employers are ultimately responsible, they need to be particularly concerned with developing strategies to prevent sexual harassment on the part of their employees.

Many employers are developing strategies to prevent sexual harassment. One such strategy includes the following steps:

- Raise affirmatively the issue of harassment, and the fact that it exists, to the rest of the organization. The HR manager should persuade top management to make it a rule that all discharges must be reviewed by a senior corporate officer or review board.
- Set up reporting (grievance) procedures for those who have been harassed. Because the employer is liable for sexual harassment, except where it can be shown the organization took immediate and appropriate corrective action (then the offending individual is guilty), it pays to have an established policy and system in place.
- Establish procedures for corroborating a sexual harassment charge. That is, the HR manager should make sure that the person charged with sexual harassment has the right to respond immediately after charges are made. Due process must be available to the alleged perpetrator as well as the alleged victim.
- Specify a set of steps in a framework of progressive discipline for perpetuators of sexual harassment. These could be the same steps used by the organization in treating any violation of organizational policies (see the progressive discipline procedures discussed earlier).
- Finally, make all employees aware of the company's position on sexual harassment. Provide support, such as training programs, for managers and supervisors.

Although implementing these steps does not guarantee the elimination of sexual harassment, it establishes a clear-cut policy in this important HR area.

Similarly, with respect to smoking, management is moving away from a short-sighted, cavalier approach toward developing and enforcing a formal smoking policy. Some of the reasons that push corporations to ban smoking, or to restrict it to certain areas, include:

- *Corporate image*: Smoking is no longer considered appropriate. The new breed of employees are more attracted to companies that restrict it.
- *Employee morale*: Smoking is a source of irritation and discomfort.
- *Liability*: Court rulings are convincing employers that they have a duty to provide a smoke-free work environment.
- *Passive smoker hazard*: Nonsmokers are affected and consequently illnesses are on the rise, absenteeism increases, and productivity diminishes.

EMPLOYEE RIGHTS TO PLANT/OFFICE CLOSING ARRANGEMENTS. Basically, employers are not legally obligated to notify employees if a facility is to be closed down or relocated. As in the question of discharge without cause, employers resist granting this right because it limits their flexibility. In addition, some employees argue that it really is better for them as well if management retains such information, because this helps the company remain operative for a while longer and they keep their jobs for this extra duration.

These arguments, however, are beyond the immediate interest of the employees involved in a potential or actual plant closing. And, despite their resistance, employers are recognizing the right to "humane" treatment when facilities are being closed. Therefore, some notify employees well in advance of the actual closing. While recognition of this right was largely initiated by the pressure of unions on management, many nonunion companies are now providing help, most commonly in the form of outplacement assistance.

Outplacement assistance is usually offered to individuals who are discharged or displaced, but it can have more dramatic value for entire workforces displaced because of plant/office closing. Outplacement assistance programs typically offer a number of benefits to employees, such as:

- Severance pay,
- Enhanced benefits,
- Four-week termination notification period,
- Training and development programs to help develop new skills and find other jobs,
- Double pay for overtime work needed to get the facility ready to close down,
- Retention bonus to encourage employees to stay until the time of actual closing.

TRENDS IN EMPLOYEE RIGHTS

Assessing Employee Rights Activities

When organizations recognize employee rights and establish programs to ensure they are observed, they achieve a match between employee rights and obligations and employer rights and obligations. In achieving this both organizations and employees benefit. Organizations benefit from reduced legal costs, since not observing many employee rights is illegal, and the fact that their images as good employers enhance organizational attractiveness. This, in turn, makes it easier to recruit from a pool of potentially qualified applicants. And, although it is suggested that expanded employee rights, especially job security, may reduce needed management flexibility, it may also be an impetus for better planning, resulting in increased profitability.

Increased profitability may also result from the benefits employees receive when their rights are observed: they feel that they are being treated fairly and with respect, and they experience increased self-esteem and a heightened sense of job security. Employees who perceive job security may be more productive and committed to the organization than those who do not. As employees begin to see the value of job security guarantees, organizations benefit through reduced wage increase demands and greater flexibility in job assignments. This is happening in many of the traditionally unionized manufacturing industries, where the protection of employee rights, especially job security, is considered as much a matter of survival as profitability. As discussed in Chapter 16, it is also a matter of concern for a new era of union–management relations.

An organization's employee rights activities can be assessed in many ways, some of which are more appropriate than others. For example, evaluating these activities by the size of legal costs is certainly appropriate in the areas of cooperative acceptance and unjustifiable dismissal. Where employee rights are not legally protected, using legal costs to assess these activities may be less appropriate. If organizations fail to observe those humane rights not now legally protected, however, they may soon find themselves using legal costs to evaluate all their employee rights activities. Many organizations recognize this and are moving to observe humane rights as well as legal rights. This seems particularly true for employee rights to privacy, access to records, and facility closing arrangements.

Considerable private information about workers exists in the computer databases kept by practically every organization. This information is available to a surprisingly wide range of people. Although data pertaining to medical history are relatively well protected, other types of data are not. Today, highly confidential information such as polygraph testing results, AIDS, drug testing, and even letters of reference can be accessed by computers.

Consequently, privacy must be a chief concern of the HR department. However, with the realities of current database systems privacy is extremely difficult to provide. Nevertheless, as database design advances, the ability to restrict retrieval by unauthorized personnel increases. In some cases, restrictions are handled on a item by item basis. For example, a mailing clerk needs to know all the employees' addresses for the engineering department. Most database systems (and especially HRIS as discussed in Chapter 4) can allow access to that individual by granting him or her "viewing only rights" to the engineering department's employee records for name and address only. In order to ensure privacy, a well-run computer application should attempt to address the following issues pertaining to privacy:

- *Access by interface*: It should not be possible to deduce the values of restricted data elements by manipulating the values of nonrestricted data elements.
- *Aggregation*: Screen access to personal data at the data element level is not sufficient, since information that is relatively innocuous at the level of the individual could be extremely sensitive at the aggregate level.
- *Executive intimidation*: A good access control system should maintain its integrity and be effective across ranks in the hierarchy.
- *Prying subordinates or co-workers*: The system should make it easy for a company to place special controls restricting employees from gaining access to the personal data of their superiors, executives, and co-workers in the same unit.
- *Absolute privacy*: Extremely sensitive personal data should be properly restricted to the single purpose for which the data were collected.[11]

Confidentiality of Employee Records on Computers

S U M M A R Y

Employee rights are gaining considerable attention in the 1990s. Though employees have won many legal rights over the years, the most controversial ones are those not legally protected or those left to the employer's discretion. Thus, the tribunals have a potentially significant role to play in the future of employee rights. Whether the courts and the legislative and executive bodies move to increase the number of legally protected employee rights depends to some extent on how employers behave in the area of unprotected employee rights. If they take a proactive position, the courts and legislative bodies may be less inclined to legislate both job security and on-the-job employee rights. At this time, a great deal of momentum has gathered to provide some type of legal protection for job security rights. Nevertheless, HR managers and employers can still have an impact in shaping the form of such legal protection.

Although many employers claim that, essentially, many of their rights have been taken away, they still retain the right to terminate workers for poor performance, excessive absenteeism, unsafe conduct, and generally poor organizational citizenship. It is critical, however, for employers to maintain accurate records of these employee actions, and to inform the employees of where they stand. To be safe, it is also advisable for employers to have a grievance process for employees so as to ensure that due process is respected.

Today it is more important than ever to keep objective and orderly personnel files. They are critical evidence that employers have treated their employees fairly and with respect and have not violated any laws. Without these, organizations may get caught on the short end of a law suit. Many employers are moving on their own initiative to give their employees the right to access their personnel files and to prohibit the file information from being given to others without the employee's consent. In addition, employers are omitting from their personnel files any nonjob-related information and avoiding hiring practices that solicit that type of information.

Although employers have the right to close down a facility without any notification, many are notifying their employees in advance of the closing. This is true even in nonunion companies. In addition to giving notification, employers are implementing out-placement assistance programs. These offer employees retraining for new jobs, counselling and aid in finding new jobs or in getting transfers, provisions for severance pay, and even retention bonuses for those who stay until closing time. Closing a facility with notification and with outplacement assistance seems to produce positive results for the organization and minimize the negative effects for the employees.

Finally, in the area of employee rights to cooperative acceptance, it is necessary for employers to prevent sexual harassment. This can be done with top-management support, grievance procedures, verification procedures, training for all employees, and appraisal and compensation policies that reward those who practise anti-harassment behaviour and punish those who do not. Where appropriate, it is also useful to develop policies in cooperation with the union in order to prevent harassment. Union cooperation should be sought on many issues, as discussed in the next chapter.

POSTSCRIPT

Firing an employee is always difficult for the HR manager. Unfortunately, he or she must be involved in this process. Not only are there legal repercussions to consider, but the sit-uation is highly emotionally charged. Recently, there has been an increase in the number of incidents in which disgruntled employees reacted violently (e.g., shooting, killing) during or immediately after the termination of their employment. Two such cases were reported in the media at the beginning of 1992. In the first case (January 1992) a fired General Dynamics worker killed his union representative and wounded his former supervisor; in another case (February 1992), three workers were shot and killed at a Waterloo, Ontario glove plant by a worker who had been suspended from his job. Although General Dynamic officials claim that the company followed a "long, deliberate procedure" before dismissing employees, it is obvious that the procedure did not work in the case mentioned above. This has set up an entirely new syndrome, "fatal retaliation" at work.[12]

In order to deal with the numerous unpleasant and often risky facets of dismissing an employee, HR managers must become more sophisticated in their approach. Some of the ingredients for the approach have been known for quite a while, others are being experimented with. HR managers know, for example, that the interview itself should be short; they also know that they should come to the interview well prepared, and armed with legal, financial, and other factual data. As for the emerging strategies intended to soften the blow, psychologists have come to the rescue of HR managers by offering a host of principles pertaining to the *art of firing*. First, a new vocabulary is being introduced, denoting a more positive approach to dismissal—we do not "fire" anymore, rather we "de-hire." Additionally, because the actual delivery of the message during the termination interview is crucial, it has to be carefully worded; some experts believe that the first two or three sentences are the key to a successful termination. Consequently, popular books and magazines containing "prepared statements to suit all occasions" are flourishing. Here is a sample:

Sally, it is with regret that I must advise you that effective today, your services will no longer be required. You have not been able to stimulate new business and your clients have been complaining that they have not seen you for months. We have discussed the situation three times in the past four months but there has been no change. The company is prepared to provide you with assistance in the form of $xxx in severance, plus benefits to September 1, xxxx. I regret that we had to take this action, but I feel it's right for both you and the company.

Or another example:

James, I have a very difficult task to perform this afternoon, which is to tell you that effective immediately you are being relieved of your position with Widgets Inc. We both know that things have not been working out for you lately. We have designed a severance package to support you as follows...

You probably have a number of personal effects to take home from your office. If you would rather do this later, let me know or contact Frank Jones who will arrange a time for you to return.

James, I'm sorry it had to come to this. I'd like to wish you the very best for the future. It goes without saying that if I can be of help, let me know.[13]

While these suggestions could be used for illustrative purposes, it is hoped that HR managers will not use a prepackaged formula as is. While no one can dismiss the difficulties encountered during the termination interview, borrowing someone else's wording risks making the situation artificial. What can be more instrumental is being correct, candid, and straightforward; this is the preference of the vast majority of de-hired employees.

REVIEW AND ANALYSIS QUESTIONS

1. What is the strategic importance to the organization of protecting employee rights?
2. Discuss some legal protection now being offered to employees that results from recent federal or provincial acts and/or court/tribunal decisions.
3. On what grounds can employees be legally discharged? What do you think the most common reason is for termination decisions?
4. Identify and discuss the consequences for the organization and its HR department resulting from laws concerning employee rights to privacy and access to records.
5. What kind of behaviour constitutes sexual harassment? How should an organization prevent those behaviours from occurring? Under what conditions can an employer be held legally responsible for sexual harassment of its employees?
6. What strategies exist for employers to ensure employee job security rights?
7. Outline and discuss what is meant by a progressive disciplinary procedure.
8. What employee rights must an employer satisfy when closing or relocating a facility?

CASE STUDY

WHAT'S WRONG WITH WHAT'S RIGHT?

Stuart Campbell, now 35, moved slowly down the front steps of the courthouse and squinted as the last rays of sunlight pierced through downtown Winnipeg. It was a long day in his life; once again he had relived, before a Manitoba Superior Court, a tortuous two years of his past. He had spent the entire day recalling the details of his past employment with Nako Electronics, a major marketer of audio tapes in Canada. Nako had a considerable stake in Stuart. Today, both sides had made concluding arguments before the court in a trial initiated by Nako to overturn a private arbitrator's ruling that it had wrongfully terminated Stuart. The arbitrator's decision and the award of $500,000 plus interest of $82,083.50 were a bitter pill for Nako to swallow for having terminated their regional sales representative.

Stuart hesitated for a moment at the foot of the courthouse steps and came back to the present; he had agreed to meet his attorney, Jim Baldwin, at the Steak and Brew for a couple of drinks and to unwind after the courtroom tension. His spirits began to pick up as he manoeuvered through the city traffic, but he could not help thinking how, within a year's time, his good job had gone so bad on him.

Five years ago, Stuart was riding high as the regional representative for Nako covering all the prairies and western Canada. Stuart, a hard driver, contracted with Nako and then boosted the sluggish sales of their audio tapes from less than $200,000 to a $1 million business in about fourteen months. In fact, business was going so well for Stuart that he began driving a Mercedes-Benz 450 SEL. But that is when Mike Hammond, vice-president of marketing at Nako Electronics, took notice of Stuart. On one of his visits to Stuart's territory, Mike commented that he really liked Stuart's car. Mike remarked that he was making a trip to Vancouver soon. "I distinctly remember Mike saying he would like to have a Buick," Stuart testified. "He didn't want anything as fancy as I had, because a new Buick would be adequate and, after all, he wanted me to bear the expense!"

Mike unfortunately could not be in court that day to defend himself; he had died unexpectedly last year of a heart attack. During the trial, though, Nako had to defend a number of allegations made against him. It seems that some of Stuart's fellow workers suffered a similar fate. Not only had Stuart refused to go along with Mike's car scheme but he had also refused to invest in a phonograph cartridge business begun by Mike, which Stuart believed was (forgive a pun) phoney. Mike, in fact, had approached all of Nako's sales representatives to invest in the cartridge company at $1,250 a share, a company in which Mike and two other associates paid $1 a share for 80 percent of the stock. Stuart's attorney made sure that two of Stuart's former fellow sales representatives testified at the court proceedings that they were mysteriously fired after refusing Mike's demands to invest in his side company.

In the year following Stuart's successful boost of sales and Mike's thwarted attempts at a commercial shakedown, Nako increased Stuart's sales quota by more than 75 percent. As Stuart further testified, Nako sabotaged a substantial proportion of his sales by refusing to give his large customers promotional assistance. In the fall of that year, Nako fired Stuart without explanation. Nako argued in court that they did not need a reason to fire Stuart, and besides, he was not meeting his new, increased sales quota. Moreover, the company argued, Mike could not very well defend himself against the charges of Stuart and the others.

Stuart had rehashed these details many times with his attorney, both during the private arbitration hearing and during numerous rehearsals for the trial. As he arrived at the Steak and Brew, he hoped he could put these memories behind him. After a few drinks, Jim summarized the day's proceedings and expressed cautious optimism for the final outcome. "But you know Stuart," mused Jim, "If you would have kicked in the 10 or 15K that Hammond demanded, you would have outlived that old son-of-a-—, you'd have a business worth over $4 million in sales today, and we wouldn't be having this drink!"

Case Question

Provide a detailed analysis of the case.

NOTES

1. The case of Clarke Transport Canada, Ltd. and L.L. Desrosiers (Secretary) is cited in *Arbitration Service Reporter* 10, 3 (March 1986): 2–3.

2. *"Report Bulletin No. 24," Human Resource Management in Canada,* February 1985, 3.

3. G. Trudeau, "Employee Rights vs. Management Rights: Some Reflections Regarding Dismissal," in *Canadian Readings in Personnel and Human Resource Management*, ed. S.L. Dolan and R.S. Schuler (St. Paul, Minn.: West Publishing Co., 1987), 367–78.

4. D. Harris, *Wrongful Dismissal* (Toronto: Richard DeBoo Publishers, 1984).

5. *Hiring and Firing Newsletter*, March 1989.

6. *Firing and Hiring Newsletter*, February 1988.

7. K. Bullock, "Termination of Employment," *Human Resource Management in Canada* (revised), August 1985, 75,000.

8. "Report Bulletin No. 37," *Human Resource Management in Canada*, March 1986, 4.

9. G. Munchus, "An update on smoking: Employees' rights and employers' responsibilities," *Personnel*, August 1987, 46.

10. L.D. Foxman and W.L. Polsky, "Ground Rules for Terminating Workers," *Personnel Journal*, July 1984, 32. See also Bullock, "Termination of Employment," 75,023–75,024.

11. D. Harris, "A Matter of Privacy: Managing Personnel Data in Company Computers," *Personnel*, February 1987, 40.

12. S. Pack, "Fatal Retaliation: Employers search for ways to stop violent outbursts at the workplace," *The Montreal Gazette*, 15 March 1992, B7.

13. *Hiring and Firing Newsletter*, May 1988.

CHAPTER SIXTEEN

LABOUR RELATIONS

KEYNOTE ADDRESS

Shirley G.E. Carr
Former President, Canadian Labour Congress

The Role and Importance of the Labour Movement in Canada

The collective bargaining system is at the cutting edge of social change. Many of the things won at the bargaining table have later been made available to all through the political system. Through collective bargaining many workers will achieve job security and the goals of affirmative action, including pay equity, will be realized for thousands of women. It is also at the bargaining table that we continue our fight against overtime, and pursue shorter working hours, better vacations, and a shorter working life as a way of reducing unemployment, especially for our younger people, many of whom face the possibility of a lifetime without steady employment.

However, what is gained at the bargaining table is often lost because of government policies that victimize workers and blame them for failures of economic policy. Even before the current recession, the federal government's policies exacerbated the adversarial relationship between management and labour. This has been happening while government and business rhetoric has espoused a more cooperative, less adversarial relationship. Legislated wage freezes and wage controls raise serious questions about the desire for a more cooperative relationship.

The dominant issues shaping the workforce today are mass unemployment, declining real wages, the growing polarization of jobs into good and bad jobs, and the alarming increase in poverty. Nearly four million Canadians are living on incomes below the poverty line. Over a million Canadian children are growing up in poverty. Among the Western industrialized countries only the United States has a higher rate of child poverty.

At the bargaining table labour sees both the public and private sectors attempt to extract concessions, and to roll back wages and working conditions, vacations, and employment levels. We see cutbacks in staff layoffs or through attrition, while demands for overtime increase. Contracting-out in the public sector has eroded job security. The replacement of full-time jobs with temporary and casual jobs has meant low wages, low benefits, and no job security.

As new technologies are introduced into the workplace, workers are called upon to adapt, adjust, retrain, and relocate. As competition for global markets increases, workers in Canada are urged to be more competitive by accepting lower wages and reducing demands on social services. This kind of approach to competitiveness, however, amounts to a fundamental attack on workers' living standards and on their basic rights. In effect, the survival of capital or the corporation takes priority over labour, people, and communities.

The labour movement shoulders a weighty responsibility in challenging narrow economic interests, and in promoting a broad social and economic agenda. From labour's perspective our economic and social goals must reflect a renewed national commitment to full employment with an emphasis on permanent and meaningful jobs, and new patterns of work with adequate personal or family income. They must also entail a commitment to providing basic social services—education, health care, social security, unemployment insurance, and child care. These social objectives, in turn, require a commitment to finding new and more effective ways of redistributing wealth and power among both the people and the regions of this country.

The labour movement will continue to press for economic equality so that all Canadians can share in the prosperity that our economy is capable of producing. Labour totally rejects the view that inequality is a necessary price to pay for prosperity or competitive advantage. This view is as groundless in economic terms as it is morally.

The labour movement recognizes that Canada's economy, not unlike those of other countries, is undergoing rapid change brought about by the increasing mobility of both financial and real capital and by technological change. This state of affairs increases the need for a mixed economy. Labour believes that democratically elected governments have a responsibility to manage the market economy. We not only accept, but welcome, the use of public authority in achieving our economic objectives by transferring income directly, by providing goods and services, and by regulating private sector economic activity.

The workplace must be subject to greater democratic control to make work life itself more fulfilling, to ensure that workers share in the benefits of economic progress, and to make our economy more productive. Unilateral management initiatives to involve employees in decisions at the workplace through techniques such as teamwork and quality of work life programs should not be confused with unionization and collective bargaining or other mechanisms designed to bring about a form of democracy in industry.

Unionization has long been viewed by industrial relations specialists as a system of workplace governance that provides a counterbalance to managerial power. Unionized workers are more likely to challenge management proposals and more apt to come up with workable solutions to problems than are employees in nonunionized firms, where any challenge is perceived as threatening to managerial authority.

Having a union involves a number of formal mechanisms for conflict resolution through which collaborative problem solving can occur. For example, negotiation between unions and management is itself a form of joint problem solving and occurs routinely in the day-to-day handling of grievances and in collective bargaining. In fact, workers' participation, instituted in the context of unionization, is likely to be more productive than participation by their nonunion counterparts.

Unionization reduces turnover as well as wage inequality within a firm and between different establishments. In so doing, it contributes to longer job tenure, and with it, the accumulation of knowledge, experience, and expertise within the workplace. By reducing wage inequality, unions promote cooperation and the sharing of tacit knowledge among workers in the same company or plant, which indirectly increases productivity. If unions are to enhance productivity, the union must be an equal partner. There is no evidence to support the view that an authoritarian, nonunion strategy is even justified on the basis of economic efficiency.

While collective bargaining must be the cornerstone of worker participation, other forms of labour–management cooperation are important mechanisms for meeting the global challenges that lie ahead for the nation. For example, at the national level, labour and management have demonstrated an ability to address important policy issues constructively. Labour is now working on training with business and community interests as partners through the Canadian Labour Force Development Board and similar boards and councils at the local sectorial level.

Such cooperation must find its way to the individual firm level. Unions have a great deal of expertise to offer management in improving the operation of the workplace to the benefit of all. In the successful workplaces of the future, the confrontational approach will have been abandoned in favour of a management approach that treats its employees, and their unions, as valuable partners rather than as the enemy.

• • • •

The Keynote Address by Shirley Carr, who was president of the Canadian Labour Congress until 1992, provides a unique opportunity to understand labour–management relationships and the objectives each group has. Ms. Carr asserts that all participants—labour, management, and government—must work cooperatively and take joint responsibility for reaching solutions. To reach that point, the participants must engage in collaborative problem solving and information sharing: processes that are integral to union–management negotiations. A labour–management partnership is the key to meeting future global challenges. The objective of the chapter is to introduce the system of labour relations in Canada, to discuss the structure and roles of unions within this system, and to present an overview of the collective bargaining process as well as describe ways and means to solve industrial conflicts.

• • • •

THE LABOUR RELATIONS SYSTEM IN CANADA

Principal Features of the Labour Relations System in Canada

An understanding of union–management relationships is facilitated by seeing them set in a **labour relations system (LRS)** or **industrial relations system (IRS)**. Using a simplified explanation of "systems approaches," it is possible to define the LRS as comprising "a complex of private and public activities, operating in a specified environment, which is concerned with the allocation of rewards to employees for their services and the conditions under which these services are rendered."[1] Exhibit 16.1 summarizes the forces and actors operating within the LRS, identifying the major components and subunits. It shows that the LRS is influenced by a number of environmental subsystems—economic, political, legal and social—as well as the goals, values, and power of the main actors: labour, management, and government.

Labour may be nonexempt employees or union members; management are the exempt employees (they may also be the owners); and governments and public agencies form the third party to the LRS (e.g., labour relations boards or public sector employees). These three components were labelled by John Dunlop, a pioneer in the field of industrial relations, as "actors" (denoting both individuals and groups). The actors, therefore, include managers, as individuals or management teams, and employees or their organizations (associations or unions formed to represent their collective concerns).

Each of the groups identified in the LRS model has traditionally had different goals. Workers are interested in improved working conditions, due process, wages, and opportunities; unions are interested in their own survival, growth, and acquisition of power, which depend on their ability to maintain the support of the employees by providing for their needs. Management's goals are concerned with profits, certainty, market share and growth; the organization also seeks to preserve managerial prerogatives to direct the workforce, to receive promotions, and to achieve personal goals. Government is interested in a stable and healthy economy, protection of individual rights, due process, and safety and fairness in the workplace.

These sets of goals, and particularly those of unions and management, are important because they explain the very essence of the union–management relationship.

ADVERSARIAL RELATIONSHIP. When the goals of union and management are seen as incompatible, an **adversarial system** emerges. Labour and management both attempt to get a bigger cut of the pie while government attempts to protect its own interests. Under adversarial union–management relations, the union's role is to gain concessions from management during collective bargaining and to see that the contract is enforced through the grievance procedure, if necessary. The union is an outsider and critic.

Historically, unions came about due to the extremely poor working conditions in pre-union times. As a result, unions have adopted an adversarial role in their interactions with management. Their focus has been on wages and working conditions, and they have continually attempted to get "more and better," respectively. This approach works well in economic boom times, but becomes difficult when the economy is not healthy. In fact, high unemployment and the threat of continued job losses have recently induced unions, as well as management, to revise their relationship. Many unions have begun to enter into new, collaborative efforts with employers.

COOPERATIVE RELATIONSHIP. In a **cooperative system**, the union is a partner, not a critic, and it takes joint responsibility with management for reaching a solution. Thus, a cooperative system requires that unions and management engage in problem solving, information sharing, and integration of outcomes. Cooperative systems have been a major LRS component in countries such as Sweden and Germany. There, they have built a cooperative mechanism (co-determination is discussed in Chapter 17) into the labour system. There have been occasions, however, when Canadian management and labour have

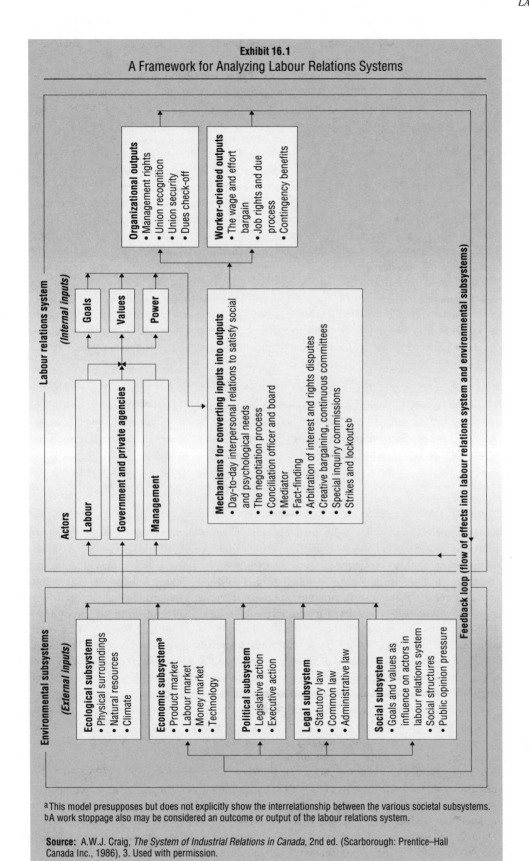

Exhibit 16.1
A Framework for Analyzing Labour Relations Systems

Labour relations system

(Internal inputs)

Organizational outputs
- Management rights
- Union recognition
- Union security
- Dues check-off

Worker-oriented outputs
- The wage and effort bargain
- Job rights and due process
- Contingency benefits

Goals · Values · Power

Actors
- Labour
- Government and private agencies
- Management

Mechanisms for converting inputs into outputs
- Day-to-day interpersonal relations to satisfy social and psychological needs
- The negotiation process
- Conciliation officer and board
- Mediator
- Fact-finding
- Arbitration of interest and rights disputes
- Creative bargaining, continuous committees
- Special inquiry commissions
- Strikes and lockouts[b]

Feedback loop (flow of effects into labour relations system and environmental subsystems)

Environmental subsystems

(External inputs)

Ecological subsystem
- Physical surroundings
- Natural resources
- Climate

Economic subsystem[a]
- Product market
- Labour market
- Money market
- Technology

Political subsystem
- Legislative action
- Executive action

Legal subsystem
- Statutory law
- Common law
- Administrative law

Social subsystem
- Goals and values as influence on actors in labour relations system
- Social structures
- Public opinion pressure

[a] This model presupposes but does not explicitly show the interrelationship between the various societal subsystems.
[b] A work stoppage also may be considered an outcome or output of the labour relations system.

Source: A.W.J. Craig, *The System of Industrial Relations in Canada*, 2nd ed. (Scarborough: Prentice–Hall Canada Inc., 1986), 3. Used with permission.

worked together to solve a problem. Typically, this has been the case in the domain of health and safety, as indicated in Chapter 14.

Successful projects in other domains, for instance, the Shell Sarnia plant (mentioned in Chapter 13), have involved unions in cooperative efforts to solve problems of concern to both parties. A dramatic example of the emerging cooperative union attitudes can be found in the country's steel industry. Since the late 1980s, top industry executives have met with the United Steelworkers' Union to thrash out common strategies for dealing with the industry's weak points. The two groups formalized their relationship by creating the Canadian Steel Trade Conference, a combination think tank and lobby organization. Because the steel firms and the United Steelworkers have agreed to set aside collective bargaining sore points, issues such as technological change and adjustment to free trade are addressed with less than the usual acrimony. In fact, the steel group's experiment has attracted attention elsewhere in the country. Among the unions said to be interested in pursuing similar arrangements are the Energy and Chemical Workers and the International Woodworkers of America.

Another cooperative approach is the use of an in-house fact-finder appointed by union–management agreement. This person develops and suggests alternative solutions to labour relations problems. The fact-finder is a neutral party who has the trust and confidence of both sides and whose primary concern is employee participation in decision making. The fact-finder is often able to alter an adversarial relationship between union and management.

A GLOBAL PERSPECTIVE OF THE LRS IN CANADA. Although traditionally the LRS in Canada was very adversarial, the economic shocks of the late 1960s, early 1980s, and early 1990s have resulted in a cooperative effort by all parties involved. Labour, management, and the government now focus more on achieving a consensus and on the expansion of workers' participation by right.

Until the early 1960s, the Canadian Labour Congress (CLC) sought to protect and enhance the terms and conditions of employment of their members via negotiations with employers. Bread and butter today rather than pie in the sky tomorrow was the primary union strategy. The labour movement had little direct influence on government policy. Canadian employers were fragmented in their approach to organized labour. Although many employers' associations existed, some on a provincial and some on a national level, there was no common strategy for dealing with unions. Because of the unwillingness of employers to bargain collectively unless forced to do so, relations between labour and management were, in general, strained and distant. During this period of adversarial relations, the government considered its primary role to be that of protecting the public from the disruptions that could result from industrial conflict. Consultation began to take place with various employees' associations, with impasses resolved unilaterally by the employer. At that time, public-sector unionism grew rapidly, and government employees who were discontented with consultation were demanding the same rights as private-sector workers. Legislation toward that end was then introduced in many jurisdictions.[2]

The LRS changed between the 1960s and the 1990s. Economic recessions and high inflation led to an increase in union militancy. For example, during the 1970s, Canada had the second highest level of time lost due to strikes in the Western world. Several approaches were tried by the Canadian government to control (or influence) the outcomes of collective bargaining during that period: policies ranged from wage–price guidelines (1969–1970), to mandatory wage–price controls (1975–1978), to complete federal public-sector compensation control; several provincial jurisdictions also controlled wages in the public sector. The unilateral imposition of wage and price controls triggered strong opposition from both labour and management. Government then searched for alternative means by which to foster consensus in the LRS. Experiments with various procedures, such as fact-finding, first contact arbitration, grievance mediation, and bargaining by objectives followed. At the same time, a great deal of new legislation was passed in order to improve substantive conditions, not only for unionized workers but also for nonunion employees, in the area of health and safety and human rights.

During the early 1980s, the Canadian LRS was again influenced by the deep recession. Employers adopted a tougher stand at the bargaining table. At the same time, Canadian unions resisted demands for concessions more effectively than their U.S. counterparts. Whereas in the U.S.A. as many as three out of four agreements during that period contained concessions, in Canada the rate was no more than one in ten. Nonetheless, wage and price increases slowed significantly during 1983–1984. Similar trends are emerging for the 1990s. Organized labour is refusing to "buy the call to get on board the competitiveness train" with management. In the face of widespread layoffs, plant closures, and downsizing, unions are placing greater emphasis on job security and income protection measures. The labour movement has taken a strong stand against concessionary bargaining.[3] However, contrary to official labour movement stands, many local unions are eager to cooperate with management in order to save their memberships' jobs.

While on the surface it looked as if the Canadian LRS remained adversarial, in fact, from the early 1960s to the 1990s, a slow but systematic shift took place toward a more cooperative relationship between the partners. This shift, labelled *tripartism*, refers to formal or quasi-formal decision-making structures in which representatives of labour, business, and government attempt to reach consensus on policy issues of mutual concern. The major features of this cooperative tripartism included:

- The increased influence of the CLC on government policies;
- The emergence of a loose national employers' organization, the Business Council on National Issues (BCNI), which has become the most influential business actor at the national level;
- The creation by the federal government of task forces composed of both labour and industry to study the problems and prospects of twenty-three Canadian industries; the Major Projects Task Force was created to develop a strategy for implementing major construction projects. The equal composition of labour and business representatives on this task force led to the issuance of a consensus report in 1981;
- The creation of a National Labour Market and Productivity Centre composed of representatives of labour and business is another example of tripartism.

While on a national level the LRS seems to be characterized by tripartism, this does not necessarily mean that the same level of cooperation is characteristic of the plant level.

Labour relations is related to many other HR functions and operates in a complex legal context. Because this context influences organizing as well as other collective bargaining activities, an entire section in this chapter is devoted to the legal considerations for unionization and collective bargaining.

Relationships to and Influences of Labour Relations

RECRUITMENT AND SELECTION. Unionization may have a direct impact on who is hired and the conditions under which that applicant is hired. Also, employers are bound by jurisdictions regarding replacement of workers during a strike. In all Canadian jurisdictions except Quebec (as per Bill 45 of 1977) and Ontario, employers are permitted to hire workers to replace striking employees. Unions can also play an important role in deciding who is to be promoted, given a new job assignment, put into training programs, terminated, or laid off. This role is facilitated by established seniority provisions in union–management contracts. It is further strengthened by court and Human Rights Commission decisions that recognize seniority provisions as part of a bona fide seniority system.[4] The "last hired, first fired" principle is still the common practice for unionized employees.

COMPENSATION. One of the most important goals of employees is an acceptable wage and adequate benefits. Because it is perceived that unions can force employers to provide these, employees are more likely to find unionization attractive. The threat of possible unionization, however, is often enough to cause employers to provide better than satisfactory wages and benefits.

EMPLOYEE RIGHTS. When employers treat individuals with fairness and respect, they may be more inclined to exhibit loyalty toward their employers. The more rights employers recognize and observe, the better employees feel and the less likely they are to form a union. Once workers are unionized, the union will help ensure that both legal and humane employee rights are observed.

QWL AND PRODUCTIVITY. As described in Chapter 13, many HR programs for QWL and productivity improvement are jointly undertaken by union and management. Although not all unions support the QWL programs, many unions do offer active support and the involvement (generally voluntary) of their members.

UNIONIZATION OF EMPLOYEES

Unionizing or **unionization** is the effort by employees and outside agencies (unions or associations) to band together and act as a single unit when dealing with management over issues related to work. The most common form into which employees organize is the **union**, an organization with the legal authority to negotiate with the employer on their behalf—over wages, hours, and other conditions of employment—and to administer the ensuing agreement.

Exhibit 16.2 shows the principal components involved in employee unionization as part of the LRS.

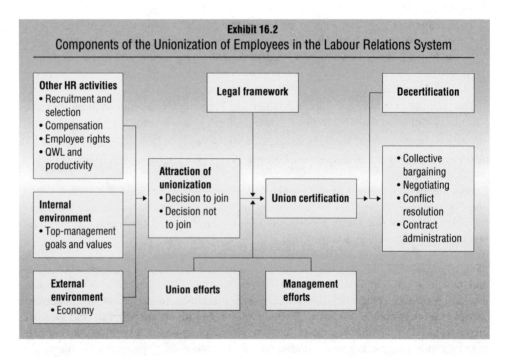

Exhibit 16.2
Components of the Unionization of Employees in the Labour Relations System

Purposes and Importance of Unionization

On the one hand, the existence of a union—or even the possibility of one—can exert a significant influence on the ability of an employer to manage vital human resources. On the other hand, unions can often help employees get what they want (e.g., better wages and job security) from employers.

IMPORTANCE TO EMPLOYERS. Understanding the unionizing or organizing process, its causes, and its consequences is an important part of HRM. Unionization often results in management having less flexibility in hiring, job assignments, and the introduction of new work methods such as automation and inflexible job structures. And, very often, unions obtain for their members rights that nonunionized employees do not legally have. This, of course, forces organizations with unions to consider their employees' reactions to many more decisions than would be the case otherwise.

There are some cases, however, in which employers who do not have to deal with unions and want to remain that way give more consideration and provide more benefits to their employees. Consequently, the claim that it is more expensive for a company to operate with unionized rather than nonunionized employees is not always true. Unions also assist employers through wage concessions or cooperation and assistance in workplace joint efforts, such as quality circles, Scanlon Plans, or safety committees, allowing employers to survive particularly difficult times and, in fact, remain profitable and competitive.

IMPORTANCE TO EMPLOYEES. Surveys show that the four most commonly expressed goals of employees (irrespective of whether or not they are unionized) are: (1) earning a living wage, (2) working in a safe environment, (3) having decent hours of work, and (4) having comfortable physical surroundings. These goals are particularly interesting in light of the recent emphasis on innovative management philosophies, such as employee participation, quality circles, and job enrichment. For many workers, having a good QWL means first having a decent income and good working conditions. Once these are provided, other dimensions of QWL may take on greater importance. By the same token, attempts at QWL improvements via more participation or quality circles are less appropriate during times when some employees are asked to make wage concessions and others are being laid off.

Three basic beliefs underlie the legal framework for labour relations in Canada:
1. Employees should be free to organize.
2. Representatives of employees should be able to engage employers in bargaining.
3. Employees and employers should be free to invoke sanctions in support of their positions, employees should be free to withdraw services, and employers to close their doors.

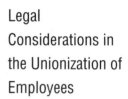

Legal Considerations in the Unionization of Employees

THE ORIGINS OF LABOUR RELATIONS LEGISLATION. In Canada a multiplicity of labour relations legislation exists at both the federal and provincial levels. Separate acts, or special clauses in the general legislation, exist for different sectors, industries, and workers. According to one expert, the Canadian constitutional division of powers has led to the most decentralized industrial relations system in the world.[5] The federal government has jurisdiction over a number of industries, such as inter-provincial transportation and communications, but manufacturing, mining, and other industries fall under provincial jurisdiction even though companies may operate plants on a national basis. During times of national emergency, the federal government may invoke the War Measures Act of 1918 to legislate in the labour relations field for industries considered to be essential to the emergency. This occurred during World War II.

After the war, labour relations legislation reverted to provincial jurisdiction, with the provinces having jurisdiction over 90 percent of the labour force. For a number of years following World War II, many of the provinces passed legislation modelled after the federal Industrial Relations Disputes and Investigation Act (IRDI Act, 1948). It specified the rights of workers to join unions, made provisions for the certification of unions as bargaining agents by a labour relations board, required unions and management to negotiate in good faith, specified a number of unfair labour practices by both unions and management, and developed a two-stage compulsory conciliation process that had to be complied with before strikes or lockouts became legal.

In the 1950s, several provinces began to move away from the IRDI Act model, introducing features into their own labour relations legislation to meet the special needs of their jurisdiction. At this time labour legislation in Canada began to evolve into eleven different policies—one federal and ten provincial. The most radical departure from the IRDI Act model was the retreat from the two-stage compulsory conciliation procedure to alternatives that included greater flexibility and a greater degree of voluntarism, and allowed more options to governments in the method of settling disputes.

LABOUR RELATIONS LEGISLATION TODAY. It would be beyond the scope of this chapter to attempt to describe the contents of the labour relations legislation in each jurisdiction. Instead, the following sections provide a cursory review of legislation that characterizes the Canadian labour laws, with special emphasis on common features as well as distinctive legislation.

Certification of Bargaining Unit. Under Canadian legislation, an employer may voluntarily recognize a union and negotiate a collective agreement. However, if the employer refuses to voluntarily recognize the union, it may apply to the labour relations board for certification. Legislation across Canada since the 1950s requires that unions have a majority of employees as members in a bargaining unit before they can apply for a **certification election**. In recent years, however, some jurisdictions have made the requirement less than 50 percent, in the sense that they require 50 percent of *those voting* rather than 50 percent of all members of the bargaining unit. Those who fail to cast ballots are no longer considered as voting against the certification of the union. Except for British Columbia, the certification process is different from that in the U.S.A. in that in Canada the majority of unions are certified without a vote if an officer of the appropriate labour relations board finds, on the basis of signed membership cards, that the union truly does have the support of a majority. In British Columbia, following a change in 1984, a vote is required in every case of union certification.

Labour Relations Boards. **Labour relations boards (LRBs)** exist in all jurisdictions except for the province of Quebec, where this body has been replaced by a group of some twenty commissioners. The boards were set up to administer the respective labour relations acts. Usually they are tripartite: composed of union representatives, management representatives, and a neutral chair (usually a civil servant). LRBs have much flexibility in their procedures, particularly those for solving conflicts.

Determination of the unit appropriate for collective bargaining is one of the more important functions of the board. It may accept the unit described in the union's application or it may alter the unit, usually by adding or dropping employees in order to ensure homogeneity, viability, and representative characteristics of the employing organization. Units may include all plant workers of one employer, plant workers of several employers in the same area, workers in more than one plant of the same employer, parts of a plant, or particular occupations or crafts. Most of the acts provide some guidelines specifying what constitutes an "appropriate" unit. For example, they may suggest that professional employees would constitute a single unit or that particular crafts or occupations such as carpenters, watchmen, supervisors, etc. may each be included in their own bargaining units.

Most acts also specify certain categories of workers that are not covered by the legislation. Generally these include management and employees working in a confidential capacity, as well as doctors, dentists, and lawyers. These employees do not have the protection of legislation, should they wish to establish unions to represent them in negotiations with their employers.

In establishing the appropriate unit, boards generally pay close attention to the wishes of the employees, the history of bargaining in similar units, the type of union organization (industrial or craft union), and the employees involved (plant, office, technical, professional, and craft). Most determinations involve a single plant, and this is a principal reason why collective bargaining operates on a local plant basis.

Considerable time may elapse between an application for certification and the determination by the LRB of the need for a vote. During this period, employees could be swayed against the certification or lose interest for one reason or another, for example, because of inaction brought on by the delay. Since these delays have little to do with the applicant union, several of the acts provide for pre-hearing votes. Under such a provision, the LRB will conduct a vote upon receipt of the application. In Ontario and Quebec and for federal employees, for example, a pre-hearing vote will be held upon request from the union, if the board is satisfied that at least 35 percent of the employees in the voting constituency are members of the trade union. A pre-hearing vote usually covers the unit specified in the application, although this may be modified by the board on the basis of an examination of its records. The resulting ballots are sealed until the certification proceedings have been completed. Depending on the outcome of these proceedings, the ballots will then be counted to determine whether the union is to be certified.

Decertification.   All acts provide orderly procedures for decertifying unions. Generally, application for **decertification** can be made if the certified union fails to bargain, or if after a certain period either another union claims majority support of the employees or the majority of employees indicate that they do not want to be represented by a union. Where an agreement has been signed, application for decertification can be made only at specified periods, generally within two months before the agreement's termination.

Applications for decertification may be made by the employees in the unit or by the employer if the union fails to bargain. Some provincial laws—for example those of Ontario and Manitoba—allow for application to the LRB to terminate a union's bargaining rights if those rights were originally acquired through voluntary action of the employer— that is, no formal certification exists in these situations. The federal statute does not provide procedures for termination of bargaining rights in these instances of voluntary recognition.

Accreditation.   A recent provision in labour relations legislation concerns the granting of **accreditation**, that is, certification rights for employer associations. Accreditation is particularly important in construction, where much of the bargaining takes place between unions and employer groups. Its purposes are to ensure the unification of employers in bargaining, to force unions to recognize majority employer associations for bargaining purposes, and to ensure the adherence of all employers to the agreement negotiated between the accredited association and the union. Procedures for acquiring accreditation are similar to those for acquiring certification.

Unfair Labour Practices.   Certain behaviours involving either the company or the unions are considered **unfair labour practices**, and rules regarding them are subject to enforcement by the LRBs or the courts. The following are examples of unfair practices on the part of employers:

- Interference with the rights of employees to select the union of their choice for collective bargaining purposes, or discrimination against employees for union activity; by law employers cannot dismiss, discipline, or threaten employees for exercising their rights to unionize. They cannot make promises that will influence an employee's choice of a union—for example, promising better benefits should the employee select one union rather than another or vote for no union. This legislation, however, does not prevent employers from making their case in support of one union or another, or for no union. What the employer can say under these circumstances, the manner in which he or she can say it, and the forum used are matters that are subject to review by the relevant LRB;

- Participation in the formation, selection or support—financial or otherwise—of unions representing employees;
- Unilaterally changing the terms of collective agreements or changing the wages and working conditions during certification proceedings or during collective bargaining if the purpose is to undermine the union; by law, employers are compelled, as are unions, to bargain in good faith—that is, to demonstrate serious intentions to bargain fairly.

Some unfair labour practices on the part of unions include:

- Interference with, or participation in, the formation or administration of an employer's organization;
- Interference with the bargaining rights of a certified union;
- Discrimination against union members or employees in the bargaining unit;
- Intimidation or coercion of employees to become or remain members of the union;
- Forcing employers to discriminate against, dismiss, or discipline union members;
- Failure to provide fair representation for all employees in the bargaining unit, whether in collective bargaining or in grievance procedure cases.

Conciliation and Mediation. In their legislation, all jurisdictions provide for conciliation and mediation services. Yet, this legislation varies in the scope and extent of government intervention. Quebec, for example, has abolished its conciliation boards, and allows employees to strike for ninety days following a union request for the appointment of a conciliation officer. Most other jurisdictions still enforce the compulsory two-stage conciliation approach.

Typically, the statute specifies that no strike action is permitted before a conciliation effort has been made and has failed. Conciliators and mediators are appointed by the federal or provincial minister of labour, at the request of either one or both of the parties involved or at the discretion of the minister. If the dispute is still not settled, a conciliation board comprising appointees of the parties and a neutral chairman may be appointed. The board will try to effect a settlement; failing that, it will report to the government its recommendations for a settlement. Again, the term of the board is set down in the legislation and may be extended by the parties. Most of the legislations require a seven to fourteen day waiting period following the delivery of the board's report before the parties acquire the right to strike or lock out. Conciliation boards are seldom used now, due to criticisms for the time lapse in their decision-making process and their lack of success.

Arbitration. All jurisdictions, with the exception of Saskatchewan, require that collective bargaining agreements include a provision for final settlement by **arbitration** (of issues relating to interpretation of the collective agreement), without stoppage of work. This means that as long as a collective agreement is in force, any strike or lockout is illegal. The arbitrator's decision is final and cannot be changed or revised, except in cases of manifest error, proved corruption, fraud, breach of natural justice, or if the arbitrator oversteps his or her jurisdiction.

ATTRACTION OF UNIONIZATION

To understand the union movement today, it is necessary to consider the reasons for which employees decide either to join or not to join unions. A great deal of research has been conducted in an attempt to analyze why workers unionize. Although no single reason exists, three separate conditions appear to be strong influences in an employee's decision to join a union. They include: dissatisfaction, lack of power, and union instrumentality.

DISSATISFACTION. When an individual takes a job, certain conditions of employment (e.g., wages, hours, type of work) are specified in the **employment contract**. A **psychological contract** also exists between employer and employee, which consists of the employee's unspecified expectations about reasonable working conditions, requirements of the work itself, the level of effort that should be expended on the job, and the amount and nature of the employer's authority in directing the employee's work. These expectations are related to the employee's desire to satisfy certain personal preferences in the workplace. The degree to which the organization fulfils these preferences determines the employee's level of satisfaction.

Dissatisfaction with either the employment contract or the psychological contract will lead the employee to attempt to improve the work situation, often through unionization. A major study found a very strong relationship between the level of dissatisfaction and the proportion of workers voting for a union. Almost all workers who were highly dissatisfied voted for a union, but almost all workers who were satisfied voted against the union.[6] In general, though, workers who perceive unions to be instrumental in improving their QWL are more likely to become union members, support union activities, and participate in union affairs.[7]

Therefore, if management wants to make unionization less attractive to employees, it should consider making work conditions more satisfying. Management and the HR department often contribute to the level of work dissatisfaction by committing the following mistakes:

- Giving unrealistic job previews that create expectations that cannot be fulfilled;
- Designing jobs that fail to use the SKAs of employees and that are compatible with their PIPs;
- Practising such day-to-day management and supervisory behaviours as poor supervision, unfair treatment, and lack of upward communication;
- Failing to tell employees that they would prefer to operate without unions and that they are committed to treating employees with respect.[8]

LACK OF POWER. Unionization is seldom the first attempt at a remedy by employees who are dissatisfied with some aspect of their job. The first attempt to improve the work situation is usually made by an individual acting alone. Someone who has enough power or influence can effect the necessary changes without collaborating with others. The features of a job that determine the amount of power the job holder has in the organization are **essentiality**, (how important or critical the job is to the overall success of the organization), and **exclusivity** (how difficult it is to replace the person). An employee with an essential task and who is difficult to replace may be able to force the employer to make changes. If, however, the individual tasks are not critical and workers can easily be replaced, they are likely to consider other means, including collective action, to increase their power to influence the organization. Labour economists refer to this phenomenon of whether to fight for the improvement of working conditions or to quit the organization as the "exit–voice" debate.

In considering whether or not collective action is appropriate, employees are also likely to consider the possibility that a union can improve certain aspects of the work environment not now provided by the employer, and will weigh those possible benefits against the costs of unionization. In other words, the employees will determine union instrumentality.

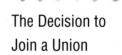

The Decision to Join a Union

UNION INSTRUMENTALITY. Employees who are dissatisfied with many aspects of a work environment, such as pay, promotion opportunity, treatment by the supervisor, the job itself, and work rules, are likely to perceive a union as instrumental in removing such negative job aspects. The more that employees believe that a union is very likely to obtain positive work changes, the more instrumental the union is for the employees. The employees then determine the value of these benefits or potential positive work aspects, and the costs of unionization, such as the bad feelings with the supervisors and managers, a lengthy organizing campaign, and the bad feelings with other employees who may not want a union. When the benefits exceed the costs, employees will be more willing to support a union.

Exhibit 16.3 summarizes the reasons that employees might have for deciding to join a union. In general, the expectation that work will satisfy personal preferences may induce satisfaction or dissatisfaction with it. As the level of dissatisfaction increases, individuals seek to change their work situation. If they fail, and if the positive consequences of unionization seem to outweigh the negative consequences, individuals will be inclined to join the union. This, however, will not always be the case. Employees may choose not to join a union.

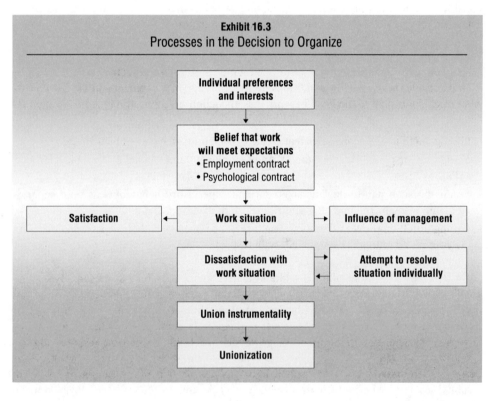

Exhibit 16.3
Processes in the Decision to Organize

The question of whether or not to join a union involves an assessment of the negative consequences of unionization. Employees may have misgivings about how effectively a union can improve unsatisfactory work conditions. Collective bargaining is not always successful; if the union is not strong, it will be unable to make an employer meet its demands. Even if an employer does respond to union demands, the workers may be affected adversely. For example, the employer may not be able to survive when the demands of the union are met, and thus the company may close down, costing employees their jobs. Or the organization may force the union to strike, inflicting economic hardship on employees who may not be able to afford being out of work, or it may, in some cases, attempt reprisals against pro-union employees, although this is illegal.

The Decision not to Join a Union

Beyond perceptions of unions as ineffective in the pursuit of personal gains, employees may also resist unionization because of general negative attitudes toward unions. Employees may identify strongly with the company and have a high level of commitment to it. They would therefore tend to view the union as an adversary and would be receptive to company arguments against it. Employees may also perceive the goals of the union to be objectionable, intending to harm the company and the free enterprise system in general. They may object to the concept of seniority or even to the political activities of the unions. Moreover, certain employees view themselves as professionals and find collective action to be contrary to such professional ideals as independence and auto-control.

The decision not to unionize can be influenced by management as well. Employers may influence the employees' decision not to join a union if they have established good management practices: fostering employee participation in planning and decision making, opening channels of communication, setting up processes for handling employee problems and grievances, developing employee trust, and offering competitive wages, are all sound HR practices discussed throughout this book.

According to a survey by Decima Research of Toronto conducted on behalf of the Canadian Federation of Labour, Canadians have mixed views about trade unions but many would join one if they could. Those most likely to think highly of unions are civil servants, teachers, part-time workers, and workers with union members in their family.[9]

The study of labour unions is enhanced a great deal by an appreciation of their historical context. A better understanding of the attitudes and behaviours of both unions and management can be gained through a knowledge of their growth and development.

THE EARLY DAYS. In the last century, Canada's economy was largely agricultural, with a few large concentrations of population and industry. However, a few labour unions existed in the early 1800s. There are, for example, records of several craft unions that existed in the Maritime Provinces before the end of the War of 1812. There is also evidence as early as 1827 of the existence of a printers' union in Quebec City, and a few shoemakers' unions in Montreal in the 1830s. Little by way of broadening the organization base among workers beyond individual local units was evident until the latter half of the last century.

The development and growth of unions in Canada have been most heavily influenced by events and developments in the United States. In the decade preceding Confederation, unions that had been operating south of the border began to form locals in Upper Canada. This was the beginning of "international unionism" as we know it in Canada today.

In subsequent decades, a number of attempts were made to establish a central labour federation. All of these failed except the Trades and Labour Congress of Canada (TLC), which was established in 1886. A close link developed between the American Federation of Labor (AFL) and the TLC. Many of the international unions that became members of the AFL also had Canadian districts that helped form the TLC. The TLC also included strictly Canadian unions at that time. In 1902, the TLC acceded to the wishes of the AFL and barred "dual unionism."

The fastest growth in the Canadian labour movement occurred between 1913 and 1920. In 1919, union membership was over 778,000. Some of the major reasons for this growth included favourable economic conditions and the population growth and economic and industrial expansion in the aftermath of World War I.

The TLC experienced an uneven pattern of growth during the 1930s and the 1940s. While the depression period led to a decline in membership, an increase followed the passage of the Wagner Act of 1935 (in the U.S.A.). This Act gave unions the right to organize and required employers to bargain in good faith. With the passage of this Act, new industry-wide unions spread into Canada and contributed to further growth in the labour movement. Initial growth was achieved in affiliation with the TLC, but these new industrial

STATE OF UNIONIZATION

Growth and Development

unions generated tension and were finally expelled from it. They were later welcomed into the more nationalistic CCL (Confederation of Canadian Labour). The merger of the two congresses (CCL and TLC) occurred in 1956, and together they formed the Canadian Labour Congress (CLC).

The evolution of the labour movement was different in French Canada. The growing militancy of the CCL resulted in discarding religious and Church ties in 1960 to become an independent militant federation (CNTU, Confederation of National Trade Unions). In 1972, a third federation, the Confederation of Democratic Unions (CDU) broke off from the CNTU, however this federation remains small.

In sum, since 1956 most unions in Canada have been affiliated with the CLC or the CNTU. In 1981, however, the CLC suspended fourteen international building trade unions with over 229,700 members for nonpayment of affiliation fees. In 1982, the expelled unions founded the Canadian Federation of Labour (CFL).

TODAY. Unions are very important in the fabric of the Canadian LRS. Although their relative power has declined in the early 1990s due to the economic hardships and the state of the economy, as suggested in the HRM in the News Vignette, the Canadian labour movement is still going strong. In order to maintain the current level of unionization, there is a trend to break away from international unions and become independent. In fact membership in national unions totalled 2.7 million in 1990 (or 68 percent of total union membership) compared to 28 percent in the early 1960s. At the same time, international unions represented a total of 32 percent of membership in 1990 compared to 72 percent in 1961.[10]

Union Membership. Although union membership in Canada is close to 40 percent (total) in comparison to only 16 percent in the U.S.A., it is to be noted that in the last couple of years growth has slowed, and in some private sector unions, it has declined. Nonetheless, Canada is one of the very few countries in the world where union membership has risen and union density has been stable.[11] At the beginning of 1990, total union membership in Canada was four million.

Distribution of Membership. Here are a few recent statistics about union membership in Canada for 1990:

- *Size*: The largest union was the Canadian Union of Public Employees (increased 11.8 percent over 1989); the second largest union was the National Union of Provincial Government Employees, and the third largest was the Public Service Alliance of Canada.
- *Affiliation:* The CLC is the largest central body with 2.4 million members (58.6 percent), followed by the Quebec-based CNTU.
- *By Province*: The highest proportion of unionized employees is concentrated in Newfoundland, British Columbia, Quebec, and New Brunswick.
- *By Industry*: The service sector is the major source of union membership. In 1987, 33 percent were in the service sector, compared to 16 percent in manufacturing and only 1 percent in agriculture and forestry.

Structure and Function of Unions in Canada

Central federations such as the CLC exist in most industrial countries. These federations have much input into public policy decisions. However, since jurisdiction over labour relations policy in Canada is primarily at the provincial level, national federations have provincial organizational entities that attempt to influence the formulation of provincial policies. At a lower level, there are the local labour councils and the local unions.

HRM IN THE NEWS VIGNETTE
Unions' Bargaining Power Weakening, Think Tank Says

The ghosts of the recession—a weak recovery, high unemployment, government deficit fighting, and business cost-cutting—will haunt labour negotiations and weaken the bargaining position of unions this year, the Conference Board of Canada said yesterday.

"Competition from beyond our borders along with government restraint are critical factors in labour–management discussions, which will focus on productivity, cost containment and employment security," said Ruth Wright, author of the board's Industrial Relations Outlook 1992.

But with very low inflation, many, though not all workers, should still leave the negotiating table as wage winners, she said in an interview. "It depends on the sector," Wright said, noting that for some companies the outcome of negotiations will determine whether they survive.

Wage gains should average more than 3 per cent this year, she speculated. That's less than expected only six months ago but still exceeds projected inflation of just over 2 per cent this year. But wages aren't at the top of labour's list at the bargaining table this year and the biggest challenges facing labour won't even be at the negotiating table, she explained.

Looking for security. At the table, unions will be looking for job security for members, while away from the table, unions will be trying to rebuild membership eroded by the recession and will focus more closely on politics. Only 17 per cent of private-sector workers in Canada are still unionized, a proportion that is sliding, though still above the 12 per cent level in the U.S. So far, unions have failed to organize the growth areas of the economy, such as the service sector's highly skilled and better-paid employees, it said.

"Labour will focus on a move towards greater politicization that is evident by its support of New Democratic Party governments in Ontario, British Columbia and Saskatchewan…and the prospect of new leadership and mergers of high-profile unions," the report says.

"Labour is increasingly concerned about government policies which appear to them to compromise Canadian culture and standard of living," Wright said, adding that labour perceives an assault on its members by policies such as free trade, privatization and deregulation.

Sees new direction. And the militancy seen in the federal public-service unions last year, such as the strike in the fall against the federal wage freeze, will likely shift to the provinces and to sectors such as health and education.

But Wright is not expecting a lot of strike action this year. It's not a heavy bargaining year for the private or federal public-service sectors. "There's a sort of contained anger that's building up over federal government policies that labour sees as promoting the corporate competitive agenda," she said. "But there's not much they can do at the bargaining table."

What we may be seeing is labour emerging from the crossroads of recent years and heading in what will be a new direction in the coming years, she explained. "We see it in a new more political and social role," she said, adding that would be more in line with the role played by unions in Europe.

Source: A feature article of the same title by E. Beauchesne, Southam News, in *The Montreal Gazette*, 4 March 1992, C3. Reprinted with permission

---

The most prominent and numerically dominant central federation in Canada is the CLC. Like the American AFL–CIO, the CLC is a loose and very weak federation. The power in the Canadian labour movement rests with the sovereign national and international unions and, in varying degrees, at the local union level. The primary function of the CLC is to look after labour's interest at the national level. Research suggests that in the past it could block negative legislation, but it did not have the power to compel legislation over the opposition of other influential groups. In addition to its political role, a central federation (such as the CLC) attempts to resolve conflicts among its constituent components and to ensure that they follow the policies adopted by the periodic national conventions. To this end they have a number of sub-bodies that meet between conventions to assess the extent to which policies are being followed and to guide the senior executive officers in the ongoing conduct of federation affairs.

The supreme governing body of the CLC is the biennial convention that develops policy and amends its constitution. The CLC attempts to achieve its objectives at the national level in a number of ways. Each winter it has traditionally presented its annual memorandum to the government of Canada. In it the CLC president outlines to the prime minister and his cabinet the objectives he or she thinks the government should pursue. Often the recommendation is very critical of federal policy.

In addition, when Statistics Canada releases its monthly figures on the cost of living and unemployment rate, the CLC frequently prepares press releases and:

- Engages in public relations to improve the public's perception of the labour movement and to make the public aware of the positive effect the union movement has had in the areas of workers' rights, for instance;
- Monitors the courts for anti-union challenges under the Charter of Rights;
- Presses the government of Canada against free trade with the U.S.A. and Mexico.

The CLC attempts to influence the formulation and administration of public policy at the national level. It suggests policies it thinks the government should pursue in light of price changes, the rate of unemployment, and other economic indicators. Another important function is that of defining, organizing, and ironing out problems of conflicting jurisdiction of its affiliates. The latter problem arose, for example, when the United Automobile Workers union and the Machinists Union tried to organize aerospace workers in the same plants.

The CLC consists of slightly over fifty Canadian branches of international unions and over twenty national unions. Each national union is usually given a mandate to organize within a particular jurisdictional area as defined in its constitution. Not only does the national (or international) branch serve its local unions, but it helps in organizing campaigns. Also, during contract negotiations, the representatives of the national union may assist the local negotiating committee in the formulation and negotiation of their demands, and even in the actual negotiations. The national unions also assist the local in processing grievances.

The **local union** is the basic unit of labour organization formed in a particular plant or locality. "The members (of the local) participate directly in the affairs of their local including the election of officers, financial, and other business matters."[12] A worker's first contact with unionism is usually with a local. It represents the basic building block of the labour movement structure. There are an estimated 13,000 locals in Canada. The number of locals per union varies. Some unions have fewer than ten locals, while others have more than 100 locals. Like unions, locals are of varying sizes, ranging from a few members to many thousands.

Activities of union locals revolve around collective bargaining and handling grievances. In addition, locals hold general meetings, publish newsletters, and otherwise keep their members informed. Typically, however, the members are apathetic about union involvement. Unless a serious problem exists, attendance at meetings is usually very low, and often elections of officers draw votes from less than one-fourth of the membership.

THE ORGANIZING CAMPAIGN

One of the major functions of the LRBs is to conduct the selection of a union to represent a group of employees. This is accomplished through a certification election to determine if the majority of employees want the union. Under Canadian labour laws, the union that is certified has sole and exclusive rights to bargain for that group.

Because unions may acquire significant power through certification, employers may be anxious to prevent this. In addition to this situation of potential union–management conflict, there may be more than one union attempting to win certification as representative of a group of employees, creating competition and conflict between unions.

Several steps in the regular certification process can be identified. These are presented in Exhibit 16.4. A union may also organize a majority of the employees and obtain voluntary approval by the employer, in which case, it would not need to follow these suggested steps

Different jurisdictions have different provisions for the percentage of support needed to either apply for certification or for a board mandate without a vote. Also, the percentages required to certify the bargaining unit are different from those required to vote otherwise.

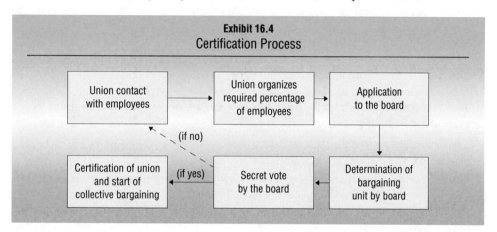

Exhibit 16.4
Certification Process

In the campaign to generate a sufficient number of memberships to be certified, unions generally contact employees directly to solicit their support. Special field organizers are used for this purpose. (The life of a typical organizer was well depicted in the movie *Norma Rae.*) Most organizers possess extremely good organizational and verbal skills and have up-to-date knowledge of all relevant laws. Their techniques vary as a function of the nature and composition of the workforce and the problems at hand. Certain organizers cater to specific populations, such as blacks, women, or white-collar professionals. In Canada the United Steelworkers, for example, at one time employed a Canadian–Italian who was specialized in organizing workers of Italian origin.[13]

The Campaign to Solicit Employee Support

ESTABLISHING CONTACT. Contact between the union and the employees can be initiated by either party. National or international unions may contact employees in industries or occupations in which they have an interest or have been traditionally involved. Most union organizing drives start with a few workers who are dissatisfied with their salaries and/or working conditions, and they call or visit the local office of a union. On initial contact, the union official will assess the situation and, if it looks reasonably promising, the official will set up a plan of action. From this time on, the organizer works as a strategist, educator, counsellor, and companion to members of the workforce in an effort to enlist enough support to secure certification.

In communities where one or two well-known nonunion companies operate amid a preponderance of unionized firms, initiative comes from the national or international union. Such was the case with the organization of the employees of the T. Eaton Co. Ltd. store in Brampton, Ontario. The concentration on this store snowballed into a historic organizing drive that eventually affected three of Canada's biggest department store chains—Eaton's, Sears, and the former Simpson's.[14]

In all campaigns, a list of all employees in the bargaining unit is needed. To obtain such a list without the employer's knowledge is difficult, so organizers resort to many alternative devices.

Some organizers obtain this by list using the information on employees' licence plates to initiate requests for ownership information through the provincial Ministry of Transportation, which is legal in Canada. Once the list is compiled, demographic and socioeconomic analyses are conducted. All of these become important during the campaign.

SIGN-UPS. Once contact has been made, the union begins to pressure employees to sign membership cards as soon as possible. Through the work of a nucleus of committed employees, many unions use tactics such as house visits. Such a strategy may help to persuade undecided workers to go along with the union. Different organizers aim for different percentages of sign-ups, although all aim beyond the minimum required by the certification law. During the sign-up campaign, many organizers try to give the impression that the union is there to stay.

EMPLOYER RESISTANCE. The employer usually resists the union's campaign. One of the best tactics for preventing unionization is to keep the employees content. This is difficult; no matter how good the working conditions, there are always going to be dissatisfied workers. Another approach used by employers is the use of consultants who resort to one or more of the following tactics:

- Use of doctored statistics, such as selective wage surveys, to make employees believe that company conditions already are superior;
- Making threats or promises contingent upon victory or defeat of the union. For example: "We may eventually close the plant and move to another province";
- Secretly promoting the formation of an employees' association and encouraging the association itself to apply for certification.

However, in most jurisdictions, employers are legally constrained from interfering with an employee's freedom of choice. The following actions by an employer are illegal:

- Promising improvement in wages or working conditions contingent on defeat of the union;
- Granting wage increases or making other HR changes that cannot be proved to be normal;
- Taking any action that the LRB believes could deceive employees as to the degree that they are able to vote freely on vital issues.

During the union campaign and election process, therefore, it is important that the HR manager caution the company against engaging in unfair labour practices, which, when identified, generally cause the election to be set aside. Severe violations by the employer can result in certification of the union as the bargaining representative, even if it has lost the election.

Determination of the Bargaining Unit

A bargaining unit is usually defined as a unit of employees who are considered "appropriate" for collective bargaining. Usually statutes are set out in broad terms and it is up to the boards to determine who should, or should not, be included in the units. A typical unit may consist exclusively of craft employees, technical employees, or workers with various skills. It is necessary to have at least two employees to form a bargaining unit.

The statute governing the definition of "appropriate unit" is rather broad in most jurisdictions in Canada. For example, in Alberta, Nova Scotia, and Prince Edward Island, excluded from bargaining units are members of the medical, dental, legal, architectural, and engineering professions. In an overhaul of the Labour Relations Act in Ontario, the NDP government passed a bill allowing engineers, surveyors, domestics, lawyers, and architects to join unions for the first time. All jurisdictions in Canada exclude employees who are considered to act in a confidential capacity in matters relating to industrial relations or who exercise managerial functions.

The core of union–management relations is **collective bargaining**. It generally includes two types of interaction. The first is the negotiation of work conditions that, when written up as the collective agreement (the contract), become the basis for the employee–employer relationship on the job. The second type of interaction relates to interpreting and enforcing the collective agreement (contract administration) and resolving any conflicts arising from it.

Collective bargaining is a complex process in which union and management negotiators both manoeuvre to win the most advantageous contract. How the issues involved are settled depends upon the following:

- The quality of the union–management relationship,
- The processes of bargaining used by labour and management,
- Management's strategies in the collective bargaining process,
- The union's strategies in the collective bargaining process,
- Joint union–management strategies.

The most widely used description incorporates four types of bargaining in contract negotiations: distributive bargaining, integrative bargaining, attitudinal structuring, and intra-organizational bargaining.

DISTRIBUTIVE BARGAINING. **Distributive bargaining** takes place when the parties are in conflict over an issue and the outcome represents a gain for one party and loss for the other. Each party tries to negotiate for the best possible outcome. Some experts refer to this process as a "zero-sum" game.

Exhibit 16.5 outlines the distributive bargaining process. On any particular issue, the union negotiators have three identifiable positions. The **initial demand point** is generally more than they expect to get; the **target point** is their realistic assessment of what they may be able to get; and the **resistance point** is the lowest acceptable level for that issue.

Management has three similar points: the **initial offer** is usually lower than the expected settlement; the **target point** is the point it would prefer to reach agreement at; and the resistance point is its upper acceptable limit. If, as shown in Exhibit 16.5, management's resistance point is greater than the union's resistance point, there is a **positive settlement range** where negotiation can take place. The exact agreement within this range depends on the bargaining behaviour of the negotiators. If, however, management's resistance point is below that of the union, there is no common ground for negotiation. In such a situation there is a **negative settlement range** and a bargaining impasse exists.

For example, in regard to wages, the union may have a resistance point of $7.40 per hour, a target of $7.60, and an initial demand of $7.75. Management may offer $7.20 but have a target of $7.45 and a resistance point of $7.55. The positive settlement range is between $7.40 and $7.55, and it is very likely that this is where the settlement will be. Note, however, that only the initial wage demand and offer are actually made public at the beginning of negotiations.

Because many issues are involved in a bargaining session, the process becomes much more complicated. Although each issue may be described using the above model, in actual negotiations there is an interaction among issues. Union concessions on one issue may be traded for management concessions on another. Thus the total process is dynamic.

The ritual of the distributive bargaining process is well established, and deviations are often met with suspicion. The following story illustrates this point:

A labour lawyer tells the story of a young executive who had just taken over the helm of a company. Imbued with idealism, he wanted to end the bickering he had seen take place during past negotiations with labour. To do this, he was ready to give the workers as much as his company could afford. Consequently, he asked some

THE COLLECTIVE BARGAINING PROCESS

Process of Bargaining

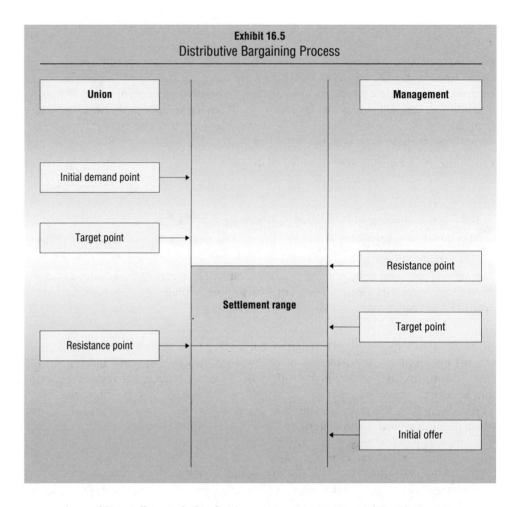

Exhibit 16.5
Distributive Bargaining Process

members of his staff to study his firm's own wage structure and decide how it compared with other companies, as well as a host of other related matters. He approached the collective bargaining table with a halo of goodness surrounding him. Asking for the floor, he proceeded to describe what he had done and with a big smile on his face made the offer.

Throughout his entire presentation, the union officials stared at him in amazement. He had offered more than they had expected to secure. But no matter, as soon as he finished, they proceeded to lambaste him, denouncing him for trying to destroy collective bargaining and for attempting to buy off labour. They announced that they would not stand for any such unethical maneuvering, and immediately asked for 5 cents more than the idealist had offered.[15]

INTEGRATIVE BARGAINING. With **integrative bargaining** management and the union work to solve a problem to the benefit of both. For example, issues of work crew size or union concerns for job security may be addressed. Most QWL changes involve integrative bargaining. The new work setting will benefit employees as well as the employer. Given the adversarial nature of labour–management relations, integrative bargaining is not common, although the recent interest in cooperative relations is changing, particularly in the field of health and safety.

The federal government, through its Department of Labour and several provincial governments, developed a wide-ranging reform in order to foster more integrative bargaining and cooperation, but it had limited success. The initiatives included steps to remove irritants that may give rise to conflicts, such as outlawing professional strikebreakers in a few jurisdictions (Ontario, Quebec, and British Columbia), eliminating the requirement that employers deduct union dues directly from paycheques and remit them to the union (the Rand formula), and introducing binding arbitration of first contracts in case of impasse by several Canadian jurisdictions. These were all intended to foster a climate of integrative bargaining.

Finally, Labour Canada QWL initiatives in the early 1980s aimed at improving employee satisfaction and enhancing productivity were an example of government tripartism on the plant level designed to foster a more cooperative LRS and bargaining climate. Not all bargaining processes, however, determine who gets how much or whether or not problems are solved. In some, either the union or management tries to influence the attitude of the other. This is referred to as "attitudinal structuring."

ATTITUDINAL STRUCTURING. The relationship between labour and management results in **attitudinal structuring**, or the shaping of attitudes toward one another. Four dimensions of this relationship have been identified: (1) motivational orientation, or tendencies that indicate whether the interaction will be competitive and adversarial or cooperative; (2) beliefs about the legitimacy of the other, or how much a party believes the other has a right to be bargaining; (3) level of trust in conducting affairs, or belief in the integrity and honesty of the other party; and (4) degree of friendliness, or the likelihood that interactions will be friendly or hostile. As the bargaining process proceeds, these attitudes may be altered. The attitudes emerging from the negotiations will have a serious impact on the administration of the contract and future negotiations.

INTRA-ORGANIZATIONAL BARGAINING. During negotiations, the bargaining teams from both sides may have to engage in **intra-organizational bargaining**, or confer with their constituents over changes in bargaining positions. Management negotiators may have to convince management to change its position on an issue—for instance, to agree to a higher wage settlement. Union negotiators must eventually convince their members to accept the negotiated contract, so they must not only be sensitive to the demands of the membership, but realistic as well. When members vote on the proposed package, they will be strongly influenced by the opinions of the union negotiators.

Within the range of these bargaining processes, unions and management can engage in a wide variety of actual bargaining behaviour. The process chosen, and the specific behaviours enacted, are often a product of strategies they choose to pursue, either separately or jointly.

Prior to the bargaining session, management negotiators develop the strategies and proposals they will use. Four major areas of preparation have been identified:

- Preparation of specific proposals for changes in contract language;
- Determination of the general size of the economic package that the company anticipates offering during the negotiations;
- Preparation of statistical displays and supportive data that the company will use during negotiations;
- Preparation of a bargaining book for use by company negotiators; typically, this contains a compilation of information on issues that will be discussed, giving an analysis of the effect of each clause, its use in other companies, and other facts.

Management Strategies

An important part of this preparation is the calculation of the cost of various bargaining issues or demands. The relative cost of pension contributions, pay increases, health benefits, and other provisions should be determined prior to negotiations. Other costs should also be considered. For instance, what is the cost to management, in terms of its ability to do its job, of union demands for changes in grievance and discipline procedures or transfer and promotion provisions? The goal is to be as well prepared as possible by considering the implications and ramifications of the issues that will be discussed, and by being able to present a strong argument for the position that management takes.

Union Strategies

Like management, unions need to prepare for negotiations by collecting information. The more thorough the investigation, the more convincing the union will be during negotiations. Since collective bargaining is the major means by which a union can convince its members that it is effective and valuable, this is a critical activity. Unions should collect information in at least three areas:

- The financial situation of the company and its ability to pay;
- The attitude of management toward various issues, as reflected in past negotiations or inferred from negotiations in similar companies;
- The attitudes and desires of the employees.

The first two areas give the union an idea of what demands management is likely to accept. The third area is important, but is sometimes overlooked. The union should also be aware of the preferences of the membership. For instance, is a pension increase preferred over increased vacation or holiday benefits? The preferences will vary with the characteristics of the workers. Younger workers are more likely to prefer more holidays, shorter work weeks, and limited overtime, whereas older workers are more interested in pension plans, benefits, and overtime. Unions normally canvass members of the local to identify which items they would like to have negotiated. Once the suggestions are received, a compilation is done by the union before proposing a negotiation package to the entire membership for approval.

Joint Union–Management Strategies

Consistent with cooperative union–management relationships and integrative bargaining are joint union–management strategies. There are three major types: productivity bargaining, concessionary bargaining, and continuous bargaining.

PRODUCTIVITY BARGAINING. A relatively recent method of negotiating is **productivity bargaining**. This is a special form of integrative bargaining. Labour agrees to scrap old work habits and work rules for the new and more effective ones desired by management, and, in exchange, management returns some of the gains of modernization and increased efficiency to labour in the form of new and better work incentives.

Most unions have been hesitant to agree to this approach, because they fear that their members will lose jobs, that the company will require excessive work, or that technological change will eventually eliminate more jobs. Despite this hesitancy, productivity bargaining has been used successfully. One notable result is that the bargaining process changes from distributive to integrative. Labour and management work together, not only to create the agreement itself, but to create an atmosphere of ongoing cooperation. Another notable result is that significant cost savings are realized, enabling the company to survive and providing continued jobs for union members.

CONCESSIONARY BARGAINING. As mentioned earlier, **concessionary bargaining** is prompted by severe economic and near-bankruptcy conditions of employers. In an effort to survive, employers seek concessions from the unions, in return giving promises of job security. Concessions sought may include wage freezes, wage reductions, work rule change or elimination, fringe benefit reductions, delay or elimination of COLAs, and more hours of work for the same pay. Although some rank-and-file union members are not pleased with concessions and many reject tentative contracts that have them, their alternatives seem to be limited. Either concessions can be made, or plants can be closed or moved, or the entire company can declare bankruptcy.

CONTINUOUS BARGAINING. Like affirmative action, OH&S requirements and other government regulations continue to complicate the situation for both unions and employers. As the rate of change in the work environment continues to accelerate, some labour and management negotiators are turning to **continuous bargaining**. Under this approach, a joint committee meets on a regular basis to explore issues and analyze and solve problems of common interest. Several characteristics of continuous bargaining have been identified:

- Frequent meetings during the life of the contract,
- Focus on external events and problem areas rather than internal problems,
- Use of outside experts in decision making,
- Use of a problem-solving (integrative) approach.

The intention is to develop a union–management structure capable of adapting to sudden changes in the environment in a positive, productive manner. This continuous bargaining approach is different from, but an extension of, the emergency negotiations that unions have insisted on when inflation or other factors have substantially changed the acceptability of the existing agreement. Continuous bargaining is a permanent arrangement intended to help avoid the crises that often occur under traditional collective bargaining systems.

NEGOTIATING THE AGREEMENT

Once a union is certified as the representative of a bargaining unit, it becomes the only party that can negotiate an agreement with the employer for all members of that work unit. This is, therefore, an important and powerful position. The union is responsible for negotiating for what its members want, and it has the duty to represent all employees fairly. The union is a critical link between the employees and the employer. The quality of its bargaining is an important measure of union effectiveness.

Negotiating Committees

The employer and the union select their own representatives for the **negotiating committee**. Neither party is required to consider the wishes of the other. Negotiations must begin and be carried out diligently and in good faith. Neither side's representatives can refuse to bargain with the other side because they dislike someone on that side or view that person as an inappropriate choice.

Union negotiating teams typically include representatives of the union local, the president, and other executive staff members. In addition, the national union may send a negotiating specialist, likely a labour lawyer, to work with the team. The negotiators selected by the union do not have to be members of the union or employees of the company. The general goal is to balance bargaining skill and experience with knowledge and information about the specific situation.

At the local level, when a single bargaining unit is negotiating a contract, the company is usually represented by the manager and members of the labour relations or HR staff. Finance and production managers may also be involved. When the negotiations are critical, either because the size of the bargaining unit is large or because the effect on the company is great, such specialists as labour lawyers may be included on the team.

In national organizations, top industrial relations or HR executives frequently head a team made up of specialists from corporate headquarters and perhaps managers from critical divisions or plants within the company. Again, the goal is to have expertise along with specific knowledge about critical situations.

The Negotiating Structure

Most contracts are negotiated by a single union and a single employer. In some situations, however, different arrangements can be agreed upon. When a single union negotiates with several similar companies—for instance, the construction industry or supermarkets—the employers may bargain as a group with the union. At the local level this is called **multi-employer bargaining**, but at the national level it is referred to as **industry-wide bargaining**. Industry-wide bargaining occurs in both the public and the private sector. National negotiations result in contracts that settle major issues, such as compensation, whereas issues relating to working conditions are settled locally. This split bargaining style is common in Great Britain, Sweden, and Israel.

When several unions bargain jointly with a single employer, they engage in **coordinated bargaining**. Although not as common as the other types, instances of coordinated bargaining appear to be increasing, especially in public-sector bargaining. One consequence of coordinated and industry-wide bargaining is often **pattern settlements**, where similar wage rates are imposed on the companies whose employees are represented by the same union within a given industry. Pattern settlements can be detrimental because they ignore differences in the employers' economic condition and ability to pay. The result of this can be settlements that are tolerable for some companies but cause severe economic trouble for others. As a partial consequence of this, pattern settlements resulting from coordinated and industry-wide bargaining now no longer occur very often. Nevertheless, there is an incentive to use these bargaining structures on account of their efficiency and the relative strength of union and management.

In multi-employer bargaining, the companies negotiate very similar contracts to eliminate the time and cost of individual negotiations. Since this also saves the union's time and money, it may be willing to accept this type of bargaining if its own position is not weakened. Where local conditions vary substantially, there may be a need for splitting the bargaining between the national and local levels—settling the major issues at the national level and leaving specific issues for the local level, where they can be adjusted to meet local needs.

Given the fact that in Canada there is a high degree of provincial jurisdiction over the private sector, it is very difficult for employers and unions to negotiate on a national basis. However, multi-provincial negotiations have taken place in a number of industries. For example, while the main negotiations for the Steel Company of Canada (Stelco) occur at the Hamilton headquarters, negotiators from other locations in Canada assist in the process. Only when the terms of the settlement in Hamilton are acceptable to negotiators from Montreal and other locations is agreement reached.

In some provinces, such as British Columbia, multi-employer bargaining takes place frequently. This is due to legislation that enables employers' associations in any industry to be accredited and to bargain on behalf of all of their members. Accreditation in the other provinces is confined mainly to the construction industry.

Issues for Negotiation

There is no typical format for negotiations. Issues may vary from traditional wages and working conditions to agreements regarding benefits, grievance handling, and other items that determine working conditions. Today's list of issues for negotiation is voluminous. An analysis by Labour Canada summarizes the most important items typically found in agreements. It includes about 164 items classified under twenty-six main headings. Some of the most prevalent items will be briefly summarized in the next paragraphs.

Although there are no formal or legal rules governing the issues subject to bargaining, there are a few exceptions in the public sector, in which the law limits the issues that can be negotiated and included in an agreement. The Public Service Staff Relations Act (PSSRA), which was introduced in 1967 and governs collective bargaining for federal public employees, allows all issues to be negotiated except matters that would require a change in statute. A fairly large number of issues may be dealt with by a conciliation board. Arbitration, the alternative to the conciliation/strike route, is severely restricted in the items that may be addressed by an arbitration board. Parties who fail to reach an agreement and choose to submit it to arbitration may submit only the following issues: rates of pay, hours of work, leave entitlements, standards of discipline, and other terms and conditions of employment directly related to those items.

WAGES. Probably no issues under collective bargaining continue to give rise to more difficult prolems than do wages and wage-related subjects. Wage conflicts are the leading cause of strikes. Difficulties here are understandable because a wage increase is a direct cost to the employer, just as a wage decrease is to the employee.

The wages that an employee is paid are primarily determined by the basic pay rate for a certain job. This pay may then be increased by several other factors, all of which are subject to collective bargaining. Although management would prefer that basic pay be related only to productivity, this is seldom the case. Three additional standards are frequently used: (1) comparative norm, where rate of pay is influenced by the rates provided for similar jobs in other companies within an industry or even by comparative rates between industries; (2) ability to pay, where the pay rate is influenced by the financial capability of the company and, especially, the amount of its profit; and (3) standard of living, where changes in the cost of living influence the rate of pay.

Recently, due to the productivity crisis and increased international competition, firms are having profitability problems. In turn, they are asking unions to forego wage increases and in some cases to take a wage reduction. As described in the section on concessionary bargaining, however, when employers ask for wage concessions, unions ask for job security in return. In turn, to facilitate being able to provide job security, employers provide early retirement incentives to all their employees.

Wages, however, comprise only one general category of payment to employees. The other is economic supplements, or indirect (fringe) benefits. Collective bargaining deliberations may include discussion of how an increase in compensation will be split between these two types of payments. This is an important question, because the cost to the company of wages and fringe benefits may differ.

ECONOMIC SUPPLEMENTS. An increasingly important part of the pay package is the section covering **economic supplements**, fringe benefits such as vacations, holidays, pensions, and insurance. These benefits run as high as 40 percent of the cost of wages and are now a major factor in collective bargaining.

Provisions written into the bargaining agreement are very difficult to remove. If the union wins a new medical plan, for example, management will have difficulty in negotiating its demand for its removal at the next bargaining session. Since management has less control over fringe benefits than over wages, it tends to be cautious about agreeing to costly benefits. Occasionally, economic circumstances are so extreme that the union will agree to reductions in fringe benefits. The general rule, however, is that once something becomes part of the agreement, it remains. Common economic supplements include:

- *Pensions*: Once management has decided to provide a pension plan, the conditions of the plan must be determined (when the benefits will be available, how much will be paid, and whether they become available according to age or years of service). Finally, the organization must decide how long employees must work for the company in order to receive minimum benefits (vesting) and whether the organization will pay the whole cost or whether employees or the union will be asked to help.

- *Paid vacation*: Most agreements provide for paid vacation above and beyond the minimum required by law. The length of vacation is usually determined by length of service, up to some maximum point. The conditions that qualify an individual for a vacation in a given year are also specified. Agreements occasionally specify how the timing of vacations will be determined. Also, employees may be given their choice of vacation time according to seniority. It should be noted that even those employees who are terminated are entitled to paid vacation on a pro rata basis depending on the amount of time worked since the last vacation. One survey conducted by Labour Canada in the early 1980s found the following paid vacation clauses in collective agreements covering 200 or more employees:
  - 60 percent of agreements provide two weeks' vacation and require a minimum of one year of service,
  - 20 percent of agreements grant three weeks' paid vacation after one year of service,
  - 20 percent of agreements grant five weeks' paid vacation for employees with more than twenty years' seniority.[16]
- *Paid holidays*: A substantial proportion of collective agreements stipulate that employees will be paid for statutory holidays. In order to be eligible for this payment, however, employees must meet certain conditions with respect to days worked before and/or after the statutory holidays. For example, about 50 percent of collective agreements stipulate that employees must work the working days preceding and following the holiday in order to be paid for it.
- *Sick leave*: Paid sick leave allows the employee to take time off for sickness without financial penalty. Paid sick leave is usually accumulated while working. Typically, one-half to one-and-a-half days of paid sick leave are credited for each month of work.
- *Life insurance*: The employer may be required to pay some or all of the costs of life insurance plans.
- *Dismissal or severance pay*: Occasionally employers agree to pay an extra amount to any employee who is dismissed or laid off due to technological changes or business difficulties.

INSTITUTIONAL ISSUES. Some issues are not directly related to jobs, but are nevertheless important to both employees and management. Institutional issues that affect the security and success of both parties include:

- *Union security*: Union security clauses define the relationship between the union and its members. There are four types of union security clauses in Canada. Under the **closed shop**, the company agrees to hire and retain union members only. Closed shops are very frequently found in construction and are often associated with "hiring halls." Closed shops are not a very popular form of union security since only 4 percent of agreements discuss them. A **union shop** agreement requires all employees to become union members. Of collective agreements in Canada, 22.8 percent stipulate this provision. A **modified union shop** exempts from compulsory membership all employees who are not union members at the time of the agreement, but requires future hires to join the union. This provision is contained in 19.2 percent of agreements in Canada. The final union security clause is the **Rand Formula,** which requires all employees within the bargaining unit, including nonunion employees, to pay the equivalent of union dues as a condition of retaining employment.
- *Checkoff*: Unions have attempted to arrange for payment of dues through deduction from employees' paycheques. Five provinces (Quebec, Saskatchewan, Manitoba, Ontario, and Newfoundland) have legislation to make the checkoff compulsory. Checkoff clauses in other provinces may contain provisions regarding the type of

checkoffs: compulsory for all employees; compulsory for union members only; voluntary revocable. About 91 percent of union contracts contain this provision.

- *Managerial prerogatives*: Over 80 percent of the agreements today stipulate that certain activities are the right of management. In addition, management in most companies argues that it has "residual rights"—that is, all rights not specifically limited by the agreement belong to management.

ADMINISTRATIVE ISSUES. The last category of issues concerns the treatment of employees at work. **Administrative issues** include:

- *Breaks and cleanup time*: Some contracts specify the time and length of coffee breaks and meal breaks for employees. Also, jobs requiring cleanup may have a portion of the work period set aside for this procedure.

- *Job security*: This is perhaps the issue of most concern to employees and unions. Employers are concerned with the restriction of their ability to lay off employees. Changes in technology or attempts to subcontract work are issues that influence job security. One agreement illustrating this point was reached by the Canadian Brotherhood of Railway, Transport and General Workers in 1985 and VIA Rail. The agreement stipulated that employees with four years or more of continuous service will be protected from layoffs caused by technological, operational or organizational changes. In return for this clause, the union at VIA agreed to overhaul the pay structure for train service employees so that workers will have to work for all the money they are paid.[17]

- *Seniority*: Length of service is used as a criterion for many personnel decisions in most collective agreements. Layoffs are usually determined by seniority. "Last hired, first fired" is a common situation. Provisions for layoff on the basis of seniority are contained in 16 percent of agreements, covering 17 percent of employees and 34 percent of agreements covering an additional 33 percent of employees include provisions for seniority with other factors such as ability, skill and knowledge, and physical fitness. Seniority is also important in transfer and promotion decisions.

- *Discharge and discipline*: This is a touchy issue, and even when an agreement addresses these problems, many grievances are filed concerning the way employees are disciplined or discharged.

- *Health and safety*: Although various Occupational Health and Safety Acts specifically deal with this issue, some contracts have provisions specifying that the company will provide additional safety equipment, first aid, physical examinations, accident investigations, and safety committees. Hazardous work is covered by special provisions and pay rates. Often the agreement will generally state that the employer is responsible for the safety of the workers, so the union can use the grievance process when any safety issues arise.

- *Production standards*: The level of productivity or performance of employees is a concern of both management and the union. Management is concerned with efficiency, but the union is concerned with the fairness and reasonableness of management's demands.

- *Grievance procedures*: This is a significant part of collective bargaining, and is discussed in more detail later in the chapter.

- *Training*: The design and administration of training and development programs and the procedure for selecting employees may also be bargaining issues.

- *Duration of the agreement*: Agreements can last for one year or longer, with the most common period being three years.

CONFLICT RESOLUTION

Although the desired outcome of collective bargaining is agreement on the conditions of employment, negotiators often are unable to reach such an agreement at the bargaining table. In these situations, several alternatives are used to resolve the impasse. The most visible response is the strike or lockout, but third-party interventions such as mediation and arbitration are also used.

Strikes and Lockouts

When the union is unable to get management to agree to a demand it feels is critical, it may resort to a strike. A **strike** is the refusal by employees to work at the company. Management may refuse to allow employees to work, which is called a **lockout**, but this is not a frequent occurrence.

In order to strike, the union must hold a strike vote to get its members' approval. Strong membership support for a strike strengthens the union negotiators' position. If the strike takes place, union members picket the employer, informing the public about the existence of a labour dispute in the hope that the public will boycott this company's products during the strike. A common practice is the refusal of union members to cross the picket line of another striking union. This gives added support to the striking union.

Employers usually attempt to continue operations while the strike is in effect. They either run the company with supervisory personnel and people not in the bargaining unit, or hire replacements for the employees. Many jurisdictions have passed "antiscab" laws that do not permit the employer to hire replacements, as in Quebec and Ontario.

The success of a strike depends on its ability to cause economic hardship to the employer. Severe hardship usually causes the employer to accede to the union's demands. Thus it is paramount, from the union's point of view, that the company not be able to operate successfully during the strike and that the cost of this lack of production be high. In addition, the timing of the strike is often critical. The union attempts to hold negotiations just prior to the period when the employer has a peak demand for its products or services, so that the strike will have maximum economic impact.

Although strikes are common, they are costly to both the employer, who loses revenue, and the employees, who lose income. If the strike is prolonged, it is likely that the cost to employees will never be fully offset by the benefits gained. In addition, the public interest generally is not served by strikes, which are often an inconvenience and can have serious consequences to the economy as a whole. All in all, work stoppages in Canada due to strikes and other reasons seem to be declining. For example, from an average of 5.7 person-days lost in 1986, they declined to 2.6 days in 1990.[18] The prolonged recession, the declining power of unions in the private sector, and the improved quality of HR practices are all factors to which this decline can be attributed.

The right to strike in the public sector is even more debatable—public services employees withhold services from the general public in an attempt to gain concessions from the public employer. The public, therefore, is held "hostage" by the public-sector union during a strike. For these reasons, all jurisdictions in Canada that grant the right to strike in the public sector, also use a "designation" process to deal with "essential services." Some jurisdictions, such as British Columbia and Quebec, specify which services are essential and must be maintained either wholly or in part. In 1982, Quebec established the Essential Services Council, which is empowered to designate the level of service to be maintained if the parties cannot agree on the number of employees required, or if the union does not designate a sufficient number of employees. Conflict resolution interventions such as arbitration, mediation, and other measures are often required.

Mediation

Mediation is a procedure in which a neutral third party assists the union and management negotiators in reaching voluntary agreement. This third party has no power to impose a solution, but only attempts to facilitate the negotiations between union and management. The mediator may make suggestions and recommendations, and perhaps add objectivity to the often emotional negotiations. To have any success at all, the mediator must have the trust and respect of both parties and have sufficient expertise and neutrality to convince the union and employer that he or she will be fair and equitable. Conciliation is compulsory in all jurisdictions in Canada (except Saskatchewan), and provides for the appointment of a mediator.

In **arbitration** a neutral third party studies the bargaining situation, listening to both parties and gathering information, and then makes recommendations that are binding on the parties. The arbitrator, in effect, determines the conditions of the agreement.

Arbitration

Three types of arbitration have developed. The first is an **extension of bargaining**: the arbitrator attempts to reach a rational and equitable decision acceptable to both parties. The second type, called **final-offer arbitration**, sees the arbitrator choose between the final offer of the union and the final offer of the employer. The arbitrator cannot alter these offers but must choose one as it stands. Since the arbitrator chooses the offer that appears most fair, and since losing the arbitration decision means settling for the other's offer, there is pressure to make as good an offer as possible. The intention of final-offer arbitration is to encourage the parties to make their best offer and to reach an agreement before arbitration becomes necessary. This is also true with respect to the use of **closed-offer arbitration**. Here the arbitrator receives information on only the parties' original positions without any information on the bargaining progress up to the point.

The process previously described, which deals with the contract terms and conditions, is called **interest arbitration**. While this is relatively infrequent in the private sector, it is more common in the public sector, because most jurisdictions in Canada force this. Most of the statutes set out fairly broad criteria for arbitrators to follow, yet some provinces request that they keep the interests of the public foremost. Ontario and Alberta require that arbitrators or arbitration boards consider the government's fiscal policies when rendering their interest arbitration awards.

Once the impasse is resolved, union and management have a contract to abide by. This is the essence of contract administration; however, there are times during contract administration when arbitration is again necessary, namely when a grievance is filed; this type of arbitration is referred to as **grievance arbitration**.

Because of the infrequency with which interest arbitration affects the private sector, it is grievance arbitration that is subject to the most attention and concern. The role of grievance arbitration and the arbitrator is considered in Step 4 of the grievance procedures in the discussion of contract administration.

CONTRACT ADMINISTRATION

Once signed, the collective agreement becomes the basic legislation governing the lives of the workers. That is, the daily operation and activities in the organization are subject to the conditions of the agreement. Since it is impossible to write an unambiguous agreement that will anticipate all the situations occurring over its life, there will inevitably be disputes over interpretation and application of the agreement. The most common method of resolving these disputes is a **grievance procedure**. Virtually all agreements negotiated today provide for a grievance process to handle employee complaints.

Grievance Procedures

Basically, a grievance is a charge that the union–management contract has been violated. A grievance may be filed by the union for employees or by employers, although management rarely does so. The grievance process is designed to investigate the charges and to resolve the problem.

Five common sources of grievances have been identified:

- Outright violation of the agreement,
- Disagreement over facts,
- Dispute over the meaning of the agreement,
- Dispute over the method of applying the agreement,
- Argument over the fairness or reasonableness of action.

In resolving these sources of conflict, the grievance procedure should serve four separate groups: the *employers* and *unions*, by interpreting and adjusting the agreement as conditions require; the *employees*, by protecting their contractual rights and providing a channel of appeal; and *society* at large, by keeping industrial peace and reducing the number of industrial disputes in the courts.

Grievance procedures typically involve several stages. The collective bargaining agreement specifies the maximum length of time that each step may take. For example, it may require the grievance to be filed within five days of the incident that is the subject of dispute. The most common grievance procedure, shown in Exhibit 16.6, involves four steps, with the final step being arbitration.

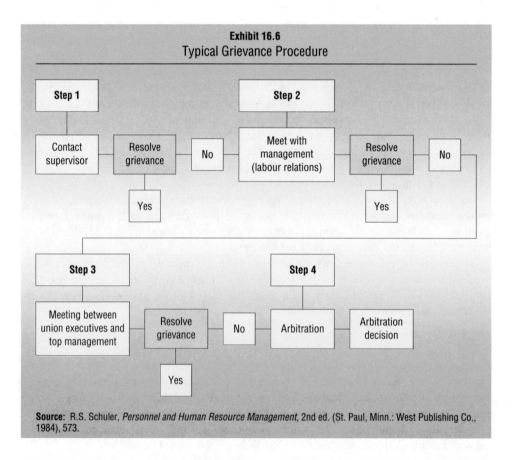

Exhibit 16.6
Typical Grievance Procedure

Source: R.S. Schuler, *Personnel and Human Resource Management*, 2nd ed. (St. Paul, Minn.: West Publishing Co., 1984), 573.

STEP 1. An employee who feels that the labour contract has been violated usually contacts the union steward, and together they discuss the problem with the supervisor involved. If the problem is simple and straightforward, it is often resolved at this level. Many contracts require the grievance to be in written form at this first stage. However, there may be cases that are resolved by informal discussion between the supervisor and the employee, and therefore do not officially enter the grievance process.

STEP 2. If agreement cannot be reached at the supervisory level, or if the employee is not satisfied, the complaint can enter the second step of the grievance procedure. Typically, an industrial relations representative of the company now seeks to resolve the grievance.

STEP 3. If the grievance is sufficiently important or difficult to resolve, it may be taken to the third step. Although contracts vary, top-level management and union executives are usually involved at this step. These people have the authority to make the major decisions that may be required to resolve the grievance.

STEP 4. If a grievance cannot be resolved at the third step, most agreements require the use of an arbitrator to consider the case and reach a decision. The arbitrator (or arbitration board) is a neutral, and mutually acceptable, individual. However, if the parties are unable or unwilling to select the members or the chair of an arbitration board, then in practically all jurisdictions in Canada the respective Minister of Labour has the right to nominate the members to the board. Also, some provinces supply the parties with a list of arbitrators and when both parties have selected the same name, that person becomes the arbitrator. The arbitrator holds a hearing, reviews the evidence, then rules on the grievance. The decision of the arbitrator is usually binding.

Since the cost of arbitration is shared by the union and the employer, there is some incentive to settle the grievance before it goes to arbitration. Moreover, given that the arbitrators' fees in Canada range from $400 to $1,500 per day, along with other fees, the parties have an incentive to resort to less expensive methods of resolving the conflict. A newly suggested method is **grievance mediation**, which is, according to some experts, cheaper, quicker, and remains confidential; hence mediated settlements are not published. Air Canada has been using this approach for some time.

Occasionally, the union will call a strike over a grievance in order to resolve it. This may happen when the issue at hand is so important that the union feels it cannot wait for the slower arbitration process. This "employee rights" strike may be legal, but if the contract specifically forbids strikes during the tenure of the agreement, it is not legal and is called a **wildcat strike**. In Canada, only Saskatchewan does not outlaw the wildcat strike. However, wildcat strikes are not common since most grievances are settled through arbitration.

Grievances can be filed over any workplace issue that is covered by the collective agreement, or they can be filed over interpretation and implementation of the agreement itself. The most common type of grievance reaching the arbitration stage concerns discipline and discharge, although many grievances are filed over other issues. It is generally conceded that management has the right to discipline employees. The grievance issue usually relates to "just cause" for the discipline and the fairness and consistency of the action taken. Because disputes can arise over the definition of "just cause," discipline and discharge actions are prone to grievances.

Grievance Issues

Although it is accepted that absenteeism, for example, can constitute grounds for discharge, the critical issue is whether the absenteeism in question is excessive. Insubordination usually is either failure to do as the supervisor requests, or the more serious problem of outright refusal to do it. If the supervisor's orders are clear and explicit and if the employee is warned of the consequences, discipline for refusal to respond is usually acceptable. The exception is when the employee feels that the work constitutes a health danger.

Since seniority is usually used to determine who is laid off, bumped from a job to make way for someone else, or rehired, its calculation is of great concern to employees. Promotions and transfers also use seniority as one of the criteria to determine eligibility, so management must be careful in this area so as to avoid complaints and grievances.

Compensation for time away from work, vacations, holidays, or sick leave is also a common source for grievances. Holidays cause problems because there are often special pay arrangements for people working on those days. Wage and work schedules may also lead to grievances. Disagreements often arise over interpretation or application of the agreement relating to such issues as overtime pay, pay for reporting, and scheduling.

Grievances have been filed over the exercise of management rights—that is, its right to introduce technological change, use subcontractors, or change jobs in other ways. This type of behaviour may also be the source of charges of unfair labour practices, since these activities may require collective bargaining.

Occasionally other activities prompt grievances. Wildcat strikes or behaviour that is considered to be a strike (e.g., mass absences from work) may result in a management grievance. The major focus of grievances, however, is usually in the administration of the conditions of the agreement.

Management Procedures

Management can significantly affect the grievance rate by adopting proper procedures when taking action against an employee. One of the areas most in need of such procedures is that of discipline and discharge. The issue of just cause and fairness is central to most discipline grievances. Employers must ensure that the employee is adequately warned of the consequences of poor performance or role violations, that the rule involved is related to the operation of the company, that a thorough investigation is undertaken, and that the penalty is reasonable. The following activities have been identified as being useful in meeting these conditions:

- Explanation of rules to employees;
- Consideration of the accusations and facts;
- Regular warning procedures, including written records;
- Involvement of the union in the case;
- Examination of the employee's motives and reasons;
- Consideration of the employee's past record;
- Familiarization of all management personnel, especially supervisors, with disciplinary procedures and company rules.

In areas outside of discipline and discharge, management can avoid some grievance problems by educating supervisors and managers about labour relations and about the conditions of the collective agreement. It has been found that the presence of supervisors with labour knowledge can significantly reduce the number of grievances.

Union Procedures

The union has an obligation to its members to provide them with fair and adequate representation and to investigate and process speedily grievances brought by its members. Thus, it should have a grievance-handling procedure that will aid in effectively processing grievances without any unfair representation.

Unions may have an additional interest in grievances as a tool in collective negotiation. They may attempt to increase grievance rates in order to influence management as collective bargaining approaches. Grievances may also be a way to introduce or show concern for an issue in negotiations. In some cases, grievances may be withdrawn by unions in exchange for some management concessions. This may be dangerous, however, since it may be an unfair representation of the employee.

The union steward has an important influence on the grievance process as the first person to hear about an employee's grievance. A steward can encourage an employee to file a grievance, can suggest that the problem is really not a grievance, or can informally resolve the problem outside the grievance procedure. The personality characteristics of stewards may, in fact, influence the number of grievances filed.[19] Because stewards are selected from the ranks of employees, and may have little knowledge of labour relations, the union should provide training to improve their effectiveness. The company should support such training as well.

Because union–management activities are enmeshed in a web of federal and provincial laws, one measure of effectiveness is how well the HR manager avoids violating these laws while maintaining productive relationships with the workforce. Moreover, HR corporate officers who are responsible for developing labour relations policies across provincial lines (in the case of multi-plant, multi-provincial locations) have the duty of closely monitoring the different labour relations statutes and complying with them. By the same token, effectiveness can be judged by how well the HR manager negotiates and administers contracts if the employees are unionized.

The effectiveness of the entire collective bargaining process and the union–management relationship can be measured by the extent to which each party attains its goals, but there are some difficulties associated with this approach. Because goals are incompatible in many cases, and can therefore lead to conflicting estimates of effectiveness, a more useful measure of effectiveness may be the quality of the system used to resolve conflict. Conflict is more apparent in the collective bargaining process, where failure to resolve the issues typically leads to strikes. Another measure of effectiveness is the success of the grievance process, or the ability to resolve issues developing out of the bargaining agreement.

EFFECTIVENESS OF NEGOTIATIONS. Because the purpose of negotiations is to achieve an agreement, this becomes an overall measure of bargaining effectiveness. A healthy and effective bargaining process encourages the discussion of issues and problems and their subsequent resolution at the bargaining table. In addition, the effort required to reach agreement is a measure of how well the process is working. Some indications of this effort are the duration of strikes, the use of mediation and arbitration, the need for government intervention, and the resulting quality of union–management relations (whether conflict or cooperation exists). Certainly joint programs for productivity and QWL improvements could be regarded as successes resulting from the quality of union–management relations.

EFFECTIVENESS OF GRIEVANCE PROCEDURES. How successful a grievance procedure is may be assessed from different perspectives. Management may view the number of grievances filed and the number settled in management's favour as measures of effectiveness. Unions may also consider the number of grievances, but from their point of view, a larger number rather than a smaller number may be considered more successful. Naturally, the percentage of settlements in the union's favour is another measure of effectiveness.

Although the views of management and the union may differ, an overall set of measures to gauge grievance procedure effectiveness may be related to the disagreements between managers and employees. Measures that might be included are frequency of grievances; the level in the grievance procedure at which grievances are usually settled; the frequency of strikes or slowdowns during the term of the labour agreements; the rates of absenteeism, turnover, and sabotage; and the necessity for government intervention.

The success of arbitration is often judged by the acceptability of the decisions, the satisfaction of the parties, innovation, and the absence of bias in either direction. The effectiveness of any third-party intervention rests in part on its ability to reduce or avoid strikes, since the motivation for third-party intervention is the realization that strikes do occur.

It is becoming more common for labour negotiators to carry portable computers to the bargaining sessions. This enables them to use spreadsheets, as well as other packaged pro-

TRENDS IN LABOUR RELATIONS

Assessing Union–Management Relationships

Assessing the Collective Bargaining Process

Computer Applications

grams, to cost out proposed contract terms so that they will be able to quickly determine the bottom line impact of each proposal. In addition, there are numerous packaged systems for grievance tracking and other systems that monitor contract administration issues, and, more specifically, disciplinary actions. Additionally, several computer simulations have been developed for training negotiators. In these systems, a scenario is provided and the player chooses the role of either union representative or management representative and the computer will assume the other party role. Results are then analyzed by expert trainers.

HRM DYNAMICS
Labour Relations Profiles in Selected Canadian Organizations

Air Canada

Approximately three-quarters of Air Canada's 23,000 employees are unionized. The 4,000 flight attendants are represented by the Canadian Union of Public Employees (CUPE). Additionally, there are three other large unions within the company: the International Association of Machinists and Aerospace Workers, representing 8,000 employees, the Canadian Auto Workers, representing 2,800 passenger agents; and the Canadian Airline Pilots Association, representing 1,725 members. In order to negotiate with this sizable unionized workforce, Air Canada employed eighteen labour relations specialists. The CUPE contract runs for three years. It defines the responsibilities of the various cabin personnel classifications, hourly pay rates for different seniority levels, other pay calculation parameters, grievance and discipline procedures, and rules for the awarding of flight blocks.

McGill University

McGill University has about 7,200 employees, of which only 500 are unionized. Nonetheless, McGill has one of the largest groups of employees under one association, the McGill University nonacademic staff association. About 1,600 people belong to this group that is similar to a union, except that the association is involved in fewer functions and does not have the same extended rights as a union. In 1976 the association signed a parity agreement with McGill, which is still in effect. This agreement allows all nonacademic, nonunionized employees to maintain a comparable level in salary and other fringe benefits with the University of Montreal.

SUMMARY

Unions are an important labour relations system element. Although they have benefited from significant growth and power over the years, the situation is changing today. Strategically, unions have had to adjust to the decline in employment in traditional industries such as steel, automobile, and mining. In addition, the labour force has shifted to services and from blue- to pink- and white-collar occupations. Unions have yet to capture new labour force entrants, particularly females. Although the fastest growing unions in the past were in the public sector, this growth has slowed in relation to population growth. Organized labour is concerned about its image and will make renewed efforts to match the geographical, industrial, occupational, and demographic shifts in the labour force.

Collective bargaining is a complex process in which union and management negotiators manoeuvre to win the most advantageous contract. This has been the process in the traditional union–management relationship. This has been changing, however, especially with the development of the productivity crisis in Canada. In addition, government intervention in the LRS at all levels is becoming much more apparent. The aim of all concerned is to safeguard the basic rights of collective bargaining, yet at the same time, move the parties from an adversarial relationship to a more cooperative one. Canada certainly seems to be shifting in this direction at both the national and local levels.

Although many obstacles exist to union–management cooperation, present economic conditions are prompting many firms to cooperate with unions for their mutual benefit. The need for more cooperation has also been recognized by some union leaders, who recommend more involvement with management.

Historically, the threat of a strike has been necessary to bring concessions by management. Without the threat, these concessions become less likely, though some managements may grant them even without threat. The strike threat is an integral part of union–management relations in the private sector. Is the public sector really different from the private sector? Arguments go both ways of course. It is hard to tell the difference, however, between irresponsible management in the private sector and its counterpart in the public sector, regardless of how essential the services are to the community.

The quality of the union–management relationship can have a strong influence on contract negotiations. Labour and management each select a bargaining committee to negotiate the new agreement. The negotiations may be between a single union and a single company or multiple companies, or between multiple unions and a single company. Bargaining issues vary in scope and content, thus issues can be grouped into wage issues, economic supplements issues, institutional issues, and administrative issues. Mandatory issues must be discussed, permissive issues can be discussed if both parties agree, and prohibited issues cannot be discussed.

Almost all labour contracts outline grievance procedures for handling employee complaints. The most common grievance relates to discipline and discharge, although wages, promotions, seniority, vacations, holidays, and management and union rights are also sources of complaints. Management can influence the results of grievances by developing a procedure that ensures management's actions are just and fair. Written records of actions taken are useful for potential arbitration. Unions have a legal responsibility to represent the employee fairly in grievances; therefore, they also need a grievance-handling procedure.

The effective HR manager should understand the history of union–management relations and the basic legal framework that guides collective bargaining in Canada. A knowledge of the role of the LRB is critical if organizations are to avoid committing unfair labour practices. In addition, an understanding of why unions appeal to workers has implications for the design of effective HR functions. Finally, the HR manager needs to know how to deal with unions and how to enforce the agreement signed with the organization.

P O S T S C R I P T

We are currently witnessing a major experiment in the Canadian labour relations system. Both federal and provincial governments are obliged to control their budgets and therefore pass the buck to their employees by imposing all sorts of freezes on salaries and employment levels. Employers in the private sector are also cutting back on personnel and demanding more and more concessions from unions just to keep operations afloat. And unions are in the centre of the crisis. Unions and their leaders, especially in the private sector, are facing a growing challenge: how to respond to members' demands in hard economic times when their options are really limited. Union leaders know that by maintaining the status quo, they will most likely vote themselves out of office. Union members who feel disgruntled with the economy in general react in two distinct ways: either they become more militant in union affairs, hoping to bring about changes, or, in the majority of cases, they fall into such despair that they become completely apathetic to unions' activities; they simply do not believe in the unions' ability to deliver. This is seen in the continuous decline in members' participation in union affairs. It is well known that many unions have been obliged to reduce the necessary quorum in their by-laws in order to enable the passage of various resolutions; members simply do not show up. Although statistics are not available, rumours have it that the average quorum needed for local unions' resolutions is about 20 percent.

Because of these mounting pressures, unions (and union leaders) are being forced to be innovative to survive. This is perhaps the best result deriving from the pressures applied to them. Here are a few innovations:

1. In order to satisfy their members, more and more union leaders pay careful attention to members' opinions, which are solicited by means of surveys. In the case of the Montreal Brotherhood of Policemen, the leadership learned that members were concerned with job content issues to the same extent that they were concerned with traditional bread-and-butter issues. However, since most police officers understood that any excessive demands for monetary and other working conditions would be rejected, the emphasis during negotiations was placed on nonmonetary issues such as the development of a career plan (there were no formal career plans available for police officers). Maybe in the future, we will witness an increase in negotiations for intrinsic rewards.

2. Some Canadian labour federations are learning how to increase their power (i.e., economic power) from the experience of their counterparts in Germany, Sweden, and Israel. There, unions are becoming involved in setting up, investing in, and even managing certain industries/organizations. In Quebec, for example, an umbrella group of labour organizations created the Solidarity Fund of Quebec, which is the main vehicle for labour's investments. After negotiating a tax exemption for investors with the government, the fund has accumulated substantial capital, which is carefully channelled and re-invested, especially in industries that are labour intensive. The experience thus far has been very good.

3. Because union organizing is at or near its saturation level in the public sector, there is an increasing awareness of the need to concentrate on the private sector, since it holds the greatest potential for future organizing campaigns, namely in finance, insurance, real estate, and the white-collar workforce in the manufacturing industries. However, these sectors are also characterized by a high proportion of women, part-time employees, and professionals, and they either consist of very large employers, where union-organizing attempts failed in the past, or small-sized firms, which have generally been harder to get to. In order to be more successful in penetrating these sectors, some unions are developing more sophisticated approaches to organizing. This goes hand in hand with an attempt to improve their image so as to cater to the professional employees. Unions also have begun hiring high-calibre employees, that is, people with more education and professionalism, to be involved in the organizing campaigns.

REVIEW AND ANALYSIS QUESTIONS

1. Identify and discuss the factors that make unionization attractive to employees. Are these factors different today than they were fifty years ago?
2. Given the similar LRS in Canada and in the U.S.A., what factors explain the significant decrease in union membership in the U.S.A. over the past few years, compared to almost no change in the percentage of union membership of the labour force in Canada?
3. Identify and explain the major steps in the certification process.
4. What are the major ingredients for a successful campaign to solicit employees' support?
5. What legal strategies could be undertaken by employers to devise a nonunion campaign?
6. What is the current trend in union–management relations and what impact does this trend have on unions, management, and employees?
7. Compare and contrast adversarial and cooperative union–management relations.
8. Discuss the strategies that managements and unions use to prepare for collective bargaining.

9. What alternatives are there for management and labour to resolve an impasse in collective bargaining?

10. What is the purpose of a grievance procedure? What are legitimate grievances, and what is the process by which grievances are resolved? What are innovative methods to resolve conflicts at work?

CASE STUDY

NEGOTIATIONS IN THE HI-TECH PLASTICS COMPANY

In union–management relations, collective bargaining is essentially a power relationship. It is through the implied and actual use of power that parties are compelled to resolve their conflicts. This was the situation when the management of Hi-Tech Plastics Company sat down with the Amalgamated Plastics Workers (APW) to negotiate a new contract.

Allen Springer, the 45-year-old president and owner of Hi-Tech, was surprised at the list of demands presented by the APW business agent, Tony Mattson. But Springer was completely taken aback by the union's tenacity. Throughout the six-hour session the union team refused to budge from their initial positions. It was not the first time the APW had caught Springer off guard; the organizing drive that had brought the union into Hi-Tech had also come unexpectedly.

Allen Springer had taken the reins of this Oshawa company following the untimely death of his father, the founder of the company. At that time, Oshawa automakers needed plastic body parts, trim pieces, and fasteners to meet government-mandated high mileage standards. Allen took full advantage of this demand and shifted his company's output from consumer to industrial lines. Under this strategy, sales volume almost tripled and the employee roster doubled to its present size of 105 employees. Measured against the industry leaders, however, Hi-Tech was still a small firm.

In the third year of Springer's presidency, a recession caused major setbacks in the auto industry; Hi-Tech's revenues declined and unsold inventory stacked up. In the midst of this bad news, Allen Springer was hit with another blow—his workers were signing cards and pressing for union certification.

Following the successful drive, the union represented seventy-five Hi-Tech employees. The first contract was easily drafted, and included a 4 percent wage hike in a one-year pact, but the renewal negotiations were more militant. Battle lines formed on three union demands:

1. A three-year agreement, with a 17 percent wage boost the first year of the contract and 13 percent for each of the following years.

Because contract negotiations were time-consuming and expensive, Springer wanted the contract to run longer than the one-year term of the first contract, but not at the proposed wage increases. He offered what he believed was a generous 6 percent wage hike.

But Tony Mattson claimed that stingy wage hikes over the preceding five years had cut severely into the union members' standard of living. A 17 percent increase, he stated, was just bridging the gap between past wage increases and the inflation rate, as measured by the Consumer Price Index.

2. A dental health plan. On this point the talks became heated. Mattson pounded on the table, jumped to his feet, and shouted: "How can management claim to care about their workers while ignoring their health?"

3. Reinstate service pins. From the time Hi-Tech had opened its doors, the elder Springer had acknowledged employee loyalty with 24-carat gold service pins for five, ten, fifteen, and twenty years of uninterrupted employment. But in the face of declining income, Allen Springer had halted the practice. The union was quick to respond with a grievance calling for the pins to be brought back. At contract negotiation time the issue was still unresolved, but the APW members were adamant—"give us our pins," they said, "or submit the entire issue to binding arbitration."

Aside from the specific demands, what troubled Springer the most was the apparent willingness of the members to strike if their demands were not met. Throughout the session the power of a strike was implied. Several times Mattson hinted that the rank-and-file members had already voted for a strike if their demands were not met to the letter.

During a break in the negotiations, Mattson confided to Springer that, although he was personally against a strike, the members were prepared. His manner was in sharp contrast to the shouting and table pounding during the bargaining. Now he was speaking in low, even tones. "The local has already rented office space across the street from the plant for strike headquarters," he said.

"The central labour union is giving advice and the other labour unions have pledged their support. I'm afraid they mean business."

This information disturbed Springer. If the unionized employees went on a picket line, he would be left with only clerical personnel, a sales staff, and six production supervisors.

As Springer reflected on the demands and the strike threat, he was at least grateful that this was only the first bargaining session with two more to go, and that the present contract had fifteen more days before it expired. He had three days to prepare for the next bargaining meeting.

Case Questions

1. What information does Springer need to prepare for the next session? How would the information be useful?
2. What past poor labour relations practices can you identify?
3. What strategy or strategies would you suggest Springer use? Should he "take a strike" or try to avert it? Why?
4. What could be done to develop more effective labour relations on a long-term basis?

NOTES

1. A.W.J. Craig, *The System of Industrial Relations in Canada*, 2nd ed. (Scarborough: Prentice–Hall, 1986). 1.

2. A.M. Ponack, "Public-Sector Collective Bargaining," in *Union–Management Relations in Canada*, ed. J. Anderson and M. Gunderson (Don Mills, Ont.: Addison–Wesley, 1982), 343–74.

3. M.L. Coates, "Industrial Relations in the 1990s: Trends and Emerging Issues," *The Current Industrial Relations Scene in Canada 1990* (Kingston: Queens University, Industrial Relations Centre, 1991).

4. G. Trudeau, "Employee Rights versus Management Rights: Some Reflections Regarding Dismissal," in *Canadian Readings in Personnel and Human Resource Management*, ed. S.L. Dolan and R.S. Schuler (St. Paul, Minn.: West Publishing Co., 1987), 367–78; and W.S. Tarnopolsky, *Discrimination and the Law in Canada* (Toronto: R. DeBoo Ltd., 1982).

5. A.W.J. Craig, "The Canadian Industrial Relations System," in *Canadian Readings in Personnel and Human Resource Management*, ed. S.L. Dolan and R.S. Schuler (St. Paul, Minn.: West Publishing Co., 1987), 339–52.

6. J.G. Getman, S.B. Goldberg, and J.B. Herman, *Union Representation Elections: Law and Reality* (New York: Russell Sage Foundation, 1976).

7. D.G. Gallagher and G. Strauss, "Union Membership: Attitudes and Participation," in *The State of the Unions*, ed. G. Strauss, D. Gallagher, and J. Fiorito (Madison, Wis.: Industrial Relations Research Association, 1991) v–xi; and H. Wheeler and A. McClendon, "The Individual Decision to Unionize," in ibid., 47–84

8. J.F. Rand, "Preventive Maintenance Techniques for Staying Union Free," *Personnel Journal*, June 1980, 498.

9. "How Canadians view unions," *The Worklife Report* 7, 5 (1990): 14.

10. For further information on the evolution of trade unions, see M.R. Coates, *Is there a Future for the Canadian Labour Movement?* "Industrial Relations Centre, Queen's University (IRC Press), 1992; and D.D. Carter, *Canadian Industrial Relations in the Year 2000: Towards a new order?* Industrial Relations Centre, Queen's University (IRC Press), 1992.

11. Coates, "Industrial Relations in the 1990s," 46.

12. *Directory of Labour Organizations in Canada*, Labour Data Branch, Labour Canada, 1982, 81.

13. D.A. Peach and D. Kuechle, *The Practice of Industrial Relations* (Toronto: McGraw–Hill Ryerson Ltd., 1975), 81.

14. T. Brodie, "Department Stores Gain Upper Hand," *Financial Times of Canada*, 24 March 1986, 4.

15. A.B. Blum, "Collective Bargaining: Ritual or Reality?" *Harvard Business Review*, Nov.–Dec. 1961, Copyright © 1961 by the President and Fellows of Harvard College. All rights reserved. Reprinted by permission of the Harvard Business Review.

16. Agreement Analysis Section, Labour Data–Labour Canada, *Provisions in Collective Agreements in Canada Covering 200 and More Employees: All Industries (Excluding Construction)* (Ottawa: Supply and Services Canada, March 1981), 31–34.

17. "Via Rail Employees Get Job Security in New Contract," *The Montreal Gazette*, 16 July 1985, D7.

18. R. Wright, ed., "The 1991 Industrial Relations Outlook," *Report 66–91*, (Ottawa: Compensation Research Centre, Conference Board of Canada, January 1991), 7. Note that data for 1990 were available for only the first nine months.

19. D.R. Dalton and W.D. Todor, "Manifest Needs of Stewards: Propensity to File a Grievance," *Journal of Applied Psychology*, December 1979, 654–59.

CHAPTER SEVENTEEN

INTERNATIONAL AND MULTINATIONAL HRM

KEYNOTE ADDRESS

Yoshida Kogyo
President and CEO, YKK Canada

Managing Human Resources in Canada Japanese Style:
Myths and Realities

Yoshida Kogyo, known as YKK throughout the world, has manufacturing and sales facilities in almost every country in the free world. In North America, we first established YKK USA and subsequently YKK Canada, which has been in operation since 1968. We have been fortunate in almost every country where we have conducted business and we have often been asked what the secret is of our success. Many feel our management system could well be the cornerstone.

I have been asked to address the experiences of YKK in Japan and North America and YKK's HRM approach. This is quite difficult to do. First, I would like to try to help form an idea of what I feel are very basic differences between the thinking of Japanese people and North American people. In North America, God is thought of and represented as "absolute," with a capital G. In Japan, God is one of many Gods.

Your Old Testament speaks of Adam and Eve being chased out of paradise and of humankind being condemned to work for the rest of their lives. When you consider paradise and all that this entails and then think of being condemned to having to work for the rest of your lives, it certainly leaves you with a heavy heart, longing for that lost paradise. In the Japanese culture, work is considered a privilege, a way of becoming closer to God. I am in no way trying to challenge the teachings of the Bible or of any church or, for that matter, anybody's religious beliefs. What I am trying to do is underline the basic differences in our cultural backgrounds and how I feel they form a part of the different management practices. For one thing, there is a substantial difference in what "work" represents, especially if we consider the cultural differences between Japan and North America.

When we speak of management practices, we have stereotyped ideas of what Japanese practices are in contrast to North American practices. If I were to stereotype American management, I would have to say that they consider their labour force a commodity, that they show very little compassion for it. During difficult times, one of the first steps considered is to trim the workforce to meet the production demands through cold-blooded mass layoffs or firings. On the other hand, if I were to stereotype Japanese management, I would say that once an employee is hired he is guaranteed lifetime employment.

Both are not quite true. In North America, and especially in Canada, union agreements and legislation provide strict guidelines that do not simplify the task of laying off or firing. As well, what happens in Japan when a company that basically offers lifetime employment runs into financial difficulties? Just how far can this burden be carried? Thus, in reality, there is no real guarantee of lifetime employment in Japan. By the same token, it is not always mass layoffs or firing that take precedence in North America.

Is YKK Canada's management system really different when compared to other Canadian manufacturing companies? Yes, there are certain differences in approach that are not really that apparent. Is the YKK Canada management system different from YKK Japan's? Yes, it is. Our Canadian system has evolved into a combination of YKK Japan's systems and those of local Canadian employers. Furthermore, we are also in a constant state of evolution. Many of the differences are not really due to the different systems; most times they are due to the expectations of our employees.

Firstly, I find that most Canadian companies do not keep their employees informed of the company's financial performance. We make regular reports to our employees on our financial situation. Our managers are active participants in our quarterly board of directors' meetings. They make no secret of what is discussed during those meetings.

Secondly, the concept of quality circles, which has been in practice for many years in Japan and which I view as the cornerstone of the Japanese success story, had mixed results in North America. While Japanese employees voluntarily work together on joint projects after the normal workday, the vast majority of quality circles in operation in Canada are conducted during the normal work hours; workers are reluctant to give of their personal time.

Peer pressure is a third factor that distinguishes the Japanese worker from his North American counterpart. I have been told of new employees in North America being warned to slow down their pace when more senior employees felt they were being over-productive. In Japan, there is peer pressure as well, but I feel it works the other way: the members of the group will normally apply pressure to an individual who they feel is not performing up to normal standards. I regret to say that there is a different "work ethic."

In Japan, when management addresses an issue and advises employees of certain facts, the vast majority do not question what is said. In Canada, there seems to be a basic feeling of distrust between management and employees, a sort of invisible line that tends to keep the two apart, each side mistrusting the other's motives.

In Canada, the employees have a strong need to have established parameters regarding their duties and responsibilities, which is the core of the job description function. In Japan, there is a great deal of ambiguity concerning an individual's duties and responsibilities. There are many overlapping areas of responsibility, and sometimes clashes in the realm of whose authority is to be exercised. This ambiguity is an extension of the Japanese cultural background. Even the language is less direct, less straightforward than its English counterpart, or even its French counterpart. Furthermore, this ambiguity in the work context obliges the subordinate to stretch his imagination. This can sometimes lead to dramatic results, surpassing original expectations....

As previously stated, our management methods have similarities to both cultures, a combination of both, basically one that is "Made in Canada." There is no "magic formula": We follow a straightforward, honest approach to problems and stress the fact that problems are mutually shared and overcome. The feeling that "we are all in the same boat" is the best basis for success.

·   ·   ·

The globalization of business is having a significant impact upon human resource management. As the world becomes more interdependent and international mobility characterizes many business organizations, Canadian managers are beginning to recognize the need to be aware of HR practices in other cultures and nations. Canadian managers continue to be fascinated by Japan's traditions and, more importantly, by its impressive economic success. The Keynote Address by K. Yoshida, who is founder and CEO of a multinational company based in Japan with subsidiaries in virtually every industrial country, is interesting in that it describes very specifically the core of the Japanese values that contribute to the company's success. According to Mr. Yoshida, he instils the same values in all his plants worldwide, while recognizing the cultural differences between Japanese workers and other workers.

·   ·   ·

Purposes and Importance

The globalization of HRM cannot be understood without focusing on the present economic situation and projecting the future behaviour of Canadian organizations within this economic climate. As this is being written, the world economic situation is in upheaval. The communist governments have tumbled in the Eastern bloc countries and new governments are attempting to establish themselves. Japan's long-established system of management is coming under scrutiny and changes are inevitable. Hong Kong will come under the jurisdiction of China as of 1997, and this prospect is already influencing a shift of capital and workforces. Western Europe is venturing into the Economic Common Market, and in North America, the free trade agreement has been passed among Canada, the U.S.A., and Mexico.

If organizations intend to operate in this new world market rather than the domestic market, the HR department will have to search for, recommend, hire, train, compensate, and negotiate with employees for the global organization. All facets of HRM will come into play in this global environment.

However, HRM is unlike any other organizational branch (e.g., accounting, marketing, or finance). There are not set formulas to follow, and no one answer provides all solutions. It revolves around people; its foundation is people. To effectively manage people in various continents and cultures is one of the most difficult tasks that multinational corporations (MNCs) are confronting. Consequently, pressures are placed on the HR corporate manager forcing him or her to adjust to constant change; business environments are in a state of continuous motion and this requires the HR manager in the MNC to be atuned, proactive, and innovative.

Businesses today are taking a great leap forward: the globalization of the world's economic activities and human resources predominates on the list of issues to consider. Failure to take an international perspective in HR policies and practices will result in the organization's inability to successfully compete. Effective HR strategies must be developed to utilize a multinational workforce. Constant change is affecting this level of management, therefore, exposure to new practices and strategies is gaining importance. Broad-based global strategies are being created due to increased communication and a greater sharing of assets throughout the world. Like all other facets of the corporation, HRM is evolving into a global operation.[1]

In the 1980s, companies were looking to countries such as Japan and Germany in search of solutions to their management problems. Today, the need to globalize human resources causes companies to turn to developing areas such as Mexico, Thailand, Korea, Singapore, and the Eastern bloc, to name a few. There, labour is abundant and relatively much less expensive by comparison to that of the multinational's home country.

During the early 1980s and 1990s, when recessions cut deep into the economy and business suffered, companies looked to other countries in search of magic solutions to their problems. This was a period when many new Japanese management tools and techniques, for example, were often mentioned by management. Quality circles and management by consensus were two hot topics. Buzzwords such as "codetermination" from Germany, were often used in Canada to denote the need for worker participation and QWL programs. Yet, when one examines many of these "new" concepts closely, it is evident that they are not so innovative. Many have been known to Canadian business for a long time.

Perhaps the most important discovery was that these ideas could be successfully implemented organization wide (or nation wide). Yet, as we further examine the reasons for the relative prosperity of Japanese or German firms during periods when the rest of the Western world suffered from high inflation and high unemployment, we may identify the missing link. Namely, that prosperity did not derive from management technologies, but rather was linked to certain cultural variables; and since we cannot import the culture of one country to another in a wholesale fashion, a more realistic view of the "importable cultural ingredients" should be taken.

This chapter includes two main themes. First, HRM in selected countries is presented; particular reference is made to Japan and Mexico, while other countries are also mentioned briefly. Because of the similarities in the values, norms, and HR practices between Canada and the U.S.A., the latter's system is not presented here. Japan and Mexico have been chosen for more elaborate presentation due to their relevancy and relative present and future impact on the Canadian economy. The Japanese are the dominant industrial force in the Pacific (and beyond), and Mexico is about to become Canada's partner in the North American Free Trade Agreement (NAFTA).

Second, given the increased role of multinational corporations, an entire section is devoted to presenting the dilemmas and challenges pertaining to HRM. One can say that the world is shrinking with the emergence of trading zones. As a result of this situation, multinational corporations (MNCs) are strategically planning their next move. So the question is: how does HRM fit into all of this? HRM is of critical importance to the MNC on account of the underlying fact that in the short run the availability of human resources imposes limits on the strategic alternatives available to the firm. In the long run if HRM is not closely involved with MNCs' strategies, problems can arise regarding the capability to develop and carry out alternatives. The HR task is like that in any domestic corporation: time and dedication must be given to recruitment, selection, training, development, evaluation, and compensation. Underlying these issues are the external and internal factors that affect the MNC.

Looking first at the *external* factors, MNCs face difficulties because they operate in a different culture, language, value system, and business environment. But what is more, they must deal with such issues as:

1. Skills, attitudes, and motivation of personnel in countries where operations are situated;
2. Government policies;
3. Labour laws governing compensation, hiring, firing, unionization, and the management–worker relationship;
4. Consideration of ethics, social responsibility, and government interaction.

Internal factors relate specifically to the management style, which is an important way for both managers and workers to identify with the corporate philosophy of the MNC. McDonald's is a good example of a highly successful global company. Although it is highly decentralized, there emerges a country-to-country consistency of their operation; this can be attributed to their notable *training systems* (e.g., Hamburger University). They comprise such things as global training efforts, travelling internal consultants, and the sharing of HR managers and data. Even for McDonald's, however, many obstacles existed prior to setting up an operation in Russia. McDonald's Canada spent fourteen years setting up its joint venture (see the case study at the end of the chapter). Another example is DOW, which has a group of eleven top managers who meet for intensive sessions during which they discuss benefit changes, legal issues, etc.

HRM IN JAPAN

Japan's emergence as a significant world power in the post-World War II economic order is remarkable. Many observers attribute this to its industrial development since the end of the war, which continues to astonish the world. How has a country that was in virtual ashes immediately after the war, been able to rebuild itself with such remarkable success, and in certain respects construct a society that has surpassed many of the so-called advanced industrial nations?

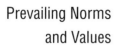

Prevailing Norms and Values

The answers to those questions are complex. Some analysts have argued that the traditions inherent in the Japanese people have contributed to Japan's outstanding position in the international community. Others have identified the structure, behaviour, practices, strategies, and composition of the Japanese corporation as the underpinnings of the country's phenomenal growth. The outstanding accomplishments of the Japanese corporation are even more compelling when one realizes that the country is not blessed with an abundance of natural resources—except for its people.

Akio Morita, the founder and owner of Sony Corporation, recounts an event that taught him the difference in management style and the values inherent in a particular system. In Morita's own words:

We had a district sales manager, who looked very promising, so promising that I sent him to Tokyo on an extended business trip to meet everybody at the home office and get acquainted with the philosophy and spirit of our Organization. He did beautifully, impressing everybody in Tokyo. He came back to the States and went to work and continued to please us until one day, without any warning, he advised me that he was leaving. I couldn't believe my ears. A competitor had offered to double or triple his salary, and he felt he couldn't refuse. I was embittered and embarrassed by this episode and frankly I really didn't know how to handle it. Months later, I went to an electronics show and there at the booth of one of our competitors was this traitor. I thought we should avoid each other, but instead of hiding from me, he rushed over to me full of greetings and conversation, as though there was nothing to be ashamed about. He introduced me around enthusiastically and demonstrated his new product, just as if there had been no breach of faith between us. Then I realized that for him, and in the American system, there had been nothing wrong with his departure with all of our marketing information and our corporate secrets.[2]

This story exemplifies one salient facet of the Japanese system, the "family." In fact, Morita alludes to his management style as "All in the family." Successful Japanese corporations believe in and implement a theoretical construct, first put forth by Tonnes, called *Gemeinschaft*. This theory states simply that Gemeinschaft is like a family, or a church, where members are held together by mutual love. Getting together is itself a source of joy. People love, help, trust, and understand one another, and share bad luck as well as good.[3]

Japanese organizations strive to implement this theory by attempting to respect the welfare of employees and give more equal treatment on a length-of-service system. In turn, employees devote themselves willingly to the organization. Given these facts, Mr. Morita's reaction is completely understandable. In his perception, the sales manager was a part of his family whose betrayal was not only a source of puzzlement, but an act that cannot be forgiven. Delving deeper into this concept of family, one cannot help but ask the question: How does the Japanese organization cultivate and sustain these feelings of loyalty and paternalism?

The answer relates to the underpinnings of Japanese society, by which we mean the culture and traditions of its people. Scholars who have investigated the heritage of Japan argue that from an economic perspective the country has been transformed from an agrarian to an advanced industrial society in just over one hundred years; however, culture changes have occurred much more slowly. As a consequence, remnants of a cultural value system born in a feudal peasant society can still be found in Japan today, especially in terms of human relations.[4]

Thus, Japanese society is characterized by a lack of legalism (i.e., impersonal, contractual relations that limit the scope and magnitude of authority, but also clearly define the lines and direction of authority and responsibility). In contrast, personalism attaches primary importance to face-to-face relations in the exercise of authority. While authority and obligations are, in principle, unlimited, duties and responsibilities are only vaguely defined and may vary significantly from situation to situation. In other words, authority relations are particularistic and diffuse rather than universalistic and specific. Personalism, then, is characterized by a rigid, hierarchical ordering of roles combined with rather relativistic and situationally defined authority relations.

In Japan, the emphasis on personalism is unusually strong because of the near absence of legalistic modes of thought. Japanese culture has been uniquely devoid of absolutes of either transcendental or legalistic nature. Traditionally there has been no law that set down what people should and should not do in clear and unambiguous terms. Instead, Japanese thought has emphasized the impermanency and mutability of the human condition; therefore, what is true today may not be true tomorrow and nothing can be absolutely certain. The Japanese have always been staunch relativists, feeling that it would be inhuman and unjust to attempt to regulate the affairs of people through the application of inflexible abstract laws. Right and wrong behaviour can be determined only by circumstances. Rules can be broken if they fail to meet human needs in a particular situation. This clear lack of universal truth means that Japanese society is based on human relations. The only inviolable rules are *chu* (loyalty), and *giri* (social obligations). These rules ensure that all debts and favours will remain in force, registered on some mental balance sheet, guaranteed by one's family, and regularly audited by one's neighbours—until they are eventually repaid.

Moving from the personalistic roots of Japanese culture to the holistic nature of Japanese society, this is a tradition in which the whole is greater than the sum of its parts, so that the highest value must be attached to the goals and interests of the group, even if that requires a great sacrifice of individual wants and needs. Since the harmony and solidarity of the group must be maintained for the sake of the collective good, great emphasis is placed on the values of *conformity*, *dependency*, and *conflict avoidance*.

The seeds of group-oriented work, sharing, and commitment are found in the rurality of the Japanese community and have been transferred to the modern industrial work team; the formation of groups is based uniquely on what is called *ba*—the frame, location, or place. For example, a male employee is identified not so much by his attributes, personal achievement, skills, or function as by the home town he comes from, the school he graduated from, and the company he works for. Thus, when that employee introduces himself, he is more likely to identify himself by whom he works for rather than what he does. The more powerful and prestigious the group he belongs to, the greater his self-esteem. As a result, it is often said that the Japanese would prefer to be employed at the middle level of a large, prestigious company than as top executives in a small organization, even at a higher salary.

The group-centred way of life that is so predominant in many Japanese firms is not only a product of cultural aspects, but is also a result of conscious strategies that Japanese management has implemented. These strategies build on the components of Japanese culture and promote a sense of "family" in the workers. Here are a few examples of this culture:

1. Sugimoto Yukio presides over a hot springs resort hotel complex located near the city of Misawa Ashiking. A striking part of Sugimoto's management is that his maintenance cost is minimal. Workers and guests alike help keep his park and complex clean. A number of years ago, he saw a lot of cigarette butts and paper strewn around the park and decided to do something about it. He did not write memos but as he strolled he used a stick or his bare hands to pick up refuse. The maids, seeing what their president was doing, imitated him. Soon, some of the guests started doing the same. Before long no one threw anything on the ground. Managing by example has proved to be a most useful vehicle for transmitting corporate values.[5]

2. Matsushita Kroosuke, another industrial giant, has utilized this identical technique by cleaning a toilet no worker wanted to touch. He completed the task in the presence of his workers. They (the workers) have never forgotten this incident. In fact, his factories are now kept meticulously clean, providing a pleasant working milieu.[6]

3. Another facet of the Japanese corporate culture is its spirit of sharing and accessibility to any member, regardless of rank, in the organization. This notion of accessibility to top management, which facilitates direct communication, has been innovatively

resolved by the YKK Corporation. In regard to its white-collar workers, YKK has designed its offices without walls, thus removing the physical barriers to communication, and promoting interaction among its members.

As we can see by these examples, Japanese management is attempting to build a sense of mutual trust and sharing of knowledge. Matsushita has publicly stated that one must share everything with the workers; they will never betray your trust and sell your secret. The important thing to remember is that you must create a relationship of mutual trust and respect.

HRM IN THE NEWS VIGNETTE

Tokyo Lawyer Sues for Those Who Died of Overwork But Some Say Japanese Only Put in Long Hours

As night falls, lawyer Hiroshi Kawahito looks out his fifth-floor conference room window at a familiar sight. Across the street, in the high-rise with the glowing Toshiba sign on top, every floor is brightly lit.

Everywhere he looks, he sees people, hundreds of them, on the phone, hunched over papers, conferring. Even at midnight, Kawahito predicts many will still be at work.

Kawahito describes this as symptomatic of what he considers a Japanese national disease that loosely translates as "working oneself to death." He specializes in suing corporations on behalf of families of men who, he says, have died of overwork.

"Karoshi is a symbol of long, long work," Kawahito says. "It is the secret reason for Japanese economic power." But while few would contest that Japanese "corporate warriors" work longer hours than their U.S. counterparts, many ask whether the Japanese really work any harder.

"The Japanese do have more productivity, so from that standpoint they do work hard," said Masami Iburi, a Japanese-born industrial sociologist who teaches at the University of Michigan. "But looking at its subjectively, from a worker's perspective, it is quite hard to say that they work harder.

"My observation is that it is important to get to work at 9 a.m. sharp. But that's not the same as working effectively. It's even common to come to work with a hangover in the morning, and it is excused."

Call for legislation

Nonetheless, for workers, the prospect of karoshi is scary. A study last year by the Tokyo-based Fukoku Life Insurance Co. found that 40 per cent of employees with 15 or more years at large Japanese companies fear that they may work themselves to death.

Yesterday, the lawyers' organization that Kawahito helped found, the National Defence Counsel for Victims of Karoshi, urged the Labor Ministry to specify karoshi as a basis for worker's compensation and called for new anti-karoshi legislation.

It is easy to have a long workday in Tokyo. Many men spend two hours jammed in subway cars commuting to work. Unpaid overtime is as customary for ambitious white-collar workers as going drinking with co-workers at night.

Many fathers, who tend to skip vacations, are such strangers to the wives and children they see only on Sundays that one television commercial shows a family driving away on a vacation but forgetting to take Dad—who's still asleep at home.

Kawahito argues that as Japanese companies become more successful and the national labor shortage more acute, the pressure to overwork has become harder for many workers to avoid. Consequently, he says, in recent years the number of claims for work-related cases of heart disease, cerebral haemorrhages and other stress disorders has grown to more than 700 a year.

But Kawahito's statistics show that in 1988, a court ruled that a death resulted from overwork in only 30 cases. Kawahito admits that karoshi is difficult to prove as a cause of death. "But recently, the study of karoshi has been very big in the medical world. We are working with many doctors, and we are studying karoshi together."

Mitsutaka Kanai, a former corporate head-hunter who now co-owns a small Tokyo advertising company, is among those who argue that many Japanese "only pretend to work hard."

And Keith Mitchell, an Australian who teaches English to Japanese corporate executives and has spent three years watching their work habits, agrees. "Don't confuse working long hours with working hard," he said. "Go to a Japanese office and you'll see what I mean. They seem to have 10 times as many people as they need. It's very, very inefficient."

Mitchell argues that the Japanese put on a good show to impress their superiors. "In a lot of cases, you can't go home before your co-workers, but you never stay later than your boss," he said. "If you leave early, you don't fit in with the group,"

Still, you could hardly call Japan a nation of slackers. Late at night, the Tokyo trains are full of men in business suits who appear to be asleep while standing. And the sight of workers at small companies doing exercise routines beside their desks in the early morning suggests an environment in which extra effort is demanded.

And one look at a typical Japanese office—the endless rows of tightly packed grey desks and filing cabinets, all devoid of family pictures or personal effects—creates a grim and intimidating impression on the Western visitor.

Even Mitchell, the Australian, admits: "People here work like bees in a hive. It creates a kind of energy. You want to fit in. There's an unspoken pressure. Outspoken people tend to conform."

"Maybe to solve the karoshi problem, long working hours must be reduced," Kawahito says. "Maybe then Japan's economic power would be down. Maybe the gross national product would be down. But in Japan, companies are rich, but the people are not rich. There are many countries where the GNP is lower but the people are happier."

Kawahito says karoshi won't remain just a Japanese problem. "I am afraid the karoshi will be exported to foreign countries," he says. "These days in the world, the Japanese management system is admired. Many foreign managers study Japanese management style."

He finishes with his guests and turns out the lights in the conference room. Across the street at Toshiba, the lights are still blazing.

Source: A feature article of the same title by R. Ratliff, reprinted in *The Montreal Gazette*, 30 November 1991, A13. Reprinted with permission from Knight-Ridder/Tribune Information Services.

The most salient aspect of this corporate culture and the feeling of family is the policy of lifetime employment; it is also referred to as long-term commitment or *shushin koyo*. Lifetime employment is a way of thinking on both sides—the employer and the employee. It is more a "cultural contract" than a legal one. Employment is guaranteed to the ages of fifty-five or sixty, but this is practised only in larger companies. Employees of subcontractors do not enjoy the same privilege. Estimates vary as to the number of employees covered under lifetime employment. The rate is probably lower than 40 percent.

Lifetime employment creates a high degree of employee stability and generates tremendous employee loyalty. A company can feel confident that the time and money invested in an employee's training will not result in the employee being hired by a competitor. Present-day lifetime employment has its roots in the traditional *zaibatsu*, according to which a youth entered the firm as an apprentice and ended up being a manager or founder of a new branch office. This system took on more significance after World War II, when workers and unions tried to improve employment security because of the crisis of the postwar period. It gained further momentum in the 1950s in large firms, mainly because the system was found to be the most effective means to make employees identify their own interests with those of the corporation.[7]

Observers of corporate Japan argue that the lifetime employment system makes the reduction of employee numbers highly problematic. Methods to cope with decreased demand for human-hours includes transfers from the departments with slack jobs to other departments with busier jobs, sometimes to sales offices and to subsidiaries. Suspension of new recruitment, early retirement with an increased rate of retirement allowance (flexible retirement system), temporary "going back to country home" with pay, are all frequently used. Voluntary retirement is also solicited from older workers. However, one major problem that the system generates is *overwork*, as can be seen in the HRM in the News Vignette.

Recruitment and Selection Process

The recruitment of graduates takes place once a year only. Recruitment on college campuses begins in October, after the summer vacation and continues throughout the remainder of the academic year. In a company's direct recruitment, college professors play dominant roles.

Company Y may ask Professor X to recommend so many students with special qualifications in certain fields. It is an old-boys network, with connections playing a key role. The selection process starts during the summer. The format depends on the students' future occupational class. Students who major in the social sciences, law, or the humanities will enter administrative (*jimukei*) jobs, such as planning, personnel, sales, or purchasing. Students majoring in technical disciplines will enter technical jobs (*gijitsukei*). The selection procedures differ for each of the two occupational classes.

Aspiring administrators are asked to apply directly to employers for jobs. Following the formal application, the candidates are asked to appear for a set of interviews with company employees, managers, and executives. The basic criteria for hiring—besides an employee's potential or ability, are a "balanced" personality and moderate views. The evaluation of job candidates is often supplemented by background checks assigned to private investigators, who interview the candidate's neighbours and acquaintances, check local police records, and examine the family history. Those who pass the last round of interviews are invited to sit for the company entrance examination. Officially this exam should determine who is best qualified for the job, but in many corporations over 90 percent of candidates are preselected on the basis of earlier interviews. The exam usually asks essay questions on such topics as family background, career/life objectives, or the applicant's strengths and weaknesses. A number of firms actually use the exam as an assessment tool to determine the career interests of new employees.[8]

The reliance on intermediaries (i.e., college professors) for selection decisions, especially when evaluating technical candidates, serves a number of purposes. Firstly, it is difficult to evaluate a student's technical potential on the basis of a short interview only, when the majority of interviewers have little up-to-date technical background. If a company waited for a written examination, it would not preselect and would risk losing the best candidates to the competition. Secondly, because of the competition for graduates, recruiters cultivate good relations with college professors, who then recommend individual firms to the students. In this way, the firms expect to get their "fair share" of talent and simultaneously prevent a self-defeating bidding war that would not only raise the starting salaries for selected jobs, but more critically would disrupt the carefully balanced compensation structures of internal labour markets. Moreover, specific seminars (courses taken with a professor's permission) are seen as more selective than others and thus develop an "elite" reputation. And lastly, college grades are not an important selection tool. What matters are the educational credentials of the school from which the student is graduating. Given the intense and rigorous competition to enter first-tier schools, the companies rely on the university entrance examination as an indicator of the employee's "latest ability."

During the 1970s, many factors in Japanese management practice demanded modification. Economic growth rates were declining and automation was broadly implemented. At this point, Japanese companies began hiring significantly fewer workers in entry-level positions. This resulted in an increase in the average age of employees as they moved up the seniority ladder. In turn, pressure was added on average wage costs. The most powerful and negative effect of this era was the low morale caused by few opportunities for real advancement.

The Japanese responded to these problems quickly rather than ignoring them. They increased their flexibility in employment. This was accomplished with temporary transfers of surplus employees and flextime systems. For the promotion of staff workers to unavailable managerial positions, a system of "specialist" and "expert" posts was created.

Training and Development

Given the "policy" of lifetime employment in Japan, training is a vital aspect of Japanese corporate strategy. This aspect is accomplished through education. The employees are promoted within the company, and consequently their job changes, as does the product and the technology associated with production; so education is necessary. This thought is expressed at Hitachi in the following phrase: "The essence of enterprise is people." "Matsushita produces capable people before it produces products," is yet another phrase that reflects the emphasis on training.[9]

Trainees can be categorized under three headings: (1) newly hired employees, (2) general employees, and (3) managers. One of the reasons why Japanese companies prefer to hire only the new school graduates is that a virgin workforce can be readily assimilated into each company's unique environment as a community. This assimilation process begins with a lecture by the owner of the corporation. This lecture attempts to instil the corporate philosophy and objectives in the new recruitees. Almost always the message is evident: "We are in this together." The phrase comes from the Japanese phrase "*ichiren takusho*"; it has taken on the meaning that, for better or worse, people must work together and share the same fate.

On-the-job training is intensive, at times taking the form of apprenticeship as well as lectures. The length of training varies from company to company, but the norm is from three to eight months. In Matsushita, the orientation and training of new employees from universities is centralized in the head office and the schedule is as follows:

- Lectures in the head office (three weeks),
- Training in retail stores (three months),
- Training in the works (one month),
- Lectures on cost accounting (one month),
- Lectures on marketing (two months).[10]

Trainees are allowed to make mistakes and their opinions are sought. Mistakes are viewed as part of the learning process; avoiding reoccurrence is what matters. In on-the-job training, learning takes place through example and initiative is encouraged, especially when the new employee is given entire responsibility for a small project.

One of the best uses of on-the-job training is demonstrated by Fujitsu, the computer manufacturer. It recruits engineers from top universities and immediately places them in the design division to design large mainframe computers. After two or three years in the design division, these young engineers are transferred to the manufacturing division to produce the computers they themselves designed. Then after three or more years in manufacturing, these engineers are sent out as systems engineers or engaged in technical sales to operate, service, and sell the computers that they designed and manufactured.

The advantage of this training is quite obvious. These engineers are involved with the product from beginning to end. They are best equipped to manufacture, sell, and service the product, because they literally know it inside out. And the feedback they get from customers in the form of complaints only helps them to design better machines.

Job rotation (in-company) is yet another method for the training and development of people. It is an ongoing process that continues until retirement, and a tremendous learning experience. The worker is trained not only at his or her job, but in other jobs at his or her job level. The on-the-job training promotes tremendous flexibility in the workforce and aids in developing the middle or upper managers into "generalists," with broader perspectives on the experience of the company's business and with the wider human contacts and friendships that are vital for generating consensus. For example, Toyota's policy is to rotate employees once every three years; Canon has an implicit policy of choosing the head of a section from among those members of staff that have served in at least three different departments.

The merits of this type of employee developmental strategy include:

1. It enables the firm to reassign production and office workers more freely.
2. Japanese employees (because of their job security) are more receptive to organizational changes and the introduction of new technology or machinery.
3. Wider experience within the firm tends to nurture the goals of the total firm, rather than those of specific subunits.
4. It can produce high-quality managers. The job rotation system allows an employee to build wider interpersonal relationships that may result in freer information exchange.[11]

Furthermore, it should be pointed out that a socialization and re-socialization process occurs at each point of entry for the employee whether he or she is a new employee or is transferring to another department. This socialization process is usually supplemented by off-the job training in the form of technical training and language classes. Managers are trained mainly by this method, the primary purpose of this instruction being to improve one's skills in negotiations, leadership ability, human relations, and conceptual skills. Needless to say, these classes are sponsored both by the divisions and by the head offices.

Rewards, Negotiations, and Promotion Systems

In most Japanese firms there are two related avenues or ladders of promotion: one is the hierarchy based on job grading, the other is the hierarchy related to status grading. (At Hitachi, for example, the promotion policy is: "Any person can be promoted to the first grade of eight grades in the formal status grading system by the age of 53 at the latest." In addition, employees are promoted on the basis of job grading. Operational jobs are graded by the formal job evaluation method. Employees are also promoted on the formal status grade according to length of service and merit. There is a minimum number of years for staying in the same status grade, and beyond the maximum number of years the employee is automatically promoted to a higher status grade.

The emphasis on seniority, or years of service, as a determinant of job promotion has led many observers of the Japanese economy to conclude that seniority promotes a slow progression of employees through the ranks. However, several Japanese scholars have argued that the impact of seniority on promotion has been exaggerated. With promotion being awarded on the basis of merit evaluation, seniority is a necessary, but not a sufficient condition of success. Most companies, such as ELCO and STEELCO (two major steel producing industries), set up minimum tenure requirements for a position or minimum tenure in a grade before the next promotion or both. As a result, career progression lines are rigid and chances to recover after a slippage in ratings and a missed promotion are limited.

There is no denying the fact that promotion is gradual when one compares this system to that of the West. In fact, one specialist found that in one company it takes sixteen years to be promoted from the lowest management position of supervisor to that of general manager. Moreover, if a supervisor is passed over in two successive years for promotion his or her chances of reaching the level of senior manager are altogether eliminated. Then again, promotions are most likely to occur in situations where the organization is expanding rapidly.[12]

The degree of competitiveness inherent in this job-promotion system can be said to undermine the cooperative effort. However, the Japanese appraisal system serves as a check on these possible negative aspects of competition, because what is rewarded most is credibility and the ability to get things done in cooperation with others. Competition with colleagues may be acute, but its focal point is cooperation building: cooperative networks with the same people who are rivals for future promotion.

In addition to the emphasis on cooperation as a significant factor in evaluation, quality of performance and technical skill are other relevant criteria. Contribution to profits is not as important as the above characteristics. For example, the evaluations for managers have four major components based on tests, presentations, and overall rating:

1. A single achievement score;
2. Six scores measuring job-related abilities such as human relations, business judgment, coordination, and planning;
3. Two outstanding job-related attributes (selected from a list of eight, such as creativity, leadership, and reliability);
4. Two outstanding personality-related attributes (selected from a list of twelve, such as sociability, flexibility, confidence).

One could conceivably argue that the above criteria lend themselves to high degrees of subjectivity in evaluation. Subjectivity is a bias that cannot be completely eradicated; yet frequent evaluations done by different supervisors reduce the error of subjectivity, as is the case in most Japanese corporations. Toyota, for example, has an implicit policy of promoting an employee to the position of manager based on six evaluations.[13]

Japan's success has been attributed to its management styles, such as lifetime employment, seniority-based promotion, the wage system, and consensus-based decision making. Yet, in the 1990s Japan's paternalistic management style faces new competition. The four major challenges are: (1) reducing labour costs, (2) restructuring without massive layoffs, (3) motivating employees and managers in the midst of changing attitudes and expectations, and (4) redesigning employment relationships in a way that will blend the traditional system with the new one that is being created.

Current Trends in Japanese HRM

A major advantage of lifetime employment is that it creates a high degree of employee loyalty; it is also congruent with Japan's paternalistic values. In the past, Japanese companies maintained lifetime employment even during the down periods of the business cycle. This was achieved by the following techniques:

1. Transferring employees from one company to another,
2. Lending workers from companies with excess labour supply to those with temporary shortages of labour,
3. Encouraging early retirement.

Even with the implementation of the above strategies, Japan is still vulnerable to the slowing economy and increased international competition. Faced with these problems, the Japanese have realized the need for a reduction in aggregate labour cost, which consequently means a reduction in their workforce. Although the Japanese have always believed layoffs to be avoidable, reality has shown them otherwise. There is no feasible financial process that could allow them to survive while continuing their current employee practices. Japan seems to acknowledge this fact, as does the younger portion of the population. Many Japanese people ages 15 and over have expressed in surveys a desire for employment change.

Although it is obvious that change is necessary, concrete steps must be taken to modify the lifetime employment principle. The Japanese are taking steps to achieve this by increasing the use of diversified hiring methods. They are hiring more part-timers and contract employees in place of school graduates. In addition, management is hiring on the basis of skills for a specific, narrowly defined job, instead of having a single generalist.

With respect to seniority-based promotion and the wage system, all regular employees used to receive higher positions and responsibilities as they reached appropriate age levels. But this system can only work if the company is growing and the economy is expanding. Nonetheless, during the past economic recession, many Japanese companies began to change their motivational system, which was based on loyalty and the maintenance of group harmony; they responded to the crisis by remodelling the motivational system. Even though retirement age in Japan has been extended, many companies continue to use various forms of early retirement incentives.

The strength of decision making by consensus lies in the participation of the workers, who will in fact be responsible for the implementation of decisions. However, many Japanese companies are confronted with difficult conditions. These difficulties require the modification of the conventional system, so that companies reduce the excess of middle management and limit the number of people involved in the decision process.

Further changes in Japanese HR practices are found in performance appraisal (PA). The Japanese style of PA, called *shikaku* classification system, was responsible for grading promotion, wages, and bonus decisions. Presently, the Japanese are looking to incorporate PA and merit rating systems. For example, if in 1978 58 percent of salary raises were based on seniority, ten years later (in 1988) only 46 percent of pay raises were attributed to seniority. "In companies which have embraced the individual merit rating system, the formula would typically look as follows:[14]

$$\begin{array}{ccccccc} \text{Individual base} \\ \text{salary or wage} \end{array} \times \begin{array}{c} \text{Average "up rate"} \\ \text{within each grade (\%)} \end{array} \times \begin{array}{c} \text{Individual} \\ \text{merit rating} \end{array} \times \begin{array}{c} \text{Seniority} \\ \text{coefficient} \end{array} = \text{Raise}$$

Because of the differing cultures and business practices, North Americans should realize that the Japanese concepts of performance and achievement are not identical to those of the West. The method of personnel evaluation most widely used in Japan is the merit rating (*jinki koka*). This is based on two factors: the level of education attained and specific job ability elements, such as communication skills, cooperativeness, and a sense of responsibility. Personnel evaluation is slowly being replaced by performance evaluation based on on-the-job performance. The concept of performance again differs from the Canadian model in that it not only includes the achievement of actual results, but the expenditure of good faith and effort.

In April of 1986, the Japanese labour ministry published a significant economic document entitled the Maekawa Report. The Report recommended that the Japanese society and economy must undertake a historic transformation of its traditional policies on economic management and of the nation's lifestyle. Moreover, the rate of direct investment overseas must be increased. In the early 1990s direct investment abroad by Japanese corporations amounted to $12.2 billion, $5.4 billion in the U.S.A., and $100 million in Canada. Consequently, if the Maekawa recommendations are implemented, a trend toward further globalization of Japanese firms can be expected.

Mitsuyo Hanada, a professor at the Sanno Institute of Business Administration is investigating this trend in Japanese corporate expansion, which eventually culminates in globalization. Prof. Handa argues that the Japanese corporation is actively progressing through various stages in its corporate life (See Exhibits 17.1 and 17.2). These phases are the export-centred phase followed by localization, internationalization, multinationalization, and globalization. He theorizes that there are two vitally important factors in this strategy: (1) the accumulation of phased experience in the company's overseas expansion, and (2) the effective use of human resources on a worldwide scale.

From an examination of Exhibit 17.2, it can be seen that the strategies regarding human resources differ at each phase. In general, the Japanese corporation is at the localization and internationalization levels of Handa's development process, with some companies approaching the multinational phase. The lines of demarcation between these levels are difficult to distinguish and even more problematic to accurately define.

The localization phase begins when companies dispatch specialists to foreign operations. At this phase, linguistic ability is secondary to specialized qualification in manufacturing technology, production start-up, or financial affairs. Specifically the onus is placed on what is termed "production-floor orientation" or the "shop-floor centred approach." This puts heavy emphasis on basic management principles that maximize the activities of

Exhibit 17.1
The Development Process of Overseas Expansion by Japanese Companies

PHASE	PATTERN	PRINCIPAL CONCERN MANAGERIAL RESOURCES	ORGANIZATIONAL FEATURES
1	Export-centred	Material objects	Export department
2	Localization	Material objects and money	Overseas operations
	Stage I	Establishment of production, sales, service facilities; assembly of knocked-down components	
	Stage II	Independence of production, sales, service facilities	
3	Internationalization	Material objects and money and people	Matrix-like integration of overseas operations department and existing operations departments; creation of an overseas personnel department
4	Multinationalization	Material objects and money and people and information	Overseas operations department is made independent; subsidiary company for controlling overseas is subsidiaries established
	Stage I: Japan-centred multinationalization		
	Stage II: Establishment of a worldwide operations central department		
5	Globalization	Material objects and money and people and information and corporate culture	Worldwide-mobile organization endowed with high flexibility

Source: Mitsuyo Hanada, "Management Themes in the Age of Globalization," *Management Japan* 20, 2 (Autumn 1987): 20, published by International Management of Japan Inc. Reprinted with permission.

production-level works through organizational effectiveness and the improvement of efficiency, which make great use of the dynamism inherent on the production floor, and which evaluate and develop human resources quickly for the long-term outlook. By having the workers fully understand the importance of such basics as strong discipline through keeping the plant clean, neat, and orderly, and by eliminating irregularities, waste, and irrationality, it is possible to have each worker identify with the principles of Japanese management.

The on-the-job training (OJT) in this type of system is to train and guide non-Japanese foremen as they interact in the shop-floor approach. As a result, Japanese subsidiaries abroad send many blue-collar workers to Japan for training, where they can learn from and have direct contact with Japanese production workers and their environment. For example: Toyota and Nissan have implemented this program, which usually lasts from several weeks to a couple of months, depending on the perceived need.[15] Moreover, OJT programs overseas are supervised by Japanese employees dispatched abroad for that purpose. Even after the start of production at a new plant, many Japanese expatriates are sent to subsidiaries as advisers on each line so as to supervise the production activities.

As the Japanese firm moves into the internationalization phase of corporate evolution, language ability and sensitivity to other cultures take on critical dimensions. At this point, Japanese managers sent abroad are more likely to be flexible, rather than seasoned specialists. It is also likely that, at this point, non-Japanese employees are given important managerial responsibilities.

Exhibit 17.2
Strategic Positioning for Human Resources for Japanese Firms

CALENDAR	STRATEGIC POSITIONING FOR HUMAN RESOURCES		CHARACTERISTICS OF MANAGEMENT
	Japanese	Non-Japanese	
1960s	Language ability important	No strategic consideration	Ingenuous; trial and error
1970s	Specialized skills		
1971–75	Dispatch of specialists	Line foremen important	
1976–80	Specialists become specialized also in a particular region	Selection and preparation of persons for top posts, through delegation of authority	Emphasis on a Japanese-like workplace
1981–85	International manager as a type of specialist	Development of middle management; development of specialists	Establishment of a strategic human resources development system
1986–90	Head company executives include men with international management records	All-around players who can also function at the head office	Improvement of the information network.
	Integration of Japanese and non-Japanese employees		Globalization of the company

Source: Mitsuyo Hanada, "Management Themes in the Age of Globalization," *Management Japan* 20, 2 (Autumn 1987): 21, published by International Management Association of Japan, Inc. Reprinted with permission.

Fujitsu, for example, has started to transfer foreign employees from its forty plus overseas subsidiaries to its Japanese headquarters on a *shukko* (temporary) basis in order to train them to be middle managers of subsidiaries.[16] Another critical facet of the Maekawa document is its focus on the domestic economy of Japan, urging the nation to produce for its domestic market and consumers, rather than to follow its current export-centred direction. The rise of NICs (Newly Industrialized Countries) in the international market is a further indication of Japan's need to transform its business style. Moreover, HR strategies are changing from a "group-centred" approach to an "individual-centred" one, with a paradigm shift from a production-oriented (productivity-centred) to a product-oriented (creativity-centred) approach.

One manifestation of this new creative spirit can be found in the slogans of the following companies: "Keeping Information Alive" (Nippon Telephone and Telegraph); "Creation of Environmental Beauty" (INAX, a leading household ceramics manufacturer). These slogans are intended to encourage the employees to think imaginatively about their meaning and to relate the underlying message to the obstacles to be overcome in accomplishing their missions. The strategic vision that serves as the foundation of the organizational missions is best served when it is created by the people who will be directly responsible for its realization.

There seems to be a movement to undermine the traditional emphasis on seniority as a means of promotion and compensation. The Nippon Telephone and Telegraph company introduced a compensation system in October 1987 to meet challenges from new telephone companies. The main salary determinant used to be the employee's position, the assignment of which was seniority based. The new system is a combination of ability and seniority. The ability-based qualification system enables younger workers to move through the ranks at an accelerated rate.

Another aspect of the compensation system is the introduction of incentive systems for managers. Nippon Steel has a compensation package that reflects this dimension, in the sense that a middle manager's business performance per half-year term is reflected in his or her bonus for that particular term.

In the area of promotion policies, many Japanese companies have resorted to a dual career ladder system. Toshiba for instance, has a ladder for managers and one for specialists. These two ladders are parallel and completely equivalent to each other. Employees are assigned to one of these ladders according to their abilities and their own choices. Research staff members generally start their careers as specialist researchers, and those who have the ability to become good managers will be transferred to the managerial ladder. But if they have a strong desire to continue their research as specialist researchers, they will be moved back to the original ladder.

In an effort to promote a sense of equal importance among its research staff, the Honda Motor Company changed all Japanese position titles in its technical research laboratory to English titles. The Honda management felt that Japanese names gave the organization a more bureaucratic structure.

To be transferred to a subsidiary of a company has been viewed by many workers as a demotion or reprimand for poor performance. However, in today's business climate, *shukko* is viewed as an excellent avenue or express lane for promotion, especially now that new business development in Japanese companies is often initiated by their newly established subsidiaries. Parent companies are transferring only truly competent staff members to subsidiaries so that they will develop these "sister" companies to become reliable customers of the parent company. For example, Nippon Chemical Condenser Co. virtually makes those employees who are to be hired by group companies first resign from the parent company in order to motivate them more strongly to work for the new companies. They are even paid a "retirement allowance" at the time of transfer. The reverse is also in use, as delineated by the actions of the Hasegawa Komutten, a leading Japanese contractor. In April of 1988, the company hired all the employees of its subsidiaries, and then transferred them to their original companies. It is expected that such personnel changes will motivate and raise the work morale of employees of its subsidiaries, wipe out feelings of inequality in the minds of staff members of the parent company who are temporarily transferred to subsidiaries, and further enable strategic optimization of company-wide human resources.[17]

It should be clear that Japanese HR systems are taking on more of a Western face. In the current system, feedback between employee and supervisor after an appraisal is minimal. The trend toward a more open appraisal system is now a characteristic of the Kyowa Bank. The evaluation cannot be completed until both the supervisor and subordinate have agreed with the results after thorough discussion. One of the essential evaluation criteria is the achievement of half-year goals pertaining to task and ability improvements. This facet of MBO (management by objectives) is displaying signs of growth among Japanese firms.

These are just a few recent changes in HR policies undertaken by Japanese firms. The extent of their implementation depends on subsequent evaluations and their relevancy to corporate objectives.

The "family" aspect that is so pervasive in Japanese corporations has been described as remarkable. The worker in this community views the company as a source of nourishment—physically and emotionally. It is no wonder that Japanese employees worked 2,110 hours last year, as compared to 1,850 hours for U.S. and British workers (i.e., Japanese workers spent an extra ten days at work). However, things are changing fast, and the loyalty to work is causing many problems in family life, as can be seen in the HRM in the News Vignette.

However, the manner in which the Japanese conduct business is changing. Globalization, the world economic climate, and the nation's economic direction are in constant alteration. As a consequence, Japanese firms will have to adapt to these new challenges. From the preceding discussion on future trends, the corporate strategy seems to be taking on Western features as it grapples with these challenges.

It was argued that Japanese management is attempting to export, not only its products, but also its techniques as it moves overseas. Attempting to transplant a technique and strategy based on unique cultural foundations is difficult, when one considers that the cultural fabric of a society and its distinctive framework may not allow for such a construct to take root. Then again, one must keep in mind that it was the Americans that attempted to graft their strategy onto Japan immediately following World War II. The ultimate result was a nation that utilized what was appropriate from the American model and created a unique entity called Japan.

Japanese society is in a process of change. The Maekawa document and burgeoning rights for women are indications of this process. Observers point quite clearly to the shift in society from a group-centred way of life, that some believe impedes initiative and creativity, to an individual-oriented culture, that would serve as a catalyst to creativity. This may be true, but whatever the shape of this new individuality one thing is certain, it will not take the form of and manifest itself as individuality in the Western sense. It will be Japanese, and as such it will differ. Corporate strategy will reflect this new paradigm. The extent of its application and longevity will depend on how efficiently it fulfils corporate objectives in the 21st century.

HRM IN MEXICO

This section focuses on HRM in Mexico, and more specifically on the maquiladora industry. This industry has not received much attention. There is a significant difference between HR practices in Canada and the U.S.A., and those of Mexico. This is due to historical as well as cultural differences in the populations; for these reasons HRM in Mexico can be characterized as extremely pro-employee and heavily government regulated. The Mexican government dictates most of what HR professionals can do there.

Mexico is an excellent source for the study of the circumstantial influence of HR practices and alliance effectiveness. In 1965 Mexico established the Border Industrialization Program (BIP) to fight high unemployment. The maquiladoras grew from the BIP. Maquiladoras are "off-shore" manufacturing plants for the assembly, processing, and finishing of foreign material and components. Most of these facilities are located along the U.S.–Mexico border. The program permits duty-free import of all tools (equipment, raw materials) required for production if the final product is to be exported.

Since its inception, BIP goals have remained the same: to increase Mexico's level of industrialization; to create new jobs; to raise the domestic income level; to facilitate the transfer, absorption, and skills of technology; and to attract much-needed foreign exchange.

A foreign firm's main reasons to have a Mexican base are the low cost of labour and the high productivity levels. The U.S. investors also cut costs of transportation and storage, since they are virtually next door. In order to better understand HR practices in Mexico, selected aspects and functions are described in this section. Additionally, the HRM in the News Vignette explains the reasons why some Canadian companies have shifted operations to Mexico.

MAQUILADORAS AT A GLANCE (1992 PORTRAIT). In 1992 there were about 1,800 maquiladoras; since 1985, the annual growth in their number approximates 20 percent. There are an estimated 500,000 workers operating in the various plants; there are only about a dozen Canadian companies, the bulk are U.S. companies. The average hourly wage of maquiladora workers is just over $1, while Canadian industrial workers average about $13.74.[18]

HRM IN THE NEWS VIGNETTE
Montreal Firm Found Cheap Labour, Lax Rules in Mexico

In a squalid neighbourhood of barefoot children and snorting pigs, a gloomy factory rises fortress-like behind bricked-up windows. Across the street, families live in sagging shacks with no indoor plumbing. Two blocks away, garbage collects in an open-air dump.

No sign indicates who occupies the factory building. But the neighbours all know. "It's los Canadienses" (the Canadians), says a teenager in a baseball cap.

The factory may look like a relic from the past, but some say it's a harbinger of the future if Canada signs a free-trade deal with the U.S. and Mexico.

The factory belongs to Montreal-based Ideal Equipment Co. Ltd. In 1978, Ideal became the first Canadian company to shift operations to Mexico's northern border zone, a kind of free-trade corridor. Since then, it has slashed its work force to 40 from 150 while increasing its Mexican staff to more than 100.

In Montreal, Ideal pays employees an average $14 an hour to produce sewing machine parts. In Mexico, it pays under $3. "Cheap labour is a motive behind 100 of the companies that have set out down here," said Michel Folacci, general manager of Ideal's plant, "Anyone who says that's not the case is a liar."

The three-way free-trade deal now being negotiated has focused attention on plants like Ideal. Ideal stands on the free-trade corridor on the U.S.–Mexican border along with 1,800 other maquiladoras—foreign-owned assembly plants. Only a dozen are Canadian owned—for now. But critics say trilateral free trade will bring more Canadian businesses to Mexico—lured by cheap wages, lax enforcement of environmental laws and even child labor.

...Canada Ave. in Matamoros is a pothole roadway flanked by weeds, so named because it featured the headquarters of Auto Trim de Mexico, owned by Custom Trim of Waterloo, Ont. Auto Trim has a modern plant, throws employees parties and publishes a glossy in-house magazine. But last month its workers were on strike, lying on the grass and sitting on car fenders while guards stood by.

The employees were generally pleased about working conditions, though a few complained about headaches from glue fumes. But they were striking to increase their salaries to about $10 a day. Their counterparts at the Custom Trim plant in Ontario make $10 an hour. "All we want is enough to pay for water and electricity," said Guadalupe Garcia Sanchez, a union delegate.

Source: Excerpts from a feature article of the same title by Ingrid Peritz, *The Montreal Gazette*, 16 March 1992, A1 and A7. Reprinted with permission.

Mexican employers in the maquiladora region determine their staffing needs. They recruit, hire, and fire personnel as the need arises. There is always an abundance of applicants, which allows employers to screen for those who are most apt for what are mostly assembly jobs. Mexican workers accept this screening because of the relatively good wages and benefits they can get at maquiladoras, compared to other manufacturing-based employment opportunities. The work week in this industry is normally forty-eight hours. Overtime at one-and-a-half times the hourly rate is paid for time in excess of forty-eight hours.

Since the cost of newspapers makes help wanted advertisements useless, recruitment is done primarily by approaching people and asking them to apply. Therefore, it is common to find many family members working at the same maquiladora.

Another significant aspect of employee retention and recruitment involves having workers feel they are part of the operation. The plant is populated by people oriented to traditional Mexican values and social structure. To achieve this, employers celebrate the

Recruitment and Selection

numerous holidays, and it is common for companies to throw parties for a variety of events.

The social structure is similar to the family structure. One of the biggest issues in Mexico, which is similar to that of Japan, is paternalism. In the Mexican mind, all institutions, whether government, business, or church, are like an authoritarian family structure. A plant manager, just as the president of Mexico, fills an authoritarian and fatherly role, rather than a mere organizational function.

Mexican law and history reflect the view that the employer has a moral and paternal responsibility for all his employees, even when there is a union. The Mexican is not just working for a paycheque. Workers tend to expect to be treated as the "extended family" of the boss, and therefore to receive a wider range of services and benefits than the ones provided north of the border. Examples of these include food baskets and medical attention for themselves and their families (apart from social security). The latter are not considered "an extra," or discretionary; in the Mexican worker's mind, they simply fulfil the employer's role and responsibilities.

The good side to this practice is the Mexican view that employees have a corresponding obligation to be loyal, to work hard, and to be willing to do whatever is requested of them. Managers who accept the Mexican outlook (that a job is more than a paycheque) and who try to fulfil their part of the "bargain" can receive the benefits of employee loyalty. There is a willingness to come to work every day and to work conscientiously. Lack of acceptance of the Mexican concept results in strikes, excessive absenteeism, turnover, and poor-quality production.

Training

Training the Mexican workforce and supervisors prior to and during start-up (as well as educating non-Mexican managers who will be working in Mexico) is probably the most critical factor in maquiladora success. One manager of a successful maquiladora said: "If the assembly process requires getting from point A to point D, you have to teach these women points A, B, C, and D, otherwise, they won't get it." A manager from another successful maquiladora observed: "Mexico is not just another state; you have to understand the culture—when to kiss and hug, and when to keep your distance; until we really got a handle on the Mexican culture (by the employment of a Mexican HR manager) we were pouring training dollars down the drain."

Mexican workers are mainly inexperienced. The willing Mexican worker is likely to follow orders without taking precautions or asking questions. This can be seen from the following example: in a maquiladora, the janitor was told to light the boiler without being told about adjustments. The boiler exploded injuring several workers. Thus, careful training is of the utmost importance in avoiding situations like this. Additionally, it should be pointed out that Mexican industry is still 75 percent state-run and profit is of no importance. Mexicans are not tuned into the profit motive, nor to the idea that if the product is not well made or produced on time, customers and jobs will be lost. Consequently, there is still a long way to go in developing a culture of responsibility and quality in the products made.

Management Style

Mexicans value status and its observance. They accept a hierarchy and their "stations" in life. For them the issue is honour, not equality. Rather than resenting their rank, workers expect respectful recognition of their status within the hierarchy.

North Americans regard status as "undemocratic," and try to minimize the difference by dressing casually and by calling everyone by their given name. They resist recognizing the importance of social hierarchy or working within it, and keep trying to bring about the equality inherent in the democratic ideal. Mexican employees, on the other hand, resent that. Here is an example that illustrates this point: in an automotive component plant, the plant manager tried to bring hourly employees and supervisors closer together by closing the supervisors' lunch room so that they would be forced to eat with the hourly employees; to his surprise, the supervisors went outside to eat under a tree. Mexican custom dictated that there is a distance between the supervisor and the worker, and thus the supervisors and the employees resented the manager's decision.

It is important to train the Mexican supervisor on various aspects of labour management relations and employees' motivation. These must be presented in terms of Mexican values. Supervisory training available through Mexican schools is mainly concerned with etiquette rituals, with little emphasis on how to identify and solve problems. A non-Mexican manager of a maquiladora was disappointed to learn that supervisors secretly threw out the bad pieces every night. He was unaware that the Mexican supervisors were too proud to confess they did not know how to adjust the malfunctioning equipment. So they chose to discard the bad pieces.

Labour Legislation and Compensation

The Mexican federal labour law governs all labour matters. The state labour boards oversee the enforcement of the law. These boards have representatives from the government, labour, and management. The law states that full-time employees should get certain fringe benefits. Among the benefits are six days' paid vacation yearly, a 25 percent vacation pay premium, seven paid federal holidays, a profit-sharing plan, and an employer-paid payroll tax that funds employee day-care centres.

The employer has twenty-eight days to evaluate the employee's work ethics. After that period, the worker is granted job security and termination becomes difficult. This is especially true in terms of financial liability. For example, an employer that decides to fire a worker who has been with the company for six months could be charged for an additional six weeks plus vacation pay and bonuses accordingly. It is therefore worthwhile to screen employees before hiring.

An employee is considered tenured after one year of employment. This worker may be dismissed only for causes specifically set out in the Mexican federal labour law, for example, falsifying employment documents, or committing dishonest or violent acts during working hours.

When a labour union declares a strike, all employees, including management, must leave the plant. If the strike is legal, workers receive pay for the duration of the strike. Employment contracts in Mexico must be in writing and normally run for an indefinite length of time. An employer can be fined heavily or put in jail if the minimum wage is not respected. In order for a dismissal to be valid, a written notice of the firing and complete documentation of the offences must be given.

Individual maquiladoras will give additional benefits to entice workers. Some of these benefits include transportation, showers at the plant, subsidized lunches (some free), on-site education, athletic activities, and make-up for female workers.

Certain border plants are short of workers because of the infrastructure of some cities. Most northern towns in Mexico have grown fast, but people do not move in because of a housing shortage and transportation problems. This shortage has not really affected the industry as yet. But people change jobs to be closer to home or for better fringe benefits. The size of the available workforce is not a problem; the problem is the infrastructure. Some maquiladoras solve this by finding a central location. This way most employees are within walking distance.

Most maquiladoras pay the Mexican legal minimum wage. This wage varies about 10 percent throughout the country. Due to the pay, turnover may range from 30 to 100 percent per annum in major cities. This turnover results in higher production costs, poor quality, and higher wages in the local industry. Some maquiladoras have to pay their employees above minimum wage because of the labour shortage. Such is the case in the Tecate area.

Another concern pertaining to turnover is the difficulty in determining the reason for leaving. Mexicans will not often give the true reason for departure. The common reasons used are better job opportunities and moving from the area.

As can be seen, a significant effort must be expended in developing wage and benefits packages that attract and keep qualified employees in the maquiladora industry. A strategy that was used to prevent high turnover was to establish a career path, which made employees feel that they could move up in the company. Seniority wage levels were created, where there would be an increase in salary after a certain amount of service time with the company. Although results have not been evaluated as yet, management believes that there has been a considerable decline in the turnover rate.

HR PRACTICES IN OTHER COUNTRIES

China

During Mao's tenure in China, the evaluation of individual performance and the use of performance-based pay systems were denounced as capitalistic and incompatible with communist ideology. Instead, job security was absolute and compensation administration was egalitarian. To be eligible for a wage increase, a worker's political standing, attitude toward labour, experience, and achievements had to be appraised democratically by colleagues. Under strict guidelines, raises were allocated in such a manner as to be equal. By the economic reforms in the 1980s, the lowest paid workers earned approximately 35 yuan a month and the highest paid official, including the premier, earned only 450 yuan, a differential of only twelve times, far less than the differential in North America or even in the former Soviet Union.[19]

With the economic revolution, it was decided that an enterprise's performance should be linked directly to the amount of profits generated. This was particularly true in the free economic zones, where capitalistic principles were encouraged. The mandated philosophy became: "from each according to his ability, to each according to his work" and "more pay for more work, less pay for less work."

There is limited evidence that the Chinese have made this philosophical shift. In one study it was reported that the Chinese relied primarily on supervisory assessment of performance to allocate pay raises. Unfortunately, peer evaluation as well as individual needs were still considered when granting raises. However, in another study, performance was the most important determinant of pay decisions.[20]

Germany

Germans are known to pay particular attention to rules and regulations, and to power and status symbols. This results in more formal management and operation styles than exist in Canada. Broadly speaking, most of the HR guidelines are translated into a web of rules and regulations. German workers and employers feel more secure this way. Nonetheless, this does not prevent many innovative HR ideas from being implemented in German firms.

Many German workers perform in "work islands" where they can avoid boredom by rotating jobs, socializing, and working in cycles of up to twenty minutes rather than a few seconds. Germans appear to be well ahead of other countries in modifying the conventional assembly line. This enlightened position in alternative job design utilization is a product of the work humanization movement in Germany, initially funded by the federal government in 1974 and maintained by the cooperative relationship between labour and management. Many companies also furnish their own funds for work design innovation projects.

An interesting work arrangement is the experimental **flexyear schedule** in Germany. Under flexyear, employees base their work schedule in terms of a year rather than a day or a week. Actual implementation of such schedules may vary across organizations, but typically employees indicate how many hours they want to work each month. Then the employer and the employee together reach agreement on the exact days and hours of the day to be worked. As with many alternative work plans in Canada, a critical advantage of flexyear schedules is the choice that it provides the employees. The results thus far are extremely favourable: reduced absenteeism, reduced conflict between work and family commitments for many employees, and increased accommodation of employees' desires for more leisure time.

A relatively unique feature of training and development in German firms is the extensive and successful apprenticeship system. This system receives financial and organizational support from both labour and management. Apprenticeship training for many German students begins at age fifteen, when compulsory schooling ends. Youths then select one of several programs that last between two and three years. Presently, an apprenticeship is required for 451 jobs in Germany. In total, almost half of German youths ages 15 to 18 are enrolled in almost half a million apprenticeships. The results of this system include training for currently available jobs and an unemployment rate among youths that is far lower than that in Canada.

The belief that worker interests are best served if employees have a direct say in the management of the company is called *Mitbestimmung* (or codetermination). The original ideas about **codetermination** were conceived in Germany and they are now spreading into many other European countries. Codetermination means, for example, that unions are given seats on the boards of directors of corporations. In addition, managers are encouraged to consult with unions before making major organizational changes, whether they be mergers, investments, plant closing, or relocations. If management disagrees with the union position, management prevails. However, unions may veto subcontracts by the company and they have access to all company records.

Under the Social-Democrat government in Germany, a consensus was reached during the early 1980s to promote international competitiveness through technological superiority and to overcome barriers to innovation by integrating the trade unions into the process of change. The German system of labour relations, with its key features of centralization, jurisdiction, and participation seem to be functioning well, even in the face of changed socioeconomic conditions. The efficiency and legitimacy of collective bargaining seems to hold, given the codetermination practice and similar system flexibility. Low levels of conflict and commitment to cooperation characterize the LRS in Germany.

Since its defeat by the fascists in the 1930s, the German labour movement has consisted of unions with unitary structures that synthesize traditional elements of the socialist and the Catholic labour movement. Although labour is dominated by social democracy, the Catholic influence on the development of such concepts as codetermination, social partnership, or capital formation for employees has become an integral part of the German trade unions' ideology. A second principle of German trade unions is that they are organized on an industrial basis. The dominant labour organizations are seventeen trade unions affiliated with the DGB (Confederation of Trade Unions). The DGB sets the pattern in negotiating for the majority of the workers. The other trade union federations (the DBB, Association of Civil Servants; DAG, White Collar Association, and the CGB, Christian Trade Unions) lack significant bargaining power, and therefore civil servants are not allowed to strike.

In the 1980s unionized employees who were members of DGB affiliates made up a third of the labour force. Nonetheless, their power and influence stretches significantly beyond their numbers. For example, employee support for unions far exceeds their readiness for unionization. In fact, during the election of workplace representatives, about 80 percent of all employees regularly vote for candidates who have been nominated by DGB unions. Another feature of the German unions is their centralized authority. Most of the internal decision making takes place in the peak echelons of union bureaucracy.

German employers are also organized and centralized. There are employers' associations in several industries, often dominated by large-scale companies. The largest employer umbrella organization is the BDA (Federation of German Employers' Association). The BDA coordinates various kinds of legally binding agreements for its members. For example, in 1978 it published a "taboo catalogue" containing rules and provisions of the association designed to strengthen its bargaining power. It limited management compromise in bargaining; among its instructions was that Saturday, usually not a working day, should remain a working day in order to maximize the use of labour and machinery. Although this instruction was reversed in 1984, it illustrates the strategy of the employers' association to establish common policies.

Due to the unification of Germany on 3 October 1990, many changes can be expected in HRM and in the labour laws. Among the thorny issues to be dealt with are the integration of a workforce raised in the communist tradition with a highly efficient western labour force, as well as the problem of a large number of foreign labourers who are no longer needed but who feel they have rights based on years of service to German industry.

Great Britain

One of the aspects that distinguishes Great Britain from North America, and even from many of the other European countries, is its labour relations system. Traditionally, the framework of labour law in Britain has been noninterventionist, fostering an essentially voluntary system of labour relations. Under this system, employers have no general legal duty to recognize and bargain with their employees, while employees have no legally protected rights to organize themselves in unions. Also, negotiated agreements signed between unions and employers are not enforceable as legal contracts. The collective agreements familiar to Canadian managers are more akin to gentlemen's agreements in Britain and are based on social rather than on legal sanctions.

This policy, however, has come under attack in recent years. Concern over the country's poor economic performance and growing international reputation for labour strife sparked a vigorous debate among the major political parties in Britain during the 1960s and eventually led to the establishment of a royal commission of inquiry (the Donovan Commission). Consequently, following a heated debate, the Industrial Relations Act of 1971 was passed. It included provisions for formalizing the process of union certification through the establishment of bargaining units. This reform was intended to replace the practice of voluntary recognition, which led to a complex pattern of multi-unionism, under which a single local management could find itself negotiating with as many as half a dozen unions at the same workplace. Additionally, the 1971 legislation defined a number of individual rights, including protection against unfair dismissal.

However, active union hostility combined with management indifference made this legislation unworkable. Consequently, the Act was replaced by a Labour government in 1974. This legislation took more positive legal action to protect and support trade union membership and entrenched a variety of individual rights, including protection from discrimination on the basis of sex or race.

The legislation took another turn with the election to office of the Conservative government. Since 1979, in a step-by-step process the labour relations laws were reformed. The reform included laws against secondary picketing, restrictions on the operation of the closed shop, and the establishment of secret union ballots before strikes. All these measures effectively shifted the balance of power back toward management. High levels of unemployment have further undermined union bargaining power.

Sweden

The Volvo QWL projects have been implemented in several plants in Sweden, but the most famous is the assembly plant at Kalmar. This plant, in operation since 1972, uses work teams instead of the traditional assembly line and allows employees to design and organize their own work. The plant was built in response to employees' absenteeism, apathetic attitudes, antagonism, and an extremely high level of alcoholism.

Volvo's QWL project received worldwide attention, and has been copied and adapted to many North American plants. Although the shift to this type of production required massive capital and technological investment, Volvo proved that it can be done successfully.

At present, the essence of Volvo's assembly line is group or team work (about twenty workers per team). Employees participate in decisions involving various aspects of their work. A technique used in many of Volvo's plants at the discretion of the workers is **job rotation**. This is done within relatively autonomous work groups. Today approximately 70 percent of the assembly workers engage in job rotation.

Since 1977, Swedish law requires full consultation with employees and full participation by their representatives in decision making from the board level to the shop floor. Swedish legislation is cultivating participation as the preferred strategy to improve quality of life at work as well as outside work. Consequently, local companies are being encouraged to participate actively in the development of public policy related to research and higher education. As such companies encourage their employees to accept appointments to university boards, education boards, and even to undertake part-time research or teaching in these universities.

The most frequent, and usually the first, HR question posed by multinationals is: "How will we pay the employees we send abroad to set up our overseas business?" In most cases, no one in the company knows the answer and a guessing game ensues. It is only after a while that a new MNC inquires about pay in other companies in order to make the first tentative compensation arrangements.

Often, the first international HR specialist is the international controller's secretary or a young promising trainee who is given the assignment to test his or her skills and potential. Another common practice is to recruit an international human resource (IHR) consultant from outside the company. In both instances the individual is rarely a member of the corporate HR staff and hardly ever has any domestic HR experience.[21]

When a company's first international ventures prove successful and management decides to continue global expansion, the need for broader IHR activity becomes clear. But how can this need be met? HR professionals with experience in IHR typically are narrowly focused in expatriate compensation. Those with broader backgrounds are generally unfamiliar with HR practices outside Canada.

All other HR activities are already present in overseas operations, albeit in different forms. For example, even though methods are often different abroad, employees are paid, pensions are offered, union agreements are negotiated, training programs are developed, and employment laws are obeyed. The primary, if not sole, essential HR activity unique to international business is expatriate compensation. As the IHR function matures, other activities are developed (e.g., selection of managers with skills to perform effectively overseas, cross-cultural training); these too are related to the expatriation process. HR specialists are among the last to be sent abroad. Most companies expatriate general managers, marketing and technical specialists, and financial professionals long before they consider sending anyone overseas to perform a HR function. While some argue that overseas experience is not necessary to an effective IHR executive, it is interesting to note that those who make this argument are invariably those without such experience.

The success of IHRM in the future will depend on the ability of companies to develop IHR executives with broad perspectives, international experience, and strong technical skills. This can be achieved by including one or more overseas assignments in the career paths of highly skilled HR managers, introducing some of the best non-Canadian HR tal-

CONCEPTS AND MODELS IN MULTINATIONALS' GLOBALIZATION STRATEGY

Making International Human Resources a Global Function

ent into Canadian-based divisions and headquarters staffs, and providing high-potential HR practitioners with international experience earlier in their careers.

An IHRM function strengthened by a combination of these approaches would have the capability of developing entirely new IHRM technologies to ensure the success of globalization. A summary of the typical international HR functions and structure is provided in Exhibit 17.3.

Exhibit 17.3
International HR Management
Typical Organization Unit Responsibility Structures

ACTIVITY	PRIMARY UNIT(S) RESPONSIBLE	OTHER UNIT(S) WITH RESPONSIBILITY	COMMENTS
Policy/Coordination			
International HR strategy and management	Corporate HR	Divisions, regions	Assumes several global divisions
Expatriate comp/benefits	Corporate HR		If international division(s) managed separately from domestic, international division(s) have primary responsibility
TCN comp/benefits	Corporate HR	Regions	
Local–national comp/benefits	Subsidiaries	Regions	
Recruiting/staffing	All		Growing corporate involvement
Management development	Corporate HR	Divisions, regions	
Training	Subsidiaries	Regions	Depends on level
Labor affairs	Subsidiaries	Regions	Courses often developed by corporate or outsourced
International coordination	Divisions	Corporate	Minimal oversight by corporate
Administration/ Implementation			
Expatriate comp/benefits	Corporate HR		Often outsourced
TCN comp/benefits	Corporate HR	Regions/subsidiaries	
Tax equalization	Corporate HR or Tax		
Relocation	Corporate HR or Traffic		Often outsourced

Source: Calvin Reynolds, *International HR Magazine*, February 1992. Reprinted with the permission of *HR Magazine* published by the Society for Human Resource Management, Alexandria, VA.

Stages in Globalizing

Once the decision is made to venture into the global marketplace, there are several steps that an organization can take. This transition from a domestic to a global organization may involve one of the following stages.

STAGE I: THE EXPORT STAGE. At this stage, the organization is cautiously testing the market. Its product will initially be handled by a middle person, such as an exporter or a foreign distributor and HR activities will probably be handled by professional firms rather than a company's own employees. For example, Peat Marwick Stevenson Kellogg is Canada's largest firm of professional advisors, and they can put you in touch with professional business advisors through a network of over 800 offices in 125 countries. This shows a definite market for these services.

If the area is closed to outside companies, then the foreign company may distribute its product through a local firm under the local firm's name until the product is established in the new area. One interesting example is that of Gennum Corporation. Gennum is a

Canadian manufacturer of silicon integrated circuits that sells its product to the Japanese market. But it took Gennum about fifteen years to develop its Japanese business. Marketing means something different in Japan, and tapping the human dimension is a matter of breaking into a complex web of business connections based more on patience, trust, and loyalty than on carefully worded documents. Gennum initially worked its way into the web by establishing a partnership with Sanshin Enterprises Co., a small Tokyo-based trading house. Gennum sold its product to Sanshin, and Sanshin resold it to its customers. As Gennum gained confidence in Japan, it wanted more direct, ongoing contact with its customers and in 1989 it opened its own Tokyo sales office.[22]

A final phase in this stage, involves the establishment of an export department with domestic staff controlling from headquarters. The domestic HR department would be involved in the administration, selection, and compensation tasks.

STAGE II: THE SALES SUBSIDIARY STAGE. At this stage branch offices are set up in the foreign market countries. The organization now decides whether to staff this branch office with parent country national's (PCNs) or most country nationals (MCNs). This decision will be based on the magnitude of the problems arising from knowledge of the foreign market, language, sensitivity to host country needs, legal issues, etc.

Canada's Kimberly–Clark has recently built plants in France and Germany, but they admit that they faced a monumental marketing challenge when trade barriers came down in 1992. The continent has to deal with a hodgepodge of cultures involving disparate tastes, various languages, and currencies.[23]

In organizations that choose to use PCNs the role of the HR department is limited to supervising the selection of staff and handling its compensation. The HR roles of performance appraisal, as well as training and development, are handled locally, although the training itself may be at corporate headquarters.

STAGE III: THE INTERNATIONAL DIVISION STAGE. This is the step from marketing a product abroad to production of the product in a foreign country. For example, the Philip Morris cigarette company first tested the market by shipping 20 billion cigarettes to the former Soviet Union during an entire year (1991).[24] This was the export stage. They then moved ahead with an ambitious overseas expansion program, including two cigarette manufacturing sites in Russia.[25]

Once the product is produced abroad, the next step is the creation of an international division in which all international activities are grouped and managed by a senior executive at the corporate headquarters. If the organization expands into several countries, it will tend to staff with PCNs because this gives more control. HR activity at this stage is concerned with management selection and compensation. All other HR activities would be handled by an expanding local HR staff.

STAGE IV: THE GLOBAL PRODUCT/AREA DIVISION STAGE. This stage develops when there is a need for national influence over standardization and diversification. Market differences, customer needs, local culture, or legal issues may cause a demand for greater local control.

A full-fledged MNC may evolve at this time if the top managers recognize the need for more local control. Major strategic planning and policy decision making must still be a headquarters function. When the company becomes a full-fledged MNC, the direction of the HR functions also change.

The HR organization changes because many of the corporate headquarters functions are now transferred to the subsidiary, as they adapt to each host country's specific requirements. These local employees are the responsibility of the subsidiary HR group and not that of the parent company. Corporate HR staff is still involved in monitoring activities, but has no direct control over human resources in each host country.

Bombardier Inc., a Montreal-based firm, earns 80 percent of its profits abroad. Its chief, Laurent Beaudoin, says that the secret of being able to compete worldwide is to choose your niche, and then exploit it by motivating people through a highly decentralized organization.[26]

HR planning becomes more complex with each stage. At this stage HRM is greatly concerned with the selection and recruitment, or the development of top managers who can function in an international environment.

STAGE V: THE GLOBAL MULTIDIMENSIONAL STAGE. At this stage the local organization functions almost as a domestic company. Its focus must constantly fluctuate between the host country regulations and corporate direction and control. The global MNC still has a tight system of control because of a shared corporate strategy and a heavy flow of products and personnel between its subsidiaries and corporate headquarters.

STAGE VI: THE TRANSNATIONAL STAGE. This stage is characterized by an interdependence of resources and responsibilities across all business units, regardless of national boundaries, together with a strong corporate identity. Chrysler Corporation has started assembling some of its cars in Mexico. With the advent of free trade, companies could be shipping cars and parts across the Rio Grande as if it were just another state line.

HR activities at this stage are further decentralized as the HR corporate function becomes primarily one of attaining and developing strong international focusing management.

These stages vary from organization to organization. The country of the parent organization, together with variables such as size of organization, management policies, etc., plays a part in the growth of each organization but the HR role is a strong influence in the way an organization develops.

Congruency, Fit, and Flexibility

IHRM practices in MNCs appear to play an additional role as mechanisms are developed that enable the firm to deal with control and cross-cultural issues that are both internal and external to the firm. Inherent in the need for control and cross-cultural sensitivity are again the concepts of *fit* and *flexibility*. However, MNCs often must address greater challenges than domestic firms in terms of geographic dispersion of operations, cross-cultural differences, global competition, and greater reliance on overseas divisions. Therefore, the concepts of fit and flexibility are expected to be even more complex when applied to the MNC.

A fundamental challenge of strategic management is to align the firm's strategy, structure, and HR dimensions. Creating effective strategic HR practices requires the management of two fits simultaneously, *external* and *internal*. The external fit involves the fit between HR activities and the organizational context at each major developmental stage (i.e., life cycle phase) of the organization; the internal fit requires that the HR components must fit with and support each other. Thus, the internal fit concerns the relationship between the various HR functions (e.g., selection, training, performance appraisal, compensation).

In terms of the external fit, a central purpose of IHRM practices is to facilitate effective cross-cultural interaction. MNCs must deal not only with the cross-cultural environment, but also with the cross-national environment, which includes the social, legal, and political settings of the various foreign countries in which they operate. Some specific elements of the cross-national environment include the nature and history of the labour unions and management, national entry barriers (tariffs, quotas, and other border restrictions), local national government effects (preference in terms of purchasing arrangements, subsidies, research expenditures, etc.), and industry regulations and associations.

HRM IN THE NEWS VIGNETTE

Globalization of Canadian Firms

Murex to establish European foothold

International Murex Technologies Corp. (Toronto, Ontario) will expand yearly revenues from $20 million annually to about $1000 million if its planned acquisition of the diagnostic unit of Welcome Foundation Ltd., a British multinational based in London, England, goes ahead. Murex develops, manufactures and sells products for blood banks and low cost diagnostic tests for infectious diseases. The acquisition would help it diversify and give it greater international expansion.

Source: A. Bradley, *The Financial Post*, 6 November 1991, 16. Reprinted with permission.

Gandalf signs South Korean deal

Gandalf Technologies (Ottawa) has signed a contract with multinational Samsung (South Korea) to distribute communications systems equipment in Korea. GT hopes the $7.7 million three-year contract will be the start towards a good share of the growing Korean telecommunications market.

Source: *The Financial Post*, 14 August 1991, 11. Reprinted with permission.

Human resource flexibility can be defined as the capacity of HRM to facilitate the organization's ability to adapt effectively and in a timely manner to changing demands from either its environment or from within the firm itself. Flexibility, an independent concept from fit, may involve such aspects as the ability of monitor the organization's internal and external environments and the capability to swiftly implement organization change, be innovative, and possess a variety of skills that are adaptive to many diverse situations. Four possible situations that may require flexibility include: (a) a dynamic environment, (b) a variety of different environmental conditions and situations, (c) rapidly changing organizational goals or strategies, and (d) two or more divergent organizational goals. International firms frequently face dynamic multiple environments; therefore, the concept of flexibility is an important complement to that of fit.[27]

IHRM ROLES IN MULTINATIONAL ORGANIZATIONS

IHRM Approaches

IHRM approaches within MNCs can be broken down into four major categories:[28]

1. *The ethnocentric approach*: Headquarters controls HR activities and subsidiaries are managed by expatriates from the home country (PCNs).

2. *The polycentric approach*: Each country is treated as a separate entity with some decision making at the local level. Although the subsidiary is managed by HCNs, they are seldom promoted to the parent organization.

3. *The regiocentric approach*: Personnel may be promoted within regions, but are not usually promoted to headquarters. More regional decision making occurs at this level.

4. *The geocentric approach*: A transnational philosophy is adopted to apply to all business units regardless of country.

Recruitment and Selection[29]

This key IHRM activity involves the searching for, and the obtaining of, potential job candidates required by the organization, together with the process of evaluating and deciding who should be employed. Staffing needs in MNCs are different from those in domestic corporations and HR personnel must be aware of these differences.

A staffing policy must be established for the MNC. Issues such as recruitment and selection of HCNs and expatriate recruitment and repatriation must also be considered.

Many universities have established international schools to train their management graduates for the expanding global market. Queen's University in Kingston, York University in Toronto, and the University of Alberta in Edmonton have strong ties to the international corporate world. McGill University in Montreal has recently established an international advisory board composed of twelve business leaders from Canada, the U.S.A., and Europe to help make McGill's Faculty of Management a world leader.[30]

The ethnocentric approach to staffing requires the HR staff to find and prepare employees, and possibly their families, for living and working in another country. The HR managers will be responsible for things such as housing, family activities, and schooling. It will be essential to prepare employees and seek candidates carefully because expatriate failure is costly to the company.

Many Japanese businesses have expanded into the world market, yet even those with extensive global operations hold a rather ethnocentric attitude toward internationalization, and they may not be regarded as truly global organizations. These companies train their own managers for positions abroad and the success of these expatriate managers will determine the success or failure of the assignment. A number of studies shows that a large percentage of the failures are blamed on family-related problems. Thus, it is essential that the candidate's family be included in preparatory programs to ensure success in placing the employee abroad.

The polycentric approach may evolve from the ethnocentric approach as HCNs become trained in managing the subsidiaries in their own countries. This eliminates problems such as language barriers, expatriate adjustment, etc. The HR function is no longer one of support to expatriates but that of support and supervision. It is essential that enough control be maintained to give the subsidiary personnel a feeling of being an integral part of the parent company and HRM can play a role in establishing some sort of career planning within subsidiary companies to give the personnel this feeling.

The geocentric approach to staffing places people above nationalities. Relocation is expensive and time consuming, but if the MNC's policy is to use this approach to give their top people an overview of the entire organization and if it is essential training in the career planning of its management, then the HR team will be heavily involved. HRM must consider many issues in an organization with this approach to staffing but one of the main concerns will be immigration laws that encourage the employment of HCNs.

IBM is a good example of the way in which the MNC can make effective use of its personnel. IBM has a policy of recruiting and developing HCNs for both research and management positions. It even decentralizes much of its R&D, using local technicians, engineers, and managers, while retaining centralized control over the ultimate use of it. IBM, until very recently, also engaged in local purchasing, and attempted to keep a balance of trade according to each nation it operated in. It had host nationals, including local political figures, on its boards, and it attempted to act as a good corporate citizen in each host nation. This geocentric concern for the social and economic welfare of all its managers and workers has resulted in an extraordinary loyalty to IBM among its personnel at all levels. There are excellent management–labour relations and a common corporate culture. Managers identify with the mission of IBM as the leader in the computer industry. Partially because of its HRM method, IBM has been successful in retaining its world market share in the face of ever-increasing global competition.[31]

The regiocentric approach is a regional policy that takes into account the executives' nationality. This requires HR managers to recruit and select experienced HCNs for the regional organization.

Performance Appraisal

The PA system in an international organization must consider competence, but attention must also be paid to such things as cross-cultural personal skills, sensitivity to foreign norms and values, and ease of adaptation to unfamiliar environments. It must ensure that the organizational objectives have been met, while at the same time recognizing local customs and laws.

Consequently, appraisal of managers of MNCs, for example, needs to consider the following major features or constraints:

- Focusing on global performance and subsidiary or regional market performance of the unit must be simultaneous.
- Comparing data for subsidiaries may not be easily applicable, since import tariffs, local labour laws, and market conditions may distort the outputs.
- Developing a market in the foreign subsidiary may be slower and more difficult to achieve, depending on the supporting infrastructure of the parent company.

One of the problems faced in managing the employees in the Moscow McDonald's, for example, was establishing guidelines for appraising employees who had never worked in a democratic organization. Soviet-designed production and incentive systems are associated with low employee motivation and low productivity.[32]

Pepsi-Cola International commissioned a study to determine the factors associated with individual managers' performances across its various subsidiaries throughout the world. The study team looked at 100 successful managers and 100 not-so-successful managers from many different functional specialties and different nationalities. Eleven dimensions emerged as pertinent to the measurement of success: (1) handling business complexity, (2) drives/results orientation, (3) management of people, (4) executional excellence, (5) organizational savvy, (6) composure under pressure, (7) executive maturity, (8) technical knowledge, (9) positive people skills, (10) effective communication, and (11) impact/influence (being able to overcome obstacles).[33]

Training and Development

Once a company has established a corporate global strategy, its next consideration will be choosing employees who fit into this expanded international focus. HR managers will have to establish the personal and professional characteristics required and find such employees. The HR focus will then be on the training and education of these employees in the culture of the host country and corporate headquarters.

Many organizations no longer have a top-heavy vertical command type of management. The new flatter structures empower management at every level with a sense of involvement and responsibility. In the MNC it is important that managers at every level be trained for international assignments. HR managers are responsible for this training, but they must be aware that to ensure its success, training must include HCNs as well as PCNs.

Training and development decisions are based on the international stage of the company:

1. At the export stage, many of the needs are met by outside groups or personnel, such as export companies, sales representatives, or professionals located in the host country.
2. A firm with national subsidiaries is at a stage where, initially, training and development includes PCNs but over time HCNs are trained to manage the subsidiary companies. When McDonald's established itself in Moscow, it sent its HCNs to the U.S.A. to train. Now the staff has eighty or so Russian managers with only a smattering of management from the rest of the global family. One of McDonald's continuing training problems is to persuade employees that the company really is interested in their input.[34]
3. A firm at the regional business stage must balance cultural and geographic differences in arriving at overall strategies. Usually the senior managers have lived in different countries within the region and they must be trained to provide the required leadership.

The key to success in today's international marketplace is knowledge of a foreign language, concern for the environment, and superb cross-cultural skills; in fact, this applies if one aspires to lead a diversified workforce at home or abroad.[35]

4. A worldwide company with several global businesses needs its HRM to emphasize worldwide information sharing on economic, social, political, technological, and market trends and to focus on teamwork across related business lines, as well as across functional and country–regional lines.

With the advent of free trade in the North American market, another HR concern should be the retraining of workers who lose their jobs. North American companies may face legal battles if they move too quickly to establish themselves in another location.

Gillette International is a company that is not just thinking about foreign talent, but recruiting it. With its International Graduate Trainee Program it has helped groom local talent in the developing nations in which the company has operations. It hires top students from prestigious universities and then trains them for six months for positions in Gillette offices in their home countries. The advantage of this is that the employees are familiar with the culture, language, etc. The key here, though, is training.

Compensation

Compensation in a global company is one of the biggest challenges facing the HR team. Successful management of compensation and benefits requires knowledge of the laws, customs, environment, and employment practices of many foreign countries. These must all be considered while also keeping in mind the parent country's financial, legal, and customary practices.

When developing the compensation policy the following objectives should be kept in mind:

1. It must be fair and consistent in its treatment of all categories of its international employees. Everyone must perceive that they are being treated equitably.

2. It must attract and retain valuable personnel.

3. It should facilitate the transfer of employees in the most cost-efficient manner for the MNC.

4. It should serve to motivate the employee.

The economic climate is changing so rapidly that HRM must be creative and diversified in developing compensation packages. A balance-sheet approach is the common system used to equalize the purchasing power of the employees regardless of the country of employment.

A typical balance sheet has five major categories of outlays that cover all types of expenses by the expatriate families.

1. Goods and services—food, personal care, clothing, etc.

2. Housing

3. Income taxes

4. Reserve—savings, pension contributions, etc.

5. Shipment and storage—for household effects

The MNC must develop packages for their expatriate managers that are competitive in all the aspects of compensation salary, taxation, benefits, and allowances. Because of the financial burden of PCNs' compensation packages, more and more companies are establishing themselves in foreign countries to take advantage of the local workforce and avoid some of these costs.

A comparison of an employee in a Mexican company and a James MacLaren Inc. employee in Thurso, Quebec emphasizes these differences. It is presented in Exhibit 17.4.

Exhibit 17.4
Comparison of Welders' Employment Status in Mexico and Canada (for 1992)

	TOLUCA, MEXICO	THURSO, QUEBEC
Work:	Welder	Welder
Pay:	$1.75 hour	$18.61–$23.53 hour
Benefits:	Mandated profit sharing, extra vacation pay, one month's bonus at Christmas, a one-cent lunch	Paid vacation, full health care, paid meal in case of emergency, income protection for layoffs
Seniority:	5 years	1 to 6 years
Education:	Jr. high	Jr. high

The challenge for the HR manager is not just how to operate in this global economy but how to treat everyone equitably. In this economic climate a commitment must be made to displaced workers when a company does relocate.

Another aspect of financial concern to a company expanding or relocating is the termination packages involved if the company downsizes when restructuring itself. The company's corporate policies must be carried out by the HR manager while considering all the legal aspects.

Some North American companies have let their managers go with little more than a few weeks' pay, while relatively high termination benefits are set by law in most European countries.

A host of complexities arise when companies move from the domestic level to compensation in an international context, but there are two very important concerns. The compensation issues should be positioned within the long-term strategic goals of the MNC, and these programs should further its international competitive standing.

Much of the literature on the labour relations practices of MNCs tends to be at a macro or comparative level, and there is a scarcity of research that examines labour relations practices at the enterprise level. However, several strategic aspects of international labour relations can be identified, particularly with regard to the role of unions.

Labour unions may constrain MNCs' choices in three ways: (1) by influencing wage levels to the extent that cost structures may become noncompetitive, (2) by limiting the ability of MNCs to vary employment levels at will (that is, at their own discretion), and (3) by hindering or preventing global integration of the operations of MNCs.

An example of the key dimensions that MNCs need to be concerned with in the years to come, specifically in Europe, is briefly discussed below. The year 1993 sees the integration of the European Community; the key question is: what are the implications for HR?

Some answers to this question can be found in the *Price Waterhouse Cranfield Project 1990*, a study compiling the findings and the insights and perspectives of front-line European practitioners on HR.[36] The main findings include:

. HR responsibility is relegated to line managers.

. Employers prefer various initiatives, such as training and overpay incentives.

. Variable pay is on the increase with bonuses being used as incentives, to ease recruitment problems

. Temporary work and sub-contracting are used.

. Trade unions remain prevalent even though employers are using a more direct line of communication with their workers.

Labour Relations and Employee Rights

Germany, Spain, and Sweden have seen an increase in trade union influence, whereas France and the U.K. have witnessed a decrease. The interesting part is to see the integration of the different HR practices in Europe. For example, in France they are just now beginning to depart from the traditional method of not needing to measure, compare, and evaluate jobs within their organization or to use job evaluation as a basis for developing broader-based HRM.

The new web of rules and regulations in Europe will be dominated by a Charter of Social Rights, which the MNCs will have to study and comply with. The Charter is provided in Exhibit 17.5.

Exhibit 17.5
EC Charter of Social Rights

The charter lists twelve basic rights including:

1. Freedom of Movement: Allowing workers to move within the EC and receive equitable treatment with regard to employment, working conditions and social protection.
2. Employment and Remuneration: Entitlement to fair and equitable wages.
3. Improvement of Living and Working Conditions: Making the Community legally bound to improve conditions of EC workers.
4. Social Protection: An inherent right for every EC worker.
5. Freedom of Association and Collective Bargaining: Mediation and arbitration are to be encouraged, but the right to strike in accordance with national practice for those choosing to join unions is maintained.
6. Vocational Training: Becomes an opportunity accessible to all workers.
7. Equal Treatment for Men and Women: Assurance of equal opportunity for all.
8. Information, Consultation and Participation for Workers: Provisions to especially address technological change, restructuring and redundancy procedures.
9. Health Protection and Safety at the Workplace: Right to satisfactory conditions.
10. Protection of Children and Adolescents: Preventing employment abuses of youths.
11. Elderly Persons: Resources for providing a decent standard of living upon retirement must be guaranteed.
12. Disabled Persons: Entitlement of measures for their assimilation into the workforce.

Source: European Community, "Community Charter of the Fundamental Social Rights of Workers," December 1989.

TRENDS IN GLOBAL HRM

Assessing Multinational HRM

It is generally recognized that HR management is a basic element of general management. However, as shown in the chapter, the practice of HR management differs from country to country. Many of these differences reflect cultural diversity among these countries. Thus, to assess the effectiveness of IHRM one must focus on the success of fitting into the local culture.

When employees from one culture are employed at an organization that is governed by another culture's management practices, the differences between the two cultures may become painfully evident. For a long time Germany recruited several million workers from foreign countries, such as Turkey and former Yugoslavia. These workers' culture was incompatible with German modern workplace management. Consequently, not only did these workers have difficulty in gaining the acceptance of their German colleagues, but the HR department, which was accustomed to dealing with a homogenous workforce, was confronted for the first time with the conflicts that inevitably arise from diversity. They found themselves largely unable to understand the foreigners' attitudes and reactions.

Many multinationals therefore recognize that the HR staff needs to be familiar with the employees' cultural background in order to manage effectively. Sometimes, the culture calls for HR practices considered to be unethical or even illegal in the home country. For example, when Kruger Inc., a pulp and paper multinational based in Montreal, set up a plant in Venezuela, a special budget was assigned to the director general for all sorts of "under the table" payments. Without such incentives, the company risked workers not showing up to work, stealing, and committing other crimes. A common practice to help fit into the culture is to hire local HR staff. An HR staff that shares the employees' cultural background is more likely to be sensitive to their needs and expectations in the work-place—and is thus more likely to manage the company successfully.

Computer Applications

The buzzword regarding computer applications in multinational and multi-divisional organizations is networking. Networks provide an efficient, more cost-effective flow of information to branches and subsidiaries in distant places. According to Evans Research, Canadian businesses invested an estimated $174 million in 1991 on network operation systems. This represents an increase of 172 percent compared to 1988 figures.[37] International Data Corp. suggests that almost 15 million North American microcomputers have been tied to Local Area Networks (LAN), with almost 21 million predicted for 1992 compared to less than 3 million in 1987. These networks can be further connected via Wide Area Networks (WAN), which facilitate communications for multinational and multi-divisional corporations. The switch from a mainframe to a network of microcomputers reduced Winnipeg-based Comcheq Services' operating costs by 6 percent.

The diversity in computer architecture requires improvements with respect to connectivity. Royal Bank has initiated a policy called Royal Information Technology Architecture to regulate buying practices. The bank has adopted a standard architecture for its computers and automated banking machines. It currently has 20,000 microcomputers tied to a network reaching across Canada and into forty-three international centres. It adds roughly 5,000 machines each year.

SUMMARY

With companies and nations increasingly dependent on events in the global market, it is becoming more important than ever to have some awareness of how other countries utilize their human resources. First, this chapter described HRM and general management practices in Japan and Mexico. Short passages were devoted to HR themes in China, Germany, Great Britain, and Sweden as well. Second, the role and HR dilemmas of the multinational corporations were presented.

It has been suggested that Japan's business success is deeply embedded in its paternalistic value system with the corresponding loyalty and dedication of Japanese workers. Nonetheless, things are changing. Japanese corporations and workers are finding themselves in situations in which they are forced to adopt HR measures already used in North America for a long time. Germany has also benefited from prosperity due to the disciplinary values of their workers. However, with the unification of the country and the introduction of workers with other sets of values, the future of many corporations is at risk. It is probable that all sorts of tune-ups will be required both at the plant level and at the national level in order to accommodate this influx of workers. Nonetheless, some principles of HR management that have produced good results in the past are likely to remain as prevailing concepts.

Mexico is the "new kid on the block" for North American corporations. Although it has been known for years that the country can provide an abundance of inexpensive labour, there has been little confidence in the level of skills of these types of workers. However, the experiments in the maquiladora region provide good incentives to corporations to establish plants there and to benefit from the manpower available. With the passage by all three governments (Canada, the U.S.A., and Mexico) of NAFTA, the North American market will be the largest in the world.

The overview of HR practices in other countries highlights the similarities and differences between practices in Canada and elsewhere. While it would be naive to suggest that foreign HR practices can be easily transported to Canada, an understanding of them facilitates a rethinking of the assumptions that underline our Canadian practices.

The second half of the chapter provides an overview of the field of multinational HRM. Emphasis has been placed on examining some of the similarities and differences between international and domestic HRM. It is evident that operating in a global environment is more complex than operating in a single country. This becomes even more difficult in view of strategic imperatives that are linked to the stages of internationalization. Strategic imperatives change according to management philosophy, the type of industry, and the type of market. Each of the five stages offers new organizational challenges that international HR planning can influence significantly.

P O S T S C R I P T

For many years Japan represented a model for North America. This chapter suggests that (a) this model worked well in the past only in Japan (or in places that share similar cultural values); and (b) the Japanese system is very stereotypical; but there are many problems with the Japanese system (and society), so it should not be looked upon as ideal. For one, the Japanese corporate system is so clogged that qualified executives and other professionals are beginning to abandon their unique loyalty and to turn elsewhere for their career. This is especially the case for executives who have spent a few years in graduate schools in North America and in the process have discovered that other systems exist. Moreover, one of the reasons for the low unemployment rate in Japan was the fact that married women were expected to leave the labour force and become housewives. With the increased numbers of women who pursue academic training, this situation is changing rapidly and may lead to a quasi-revolution. But the most problematic aspect of the Japanese system, when compared to the North American system, is a culture that places high value on conformity. The latter is counter productive to innovativeness. In North America, we are experiencing multiple problems in the production process due to lack of mutual consideration and discipline on the part of managers and workers alike; but the high emphasis placed on *individualism* is also very helpful to creativity and innovation. As suggested in Chapter 13, some companies such as 3M even encourage "bootlegging," which would be unthinkable in the Japanese system. It is for these reasons that the North American system has relatively more new ideas, new inventions, and individual vision. Nonetheless, the economic rivalry between the three industrial leaders, Japan, Germany, and the U.S.A., will probably force each partner to adapt its style in order to gain the competitive edge. Consequently, while Japanese and German corporations are beginning to trade off cultural rigidity in order to foster R&D and creativity, U.S. companies are beginning to introduce systems that will render individual employees accountable for their service and/or product.

This competitive rivalry will most likely increase in the future as new elements are introduced. Japan is beginning to feel the competition from neighbouring countries, such as Korea, Thailand, Taiwan, Malaysia, and Singapore, which have similar (but not identical) work ethics, but which still enjoy a competitive edge in the form of cheaper labour due to their lower standard of living. In Europe, other forces currently taking shape will have far-reaching consequences for management. Once the European market becomes unified, the competition for the labour force will be fierce given the mobility of employees within this market. In order to facilitate this economic unification there is also to be a shift to a single currency. Additionally, many of the former communist countries, with their advantageous low-cost labour, are entering global competition and will most certainly have an impact on the world market in general and the European one in particular. Likewise, the expansion of free trade to include Mexico will most likely produce similar results. All these changes will create a challenge on a scale never experienced before for North American corporations. Those who are unable to grasp the implications of these international changes, and those who are unwilling to adapt, sometimes by taking risks, will probably not survive.

Another issue pertains to semantics in the field of HR. Semantics and key terms are very important to every field. They show that the field has matured and the terms are here to stay. A term such as "globalization" is relatively new. It has become increasingly popular in the course of the past several years. However, very few dictionaries will include it. Globalization has resulted from changes that have occurred (and are occurring) in the world. What makes things more complicated for the HR specialist is the phenomenon that before a new term "sinks in" and everyone is comfortable with it, allied terms emerge, often confusing the understanding of the initial jargon.

One such emerging term is "global localization." With the economic difficulties currently experienced by Japan, it has been suggested that the country is moving to a new stage of economic development. Sony Corp. chairman, Akio Morita, has labelled it " global localization." It involves allowing foreign subsidiaries with established sales and distribution networks to become autonomous companies. The parent company benefits from global localization because the latter eases trade frictions. The parent becomes an insider in local markets, participates in international research projects, and demonstrates good corporate citizenship through a higher level of investment.[38] So, the difference between the "global" company and the "local-global" company resides in what they do with profits and how they contribute to employment and the local economy. For example, the Chateau Whistler Hotel in British Columbia, which is 80 percent Japanese-owned, channels all profits back to Japan. Moreover, though most employees are Canadian, management is Japanese.

REVIEW AND ANALYSIS QUESTIONS

1. What are the strengths of the traditional HR practices in Japan? Discuss.
2. What are the current challenges confronting Japanese corporations?
3. What principles of the Japanese model can be borrowed and successfully applied in Canada? Elaborate your answer.
4. Why is Mexico an attractive place for Canadian corporations to set up business?
5. What are some typical Mexican-style HR activities that Canadian managers should be aware of?
6. What are the main similarities and differences between domestic and international HRM?
7. What are the stages an international business goes through before it finally develops into a true MNC?
8. What are the different practices associated with ethnocentric, polycentric, regiocentric, and geocentric HR approaches?
9. How are "fit" and "flexibility" tied into IHRM practices?
10. Outline the main characteristics of the ethnocentric, polycentric, regiocentric, and geocentric approaches to international staffing.

11. "Training and development decisions are based on the international stage of the company." Develop this idea.

12. Identify key compensation parameters to be considered in respect of MNCs.

CASE STUDY

MCDONALD'S MOSCOW: A CANADIAN SUBSIDIARY

A few years ago George Cohen, president of McDonald's Canada, decided that his firm should be amongst the first MNCs to open a subsidiary in Russia. Opened in 1990, the Moscow McDonald's is one of the largest in the world. It has 860 seats indoors and out, and is capable of serving 12,000 to 15,000 customers a day. Presently, there are over 400 local employees involved in the operation. When McDonald's placed an add to recruit employees thousands showed up for the interview.

In order to sell Big Macs for 1.50 to 2.50 rubles (which was about $3.50 to $4.00 in 1992), the company decided to obtain all its supplies locally. However, in order to minimize problems pertaining to shortages and spoilage that affect the average Russian consumer, the company decided to assume control over the quality and flow of its key raw products: beef, potatoes, and lettuce. These were supplied by local sources, although a few initial steps were undertaken: (a) before the opening of the restaurant, McDonald's shipped its own seed potatoes and taught Russian agronomists and farmers how to grow them; (b) it also taught Russian farmers how to raise the beef, and the corporation built its own process-ing plant in order to comply with its own health and sanitary standards; (3) lettuce was grown in greenhouses; (4) buns were also made in a special bakery in Moscow.

McDonald's is facing a number of problems. These need to be addressed before they move to the second phase, building another nineteen restaurants in Moscow. Not only is McDonald's standard of a quick meal in a clean restaurant an alien concept in Russia, but the work-related habits and values of the average Russian employee are very different from those of the North American or even the West European worker. However, the recruitment experience with the first restaurant was very encouraging. For the 400 positions available thousands of people (old and young) applied.

After having taken care of the other aspects of the operation, McDonald's has decided to concentrate on the HR aspects of it. While its overall strategic objective is to provide the same quality service as in the other restaurants in Canada (and around the globe), it has been recognized that some preparatory steps and several changes will be required in HR functions and activities.

Case Questions

1. Identify (to the best of your knowledge) some key external environment factors that may impact on McDonald's management of human resources (i.e., economic, social, cultural, and political).

2. Can McDonald's Canada simply extend its HR policies and practices to its Russian operations? Elaborate on your answer.

3. With the help of the following grid, link the various external environmental factors to HRM at McDonald's. Identify how domestic HR functions are altered when an organization such as McDonald's goes international.

GRID OF ENVIRONMENTAL IMPACT ON INTERNATIONAL HRM					
HR FUNCTIONS	SOCIAL	POLITICAL	CULTURAL	ECONOMIC	LEGAL
Recruitment and selection 1. 2. 3. 4.					
Performance appraisal 1. 2. 3. 4.					
Training and development 1. 2. 3. 4.					
Compensation 1. 2. 3. 4.					
Labour relations 1. 2. 3. 4.					

NOTES

1. E. Brandt, "Global HR," *Personnel Journal*, March 1991, 38–44.
2. A. Morita, *Made in Japan* (New York: E.P. Dutton, 1986), 151–52.
3. T. Kono, *Strategy and Structure of Japanese Enterprises* (New York: M.E. Sharpe Inc., 1984), 318.
4. B. Richardson et al., *Politics JAPAN* (Little, Brown & Company, 1984), 50.
5. D. Lu, *Inside Corporate Japan: The Art of Fumble* (Stamford, Conn.: Free Management (Productivity Press), 1987), 66.
6. Ibid., 68.
7. S. Sethi et al., *The False Promise of the Japanese Miracle: Illusions and Realities of the Japanese Management System* (Pitman Publishing, 1985), 43.

8. V. Puick, "White collar human resource management in large Japanese manufacturing firms," *Human Resource Management* 20, 2 (1984): 264.

9. Kono, *Strategy and Structure*, 320.

10. Ibid. 320.

11. Sethi et al., *The False Promise*, 46.

12. Puick, "White collar human resource management," 277.

13. Kono, *Strategy and Structure*, 324.

14. T.W. Johnson and G.H. Maroochehsi, "Adopting JIT: Implications for Walker Rules and Human Resource Management," *Industrial Management* 32, 3 (May–June 1990): 2–6.

15. M. Hanada, "Management themes in the age of globalization: exploring paths for the globalization of the Japanese corporation," *Management Japan* 20, 2 (Autumn 1987): 19–26.

16. I. Nonaka, "Self renewal of the Japanese firm and the human resource strategy," *Human Resource Management* 27, 1 (1988): 45–61.

17. *Ibid.* 57.

18. Data compiled from the Conference Board of Canada documents, Statistics Canada and *The Montreal Gazette* 17 March 1992, A7.

19. R.L. Tung, "Patterns of motivation in Chinese industrial enterprise," *Academy of Management Review* 6 (1981): 481–89; see also M. Warner, "Managing human resources in China: an empirical study," *Organizational Studies* 7 (1983): 353–66.

20. G. Northcraft, M. Neale, and V. Huber, "Behind the Great Wall: A Comparison of Pay Allocation Values of Americans and Chinese" (Paper presented at the 1987 National Meeting of the Academy of Management, New Orleans); and V. Huber, G. Northcraft, M. Neale, and X. Zao, "Comparison of appraisal and pay decisions of Chinese and Americans: A management revolution in the making" (Paper presented at the 1987 Eastern Academy of Management's International Conference, Hong Kong).

21. The ensuing discussion is based on C. Reynolds, "Are you ready to make IHR a global function?" *HR News—International HR*, February 1992, Section C.

22. W. Gooding, "Fear of Trying," *The Globe and Mail Report on Business Magazine*, April 1992, 40.

23. S. Anderson, "Kimberley–Clark's European Paper Chase," *Business Week*, 16 March 1992, 94.

24. D. Greising, *Business Week*, 16 March 1992, 134.

25. *The Financial Post*, 21 February 1992.

26. *The Globe and Mail World, Report on Business Magazine*, 1990, 30.

27. For more information, see J. Milliman, M.A. Van Glinow, and M. Nathan, "Organizational Life Cycles and Strategic International Human Resource Management in Multinational Companies: Implications for Congruence Theory," *Academy of Management* 16, 2 (1991): 319–39.

28. This section is based on P.J. Dowling and R.S. Schuler, *International Dimensions of Human Resource Management* (Boston: PWS–KENT Publishing Co., 1990), Chapter 3; and D.A. Ondrack, "International Human Resources Management in European and North-American Firms," *International Studies of Management and Organization* 15, 1 (1985): 6–32.

29. The ensuing discussion is based on Dowling and Schuler, *International Dimensions*.

30. A.D. Gray, "McGill Goes Global," *The Montreal Gazette*, 16 January 1992, 3.

31. Gugaman, Lecraw, and Booth, *International Business Firm & Environment* (New York: McGraw–Hill, 1990), 400.

32. F. Heller, "Human Resource Utilisation: A Model Based on East–West Research," *The International Executive* 34 (January–February 1992): 16.

33. For more information on this study, see J.R. Fulkerson and R.S. Schuler, "Managing People Worldwide: Diversity at Pepsi-Cola International," in S.E. Jackson and Associates, *Diversity in the Workplace: Human Resource Initiatives* (New York: Guilford Press, 1992), Chapter 11.

34. "McKapitalism," *Canadian Business*, January 1992, 16.

35. P. Aburdene, "A CEO for the 90's," *Working Women*, September 1990, 134–37.

36. G. Prindle, "Ticking Toward EC '92," *HR Magazine*, December 1991, 66–70.

37. B. Gates, "Networks link computers across world," *The Financial Post*, 9 March 1991, 12.

38. C. Leitch, "Japan Inc. expands corporate borders around the world: companies are fine-tuning their operations to suit local markets," *The Globe and Mail*, 11 June 1991, B13 and B18.

CHAPTER EIGHTEEN

HR EFFECTIVENESS: RESEARCH AND PRACTICE

KEYNOTE ADDRESS

Peter A.W. Green
President and CEO, Alcatel Canada Wire Inc.

Emerging Perspectives in Managing Human Resources:
Building Organizational Capabilities

To compete globally a company must strive for continuous improvement in customer value delivery and strategic organizational renewal. A company must simultaneously be responsive to local markets, derive the benefits of global-scale efficiencies, and pursue worldwide innovations. This is no mean task.

The accomplishment of these objectives requires HR professionals who work as equal partners with senior line managers to create a sustained competitive advantage. The common purpose of this partnership is to build those organizational capabilities that will empower the employees of the organization to champion programs leading to high quality customer satisfaction, low cost, timely responses, and product/process innovations.

There are four areas in which the HR manager must make a major contribution.

1. As Coach of Senior Managers

The HR professional and the senior manager work together in planning, implementing, and reviewing action programs. They jointly address the essential issues facing the organization today and prepare for its successful continuity.

The achievement of organizational goals requires effectiveness on a number of dimensions that are the direct area of competence of the HR professional. The educator and manager become partners in learning how to think in terms of multi-dimensional processes, how to act within interdependent systems, and how to monitor and evaluate both the outcome states and performance processes....

2. As Facilitator of Team Competence

High-performance teams are becoming the unit of work at all levels, from work teams in a production setting to self-directed top-management groups. A company relies heavily on inter-functional teams, cross-divisional task forces, and transnational networks.

HR professionals are active facilitators of the teams in which they participate. They cooperate with the team members and their leader to achieve outputs that satisfy the team's customers via a process that builds cohesion. They enable productive teams to set clear goals, identify member roles and responsibilities, and establish norms for making decisions and managing conflict.

A major concern for a dynamic company is to overcome regionalism and unify the efforts of people from different national backgrounds. The face-to-face interaction in teams and networks builds trust and cooperation when guided by a competent facilitator.

3. As Change Agent for Systems Improvement

Change agents are catalysts in creating favourable performance conditions for continuous improvement. They concentrate on the systems and procedures used to coordinate and integrate the organization. They mobilize energy by creating a unity of purpose amongst a wide range of stakeholders....

The system for developing product and/or process innovations can illustrate the role of the HR professional as change agent. Transnational companies recognize that a worldwide innovation system can start anywhere, but must be leveraged beyond its point of origin and linked to all pertinent operations. The HR professional collaborates with senior managers in building the required knowledge links and creating a culture that endorses interdependence and resource sharing.

4. As Architect of Corporate Renewal

An architect of corporate renewal treats the domains of corporate strategy, structure, and culture as one dynamic entity. Such social architects are in the forefront in designing the desired future and in shifting the company from its current state toward the preferred ideal.

The architect role comes to the centre stage every time an acquisition or merger is undertaken. It has generally been recognized that the process of managing the acquisition is a major determinant of its success. Whatever the degree of integration with the acquiring company that has been strategically decided, from autonomy to absorption, the creation of value from the acquisition rests upon synergies and capability transfers....

These are four roles of HR professionals in a high performance firm. All four will be performed by the same person at different times. They illustrate that the role of HR professionals is changing and expanding to meet today's needs of global business. Their traditional focus on individual performance must be supplemented with expertise in team, system, and organizational effectiveness.

. . . .

In order to enhance the effectiveness of HRM, organizations need to look continuously for ways and means to improve HR practices. The Keynote Address by the president of Alcatel provides the framework for the continuous changes in emphasizing the role of senior managers as coaches, promotion of team competence, and finally a striving for corporate renewal. The message is very clear: if a company wishes to improve its HR effectiveness, it should never be content; contentment leads to stagnation. The chapter describes the theory and practice of HR research and evaluation.

. . . .

HRM EFFECTIVENESS

Purposes and Importance

Many organizations do not appreciate the magnitude of the investment in their HR activities unless they adopt a systematic framework for assessing and controlling them. At present, only very large organizations in Canada engage in some formal HR assessment. Many managers consider the HR contribution as "intangible" and thus see little need to conduct a formal evaluation. By failing to develop a rigorous and systematic assessment, they do not recognize the real input of the HR department into the organization's overall productivity.

Every organization (and department) needs to undertake a periodic analysis to pinpoint its existing strengths and weaknesses. In turn these results must be compared with predictors about conditions inside and outside the organization. Together this information provides the basis for HR control, in the sense that it helps to select a strategic HR plan.

Research and analysis in the area of HR effectiveness is scant. The evaluation of the HR function and its relationship with organizational effectiveness results in an understanding that is useful when modelling the path toward strategic HRM. Progress in this direction is ultimately a result of the perception that changes should be justified by bottom-line considerations and increased organizational effectiveness. Thus, evaluation and control mechanisms are a requisite and contributing factor to the credibility and acceptance of HRM in the eyes of corporate management.

In a broad sense, performance control is felt to be necessary to control costs and as a basis for auditing/evaluating the effectiveness and efficiency of different HR practices.

Senior managers are quick to proclaim that the major strength of their organization is their employees, but when asked to justify the HR budget, or even to explain HR budget cuts (at times of economic difficulty), they are unable to provide a practical rationale.

Many HR managers themselves face a similar dilemma when they are asked to justify the economic rationale for the introduction of a new HR program or service. How do they present the anticipated tangible outcomes of an attitude survey? A new stress management program? A new PA procedure? Most business people understand and respect HR activities when their costs and benefits are translated into dollars and cents. Thus, the need arises to develop a systematic framework with a coherent logic for estimating, monitoring, and assessing these activities. Without such a framework, an HR manager not only encounters difficulty in justifying the department's activities to others, but he or she does not have a criterion against which to assess the effectiveness of the programs for HRM's own use.

There are four general reasons for the importance of carrying out an HRM effectiveness assessment:[1]

1. The renewed recognition that *people* make the difference between the success and failure of an organization;
2. People are expensive, and their wages are often an organization's largest controllable cost;
3. Society, through social and labour legislation, requires organizations to produce an HRM effectiveness report in compliance with the law (e.g., employment equity);
4. So little is known about what it really takes to manage human resources, that it requires constant assessment in order to advance our understanding.

On a more concrete level, the assessment of HRM effectiveness serves the following purposes:

- It helps evaluate the state of health of the HR system and identify problem areas.
- It helps evaluate and monitor the various HR activities in terms of tangible criteria (bottom-line contribution to the organization).
- It helps anticipate future problems and initiate interventions.

At present, there is a growing interest among organizations to learn how to conduct a systematic HRM assessment. With the significant rise in labour costs and the increased importance attached to human assets, the search for evaluation methodologies intensifies. Although management understands the need for assessing the effectiveness of their HR services, the approaches and valid instruments available to carry out this task are not very developed.

Furthermore, recent research suggests that strong correlations exist between organizational effectiveness and the use of *objective* measures of *outcomes*.[2] While many approaches exist for conducting an HRM control and evaluation, very few companies in Canada have formal systems in place. Only one-third of the companies surveyed, reported having one form or another of audit or other method of assessing of their HR activities.[3]

The underlying rationale for conducting an evaluation is that, in addition to finding areas for improvement, the use of valid controls and effective mechanisms by the firm boosts the image of its HR staff, since it can demonstrate the latter's tangible contribution to the overall effectiveness of the organization.

The proliferation of HR activities, policies, and programs over the last decade has led to a situation where a natural tendency persists for each of these programs to generate continuous demands for change and for autonomous growth in their specific budgets. But adding more new money just generates further needs, which justify further disbursements in exponential leaps and bounds. The pressure for an endlessly growing HR budget has to be dealt with, together with the even greater difficulty of allocating the resources among various HR activities. Criteria are needed to be able to judge their relative importance and this requires the systematic development of quantitatively based audits and performance measures so as to judge the relative worth of investments in the respective programs and the deployment of the requisite resources by the HR department.

Assessment of various programs and activities has already been mentioned in the preceding chapters that discussed HR functions. Similarly, some advantages and disadvantages of various program approaches have been reviewed. This chapter draws together the preceding discussions of evaluation and presents a more macroscopic approach to it.

The choice of assessor/auditor depends on the type and scope of HR assessment. Some companies prefer *external assessment*, normally by a well-established HR consultant or consulting firm, while other companies require their HR department to periodically conduct a selective *internal assessment*. Obviously, each method has its advantages and disadvantages.

Who Assesses?

EXTERNAL ASSESSORS. If the target for the assessment is to compare the HR department to others in the industry or to those of major competitors, an external analysis by a consultant is preferred. Similar to the case with a financial audit, an external consultant may bring a fresh and unbiased examination of the HR department's practices and policies. Should this be undertaken by insiders, there is always the risk of justifying or rationalizing existing policies and procedures. An outside consultant may be more critical and may be in a better position to detect discrepancies and variations by comparison with other organizations, as well as by reference to his or her own beliefs and knowledge.

INTERNAL ASSESSORS. Assessment based on research and statistical analysis of specific HR problems, such as costs of grievance, absenteeism, tardiness, and accidents, can best be carried out by insiders. In order for such an analysis to occur on a regular basis, the insider (normally an HR staff member) needs to be able to easily tap into the HRIS. Without it, the task becomes formidable. Other types of assessment that could be delegated to insiders pertain to compliance with laws, rules, and regulations primarily in such areas as employment equity, OH&S, and employment law in general. Assessors can create a simple checklist of the government requirements applicable to the firm and then compare actual practices and policies to those required.

What to Assess?

An HRM effectiveness assessment can vary greatly in scope and focus. It can centre around the purpose, goals, objectives, structures, activities, and results of the HR department. It can also examine a single HR function, such as training, recruitment, or compensation. Another focus can be on an issue such as how the HR department is controlling turnover, promoting health and safety, or handling disciplinary problems.

There are two general perspectives for assessing HRM effectiveness: (a) one assumes a "universal excellence" according to which there is one best way of carrying out effective HRM; and (b) the second, often labelled a "fit" model, argues that effective HRM is not universal but rather involves matching the HR policies and practices with those of the organization's strategy.[4] The essence of the fit model was discussed in Chapter 2 (strategic aspects of HRM). A combined approach is presented in the ensuing paragraphs.

Due to the diversity of approaches to, scopes of, and perspectives on HR assessment and control, an attempt has been made to develop a typology. It is presented in Exhibit 18.1. In this typology the different methods and approaches to be dealt with in the remainder of the chapter are presented. On the vertical axis of the exhibit, the methods are listed; on the horizontal axis the target and scope for the assessment as well as the principal authors/advocates for each approach are listed. Targets and scope are divided into three categories: HR functions (i.e. staffing, training, etc.); HR services (quality of service to customers); and HR outputs (i.e., absenteeism, ratio of HR department, number of grievances, etc.).

Exhibit 18.1
Typology and Scope for Assessing Human Resources in Organizations

METHOD/APPROACH	HR FUNCTIONS	HR SERVICES	HR OUTPUTS	PRINCIPAL AUTHOR(S)/ADVOCATE(S)[5]
Qualitative Approaches				
Audit	X	X	X	Biles & Schuler (1986); Mahler (1979)
Work Analysis/Budget	X		X	Carroll (1960)
Quantitative Approaches				
HRM Indexes	X		X	Fitz-enz (1984)
Costs/Benefits and Utility Analysis			X	Cascio (1987); Dahl (1988)
HR Accounting			X	Flamholtz (1985)
Emerging Approaches				
Multiple Constituency		X		Tsui & Gomez-Mejia (1987); Tsui & Milkovich (1985); Tsui (1987)

QUALITATIVE APPROACHES TO CONTROL AND ASSESSMENT

The most simple and straightforward approach to assessing HR effectiveness is the audit. This is a *systematic, formal evaluation of all HR policies and programs in an organization*. It may focus on different issues, for example: (1) how well the HR department's structure enhances its ability to function, or (2) how well the HR department's present purpose and strategy support those of the organization, or (3) how well the HR department carries out various HR functions such as staffing, performance appraisal, handling grievances, etc. In its pure form, an audit is simply a review of the many available HR records to determine if key HR policies and procedures are in place and followed. Similar to financial audits, HRM audits rely on existing records, such as HR budgets and allocations, grievances, type and number of training and development programs, and performance evaluation records.

Thus, it is clear that the audit can be very comprehensive and encompass all the issues, or can be targeted to selected issues. In order to carry out the audit, the auditor needs to:

HRM Audit Approach

- Decide what to examine in an HR audit.
- Tentatively decide how to conduct the audit by drafting a rough audit plan.
- Select the staff to be involved in the audit.
- Engage in pre-audit research, which primarily involves collecting background information about the HR department, the organization, and specific problems considered to be acute in the latter.
- Finalize the audit plan by refining the audit tools/measures and developing a clear timetable for its conduct.
- Collect audit information.
- Compile audit results and use them to identify present strengths and weaknesses of the HR department and pinpoint fruitful areas for long-term action in order to improve its status.

There are two kinds of HRM audits: strategic and operational. The focus of the *strategic audit* is to assess the appropriateness of the HR policies and practices in supporting the organization's overall business strategy. It should be remembered that the HR grand strategy should support and complement organizational strategy but need not be driven by it. Some of the factors to be assessed in the strategic audit, include:[6]

- *Environmental factors*: The question to be asked is: How does the HR function contribute to the organization's dealing with the external environment? or, To what extent does the HR subsystem contribute to the achievement of the long-term goals?
- *Industry factors*: What HR issues are of key concern in the industry? For example, compliance with special laws or regulations applicable to it.
- *Strategy implementation factors*: What key HR issues are involved in implementation of the HR grand strategy? For example, the state of relations between the HR department and line departments.
- *Company factors*: What are the organization's existing HR strengths and weaknesses? For example, what HR practice areas match up particularly well with desired future needs as envisioned in the strategy? Which ones do not match up so well?

The focus in the *operational audit* is to guide short-term decisions and actions so that they do not conflict with long-term ones. Two different methods of conducting an operational audit are illustrated in Exhibits 18.2, and 18.3. In both methods, items are usually grouped by HR activity, and the person who normally provides the information through an interview or a structured questionnaire/inventory is the senior HR officer. The actual audit is much longer; the questions/items selected for illustration in Exhibits 18.2 and 18.3 are only a sample.[7]

As can be seen in Exhibit 18.3, a checklist is a very simple, elementary approach to assessment, but its interpretation is quite difficult due to the subjectivity of the information. In order to overcome some of the difficulties in interpretation, audits are often conducted by a team. Multiple audits designed for sections or units in the organization are conducted by a joint team of HR specialists and line managers representing the unit. Some organizations conduct this audit on an annual or bi-annual basis. In order to facilitate interpretation, the unit's audit results could be compared with results from other units in the organization or from similar units/sections in other organizations.

Exhibit 18.2

Selected Questions for an HR Audit via Interview

A. Questions of general nature

1. What would you say are the principal objectives of your organization?
2. As you see it, what are the major responsibilities of the HR department?
3. What are some current critical problems/difficulties in the organization? Causes? How widespread?
4. Do you have any specific HR objectives for this year? What about in the long term?

B. Job analysis

5. Do you have an updated job description, specifications?
6. What are the methods used to create job descriptions/specifications for exempt and nonexempt employees?

C. HR planning

7. What kind of plans do you have for meeting the future HR needs of your own component? Indicate plans for hourly, nonexempt. How far do your plans extend to the future?
8. What methods/means/models do you use for carrying out HR planning? What is your experience with the methods/means?
9. What do you expect other managers in the organization to do in order to facilitate your HR plans? How should they do it? What policies are in place to motivate other managers to collaborate in this regard?

D. Staffing

10. How do you recruit different categories of personnel, and what is the average time that it takes to fill a position?
11. What are the easiest/most difficult positions to fill? What innovative strategies did you undertake to fill the most difficult positions?
12. What policies do you have in place for internal vs. external recruitment? Why? Are you satisfied with the current practice?
13. What are the common methods used to select key categories of employees? Do you have any statistics about their success/failure? Do you have some idea of their costs?

E. Compensation

14. What is your responsibility for exempt employees' salary administration? How do you determine job evaluation/salary increases?
15. Do you have any merit- or incentive-based pay? If yes, elaborate on the rationale for using it/them. If not, explain why not.
16. What is your major problem in salary administration?
17. Apart from benefits that you are required to pay by law, what other benefits do you provide to employees? Why (what is the rationale behind the benefits?)?

F. Performance appraisal

18. Are you satisfied with the PA forms used for different categories of personnel? What are the principal reasons for dissatisfaction?
19. What purpose does PA serve? Why?
20. How often do supervisors conduct a formal performance review of their employees? Do they like the system? Do subordinates like the existing system?

G. Training and development

21. Do you conduct training needs analysis on a regular basis? How is it done? How do you decide which employees will be trained?

Exhibit 18.2
Selected Questions for an HR Audit via Interview (continued)

22. How are training programs designed (in terms of content)? What is their rationale?

23. How do you evaluate the effectiveness of the various training programs?

24. What changes or improvements do you think should be made in the on-the-job training?

25. Are there any systems in place to encourage superiors to help employees develop their potential?

H. Career planning and management

26. Are there any career planning policies in the organization? What do you like/dislike about them?

27. Are there any policies for assisting employees who have reached a career plateau?

28. Is the organization encouraging informal career counselling (mentoring for example)?

I. Quality of work life and productivity

29. Are there any particular productivity enhancement programs in place (quality circles, job enrichment, total quality management, etc.)? What is your impression of the effectiveness of these programs?

30. Do you have any programs in place for a "troubled employee" (EAP, counselling)? How effective are these programs?

31. How do you keep employees informed about what is going on in the organization? Do you have regular communication activities? Any particular problems?

32. How do you go about finding out information about employees? Channels and methods? Frequency?

J. Health and safety

33. What are the principal mechanisms for maintaining health and safety in the organization? Are there any particular problems?

34. What are the company's policies with regard to prevention of accidents and occupational illnesses? Are you pleased with the current systems in place?

35. Do you compile and analyze the health and safety data on a regular basis? In addition to making reports to the workers' compensation boards, what else do you do with the information?

36. Are there any other comments/suggestions about health and safety that you wish to make?

K. Labour relations

37. How would you characterize the relations the HR department has with the unions in the organization? Can you comment on how you see improvements in the future?

38. Do you keep statistics on the number and nature of grievances? Do you estimate the cost per grievance?

39. Do you encounter particular difficulties in enforcing the collective agreement?

40. Do you have any difficulties in disciplining employees?

L. Miscellaneous HR functions

41. What are managers and other senior professionals expected to do about community relations?

42. How do you view your budget? Elaborate.

43. How do you view the quality of the personnel in the HR department? Comment.

44. How do you view the role of the HR department in the organization? Comment.

Source: MDS Management Inc., Montreal.

Exhibit 18.3
A Checklist Approach to HR Audit

CODE	THEME/AREA FOR AN AUDIT	YES	NO		COMMENTS
1.0	**Job Analysis**				
	1.1 Was job analysis conducted?				
	1.2 Are there written documents of job analysis?				
	1.3 Is the job analysis format satisfactory?				
	1.4 Are job analyses being updated?				
	1.5 Are job analyses being used for:				
	1.5.1 Staffing?				
	1.5.2 Performance appraisal?				
	1.5.3 Training?				
	1.5.4 Career planning?				
	1.5.5 Promotions?				
	1.5.6 Compensation?				
	1.6 Is job analysis linked to HRIS?				
2.0	**HR Planning**				
	2.1 Are there any HR forecasts made in regard to:				
	2.1.1 Overall HR needs?				
	2.1.2 Replacement of existing personnel?				
	2.1.3 Key positions (i.e., succession planning)?				
	2.2 Are there enough multiskilled employees for cases of emergency?				
3.0	**Recruitment**				
	3.1 Are there difficulties in recruiting employees?				
	3.2 Are the following media used for recruiting scarce employees:				
	3.2.1 Employment Canada offices?				
	3.2.2 Mass media (newspapers/radio)?				
	3.2.3 Employee referrals?				
	3.2.4 Head hunting firms?				
	3.3 Was cost/benefit analysis pertaining to recruitment media conducted?				
	3.4 Is there sufficient notice for recruitment?				
	3.5 Are lists of potential candidates prepared in advance?				
	3.6 Are there established procedures for first contact with potential candidates?				
4.0	**Selection**				
	4.1 Are selection decisions made in clear understanding of the job descriptions?				
	4.2 Are selection officers trained in selection interviews?				
	4.3 Are application blanks complied according to legal requirements?				
	4.4 Were items/questions on the application examined for their validity and reliability?				
	4.5 Are interviewers being trained?				
	4.6 Are realistic job previews being practised?				

Exhibit 18.3
A Checklist Approach to HR Audit (continued)

CODE	THEME/AREA FOR AN AUDIT	YES	NO		COMMENTS
4.0	**Selection**				
	4.7 Are standardized psychological or other paper-and-pencil tests being used?				
	4.8 Were selection devices examined in terms of their validity and reliability?				
5.0	**Orientation and Placement**				
	5.1 Are there written procedures for placing new employees?				
	5.2 Does basic information include:				
	5.2.1 Information about the company?				
	5.2.2 Organization chart/structure?				
	5.2.3 Individual contract or collective agreement?				
	5.3 Are explanations about the place and role of the new employee being provided?				
	5.4 Is the new worker being told who to refer to in case of questions/problems?				
	5.5 Is there any follow-up on the success of the orientation/placement?				
6.0	**Direct Compensation**				
	6.1 Is direct compensation based on job evaluation?				
	6.2 Is job evaluation being revised periodically?				
	6.3 Are there any performance-based pay plans:				
	6.3.1 Individual?				
	6.3.2 Group?				
	6.4 Are there any problems pertaining to pay differentials:				
	6.4.1 Internal inequities?				
	6.4.2 External inequities?				
7.0	**Indirect Compensation**				
	7.1 Are benefits plans communicated to employees?				
	7.2 Are flexible benefits offered to employees?				
	7.3 Are satisfaction surveys pertaining to benefits conducted?				
8.0	**Performance Appraisal**				
	8.1 Are performance appraisals in place for all categories of personnel?				
	8.2 Are performance appraisals based on:				
	8.2.1 Personality traits?				
	8.2.2 Actual behaviours?				
	8.2.3 Output?				
	8.3 Were performance appraisal methods revised recently?				
	8.4 Are existing performance appraisals liked by:				
	8.4.1 Managers?				
	8.4.2 Employees?				
	8.5 Were appraisers trained in conducting the appraisal interview?				

Exhibit 18.3
A Checklist Approach to HR Audit (continued)

CODE	THEME/AREA FOR AN AUDIT	YES	NO		COMMENTS
8.0	**Performance Appraisal Con't**				
	8.6 Is the frequency of the appraisal interview satisfactory?				
9.0	**Training and Development**				
	9.1 Are there training programs for:				
	9.1.1 Managers?				
	9.1.2 Professionals?				
	9.1.3 Workers?				
	9.2 Are training programs offered based on training needs analyses?				
	9.3 Is there an annual budget for training and development?				
	9.4 Is training conducted primarily by:				
	9.4.1 Inside trainers?				
	9.4.2 Outside trainers?				
	9.5 Is most training conducted:				
	9.5.1 On the job?				
	9.5.2 Off the job but on site?				
	9.5.3 Off the job and off site?				
	9.6 Is training success being measured/monitored:				
	9.6.1 In the training?				
	9.6.2 On the job?				
	9.7 Is training effectiveness being measured satisfactorily?				
10.0	**Career Management and Planning**				
	10.1 Are there career planning programs for:				
	10.1.1 Managers?				
	10.1.2 Professional and skilled employees?				
	10.1.3 Semi-skilled employees?				
	10.1.4 Unskilled labour?				
	10.2 Are employees encouraged to conduct self-assessment and develop careers?				
	10.3 Are managers encouraged to assist their subordinates to develop careers?				
11.0	**QWL and Productivity Improvements**				
	11.1 Are surveys of job satisfaction conducted?				
	11.2 Are there any programs for:				
	11.2.1 Job enlargement?				
	11.2.2 Job enrichment?				
	11.2.3 Quality circles?				
	11.2.4 Total quality programs?				
	11.3 Is there any employee suggestions system?				
12.0	**Health and Safety**				
	12.1 Are there any plans for accident prevention?				
	12.2 Are statistics on injuries and occupational illnesses being analyzed systematically?				

Exhibit 18.3
A Checklist Approach to HR Audit (continued)

CODE	THEME/AREA FOR AN AUDIT	YES	NO		COMMENTS
12.0	**Health and Safety**				
	12.3 Are any outlets/facilities to aid employees in case of:				
	12.3.1 Accident/illness?				
	12.3.2 Emotional problems?				
13.0	**Training and Development**				
	13.1 Are there clear policies regarding:				
	13.1.1 Grievances?				
	13.1.2. Disciplinary actions?				
	13.1.3 Dismissals?				
	13.2 Are attempts made between negotiations to improve the labour relations?				
	13.3 Are statistics/information about costs of grievances being compiled?				
14.0	**Miscellaneous**				
	14.1 Is there a Human Resource Information System in place?				
	14.2 Are personnel files being updated?				
	14.3 Are exit interviews conducted for employees who quit?				
	14.4 Is the HR staff systematically following developments in the field?				

Source: MDS Management Inc., Montreal.

Work Analysis and Budgeting Approaches

Although work analysis and budgeting approaches involve actual figures, they are in the qualitative category since each approach calls for a subjective evaluation of the appropriateness of the budget or of a selected service. *Work analysis* is based on work sampling techniques that randomly examine HR staff activities with the purpose of drawing inferences about the total activities of the department. For example, using this technique one study concluded that the HR department spent over 50 percent of their time on staffing and benefits, which was consistent with the department strategy.[8]

Budgeting could provide another clue by which to assess HRM effectiveness. Accordingly, HR activities can be evaluated in terms of the percentage of budget allocated to each major activity. The amount of money allocated reflects the strategic importance of the activity. Changes in direction and magnitude of HR policies can be assessed over time as well as compared with other HR activities. Additionally, the evolution of the HR department budget compared to other departments in the organization, or compared to other HR departments in similar organizations (in size and mission) can provide a clue to the effectiveness of the department. For instance, the provision in the HR budget to pay professional HR staff is an indirect indication of the importance the organization is attaching to its HR services. One measure that is often used to indicate the latter is the *PAHR ratio* (Personnel and Human Resources), which divides the total number of staff in the HR department by the total number of employees, and the *refined PAHR ratio*, which divides the number of professional HR staff (excluding secretarial and technical personnel) by the total number of employees. These ratios can be compared to those of other organizations. For example, in a study recently completed it has been found that PAHR ratios are higher in large organizations (over 2,000 employees) as compared to medium-sized and smaller organizations (less than 2,000 employees); the same study found that in relative terms, Canadian simple and refined PAHR ratios are significantly higher than those reported for U.S. firms: based on 100, it was 1.4 (simple) and 0.7 (refined) for Canada, and 1.2 and 0.46 respectively for the U.S.A.[9] One plausible explanation for the higher PAHR ratio in Canada is the higher union densities in Canada, which require more HR staff to service agreements and to negotiate settlements.

QUANTITATIVE APPROACHES TO CONTROL AND ASSESSMENT

HR Indexes

Many organizations develop in-house HR indexes to be used in assessing the efficiency of the HR unit. These indexes and ratios are usually grouped to correspond to the major activities of the HR department. They can also be grouped according to strategic HR concerns such as: accidents, turnover, absenteeism, productivity, etc. Examples of typical HR indexes are provided in Exhibit 18.4.

Exhibit 18.4
Sample of Quantitative HR Indexes

Planning
- Number of unpredicted new jobs opening
- Deviation between forecasted and actual needs

Staffing
- Average age of workforce
- Ratio of exempt to nonexempt employees
- Average amount of time it takes to recruit employees by skill types
- Advertising cost per hire/per referral
- Turnover and absence rates
- Ratio of various selection devices (application blanks, tests, etc.) to performance indexes

Compensation
- Number of employees above or below the standard wage rates
- Ratio of promotion by merit vs. promotion by seniority
- Mean wage differential between departments, divisions, and/or critical categories of employees
- Number and types of employees participating in profit sharing
- Number and types of employees using services provided by the company (insurance plans, recreation facilities, etc.)

Training and Development
- Proportion of eligible employees who received skills training in the past year; new supervisors who received supervisory training
- Proportion of employees fully qualified for their jobs
- Product and service quality before and after training
- Training costs per employee and employee salary level

Health and Safety
- Frequency of accident rates
- Number of days/hours lost due to accidents
- Accidents by type
- Accidents/professional diseases by department/division or category of employees

Labour Relations
- Proportion of grievances won in the last year
- Average cost of a grievance per employee
- Number of grievances and complaints filed
- Grievances by subjects

Most organizations compare these indexes to the unit's own past data or to some desired objectives. Data could also be compared to the industry average. The results of these comparisons can indicate whether the unit is stable, improving, or declining. Analysis of the trend can certainly provide insights into the relationship between HR activities and unit performance.

COST–BENEFIT ANALYSIS. The term cost–benefit analysis has taken on a variety of meanings. Overall, however, it reflects a set of procedures with various degrees of mathematical sophistication that help management (1) justify existing programs, (2) reduce program costs while maintaining program effectiveness, (3) achieve better control over program costs while obtaining equal program effectiveness, (4) determine how to improve program results without increasing costs, and (5) evaluate the feasibility of proposed programs. Although the reasoning is very sound, cost–benefit models have not been as widely used in HRM as they have been in other management areas. Nonetheless, the increasing demand for HRM accountability will most likely be accompanied by an increase in their future use.

The definition of the cost of all HR functions includes two major cost parameters: *controllable* vs. *uncontrollable*, and *direct* vs. *indirect*. Therefore, it is necessary to recognize the impact of situational factors in developing costing formulas. For instance, consider employee absenteeism: the extent to which people are absent due to real illness or a child's sickness or even the weather represents an uncontrollable cost. However, employees' use of their bank of sick-leave days because they are discontented with their salary or as a stress-reduction strategy, can be controlled by the organization.

Direct measures are actual costs, such as the accumulated direct cost of replacing an absent employee. Indirect measures are usually expressed in terms of time, quality, or quantity. In many cases, indirect costs exceed direct costs in terms of dollars and cents, although rarely are they seriously recognized in many organizations. For example, the indirect cost associated with replacing an absent employee may include:

- The administrative cost of searching for a replacement,
- The cost in productive time of the supervisor responsible for orienting the replacement,
- The short-term cost of training and orienting the replacement,
- The cost associated with low morale on the part of other employees.

Thus, indirect measures are valuable in that they supply part of the data needed to develop a direct measure. Estimating the dollar values associated with outcomes can be very instrumental in calculating the benefits associated with the programs intended to reduce these costs. The programs may include offering training, changing control systems in the organization, or changing the compensation policies. The real payoff to be gained from determining the cost of employee behaviours lies in being able to demonstrate a financial gain from an intelligent application of HR methods.

UTILITY ANALYSIS. Utility analysis is a method of balancing the costs and benefits of HR programs. Usually, HR specialists can specify the effectiveness of their activities, but they have a harder time determining whether those activities are worth what they cost the organization. For example, selection specialists can specify the effectiveness of a selection method by computing the validity coefficient, but they have a harder time translating that validity coefficient into a statement of the dollar value of the resulting improved productivity. Utility analysis is a method of calculating that dollar value. One author, for example, calculated savings in the millions of dollars to Canadian industry if companies would use scientific methods in selection, rather than intuition or other nonscientific approaches.[10]

Although utility analysis is based on a single set of principles or ideas, it uses different methods for determining the financial value of a program in respect of different HR functions. Consequently, the formula for selection programs is different from that for training

Cost–Benefit and Utility Approaches

or performance appraisal. Consider training for example. If financial return constitutes the criterion, then the decision to adopt a training program should depend on whether the improvement in productivity that results from training exceeds the increased costs of training. To determine that, the assessor must compare the dollar value of the new training program with that of whatever approach it would replace. This might be influenced by four factors:[11]

1. *Productivity difference*: The average productivity of those trained by the new program minus the average productivity of those trained with the old program;

2. *Variability*: How much individuals differ in the dollar value of their performance for the year;

3. *Number of trainees*;

4. *Cost differences*: The cost of the new program minus the cost of the old approach.

The following formula relates these four factors to determine the utility of adopting the new program:

$$\text{Utility} = (\text{Productivity difference}) \times (\text{Variability}) \times (\text{Number of trainees}) - (\text{Cost difference})$$

Human Resource Accounting

What makes this approach different from others is the quantification, in financial terms, of a set of common behavioural and performance outcomes. Although there are no generally accepted accounting procedures for employee valuation, an attempt has been made to apply standard accounting principles to employee behaviour. Behaviours that are measured in this approach are those associated with the HR functions of attracting, selecting, retaining, developing, and utilizing employees.

HR accounting represents an attempt to treat human resources as assets rather than expenses. Under this approach, the accounting conventions applied to capital assets are also applied to the workforce. Consequently, the asset value of human resources may be estimated by its replacement costs and/or acquisition costs, and depreciation is possible.

Often HR accounting resembles utility analysis. In many instances HR costs are measured by soliciting managers' estimates of the dollar values to be attached to the results expected from HR activities. For example, in one study managers were asked to estimate the dollar value of different performance levels of computer programmers. By pointing out the improvement in performance attributed to a new selection program, HR officers were able to estimate the dollar value of its results.[12] A few employers such as General Motors and IBM are beginning to experiment with HR accounting approaches.

EMERGING APPROACHES

The Multiple Constituency Approach

Recently, the quantitative and qualitative approaches to assessing HR activities have been complemented by data generated through interviews and/or surveys of principal clients/customers. The premise for this approach is that the effectiveness of the HR department is determined by its reputation with its constituents or clients. It should be noted, however, that if constituent satisfaction is used exclusively in the assessment process it could lead to erroneous results. The attitudes of the various users should be considered in conjunction with any of the other methods listed previously in this section.

The multiple constituency approach is on the rise, given the importance that is accorded in the general management literature to customer satisfaction. With the rise in general concepts such as "total quality management," zero defects" and the like, there has been an attempt to measure constituent satisfaction as an indicator of the effectiveness of the HR department. Obviously, the HR department cannot satisfy all of its internal customers. Consequently, given the notion of limited resources, an effective HR department is one that is able to identify the critical constituents in an organization and attempts to satisfy these groups first and foremost. Identifying the most important individuals or groups in an organization is not an easy and straightforward task. Nonetheless, an organization that neglects to address these "core human elements" may allocate time, money, and other resources to the less important constituents and consequently may have less impact on the organization's bottom line. A few studies have been undertaken recently that support this line of logic.[13]

The value of research in HRM is twofold: first, familiarity with the principles of sound research methods may assist the HR specialist in deriving relevant information in particular areas and, secondly, it increases the chances of addressing a given problem with its proper remedy. In other words, familiarity with research methodology may increase the certainty of decision making and thus contributes to expanded control.

Research can be used for description, prediction, and/or understanding. Research can also be used to increase control. Academics and practitioners often conduct research for different purposes. For example, academic-based research in HRM might be aimed at: developing a new theory, testing or refining an existing theory, comparing or evaluating two or more theories, reconciling discrepancies reported in published research, etc. Practitioners or professional HR staff, on the other hand, may have other reasons to conduct research; often they need to provide answers to immediate or long-term organizational problems. For example: assessing organizational needs for HR programs or interventions (e.g., training needs, counselling needs); studying the impact of newly implemented programs on employee behaviour and productivity (e.g., EAP, new benefits program); assessing the timing and appropriateness of changing HR policies and reducing resistance to change (e.g., new job evaluation methods, introducing new technologies); evaluating current programs, policies, and practices (as discussed in the first half of the chapter); diagnosing the causes for organizational problems (e.g., high turnover rate, high absence rate).

Regardless of who conducts the research and for what purpose, there are a number of common considerations, or common "rules," in conducting quality research. Quality research is the process of investigation in which data are collected in a systematic and relevant manner, properly coded, and analyzed; limitations are recognized; and finally, a certain degree of confidence can be attributed to the findings. Thus, research involves a series of well-thought-out and carefully executed activities that enable the HR professional to know how organizational problems can be solved, or at least minimized. The research cycle encompasses inquiry, investigation, examination, experimentation, and analysis. These processes have to be carried out systematically, diligently, critically, objectively, and logically.

The difference between a sensitive observer who uses common sense to arrive at some analysis and make a decision in a given situation and the researcher who uses a scientific method is that the latter conducts a systematic inquiry into the matter and tries to describe, explain, or predict phenomena based on data carefully collected for the purpose.

Any scientific investigation has several common characteristics. These include:[14]

- *Purposiveness*: Research needs to have a definite reason or purpose for being conducted.
- *Rigour*: A good theoretical base and a sound methodological design would add rigour to any investigation. Rigour means being careful, meticulous, and precise before, during, and after the study.
- *Testability*: Scientific research lends itself to testing logically derived hypotheses. The latter are normally developed after prudent examination of other published research in

RESEARCH IN HRM

Why Research?

The Logic and Process of Scientific Investigation

the area of investigation. Hypotheses can normally be tested by applying certain statistical tests.

- *Replicability*: The results of research that was carefully conducted should yield similar findings when repeated under similar circumstances. Replicability assures the researcher that the results were not merely obtained by chance.

- *Precision, confidence, and generalizability*: Because most applied research in HRM is rarely conducted in laboratory settings under controlled conditions, and further, because most research is based on studying a sample of a population, conclusions are normally stated in probabilistic terms. Measurement errors and other problems are also bound to introduce biases or errors in the findings. Consequently, *precision* refers to how close the findings, based on the sample, are to the "real phenomenon" about which we are trying to reach general conclusions. Some researchers label precision as *validity*. *Confidence*, on the other hand, refers to the probability that the estimations based on the sample findings are correct. In HRM research, as well as in social and behavioural science in general, the norm is to be able to conclude that 95 percent of the time chances are that results will be true (5 percent is left as the margin of error).

- *Objectivity*: The methods of data gathering as well as the conclusions drawn through the interpretation of the results should be objective; there are many principles by which researchers can attempt to collect data in an unobtrusive manner.

- *Parsimony*: Simple explanations of the problem at hand are always preferred to complex research frameworks that consider an unmanageable number of factors.

In order to adhere to a scientific investigation, there are a number of steps a researcher must follow:

1. *Define the problem at hand.* The first step is to define, in a clear and precise way, the problem to be investigated. Often, HR professionals ignore the real problem and instead concentrate on the *symptoms* of a problem. Chronic absenteeism, for example, may cost the organization a fortune. However, in many instances absenteeism is symptomatic of other HR problems, such as a poor labour relations climate, poor supervision, career dead-ends, etc. Thus, when studying absenteeism, there is a need to define the scope, aim, and level of analysis (absenteeism as an individual phenomenon might be different from unit or department absenteeism).

2. *Observe and gather preliminary information.* After the problem is defined, preliminary information needs to be gathered about it. One has to know more about what one has observed. This could be done by talking to several knowledgeable people at work. Additionally, by doing library research the investigator would find out how similar problems/issues have been tackled in other situations. With the help of computers, library search information can be obtained quickly and efficiently.

3. *Form a theory and state your hypotheses.* Theory formulation is an attempt to integrate the information gathered through the multiple means (i.e., observations, interviews, and literature review) into a coherent conceptualization. Key variables and suggested associations are depicted in some sort of model. From these, certain testable hypotheses can be deduced. Research may concentrate on a single hypothesis or on a set of complementary hypotheses.

4. *Develop and refine the methodologies for systematic data collection.* Following the development of the theoretical model and the hypotheses, data pertaining to each variable included in them must be obtained. Systematic data collection can be done through structured interviews, questionnaires, examination of company records, and the like. What is important is to understand the inherent scientific quality of the instruments and methodologies used for the data collection. Each has its strengths and weaknesses. The two most critical qualities of data collection or of measuring devices are their reliability and validity.

Measures in the physical sciences usually are more precise than those in the management sciences. The extent to which the measure provides consistent and systematic observations is referred to as its *reliability*. Conversely, an unreliable instrument is sensitive to factors in the environment and may change from one measurement situation to the next. The concept of reliability was discussed in more detail in Chapter 6. *Validity* refers to the degree to which an instrument actually measures what it is supposed to measure, or more formally, the degree to which inferences from an instrument are correct or accurate.[15] Types of validity were discussed in Chapter 6.

5. *Analyze data.* In this step, the data gathered are analyzed. Both quantitative and qualitative data can be analyzed to test the hypotheses. Quantitative data analysis is usually done through the selection of appropriate statistical analyses.

6. *Draw conclusions and consider limitations.* The final step in the process is to interpret the results obtained and to put them in a proper perspective. It is important to consider the limitations of the study when drawing conclusions. A respectful HR investigator is careful about the wording and conclusions derived form the data analysis. Normally, in an applied setting, the researcher would make recommendations on how the problem can be tackled.

There are diverse problems that represent worthwhile research for an HR professional. The next section will briefly illustrate some typical areas for research related to the control and effectiveness of the HR department.

An important application of validity and reliability is in selection decision making. By examining the interaction between validity and reliability, as well as the selection ratio and cutoff scores, the usefulness of one given selection device as compared to another can be assessed.

A FEW ILLUSTRATIONS OF RESEARCH INTO HRM EFFECTIVENESS

Staffing Example

UTILITY CONSIDERATIONS: BASE RATE VS. PREDICTOR RATE. As long as the predictor used for selection decisions has less than perfect validity (r = 1.00), all HR selection will entail some errors. The objective, of course, is to minimize these errors as much as possible. While using predictors, HR managers operate on the following premises:

1. Some job applicants will perform better than others.

2. The better performers can be identified.

3. The use of predictors will result in a greater success rate than not using them at all. In other words, it is assumed that the **predictor rate** (i.e., the number of true decisions relative to the total number of decisions) will significantly exceed the **base rate** (i.e., the proportion of applicants who would succeed on the job in any event if they are selected randomly).

The concepts of **false negative decisions**, **false positive decisions**, true positive, and true negative are useful in assessing these utility considerations. What an organization wants to do in selecting employees is to make as many true decisions as possible (both positive and negative) and to minimize the number of false ones. Using a test with a predictor rate higher than the base rate does this. For example, if the base rate is .5 (half the applicants who are randomly hired turn out to be good performers) and the predictor rate is .8 (80 percent of the selection decisions are effective), many more true decisions will be made using the predictor. This can be illustrated using two scattergrams, each plotting one hundred applicants hired, with one showing a .5 base rate and the other a .8 predictor rate. A *cutoff score* is used to categorize the employees as good or poor performers, those who would be hired or rejected if the predictor was used. The two scattergrams are shown in Exhibit 18.5.

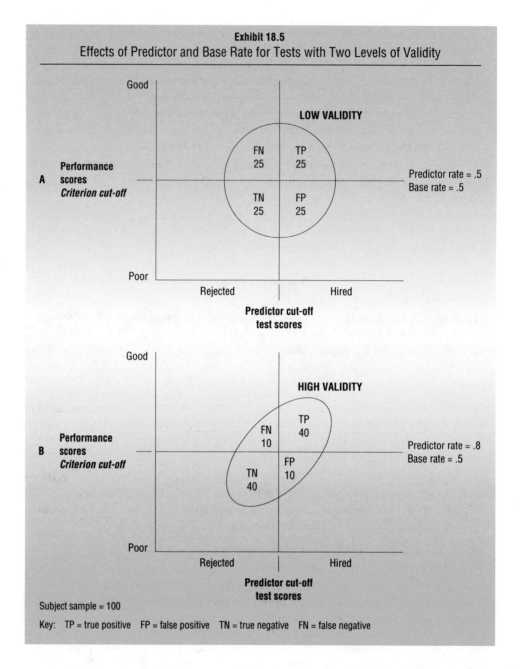

Exhibit 18.5
Effects of Predictor and Base Rate for Tests with Two Levels of Validity

A

Performance scores
Criterion cut-off

Good

LOW VALIDITY

| FN 25 | TP 25 |
| TN 25 | FP 25 |

Predictor rate = .5
Base rate = .5

Poor

Rejected | Hired

Predictor cut-off test scores

B

Performance scores
Criterion cut-off

Good

HIGH VALIDITY

| FN 10 | TP 40 |
| TN 40 | FP 10 |

Predictor rate = .8
Base rate = .5

Poor

Rejected | Hired

Predictor cut-off test scores

Subject sample = 100

Key: TP = true positive   FP = false positive   TN = true negative   FN = false negative

In scattergram A there is essentially no relationship between test score and total performance. Note that an equal number of applicants turned out to be true positive (TP), false positive (FP), true negative (TN), and false negative (FN) (in all cases the number of applicants (n) = 25). The number of correct decisions is 50. The predictor rate does not exceed the base rate of .5.

In scattergram B, however, the number of individuals in the four categories is not equal. In fact, FP and FN are each 10, and TP and TN are each 40. Thus, 80 correct decisions were made in this case, as opposed to only 50 in the previous case. Thus, using tests with predictor rates exceeding base rates tends to improve the utility of the selection process. Final evaluation of the real utility, however, must incorporate a number of additional variables. These will be discussed next.

SELECTION RATIO.   A further important concept in evaluating selection and placement procedures is the **selection ratio**, which is defined as the proportion of individuals actually hired to those who applied. For example, only 10 individuals out of 200 applicants might be hired. This would represent a selection ratio of 10/200 or 5 percent.

Generally speaking, a selection system has greater value when the selection ratio is small—that is, when there are many more applicants than jobs. The fewer the applicants, the lower the chance that this pool contains the best possible applicant. With few applicants, more care must be taken in matching them to the jobs available. If an organization must hire anyone who applies because there are so few applicants, the validity of the selection and placement devices becomes irrelevant. This is particularly true when there is only one type of job available.

In these situations the chance is low that all people hired will perform well. Consequently, the organization may need to establish extensive training programs (which may be costly). The organization could also try to attract more job applicants by raising wages, but that may only cause many of the current employees to be unhappy if they detect pay inequities. Therefore, it pays an organization to attract as many potentially qualified applicants as possible and reduce its selection ratio. Without choice, the utility of selection devices is minimal; with choice, utility may be high and there is a greater probability that the applicants chosen will do well and be satisfied.

UTILITY AND COST.   Organizations should use specific selection and placement procedures that result in the highest gain in relation to costs. Generally those procedures that produce potentially greater gains tend to be more job-related and more costly. Consequently, it is important to consider both the benefits derived from effective selection decisions and the costs of the more effective procedures. The costs to consider include both actual and potential costs, as detailed below:

1. *Actual costs* (costs actually incurred in hiring applicants):
   a. Recruiting and assessment costs—salaries of staff, advertising expenses, travel expenses, and testing personnel evaluation costs.
   b. Induction and orientation costs—administrative costs of adding the employee to the payroll and salaries of the new employee and of those responsible for orienting him or her to the new job.
   c. Training costs—salaries of training and development staff; salary of the new employee during training; and costs of any special materials, instruments, or facilities for training.
2. *Potential costs* (costs that might be incurred if a wrong selection decision is made):
   a. Costs associated with hiring a person who subsequently fails—recordkeeping, termination, costs of undesirable job behaviour, such as materials or equipment damaged; loss of customers or clients; loss of good will; and costs incurred in replacing a failing employee.
   b. Costs associated with rejecting a person who would have been successful on the job—competitive disadvantage if he or she is hired by another firm (e.g., loss of a top sports celebrity to a competing team), and cost of recruiting and assessing an additional applicant to replace the rejectee.

In addition to comparing the costs and benefits of alternative selection and placement procedures, HR researchers should also compare the costs and benefits of techniques other than selection and placement to obtain increases in job performance and employee retention.

Recently, utility analysis has been applied to training and career development. Because of the large sums of money invested in training and development programs, companies are

Training and
Development
Example

trying to assess the benefits of these programs, or more specifically how they affect the bottom line. In Chapter 11, we discussed more traditional training evaluation designs aimed at assessing whether or not real learning took place as a result of the training. In this section we will examine recent research that looks at the economic impact of training and development efforts. HR professionals are interested in applying methods and models that will permit them to quantify the information in terms of dollars.

One HR researcher presents a three-step process by which to estimate the utility of training and development programs: (1) the use of *capital budgeting* methods to analyze the minimum annual benefits, in dollars, required as the return on investment for training; (2) the use of *break-even analysis*, which employs the general utility equation to estimate the minimum effect size (degree of departure from the null hypothesis) for a proposed training program so as to produce the necessary returns; and (3) the use of *meta-analysis*[16] results from similar programs to estimate the expected actual payoff from the proposed training program.[17] The approach taken here integrates expected payoffs from training with the firm's capital investment decisions. Computational models can be computerized, so that the HR manager needs only to input values corresponding to each of the critical parameters, which include:

- Cost (the present value of the after-tax cash outlays incurred over the life of the program),
- Benefits (the incremental cash flows generated as a result of the program; these are derived from the utility parameters),
- Number of employees trained,
- Expected effect size determined by meta-analysis,
- Estimated standard deviations from the program,
- Duration of the program and its benefits,
- Discount rate representing the organization's minimum required return on investment,
- Corporate tax rate,
- Percentage of variable costs associated with the program.[18]

Once the above are specified, the minimum payoff required by the firm (from the perspective of capital budgeting), the minimum effect size necessary to yield the required payoff (determined by the break-even analysis), and the expected payoff of the training program over the duration of the program's effects can be calculated. If the expected payoff exceeds the minimum payoff, then the HR manager can submit (with economic justification) a proposal for a training and development program.

Compensation Example

A research question often raised by compensation specialists is: How do variations in systems design and scope affect the bottom line? Recent writings argue that because compensation has traditionally been investigated through a micro-perspective within the HR field, the connection between pay strategies and the firm's performance has been neglected.[19]

Exhibit 18.6 depicts the key theoretical variables that help explain how and why pay strategies affect a firm's performance. The model suggests a contingency approach in which the relative contribution of pay strategies to the firm's performance increases as a result of a fit between various compensation strategy components and certain organizational conditions. The following are suggested:[20]

- The greater the integration among pay strategies, corporate strategies, business unit strategies, organizational idiosyncrasies, and the dominant logic of the top-management team, the greater the contribution to the firm's performance.
- The more pay that strategies serve to erect barriers of entry for competitors, the greater the firm's performance.

- The more that a firm's pay strategies enable it to capitalize on its distinctive competencies, the greater the firm's performance.
- The more that pay strategies can reduce transaction costs between organizational subunits, the greater the firm's performance.
- The more that the pay system is capable of securing and maintaining strategic employee groups critical to the accomplishment of a firm's mission and integral to its technical core, the greater the firm's performance.

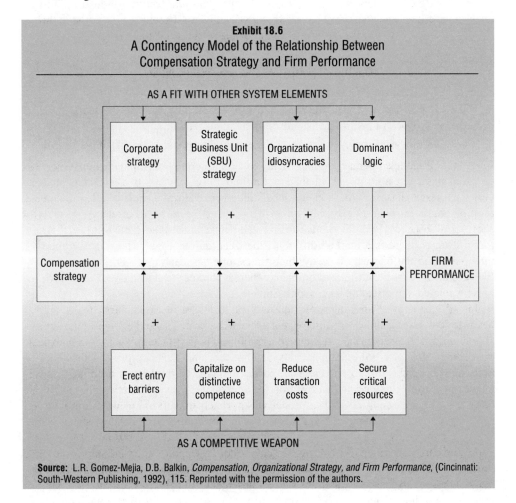

Exhibit 18.6
A Contingency Model of the Relationship Between Compensation Strategy and Firm Performance

Source: L.R. Gomez-Mejia, D.B. Balkin, *Compensation, Organizational Strategy, and Firm Performance*, (Cincinnati: South-Western Publishing, 1992), 115. Reprinted with the permission of the authors.

ABSENTEEISM.   Absence from work is a major cost and concern for many HR organizations. Although it is difficult to place an accurate figure on its cost, estimates range from $3 billion to $10 billion per year. Obviously, the costs for an individual organization will differ according to a wide range of variables. However, most estimates of the cost of absenteeism include some combination of the following:

- Value of lost productivity,
- Salary or wages paid to absentee (if the absence is paid),
- Fringe benefits paid to the absentee, including accrued vacation, disability insurance premiums, etc.,
- Overtime paid to replacement personnel,
- Salary or wages and benefits paid for overstaffing to compensate for a chronic level of absenteeism.[21]

Absenteeism and Turnover

Additionally, absenteeism incurs indirect costs, such as: (1) quality of work—usually it declines when a job is being performed by a replacement; (2) administrative costs—each unscheduled absence triggers a chain of events forcing the supervisor to reassign other personnel, or find a replacement, or orient the new replacement, or closely supervise the replacement, all of which take up time.

The key question often asked by employers is: What is the average or typical amount of scheduled time lost due to absenteeism? The answer to this question is complicated by the general lack of consistent reporting systems both within and between industries. But an even more critical question is: Why are employees absent? The answer is not straightforward. Of the many alternative models suggested in the literature, the principal ones include:

1. *Medical models*: A significant portion of absences is attributed to illness or injuries.
2. *Withdrawal models*: Absences are symptomatic of dissatisfaction and stress.
3. *Cultural models*: Absences are attributed to the general culture in the work environment and to lack of control and monitoring by management.
4. *Economic models*: Employees compute the economic costs and benefits of being absent.

In reality, all models operate simultaneously to explain complex employee behaviour. No research has been able to affirm the predominance of any one of the above models. However, research on absenteeism could be strengthened if researchers decided to employ multiple measures of it. For example, a measure of the *frequency* of absence, particularly short-term absences, is more subject to management control than a measure of the *time lost*.[22] That is, there is a marked difference between an employee who is away once for three days and the one who is away three times, one day each time. The former is more likely to have had a health-related problem, whereas the second may have missed work for reasons related to motivation, stress, or attitude.

In order to control absenteeism, a number of steps are required. First, the company needs to have a clear policy on employee absence. The policy should explicitly list acceptable grounds for absence, the requirement to promptly notify the employer of an unexpected absence, the pay policy for periods of absence, and the disciplinary procedures, particularly for chronic absentees. The current trend is to implement a "mixed consequence system," which combines rewards for attendance with systematic, rigorous discipline for absence, coupled with a proactive approach to improving work climate and reducing stress, and continuous training of management (especially first-line supervisors). When managers know how to reward good attendance and also know how to confront poor attenders, this results in a lower absence rate. A second important step in absence control is a good diagnosis. The company needs to analyze and identify the magnitude/severity, patterns, and costs of its absenteeism. This requires careful compilation and recording of information. If such are nonexistent, surveys in various units might be substituted for hard core data.

TURNOVER. In many respects, voluntary turnover is similar to absenteeism. However, excessive turnover is very often considered a symptom that something is wrong in the organization/unit. Most research uses turnover (for any reason) as an indicator of organizational health. In addition, however, there are the costs to an organization. The most visible costs come from recruiting, selecting (interviewing, testing, medical), placing, orienting, training, and supervising newcomers. For example, a newly hired secretary may cost between $1,500 and $2,000, the loss of a computer programmer may vary between $5,000 and $9,000. Generally, the cost of losing a staff member correlates positively with his or her position within the firm. There are, of course, other costs associated with an employee joining the competition.

The prime cause for employees quitting is disillusionment and dissatisfaction; the first step in reducing turnover is understanding its roots and finding out if there are common denominators amongst staff who quit. In order to research turnover, companies need to engage in periodical attitude surveys and address the problems detected by analyzing the responses. Additionally, companies need to conduct an exit interview with departing employees. These need to be recorded and analyzed in an aggregate form at a later date.

Both voluntary and nonvoluntary turnover represent costs to organizations. If the organization selected the wrong employee and a few months later it was forced to de-hire him or her, it would incur similar costs to those deriving from an employee who decided to quit a few months later. All in all, most formulas that calculate the costs of turnover, consider three major categories: separation costs, replacement costs, and training costs. Both direct and indirect parameters can be included in these three categories.

Procedural Justice

An HR research area that is gaining popularity concerns perceptions of justice and fair treatment at work. This line of research is important since a perception of injustice (inequity) by employees may result in low morale, high absenteeism, and high turnover. Thus, the research focuses on the process by which evaluation decisions (selection, performance appraisal, layoffs) or reward allocation decisions are made. The underlying assumption is that, even when employees are satisfied with an HR outcome, they may or may not be satisfied with the process or procedures that were used to make the decision.

While research on procedural justice is in its infancy, initial findings suggest that procedures that are open, are specified in advance, treat situated people similarly, and allow input from employees are more likely to be perceived as fair than are those violating these principles. Procedural justice is of the greatest concern when outcomes are unfavourable (e.g., layoffs, disciplinary actions, bumping, etc.)

Early research on procedural justice was conducted in laboratory settings. Field research may be helpful to HR practitioners since it might help the organization to better compete in a global competitive economy. Fairness of procedures will become even more important because allocation decisions will more often be unfavourable to employees in several ways.

Mergers, Acquisitions, and Downsizing

As noted in previous chapters, many Canadian firms have been forced to cut costs and reduce size, to become "lean and mean" in order to survive. At the same time, the rate of mergers and acquisitions has greatly increased. Both these trends have important implications for HR practices and strategies. Because of the speed of these changes, HR research has lagged behind, rather than led, actions in the real world. Still, some knowledge has been acquired, and more can be expected about the changing structure of organizations.

Articles in practitioners' journals on outplacement activities surfaced in the early 1980s and stimulated academic research on the consequences of job loss and job change. Some of this research has identified the conditions under which job loss is positive, leading to personal and career growth. Other research has focused on what organizations can do to reduce the stress associated with job loss or change through mergers and acquisitions.

On the flip side of layoffs, knowledge is beginning to be amassed regarding the reactions of retired employees to reductions in the labour force. Several studies have shown that "survivor guilt" can lead to increased performance among the survivors of layoffs.

Other research has identified the strategies used by organizations to reduce the size of the workforce. For example, one study found that layoffs were by far the most common downsizing strategy used, because HR managers had less than two months, on average, in which to plan and carry out the reduction in employment levels. It would seem that if the phenomenon was better researched and understood, HR managers could become more expert and proactive in monitoring product life cycles, the business environment, and organizational strategy in order to anticipate needed staff changes. Consequently, more research on how downsizing can be accomplished and how employees respond before, during, and after the fact is needed.

S U M M A R Y

Like any other managers, the HR manager needs to be accountable for his or her behaviour, and must be able to demonstrate a contribution to the organization. Pressures are mounting for professionals in the organization to show greater efficiency. For the HR function to show its effectiveness, it needs to be able to control, evaluate, and research its areas of responsibility. In the past, HR inputs and outputs were treated with more understanding by corporate executives, primarily due to the nontangibility of either inputs or outputs. In fact, however, the control of human resources is perhaps one of the most subtle and complex of all management tasks, the more so since times are changing.

Today, an array of approaches, measures, inventories, and tools is available for the HR manager to use in assessing his or her work, as well as the effectiveness of the entire HR department. A variety of quantitative and qualitative approaches, each with a different scope, aim, and degree of precision, have been presented. An intelligent strategy by senior HR executives will be to combine and complement these approaches, as well as to use internal and external resources to conduct a thorough HRM audit.

Although HR managers are not expected to become qualified researchers, basic research in HRM is feasible and valuable. It is feasible because an understanding of the basic universal principles of the scientific research process can lead to initiatives that will save the organization money. Even if the research cannot be performed by the HR department, an understanding of HR problems is necessary to make an intelligent decision regarding the identification and solution of problems pertaining to human work.

P O S T S C R I P T

You will notice that this chapter's Keynote Address does not refer directly to the issue of assessing HR effectiveness. Rather, Mr. Green, president and CEO of Alcatel Canada, was kind enough to concentrate on the factors that contribute to HR effectiveness in the global economy. We asked twenty-two large Canadian organizations to share with the readers of this text their practices in the area of HR effectiveness. All of them politely and skillfully declined the invitation. Our conclusion, unfortunately, is very simple: most of these organizations do not have a formal and rigorous HR control and evaluation system in place. Perhaps the activity is seen as being too costly or really not necessary. None of these organizations was prepared to admit this fact. This is only our speculation. Perhaps we are wrong.

It is hoped that by the time the third edition of this book is prepared, many more companies, and particularly their HR departments, will have a system in place for controlling and evaluating their contribution to the organization. In this day and age, where accountability is expected of each service, HR departments will not be able to escape it. Although this task is not an easy one it is becoming a necessity; many options for conducting research and evaluation are in fact available. In addition to subscribing to sound principles of management, additional positive consequences of applying such measures will be significant boosts to HR staff image, professionalism, and influence in corporate affairs.

R E V I E W   A N D   A N A L Y S I S   Q U E S T I O N S

1. What are the purposes of assessing HR activities? Why are they important?
2. What are some advantages and disadvantages of internal vs. external assessors?
3. Describe the essential elements in conducting an HRM audit. What are the strengths and weaknesses of this approach?

4. Select any quantitative approach to control and assessment of HRM and describe its main features.

5. Why is the multiple constituency approach gaining popularity?

6. What are the main steps of a scientific investigation? How different is it from common sense?

7. Choose any area in HRM and illustrate why and how it can be controlled/assessed.

C A S E   S T U D Y

ABSENTEEISM AND BEYOND

Morag Kavanagh of Management Decisions Systems Inc., a highly respected management consultant firm, had been asked by one of her clients to assess the feasibility of implementing a program designed to reduce the alarming rates of absenteeism among certain groups of employees. Her client, Teletalk, was a large public utility that provided telecommunication services.

Teletalk had been contending with problems related to technological innovations in the telecommunications industry, which had resulted in two major reorganizations and a threatened strike by the union over automation.

After meeting with Victor Vigdorhouse, VP human resources, and his staff, Morag arranged to interview some of the Teletalk employees, including workers from four different departments, their supervisors, a member of the support staff, the medical director, and the union. While Morag wanted to get a reading on the worker reactions to the implementation of a new program (she had in mind combining quality circles with team award programs), she was equally interested in finding out the workers' explanation for the singular increase in absenteeism at Teletalk.

The first group with which Morag met comprised three young women who had recently undergone training for craft positions (installer, line repairperson, switch equipment technician) and had completed six months in their new jobs. The positions, which had been previously male-occupied, paid considerably more than the jobs of operator or service representative that women had traditionally held with Teletalk. When questioned about the absenteeism rates, particularly the significantly higher rates observed for female Teletalk employees, all three agreed that the problem was that women were victims of occupational segregation by Teletalk. The skilled, better-paying, and more challenging jobs had not been available to the women until very recently. Furthermore, in response to Morag's question about possible quality circle and team award programs, Jacqueline Gautier, the most articulate of the three, said: "Frankly, we don't need this program; we don't want it, and moreover, if human resources sends us one more survey to fill out, we're going to throw up! We're sick of it!"

The next group was made up of four supervisors drawn from the largest departments, who gave Morag an entirely different perspective on the problem of absenteeism. According to the supervisors, absenteeism was not their problem and they had the data to support their argument. For reporting purposes, Teletalk divided absenteeism into two categories: incidental and medical. Incidental absences were any episodes of seven days' duration or less. Medical absences, by definition, were any episodes of greater than seven days' duration, and therefore required a clearance from the medical department before the absent employee could return to work. The supervisors then showed Morag graphs of a five-year trend of incidental and medical absences. For each of their departments, the trend was unmistakably consistent: incidental absence exhibited a gradual decline while medical absence was showing a marked increase. The supervisors agreed that Morag should forget the intended intervention because the problem was the medical department's fault.

Morag's next stop was Dr. Virgil Gangstead, the medical director of Teletalk. While Virgil was sympathetic to the supervisor's viewpoint, he felt that they were misguided. In fact, Virgil challenged Management Decision Systems Inc. to do a job-attitude study of the correlations of incidental to medical absenteeism and, he predicted, they would discover that incidental and medical absences shared the same work-related causes. Virgil also felt that the medical department was the victim of poor assessment and gamesmanship by the organization. He explained: "Your intended project is no different from the other programs management has tried in the past; it will roll in like a large wave and then regress to the ocean to be swallowed up, just like all the other programs!"

According to Virgil, the real problem was management's belief in the infallibility of the absenteeism recording system. Supervisors were rewarded for holding down incidental absence, which represented an insignificant amount of the total lost time. Moreover, each department interpreted differently the absenteeism coding scheme, created by the accounting department for payroll purposes.

"The problem is so bad that the craft departments won't even consider transfer applications from the service departments, because they simply don't trust their absenteeism records. And I must admit that in some departments, we have cultivated an absence 'culture' for years," Virgil said. Finally Virgil suggested that if Morag really wanted to identify the problem she should talk to the union representatives who had negotiated the last contract. Not a bad idea, decided Morag, and she scheduled the union president, John Mobley, for an interview that afternoon.

Morag had been warned that John could be feisty but, on the contrary, she found him to be quite gracious and informative. When asked about the contract provision that permitted any worker with five or more years of seniority to be paid for the second through seventh day of an absenteeism, John explained without the slightest hint of defensiveness or apology: "Our workers are not stupid. They know that under this arrangement it pays, to a limit, to take more rather than less time off the job if you choose to be absent. For some of our workers, this compensates for below-standard wages. For others, it simply legitimizes the worker's right to be absent for whatever reason without undergoing an interrogation. Besides, I think management has learned from its previous attempts at absenteeism control that the workers can always invent an antidote to the poison of a new absence-control program."

As for the idea of intervention, John just laughed. "Listen, Morag, management better wake up. Absenteeism is not the exclusive domain of the nonexempt employees. We all have a need for leisure, including management. The quality circle approach combined with team award is fine, but you won't find us supporting it. Our members want more paid time off to pursue their leisure activities."

Morag concluded the interview with John and drove to her office to prepare a report. She certainly had obtained more data than she expected.

Case Questions

1. What is the core of the problem at hand? What did the research reveal?
2. Was the research undertaken by Morag to reach a diagnosis appropriate?
3. How does absenteeism relate to various HR policies? What seems to be the problem with them?
4. Speculate on the kind of recommendations/report that Morag is about to prepare. What kind of intervention will be effective? Why?
5. After you have chosen a type of intervention, elaborate on the methods to be undertaken in order to assess its effectiveness.

NOTES

1. A. Templer and J. Cattaneo, "Assessing Human resource management effectiveness: how much have we learned?" *South African Journal of Labour Relations* 15, 4 (December 1991):23–30.

2. D. Koys, S. Briggs, and S. Ross, "Organizational Effectiveness and Evaluation of the Human Resource Function" (Paper presented at the Academy of Management Meeting, New Orleans, August 1987).

3. S.L. Dolan and J.G. Harbottle, "Results of Survey amongst Senior HR Managers" (Paper presented at the Annual Meeting of the Professional Association of Human Resource Managers of the Province of Quebec, April 1989).

4. Templer and Cattaneo, "Assessing human resource management," 24.

5. See G.E. Biles and R.S. Schuler, *Audit Handbook of HRM Practices* (Alexandria: ASPA, 1986); S.J. Carroll, "Measuring the work of a personnel department," *Personnel*, July–August 1960, 49–56; W.F. Cascio, *Costing Human Resources: The financial impact of behavior in organization*, 2nd ed. (Boston: Kent Publishing, 1987); H.L. Dahl, "Human resource cost and benefit analysis: new power for human resource approach," *Human Resource Planning* 1, 2 (1988): 69–77; J. Fitz-enz, *How to measure human resource management* (New York: McGraw–Hill, 1984); E.G. Flamholtz, *Human Resource Accounting* (San Francisco: Josey–Bass, 1985); W.R. Mahler, "Auditing PAIR," in *ASPA Handbook of Personnel and Industrial Relations*, ed. D. Yoder and H. Henneman (Washington, D.C.: ASPA, 1979), 2–103; A. Tsui, "Defining the Activities and Effectiveness of the Human Resources Department: A Multiple Constituency Approach," *Human Resource Management* 26, 1, (1987): 35–69; A.S. Tsui and L.R. Gomez-Mejia, "Evaluating the human resource effectiveness," in *Human resource involving roles*

and responsibilities (ASPA\BNA handbook of HRM), Vol. 1, ed. L. Dyer (Washington D.C.: ASPA, 1987), 187–227; A. Tsui and G.T. Milkovich, "Personnel department activities: Constituency perspectives and preferences," *Personnel Psychology* 40 (1987): 519–37.

6. Discussion is based on W.J. Rothwell and H.C. Kazanas, *Strategic Human Resources Planning and Management* (Englewood Cliffs, N.J.: Prentice–Hall, 1988), 423–26.

7. A number of management consulting firms have developed an extensive HRM audit, which in the near future will be available in a computer-aided form. The sample audit provided in this exhibit was developed by MDS Management Inc. of Montreal (P.O. Box 116, C.S.L. Station, Montreal H4V 2Y3), and is used with their permission; A different approach to conducting an HR audit was developed by a British consulting firm, MCP Management Consultants (11 John Street, London WC1N 2EB).

8. S.J. Carroll, "Measuring the work of a personnel department," *Personnel*, July–August 1960.

9. Dolan and Harbottle, "Results of a Survey."

10. T. Janz, "Forecasting the Costs and Benefits of Traditional versus Scientific Employment Selection Methods in Canada to the Year 1990," in *Canadian Readings in Personnel and Human Resource Management,* ed. S.L. Dolan and R.S. Schuler (St. Paul, Minn.: West Publishing Co., 1987), 103–11.

11. Example cited in V.G. Scarpello and J. Ledvinka, *Personnel/Human Resource Management Environments and Functions* (Boston: PWS–KENT, 1988), 741.

12. J.E. Hunter et al., "Impact of valid selection procedures on work force productivity," *Journal of Applied Psychology* 64, 1 (1979): 107–18.

13. See Tsui, "Defining the Activities," 35–69; Tsui and Gomez-Mejia, "Evaluating the human resource effectiveness," 187–227; and Tsui and Milkovich, "Personnel department activities," 519–37.

14. For more information, consult U. Sekaran, *Research Methods for Business*, 2nd ed. (New York: John Wiley and Sons, 1992), 9–14.

15. For an excellent discussion on determining the quality of measures in HRM, see N.W. Schmitt and R. Klimoski, *Research Methods in Human Resources Management* (Cincinnati: South-Western Publishing Co., 1991), Chapter 3.

16. The essential character of meta-analysis is that it represents an attempt to statistically analyze the summary findings of many empirical studies. The key to the conduct of valid analysis is the method chosen to describe and code the empirical studies on relevant dimensions.

17. For more information about these approaches, see W.F. Cascio, "Using utility analysis to assess training outcomes," in I.L. Goldstein and Associates, *Training and Development in Organizations* (San Francisco: Jossey–Bass Publishers, 1989), 63–88.

18. Ibid., 85.

19. L. Gomez-Mejia and D. Balkin, *Compensation, Organizational Strategy, and Firm Performance* (Cincinnati: South-Western Publishing, 1992).

20. Ibid., 114.

21. G. Johns, "Understanding and Managing Absence from Work," in *Canadian Readings in Personnel and Human Resource Management*, ed. S.L. Dolan and R.S. Schuler (St. Paul, Minn.: West Publishing Co., 1987), 324–35.

22. For more information on the causes and measures of absenteeism, see A. Arsenault and S.L. Dolan, "The Role of Personality, Occupation and Organization in Understanding the Relationship between Job Stress, Performance and Absenteeism," *Journal of Occupational Psychology* 56, 2 (1983): 227–40; and C. Leonard, S.L. Dolan, and A. Arsenault, "Stability and Variability of Two Common Measures of Absence," *Journal of Occupational Psychology* 63, (1990): 309–16. For information on calculating the cost of absenteeism, see Cascio, "Using utility Analysis," 63–88.

ABILITY A physical or intellectual quality or capability or capacity. In HRM, ability is often equated with skills.

ABSENTEE An employee who is scheduled to be at work but is not present.

ABSOLUTE STANDARDS An approach that allows superiors to evaluate each subordinate's performance independently from that of other subordinates, and often on a number of dimensions.

ACCOMPLISHMENT RECORDS A performance-appraisal form used by professionals to describe their achievements relative to appropriate job dimensions. Suitable for professionals who claim their "record speaks for itself."

ACCREDITATION/CERTIFICATION The process by which the standards and credentials for members of a profession are established. Also, the process used to certify an organization of employees as the bargaining agent for a unit of employers/employees.

ACHIEVEMENT TESTS Measures of an individual's performance based on what he or she knows. These may be actual work samples of the job or paper-and-pencil measures.

ADMINISTRATIVE ISSUES Issues concerning the treatment of employees at work, such as breaks and clean-up time.

ADVERSARIAL SYSTEM A view of labour and management that depicts the parties in conflict over achieving incompatible goals.

ADVERSE IMPACT The reflection of a significantly higher percentage of a protected group for employment, placement, or promotion.

AFFIRMATIVE ACTION PROGRAMS (AAP) Programs designed to ensure proportional representation of employees and undo the result of past discrimination on grounds of race, creed, sex, or national origin.

ALTERNATIVE RANKING A comparative approach in which the superior alternates between ranking the best and the worst until all subordinates are ranked.

ALTERNATIVE WORK ARRANGEMENTS Making available hours of work and days of work that differ from the more traditional eight-to-five, Monday-to-Friday schedule.

APPLICATION BLANK A form seeking information about the job applicant's background and present conditions, used to make hiring decisions.

APPRAISAL BY CUSTOMER A service rating by customers or clients of the job incumbent who dealt with them on such features as courtesy, promptness, and ability to resolve the problems.

APPRAISAL BY SUBORDINATES Evaluation of their superiors by subordinates on the basis of the needs of the organization.

APPRENTICESHIP TRAINING A training format based on learning while doing that takes a long time before the trainee is recognized as competent to be a full-fledged employee.

APTITUDE TESTS Measures of an individual's potential to perform. Intelligence tests are aptitude tests.

APTITUDE–TREATMENT INTERACTION (ATI) The fitting of each trainee with the most appropriate model of instruction based on the trainee's aptitude level.

ARBITRATION A procedure in which a central third party studies the bargaining situation, listening to both parties and gathering information, and then reaches a decision that is usually binding on the parties.

ASSESSMENT The process of measuring and comparing the costs and benefits to determine effectiveness or value, especially as it relates to each HR activity and the entire HR department in a company.

ASSESSMENT CENTRE METHOD A process used to determine the managerial potential of employees. It evaluates individuals as they take part in a large number of activities conducted in a relatively isolated environment. It is also useful for identifying potential training needs.

ASSISTANTSHIP A type of on-the-job training that involves full-time employment and exposes the individual to a wide range of jobs through assisting other workers.

ASSOCIATION A formal group that represents employees before the employer; in many ways similar to a union except that an association is often involved in fewer functions than a union.

ATTITUDE SURVEY A systematic method of soliciting employees' opinions about different aspects of work.

ATTITUDINAL STRUCTURING The relationships between labour and management during collective bargaining that result in shaping their attitudes toward one another.

ATTRIBUTION PROCESS The psychological condition of assigning an explanation to an event.

ATTRITION The loss of employees due to their leaving the organization.

AUDIT An in-depth critical analysis of the activities carried out by a unit with the aim of determining its effectiveness.

AUTHORIZATION CARDS Cards to be signed by employees to indicate that they want to be represented by a particular labour organization; signed after initial contact between unions and employees.

AUTONOMOUS WORK GROUPS A variety of arrangements that allow employees to decide how they will complete their job assignments.

AUTONOMY The degree to which the job provides substantial freedom, independence, and discretion to the worker performing the job.

AVAILABILITY ANALYSIS The process of determining how many women and other visible minorities are available to work in the relevant labour market of an organization.

AWARD In labour–management arbitration, the final decision of an arbitrator, binding on both parties to the dispute.

BAND WIDTH The maximum length of work day from which an employee can choose the hours he or she will work; connected to the concept of flexible working hours.

BARGAINING UNIT The heart of the labour–management relationship. A group of employees certified by the Labour Relations Board to be included in the union.

BASE RATE   The ratio of applicants who would succeed on the job relative to the total number of applicants when the test is not used for selection.

BASE SALARY   The amount of pay that is stable or constant over a period of time and is received regardless of performance level.

BEHAVIOURALLY ANCHORED RATING SCALE (BARS)   A quantitative absolute form that expands upon the conventional rating form by more extensively specifying the anchors on the behavioural dimensions used to evaluate the subordinate.

BEHAVIOURAL DESCRIPTION INTERVIEW   An interview based on the assumption that past behaviour is the best predictor of future performance, and consequently requires the candidate to give specific examples of how he or she solved problems or performed job duties in the past.

BEHAVIOURAL OBSERVATION SCALE (BOS)   Similar to BARS except in development of the dimensions, scale format, and scoring.

BENCHMARK JOBS   Jobs against which the worth of other jobs is determined by an analysis of the compensable factors and their dollar values in the benchmark jobs and by extant factors existing in the other jobs.

BENEFIT CRITERIA   Indicators used to show the positive impact of HR activities.

BIOGRAPHICAL INFORMATION BLANK (BIB)   A form on which an applicant may provide information about past accomplishments, interests, and preferences that can be used to supplement an application blank. Often referred to as **bio data**.

BONA FIDE OCCUPATIONAL QUALIFICATION (BFOQ)   A defence for adverse impact. For example, hiring only males to play male roles in theatrical productions is a BFOQ.

BONA FIDE SENIORITY SYSTEM   A formal system of seniority that has been and is maintained with the intent or purpose not to discriminate on the basis of the various Human Rights Acts.

BOULWARISM   A bargaining practice occurring when management extends a contract offer to a union and holds fast to that position. Modifications in the proposal may result only when additional "facts" are presented that contribute to a clearer view of relevant issues for negotiation.

BSG   Basic skills of grammar, math, safety, reading, listening, and writing; these represent one of the four categories of skills and abilities that can be increased by training.

BST   Basic skills of a technical nature required to do the specific job. These represent one of the four categories of skills and abilities that can be increased by training.

BUSINESS GAMES   A kind of work sample test used in managerial selection. Business games may be similar to in-basket exercises or simulation tests; however, they are called games because there are generally rules for play and there is a winner.

BUSINESS NECESSITY   A defence used for adverse impact. Business necessity suggests that the "essence" of the business operation would be undermined by hiring members of the protected group.

CAFETERIA BENEFIT PLAN   A plan that allows an employee to select the mix of benefits and services that he or she prefers.

CANADA EMPLOYMENT CENTRES (CECs)   Centres administered by the Canada Employment and Immigration Commission that match job seekers with employers who have job openings.

CANADA LABOUR CODE   The main act regulating labour relations for the federal jurisdiction.

CANADA LABOUR RELATIONS BOARD   A board whose powers and duties include the determination of the appropriate bargaining unit, the certification and decertification of unions, decisions as to unfair labour practices, etc.

CANADA PENSION PLAN (CPP)   A mandatory, contributory pension plan applicable to all self-employed individuals and to employees in Canada (except those who work for the federal government and those covered by the Quebec Pension Plan).

CANADIAN CLASSIFICATION AND DICTIONARY OF OCCUPATIONS (CCDO)   A publication of the federal government providing detailed definitions for all jobs in Canada.

CANADIAN LABOUR CONGRESS (CLC)   A central labour congress in Canada, formed in 1956, representing more than half of organized labour in Canada.

CANADIAN HUMAN RIGHTS ACT   A federal law, enacted in 1977, prohibiting discrimination on the basis of race, national or ethnic origin, colour, religion, age, sex, marital status, or physical handicap.

CAREER   A patterned sequence of attitudes and behaviours associated with work-related experiences that span a person's life.

CAREER DEVELOPMENT PROGRAMS   Organizational programs designed to match an employee's needs, abilities, and goals with current or future opportunities and challenges within the organization.

CAREER MANAGEMENT PROGRAMS   Organizational programs that represent concerted efforts in career planning and development aimed at satisfying a dual match between employee ability and job demands and employee needs and job rewards.

CAREER PATHING   Comprised of identifying employee abilities, values, goals, strengths, and weaknesses (career planning), and providing a set of job experiences that aid the employee in satisfying those attributes (job progression).

CAREER PLANNING ACTIVITIES   Offered by the organization to help individuals identify strengths, weaknesses, specific goals, and jobs they would like to attain.

CAREER PLATEAU   A situation in which career progress slows and the prospects for promotion decrease; deadended in a career.

CARPAL TUNNEL SYNDROME   An illness characterized by numbness, tingling, soreness, and weakness in the hands or wrists often resulting from the job.

CASH PLAN   A type of profit sharing plan that provides for payment of profit shares at regular intervals.

CENTRALIZATION   A term applied to organizations where essential decision making and policy formulation are done at one location (i.e., headquarters).

CENTRAL TENDENCY BIAS   To evaluate ratees as average, even when their performance actually varies.

CERTIFICATION ELECTION An election conducted to determine if a majority of the employees in a bargaining unit want the union to represent them as a group.

CLASSIFICATION METHODS Methods used to determine job families, such as clerical and secretarial; many job families consist almost completely of women employees and are often allotted low wage rates.

CLASSIFICATION POINT SYSTEM A method combining the point ranking method with the job classification method.

CLOSED-OFFER ARBITRATION A type of arbitration in which the arbitrator receives information on only the parties' original positions without any information on the bargaining process up to the time the arbitrator is selected.

CO-DETERMINATION A system of governing an organization where the employees in addition to management help run the company through union representation on the board of directors.

COGNITIVE JOB ELEMENTS Specific parts of a job, such as communicating, decision making, analyzing, and information processing.

COLLECTIVE BARGAINING Bargaining or joint discussion over wages, hours, and conditions of employment between management and a formal representative of the employees.

COMMISSIONS Individual incentive pay plans for salespeople.

COMPANY UNION An employee organization, usually occurring in a single company, that is dominated or strongly influenced by management.

COMPARABLE WORTH A compensation issue relating to the fact that while the "true worth" of jobs may be similar, some (often held by women) are paid at a lower rate than others (often held by men). Resulting differences in pay that are disproportionate to the differences in the "true worth" of jobs amount to wage discrimination.

COMPARATIVE STANDARDS or **COMPARATIVE APPROACH** An approach to performance evaluation, according to which subordinates are all compared against each other to determine their relative performance.

COMPENSABLE FACTORS Yardstick factors against which to compare or measure jobs to determine their relative worth.

COMPENSATORY APPROACH A hiring approach where an applicant's weak point can be made up (compensated) for by a strong point.

COMPA-RATIO The measure of the average salary for a given pay grade relative to the midpoint of that pay grade.

COMPRESSED WORK WEEK A work week of fewer than the traditional five days yet equal in time to a work week of five days.

COMPUTER-AIDED JOB EVALUATION (CAJE) A system that speeds up evaluations and improves the objectivity and consistency of the evaluation process.

COMPUTER-BASED TRAINING (CBT) Training that is accomplished by using computer technology.

COMPUTER MONITORING A performance appraisal that uses performance data gathered by computers.

CONCESSIONARY BARGAINING Bargaining by unions where they give up or concede issues or positions to management.

CONCILIATION A process by which a third party (usually the government) attempts to bring parties in conflict toward a resolution.

CONCURRENT VALIDATION Measuring the relationship between a predictor (test) and a job criterion score (job performance), whereby the predictor and criterion are collected at the same time.

CONFIRMATION APPROACH An approach by which a manager "loads the deck" to favour a particular candidate by selecting several candidates for final consideration who are far less qualified.

CONSTRUCT VALIDITY A measure of how well a test measures constructs or dimensions that are judged to be critical for job performance.

CONTAMINATED The degree to which a measure of performance measures or taps dimensions that are unrelated to the actual performance of an individual.

CONFEDERATION OF CANADIAN UNIONS (CCU) A federation of unions dedicated to independence from international unions.

CONFEDERATION OF NATIONAL TRADE UNIONS (NTU) A Quebec-based central labour body.

CONTENT VALIDITY An estimate of how well the test mirrors or reflects elements of the job domain.

CONTINGENT REWARDS Extrinsic rewards given to reinforce a particular behaviour. Reinforcement is an essential component of the training process.

CONTINUOUS BARGAINING When unions and management representatives meet on a regularly scheduled basis to review contract issues of common interest.

CONTRACT PLAN An informal agreement written by each training participant, specifying one aspect of the training that will be most beneficial when back on the job and agreeing to effect that aspect once back on the job. An important dimension of the contract is selecting a "buddy" to follow-up or check on the trainee's success in implementing that aspect of the training.

CONTRAST EFFECT The theory that a good person looks even better when placed next to a bad person, and a good person looks not as good when placed next to a great person.

CONTRIBUTORY PROGRAM A type of retirement plan in which both the employee and the organization contribute for benefits to be obtained at retirement.

CONVENTIONAL RATING A quantitative absolute method in which a superior evaluates subordinates by checking off how well they are doing on a form listing several dimensions (traits) and number grades for each dimension.

COOPERATIVE ACCEPTANCE Ensuring that employees have a work environment free from sexual harassment.

COOPERATIVE SYSTEM A view of labour and management that depicts each of the two parties engaging in reciprocal problem solving, information sharing, and integration of goals.

COORDINATED BARGAINING Several unions bargain jointly with a single employer.

CORE PLUS OPTIONS A general core program offered to all eligible employees. In addition, an option is granted to either increase or expand coverage and, in some instances, employees may elect to receive cash amounts rather than benefits.

CORE TIME The time during which everyone must work; there is no choice about working at this time.

CORPORATE CULTURE The values, norms, and statements about what is important to a company and how its employees should be treated.

CORRELATION COEFFICIENT A measure of the degree of relationship between two variables (a test and job performance).

COST–BENEFIT ANALYSIS It reflects a set of procedures with various degrees of mathematical sophistication that help management.

COST-OF-LIVING ADJUSTMENTS (COLAs) A salary or compensation variation that is related to economic conditions.

COST REDUCTION STRATEGY A method of being competitive by reducing the costs of the firm.

CRITERIA Measures of job success against which selection of new employees is made.

CRITICAL INCIDENTS An absolute form in which the superior records the critical or important events exhibited by a subordinate on a predetermined list of critical incidents.

CRITICAL INCIDENT TECHNIQUE (CIT) Method of job analysis whereby behavioural descriptions that have a critical or essential impact on the performance of a job (good, average, or bad) are recorded.

CUSTOMERIZATION Designing, structuring, and orienting the HR department to serve the needs of its customers, especially line managers and the employees.

CUTOFF SCORES Scores on a test or predictor below which one decision is made (not to hire) and above which another decision is made (to hire).

DECENTRALIZATION A term applied to organizations where essential decision making and policy formulation is done at several locations (i.e., in the divisions or departments of the organization).

DECERTIFICATION An election conducted to remove a union from representation if the employees currently represented by the union vote to do so.

DEFICIENT The degree to which a measure of performance fails to measure or tap all the essential elements in the actual performance of an individual.

DELPHI TECHNIQUE A technique according to which a number of experts take turns at presenting a forecast statement. As the process continues, the forecast is subject to other members' revisions until a viable forecast emerges.

DEPTH INTERVIEW An interview where the interviewer has only a general set of questions to ask and where the interviewee is asked to go into detail in answering.

DESIGN STAGE PARTICIPATION A type of participation whereby the employees are responsible for designing a pay plan, so they are more likely to understand and accept a plan they have helped to design.

DICTIONARY OF OCCUPATIONAL TITLES (DOT) Source for obtaining the job descriptions for almost 30,000 different jobs in the U.S.A.

DIFFERENTIAL VALIDITY A comparison of validity coefficients or prediction models for two or more subgroups of individuals.

DIRECT COMPENSATION The basic wage and performance-based pay, including merit and incentive pay.

DIRECT INDEX An assessment approach that tends to be more objective because such things as actual units sold, scrap rate, absenteeism, and units produced are used to evaluate performance.

DISCRIMINATION (at work) Unequal treatment of persons, whether through hiring, promoting or discharging, on the basis of sex, age, marital status, race, creed, or other traits not related to direct job performance.

DISTRIBUTIVE BARGAINING A type of collective bargaining where both labour and management try to attain goals that would result in a gain for one party but a loss for the other.

DOWNSIZING Reducing the size of the company's workforce.

DUAL CAREER An approach that tends to emphasize occupation as a primary source of personal fulfilment.

DUTIES The specific activities that comprise a job and form its essence.

EARNED TIME A positive behavioural control strategy to reduce absenteeism through a "no-fault" approach that provides employees with potential days off, which they use as (if) needed.

ECONOMIC SUPPLEMENT A type of compensation for employees that includes: pensions, vacations, paid holidays, sick leave, health insurance, and supplemental unemployment benefits.

EFFECTIVE FEEDBACK Information given to employees in an appraisal context that enables them to use the information effectively to improve performance and to accept evaluation.

EFFECTIVENESS An indication of contribution or value to the organization, such as personnel's contribution by improving the organization's productivity, QWL, and legal compliance.

ELECTRONIC COTTAGES Homes of employees equipped with computers and other means by which they can communicate with the main office or plant.

EMPLOYEE ASSISTANCE PROGRAMS (EAPs) Programs specifically designed to assist employees with acute or chronic personal problems (for example, marital dysfunctions, alcohol abuse) that hinder their job performance, attendance, and corporate citizenship.

EMPLOYEE CONTRACT A formal and, frequently, written agreement between employer and employee specifying the wages, hours, and type of work conditions.

EMPLOYEE PACING A condition in which the pace or rate at which the employee works is determined by the employee and not the machine, as under machine pacing.

EMPLOYEE REFERRAL PROGRAMS (ERPs) Essentially word-of-mouth advertising involving current employees recruiting (informally) potentially qualified job applicants.

EMPLOYEE RIGHTS Rights desired by employees regarding the security of their jobs and the treatment administered by their employers.

EMPLOYEE SERVICE AND PERQUISITES A form of indirect compensation that varies depending on employee type and organization to offset the problems associated with working (e.g., day care) or used to symbolize a status differential (e.g., company-paid memberships to country, athletic, and social clubs).

EMPLOYEE TRAINING AND DEVELOPMENT Any attempt to improve current or future employee performance by increasing, through learning, an employee's ability to perform, especially by changing an employee's attitudes and increasing his or her skills and knowledge.

EMPLOYMENT-AT-WILL A common law doctrine stating that employers may dismiss their employees for any reason. Recently, court decisions and legislation have created some exceptions to this rule.

EMPLOYMENT CONTRACT An agreement between the employee and the employer regarding certain conditions of employment (e.g., wages, hours, and the type of work).

EMPLOYMENT EQUITY A comprehensive process adopted to ensure equitable representation of designated groups throughout the workplace and to remedy and prevent the effects of intentional and systemic discrimination.

EMPOWERING Passing on to employees the power and authority to make decisions and giving them the ability to know how to do so.

ERGONOMIC APPROACH An approach to job design concerned with designing and shaping jobs to fit the physical abilities and characteristics of individual workers.

ERROR OF CENTRAL TENDENCY A type of halo error where all dimensions are rated average or all individuals are given a more lenient rating.

ERROR OF LENIENCY In order to avoid potential conflict with subordinates, a manager rates all employees in a particular work group higher than they should be rated objectively.

ERROR OF STRICTNESS A type of halo error where all dimensions are given an unfavourable rating or all individuals receive a stricter rating.

ESSAY METHOD A performance evaluation method in which the superior describes in writing (essay form) the performance of the subordinate.

ESSENTIALITY The amount of power a job holder (any employee) has, which is determined by how critical the job is to the organization and by exclusivity.

EVALUATION DESIGNS Methods by which training programs can be evaluated to determine how effective the programs are (i.e., how much change is made).

EXCLUSIVITY The difficulty in replacing a job holder. Also, in a labour relations context, the right acquired by an employee organization to be the sole representative of the bargaining unit.

EXEMPT EMPLOYEES Job incumbents not paid overtime for working overtime; they are exempt from the wage–hour laws requiring overtime pay.

EXIT INTERVIEW A conversation that takes place with departing employees to learn the reasons for their departure.

EXTENDED CIT The application of the critical incident technique to a variety of job domains identified by job incumbents.

EXTENSION OF BARGAINING An attempt on the part of an arbitrator to reach a rational and equitable decision acceptable to both parties in arbitration.

EXTERNAL EQUITY The determination of wage rates for different jobs made on the basis of what other companies are paying for those jobs.

FACE VALIDITY A *subjective* assessment of how well a test will predict job success by examining the test items.

FACT FINDING A formal/informal dispute resolution procedure used for investigating and reporting on the facts of a situation.

FACTOR-COMPARISON METHOD A method similar to point rating in that it has compensable factors, but in factor comparison the factors have dollar not point values.

FAIR EMPLOYMENT PRACTICES The practice of employers (or unions) offering workers equal employment opportunities.

FALSE NEGATIVE DECISIONS Incorrect predictions that applicants will perform poorly, when in fact applicants will perform successfully.

FALSE POSITIVE DECISIONS Incorrect predictions that applicants will perform well, when in fact applicants will perform poorly.

FEASIBILITY ASSESSMENT An estimation of the value of using a predictor by examining its costs and benefits and by comparing it to alternative ways.

FINAL-OFFER ARBITRATION A type of settlement where the arbitrator chooses the final offer of either union or management.

FLEXIBLE COMPENSATION An approach to compensation that gives individuals a chance to choose what types of compensation they prefer, as opposed to the organization just handing them a fixed compensation package.

FLEXIBLE SPENDING PLANS Plans that provide some form and level of pay to employees that is nontaxable to some extent.

FLEXIBLE TIME The time a worker can choose to work within the band width, yet outside of the core time.

FLEXYEAR SCHEDULES A work system where employees think and schedule work time in terms of a year rather than a day or week, as in the case of flextime schedules.

FLEXTIME A work schedule that gives employees daily choice in the timing of work and nonwork activities.

FOLLOW-UP Once a person leaves a training program, finding out (in order to evaluate the effectiveness of the training program) how well the person is doing back on the job.

FORCED CHOICE FORM An absolute form on which the superior evaluates the subordinate by choosing which item in a pair of items better describes the subordinate.

FORCED DISTRIBUTION METHOD A comparative approach in which the superiors are forced to place subordinates in ranks that represent groups or percentage clusters.

FORMAL COURSE METHOD An off-the-job training program that includes self-training and formal classrooms and lectures.

FREQUENCY RATE A formula used to determine the amount of accidents and diseases similar to the incidence rate, except that it is calculated using the number of hours worked rather than on a per annum basis.

FUNCTIONAL JOB ANALYSIS (FJA) A description of the nature of jobs, job summaries, job descriptions, and employee specification.

GENETIC SCREENING A process of selecting people, or not selecting them, on the basis of gene tests.

GOALS A basis against which to evaluate how well employees are performing, especially managers.

GOAL SETTING The setting of specific, hard, and clear objective so that people learn quickly and perform better.

GOLDEN COFFINS Benefits designed to provide financial assistance, generally to top executives, in case of death in the family. All funeral costs and other related expenses are paid.

GOLDEN HANDCUFFS Extremely favourable monetary arrangements that build up over time, making it more and more costly for an employee to leave an organization.

GOLDEN PARACHUTES Extremely large sums of money made available to executives if their jobs are lost due to mergers and acquisitions.

GRIEVANCE ARBITRATION Arbitration that takes place during the life of a contract and relates to a grievance filed by either party.

GRIEVANCE PROCEDURE The most common method of resolving disputes between union and management over the application and interpretation of an agreement or contract.

GUIDELINES-ORIENTED JOB ANALYSIS (GOJA) A person-focused job analysis technique. The process involves six steps and produces helpful information for the development of performance appraisal, training, and selection procedures.

HALO ERROR The tendency (and error) to rate an individual on several dimensions by how well they do on just one dimension.

HANDICAP An impairment that substantially limits one or more of a person's major life activities.

HAY PLAN A structured procedure for analyzing jobs that is systematically tied into a job evaluation and compensation system. The Hay Plan includes information about the nature and scope of a position as well as how to reward the position.

HEALTH INSURANCE PLANS Health and medical insurance provided by the various provincial governments.

HISTORICAL RECORDS Organizations often use information on how well employees have done in the past (to determine what is actually possible) to establish what is average performance or excellent performance.

HONESTY TESTS Paper-and-pencil tests used to measure the extent to which a job applicant is likely to be honest and not lie or cheat on the job.

HORIZONTAL LOADING The addition of similar duties to those already present in the job and that require the same skills, knowledge, and abilities (SKAs).

HORN ERROR An error where negative performance in one dimension supersedes any positive performance.

HUMAN RESOURCE FLEXIBILITY The capacity of HRM to facilitate the organization's ability to adapt effectively and in a timely manner to changing demands from either its environment or from within the firm itself.

HUMAN RESOURCE INFORMATION SYSTEM (HRIS) A method that allows more rapid and frequent data collection to back up a forecast of personnel needs.

HUMAN RESOURCE MANAGEMENT SYSTEM (HRMS) See **HUMAN RESOURCE INFORMATION SYSTEM (HRIS)**.

HUMAN RESOURCE PLANNING (HRP) The process of developing and implementing plans and programs to ensure that the right number and type of individuals are available at the right time and place to fulfil organizational needs.

HUMAN RESOURCES STRATEGIC PLANNING The identification of strategies and HR needs covering a three- to five-year planning horizon.

HUMAN RESOURCES TACTICAL PLANNING The identification of the major thrusts, key objectives, and deliverables needed to support the HR strategic plan.

HUMAN RIGHTS LEGISLATION Laws enacted by the federal and provincial governments against discrimination.

IN-BASKET EXERCISE A simulation training technique in which the solitary trainee sits at a desk and works through a pile of papers found in the in-basket of a typical manager, prioritizing, recommending solutions to problems, and taking any necessary action.

INCENTIVE PAY PLAN A method of monetary and nonmonetary compensation related to direct indexes of performance for the individual group or organization. It generally represents a substantial proportion of an individual's direct compensation.

INCENTIVE STOCK OPTION An individual incentive plan that awards stock, such as stock option plans for junior stocks.

INCIDENT RATE An explicit formula for determining the number of accidents and cases of disease per year according to the number of employee exposure levels.

INDIRECT COMPENSATION Rewards or benefits provided by the organization to employees for their membership or participation (attendance) in the organization; also known as fringe benefits or supplemental compensation.

INDIVIDUAL CONTEMPORARY DESIGN A major classification of approaches to job design that focus on the individual worker–job design interface (or relationships).

INDUSTRIAL COTTAGES Small manufacturing operations that are set up in the homes of individuals who then work at home.

INDUSTRIAL RELATIONS SYSTEM (IRS) See (**LABOUR RELATIONS SYSTEM**)

INDUSTRYWIDE BARGAINING Where employers bargain as a group with the union at the national level.

INITIAL DEMAND POINT A demand by the union for a wage settlement that is higher than what is expected to be granted.

INITIAL OFFER Management's first offer, representing what wages and conditions it will grant to the union during the current round of negotiations.

INJUNCTION A court order restraining one or more persons, corporations, or unions from performing certain acts that the court thinks will result in injury to property or to other rights.

INSTITUTIONAL ISSUES Issues not directly related to the job that affect the security and success of both union and management, such as strikes and union security.

INTEGRATIVE BARGAINING A type of collective bargaining where labour and management work to solve contractual problems to the benefit of both.

INTEREST BARGAINING Arbitration that deals with the terms and conditions of the contract.

INTEREST TEST A kind of personality, interests, and preferences test given to an individual. These tests are not necessarily predictive of job performance, but they can predict which job will be more in line with a person's attributes.

INTERNAL EQUITY Wage rate determination for different jobs within one organization on the basis of the relative worth of those jobs to the organization.

INTERNAL CONSISTENCY RELIABILITY A measure of the extent or degree of relatedness or similarity that exists among items, dimensions, or statements that are supposed to refer to the same thing, such as a ten-item test of mechanical aptitude or a ten-item supervisory measure of job success.

INTERNSHIP A training period that often forms part of an agreement between schools and colleges and local organizations.

INTERRATER RELIABILITY A measure of the consistency or agreement that exists for two or more people (raters) evaluating the same event or person.

INTERNSHIPS Training programs (often part of an agreement between schools, colleges, and universities and organizations) where an individual may work full time but only for a short time.

INTERPERSONAL COMPETENCE TESTS Measures of social intelligence. These include aspects of intelligence related to awareness of nonverbal and social information.

INTRAORGANIZATIONAL BARGAINING The process whereby negotiating teams influence their constituents over changes in bargaining positions.

IPS A term referring to a category of learning involved with the acquisition of interpersonal skills including communications, human relations, decision making, leadership, and labour relations.

JOB ANALYSIS The process used to describe or record the purposes, task characteristics, and task duties of a job in a given organizational setting to determine a match for individual skill, experience, knowledge, and needs.

JOB BANKS Places where computerized listings of jobs and their characteristics are maintained. These banks are generally associated with public employment agencies.

JOB BURNOUT A specific set of symptoms brought on by severe or chronic stress directly related to the career rather than personal difficulties. Related symptoms are chronic fatigue, low energy, irritability, and a negative attitude toward job and self.

JOB CLASSES Used interchangeably with **JOB FAMILIES**.

JOB CLASSIFICATION METHOD Similar to ranking except that classes or grades are established and then the jobs are placed into the classes.

JOB DESCRIPTION A detailed statement of the duties, purposes, and conditions under which a job is to be performed (cf. **JOB ANALYSIS**).

JOB DESIGN A process that results in a set of purposes, task characteristics, and task duties in a given organizational setting based on a set of unique organizational and personnel qualities.

JOB ELEMENT INVENTORY (JEI) A form designed for completion by job incumbents.

JOB ENLARGEMENT An approach to job design that loads a job horizontally, that is, it adds more of the same types of duties requiring the same skills.

JOB ENRICHMENT An approach to job design that loads a job vertically, that is, it increases the number of skills needed and the sense of significance.

JOB EVALUATION A comparison of jobs by the use of formal and systematic procedures to determine their relative worth within the organization.

JOB FAIRS Events where many employers gather to talk with potential job applicants, often students, about job opportunities.

JOB FAMILIES The grouping together of all jobs of nearly the same value to the organization for the purpose of establishing a wage structure that reflects internal equity.

JOB FEEDBACK The degree to which the job itself provides the worker with information about how well the job is being performed.

JOB IDENTITY The degree to which a job requires completion of a "whole" and identifiable piece of work.

JOB INFORMATION MATRIX SYSTEM (JIMS) A system designed to collect information on such issues as what the employee does on the job; what equipment or tools the employee uses; what the employee has to know; what the employee's responsibilities are; and the conditions under which the employee has to perform.

JOB INSTRUCTION TRAINING (JIT) A systematic technique for on-the-job training consisting of four steps: (l) careful selection and preparation of both trainer and trainee for the learning experience to follow; (2) full explanation and demonstration by the trainer; (3) a trial on-the-job performance by the trainee; and (4) a thorough feedback session highlighting job performance and job requirements.

JOB MATCHING PROGRAM An essential function in effective recruiting that entails fitting the needs of people to the requirements of the job.

JOB NEEDS ANALYSIS An examination of the organization that provides information on the tasks to be performed on each job, the skills necessary to perform those tasks, and the minimum acceptable standards of performance.

JOB POSTING A procedure of posting a list of what jobs are available within the organization.

JOB PROFILE A major component of a job matching system that contains the descriptions of jobs that are available.

JOB PROGRESSION A systematic effort by companies to tie individual career needs to the practical needs of the organization by identifying what individuals want and what the organization needs and can offer.

JOB-RELATEDNESS   Refers to selection tests and qualifications being related to an employee's success on the job. If a test or qualification is shown to be job-related, an adverse impact charge can be defended.

JOB ROTATION   An approach to job design that does not change the job, but rather rotates the worker from job to job.

JOB SEX–ROLE STEREOTYPING   The process of associating jobs and roles according to a male or female suffix (e.g., male–foreman; female–seamstress) generally reflecting a traditional sex–role bias.

JOB SHARING   Arrangements for two people or more to share (split) the hours of one job, e.g., two people will take one job and each will work four hours daily.

JOB SIGNIFICANCE   The degree to which the job has a substantial impact on the lives of other people.

JOB SPECIFICATION   A detailed statement of the skills, knowledge, and abilities (SKAs) required of a person doing a given job (cf. **JOB ANALYSIS**).

JOB TITLE   A group of positions that are identical with regard to their significant duties.

JUDGMENTAL FORECAST   A human resources planning forecasting technique that relies on the personal judgments of selected experts.

JUNIOR STOCK   An individual incentive plan involving the awarding of a special nonvoting common stock at bargain prices.

KNOWLEDGE OF RESULTS   An important reinforcement is the knowledge of how well a task was done, or having the knowledge of results.

LABOUR RELATIONS BOARD (LRB)   A board set up in the federal and all provincial jurisdictions to administer labour relations legislation.

LABOUR MARKET   The number and characteristics of the persons in the workforce who are either working or looking for work.

LABOUR RELATIONS SYSTEM (LRS)   A conceptual paradigm used to elucidate the interrelationships among management, union, and employees.

LEADERLESS GROUP DISCUSSION (LGD)   A type of work sample test used in managerial selection where applicants sit around and discuss a topic for a given period of time.

LEARNING PRINCIPLES   Guidelines to the ways in which people learn most effectively.

LEGAL COMPLIANCE   The many laws, regulations, arbitrators, and court decisions with which organizations must comply in managing their employees.

LENIENCY (ERROR)   An often-committed error by appraisers of being too easy when doing performance appraisals.

LIE DETECTOR TEST   A polygraph exam used in the selection procedure to predict which employees are likely to lie or steal.

LOCAL UNION   The basic unit of union organization formed in a particular plant or locality.

LOCKOUT   A refusal by management to allow workers to work.

LOW QUALITY OF WORK LIFE   A sociopsychological work environment component characterized by one-way communications, lack of respect for employee rights, poor personnel, and policies that produce unfavourable psychological conditions and outcomes.

LUMP SUM BONUSES   Salary increases paid in one payment rather than being divided into several smaller increases.

MACHINE PACING   A condition under which the machine determines how fast the work must be done; therefore, the pace at which the employee works is determined by the machine.

MANAGEMENT BY OBJECTIVES (MBO)   An approach that evaluates the performance of managers (typically) on the basis of how well they have attained their predetermined goals or objectives.

MANAGEMENT POSITION DESCRIPTION QUESTIONNAIRES (MPDQ)   A method of job analysis that relies upon the checklist method to analyze jobs, especially management jobs.

MANAGEMENT RIGHTS   As used in industrial relations, those aspects of the employer's operation that do not require discussion with or concurrence of the union.

MANAGER   The person who directs and is responsible for other employees who are either supervisors or managers.

MANAGERIAL ESTIMATE   Estimates of staffing needs made by either the top-down version or the bottom-up version.

MANAGERIAL INCENTIVE PLANS   Incentive plans for managers that generally take the form of cash bonuses for the good performance of the department, division, or organization as a whole.

MANDATORY ISSUES   Wages, hours, and other terms and conditions of employment for which management must bargain according to the law.

MATURITY CURVES   In the context of compensation, the determination of compensation as a function of years of experience in a profession; in the context of training (and learning), the suggestion that people learn more and improve with time.

MEASURED DAY WORK   An incentive pay plan where production standards are established, although not as precisely as in piecework plans, and employees are paid according to those standards.

MEDIATION   A procedure in which a central third party assists union and management negotiators in reaching a voluntary agreement.

MENTOR   Someone who offers informal career guidance and support to an employee on a regular basis.

MERIT PAY PLANS   Methods of monetary compensation (generally related to subjectively evaluated performance) that represent only a small percentage increment in an employee's direct compensation.

METHOD ANALYSIS   The use of individual activity units to describe the way a job is to be performed and evaluated. Also known as motion study. The best application is to nonmanagerial jobs.

MIDLIFE TRANSITION   Re-examination of one's accomplishments relative to initial career goals, which occurs between the ages of forty and fifty-five.

MINIMUM WAGE   The rate of pay established by statute or by minimum wage orders as the lowest wage that will be paid to an employee.

MIXED INTERVIEW   An appraisal interview in which the rater combines the tell-and-sell with the problem-solving interview types.

MODULAR APPROACH   A method that allows employees to select a preferred package from various existing modules. These modules are structured in such a way so as to satisfy common situations within the workforce.

MULTIEMPLOYER BARGAINING   A type of collective negotiation where employers bargain as a group with the union at the local level.

MULTILATERAL BARGAINING   A type of collective negotiation wherein more than two parties are involved in the negotiation and there is no clear union–management dichotomy.

MULTINATIONAL CORPORATION   A firm that operates in several countries.

MULTIPLE CUTOFF MODEL   A hiring process where an applicant must exceed fixed levels of proficiency (do well on all tests) but in no particular sequence.

MULTIPLE HURDLE MODEL   A hiring process where an applicant must do well on several tests or predictors and must do well in sequence.

MULTIPLE LINEAR REGRESSION   An extension of simple linear regression, where several independent variables (Xs) are used to more accurately predict or forecast future events. For example: productivity is predicted by an equation relating absenteeism (X_1), turnover (X_2), and waste (X_3) to the dependent variable productivity (Y).

MULTIPLE MANAGEMENT PROGRAMS   Training programs for managers where lower- and middle-level managers get an opportunity to work with top-level managers.

MULTIPLE PREDICTORS APPROACH   Combining several pieces of information or predictors to make a selection decision.

NARRATIVE ESSAY   A written, open-ended statement of evaluation or appraisal of an employee.

NATIONAL UNION   A basic unit of labour unions that organizes, charters, and controls member union locals and develops general policies and procedures by which locals operate.

NEGATIVE SETTLEMENT RANGE   When there is no overlap between union demands and management's concessions, thus resulting in no grounds for settlement.

NEGOTIATING COMMITTEE   Representatives from the union and management who meet to negotiate a contract.

NETWORK   A collection of friends, acquaintances, and colleagues, both inside and outside one's workplace, that can be summoned to provide some kind of help or support.

NEUTRALIZING   The process of putting aside an employee whose performance is marginal at best, in order to prevent influencing others.

NOMINAL GROUP TECHNIQUE   A structured group process where several individuals list and identify their ideas. All ideas are considered by all members and action is decided upon after a structured evaluation is completed.

NONCOMPENSATORY APPROACHES   Hiring processes where weak points cannot be made up for by strong points.

NONCONTRIBUTORY PROGRAM   A type of retirement plan in which the employee is the sole contributor for benefits to be obtained at retirement.

NONEXEMPT EMPLOYEES   A category of employees who are not exempt from wage–hour laws regulating payment for overtime; incumbents are paid overtime for working overtime.

NONVERBAL CUES   Behaviour that does not involve words or speech. Examples include body movement, gestures, handshake, eye contact, and physical appearance.

NORM-REFERENCED APPROACH (APPRAISAL)   A performance appraisal method where employees are compared to each other in terms of overall performance.

OBJECTIVE FORMS   Appraisals where the evaluation is done against specifically defined behaviours or outcomes, such as levels of output, level of specific goal attainment, or number of days absent.

OCCUPATIONAL ACCIDENTS   Accidents such as loss of limb, loss of hearing or sight, or even loss of life as a consequence of the physical environment of an organization.

OCCUPATIONAL ANALYSIS INVENTORY (OAI)   A technique that integrates job-oriented elements with person-oriented elements. It also covers work goals.

OCCUPATIONAL DISEASES   Diseases or illnesses, such as cancer and leukemia, that result from aspects of the physical work environment.

OCCUPATIONAL HEALTH AND SAFETY (OH&S)   Physical/physiological and sociopsychological conditions of an organization's workforce.

OFF-THE-JOB TRAINING PROGRAMS (OFFJT)   Training programs that are taught outside the work organization.

ON-THE-JOB TRAINING PROGRAMS (OJT)   Training programs that are conducted on the job or where the people are working.

OPEN SHOP   A shop in which union membership is not required as a condition of retaining employment.

ORDER EFFECTS   Where the order or arrangement of information or job applicants influences the evaluation they receive.

ORGANIZATIONAL NEEDS ANALYSIS   An examination of short- and long-term objectives of the organization, HR needs, efficiency indexes, and organizational climate as they relate to the training and development needs of the organization.

ORGANIZATION STRESS   A sociopsychological work environment component characterized by organizational changes, work overload, poor supervision, unfair salaries, job insecurity, and physical insecurity, all of which produce uncertainty.

ORGANIZATIONAL SURVEYS   Gathering data from individuals in a company to determine how they feel and how things are going.

ORIENTATION PROGRAMS   Activities used by employers to help familiarize new employees with the work environment and the culture of the firm.

OUTPUT APPROACH (IN APPRAISALS)   A performance appraisal approach using hard or direct measures of output, such as goals, against which to evaluate employees.

PAIRED COMPARISON METHOD   A comparative approach in which the superior compares each subordinate with every other subordinate in order to evaluate the subordinate's performance.

PANEL INTERVIEW   An interview where there are several interviewers for just the one interviewee.

PAPER-AND-PENCIL ACHIEVEMENT TESTS   Measures of job-related knowledge rather than work samples of the job itself.

PARTIAL REINFORCEMENT   Providing immediate reward or follow-up to individuals on an intermittent basis rather than on a continuous basis.

PATTERNED OR STRUCTURED INTERVIEW An interview that has a specific set of questions in a fixed order.

PATTERN SETTLEMENTS A settlement between a union and management that is based upon and similar to an agreement made by another company with its union.

PAY ADMINISTRATION PRACTICES A practice by which an employer attracts new employees and keeps them satisfied with their pay. The wages and salaries offered should approximate the wages and salaries paid to other employees in comparable organizations.

PAY EQUITY What people feel they deserve to be paid in relation to what others deserve to be paid.

PAY FAIRNESS Ensuring that what employees are paid is in relation to what they and others give to the organization.

PAY FOR TIME NOT WORKED A form of indirect compensation received by an employee for time not spent working. There are two categories: *off-the-job*, e.g., vacations, sick leave, holidays, personal days, comprising the major portion of costs of indirect benefits, and *on-the-job*, e.g., lunch and rest periods, physical fitness facilities.

PAY GRADES A range of pay for a particular job family or class. Grade structure is based upon job evaluation points associated with a point–factor evaluation.

PAY LEVEL The absolute pay or wage that employees receive.

PAY SECRECY The issue of whether employees should or should not have access to the organization's compensation schedule.

PEER APPRAISAL A useful predictor of subordinate performance that is particularly useful when superiors lack access to some aspects of subordinates' performance.

PERFECTLY NEGATIVE VALIDITY Where the degree of relationship between two variables is one-to-one and negative.

PERFECTLY POSITIVE VALIDITY Where the degree of relationship between two variables is one-to-one and positive.

PERFORMANCE APPRAISAL (PA) A system of measuring, evaluating, and influencing an employee's job-related attributes, behaviours and outcomes, and level of absenteeism to discover at what level the employee is presently performing on the job.

PERFORMANCE APPRAISAL SYSTEM (PAS) The entire system that incorporates the following: method used to gather the appraisal data, job analysis, establishment of validity and reliability of the method, characteristics of the rater and ratee that influence the process, use of the information for development and evaluation, evaluation of appraisal in relation to its stated objectives.

PERFORMANCE-BASED PAY SYSTEMS Pay systems that relate pay to performance, including incentive pay plans and merit pay plans.

PERFORMANCE CONTRACT An employment agreement with clearly specified objectives for a given period of time and the appropriate rewards or disciplinary action for meeting or failing to meet agreed upon goals.

PERFORMANCE CRITERIA Dimensions or factors used to judge an individual in performing a particular job.

PERFORMANCE RATIOS Ratios that indicate where the performance rating of any employee stands relative to the other employees.

PERFORMANCE SHARES A managerial incentive plan whereby managers receive shares or stocks in a company as a performance reward based upon how well the company is doing.

PERFORMANCE STANDARDS Indicators or levels attached to the performance criteria to enable a judgment to be made about how well an individual is performing.

PERMANENT PART-TIME Fixed arrangements for regular employees to work fewer than five days per week or forty hours per week.

PERMISSIVE ISSUES Those issues over which it is not mandatory to bargain but that are not specifically illegal.

PERSON NEEDS ANALYSIS An examination of the deficiencies between an employee's actual performance and the desired performance or between an employee's proficiency on critical job dimensions and the desired proficiency required on the job dimensions.

PERSONAL APPRAISAL Identification of the abilities, values, and goals across several life dimensions that are important to you. Strengths and weaknesses are also noted.

PERSONAL COMPETENCE TEST A test designed to measure whether individuals know how to make appropriate and timely decisions for themselves and whether they put forth the effort to do so.

PERSONALITY INVENTORIES Tests that tap individual traits or characteristics, for example, California Psychological Inventory, Minnesota Multiphasic Personality Inventory.

PERSONNEL GENERALIST (also **HR GENERALIST**) Personnel staff with moderate experience of the language, needs, and requirements of the line. Generally found in organizations characterized by centralization.

PERSONNEL MANAGER An old title for the person or position heading the personnel department. Today most individuals occupying these positions are called human resource managers.

PERSONNEL SPECIALIST (also **HR SPECIALIST**) Staff with specific skills related to the personnel area or department of the organization. Generally found in organizations characterized by decentralization.

PHYSICAL ABILITIES ANALYSIS (PAA) A person-focused method of job analysis that uses nine abilities to analyze the physical requirements of tasks.

PHYSICAL JOB ELEMENTS The specific physical properties of a job, such as lifting, lighting, colouring, sound, speed, and positioning.

PHYSICAL WORK ENVIRONMENT Composed of the building, chairs, equipment, machines, lights, noise, heat, chemicals, toxins, and the like that are associated with occupational accidents and diseases.

PHYSIOLOGICAL/PHYSICAL CONDITIONS The conditions of the work environment that lead to occupational diseases and accidents.

PIECEWORK PLAN The most common type of incentive pay play. Under this plan employees get a standard pay rate for each unit of output.

PLACEMENT An activity concerned with ensuring that job demands are filled and that individual needs and preferences are met.

POINT FACTOR METHODS Wage scales normally adjusted to reflect both labour market rates and the subjective assessment of raters as to the relative importance of the job.

POINT RATING or POINT FACTOR METHOD A job evaluation strategy that assigns point values to previously determined compensable factors and adds them to arrive at a total score used to determine wage levels.

POLYGRAPH TEST See **LIE DETECTOR TEST.**

POSITION ANALYSIS QUESTIONNAIRE (PAQ) A structured procedure used in job analysis that describes jobs in terms of worker activities. The PAQ is based on a person-oriented trait system that allows it to be applied across a number of jobs and organizations without modification. A salient disadvantage is its length.

POSITION DESCRIPTION A description of a collection of duties performed by a single person.

POSITION DESCRIPTION QUESTIONNAIRE (PDQ) A technique that lends itself easily to quantification of results and thus to computer analysis.

POSITIVE REINFORCEMENT SYSTEM An incentive system based on the notion that behaviour can be understood and modified by its consequences. The system lets employees know how well they are meeting specific goals and rewards improvements with praise and recognition. No money is involved.

POSITIVE SETTLEMENT RANGE The overlap area between management's resistance point and the union's resistance point, which facilitates an acceptable settlement.

PREDICTIVE VALIDATION Similar to concurrent validation except that the predictor variable is measured some time before the performance variable.

PREDICTOR RATE The proportion of correct decisions (true positive plus true negative) relative to the total number of decisions when a test is used for selection.

PREDICTORS The tests or pieces of information used by personnel departments to predict how well an applicant is likely to do if hired.

PREFERENCE TEST A kind of selection test used to match employee preferences with job and organizational characteristics.

PRERETIREMENT COUNSELLING Counselling given to employees before retiring in order to facilitate their transition from work to nonwork. This may result in early retirement decisions but it need not always.

PRIMACY EFFECT An order effect where first information is given greater weight—the notion of a first impression.

PRIMARY AND RECENCY EFFECTS The fact that raters will use initial information to categorize a ratee as either a good or a poor performer.

PRIVATE EMPLOYMENT AGENCY An external recruiting source that caters primarily to two types of job applicants: professional and managerial workers and unskilled workers. These agencies charge a fee for setting up connections between applicants and employers.

PROBLEM-SOLVING INTERVIEW A participative appraisal interview in which the ratee and rater try to understand and solve performance problems.

PRODUCTIVITY The outputs of an individual, group, or organization divided by the inputs needed by the individual, group, or organization for the creation of outputs.

PRODUCTIVITY BARGAINING A special form of integrative bargaining where labour agrees to scrap old work habits for new and more effective ones desired by management.

PROFIT-SHARING PLAN An organization-wide incentive plan involving the awarding of money to employees if some level of company profit is attained.

PROGRAMMABLE AUTOMATION The increased use of new technologies, such as computer-aided design (CAD), computer-aided manufacturing (CAM), computer-aided engineering (CAE), and computer-integrated manufacturing (CIM).

PROGRAMMED INSTRUCTION (PI) A systematic and stepwise presentation of skills and tasks broken down into "frames," where each frame must be successfully completed before going on to the next. Feedback concerning the correctness of response for each frame is provided immediately and allows individuals to pace themselves.

PROGRESSIVE DISCIPLINE A system whereby employees are increasingly and more severely disciplined or punished with the repetition of offences.

PROHIBITED ISSUES Issues about which it is illegal for unions and employers to bargain.

PROMOTION-FROM-WITHIN A practice and policy of using promotions from within a company to fill vacant positions and not hiring people from the outside.

PROTECTION PROGRAMS Indirect compensation designed to protect the employee and family if and when the employee's income (direct compensation) is terminated and to protect the employee and family against the burden of health-care expenses in the event of disability.

PSYCHOLOGICAL CONTRACT An informal and unwritten understanding between employees and employer about what is reasonable to expect to get from an employee in exchange for what is in the employment contract.

PSYCHOMOTOR TESTS Aptitude tests that combine mental and physical aspects of individual ability, for example, the MacQuarrie Test for Mechanical Ability, the Tweeser Dexterity Tests.

PYGMALION EFFECT The self-fulfilling prophecy of telling someone they will succeed and then observing that person succeed.

QUALITY The level of appreciation shown by the customer for the goods and services provided by an organization.

QUALITY CIRCLE An innovative management concept that helps contribute to an organization's growth and well being, based on the philosophy that a company's workforce participation is its most valuable resource because they are often the most qualified to identify and solve work-related problems.

QUALITY IMPROVEMENT STRATEGY A plan by which to improve the competitiveness of an organization by improving the quality of its products and services.

QUALITY OF WORK LIFE (QWL) A process by which all members of the organization, through appropriate channels of communication set up for this purpose, have some say about the design of their jobs in particular and the work environment in general to satisfy their needs.

QUOTAS Specific numbers of percentage goals established by an organization for minority hiring to correct underutilization or past discrimination in employment.

RAND FORMULA A union security plan developed by Judge Rand in an arbitration decision handed down in 1946 that requires the employer to deduct union dues from the pay of all employees.

RANKING METHOD A hierarchy or ladder of jobs constructed from the job analysis to reflect the relative value of the jobs to the organization.

RATEE The person being appraised in an appraisal. See also **SUBORDINATE**.

RATER The person doing the appraising in an appraisal. See also **SUPERIOR**.

REALISTIC JOB PREVIEW A recruitment technique where the potential applicant is made aware of the positive and negative aspects of the organization. An applicant is encouraged to approach current employees and the line manager and ask questions about the appropriate fit between his or her needs and the organization's needs.

REALITY SHOCK The career disappointment from having higher expectations of jobs than what jobs can really fulfil.

RECALL POLICY Statement of how laid-off employees are to be brought back to work.

RECENCY EFFECT An order effect where the last or most recent information is given greater weight.

RECENCY-OF-EVENTS ERROR See **RECENCY EFFECT**.

RECOGNITION TESTS Examples of past behaviour or performance that indicate the quality of an individual's work, for example, portfolios.

RECRUITMENT The set of activities and processes used to legally obtain a sufficient number of the right people at the right place and time, so that the people and the organization can select in their own best short-run and long-run interests.

REDUNDANCY PLANNING Developing alternative strategies for obsolete employees to acquire skills necessary for other types of work. Planning includes counselling, training, and part-time employment.

REFERENCE VERIFICATION A method for validating information provided on the application, for example, using school records and transcripts, calling previous employers.

REINFORCEMENT Giving people immediate follow-up on their performance based on the premise people will do what is rewarded and avoid doing what is punished.

RELIABILITY The consistency of a test or test item upon repeated measurement. See also **TEST–RETEST RELIABILITY**.

RELOCATION PROGRAM A company sponsored termination benefit that assists employees who must move in connection with either transfer or discharge.

REPLACEMENT PLANNING The use of replacement charts to help plan who will be able to replace whom in the event of a position becoming vacant.

RESISTANCE POINT The lowest acceptable bargaining level that the union can take on behalf of its members or the highest acceptable bargaining level for management.

RESPONSIBILITY CENTRES A method to appraise managers by measuring how well they do in relation to costs, profits, or revenues for a given unit or division.

RESULTS MANAGEMENT An ongoing mechanism for monitoring the implementation and results of strategic and tactical plans.

RIGHT TO PLANT/OFFICE CLOSING OR RELOCATION NOTIFICATION The right to be informed before a company closes a plant or office or before it decides to move it.

ROLE AWARENESS The degree to which an individual knows what is expected and what authority he or she has.

ROLE CONFLICT The extent of conflict or incompatibility between doing what is expected and what is possible.

ROLE-PLAYING Off-the-job training, where a realistic situation is created and individuals learn by playing roles in the situation.

SAFETY COMMITTEE A strategy for accident prevention that involves employees in safety policy formulation and implementation.

SALARY COMPRESSION A decrease in the range of pay between various positions (levels) in the organization.

SALES INCENTIVE PLANS Administered for individuals engaged in selling; generally called commission plans.

SANDWICH APPROACH Used in a performance appraisal interview when negative feedback is squeezed between "two slices" of positive feedback.

SCANLON PLAN A type of company-wide incentive program emphasizing management–employee relations, especially employee participation, and underscoring efficient operations through cooperation. In effect, employees share in organization profits as a result of contributing and cooperating to attain higher productivity.

SCATTERGRAM A plotting or visual display of the relationship between two variables for several individuals.

SCIENTIFIC APPROACH An approach to designing jobs that minimizes the skills needed by the worker to perform the job. The result is often a job that is simple and repetitive.

SELECTION The process of gathering information for the purpose of evaluating and deciding who should be hired, under legal guidelines, for the short- and long-term interests of the individual and the organization.

SELECTION RATIO The proportion of individuals actually hired to those who applied.

SELF-APPRAISALS Often effective tools for programs focusing on self-development, personal growth, and goal commitment. Self-appraisals are subject to systematic biases and distortions when used for evaluative purposes.

SELF–ASSESSMENT Evaluating oneself in the career planning or the performance appraisal process.

SELF–FULFILLING PROPHECY Something becomes reality because it was predicted to occur.

SELF-MANAGEMENT A relatively new approach to resolving performance discrepancies. It teaches people to exercise control over their own behaviour.

SEMI-AUTONOMOUS WORK GROUP A permanent collection of workers whose objective is to produce a final product.

SENSITIVITY TRAINING A method of training and development conducted in a group setting that aims to give individuals insight into how and why they and others feel and act the way they do.

SEVERANCE PAY A lump sum payment by an employer to a worker whose employment has been terminated.

SEVERITY RATE Reflects the hours actually lost due to injury or illness by differentially weighting categories of injuries and illnesses.

SEX–ROLE STEREOTYPING When in society a role becomes defined as being or having a sex type, e.g., traditionally the role of housekeeper was defined as being female and the job of breadwinner as being male.

SEXUAL HARASSMENT Physical violation or verbal abuse of employees particularly by managers and supervisors.

SIMILARITY ERROR When the rater evaluates more positively those whom they perceive to be similar to themselves.

SIMPLE LINEAR REGRESSION A quantitative formula used to relate an independent variable (X) to a dependent variable (Y). For example, a forecast of future events such as sales (Y) is predicted by demand (X).

SIMULATION A training program that presents individuals with situations that are similar to actual job conditions; this occurs off the job.

SIMULATION TESTS A kind of achievement test used in the selection process. The applicant is given a task to perform, although the situation in which the task is performed is not necessarily recreated.

SINGLE PREDICTOR APPROACH The use of one test or piece of information to choose an applicant for the job.

SKILL-BASED EVALUATION A job evaluation strategy where the organization compensates the employee by paying the person for skills and experience relative to the organization's mission.

SKILL VARIETY The degree to which a job requires that an employee should have a number of different skills to do it correctly.

SOCIAL INSURANCE A public protection program devised by governments to provide wage earners and their dependents with a minimum income during periods of disability, unemployment.

SOCIALIZATION A process of bringing an individual into an organization and of transmitting norms, values, and skills to that individual.

SOCIAL SUPPORT GROUP Individuals who provide unconditional support for the individuals in the group.

SOCIOPSYCHOLOGICAL CONDITIONS Conditions in the workplace that lead to perceived stress and low quality of work life.

SOCIOPSYCHOLOGICAL WORK ENVIRONMENT The nonphysical parts of the work environment, including such things as relationships with supervisors, company policies, structure of the organization, organizational changes, uncertainty, conflicts, and relationships with co-workers.

SOCIOTECHNICAL APPROACH A productivity program under the heading of task redesign that is based on the notion that jobs are man-made inventions related to a number of technical and social systems that are themselves constantly changing. The concept reflects a sensitivity to bridging technical and social systems in such a way as to be optimally productive.

SPILLOVER EFFECT A typical error in performance appraisal. It occurs when past performance appraisal ratings, whether good or bad, are allowed to unjustly influence current ratings.

STAFFING ACTIVITIES The process of recruiting job applicants (candidates), selecting from among them those most appropriate for the available jobs, and orienting and placing the new employees.

STANDARD HOUR PLAN This second most widely used incentive pay plan pays on the basis of time per unit of output rather than on the quantity of output.

STANDARD RÉSUMÉ An organized chronological documentation of work and educational experience relating to one's career and qualifications. Generally prepared by an applicant for a position.

STATISTICAL PROJECTION A forecasting technique used in personnel planning that, for example, uses simple linear regression to predict employment growth as a function of sales growth.

STEEL-COLLAR WORKERS Refers to machines, especially robots, that can be used to do the work instead of people.

STEWARD An employee elected by the work unit to act as the union representative on the worksite and to respond to company actions that violate the labour agreement.

STOCHASTIC ANALYSIS Where the likelihood of landing a series of contracts is combined with the HR requirements of each contract to estimate expected staffing requirements.

STOCK OPTION A managerial incentive plan where the manager is given an opportunity to buy stocks of the company at a later date but at a price established at the time the option is given.

STRAIGHT RANKING A comparative approach in which the superior lists the subordinates from best to worst usually on the basis of overall performance.

STRATEGIC HUMAN RESOURCE MANAGEMENT All those activities affecting the behaviour of individuals in their efforts to formulate and implement the strategic needs of the business.

STRATEGIC LEVEL HR activities that take a longer time to implement and often are for the benefit of the entire firm.

STRATEGIC PLANNING Planning that involves long-term planning and synchronizing the HR needs with the corporate strategic needs.

STRESS INTERVIEW An interview where an applicant may be intentionally annoyed or embarrassed by the interviewer to see how the applicant reacts.

STRICTNESS (ERROR) The error of being too hard when evaluating the performance of employees.

STRIKE A refusal of employees to work at the company.

STRIKE BENEFITS Union payments, usually a small proportion of regular income, to workers during a strike.

STRUCTURED JOB ANALYSIS The use of a standard format for job descriptions so that all organizations can use the same job categories.

SUBJECTIVE FORMS Appraisal forms on which the raters evaluate an employee on the basis of "subjective" attributes such as leadership, attitude toward people, or loyalty.

SUBORDINATE The person whose performance is being appraised.

SUCCESSION PLANNING Like replacement planning but tends to be longer term, be more developmental, and offer more flexibility.

SUGGESTION SYSTEMS A form of incentive compensation paid to employees who are responsible for money-saving or money-producing ideas for the organization.

SUPERIOR The person doing the appraising of another's performance.

SUPERVISOR The person who directs and is responsible for other employees who are nonsupervisors and nonmanagers.

SUPERVISORY ASSISTANCE An informal method of training often being discussed between a supervisor and his or her employee.

SUPPLEMENTAL UNEMPLOYMENT BENEFITS (SUB) Benefits received by employees who are on layoff from their company until returning to work or until the benefits expire.

SYSTEMIC DISCRIMINATION A seemingly neutral policy that has an adverse effect on one of the groups protected under human rights legislation.

TARGET POINT A realistic assessment of what wage and conditions of employment the union is likely to get from management.

TASK LEVEL ANALYSIS Analysis providing information about the tasks to be performed on each job, the skills necessary to perform those tasks, and the minimum acceptable standards of performance.

TEAM CONTEMPORARY APPROACH A major classification of approaches to job design that focus on the group–job design interface (or relationships).

TEAMWORK Cooperation among individuals in solving problems and in performing at work.

TECHNOLOGICAL SYSTEM The machines, methods, and materials used to produce the organization's output.

TELL-AND-LISTEN INTERVIEW A performance appraisal interview in which the rater informs the ratee of the evaluation and then listens to the ratee's comments on the evaluation.

TELL-AND-SELL INTERVIEW A performance appraisal interview in which the rater informs the ratee of the evaluation and sells the ratee on the evaluation.

TERMINATE FOR GOOD CAUSE The practice or doctrine of firing employees only for good reason or for reasonable reason.

TEST-RETEST RELIABILITY The relationship between the results of the same test given at two different times.

TESTS Any paper-and-pencil performance measure or other information used as a basis for making an employment decision.

THEORY Z MANAGEMENT A current management philosophy modifying some of the more traditional American management concerns (Theory A) and integrating some of the ideas from conventional Japanese management (Theory J).

TIME SERIES ANALYSIS Where past staffing levels are used to project future HR requirements.

TIME STUDY See **WORK MEASUREMENT**.

TIMETABLES Specific dates when AAP goals and quotas are to be met.

TOTAL COMPENSATION The total of direct and indirect compensation paid to an individual.

TRAINING AND DEVELOPMENT Any attempt to improve current or future performance by increasing an employee's ability to perform through learning. It can be accomplished by changing the employee's attitude or increasing his or her skills or knowledge.

UNCERTAINTY A lack of predictability or an inability to tell what things are or will be like; a state of unpredictability.

UNFAIR LABOUR PRACTICE A practice on the part of either union or management that violates provisions of federal or provincial labour laws.

UNFAIR REPRESENTATION Breach of duty by a union to fairly represent all employees covered by the union–management contract.

UNION An organization with the legal authority to negotiate with the employer on behalf of the employees and to administer the ensuing agreement.

UNION LOCAL The grass-roots unit of the labour organization that represents the employees who are in the same union unit at a given workplace.

UNION SHOP A provision that says that employees must join the union (if the company has one) after a set number of days from initial employment.

UNIONIZATION or UNIONIZING The effort by employees and outside agencies (unions and associations) to band together and act as a single unit when dealing with management over issues related to their work.

UTILIZATION ANALYSIS Process of determining the number of women and minorities in different jobs within an organization.

VALID PREDICTOR Any test used for staffing that correlates with or predicts actual job performance.

VALIDITY The degree to which a predictor or criterion measures what it purports to measure, demonstrating the job-relatedness of a test by showing how well an applicant will perform based on the test predictions.

VALIDITY GENERALIZATION Demonstrating that the job-relatedness or validity of one test in one situation applies equally in other situations.

VERTICAL LOADING The adding to a job of duties that are different from those already in the job and that require different skills, knowledge, and abilities.

VESTED   Pertains to qualifications required to become eligible for an organization's pension benefits.

WAGE–DIVIDEND PLANS   A special type of cash plan where the percentage of profits paid to employees is determined by the amount of dividends paid to stockholders.

WAGE SURVEYS   Published reports of what several different companies are paying for different types of jobs.

WEIGHTED APPLICATION BLANK (WAB)   An application blank in which some information is given more importance or weight as a predictor of future success.

WEIGHTED CHECKLIST   Identical to a critical incidents format but with various points to differentiate the varying importance of different incidents.

WELLNESS TESTS   Health assessments of employees, which include measures of blood pressure, blood cholesterol, high density cholesterol, evaluation of diet, life change events, smoking, drinking, and family history of chronic heart disease.

WHIPSAW   The process where unions use one contract settlement as a precedent for the next and force the employer to settle all contracts before work is resumed.

WIDE-AREA AND MULTICRAFT BARGAINING   A negotiating structure that exists in the construction industry where several separate construction unions may settle a contract together.

WILDCAT STRIKE   A strike that is not legal because the contract forbids it, yet the union strikes anyway.

WORK MEASUREMENT   The determination of standard times for all units of work activity in any task. Includes the assessment of the "actual effort" exerted and the "real effort" required to accomplish a task (cf. **METHOD ANALYSIS**).

WORK PACING   The rate or flow of work and who controls the rate or flow. See also **MACHINE PACING**.

WORK SAMPLE TEST   A test that is an actual simulation of the job or critical tasks associated with the job. An example would be a typing test used to select a secretary.

WORK SAMPLING   The process of taking instantaneous samples of the work activities of individuals or groups. Activities are then timed and classified according to predetermined categories. The result is a description of the activities by classification of job and the percentage of time for each activity (cf. **METHODS ANALYSIS**).

WORK SHARING   Plan by which available work is distributed as evenly as possible among all workers when production slackens, or by which working time is generally reduced by layoffs.

WORK SIMULATIONS   See **WORK SAMPLE TEST**

WORK STANDARDS APPROACH   A type of goal-oriented evaluation, similar to management by objectives, except that the predetermined goals are dictated by management and often established by work measurement.

WORKERS' COMPENSATION   A program offered to cover worker sickness and disability.

YELLOW-DOG CONTRACTS   Contracts signed by employees upon employment agreeing not to join a union.

NAME INDEX

SUBJECT INDEX

To the owner of this book

We hope that you have enjoyed *Human Resource Management: The Canadian Dynamic*, and we would like to know as much about your experiences as you would care to offer. Only through your comments and those of others can we learn how to make this a better text for future readers.

School _____ Your instructor's name _____

Course _____ Was the text required? _____ Recommended? _____

1. What did you like the most about *Human Resource Management: The Canadian Dynamic?*

_____
_____
_____

2. How useful was this text for your course?

_____
_____
_____

3. Do you have any recommendations for ways to improve the next edition of this text?

_____
_____
_____

4. In the space below or in a separate letter, please write any other comments you have about the book. (For example, please feel free to comment on reading level, writing style, terminology, design features, and learning aids.)

_____
_____
_____
_____

Optional

Your name _____ Date _____

May Nelson Canada quote you, either in promotion for *Human Resource Management: The Canadian Dynamic* or in future publishing ventures?

Yes _____ No _____

Thanks!

FOLD HERE

MAIL ▶POSTE

Canada Post Corporation/Société canadienne des postes

Postage paid
if mailed in Canada

Port payé
si posté au Canada

Business Reply

Réponse d'affaires

0107077099   01

Nelson

0107077099-M1K5G4-BR01

Nelson Canada
College Editorial Department
1120 Birchmount Rd.
Scarborough, ON M1K 9Z9

PLEASE TAPE SHUT. DO NOT STAPLE.